INVENTING
Irish
AMERICA

THE IRISH IN AMERICA

Studies Sponsored by
the Ancient Order of Hibernians and
the Cushwa Center for
the Study of American Catholicism

INVENTING

Irish

AMERICA

Generation, Class, and Ethnic Identity
in a New England City, 1880–1928

TIMOTHY J. MEAGHER

UNIVERSITY OF NOTRE DAME PRESS
Notre Dame, Indiana

Designed by Wendy McMillen
Set in 11/13.2 Stone Print by Stanton Pub. Services, Inc.
Printed in USA by Edwards Brothers, Inc.

Manufactured in the United States of America

Library of Congress Cataloging-in-Publication Data

Meagher, Timothy J.
    Inventing Irish America : generation, class, and ethnic identity in a New England
city, 1880–1928 / Timothy J. Meagher.
        p.   cm. — (The Irish in America)
    Includes bibliographical references (p.) and index.
    ISBN 0-268-03153-3 (cloth : alk. paper) — ISBN 0-268-03154-1 (pbk. :
alk. paper)
        1. Irish Americans—Massachusetts—Worcester—Ethnic identity. 2. Irish
Americans—Cultural assimilation—Massachusetts—Worcester. 3. Generations—
Massachusetts—Worcester—History. 4. Social classes—Massachusetts—
Worcester—History. 5. Worcester (Mass.)—Ethnic relations. I. Title. II. Series

F74.W9 M38   2000
305.891'6207443—dc21

                                                                00-030255

To my mother

ELIZABETH CHRISTINE MCDERMOTT MEAGHER

and my late father

JOHN HENRY MEAGHER

I hope this book recaptures some of the world that you inherited.

Contents

Acknowledgments   ix

Introduction   1

One
The Immigrant Irish   17

Two
The Second-Generation Irish   67

Three
The Search for Accommodation: The 1880s and Early 1890s   133

Four
Ethnic Revival: The 1890s and Early 1900s   201

Five
The Triumph of Militant, Pan-Ethnic, American Catholicism:
The Early 1900s to the 1920s   269

Conclusion   373

Notes   387
Bibliography   487
Index   503

Acknowledgments

Worcester is my hometown and, being Irish American, this community is my community. It is the one I grew up in, and the one I will always remember as my own. I want to acknowledge the men and women who made up this world that I tried to recreate, the immigrants and American-born Irish who built the community that my parents inherited and then passed it on to me. When I walk in St. John's Cemetery in South Worcester, I feel like I am walking among friends, Monsignor Griffin on one side, Peter Sullivan on another, George McAleer, Walter Drohan, even the intriguingly named Eneas Lombard. I am particularly indebted to Richard O'Flynn, the Waterford-born bookseller and ticket agent, whose sense of responsibility for the community's history led him to take extensive notes and keep a rich trove of records, clippings, and pamphlets documenting the history of the Worcester Irish. I feel a special obligation to him for he left those papers, he said, "for the future historian of the Irish in Worcester." Yet I feel responsible to all of those Irish in Worcester, and I hope that I have recaptured something of their lives. I especially want to acknowledge my own grandparents, who played a crucial role in this history: James Andrew McDermott, Katherine Agnes Lavin McDermott, John Henry Meagher, and Margaret Ronayne Meagher.

This book, however, is not only an attempt to recover a forgotten slice of a community's history, but it is also an attempt to explore new ground in how historians think and write about the history of the Irish in America and, indeed, about American ethnic groups generally. I want to thank the scholarly colleagues who helped me understand about how to write history, and more particularly, the history of Irish Americans in this era: my mentor and friend, Howard Chudacoff, and James Patterson, Elmer Cornwell, and L. Perry Curtis from Brown University; my colleagues who love Worcester history, Kenneth Moynihan, John McClymer, Charles Esthus, Kevin Hickey, Ronald Formisano, Robert Kolesar, Ronald Petrin, Bruce Cohen, Vincent Powers, and James P. Hanlan. I would also like to thank my fellow historians but also good friends James M. O'Toole, Brian Mitchell, Marion Casey, Kevin O'Neill, Colleen McDannell, Elizabeth McKeown, Christopher Kauffman, Theresa McBride, James Gilbert, Gary Gerstle, David O'Brien, and especially Lenard Berlanstein, who heard more about the Irish in Worcester over the last ten years than any sane person would want to hear. I want to thank Roy Rosenzweig in particular, who was essential to the early research on this project, sharing his information, his sources, and his ideas, and who has remained both a great source of insights into American ethnic history and a good and generous friend long after he left Worcester behind. I would also like to thank Kerby Miller and Philip Gleason, who read this manuscript for the Press, recommended it for publication, and suggested some very useful revisions. I want to thank Dr. Scott Appleby of the University of Notre Dame for beginning the publication process and the staff of the University of Notre Dame Press including Dr. Barbara Hanrahan, Ann Rice, Rebecca DeBoer, John McCudden, and Ann Bromley for seeing it through so expertly and patiently.

Many librarians and archivists made this work possible, and, having toiled in that work myself, I appreciate how critical they are to all historical research, not just mine. I want to thank Nancy Gaudette at the Worcester Public Library, Mary Brown, Nancy Burkett, and Joyce Tracy at the American Antiquarian Society, James Mahoney from Holy Cross College Library, and William Wallace and especially Dorothy Gleason from the Worcester Historical Museum. Many of the sources I used remain in private hands and I want to thank the people who made them available to me: Ancient Order of Hibernians Division 36, the Knights of Columbus Alhambra Council no. 88, Msgr. Thomas Daley of St. Stephen's parish, Msgr. David Sullivan of St. Peter's, Msgr. John Martin of Our Lady of the Angels, Msgr. Frank Scollen of St. John's, Fr. John Burke of St. Paul's, and Msgr. Roger Vian of the Springfield Diocese. A number of people also graciously shared their memories of this time with me, including Lawrence O'Connell, Peter Sullivan Jr., Eleanor O'Donnell, William Kelleher, Fr. Thomas McDermott, Arthur Sheedy, F. A. Jacques, and Mary O'Reilly.

Finally there are the people who encouraged me in this work. Among my friends they include Andrea Anderson, Cynthia Robinson, Warren Leon, Suzi Jones, Frederic Miller, Arthur Y. M. Chen, Hassan Abouseda, Eric H. F.

Law, and Victor Souvanpong. They also include members of my family: my father's sister, Aunt Margaret Meagher Costello, who steered me to the Richard O'Flynn papers the day I started this research, as well as my mother's sisters and brothers, my Aunt Louise McDermott Salisbury and Uncle Charles McDermott and especially my Aunt Katherine McDermott and Uncle Andrew McDermott. Their stories and memories have inspired, illuminated, and informed this work and reminded me that it was always a story of real people. I also want to thank my sister, Mary, and my brothers, Patrick, Andrew, Dermot, and Sean, and particularly my mother, Elizabeth McDermott Meagher. She has believed in this project from the beginning and never wavered.

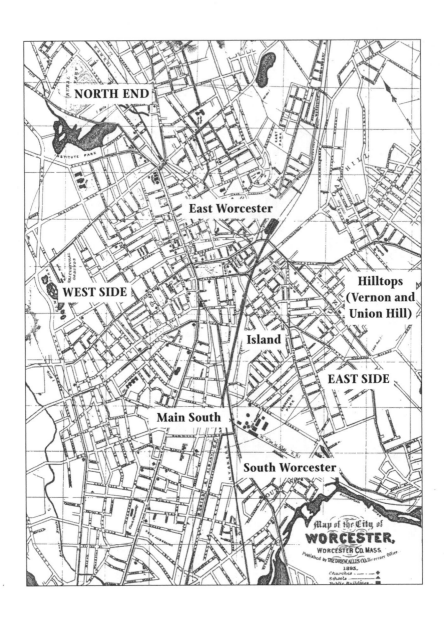

NORTH END

East Worcester

WEST SIDE

Hilltops
(Vernon and
Union Hill)

Island

EAST SIDE

Main South

South Worcester

Map of the City of
WORCESTER,
WORCESTER CO. MASS.
Published by THE DREW ALLIS CO. Directory Office
1895.
Churches
Schools
Public Buildings

Introduction

On the morning of March 17, 1890, the members of the St. Paul's Lyceum gathered in their clubhouse on Front Street in the heart of Worcester, a small but growing industrial city in central Massachusetts. They were trying to decide whether they should join a parade that afternoon honoring St. Patrick, Ireland's patron saint. The debate, Worcester's daily papers reported, was "hot."[1]

These were young men, most of them were American-born, and they were almost painfully eager to prove that they were good Americans. They had abjured drinking liquor, the "curse" of their Irish race as their pastor called it, for their Lyceum was a Catholic total abstinence society. They had also made a name for themselves locally as baseball players, and their minstrel shows were famous throughout Worcester. To many of them the parade was a waste of time and money, both better spent on building an Irish meeting hall with a gymnasium, lecture rooms, and a library that could be both a tangible symbol of their people's progress and a practical aid to its achievement. To some of them, the parade was worse than the frittering away of precious resources, it was a provocation or excuse for the drinking and brawling that besmirched the name of the Irish people of Worcester and everywhere.[2]

Yet most, if not all, of these men did not wish to abandon their past. Many remained unmarried even into their late twenties and thirties and lived at home with their parents, dutifully emptying out much of their earnings on the kitchen table each week for the good of the family. Moreover, they were good Catholics, better-instructed certainly, probably even more regularly faithful to the official rituals of their church than their parents or certainly their grandparents had been as youths. And tales of Ireland and its heroes still moved them. That was why the debate was so "hot."

Finally, Daniel Boyle rose from among them and in a passionate speech he urged the members "not to let their mothers and fathers come on the street this afternoon and find them ashamed to call themselves Irishmen." His Lyceum mates "loudly applauded"; Boyle had settled the issue. They would march that afternoon in their Sunday-best suits and bowlers, displaying proudly the big badges with trailing ribbons that testified to their commitment to total abstinence. They would not be "ashamed to call themselves Irishmen."[3]

And yet it had been a close call for the young men of the St. Paul's Lyceum. Indeed, it had been a close call for the parade itself. Back in January, when Worcester's Convention of United Irish Societies had met to consider the parade, the Lyceum delegates had voted against it. Many other Irish temperance men had also voted against it out of opposition, or had abstained from voting out of indifference. As a result, there were no parades many years in the 1880s and early 1890s; between 1881 and 1896, Worcester's Irish marched only nine times on St. Patrick's Day.[4]

In the late 1890s and early 1900s St. Patrick would suffer no such indifference on his day in Worcester. Every year from 1897 to 1904, row after row of men in green tunics and trousers, puttees, spiked and plumed helmets, marched down Worcester's Main Street on March 17. They were members of the Ancient Order of Hibernians' militia companies: The Hibernian Rifles and Guards. It was an impressive sight. The Hibernians and their allies meant it to be, for they meant it to be a powerful symbol of Irish pride and power. Members of the Ancient Order of Hibernians had always been ardent supporters of the St. Patrick's Day parade. The Hibernians were largely composed of recent immigrants from Ireland who still looked back to their native land as their real home. They were also mostly workingmen, many of them laborers or factory operatives, teetering on the brink of poverty. The parade was a reminder of their Irish home, but also a ritual reaffirmation of the community solidarity they depended on to survive in the alien and often bewildering new urban world where they now lived. It was also an opportunity to demonstrate the community's power to hostile neighbors. They were impatient with the temperance men's concerns about drinking and the parade's expense, but in the 1880s and early 1890s the Hibernians had been too weak, had too few members to make a presentable showing marching alone. They thus found themselves in those years beseeching, cajoling, and threatening the reluctant, young temperance men into marching with them. By the late 1890s, however, the local Irish temperance movement had foundered, and it was the Hibernians who were waxing strong. As its membership skyrocketed, the Ancient Order added several new branches or divisions and even built a grand new hall in downtown

Worcester as testament to its new power. The Hibernians no longer needed the temperance men, or anyone else for that matter, to honor St. Patrick with the pageantry and enthusiasm they felt that he deserved.

In 1911 Worcester's Irish community staged its last St. Patrick's Day parade for more than seventy-two years. That did not mean, however, that Irishmen in Worcester no longer marched to honor their heroes. Indeed, they turned out by the thousands in that year of 1911 and many years after that to honor a different man, one who seemed an odd choice for celebration by Irish Catholics: an Italian explorer sailing on behalf of a Spanish queen, Christopher Columbus.

Yet Columbus served these Worcester Irish well in the 1910s and 1920s in ways that St. Patrick could not. He was an American—indeed, the first American if you dismissed the native peoples who greeted him on the shores of Santo Domingo, as the Worcester Irish did. He was, however, also Catholic and a representative of a Catholic empire. His holiday was thus a perfect opportunity to demonstrate the power and solidarity of a new group in the city, a Catholic American group—militantly Catholic, if patriotically American.

Chief among the Worcester Irish struggling to create that group were the Irishmen whose society took Columbus as their patron, the Knights of Columbus. Drawing largely from the American-born and middle-class Irish, this society's numbers were growing rapidly in the early 1910s in Worcester; in a few years, after their work on behalf of American troops in World War I, their membership would soar. The Knights were eager to make these Columbus Day parades broadly representative of Worcester's entire Catholic community, and so they enticed the city's Polish Catholics to sponsor a float in 1911 and both French Canadians and Italians to march with the Knights in the same year. The Knights, like the Hibernians, were suspicious of their Protestant neighbors and they understood the value of parades to demonstrate their community's strength to suspected enemies. But the group this parade was meant to represent was not the Irish alone but a diverse array of Catholic ethnics melded into a single people, united by their faith.

At the turn of the century, the attitudes of the Worcester Irish about parades changed radically because their understanding of how to deal with their neighbors, even how to identify themselves and define the boundaries of their group, changed radically at that time. The succession of dominant societies or associations—the temperance men in the 1880s, Hibernians in the 1890s and early 1900s, and the Knights of Columbus by the 1910s—was one sign of these broad changes, but there were others. In the 1880s, when the temperance societies were popular and St. Patrick was often slighted on his day, the Worcester Irish deliberately avoided building separate Catholic institutions such as schools. They also self-consciously cultivated Yankee Protestant help in forging a moderate, safe nationalist movement to free Ireland. The watchword among the Worcester Irish in the 1880s and 1890s was accommodation. In just a few years, however, accommodation became an epithet, not a watchword, among them. Beginning in the late 1890s and carrying through to the middle of the first decade of the twentieth century, the Hibernians, now in the ascendant, marched every March 17 to trumpet the rise of a new spirit of ethnic chauvinism and belligerence in Worcester's Irish community. Yet they did more than simply march on Patrick's day. With allies like the Clan na Gael, they revived the Gaelic language and Gaelic sports in Worcester; remade the local nationalist movement into an instrument of their revolutionary dreams of Ireland's violent liberation; and challenged Yankee power and prejudice at every turn. Ethnocentrism flourished, an ethnic revival reigned, among the Worcester Irish in the decade straddling the turn of the century. By the 1910s this revival had collapsed. In that decade and the next, as the Knights of Columbus grew and organized homage to their patron, Christopher Columbus, on his October day, once Irish-dominated institutions, clubs, and parishes began to seek out French Canadians, Italians, and Poles as clients, members, or patrons. Accommodation and narrow, exclusively Irish ethnocentrism had now all but disappeared in Worcester's Irish community. Irish Catholics would make no more overtures to their Yankee neighbors as they had in the 1880s, or remain in belligerent ethnic isolation as they had in the 1890s and early 1900s. Instead they would try to forge all Catholic ethnics into a new militantly Catholic, patriotically American, pan-ethnic, American Catholic people, with themselves as leaders of this new group, arbiters of this new identity.

Throughout the turn of the century era the Irish in Worcester, Massachusetts, thus lurched from one strategy of relating to their neighbors, one conception of their identity, one definition of their community's boundaries, to another. Why?

In 1963, William Shannon, a successful journalist for the *New York Post* (Shannon later worked for the *New York Times* and, later still, became ambassador to Ireland), published a history of the Irish in America called *The American Irish*. Shannon's book proved very popular; it was well timed to take advantage of the election of America's first Irish Catholic president, and was rich and readable, filled with lively stories and dramatic biographical vignettes. Yet Shannon, the former history graduate student, was intent on probing into the heart of the Irish American experience, not just exploiting its marketability. He tried to give the long history of the Irish in America some shape and structure, to identify turning points and trace out themes.[5]

The turn of the century period in Irish American history, in particular, intrigued him. Shannon was a native of Worcester, and though he was born of a later generation, some sense of the lurches and shifts of his own community at the turn of the century may have been passed down to him. More likely, he recognized that the maturing of a new Irish generation, the first generation born in America, and the consequent expansion of the Irish American middle class had worked a fundamental revolution in the lives of Irish communities all across America at the turn of the century. In any event, he identified the forty years from 1880 to 1920 as a crossroads of sorts, a transitional period, in the history of the American Irish. The Irish, Shannon believed, were leaving behind their ghettos, seizing power in American cities, and searching for respect, but they did not, he argued, simply assimilate or merge easily into the American mainstream. "This was still a Protestant country," he pointed out, and Irish Americans at the turn of the century were very aware of the "distance that separated them from the American inner group."[6]

The Irish at the end of the nineteenth century, he contended, were caught in an "ambiguous indeterminate state" as they "reached toward a definition of themselves within an American context.... they were, in effect, asking themselves who am I?" The reason for their identity crisis, Shannon argued, was that the Irish "found themselves with a foot in both worlds ... the desire to join the ins conflicted with the desire to lead the outs." Their options, Shannon suggested were "numerous," if confusing: "conventional success or frustrated insurgency, individual assimilation or the chauvinisms of the Irish community, bleached-out respectability or labor radicalism." The American Irish had changed in that era and were still changing, Shannon suggested, but precisely how and why was not clear to them, and he himself could do no more than sketch a broad range of alternative paths that Irish men and women had followed then.[7]

William Shannon merely hypothesized about the turn of the century era as a transitional period in the history of the American Irish; he did not investigate or test his hypothesis. Nor has anyone else done so since he wrote. Scores of historians, of course, have written about the Irish at the turn of the century since Shannon's time. They have been attracted to it to examine Irish participation in a broad range of critical movements and events during that period. What Daniel Patrick Moynihan said of the Irish in New York City could well be said of Irish men and women throughout America: "there were sixty or seventy years [straddling the turn of the century] when the Irish were everywhere."[8] Pieces of the story—the Land League, liberal Catholicism, the Irish takeover of municipal politics and labor unions, or the birth of the Catholic ghetto—have thus been told before. Yet no one has addressed Shannon's questions about the importance of the era as a critical watershed in the history of the Irish in America. Indeed, in the long and rich tradition of writing American ethnic history few historians have seriously probed critical generational junctures as important crossroads in the history of any white ethnic group or community.

In large part that neglect has been because there has been no appropriate theoretical framework, no useful language, to help conceptualize and explain the historical evolution of ethnic communities or groups in transition, like the Worcester Irish at the turn of the century. Linear conceptions of ethnicity stressing either quick assimilation or its opposite, stubborn cultural persistence, have been the most common ways to understand ethnic group or community history. Such conceptions provided little reason for studying second or "middle" generations of ethnic groups or communities, since such generations either assimilated, and thus the ethnic group or community ceased to exist, or they merely held doggedly to the culture they had inherited, and thus the group or community was no different in its essentials than the ones their parents, the immigrants, had created. Marcus Lee Hansen was one of the few historians to try to explain how ethnic loyalties or cultures could change and yet persist or revive in later generations of ethnics. Hansen suggested in his "law of the third Generation" that "interest" in ethnicity varied dramatically over the course of generations: what the "son [second generation] wishes to forget, the grandson [third generation] wishes to remember."[9] Hansen's theory seems too simplistic, however, to account for the kind of complex changes among ethnics that Shannon sensed among the turn of the century Irish and that his Celtic forerunners in Worcester seemed to embody.

Recent work by historians as well as anthropologists and folklorists provides more promising, nuanced conceptions of ethnicity and ethnic change that help explain the complicated histories of ethnic groups or communities in transition. Labor historians like Roy Rosenzweig (in his classic study of Worcester's workers), Liz Cohen, Gary Gerstle, James Barrett, and others have restored the notion of change from one generation to another, ignored by emphases on cultural persistence in the 1960s and 1970s, but they have done this without the ahistorical oversimplifications of the old linear assimilationist theories. They have placed the cultural transformations in everyday life of second-generation ethnics within a historical context, emphasizing that the American culture embraced by these and other ethnics was dynamic and concrete, not timeless and abstract. Rosenzweig, for example, has delineated in detail the fundamental revolution in Worcester workers' leisure culture wrought by new commercial recreational opportunities such as movies and amusement parks in the early twentieth century. Labor historians like Gerstle and Barrett have also demonstrated the ability of second-generation ethnics to create their own meanings for their American loyalties as well as their own versions of American culture.

There are limits, however, to the usefulness of these new labor history perspectives and insights in understanding the evolution of ethnic communities. Simply put, most of these labor historians have been interested primarily in second-generation ethnics as members of the working class: when, how, and why American workers of varied ethnic backgrounds have, or have not, been able to act in concert on behalf of their own interests as workers; not when, how, and why ethnic groups or communities evolve over time. The two questions can, of course, be related, but they are not necessarily the same question. Merger into a class-conscious working class was always a potential alternative path for all ethnic workers, but it was only one of many paths.[10]

Recent research in anthropology, folklore, and political science has focused more directly on the evolution of ethnic identity and culture. This research suggests the adaptability of ethnic groups, of defining and redefining group identities, expanding or contracting group boundaries, and inventing and reinventing cultural rituals or customs to mark those boundaries. Several recent studies have noted the creation of broad pan-ethnic identities among American Hispanics ("the invention of Latinismo") centering on language, or among Asian Americans or even Native Americans focused on race. Theorists, such as Donald Horowitz, warn that these options for changing identities are limited: ethnic groups or communities are not "infinitely malleable." Nevertheless, as Horowitz points out, members of ethnic groups or communities may follow many possible paths in their historical evolution: moving backward into ethnocentric isolation, or sideways into alliances with other outsiders, as well as forward into some form of merger into a larger group. Internal trends, such as the passage of generations, are important in causing those changes, but also key are the changing circumstances of the environment, particularly, as Abner Cohen notes, an ethnic group or community's perception of its changing economic or political interests amid shifts in the balance of power among its neighboring groups.[11]

In a 1992 article in the *Journal of American Ethnic History*, several leading historians of American ethnic groups, including Kathleen Conzen, David Gerber, George Pozetta, and Rudolf Vecoli suggested how these concepts might be applied to the study of American ethnic history. Their principal point was the fluidity of ethnic identifications, boundaries, and cultures: the capacity of ethnic groups or communities to continually reinvent themselves through new definitions of identity, expansion or contraction of group boundaries, and the creation of new traditions or rituals to mark the transformed group. They pointed, as Shannon did over thirty years earlier, to the emergence of a second generation as a critical moment in the processes of ethnic invention, as the "established defenses of boundary maintenance (language, gender roles, endogamy, deference patterns) so painstakingly created by immigrants were questioned and challenged by the American born." Yet though they identified the emergence of new generations as important junctures in ethnic group or community evolution, they rejected the "passive, unconscious" adaptation of individual group members in the transition of generations— "as in the assimilation model"—as the sole cause of ethnic change. Ethnic groups and communities are historical phenomena, embedded in concrete historical processes, they argued. Ethnic group members self-consciously and actively "renegotiated traditions" or created and recreated institutions as they coped with the shifting circumstances of the environment outside the group, as well as with broad cultural adaptations within it. Wars, depressions, major political shifts could all be critical elements in those changing environmental conditions, but the "essential components" of an ethnic group or community's "process of formation and definition" are its relationships with the "dominant" or host group and other neighboring immigrant or ethnic groups.[12]

Conzen and her colleagues have offered a promising perspective for understanding ethnic change, but they appear to dismiss too easily the point made so tellingly by recent labor historians, namely, the powerful impact of America's popular culture and its industrial economy on the American-born children of immigrants. Though they recognize the critical importance of generational junctures, they seem to underestimate how that culture and economy produced such profound differences in perspectives between immigrants, natives of a foreign, rural land like Ireland, and their second-generation children, who were born and bred in the American city. One need not accept Hansen's simple and ahistorical polarities between generations (the "forgetting" second generation) to recognize such differences in outlook. Rather than a group's or community's changes through historical time alone, it is those changes combined with the silent, gradual revolution in everyday life that shapes and reshapes the community's life.[13]

The promise of the concepts argued by Conzen and her colleagues, nonetheless, cannot be denied and, indeed, seems self-evident in writing the history of ethnic groups and communities. The heart of this conception of ethnicity is fundamentally historical (in the authors' words ethnicity "is restored to the province of history") with an emphasis on change over time, the importance of contingency, real events, and "active decision making." "Ethnicity" as the authors note, "is a cultural construction accomplished over time."[14]

Historians of American ethnic groups have been surprisingly slow to take up such ideas. Particularly noteworthy is the virtual absence of such studies focusing on later generations or eras in the histories of ethnic groups or communities. It is in these periods, as Conzen and her colleagues state, that the changes seem to be most significant and dramatic. Nevertheless, as Russell Kazal suggests, the most ambitious work to date employing the concepts of Conzen and her co-authors is David Gerber's study of immigrant communities in Buffalo in the middle of the nineteenth century. Conzen and her colleagues, themselves, could cite only Deborah Dash Moore's study of second-generation Jews in New York, *At Home in America*, in discussing the importance of the transition from immigrant to American-born generations in their essay, and there have been almost no studies of that critical juncture in ethnic group evolution since the Conzen article. Despite the call in that article to examine ethnic groups and communities "over time," the writing of American ethnic community or group history remains largely fixated on immigrants, as it has been almost since its inception.[15] And thus Shannon's speculation about the turn of the century Irish in America, that the emergence of a new generation dramatically transformed their culture and identity, has never been tested.

This study proposes to finally address Shannon's speculation by focusing on the people of his own Irish community in his native city at the turn of the century. It reveals that rather than confronting a number of alternatives at once, as Shannon implied, Irish Americans moved through them in turn, in a chronology of change from accommodation to ethnic revival to the forging of a new, broader group. It also suggests that the range of options open to Irish Americans became more constricted over time. In the 1880s much seemed possible for the Worcester Irish, including even a detente or rapprochement with their longtime Yankee Protestant antagonists. By the early twentieth century that was no longer possible, and Irish American life in Worcester had frozen into a mold of militant American Catholicism that would last until the middle of the century.

Perhaps as important as laying out this chronology, this study explains why these changing definitions of identities and boundaries unfolded as they did. It reveals that the second generation's emergence did cause a revolution— quiet, gradual, but powerful—in the everyday life of the local Irish community. Yet it argues that this "passive, unconscious" change, while important in shaping the history of the Worcester Irish at the turn of the century, does not fully explain either its erratic course or even its outcome. It suggests that it is important to look at another process, at how the Worcester Irish self-consciously defined and redefined their identities and boundaries through their creation or transformation of institutions, societies, and community rituals. These efforts were shaped principally by the changing configuration of local group relations in Worcester but also by events and trends taking place throughout the nation and even around the world. This history argues, therefore, that the evolution of the Worcester Irish at the turn of the century—and any other ethnic group or community at a similar critical juncture in its history, for that matter—can best be understood not through examination of one historical process but two related processes measured in different kinds of time: the transformation of everyday life measured in generations; and the community's negotiation of its relations with its neighbors and the creation and recreation of its social and cultural life traced through the events of historical time.

The first process, the transformation of everyday life, was so slow that it was imperceptible day by day, but powerful and revolutionary when measured in generations. Ireland changed dramatically after the Famine and thus the Irish newcomers of the late nineteenth century differed from their Famine-era predecessors in many ways. The vast majority of Irish immigrants, however, were still rural peasants, like the earlier immigrants, and they shared the Famine refugees' intense communalism, the sense of themselves as exiles, and, alas, their economic fate as lowly workers at the bottom of the city's occupational hierarchy. They would thus make eager recruits for the Hibernians and would prove to be the strongest supporters of the aggressive ethnocentrism that the AOH preached. The American-born Irish, maturing in greater and greater numbers from the 1880s through the end of the century, were very different people. They were like Boyle and his Lyceum contemporaries, proud of their American birthright, passionate devotees of American popular culture, experienced in the ways of urban industrial life, and more successful than their immigrant parents or Irish-born "cousins" newly arrived from the old country. They would, of course, provide most of the members of the temperance societies, but they would also make up the bulk of the Knights of Columbus, who were, if anything, even more intensely proud of their native American birth than were the total abstinence men. The emergence of this new generation, and the attendant consequences of its emergence such as the expansion of the Irish middle class, worked a slow, unconscious, but powerful revolution in the everyday life of the Irish in the turn of the century era.

If it was a revolutionary change, however, it is important not to misunderstand it. It was not a simple process of assimilation from one timeless essence to another: from "Irishness" to "Americanness." Second-generation Irish men and women, as we have noted, had not abandoned loyalties to Ireland, and they were probably as devoutly Catholic as their Irish ancestors—at least undoubtedly more faithful to Catholicism's institutional mandates and prescribed rituals. Change among the Worcester Irish was a complicated process and was embedded in the historical concretes of its time. The American popular culture the American-born Irish reveled in, for example, was dynamic, changing, and, indeed, something they themselves were helping to make at the turn of the century. Even their Catholic religion was not simply an ancient faith handed down to them whole, but a religion revived, renewed, and transformed by a profound nineteenth-century "Devotional Revolution."

Furthermore, if the transition in generations that revolutionized everyday life explains some of the changes in Worcester's Irish community at the turn of the century, it does not explain all of them, or the important ones fully. It does not explain the puzzling *sequence* of changes in the Irish community's conceptions of identity and group boundaries as well as in its strategies for relating to other groups: why, for example, was accommodation and the embrace of American culture so pervasive in Worcester in the 1880s when most American-born Irish were still in short pants or pinafores? And why did it give way to an Irish ethnic revival even as the immigrant population's proportionate power was fading and the American-born began to mature and dominate the city's Irish community? Moreover, the generational transition does not explain why Worcester's largely second-generation Irish Catholic Americans sought a rapprochement with their Yankee Protestant neighbors and were indifferent to fellow Catholic ethnics in the 1880s, while their similarly second-generation Irish Catholic American counterparts in the 1910s and the 1920s turned their backs on the city's Protestants and sought to incorporate fellow Catholic ethnics into a broad new pan-ethnic Catholic Americanism.

The answers to these questions do not lie in the process of change in the everyday life of the Worcester Irish over the *longue durée* wrought by a new generation, or at least not in that process alone. Rather, these answers can be found in another process, the process of how the Worcester Irish negotiated day-by-day their relations with their ethnic neighbors. The central dynamic of these relations was Irish competition for power and resources with Worcester's many ethnic groups. Those groups included the "host group," the city's Yankees, who themselves were changing rapidly as they responded to the seismic economic and cultural changes of the turn of the century period, and other immigrants and ethnics, particularly the Swedes, French Canadians, and British, who arrived in Worcester in great numbers in the 1870s and 1880s, and the Italians, Poles, and Lithuanians who flooded the city in the 1900s and 1910s. Alignments among these groups are not easy to summarize simply. They shifted often as older groups broke open over political, cultural, or economic issues and reunited as those issues disappeared or members felt more threatened from outside; or as new groups arrived in the city upsetting old balances of power; or even as the rules of competition, like city charters or state election laws, were revised. Moreover, relations among ethnic groups in Worcester were never forged in local isolation. They always took place against a larger backdrop, shaped and reshaped by trends, events, and power struggles occurring on a national or even international level: economic booms and busts, wars, and decisions by presidents, popes, and even British parliaments. As Worcester's Irish changed their strategies for relating to their neighbors to take account of these contingencies, they were compelled, in turn, to rethink conceptions of their own identity or even of their own community boundaries. Who they thought their enemies were and who they thought their friends were, powerfully influenced who they thought they were; as the identity and alignments of their enemies and friends changed over time so did their conceptions of their own identity.[16]

Hence, the Worcester Irish displayed confusion in their search for practical approaches to relate to their neighbors and appropriate definitions of who they were. In the 1880s, liberal currents in their church, Parnell's ascendancy in the Irish nationalist movement, and, most importantly, local political alliances with Yankee factions encouraged Worcester Irishmen eager to embrace American culture and reconcile differences with their Protestant neighbors. The Worcester Irish at that time had little use for their "foreign" French Canadian coreligionists, who were too few to be useful allies and seemed merely an obstacle to Irish efforts to create an Americanized Catholicism acceptable to non-Catholics. The American-born, as noted, despite still being a minority of the community's adult population, felt most comfortable with the trends of the 1880s and were thus the most energetic participants in them through their temperance societies. Immigrant advocates of an aggressive ethnocentrism, whether Hibernians or militant nationalists, could never mount a sustained challenge to the largely American-born accommodationists in this atmosphere.

But in the 1890s the Vatican cracked down on Catholic Liberalism, Parnell was disgraced and then died, a brutal depression intensified economic competition, as new groups moved into Worcester threatening Irish neighborhoods and jobs, nativism revived, and the local Irish alliance with Yankees fell apart. In these circumstances, the spirit of accommodation died, and the disillusioned second-generation temperance men abandoned their societies. Such conditions, however, roused the immigrant Hibernians, whose arguments for Irish ethnic assertion and efforts to revive Irish culture seemed now to make better sense.

In the twentieth century the tide shifted within the community again. Persisting local Irish political rivalry with Yankees and other Protestants, hardening lines of social and economic exclusion protecting the Protestant elite, continued Vatican suspicions of non-Catholics, and revivals of nativism in the 1920s kept the religious battle between Catholics and Protestants alive in the twentieth century. Irish cultural ethnocentrism, however, had little appeal for the American-born Irish as the new generation began to dominate the Irish community. It also made little strategic sense to them as they struggled to compete with Yankees and other Protestants for control of the city and needed new Catholic ethnics like the French, Italians, and Poles as allies in this struggle. Led by the American-born generation, the Worcester Irish thus began to construct a pan-ethnic, militant American Catholicism that seemed to better fit the circumstances of an environment that had changed yet once again. A stunning explosion of Irish American nationalism at the end of World War I that drew on all generations of the Worcester Irish did not slow the broadening pervasiveness of this new pan-ethnic militant American Catholicism in Worcester's Irish community. Irish nationalism faded quickly as the unique circumstances that caused its rise disappeared, and it would never again be as important to the Worcester Irish. Militant American Catholicism would remain, more or less, the dominant definition of strategy, identity, and boundaries for the Worcester Irish until social, political, and economic changes swept it, and much else in American life and culture, away in the 1960s.

Because the two processes—changes in everyday life over generations and changes in relations between groups that unfolded daily—are better measured over different units of time, they are more easily analyzed separately. This book is organized, therefore, in two sections. The first section's two chapters, on the immigrant and second-generation Irish respectively, document and analyze the numbers, economic achievements, family life, residential patterns, and cultural perspectives of the two generations. These chapters reveal the differences between the two generations and point out the important influences shaping their varying customs and norms. The next three chapters in the second section explore changes in Irish life in Worcester through the events of "historical time." These chapters depict how the economic and political environment the Worcester Irish confronted changed over time, and how they responded to its opportunities and constraints and crafted strategies and definitions of themselves in response to changing circumstances. These chapters trace these strategies and definitions by examining Irish institutional and associational life, community rituals such as holiday parades, and the participation of the Worcester Irish in efforts to free Ireland in the three periods of accommodation, ethnic revival, and the building of the new militant Catholic Americanism.[17]

One question remains, however. How much can the experience of the Irish in Shannon's native city tell us about the larger history of the entire group in the United States? Put another way, how typical was the experience of the Worcester Irish of the American Irish experience generally?

It is clear that the Worcester Irish participated in the broad array of major movements that marked Irish American life in the late nineteenth and early twentieth centuries. As noted, the Land League, the Friends of Irish Freedom, liberal Catholicism, and militant American Catholicism all took root at one time or another in Worcester. The Irish there, like Irish men and women in many cities across the country, were also fighting their way to leadership in municipal politics and labor unions.

The experiences of the Irish in Worcester were similar to those of Irish elsewhere because the Irish in Worcester confronted many of the same economic trends and reacted to the same political events and movements as Irishmen in other cities and towns across the nation. Like most other cities and towns in America, Worcester was being integrated into a broad national, and even international economy in the late nineteenth century. The people of Worcester were part of a national political system as well as a local one, and, indeed, Irish Americans in Worcester as elsewhere also participated in two international political systems: Irish nationalist politics and struggles for power within the Catholic church. In both cases the Worcester Irish, like their Celtic contemporaries in cities and towns as nearby as Boston and as distant as Butte, Montana, had to respond to shifts in power balances or policy decisions made very far away from the United States of America.

Though Irish Americans in all parts of the country had much in common at the turn of the century, the specific environment of turn of the century Worcester clearly had a profound effect on the experience of its Irish people. Recent research suggests that the key environmental influences on ethnic development are the vitality of local economies and the breadth of opportunities that they afforded; the rules of politics; the ethnic origins, power, and endurance of local elites; and the time of arrival, cultural predilections, and numbers of other immigrant or racial groups. The Irish in Worcester, for example, suffered from a local economy that was reaching maturity and thus growing more slowly and providing fewer opportunities for mobility than cities with more dynamic economies in the west and elsewhere. The Irish in Worcester also encountered an entrenched Yankee population already rooted in the town for a century or more before the first Irish Catholics appeared. Irish experiences in Worcester were profoundly influenced by their relations with these Yankees. In the 1880s the Irish were able to exploit divisions in the ranks of the Yankee elite. That elite became more unified through the early twentieth century, however, as it tightened its grip on the city's economy and society despite a vast expansion of markets and a revolution in industrial production techniques and management systems in Worcester as in the country generally. By the 1920s the Yankee elite itself proved very adept in exploiting Irish factions to control growing Irish political power. The mix of other ethnic groups in the city would also prove critical in influencing the evolution of the Worcester Irish. Thousands of Swedes and French Canadians poured into Worcester in the late nineteenth century, giving the city's ethnic composition a distinct cast very different from that in nearby Boston, and thus creating a complicated political and social dynamic that was unique as well. The large number of Protestant Swedes, favored by Worcester's Yankee manufacturers and bitterly antagonistic toward the Irish, made it difficult for union men to build a unified labor movement in Worcester. The Swedes and French Canadians as well as the large numbers of new immigrants who flooded the city in the early twentieth century from Italy, Poland, and Lithuania also made it necessary for Worcester Irishmen to negotiate their way to political power among a number of different ethnic groups, rather than simply seize control of the city, as their Boston Irish contemporaries did, through the mobilization of their own people.[18]

The environment of the Worcester Irish was important not only for who was there, but also for who was not there—or not there in great numbers. In cities like San Francisco with large nonwhite Asian populations or St. Louis, or even New York, where African Americans became increasingly important presences, the advantages of whiteness and a white identity loomed large for Irish Americans. Worcester had a tiny Chinese population and a long-established but small, and only slowly growing, African American one. Thus, though the Worcester Irish understood the advantages that their whiteness bequeathed them, they rarely talked about it and even more rarely acted to assert it. Being white, and the boundary between black or yellow and white, had less meaning for the Irish in Worcester, where few nonwhite "others" lived and could not even be imagined as significant competitors.[19]

Was the experience of the Worcester Irish, then, typical of turn of the century Irish America? No, if only because the experience of the Irish in no city was, or could have been, typical. The contrast between the experience of the Irish in Worcester at the turn of the century depicted here and of the Irish in Butte, Montana, in the very same period, superbly recounted by David Emmons in his *Butte Irish*, makes this point very clear. Some of the broad trends affecting the two cities were the same, most notably the economic revolution in markets and corporate structures, and the influx of thousands of new immigrants. Yet the local environments were very different and thus the experience of the Irish in the two cities differed too. In Butte, Irish owners of the major local industry, the copper mines, created an ethnic economic niche for loyal Irish workers and nourished that loyalty with a fierce Irish American nationalism that helped bind owner and permanent workers closer together through the early twentieth century. That niche, undermined by corporate changes and overwhelmed by new immigrants in the 1900s and 1910s ultimately cracked and threw the Irish community into confusion. In Worcester control of the economy was in Yankee hands from the outset and thus group relations took a very different path in the Massachusetts city. The Worcester Irish, as noted, went through a variety of strategies and conceptions of their ethnic identity, including Americanist accommodation and efforts to forge a militant Catholic Americanism that never appeared in Butte.[20]

The contrast between the Butte and Worcester Irish points up, once again, that there was no typical Irish American experience—as the experiences of the Irish in all the other "untypical" cities like New York, Chicago, Lowell, or Denver also make clear. Nevertheless, it also underlines a more important point: that the history of ethnic groups is understood best by exploring the complicated ways in which broad national trends interacted with unique local circumstances to shape ethnic adjustments. It is there that we are most likely to find out what it meant to be Irish, or, as the history of the Worcester Irish at the turn of the century teaches us, what the changing meanings of being Irish were in changing environments. It is there in William Shannon's hometown, and in the experiences of his parents and their fellow Irish Americans, that we can begin to find the answers to some of the questions he left unanswered over thirty years ago.

One

The Immigrant Irish

It should have seemed the same. On a relief map the hills and ridges rise in the same darkening colors, the myriad streams and rivers trace similar spider webs and squiggles of blue. Traveling through the countryside, the streams and small rivers splashing down hillsides into valleys and ravines, ridges and low mountains, thickets and bright wildflowers, green grass and the rocks, rocks everywhere, outcroppings hinting at vast hidden mountains of stone, or boulders scattered about fields—it should have looked like home to them. This was central New England in the United States of America but there should have been hints of the Slieve Mish mountains of west Kerry here, the flood plain of the Main river, the rolling country east of Lough Corrib in Galway, or parts of Sligo or Mayo in the west of Ireland, or Louth or Longford further east. As anxious Irish immigrants peered out the windows of their cars on trains chugging north from New York through the hills and over the small streams of Connecticut and Massachusetts they should have found something familiar and reassuring here.

It was not the same, however, and they knew it, and many spent their lives mourning the differences that reminded them of their loss. It was not just the bogs they missed, or the clouds that gathered and hugged Ireland's small mountains or the yellow gorse and the jackdaws. And it was not just the new country's abundance of trees (Ireland had long lost most of its trees, but New England, shorn of much of its forests by 1830, was enjoying the spread of a new growth fifty years later), or the heavy snowfalls (life in Worcester came to a virtual halt when three to four feet of snow, drifting to eight feet, fell in a massive blizzard in March of 1888), or even the sharply fluctuating temperatures, colder than the Ireland they remembered in winter, and far hotter than their homeland in the summer.[1]

It was not any of that so much, for the natural differences were not that dramatic, certainly not as sharply different as the Rocky Mountains that closed in around the Celts in Butte or Denver, or the vast prairies that lapped up around the urban neighborhoods of the Irish in Chicago or St. Paul (not to mention the veldt in South Africa or the dusty outbacks of Australia). Irishmen went everywhere in the world in the nineteenth and twentieth centuries and the natural environments of many parts of the world or even America must have seemed exotic to them, but Worcester County in the center of Massachusetts and New England should not have been one of them.

It was not the physical differences or the climate, or perhaps it was them, but only because they symbolized the deeper difference, the difference between home and exile. Ireland was home; their claim to it extended far back into the mists of some ancient unknown time (mists that obscured that the Irish in Ireland were themselves the descendants of many migrant groups still reflected in their names: the Celtic Meaghers and the Norman Burkes, for example). The markers of their history, of their possession, were back there in Ireland, sharpened by distance into hallowed icons of poignant, aching memory. For Eugene Moriarty, born in Castlemaine in west Kerry there were the battered walls of the castle of the Moriartys just off the road from Castlemaine to Dingle. For Henry McDermott from Louth there was the graveyard high up on the hill at Faughart that looked far to the east over the port of Dundalk and the sea. McDermott's ancestors were buried in that graveyard, set down in the earth around a church founded by St. Bridget in the sixth century and lying in graves next to the tomb of William Bruce, slain in battle at the foot of the hill in 1317. It was a landscape littered with pieces of an ancient past and suffused with the myths and stories of history, their history.[2]

Ireland and Worcester: Background to an Encounter

It was not just the difference between home and exile that separated Ireland and New England for them, not just the difference between a landscape filled with thousands of years of their history and an alien place with no meaning or associations for Irishmen. It was not just the traces of the past embedded in those landscapes. It was how the two cultures inhabited, used, and built upon those landscapes in the present that also made them radically and profoundly different and made Irish newcomers to New England feel so out of place.

Those differences in turn were rooted in how Ireland and New England were being made and remade by a vast economic revolution that had been transforming Western civilization. Though that revolution originated just across the Irish Sea in England, Ireland was drawn into it slowly. Throughout the eighteenth century only parts of Ireland participated, but over the course of the nineteenth century more and more of the island was drawn into the larger English market. New roads and railroads began crisscrossing Ireland, poking into remote valleys, cutting through ridges and mountain passes, slowly but inexorably tying the Irish people ever more tightly into the English economy. By the late nineteenth century, much of Irish agriculture had become set in a pattern of provisioning England with cattle and dairy products, and receiving in return English manufactured goods like clothes and furniture, or overseas goods like tea or tobacco, imported and processed through English ports.[3]

This integration touched off enormous changes in Irish life—erosion of the old Gaelic culture, changes in Irish inheritance and marital customs, even a religious revival—but what is more striking is the change that did not happen. Except for the Belfast area in eastern Ulster, Ireland's integration into the English market did not drag the island into the growing ranks of the urbanizing, industrializing countries of the West. Indeed, it had the opposite effect on southern Ireland; it drowned backward Irish industries there in a sea of cheap British goods and reduced most of southern Ireland to a permanent agricultural colony of industrial England. As industries stagnated in the south, cities there did too. Only Belfast in the north grew at the rapid rates enjoyed by most English and American cities in the nineteenth century; the populations of Cork, Limerick, Waterford, even Dublin in the south increased much more slowly, where they increased at all. The southern Irish landscape—its crude peasant homes and mean villages were hardly the pastoral idyll that its Worcester exiles would remember—remained a rural landscape.[4]

New England, particularly central New England, followed a very different path. Roads and canals cut through Middlesex and Worcester counties at the end of the eighteenth century and linked the regions and towns into an ever widening market. At the same time, local farmers, eager for new sources of cash, became increasingly aware of the limited profitablity of agriculture dependent on stony New England land. The lure of markets and the need to find new sources of income inspired local artisans and farmers working as part-time craftsmen to vastly expand their production of all sorts of goods. Carrying their chairs, clocks, shoes, books, and other products to new customers, these artisans or farmers turned craftsmen clogged Worcester County's new roads at the turn of the nineteenth century. Soon small carding or spinning mills appeared on the Quinnebaug, the Blackstone, the Nashua, and a host of other streams and rivers throughout central Massachusetts. Lowell, Lawrence, and Holyoke, instant cities and important centers of textile or paper production erected de novo on the flood plains of the Merrimack or the Connecticut rivers by Boston capital, attracted more attention. The hundreds of carding, spinning, and other mills churning away in Worcester County towns and villages like Leicester, Webster, Millbury, Uxbridge, and Sturbridge, however, better exemplified the revolution that propelled New England to the forefront of industrial development in the Western world.[5]

The town of Worcester participated in this revolution, but no more or less than neighboring villages, until the 1820s when merchants from Providence with the enthusiastic support of their counterparts in Worcester contracted to build a canal linking the two communities. In the next decade one of the nation's first railroads, the Boston and Worcester, represented at its opening in 1835 by a tiny steam locomotive imported from England and a converted stagecoach mounted on iron wheels, began an even more important transportation revolution. By the late 1840s Worcester was already the hub of a rail network that extended to almost all important points of the compass, a network that would one day win it the nickname of the "Chicago of New England." Industrial and commercial development kept pace. Growth was so rapid that Charles Dickens remarked after visiting Worcester in 1842 that "all the buildings looked as if they had been built and painted that morning and could be taken down on Monday with very little trouble . . . it would have been the better for an old church, better still for some old graves." By 1890 the city was the thirteenth largest manufacturing city in America, its population had risen to nearly 85,000, and it dominated central New England.[6]

Still, visitors from more cosmopolitan cities like Boston or New York might have found Worcester little more than an overgrown small town then. The downtown was undistinguished, an embarassment to its boosters, who lamented its rutted streets and the absence of first-class hotels. The city was also small in area, densely packed into a circle with a diameter of less than four miles through the 1880s and 1890s. There were still many farms in the city of Worcester in those days, and open fields and woods abounded within the official city limits outside that tight circle of settlement.[7]

Irish immigrants travelling to Worcester, however, had different points of comparison than did visitors from Boston or New York. After arriving in Worcester and descending from the train, they could see that they had entered a new world. It was not the hilly terrain—they knew hills—but what had been done to it that would be most striking to them. Built almost always of red brick, two or more stories high, mills and factories seemed everywhere. Most of them ran along the city's north-south railroad spine and were clustered at the head of the old abandoned canal in the center of the city just east of Main Street, and then ran east again along the railroad tracks that went on to Boston. Worcester's early factories had run on water power, but the city's few streams were too small to support any but the smallest factories. Steam was the motive force that made Worcester's industry possible, and the acrid smoke lifting out of thickets of smokestacks testified to it. Surrounding the mills on the east side of the city or packed in among them were the houses of the city's workers. Almost all were wooden: in the early 1880s most were small, shoebox-like workingmen's cottages; by the late 1880s and 1890s "three-deckers," three apartments stacked on top of each other in a single detached tenement, had become numerous. Most streets were unpaved (Worcester had only two miles of streets paved by hard block in 1880), muddy and lumpy in rain or snow and choked with dust in sunshine. They were also crowded with wagons, carriages, and omnibuses. Horsecars appeared in the 1860s but the lines did not extend very far even as late as 1885. The city's transportation revolution would wait on electric streetcars in the 1890s.[8]

It was, in all, an average industrial city by American standards, dynamic and earnest but small and provincial. Yet to Irish immigrants, the crowds, energy, and dense settlement were a striking and perhaps fearful change from the quiet countryside of their youth. For them, life would be very different here.

Irish immigrants streamed into Worcester all through the nineteenth century. They left an Ireland that was rapidly changing. Much of an older Celtic Ireland seemed to be disappearing as the Gaelic (or Irish) language eroded, education improved, and religious discipline tightened. The Irishmen who arrived in Worcester, then, seemed different from the Famine immigrants, and to some observers not much different from most of the city's longtime residents.

Yet they had much more in common with earlier immigrants than was immediately apparent, and remained very different than Worcester's Yankees or even its American-born ethnics. As much as Ireland changed, it remained the same in many essentials. Those essentials, an enduring Irish sense of a separate national identity and a persistent peasant agricultural economy and society, proved more important than all of Ireland's changes in shaping how the immigrants adapted in America. Their sense of being Irishmen in exile would indelibly stamp their identity. Their lack of useful industrial skills and their peasant communal ethos would shape almost every part of their every-day lives from their journey and arrival through their efforts to find work, es-tablish families, and build neighborhood communities. Perhaps in a differ-ent place, like Australia, where opportunities in agriculture were bountiful and easy to grasp, their lack of industrial skills would have been irrelevant, and their communalism, less critical to survival, would have faded into a mere conviviality. But in this place at this time—Worcester, Massachusetts at the turn of the century—a maturing industrial economy and throngs of better-skilled, wealthier competitors made it hard for them to find an easy purchase in the local economy. Their lack of industrial skills was an unqualified handi-cap in Worcester and would hinder their adjustment there at every turn. Their communal ethos was a mixed blessing. Communalism was not very helpful in a society that favored individual ambition and risk-taking, but it softened the blows of a harsh urban industrial world as well, offering family or com-munity strategies for survival even as it helped retard individual mobility.

Three Waves of Green to Worcester

Perhaps no fact about Irish immigration to the United States was more im-pressive than its constant flow throughout the nineteenth and early twentieth centuries. In no year between 1841 and 1914 did the number of Irish immi-grants arriving in America fall below 20,000. Yet this was not an unbroken, un-differentiated stream of exiles. There was a distinct periodization in the Irish emigration to America, a periodization apparent in the types of immigrants, their reasons for leaving, their numbers, and the culture they brought to the United States. Those periods include: 1820s to 1845, the first wave of emigrants from Ireland to contain a large number of Catholics; 1846 to 1870, the Famine and post-Famine emigration; and 1870 to 1922, the modern migration.[9]

The first wave is, perhaps, less well known than the others, obscured espe-cially by the more dramatic Famine flight that came immediately after it. Through the eighteenth century emigration from Ireland to the United States had been largely an Ulster Protestant migration. It was not until the 1820s that the penetration of the market into reaches of southern Ireland, the establish-ment of new transportation connections between Liverpool and America, and the downturn in agricultural prices following the Napoleonic wars pro-voked the Catholic Irish to uproot themselves and move to America in large numbers.[10]

The first Irish Catholics came to Worcester in 1826 to build the Blackstone Canal. They were seasoned construction workers, most of them having labored on the Erie Canal in New York and on major public works in England. Originally, however, they had come from moderately prosperous farming families in the English-speaking counties of eastern and southern Ireland. After completing work on the canal, many of them settled in Worcester, to take advantage of the city's growing commercial and industrial prosperity or to use the town as a base for ventures in railroad construction work throughout New England. By the late 1830s or early 1840s, the 500 to 600 "pioneer" Irish had established a thriving little community in Worcester, which included their own church, clubs, schools, and even a small symphony orchestra.[11]

By the end of the 1840s, however, a natural disaster struck Ireland, and the subsequent wave of immigrants transformed Irish America. A blight, probably originating on the east coast of Canada, swept across the North Atlantic and ravaged the potato crops of Ireland. Estimates of deaths from the ensuing famine range from 600,000 or 700,000 to 1.2 million. Many, perhaps most, died officially of diseases such as typhus, dysentery, scurvy, or "famine dropsy," but the root cause in almost all instances was a lack of food. Those that could escape, did. One and a half million fled to North America and cities like Worcester between 1845 and 1855.[12]

Between 1840 and 1850, the city's Irish population increased nearly five times, from 600 to over 3,000. Nearly 200 of the famine immigrants arrived in the city mortally afflicted by typhus or dysentery. The others were little better off, ill-fitted by Irish experience for city life or anything but the rudest kind of labor. The old Irish immigrants, the canal workers and most of those who had followed them to Worcester in the 1830s and 1840s, had come from the modernizing eastern and southern coastal regions of Ireland. Even in 1845, two-thirds of Worcester's Irish immigrants were from Ireland's eastern or southern counties of Cork, Tipperary, Wexford, or Waterford and most of the rest were from West Meath, Kildare, Dublin, and Carlow. Just five years later, half of Worcester's Irish-born came from the very poorest and most traditionally Gaelic counties of Mayo, Galway, and Sligo in the western province of Connaught, or from the remote western reaches of Donegal in Ulster and Kerry in Munster. Mayo on the northwest coast counted more Irish immigrants in Worcester than any other county by the 1850s. It was these immigrants, many of them Gaelic speakers steeped in a traditional peasant culture, who were uprooted by the Famine, demoralized by its devastation, and launched on a tide of emigration that deposited them in Worcester, a booming industrial city that had no use for their meager skills.[13]

It is no surprise, then, that their adaptation went badly. The Famine refugees struggled not only with Worcester's unfamiliar industrial economy, urban

living conditions, and Yankee hostility, but with their fellow Irishmen, the pioneer Irish. The newcomers, alienated from the older Irish immigrants by cultural differences, also found themselves dependent on these same Celtic pio-
neers for construction jobs and tenement housing. There were differences,
too, over how to help the old country in the midst of the Famine crisis. Resentment built quickly in the middle 1840s, and on Palm Sunday in 1847 Worcester's new Irish immigrants erupted in a rebellion against the old Irish settlers.
Throughout that day, the newcomers rampaged through Worcester's Irish
neighborhoods, attacking the homes of their pioneer Irish landlords and
bosses. Over the next four or five years, Worcester's Irish community dissolved into anarchy, as gangs, most of them rooted in loyalties to counties or
regions in Ireland, roamed the streets of the city's east-side Irish slum.[14]

By the mid-1850s the conflicts within Worcester's Irish community had
played themselves out, but the Famine immigration had transformed Worcester's Irish community. Many of the pioneer Irish left the city, but new Irish immigrants continued to pour into Worcester. By 1870, there were 8,589 Irish-
born in the city, a little over one-fifth of Worcester's 41,000 people.[15]

Depression in the United States and rising agricultural prosperity in Ireland reduced the rush of immigrants to the United States and Worcester in
the 1870s, and it would never again be as large as in the Famine and post-
Famine years, from the 1840s through the early 1860s. As late as 1900, nearly
a third of Worcester's Irish-born were old immigrants who had arrived in the
United States during the 1840s, 1850s, and 1860s. Moreover, Worcester's Irish-
born population grew steadily older in the late nineteenth century. Overall,
nearly a third of Worcester's Irish immigrants in 1880, and over two-fifths in
1900 were age 45 or older.[16]

If Irish immigration into Worcester slowed in the late nineteenth century,
however, it did not stop. At the beginning of the twentieth century, half of
all the Irish immigrants in Worcester had emigrated to America after 1880.
Migration to America had become a routine necessity forced by permanent
changes in Irish agriculture. Changes in the market for Irish agricultural
products, following transportation improvements and accelerated by the
Famine, wiped away the farmers on tiny plots who had grown grain and the
agricultural laborers who were needed to harvest it. Irish peasants who could
adapt turned from producing grains to raising dairy cattle, a change that required larger holdings and little labor. No farmer could continue the practice
of partible inheritance, splitting up their farms for all their sons, as many had
done in the old tillage economy. Nor could those sons or other landless men
find work nearby. There was, therefore, a constant exodus of young men to
America. Irish immigration had become institutionalized.[17]

Most women, as well, had limited opportunities in Ireland. Indeed, they were, perhaps, worse off than their brothers, for only a few could find marriageable men or at least men with prospects of inheriting land, and Ireland's largely agricultural economy could not provide them with jobs. Irish women thus emigrated to America in great numbers; in some years in the late nineteenth century more Irish women left for America than Irish men.[18]

These changes did not occur all at once all over Ireland, and migration patterns therefore varied across the island. As in virtually all other changes in Ireland's economy and society, the conversion of Irish agriculture from tillage to pasture and the consequent transformation of inheritance practices began in the east and spread slowly west. Yet inexorable expansion of the market through railroads and new roads slowly dragged all of Ireland into the new economy. When the agricultural market collapsed in the late 1870s, emigration also rose dramatically again. This time vast numbers fled from the western province of Connaught and west Munster, areas that had been particularly hard hit by the new agricultural distress. Those areas became a principal source of the new emigration over the last two decades of the nineteenth and much of the twentieth century.[19]

The stream of Irish emigrants to Worcester after 1870 reflected most of the general trends in Irish migration to America in that period. Most left Ireland in their late teens or early twenties and came to America alone or with friends or siblings: Irish immigrants living in Worcester in 1900 had left Ireland at the age of twenty, on the average. Presumably, then, they were the sons who would not inherit the family farm and the daughters who could not find an heir to wed. As in emigration generally, women also made up a substantial proportion of Worcester's recent Celtic exiles. Indeed, because of the influx of new female immigrants and high mortality among older Irish-born males, Irish-born women outnumbered Irish-born men in Worcester by 56 percent to 44 percent by 1900. Finally, scattered sources suggest that Irish immigration to Worcester in the late nineteenth century drew heavily from the western regions of Ireland, particularly west Kerry, Mayo, Sligo, and Galway.[20]

"They Seem a Part of Us":
Change in Irish Immigrant Culture in Worcester

By the beginning of the twentieth century, Irish immigration to Worcester had gone on for so many years that some Yankee observers no longer seemed to notice the arrival of Celtic newcomers. The Board of Trade's *Worcester Magazine* suggested in 1901 that Irishmen seemed little different from the natives: "our Irish friends have been with us so long that they seem a part of us." In mid-century the Irish had, of course, been very visible in Worcester, but Irish immigrants in the late nineteenth century appeared to be different people than their predecessors of a half century earlier. The new immigrants came from a different Ireland where the vestiges of an older Gaelic, peasant culture were being washed away by the relentless spread of English mass culture.[21]

One of the most notable changes in Irish culture was the change in language. English usage became common throughout most of eastern Ireland by the early nineteenth century. The Famine cataclysm uprooted many Irish peasants from areas in the west and elsewhere where English had made few or only recent inroads. Many of the Irish who came to Worcester in the 1840s may have understood a smattering of English, but they were still Gaelic speakers. Over the course of the nineteenth century English spread progressively over almost all of Ireland. By 1901, only one in seven men and women in Ireland spoke Gaelic and all but a tiny proportion of them understood English. Not surprisingly, then, census records suggest that virtually all Irish immigrants in Worcester spoke English.[22]

Much of the old Gaelic folk culture also declined in the late nineteenth century. Traditional music and dancing flourished in early nineteenth-century rural Ireland, and a kind of raucousness, punctuated by violence, also marked life in rural Ireland in the early nineteenth century. Fairs were particularly infamous for drinking and fighting. Such scenes contrasted sharply with the quieter, or what some observers thought, starchily respectable, even culturally impoverished, rural Ireland of the late nineteenth century. Sir Horace Plunket observed wistfully in 1905 that "the national customs, culture and recreations which made the country a pleasant place to live have almost disappeared." In their place as Kerby Miller notes, "English middle class standards of music, sports and pastimes" had seemed to take hold. Lawrence McCaffrey has argued that the raucous joviality of Irish rural life, its "zip and flamboyance" had gone out of the Irish character by the end of the nineteenth century as well, yielding to a "more refined and controlled Irish personality."[23]

Once lost or weakened in Ireland, the older folk culture could scarcely flourish in American industrial cities like Worcester. Irish sports in Worcester revealed the decline of the old folk culture well. Before the 1890s, games like hurling took place infrequently in Worcester. To revive interest in the old sports, Richard O'Flynn and other Irish immigrants organized a great Gaelic sports day in July of 1880. The climax of the day was a hurling match, Ireland's traditional sport. Thirty-two players represented Ireland's thirty-two counties on two teams. The symbolism was perfect; the game was not. The Worcester correspondent for the *Boston Globe,* Irish-born Eugene Moriarty, reported that none of the players could have hit the "side of a mountain" with a hurley ball, much less score a goal. Unsure of what to do, the men seemed to wander about or "pile up in heaps" on the field. Moriarty found it comical, but the players were indignant at his criticism. One of them, Jerry Horan, an immigrant himself, complained that he and the other participants did not pretend to be great hurlers, "but when the game was talked of as a game that was played by their great-grandfathers they came up manfully."[24]

One reason for the decline of the old Gaelic folk culture in Ireland was the dramatic change in the Irish educational system. The penal laws of the early eighteenth century banned all but Protestant forms of education for Catholics in Ireland. These laws were rarely enforced, but because some Catholic children and their schoolmasters met in fields behind hedges or clusters of boulders to escape government detection such schools were called "hedge schools." Richard O'Flynn, who emigrated from the township of Grenane in Waterford to America in 1851 and to Worcester in 1858, remembered his grandmother showing him where she claimed she went to school behind the shelter of some bushes. She also pointed out a rock where she told him one of the children acted as a lookout to warn against the approach of British authorities. By the late eighteenth century official bans on Catholic schools had been repealed, but through the first few decades of the nineteenth century most schools for Catholics in Ireland continued to be privately run, makeshift affairs, holding their classes in rude quarters and pursuing irregular curricula. Historians estimate that 300,000 to 400,000 children were being educated in such schools in the mid-1820s.[25]

Richard O'Flynn himself attended one of these schools as a boy in Waterford, and his experience was probably typical. Writing in 1900 he remembered his school as a rectangular, roughhewn cottage, benches set against the wall and heated by a turf fire (students were expected to bring turf with them to school each day). The master tried to separate girls and boys and was "quick to knock down boys, rap them on the open palm or even kick them in the shins" to maintain order. The classes remained chaotic, however, with a cacophony of simultaneous recitations from a variety of lessons, the barefoot children in their tattered frieze and corduroy trying to elbow past each other to get close to the fire, and the exasperated master alternately pleading and screaming at his young charges in both Gaelic and English. Under such circumstances it is probably not surprising that one of O'Flynn's classmates took six months to learn his ABCs. O'Flynn himself could attend school only for the three years between ten and thirteen. Still, the peasant children and their parents made significant sacrifices to pick up even this little bit of learning. O'Flynn reported, for example, that several poor children "who lived far away . . . did not eat until evening" every day that they attended school.[26]

In 1831 the government of the United Kingdom worked a revolution in Irish education when it instituted a national system of publicly financed local schools. The growth of the new system was slow at first, but in the ten years between 1838 and 1848, the number of students attending the new national schools tripled, from 169,000 to 500,000. By the last decades of the nineteenth century, the national schools dominated education in Ireland. The Irish national system was not uniform, but it gave the Irish masses a grounding in basic educational skills. Dramatic improvement in the literacy rate was proof of their effectiveness, rising from about 50 percent in 1851 to over 85 percent in 1901; the literacy rate in Ireland by the latter date was higher than in either Britain or the United States. Worcester's late nineteenth-century Irish immigrants reflected these improvements in Irish education. Between 1880 and 1900, for example, the literacy rate jumped from 70 percent to 88 percent among Irish-born adults over age eighteen in Worcester.[27]

Changes in the Catholic church contributed to this transformation of Irish culture as well. Before the Famine, the church, only recently released from the oppressive restrictions of the penal laws, had few chapels or priests and little discipline or organization. The people's faith mixed folk belief, superstition, magic, and agrarian customs and festivals freely with Catholic tenets and rituals. Only a minority of peasants attended mass regularly in Ireland before the Famine. In 1834 church attendance in Irish-speaking districts in the west rarely exceeded 40 percent and more often averaged only 20 percent or 30 percent. Priests were often hailed as local symbols of opposition to the British oppressor, or feared or venerated for their magical or spiritual powers. In the 1850s, peasants in Faughart in Louth spoke of the ability of a local curate, Henry Doogan, to freeze men like stones or chase away apparitions of monkeys hanging in the trees.[28]

About the middle of the nineteenth century, Catholicism in Ireland began to change dramatically. Indeed, in the phrase of Emmet Larkin, the church experienced a "devotional revolution." The Famine's horrors and effects on the old Gaelic culture may have helped provoke it, but a rigorous self-discipline (at least sexual self-discipline) demanded by the new agricultural system made it permanent. Led by the zealous ultramontane archbishop of Dublin, Paul Cullen, the Irish were also inspired by Rome's new interest in devotions. Church attendance shot up throughout Ireland; the discipline of priests tightened; and lay devotional sodalities and confraternities multiplied. An important index of the change was a vast increase in the number of vocations. Between 1840 and 1900, the proportion of priests in the Irish population rose from one in 3,000 to one in 900 and the proportion of nuns from one in 6,500 to one in 400.[29]

The relationship of Irish immigrants to the church in Worcester reflected these trends in the Catholicism of the old country. Many of the immigrants from the west of Ireland who poured into Worcester in the 1840s were steeped in the traditions of their region's folk Catholicism. In Worcester, however, they found an English-born pastor, Matthew Gibson, who knew little and cared less for their cherished customs. In the battle between the eastern Irish and the westerners which convulsed Worcester's Irish districts in the 1840s, Father Gibson would be a principal focus of antagonism. Loudly decrying the "landlord priest," the recent, western Irish immigrants dragged him from his rectory into the street and manhandled him during the Palm Sunday riot of 1847.[30]

The tumult of the 1840s subsided, however, and never again would Worcester's priests face the same kind of open rebellion from factions in their Irish congregations. Famine immigrants became accustomed to institutional Catholicism in America, and later Irish immigrants, who had some exposure to the devotional revolution at home, were already familiar with the rules of the institutional church and were less disposed to rebellion. Thus though Worcester Irishmen sometimes complained about the cost of supporting their churches, and their priests complained of inattention at mass, there was little open conflict between pastors and their flocks after the 1850s.[31]

Not only did Worcester's Irish immigrants become more docile and devout Catholics over the course of the nineteenth century, the religious life of their churches became less distinctly Irish during that time. The sacred landscape of Ireland, the pilgrimage sites, the holy wells and ruins of old churches that served as sites for "patterns" (devotions to local saints) could not be carried to America. Except for St. Patrick, few local or even national saints from Ireland won any special recognition in the Irish Catholic churches of Worcester, and many immigrants felt that even he was slighted. In 1878 the local clergy refused to name a new church in South Worcester after Patrick or Bridget despite the protests of Irish immigrants like Richard O'Flynn. O'Flynn rose at a Father Mathew Temperance Association meeting to complain that "the money to carry on all the building of Catholic churches in this city comes from the sweat and toil of Irish Catholics [and] yet not one church . . . [is] called after any of their saints, Patrick, Bridget, Columkille. It would appear as if it would be a reproach to so name them." By the turn of the century, devotions to St. Anthony of Padua, St. Theresa of Lisieux, or St. Francis Xavier would become more important in Worcester's Irish churches than prayers to Bridget, Columba, or any Irish saint besides Patrick.[32]

All of these trends, the decline of Gaelic folk culture, the improvement of education, and the Catholic devotional revolution were bound up together and inextricably linked to the integration of Ireland into the British market that transformed Irish agriculture. Trains brought the English language and English games, sports, songs, dances, books, and magazines, as well as British furniture and clothes, into previously isolated parts of Ireland. Economic change thus worked hand in hand with the educational system to alter the cultural tastes and the leisure customs of the Irish peasantry. Schools, often run by the church, instilled the discipline of the new devotional Catholicism. And that discipline, in turn, had been made necessary by an agricultural economy that made some sons wait patiently for years to inherit a farm and marry (and some daughters to await their dowries for the same purpose) and caused other children to dutifully sail away to America. The changes occurring in Ireland were happening on a broad front, dragging the island into some version of modernity and minting a new Irish man and a new Irish woman in the process.

"O My Heart's in Old Ireland Wherever I Go": Continuity in the Identity and Culture of Irish Immigrants

Yet if late nineteenth-century Irish immigrants to Worcester differed from their Famine and pre-Famine predecessors, they felt no more at home in central Massachusetts. The ache of longing and loss and the bitter sense of exile plagued the Irish-born of the late nineteenth century just as it had the Famine emigrés. Richard O'Flynn never forgot his native Waterford. He filled his journals with recollections of his Irish home, and in some forty-odd years after he had left for America those memories still moved him. In 1890 he wrote a poem into the records of the United Irish Societies Convention (O'Flynn was the Convention's secretary):

> Who that has not wandered far
> From where he first drew vital air,
> Can tell how bright the visions are,
> That still surround his fancy there.
> The shamrock, the hawthorne, the white blossom's glow
> For my heart's in Old Ireland wherever I go
> O my heart's in Old Ireland wherever I go

Thomas Kiely, the Irish-born editor of Worcester's local Irish weekly, the *Messenger,* also recalled the old country with a rush of similar pastoral images in

1904: "the scenes and early associations, the sod, hedgerow, thrush, black-bird . . . whitewashed chapel."[33]

The sentiments of O'Flynn and Kiely reflected the tight links and constant reminders of the homeland that filled the lives of Worcester's Irish immigrants. The local Irish weekly, the *Messenger,* carried detailed news of Ireland, county by county, until the 1920s. Priests in Worcester's Irish parishes like Sacred Heart or St. John's also frequently listed relatives and friends from Ireland in the prayers for the dead at Sunday mass in the 1880s and 1890s. Representations of Ireland, especially rural Ireland, appeared often in Worcester entertainments, both those sponsored by the community's institutions or societies and those staged by commercial theaters. Ladies at a Sacred Heart Fair in the 1880s, for example, dressed as Irish peasant maids, and other parishes sponsored stereopticon shows of Irish scenes in the 1890s and 1900s or plays like the "Colleen Bawn" or "The Man from Killarney" set in rural Ireland. These plays also appeared in the commercial theaters. Songs about Ireland filled every church and organization entertainment. Such songs were almost always the melodies of nineteenth-century composers and not ancient Irish folk tunes, but they were songs that wept for the homeland or marched to its cause of national liberation. Thomas Moore's music was especially popular. His works inspired the formation of a Tom Moore club in the city in 1861 and dominated virtually every public concert of Irish music in Worcester through the late nineteenth century. A St. John's parish concert in 1879 was devoted entirely to his music and his songs were featured at a concert of Irish songs in 1888, a Sacred Heart parish concert in 1890, and the citywide St. Patrick's Day celebration of 1895 (four of the seven songs at the latter had been written by Moore).[34]

Nostalgic reminiscences of home might seem natural, but there was a bittersweet quality to the recollections of Irish immigrants that seemed to intensify the passion of their devotion to Ireland. As Kerby Miller has observed, Irish emigrants even in the late nineteenth century often saw their emigration as involuntary, a drastic step forced upon them. This sense of Irish immigrants as "exiles" certainly appeared often among the Irish in Worcester. It seemed common usage even for the American-born Irish editor of the *Worcester Daily Times,* James Mellen, who employed the terms "immigrant" and "exile" interchangeably in describing the feelings of the Irish-born on St. Patrick's Day in 1882. Kiely's reverie on "early associations" in 1904 also sounded the exile theme. Indeed, it was entitled "Exile's Musings."[35]

How many Irish immigrants in Worcester saw themselves as exiles is difficult to determine. The ease with which both first- and second-generation

Irish newspaper editors fell into using the term might suggest its pervasive-ness. In the 1880s and 1890s, particularly, the Irish in Worcester also seemed to describe the Irish-born exclusively as "Irishmen," not Irish Americans, a term apparently reserved for the American-born Irish, or Americans, a definition applied to native-stock Yankees. It seems, then, that the Irish-born were de-fined, and also defined themselves, as different from even their American-born Irish children or cousins.[36]

Irish immigrants to Worcester at the end of the century felt no less tied to their homeland and no less different from their native-stock Yankee hosts than Irish men and women who had arrived fifty or even seventy years before. Yet Ireland had changed dramatically during that time; why then did Irish im-migrants still feel like exiles and outsiders?

For one thing it was politics and economics as much as culture that defined that identity or at least sharpened the edges of its borders, drove down its roots, and fired its intensity. Irish peasants might play English games, read English books, or speak English, but they did not share English interests. The tremendous changes that rocked Ireland through the middle of the nine-teenth century did not immediately or substantially change who governed it. A small aristocracy, largely English in origin and Protestant in religion, and planted on the land at one or another of the many phases of the English conquest, owned most of Ireland's land, represented it in Parliament, and presided over its local government through much of the nineteenth century. Even when the old aristocracy no longer governed in Ireland, British politicians still set policy for Ireland in the Parliament at Westminster and enforced it through the government's bureaucracy in Dublin with the aid of the United Kingdom's army, when it was needed. The imbalance of power in Ireland be-tween English rulers and Irish ruled thus persisted through the changes wrought by the integration of Ireland into the British market. In some re-spects that integration created—or, perhaps, simply worsened—a broader distinction and imbalance between Ireland and England. As Michael Hechter has suggested, as southern Ireland became more, not less, agricultural and England industrialized at a rapid rate the divergence of their interests became increasingly clear. Yet this was a divergence of interests within a relationship of increasing dependency: the colonial, agrarian southern Irish becoming ever more dependent on the industrial metropolitan economy that made the goods they needed and controlled the markets and prices for the crops and cattle they raised.[37]

Mixed in with memories of conquest, rebellion, and suppression, these conflicting interests provided rich nourishment for Irish nationalism. In the second half of the nineteenth century this Irish nationalist sentiment exploded twice. The Fenian conspiracy in the 1860s failed to free Ireland, or even mount a credible threat to English power, but the "incurably verbal" Fenians with their memoirs, speeches, songs, and verses "made republican separatism a vital part of the mid nineteenth century's political language," Roy Foster has suggested. By the 1880s, the nationalist movement would revive on an even grander scale in the Land League and the Irish Parliamentary Party.[38]

Irish immigrants thus came to Worcester acutely conscious of their separate identity and nursing resentments of English oppression at home. Indeed, in their understanding, it was English oppression that had forced them to leave their real home. Andrew Athy, one of Worcester's most prestigious Irish politicians in the late nineteenth century, claimed that he and his family had been forced out of Galway for plotting revolution, and offered himself as living proof of English responsibility for Irish exile. "Downtrodden and despoiled Ireland" had been forced to give up her sons and daughters, James Mellen of the *Times* charged in 1882. Thomas Kiely of the *Messenger* was more specific in 1904: "Saxon oppression" had created exiles "all over the world." "They wept those exiles," Kiely contended, when they thought of their country and their forced departure.[39]

Nevertheless, it was not just a self-conscious sense of an Irish national identity that set Worcester's late nineteenth-century Irish immigrants apart from their Yankee hosts and made them feel different and alien. Despite the deluge of British goods, tastes, and fashions, educational reform, and the spread of the new piety, Gaelic culture had not entirely disappeared in Ireland and not all the "zip" had gone out of the personalities of late nineteenth-century Irish immigrants, as McCaffrey has contended.

The erosion of Gaelic culture had been less complete than it seemed. Though the Irish language had declined in Ireland over the course of the nineteenth century it had not disappeared. Kerby Miller estimates that one-fifth to one-quarter of all Irish immigrants to America in the middle and late nineteenth century (and more from the western provinces) were at least bilingual in Gaelic and English. Undoubtedly, there were many bilingual immigrants among the Irish who came to Worcester in the latter half of the nineteenth century, perhaps a higher proportion than the overall percentages for all Irish immigrants to America, since Worcester seemed to attract a disproportionate number of western Irishmen in that era. In County Kerry, which sent many immigrants to Worcester in the late nineteenth century, 41 percent of the population, for example, were still Gaelic speakers at the end of the nineteenth century. In 1898, a branch of the Gaelic League was founded in Worcester and though it attracted many English speakers who honored the language for its symbolic value, most of the branch's supporters, it appears, were immigrants who had been familiar with Gaelic in the old country. There were other examples of the folk culture's persistence. In 1907 the Ancient Order of Hibernians hired fiddlers and pipers for a summer picnic. Even when expert pipers could not be found, the Worcester Irish improvised. In 1900, women in the AOH Auxiliary convinced violinists and a piccolo player to imitate pipes so they and their escorts could enjoy "fair day" dancing at the club's "Calico Ball." Between the hardy surviving remnants of the older Gaelic culture and the cultural inventions and self-conscious inventions of the nineteenth century, such as Moore's songs, Gaelic sports, and even the revival of the language itself, Worcester's late nineteenth-century Irish immigrants found or made the cultural substance needed for a distinct identity.[40]

The persistence of less self-consciously preserved, fundamental customs such as drinking testified in an even more powerful way to the enduring essentials of rural Irish culture and thus the limits of Ireland's transformation in the latter half of the nineteenth century. The rising living standards and tightening personal discipline that accompanied the development of the new agricultural economy, improvements in education, and the Catholic Church's increasing authority and institutional reach, had worked important changes in the leisure pastimes of rural Ireland over the course of the nineteenth century. "By the end of the century," Elizabeth Malcolm writes, "the prolonged drinking, extending over several days, which had once characterized festivals and fairs was very much a thing of the past." Some anthropologists have argued, however, that changes in Irish agriculture in the nineteenth century made drinking more, not less, essential to rural Irish males. As more and more Irish men postponed marriage through their twenties and even early thirties while waiting to inherit farms, the pub or the tavern became a critical, sometimes the only, source of solace during this prolonged adolescence. Whether for this reason or others, the number of pubs per capita more than doubled in Ireland, and the country's per capita consumption of alcohol increased dramatically relative to other countries over the latter half of the nineteenth century and early years of the twentieth. As Malcolm notes, Ireland remained a rural society and drinking—cleaned up and institutionalized in legal public houses though it might have become—was still tightly woven into rural, peasant culture.[41]

In Worcester Irish immigrants were notorious for their drinking. State statistics reveal that although the Irish-born made up only 6.7 percent of Massachusetts' population in 1908, they comprised 27.3 percent of the people arrested for public intoxication. Some of these Irish drunks achieved a degree of local notoriety in Worcester, a source of ridicule for local Yankees and shame for respectable Irishmen. Richard O'Flynn kept notes, for example, on the career of Jim Daly, a "tough customer" in the 1880s who made policemen "see stars" when they tried to arrest him. One day, Daly fell nearly five flights of stairs after a drunken spree, but got up, dusted himself off, and proceeded to the nearest saloon to begin drinking anew.[42]

Irish men and women not only drank in saloons; they ran them. The Irish dominated the saloon trade in Worcester throughout the latter half of the nineteenth century. In the 1860s and 1870s Massachusetts' "Maine Law" prohibited the sale of liquor, but illegal dives flourished in the basements and kitchens of Irish immigrants in the Island and Washington Square. Legalization and regulation changed saloons and drove out most of the women liquor sellers but it did not affect Irish dominance of the liquor trade. In 1880, half of Worcester's saloonkeepers were Irish immigrants and in 1885 nearly two-thirds of the applicants for liquor licenses in Worcester were first- or second-generation Irishmen.[43]

The appeal of the saloon and drinking thus persisted in the new environment. Indeed, conditions in the new urban industrial culture seemed to encourage Irish drinking. The Irish-owned *Worcester Daily Times* emphasized the saloon's utility as a place of escape for those young workers living in mean and sometimes squalid tenement apartments crowded with children and fellow boarders. Dreary jobs as laborers or factory operatives also seemed an obvious spur to seek out the saloon and its "pleasure." Saloons not only provided escape in the warming effects of alcohol for their customers but also in entertainment. Patrick Curran, who ran the "Little House Round the Corner" was known as "a very good comic singer" who attracted "many gay sports to his place." Other Irish saloonkeepers in Worcester were known for their comic wit, their card tricks, or their sports stories. Gambling was also common in Worcester saloons, and in the 1880s saloonkeepers like Tim Delaney organized surreptitious trips to secret cockfights in neighboring towns.[44]

Yet saloons or pubs were not merely a means of escape. In Ireland, drinking was a central ritual confirming the bonds that tied the men of rural Irish communities together. In Worcester, too, saloons flourished among the Irish, as Roy Rosenzweig has argued, not just as remnants of rural life in Ireland or because they offered an escape from the drudgery of the industrial world but because they were "workingmen's clubs" that embodied, celebrated, and reinforced the ethos of communalism and reciprocity. As Rosenzweig has noted, the dives and shebeens that sprouted throughout Irish neighborhoods in the 1860s and 1870s, with their tables set up in the kitchen or the parlor and their patronage drawn from friends, were more extensions of familial and friendship networks than modern business establishments. When raided by police, owners of these dives like John Mehan or Bridget McCarty invariably protested that they were merely "treating some friends" or enjoying familial company. Such "treating," which lay at the heart of pub life in Ireland, persisted in Worcester even after saloons were transformed into larger, more respectable businesses through government regulation and high license fees. Many saloons were headquarters or centers of long-standing friendship networks that sometimes became formalized as branches of Irish ethnic associations such as the Ancient Order of Hibernians, but saloonkeepers also worked hard to integrate newcomers into the saloon's fellowship. Richard O'Flynn, a teetotaller, grudgingly admitted the genuine affability and generosity of many of Worcester's Irish saloonowners. He described Dennis Leonard, for example, as "honest and upright . . . charitable, generous to the needy," William Molloy as "a warmhearted, genial man, a harmless man obsessed with St. Columkille's prophecy for the redemption of Ireland," and Jeremiah Foley as a "genial, good natured and patriotic" backer of Irish causes and devout supporter of Catholic charities. Even some of the Irish women shebeen owners won O'Flynn's praise. He described Margaret Long, keeper of a "rum shop" as "well liked for her kind and genial manners," and Mary Cassidy as a heavy drinker, but "in other respects, she was a good neighbor and friend."[45]

Communal values persisted not just in Irish pubs but in Ireland's Catholic churches through the late nineteenth and early twentieth centuries as well. The devotional revolution exorcised some of the more extreme remnants of peasant superstitions in Ireland, but like all other changes in Irish life the revolution spread gradually and unevenly from east to west. It thus left many areas where traditional religion was only partially reformed even by the end of the century. Moreover, even in most areas where the revival had full effect the church remained committed to the values of a rural, communal society. For all the new reforms, Ireland's Catholic priests continued to preach a Catholicism that questioned excessive individual ambition as a potentially dangerous materialism, underscored the sanctity of the cohesive family unit and its assigned roles, and looked suspiciously on the threats of the modern, industrial world to a "Holy Ireland" steeped in the simple virtues of premodern times. Irish people continued to believe in the power of sacramental ritual; to look to otherworldly beings—the saints—to intervene with God on their behalf and help them negotiate the uncertainties of life in a peasant agricultural economy; and to mark the rhythms of their agrarian calendar with saint's day feasts. It was a different kind of Catholicism at the end of the nineteenth century, perhaps, from the faith of most Irish Catholics before the devotional revolution swept the country, but it was still a communal faith well suited to a peasant people.

The establishment of a shrine and special devotion to St. Anthony of Padua in St. Paul's parish in Worcester offers a good example of how Irish immigrants held to those older communal religious perspectives albeit in new forms and in the new urban environments of America. Anthony was born in Lisbon in 1195 A.D. and spent most of his short life as a monk in northern Italy; he seemed a very unlikely candidate for devotions by Irish immigrants or their children. Indeed, a story published in the *Annals of St. Anthony's Shrine* in 1900, seemed to recognize the seeming incongruity between the saint and his potential followers. In the story, set in Ireland, a peasant named Dinny comes to appreciate St. Anthony, yet only after acknowledging that he had heard about saints named Patrick and Joseph but never about one named Anthony. In the late nineteenth century, however, Rome had singled out St. Anthony for special devotion and in 1891 formed an association to encourage his veneration. A group of largely Irish-born Sisters of Mercy decided to establish a devotion to the saint at St. Paul's parish in 1898 to help them raise funds for an orphanage and a home for working girls that they ran there. After receiving the "approbation" of Bishop Beaven, they imported a statue of St. Anthony, which they placed along with candles and a donation box in a small oratory near the church. Despite Irish unfamiliarity with Anthony, the devotion quickly became very popular. Within three years, over a thousand people turned out for an annual mass and pilgrimage on St. Anthony's feast day, and the shrine drew numerous visitors daily.[46]

The appeal of the shrine and the devotion, as Reverend Bernard S. Conaty predicted at its blessing, was that it became a "center for countless benefits, a center for prayers for needed favors, a center of consolation for the poor." Every year the sisters published letters of thanksgiving for benefits in the shrine's *Annals*, carefully noting that they had received far more than they could publish. The letters were a catalogue of the vulnerabilities of the immigrant Irish and their children. Most of the petitioners had sought out St. Anthony to help them find work or to heal illnesses: "a father who was without work in the beginning of the summer was very anxious to get it back again as his children needed his help very much"; "a girl . . . had been sick for six months and doctors could provide no relief." There were, however, a wide range of needs: a servant expressed thanks for finding her mistress's pearls that she had lost, a wife sought help in reforming an alcoholic husband, a mother asked for a happy death for a fatally ill child. St. Anthony offered a source of power for meeting all those needs, perhaps a last source of power for people without many alternatives. He was, as the Reverend John Conlin suggested in a sermon in 1900, "especially loved of God and is powerful with God, so it is that we seek his intercessions in our behalf."[47]

But if he was powerful, then so were the immigrants and other intercessors, because they could move him to work on their behalf through prayers, sacrifices, and small donations. Irishmen in Worcester saw the saints as friends tied to petitioners by links of reciprocity and mutuality, just as with other friends and relatives. It seems clear from the language they employed to describe Anthony and his fellows that Irish immigrants and other petitioners saw the saints as an invisible but powerful extension of the communal or patronage network. God, a writer noted in the *Annals* in 1900, can help us without the saints, but "a patron or a friendly saint can make easy our access to the divine treasure of Christ's merit, just as in life those nearest and dearest to the dispensers of the earth's goods and honors can procure them for those who stand in need." Two years later, an *Annals* article entitled "Friends in Need" echoed those sentiments and pointed out that for most people, poor people especially, when we turn to an earthly friend, "we find that they are overloaded with wants of their own," but in the saints we have friends "beyond the reach of want or care . . . but who will always remember that they are still our brethren."[48]

Kerby Miller has stated that "a traditional Irish Catholic world view with its emphases on communalism as opposed to individualism, custom versus innovation, conformity versus initiative . . . remained prevalent [in Ireland] and continued to shape attitudes until the end of the nineteenth century." This communal tradition and the paucity of useful skills Irish immigrants inherited from their rural peasant past shaped every aspect of their adjustment to American life, from making the journey, finding lodgings, securing work, deciding when and whom to marry, and where to settle. Throughout their American lives both men and women depended on family, friends, or community to help them overcome the harsh realities of an urban industrial world that they only barely understood and in which they had to compete with Yankees or other ethnics with advantages of wealth, position, or skills that they could never match. Perhaps if they had gone elsewhere in the world or even to the western parts of the United States, an abundance of opportunities and/or an absence of competitors would have made them less dependent on one another. Here in Worcester, however, the exigencies of the new environment ironically reinforced the peasant communalism and familism of the old country. Yet this was not the old country. It was a new world with its own set of demands and opportunities. In a cruel paradox, if communal solidarity helped soften the hardships of urban industrial life for Irish immigrants in Worcester, communal values would not encourage the newcomers to overcome the lack of useful skills that condemned them to the lowest rungs of the economic order.[49]

Tickets to Louth: Going to America

Though Irish immigrants migrated to Worcester as unmarried young adults alone or with a few friends or siblings, they depended heavily on kin and friends to make that journey possible, to find places to stay when they arrived, and to provide a comforting, nourishing community once they had settled. The dependence on friends and family actually began before the immigrants left Ireland. Between 1848 and 1900, the overseas Irish sent £52 million or $260 million home to Ireland. Forty percent of that sum was in prepaid tickets. Many, perhaps most, Irish immigrants thus had their passages to America paid by relatives or friends already in the United States. Richard O'Flynn who served as an agent for steamship lines to supplement the meager income of his bookstore did a lively business in sending remittances and prepaid tickets to Ireland. On March 20, 1882, for example, he sent £10 to families in Sligo, £9 to Kerry, and £7 to Waterford from relatives in Worcester. O'Flynn did an even bigger business in prepaid tickets. In the same month of March he sent £31 to Louth for tickets for travel from Liverpool to New York City and then to Worcester. From December 4 to December 31, 1884, O'Flynn sold sixty tickets on the White Star Lines and sent them overseas. Forty-three of the sixty tickets he sold had been paid for in Worcester by people with the same last name as the prospective passenger, presumably fellow family members: John O'Connor, for example, purchased four tickets on December 12, for Jeremiah O'Connor; Bridget McNamara bought two on the same day for Andrew McNamara; and Sara Gleason two for Maurice Gleason on December 16.[50]

   Dependence on relatives and friends undoubtedly continued for the immigrant through the journey to America and arrival in Worcester. For newly arriving men that dependence on friends, family, and ethnic community is clear. New immigrant men almost always lived in all-Irish households and many stayed with friends or family when they arrived in the city. Over 15 percent of newly arrived Irish males lived with siblings, according to the 1900 census sample. Most of the rest of the recent immigrant men boarded out, but the younger, most recent immigrants usually avoided large multiethnic boarding houses and attached themselves to Irish immigrant families, where they lived with only a few other Celtic immigrant boarders. Many probably knew their hosts from the old country or had learned about them from friends in America. Moreover, sometimes their fellow boarders were also relatives or intimates. In 1900 Thomas B. and John B. Trainer (who arrived in America in 1895 and 1893 respectively) and Michael and John Mostgeen (who arrived in 1894 and 1900), both pairs presumably relatives, boarded together in the home of William and Ann B. McNally at Jefferson Street in an Irish neighborhood on Worcester's east side. Not far away Francis McHugh and Michael Early, who had both arrived in America six months earlier, boarded together in the home of the immigrants Martin and Mary Dowd. Recent Irish immigrant men thus also almost always lived in all-Irish households located deep in heavily Irish neighborhoods.[51]

Boarding out was essential to the adaptation of Irish immigrant males to life in Worcester but was not critical to the experiences of most Irish-born females. A few married quickly, boarded out or moved in with siblings, but the majority of young Irish immigrant women became domestic servants soon after they had settled in Worcester. The Irish immigrant women's choice of service can be seen—at least in part—as a practical resolution of her problem of finding a healthy, safe place to live as well as a secure, paying job. Most of the 14.1 percent of single Irish immigrant women toiling in manufacturing jobs in 1900 were among the few immigrant women who had emigrated with their parents or moved easily into the households of siblings. Most Irish women emigrated alone or with a few friends, however. Their alternative to finding a place as a servant in a respectable home was boarding out, an expensive and sometimes risky proposition for young girls with few skills when most manufacturing jobs for women paid less than eight dollars a week. As a number of historians have pointed out, service could also provide unique opportunities to learn American ways. [52]

Yet if most Irish women lived apart from friends, family, and Irish neighborhoods, it is not clear that their links with family, friends, and community were broken. To find jobs themselves or even to learn which employment agents to trust, many immigrant women depended on informal networks of friends and relatives for help. In 1881 the *Worcester Daily Times* reported the plight of a frantic Irish immigrant woman at the police station who had lost her lists of friends' addresses on her way to America. Frances Kellor, who investigated domestic service in the northeast and midwest at the turn of the century, found that securing a position "through friends or acquaintances [was] universally preferred" by prospective servants as well as by their mistresses. Those without friends to get them positions might still seek help from people within their own community. Father John J. Power, the pastor of the city's sole Catholic parish in the "bon ton region" of the west side, St. Paul's, boasted numerous friends among Yankee "swells"; he might well have acted as a broker between the servant girls of his parish and Worcester's rich west side families. Indeed, in 1895 he established the House of Mercy, later the St. Joseph's Home for Working Girls, to train single women in the arts of domestic service, provide them with a place to stay while they were searching for work, and help place them in domestic positions.[53]

However Irish domestics found their places, they appeared to remain fiercely loyal to the Irish community. In the small snatches of O'Flynn's steamship records that survive, women were more likely than men to purchase passages to America for friends and relatives from home. Their contributions were also essential to the building of St. Paul's and Immaculate Conception churches where most of them worshiped. Father Robert Walsh of Immaculate Conception was particularly effusive in his praise of the servant girls for their generosity to his parish. Observers also suggested that servants may have made up half the audiences at the city's principal St. Patrick's Day lectures and entertainments in the late nineteenth century.[54]

Irish domestic servants probably also spent much of their limited leisure time socializing with other Irish men and women. Parishes called on women to organize fairs, bazaars, and a host of other entertainments, and many parishes organized sodalities for unmarried women. In the 1890s and early 1900s several Irish fraternal societies for women appeared in Worcester, such as the Ancient Order of Hibernians auxiliaries and the Irish National Foresters ladies branches. Both drew their members largely from unmarried Irish immigrant women and thus included domestic servants. Such societies frequently sponsored balls, dances, picnic outings, and even mock marriages.[55]

"O'Somebody": Irish Immigrants Earning a Living in Worcester

In 1894 the Charity Organization Society described the city's typical charity case as an "O'Somebody . . . whose garments indicate that they have been collected from every age and clime and have suffered in the transportation." Most telling about that statement was not what was said so much as when it was said. Some seventy years after the Irish first arrived in Worcester, and nearly half a century after the Famine refugees flooded the city, it appeared that the Irish-born had made little economic progress; Irish and poor were still synonymous in Worcester as they had been for most of the nineteenth century.

Irish immigrants in the late nineteenth century, as earlier, relied on friends and kin to find them jobs, but Irishmen were never able to carve out a niche in Worcester's economy (except a small foothold in government employment that paid meager rewards) that would permit those networks of friends to be effective. Hindered by the rise and fall of local industries, ethnic competition and discrimination, a lack of useful skills, and even their own communal values, Irish-born men and women remained at the end of the nineteenth century much like Irishmen fifty years before: Patrick and Bridget O'Somebodys at the bottom of Worcester's economic ladder, toiling at the city's worst jobs.[56]

Irish immigrants, so used to relying on friends and kin to negotiate the new world, looked to those resources again to meet the challenge of finding work in this new economy. Women, as noted, probably relied on a combination of agencies, friends, and leaders of their own community to find jobs as domestics. Many men, too, it appears, sought help from their friends. Among the 42 Irish names of the 199 men on the rolls for work rooms at the Washburn Moen Company's North Works in the spring of 1882, there were two Butlers, three Barrys, four Sullivans, two Gaffneys, two Mulcahys, two Conners, and two Kellehers. Seventeen of the 42 men thus shared a surname with at least one other worker. Evidence of a different sort suggests a similar pattern of family connections in Irish efforts to secure work. In 1896, a new division of the Ancient Order of Hibernians, a largely immigrant organization, was formed in Worcester. Of the 44 men who joined the new division and can be traced in the city directories, a fourth worked at either of the city's two biggest breweries: M. J. Finnegan Company or Bowler Brothers. Family ties clearly helped young Irish immigrant men to secure work at Finnegan's. John and Michael Coakley of the new Hibernian division as well as Patrick C. and Patrick H. Shea worked at Finnegan's in 1900. Michael Hurley and Dennis Melican, brothers-in-law, members of Division 36, and both recent arrivals from Ireland, also worked there in the same year.[57]

Politics seemed a potentially fruitful means for enabling Irish immigrants to turn friendship into economic rewards. The immigrants, who had so little to offer an industrial economy, appeared to have several advantages in the pursuit of government employment. From participation in political movements such as Catholic Emancipation in the 1820s, or Repeal in the 1840s, or the Land League and Home Rule of the 1880s, many of the immigrants brought to Worcester a familiarity with political organization that was remarkable for a peasant people.[58]

In Worcester as throughout America, Irish immigrants not only recognized an Anglo-Saxon-based governmental system not unlike the one they had left, but they had the added advantage of universal male suffrage, which permitted them to profitably employ the sheer numbers of their people to good effect in political contests. In America, and specifically Worcester, the political rewards of public employment and contracts were also growing rapidly in the late nineteenth century. Between 1880 and 1900 the number of policemen rose from 58 to over 120. Worcester also built a municipal hospital in 1872, constructed 25 schoolhouses between 1888 and 1898, spent over $2 million developing a public water supply by 1893 and over $6 million on its sewer system before 1910.[59]

For some of Worcester's Irish immigrants this mix of familiarity with politics, the American democratic system, their group's numbers and the ever-expanding opportunities for public employment proved very beneficial. Andrew Athy was elected state legislator in 1874 and alderman in 1881. Matthew McCafferty served in the state legislature in 1866 and the late 1870s; David F. O'Connell was a state representative in the 1880s, an alderman in the late 1890s, and became the city's first Irish immigrant mayor in 1911. Peter Sullivan and John C. Mahoney, both Irish-born, followed O'Connell into that post in the 1920s and 1930s.[60]

Irish political success also proved rewarding for immigrant men and women of less renown. Worcester's Irish Catholic weekly, the *Messenger*, wryly noted in 1905 that large numbers of Irish immigrants in America were "saving life and property on the fire departments . . . and arresting newly arrived Englishmen who go on a spree and fancy that they are still being protected by the Royal Irish Constabulary." Five years earlier, 21 policemen, nearly a sixth of Worcester's force, had been Irish-born. The samples of Irish immigrants from the 1880 and 1900 census manuscript schedules also reveal the importance of public employment to Irish natives as a route of upward mobility. Over 30 percent in 1880 and 40 percent in 1900 of Worcester's Irish-born clerical workers were government employees.[61]

Beyond direct municipal employment, the city's thousands of dollars of construction contracts offered further work opportunities. Jeremiah Murphy, a native of Bere Island in Cork, served several terms in minor city posts in the 1880s and sedulously cultivated connections that produced city contracts for his construction company. Yearly votes on whether the city should permit the sale of liquor, and the granting of licenses by the city government (through the board of aldermen up to 1893 and thereafter by a commission appointed by the mayor), insured that this important industry for Irish immigrants would remain highly politicized throughout the turn of the century era. Finally, a whole host of city companies providing such services as streetcars, electricity, and gas became potentially large sources of employment by the turn of the century and were inextricably enmeshed in the political process.[62]

Old-country experience and American opportunity thus combined to make politics a virtual obsession for Irish immigrants in Worcester. By 1885 over 2,800 Irish-born males were naturalized citizens and voters. They made up nearly two-thirds of the Irish immigrant men eligible, a proportion far larger than for any other immigrant group in Worcester that year. Only 284, or 22 percent, of the French Canadians, and 142, or 17 percent, of the Swedes, had become naturalized by that time. Irish men often rallied behind Irish candidates, but the desperate desire to reap the rewards the political system offered often provoked bitter factional stuggles within the Democratic party. In the late 1890s, for example, formal county societies, a Sligo Club and a Thomas Francis Meagher Club for Waterford natives, helped mobilize county members to claim their share of patronage. Even without the benefit of formal organization, Kerrymen managed to capture six slots on the police force in 1900. More to the point, all six of the peace officers were from West Kerry and five were from Killarney, which had been the birthplace of a succession of important Worcester Irish politicians from Daniel Courtney to D. S. Scannell to Peter Sullivan.[63]

In the end, however, politics offered Irish immigrants only meager rewards in the late nineteenth century. The fierce infighting of the immigrants for political patronage was more a sign of their desperation than of the potential of politics for economic mobility. Ultimately only 3 percent of all male immigrants and one-fourteenth of all male laborers found jobs with the city in 1900 and local contractors working on city jobs could not have employed many more. Irish immigrant women got even less out of politics (though not their second-generation daughters, as we shall see). The numbers might have gone up for both men and women when the Irish took control of the city for good in the 1920s, but that would not be until the second decade of the twentieth century, after Irish immigration began to dwindle down from a river to a small stream. For Irish men and women at the bottom of the ladder, government was an economic niche, virtually their only one, but a small one.

That proved tragic for Irish immigrants because they found few other niches in Worcester's economy that they could dominate and thus few industries where friend or family connections could be translated into jobs. In part their difficulties stemmed from landing in Worcester rather than in a city with richer opportunities. Irishmen who migrated to Butte, Montana, for example, found work there in mines owned by Irish bosses, but almost no Irishmen owned factories, banks, major retail or wholesale stores, or transport companies in Worcester. Butte may have been an exceptional case, but it seems clear that opportunities for Irish immigrant upward mobility, were, indeed, better in other parts of the country. Several historians have suggested that Irish immigrants enjoyed far greater success in the open, dynamic economies of the west, for example, than in the stratified, sluggish economies of the northeast, especially those in New England. Like many New England cities such as Springfield or Hartford, but unlike Lowell or Lawrence, Worcester had grown out of an old town founded a century before the first Irish arrived. The native-stock Yankee population thus was well established in Worcester at the outset of industrialization and retained tight control of the city's economy throughout the twentieth century.[64]

The city's economy was, however, atypical of New England cities in many respects. In a region where many cities were devoted almost exclusively to the manufacture of a single item, such as textiles, paper, or shoes, Worcester's economy was diverse, producing everything from leather belts and barbed wire to corsets and breakfast cereal. The largest industries by the late nineteenth century were wire-making and machinery manufacture, but Worcester was never a single-industry town.[65]

How did these characteristics of Worcester's economy translate into concrete opportunities for the city's Irish immigrants? A survey of the growth in selected occupations in Worcester over the twenty years from 1880 to 1900 reveals that male clerical positions grew by almost double the growth of the overall male workforce in those two decades. Skilled blue-collar occupations such as plumbers, printers, and machinists also increased more than the male workforce in that time. By contrast, the number of laborers failed to keep pace with the overall increase. For women too the Worcester economy seemed to be providing a wide array of opportunities. The number of female clerical positions, bookkeepers, clerks, saleswomen, and stenographers, increased by an astonishing 928 percent, seven times the proportionate growth in the female workforce from 1880 to 1900. Yet the number of female servants and textile operatives fell behind the general increase in the number of working women.[66]

Opportunities thus were increasing in Worcester for skilled or white-collar work, but Irish immigrants did not seem to take advantage of them. Indeed, it is striking how few of the Irish-born seemed to find jobs in the fastest growing trades or occupations. The few Irish-born men who wore white collars were almost as likely to be small shopkeepers as they were clerks, even though the number of small retailers in Worcester was increasing far more slowly than the number of male clerical workers. Irish-born men also did not move into the fastest-growing skilled blue-collar trades such as plumbing. In 1900 only one of the 111 skilled blue-collar workers in the census sample of immigrants was a plumber. Irish-born women also seemed incapable of exploiting opportunities among the city's fastest-growing female occupations. Almost none became clerks, bookkeepers, or saleswomen despite the enormous increase in the number of such female occupations.[67]

The nature of opportunity in Worcester at the turn of the century deserves closer scrutiny, however. Though its economy was diverse, Worcester was primarily a center for heavy industry: iron and steel products, machinery, and tools. Light industries, such as textiles or clothing manufacture, which in other cities employed larger numbers of women were relatively unimportant in Worcester. Textiles employed but 4 percent of all workers in the two census years, 1880 and 1900 (only 10 percent and 7 percent of all women workers, respectively). The city did have a number of corset and envelope-making factories, but envelope manufacture employed less than 3 percent of the female work force in both 1880 and 1900. Only a little over half of Worcester's women worked in manufacturing in 1880, falling off to a third in 1900. For Irish-born women arriving in Worcester at the turn of the century, their Irish inheritance combined with the constraints of the new environment to direct them towards domestic service. Furthermore, though hardly depressed, the city's economy was reaching maturity by the late nineteenth century and its growth had slowed. The decennial rate of increase in the value of the city's manufactures fell from more than 50 percent from 1865 to 1875 to less than 25 percent from 1875 to 1885. More important, certain industries which had long been major sources of employment among Irish immigrants had either begun to decline or had been invaded by ethnic competitors such as the Swedes who enjoyed the favor of Worcester's Yankee managers.[68]

Boot- and shoe-making had long been a major source of employment among Irish immigrants, but in the late nineteenth century it fell on hard times. In 1880 the city's boot and shoe shops employed 10 percent of all Worcester's workers; no other branch of manufacture in the city employed as many. In just ten years, however, the local boot and shoe industry would collapse, the victim of technological obsolescence, style changes, and aggressive competitors elsewhere: by 1890 only 3 percent of Worcester's workers labored in the boot and shoe shops; by 1900 the number was 2 percent. For Worcester's Irish-born workers the collapse of the boot and shoe trade was a considerable catastrophe. Between 1880 and 1900, the proportion of Irish-born men working in the industry declined from 11 percent to only 2.2 percent. Here was a potential niche that disappeared in the heat of industrial competition in the late nineteenth century.[69]

While Irish immigrants struggled to escape this dying industry, Irishmen in more prosperous trades suffered from discrimination and ethnic competition. It seems clear, for example, that a number of Worcester manufacturers preferred to employ Swedish workers over Irish ones. Charles Washburn, scion of one of Worcester's most important manufacturing families, wrote glowingly about Swedish immigrants in his history of industry in Worcester, concluding four paragraphs of praise by exclaiming that "they are thrifty, industrious, capable and law abiding people who have come to make this country their home." Washburn dismissed the city's far more numerous Irish with a terse three lines, simply reporting that "as the heavier kinds of manufacture were introduced the Irishman became an important factor in our industrial development."[70]

That Washburn's opinion was widespread among the managers and owners of Worcester's industry seemed clear from his note that the "Swedes are found in most of our shops and employed exclusively in some of them." Worcester's largest company in the nineteenth century, the Washburn Moen Wire Manufacturing Company, and the largest in the twentieth century, the Norton Company, a manufacturer of abrasives, openly favored Swedish workers. It was Worcester's Swedes not its Irish, then, who established the kinds of links with factory owners and managers that provided a consistent flow of jobs for friends and family.[71]

Irish immigrant women also suffered from competition and prejudice. The most noticeable evidence of discrimination against Irish women were classified advertisements seeking domestic servants. On November 19, 1894, one of eight advertisements appearing in the *Worcester Spy* read: "Wanted a Young Swede Girl to assist in general housework." The next week, on November 24, an advertisement in the paper asked: "Wanted 50 good Swede girls." On December 6, a family in the newly opened residential districts on the city's west side sought a "Swede or English girl" and another from a wealthy area wanted "strong capable Swedish girls." Other advertisements in the 1880s and 1890s specified American, Nova Scotian, or German girls; none sought Irish domestics.[72]

Competition and discrimination compounded the economic problems of Irish immigrants, but even in a free field natives of Ireland would have had some difficulty adjusting to Worcester's economy. Southern Ireland's declining manufactures, stagnating cities, and enduring peasant agricultural economy bequeathed them no useful skills, little money, and values antithetical to the ideals of late nineteenth-century American capitalism. Indeed, it may well be true that even more of Ireland's emigrants at the end of the century were unskilled workers than during the flood of Famine refugees. In 1851, 79 percent of Ireland's emigrants declared themselves common laborers, farm laborers, or servants; by 1900, the proportion was 91.2 percent.[73]

Irish immigrants, both men and women, thus had to learn their trades in America, or more specifically Worcester, and that learning process was very slow. In both 1880 and 1900 only about 20 percent of all Worcester's Irish-born males were skilled workers. In 1900, only among the very oldest and most seasoned immigrant men (those who had been in the country for more than thirty-five years) was the proportion higher. Presumably skills learned in school and the ability to speak English would have offset the Irish lack of industrial skills and proved useful in white-collar jobs which required interaction with an English-speaking public, figuring sums, and keeping records. Yet only a tiny number of either Irish immigrant men or women secured jobs in the lowest echelons of the white-collar hierarchy, positions in sales or as bookkeepers or clerks. This absence is surprising because the fundamentally sound education of many Irish immigrants would seem most appropriate for such posts and because clerical jobs for men and women were the fastest growing occupations in the Worcester economy. The advantages of a sound elementary education and fluency in English, however, were not especially helpful to peasant farm boys and girls unfamiliar with an urban industrial economy or even entrepreneurial ways. Most Irishmen seeking to open small shops or to clerk in bigger ones were probably more like the former factory operative struggling to maintain his grocery store who was described by a Dun and Bradstreet reporter in 1886 as "strong and honest but totally lacking in business experience." Indeed, a study of social mobility among Worcester's shoeworkers found that the vast majority of Irishmen from that trade who moved up to found a small shop or grocery slipped back into the blue-collar ranks after only a few years.[74]

"Lack of business experience" denotes more than concrete knowledge of accounting practices or management methods. It suggests the lack of the kind of individual ambition and entrepreneurial values that were vital to workers trying to move up in a capitalist industrial economy. The very communal reciprocity that sustained Worcester's Irish-born may have discouraged them from taking up those values. Father John J. McCoy of Worcester's St. Anne's parish lauded his people in 1905, for example, for their virtues of neighborliness: "We are not a money saving people, but we are glad in our course because we never oppressed the sick nor have done injury to any nation." The Ancient Order of Hibernians, a largely immigrant organization, made a similar point in 1915: "The mere pagan idea of attaining happiness is gaining wealth. The Irish people have higher and nobler conceptions of happiness. We cannot hope to reorganize the industrial system, but we can refuse to permit the in-dustrial system to reorganize our family life." As some of McCoy's colleagues realized, however, expressions of this communalism were not always virtu-ous. The ambitious who broke ranks, became rich, and forgot their former comrades were suspect and reviled, as by the Ancient Order of Hibernians in 1901, for being "the incarnation, the very embodiment of heartlessness and selfishness." Envy of the successful and criticism of the ambitious seemed en-demic to the Worcester Irish. Father McCaughan, a curate at Worcester's oldest Irish parish, St. John's, complained in 1891 that his parishioners frequently "try to pull a man down from a position he has attained by true worth, ability and hard work . . . they made him look ignominious in the eyes of others be-cause he has pulled ahead of them and is desirous of being somebody in this world." Five years later, "Cousin Ruth," writing in Worcester's *School and Home Magazine* echoed McCaughan's sentiments: "Because a friend succeeds, his neighbors trace his ancestors back to the seventh generation subjecting their failings to the fierce light of worldly success and see nought but evil in them."[75]

Without a niche of their own that they could exploit or the skills or even the values to help them carve one out, Worcester's late nineteenth-century Irish immigrants inevitably ended at the bottom of the city's economic hier-archy. Statistics confirm the low economic status of Worcester's Irish immi-grants throughout the nineteenth century. In 1850 over half the Irish immi-grant men in Worcester were general laborers. By 1900 the proportion of laborers had fallen, but even then nearly 70 percent of Worcester's Irish im-migrant men were unskilled or semiskilled workers. In the same year, nearly half of all single immigrant women were servants and the rest, unskilled or semiskilled factory or service workers.[76]

These statistics perhaps exaggerate the bleakness of poverty among the Irish and obscure their economic achievements. Many immigrant families had managed to accumulate property through years of penny-pinching and saving. As early as 1870 15 percent of Worcester's Irish laborers and 12 percent of its Celtic immigrant bootworkers owned property; half of the property-owning laborers had holdings worth $2,000 or more. By 1900, moreover, over one-fifth, 22.8 percent, of Irish immigrant household heads owned their own homes.[77]

There were many success stories among the immigrants. Eugene Moriarty from west Kerry parlayed a successful political career into ownership of Worcester's second largest daily newspaper and a grand house on Worcester's posh west side. Richard Healy, who came to America in 1864, spent nearly twenty years learning the dry goods trade before he came to Worcester. In the 1880s he established very fashionable clothing stores in Worcester and Albany, New York. By the 1890s, Worcester's Irish immigrants had produced a small but noticeable class of such successful men, largely engaged in politics, retail trade, or accumulating and managing real estate.[78]

With all of these qualifications, however, it is clear that there was little substantial change in the economic status of Irish immigrants over the course of the nineteenth century. Some men may have established their own businesses or gained success in politics but, in all, less than a tenth of the men and virtually none of the single Irish immigrant women had become white-collar workers by 1900. Furthermore, though older immigrants fared better than recent ones in Worcester's job market, the differences seemed small. In 1900 38.6 percent of the men who had been in America as long as twenty to twenty-four years were still unskilled workers, a barely smaller proportion than the 43.1 percent of those who had been in America only five to fourteen years. Even the accumulation of property seemed less the achievement of the immigrants than of their children. In 1900 a substantial proportion of the household heads who owned their own homes counted on the income of two or more working children.[79]

Mired at the bottom of the economic hierarchy, most of Worcester's Irish workers earned too little to meet the needs of their families. Perhaps the most compelling evidence of the inadequacy of wages for workers in Worcester came from the surveys of working-class budgets conducted in 1875 and 1902. In 1875, the investigators found that heads of household in the lowest category, earning between $450 and $600 (the average yearly earnings for men in Worcester in 1880 was $400) brought home only two-thirds of their families' income. The Massachusetts Bureau of Labor determined that the wages of the children usually made up the rest of the family's budget. Even with these additional sources of money, 90 percent of the expenditures of such households went to food, clothing, and shelter; 60 percent was spent on food alone. And even with that proportion, the diets were mean. For the families of most outdoor laborers in Massachusetts in 1875, meals consisted of bread, butter, potatoes, and occasional salted fish or meat. The living standard of case 164, an Irish laborer's family living in Worcester, was typical. This family spent over $450 out of a $716 annual income on meals but regularly ate only corned meat, salt fish, and potatoes. After rent, fuel, and food, only $6.31 was available for clothes for the laborer, his wife, and six children. Nearly thirty years later the situations of Massachusetts' poorest had improved, but only marginally. Heads of households falling into the $450 to $700 range still earned but two-thirds of their families's wages (the average yearly earnings for men in

Worcester had increased to $553 by then), and these families too spent an enormous proportion of their income, 83 percent, on the basic necessities of food, clothing, and shelter.[80]

Since they could not support their families even with steady work, the problems for laboring men and women were severely compounded when they lost their jobs even for brief periods. Their jobs at the bottom of the economic hierarchy were not only the worst-paying but often the most dangerous positions available in Worcester's economy. Machine belts and gears in shoe shops, furnaces and rivers of molten metal in the wire mills, and wool or cotton dust in the textile mills all took their toll on the Irish and other workers. Construction also had its hazards. In 1882, for example, a cave-in suffocated one city laborer, Humphrey Sullivan, and injured another, Patrick Quinn, a recent immigrant from Ireland, as they worked to widen one of the city's streets.[81]

The most frequent cause of unemployment, of course, was being fired or laid off. Worcester's economy, like America's generally, rocked between boom times and depression throughout the late nineteenth and early twentieth centuries. Even in a relatively mild depression year such as 1885, 71 percent of the city's laborers and 44 percent of Worcester's wireworkers were unemployed for at least three months. Yet unemployment stalked Worcester's Irish workers even when the city's economy was healthy. Most industries had seasonal cycles of boom and bust even in normal or good years. Building-trade workers were idle for most of the winter. According to the *Worcester Daily Times* the boot and shoe shops also laid off substantial numbers of workers in the winter. In the relatively prosperous years of 1880 and 1900, nearly 27 percent and 17 percent of Worcester's Irish-born workers, respectively, were unemployed for at least a month.[82]

The lack of institutional support for those who lost their jobs or businesses made this insecurity all the more treacherous. Worcester's city government gave little outdoor relief or cash payments to the poor. Between 1900 and 1903 the city clerk distributed no more than $11,570 in aid to the poor. With little outdoor relief available, the truly destitute were relegated to the ignominy of the poor farm, which was a loathsome alternative for most Worcester residents but especially painful for the Irish throughout the 1880s and 1890s. An investigation by the *Worcester Daily Times* in the early 1880s turned up testimony about women and children clothed in rags and fed on bread and water. One resident of the farm told the *Times* reporter that a worker at the institution had threatened to "cut her Irish heart out." Private charities offered little more help. The Associated Charities, founded in 1890, billed itself as a "businessman's proposition" which preferred to "give careful and sympathetic advice" rather than physical aid or, as its motto ran, "Not alms but a friend." Between 1901 and 1905 the organization gave out only a little more than $11,000 to the impoverished. Irish immigrants would have to look elsewhere to weather the storms of illness, injury, and unemployment in turn of the century Worcester.[83]

The "Earning Capacity" of Children: Irish Family Strategies of Survival

The most reliable source of such help, Irish immigrants knew from the old country, was their families. Yet they had left their immediate families back home in Ireland. Here in America they could count on brothers and sisters, cousins, aunts and uncles, perhaps, but such help, even from siblings, had limits. Their best hope was to create their own families—sons and daughters—who might earn enough to make them comfortable in middle age and offer them their best chance for security in old age. Yet while Irish immigrants in Worcester and America needed to marry as early as practical, their friends and relatives who stayed home in Ireland needed to delay marriage as long as possible, or even not to marry at all. The Irish in Worcester, perhaps reflecting the influence of Irish culture, would marry later than native-stock Yankee Americans in Worcester. The pressing need for the help that only a family could provide, however, would make them marry earlier than their countrymen and women who stayed at home.

At the end of the nineteenth century, Ireland's marital and fertility customs were a distinctive exaggeration of a broad Western trend. In no other country in Europe was the average age of marriage so high or the proportion of permanently single, the celibate, so large. Between 1895 and 1914, the average age of marriage for men rose from 25 to 33, and for women from 21 to 28, and the proportion of permanently single or celibate (still single at age forty-five to fifty) grew from 12 percent to 36 percent from 1845 to the 1940s. Yet while the proportions of Irish who married, and who married young, declined, those who did marry produced extraordinarily large numbers of children. By the early twentieth century Irish marital fertility rates were far higher than those of other Western European countries.[84]

The causes of this extraordinary behavior have long been debated by historians and other observers. Some have ascribed the late age of marriage among the Irish to sexual shyness or prudery bred into the bone of Irish culture as early as the first Christian monks. Others have blamed France's puritanical seventeenth-century Jansenists for introducing antipathy toward sins of the flesh into Irish culture through their influence on Irish priests trained in French seminaries. Neither theory seems very helpful, for it appears that Irish

devotion, such as the Sacred Heart, or Mary of the Immaculate Conception. Rules of the organizations also enjoined individual members to say special prayers by themselves daily. In 1891, for example, the rules of the Men's League of the Sacred Heart stated that each member should say a decade of the rosary every morning.[33]

As the League's injunctions to its members reveal, the new devotionalism placed heavy stress on private worship and prayer as well as public or communal ritual. Colleen McDannell has recently pointed out the importance of images, statues, and other forms of material culture to such private or domestic devotions. In Worcester, Irish Catholic publications frequently advertised pictures of the Sacred Heart or various saints for their readers to hang on the walls of their homes or carry with them every day. Crucifixes were deemed especially important for creating the proper Christian domestic atmosphere. "The crucifix," the *Annals of St. Anthony's Shrine* stated in January of 1900, "is and always will be the most beautiful book of devout souls; it speaks to the senses, it speaks to the mind, it speaks to the heart . . . it teaches everything , it answers everything . . . it attracts us to recollection, to prayer, to the interior life." Every Catholic, the *Catholic Messenger* argued in 1920, should have a crucifix in his or her bedroom. Priests and other partisans of devotions also urged Catholics to wear medals or scapulars linked to specific devotions, such as St. Anthony or the Sacred Heart. Making sure that the church kept pace with changing technology and culture, the *Messenger* began to offer St. Christopher medals for drivers to hang in their cars in 1920. Pictures, statues, and other artifacts were not ends in themselves, Catholic leaders believed, but rather means to create the proper environment for prayer and sacrifice. The purpose of having a crucifix in the home, the *Annals* pointed out, was to prompt family members to spend a "little time" every day in prayer before it.[34]

No devotion was more important to the Irish in Worcester than saying the rosary. In 1920, while reviewing artifacts useful for home worship, the *Catholic Messenger* remarked almost in passing, "a rosary of course we always carry about with us." From at least the 1880s on, Worcester's Irish priests urged their parishioners to gather the family and say the rosary every evening. In May of 1919, the *Catholic Messenger* argued that the rosary was not like any other prayer or ritual for the Irish: "clinging to the beads " had been the instrument of their salvation and was an essential marker of their fidelity to Catholicism.[35]

The devotional revolution embodied in the proliferation of rituals, the spread of mission revivals, and the multiplication of sodalities affected all segments of the Irish population in Worcester, but there is reason to believe that it may have had a particularly powerful effect on the new generation, the American-born Irish. Several of the sodalities at St. John's and Sacred Heart were aimed at the young. The boys of St. Aloysius were all under age eighteen. The girls in the first section of the Children of Mary were between the ages of fifteen and twenty, and the parishes sponsored Unmarried Ladies Sodalities for young women as well. The scattered membership lists which remain from the organizations of other Irish parishes also suggest the new generation's religious devotion. The most popular male Catholic organizations in the late nineteenth and early twentieth centuries, the parish temperance societies and the Knights of Columbus, were dominated by American-born Irishmen, and women of the new generation made up the bulk of the members of organizations like the Catholic Young Women's Lyceum and the Catholic Women's Club. No lists of those "converted" by parish missions remain in Worcester. In 1884, however, the Paulists noted that their "Retreat for Young Men" at St. John's was "excellently attended" and in 1892 they were impressed by the vast numbers of "young men and women" who attended their mission at the same church. Just the year before, in 1891, Father Conaty of Sacred Heart, exclaimed that "all our young people were among the most fervent at all the services. There were very few absent from the mission."[36]

Furthermore, devotional fervor seemed to increase, not peter out, as the immigrant generation passed away and new American-born generations came to dominate the Irish community in the twentieth century. Parish missions occurred less frequently after 1900, perhaps, but they were still common enough, in old churches like St. Anne's, St. Stephen's, or Immaculate Conception, as well as Sacred Heart and St. John's, and in newly formed parishes like Ascension. Older devotions, like the devotion to St. Anthony, continued to flourish as the twentieth century progressed, and new shrines, novenas, and pilgrimages multiplied in the twentieth century. In 1903, the Sisters of Mercy, who had established the devotion to Saint Anthony in St. Paul's church, built a shrine to Our Lady of Lourdes next to their new orphanage in the nearby town of Leicester. An annual pilgrimage from Worcester to the shrine, including contingents of uniformed K. of C. members, children carrying banners and papal and American flags, altar boys bearing "gleaming candles and glowing torches," the nuns, and thousands of men, women, and children reciting the rosary, grew from 3,000 participants in the early twentieth century to 5,000 pilgrims by 1920. Novenas to St. Rita, St. Francis Xavier, St. Jude, and St. Theresa of Lisieux also took place for the first time in Worcester churches in the 1910s, 1920s, or 1930s and became annual, well-attended events. In 1927 and 1929 over 7,000 people attended the annual novena for St. Theresa conducted by Carmelite priests at St. John's parish and in the latter year the parish had to turn hundreds of people away at the door for lack of space.[37]

Church organizations also flourished in the new century. In the late nineteenth century, Sacred Heart and St. John's parishes were the most thoroughly organized Irish parishes in the city. In the twentieth century many of the older parishes that had lagged behind those two began to catch up. In the late 1890s, for example, Father Daniel F. McGillicuddy, Worcester-born of Irish immigrant parents, took over St. Stephen's church and organized many new sodalities. By 1900, the *Messenger* claimed, nearly all the women of the parish had joined the Married or Unmarried Ladies sodalities. St. Paul's, long ruled by Father John J. Power, whose vision of Catholicism harkened back to the plain style of the early nineteenth-century church, had seemed immune to the devotional fervor. But after his death in 1902, subsequent pastors of the parish created two new children's sodalities, a Holy Name Society, and reenergized the older Unmarried Ladies and Rosary sodalities and a branch of the Children of Mary. New parishes quickly formed sodalities and devotional clubs as well. One year after it was founded, Blessed Sacrament parish on Worcester's west side boasted a Rosary and a Holy Name society enrolling a combined 150 members, or one-sixth of the new church's 900 parishioners.[38]

Holy Name Societies, male sodalities devoted to reverence for the name of Christ, became particularly popular in early twentieth-century Worcester. Before 1900, only St. John's and Sacred Heart had Holy Name Society chapters, but within the next decade Immaculate Conception (1900), St. Anne's (1903), St. Peter's (1904), St. Paul's (1907), and St. Stephen's (1910) all established Holy Name Societies. Many of these societies emerged from missions: the pastor of St. Paul's, Father William Goggin, brought the Vincentian Fathers to conduct a mission at his church with the express purpose of founding a Holy Name Society; a "long" mission by the Jesuits at St. Stephen's inspired 200 men to sign up for the Holy Name Society there.[39]

Catholic organizations outside the parishes, like the national fraternal society, the Knights of Columbus, or the local Catholic Women's Club, also grew enormously during the twentieth century. In the century's first two decades, the membership of Worcester's K. of C. branch rose from a few hundred to over 5,000 men, dwarfing any other Irish or Catholic club in the city. Such organizations were not strictly devotional societies, but since they were clearly committed to advancing the church's interests, encouraged their members to a better practice of their faith, and organized retreats and other activities, their success provides another index of the broadening popular devotional sentiment among the American-born Irish in twentieth century Worcester.[40]

Evidence of the second generation's personal commitment to their faith and religious testimony reveal both the intensity and breadth of Catholic devotion among the men and women of the new generation. Large numbers of American-born Irish chose religious vocations, for example. Notices of men entering the seminary or women the convent appeared regularly in the local Irish weekly, the *Messenger*. In October of 1900, for example, the paper reported that Annie Rooney and Annie Carmody, both working in an envelope factory had joined the Sisters of Providence and in December of that same year revealed that Delia McLaughlin, clerk in a department store, had joined the Sisters of Notre Dame. The correspondence of Bishop Beaven, bishop of Springfield (Worcester was part of the Springfield diocese until 1950), suggests that his diocese may have had so many priests by the 1890s that it was exporting clerical personnel. Similar growth occurred among the religious orders of women in the Springfield diocese over the forty years of the turn of the century period. For religious orders of women as for priests the increase came largely from the American-born. By 1900, most of the pastors and all of the curates in the city's Irish parishes, and solid majorities of the nuns in local convents of religious women, were American natives. Irish immigrants were a majority only among the Sisters of Mercy.[41]

Religious fervor was powerful among young lay American-born men and women as well. Through the 1880s and 1890s Irish parishes published a number of magazines and journals. Some of these were no more than elaborate parish bulletins, but they often contained poems, articles, and prayers written by parishioners. Most of the identifiable authors of these pieces were American-born Irish men or women who poured out their longing and gratitude for God's love and celebrated the church's enlivening of a cold and dead material world. John F. O'Connor, a second-generation schoolteacher and lifelong community leader, pointed to the unique solace that Christ and his saints offered in times of loneliness or stress. "When I am alone," he wrote in *Catholic School and Home Magazine* in 1896, "'tis then I see the farthest into heaven; 'tis then I feel God's presence; then remorse will steal into my hardened heart reminding me of what I am and what I ought to be. . . . But one ambition—my sad soul's weal, a simple child, dear God, who sighs for thee." Francis McKeon, American-born schoolteacher, principal, and later candidate for mayor, found love closer to home in Pope Leo XIII, "all mankind's true lover to the end. . . . O that the world would turn to thee, to live beloved by thee."[42]

The diary of Stephen Littleton, a young American-born Irish Catholic from the South Worcester neighborhood who worked on one of these magazines, provides unique insight into the extraordinarily significant and large role the church played in the lives of many second-generation Irish lay men and women. Littleton was born in 1868 in Rutland, a town just north of Worcester. His family moved to Worcester (perhaps because of his father's death) in the late 1880s where he attended the public schools. After spending a year in high school, he followed a somewhat inconsistent career as a journalist, accountant, and clerk. In 1888, just before, as he put it, "attaining my majority," he began a diary, which he kept more or less regularly for the next three years. That diary reveals a man deeply involved in the devotional and religious life of Worcester Catholicism, but one who was also eager for entertainment and pleasure. He enjoyed meeting girls, stayed up late to walk Worcester's streets, bet on cards and crew races, and liked to dance; Littleton was religious, but he was no saint.[43]

Over the course of the three years covered by his diary, Littleton was a member of at least two, possibly three, parish temperance societies, and the choir of his home parish, Sacred Heart. He also meant to join the parish St. Vincent De Paul Society and berated himself for not carrying through on that intention. More noticeable was his constant attendance at church-related events and functions. In March of 1890 he went to Lenten services at Sacred Heart on the fourth; the stations of the cross at St. John's on the seventh, where the church was so crowded that he had to stand up throughout the entire service; an evening session of a mission run by the Jesuits at St. Stephen's church on the ninth where he heard a sermon on "What doth it profit a man to gain the whole world and lose his own soul"; a funeral mass of a well-known Irishman on the tenth; and the mission at St. Stephen's again on the twelfth, this time with three friends, Charles Callahan, Jim Healy, and Danny Lonergan, to hear the Jesuit missionary priest speak on "Death: Be Always Ready." Such unrelenting religiosity was unusual even for Littleton; his religious involvement rose in Lenten Marchs and Advent Decembers and fell in summer Julys and Augusts. Yet with his faithful attendance at mass and vespers, meetings of his parish societies, missions, and other church events, the central place of Catholicism in Littleton's life was fully evident.[44]

The church services he attended seemed to nourish this faith, inspiring often emotional bursts of devotion. In April of 1891, he reported the "grandest" ceremony he had ever seen: a priest at Sacred Heart's parish mission asked the married women to renew their nuptial vows, and as the women stood and recited them, the sun broke through some clouds and streamed through the windows, momentarily lighting up the church and prompting some of the women to cry. He was even more moved when he himself was a participant in church ritual. On Easter of 1890, Littleton noted in his diary the "large number partaking of the sacrament of the Eucharist [receiving communion] and I felt proud of myself being among their number." Inspired by his faith and its reinforcement by the church's liturgy, his New Year resolutions often took on a religious cast. On December 31, 1890, he resolved to never forget his morning and evening prayers and to confess and receive communion at least once every three months.[45]

Littleton also felt a strong attachment to his parish and its pastor, Thomas J. Conaty. Indeed, his pride in both sometimes sounded like parish boosterism. On January 4, 1891, he regretted his failure to contribute more to his parish of Sacred Heart, noting that Conaty "is untiring in his endeavors to elevate and beautify his parish surroundings." Another parish, Littleton thought, would "idolize" Conaty. If the bishop should transfer the pastor, he wrote, then "we would see our mistake" and realize we had "as beautiful a parish as can be found anywhere."[46]

Immersion in Worcester Catholicism did not merely reflect his faith commitment or parish loyalty, it provided him with entertainment and recreation. He enjoyed the music at church services, for example. On Christmas in 1890, he spent the day "almost entirely in church services" at least in part because of the music, and he was quick to note in his diary every "excellent programme of music." Littleton also sought and found company in his participation in Catholic life. His membership in parish societies helped him make friends, and he frequently stopped by the clubhouses of local parish societies to play cards or pool and often visited the houses of fellow choir or sodality members. Yet what is most striking from the notations in his diary is how attendance at church services helped Littleton to meet girls. Entries like the following literally fill the pages of his diary: March 7, 1890, "Went to the stations of the cross, met two girls walked them to Comerford and Burns Tea Store"; February 2, "attended lecture of Father Walter Elliott, accompanied them [three girls] home"; April 3, 1890, attended Lenten services, met girls after, then left in a group of boys and girls; January 4, 1891, "Went skating with girls after Vespers"; February 11, 1890, visited St. Stephen's Church fair, small crowd, only two young men, "We had quite a time with the ladies." It was a rarity when Littleton could record in his diary, as on January 4, 1891, that he attended a church event but met no one and had to walk home alone. For Littleton and perhaps other members of his generation the church was almost as much the center of their social lives as their spiritual ones.[47]

The centrality of religion in Littleton's, O'Connor's, and McKeon's lives points up another aspect of the new generation's embrace of Catholicism: religion may have been as important to males as to females. Such a conclusion contradicts interpretations of the gendered appeal of religion in nineteenth-century America. Historians have long noted the feminization of mainstream American Protestantism in that era, but Jay Dolan has also emphasized the feminine nature of Catholic piety: "Catholic devotions," he notes, "were riddled with emotionalism and sentimentalism, qualities identified as feminine." Sodalities for women, he also points out, predominated over societies for men in most parishes throughout most of the nineteenth century. Men may have been on the altar, the argument runs, but, as in Protestant churches, most of the faithful in the pew were women.[48]

Priests and church leaders at the turn of the century did, in fact, worry constantly that the temptations of the streets and saloons would lure boys and young men from the practice of their faith. Father John J. McCoy talked, for example, of the men who clapped boys on the shoulder and tried to the lure them into gangs or streets: "good boys . . . handsome fellows . . . brave lads . . . come on, don't be an old fossil of a fellow and be stuck about home or the church all the while . . . be something of a man." Despite the church's advocacy of temperance, drunkenness remained a problem for second- as well as first-generation men. In 1910, the proportion of second-generation men arrested for drunkenness in Massachusetts far exceeded their proportion in the population. Gangs of young men, the "Alcohol Gang" and "Moonlight Boys" for example, roamed Worcester's Island and East Worcester neighborhoods in the late nineteenth century.[49]

Nevertheless, the gender dynamics of Catholic devotion among the Worcester Irish were complicated. It was true that women's sodalities were more numerous in Worcester's parishes and from scattered accounts seem to have had larger memberships in the nineteenth century. The number of men's societies and the size of their memberships were impressive, however. In the early 1890s, for example, Sacred Heart had a Mutual Benefit Society that demanded religious observances from its male members, a thriving Men's League of the Sacred Heart, a St. Aloysius society for boys, and a popular male temperance organization, the Catholic Young Men's Lyceum. There were parish temperance societies like the Lyceum, organized by priests and incorporating church devotions into their regular activities, in almost every parish in Worcester at that time, and they enrolled a total of nearly a thousand young men. Men also played prominent roles in the liturgical life of their churches. In 1891 the "men of the congregation" paraded with the church's altar boys and first communion class to begin the Forty Hours devotion at Sacred Heart. According to Paulist reports, women probably predominated at parish missions since the number of women making confessions almost always exceeded the number of men. Yet the differences were often small: at St. John's in 1892, 3,680 women's confessions to 3,520 by men; at Sacred Heart in 1891, 1,375 women to 1,200 men. At Sacred Heart in 1888 the confessions by men actually outnumbered the number by women. Male participation in church life in nineteenth-century Irish Worcester thus seems greater than what might be expected from older historical interpretations.[50]

Irish male participation in church life also appeared to grow substantially in the twentieth century. As noted earlier, Holy Name Societies and the Knights of Columbus grew enormously in Worcester during the first few years of the new century. Such growth was part of a broad trend of expansion by those two and other Irish-dominated male Catholic societies that occurred not only in Worcester, but across the country and in Canada at that time and signaled a decisive upsurge in Catholic male piety or, at the very least, Catholic male identification with the church. Leslie Tentler has argued recently that new research "suggests that males from many ethnic backgrounds were gradually habituated to a relatively disciplined religious behavior" through the church in America. The pattern of Worcester Irishmen's religious behavior seems to support Tentler's contention.[51]

American-born women, as might be expected, were religiously active, too, but the nature of their participation in the church—at least as reflected in the kinds of organizations they joined—began to change in the late nineteenth and early twentieth centuries. In the late nineteenth century sodalities for young ladies and unmarried ladies as well as other women's religious organizations flourished in all of Worcester's Irish parishes. In the twentieth century women's sodalities continued to thrive, but new organizations also appeared that moved beyond exclusive dedication to devotions or Catholic ritual to offer Irish Catholic women opportunities for education in art, culture, or even important issues of the day. The first was the Catholic Young Women's Lyceum at Sacred Heart parish The women's Lyceum paralleled the parish's men's group of the same name: it imposed a temperance pledge on its members; organized lectures, debates, and educational discussions; and even fielded some sports teams. Members of the Lyceum would remember later the "many changes and upsets" that plagued their society in its early years as they battled "many prejudices."[52]

It would not be until the twentieth century that the changes in Catholic women's associations reached full flower. The Catholic Women's Club founded in 1906 was the first women's organization to draw members from all of the city's parishes. Some pastors who feared a public role for women or losses to their own sodalities objected to the new organization, but within a few years it was flourishing. Like the Lyceum, and its Protestant-dominated counterpart, the Worcester Women's Club, the Catholic Women's Club organized lectures, programs, and educational demonstrations for its members. A few years later, local Irish Catholic women organized the St. Agnes Guild to provide social services for young women in Worcester, and a Worcester resident, Katie Boyle, helped form several branches of the national women's benefit society, the Ladies Catholic Benevolent Association. The LCBA "aimed to prevent the affiliation of Catholic women with nonsectarian societies, while helping them to cement a stronger union with those of their own creed and sought to educate its members in piety by means of Catholic literature." Yet it was, as Leslie Tentler has pointed out, also an important new kind or organization for women, for it provided them with insurance benefits, and thus recognized their economic importance.[53]

Whether American-born Irish men and women practiced their faith with equal fervor, it nonetheless seems clear that religion played an important role in the lives of both. But why? Why did the American-born hold to a faith carried over from a foreign and impoverished past, a faith that often set them apart from countrymen, fellow Americans?

In part, the members of the new generation were religious because they learned to be so at their mothers' knees. As noted, many parents of Worcester's turn of the century second-generation Irish fled Ireland during or shortly after the Famine, before the devotional revolution had become all-pervasive and powerful there. The Catholicism these immigrants grew up in was likely to be a pre-Famine peasant religion only recently undergoing reforms. Yet as Bryan Clarke argues in his study of the Irish in Toronto, such immigrants were clearly exposed to the Catholic devotional revolution in North America. Immigrant women in particular, Clarke argues, participated in the new revived Catholicism and when they married they raised their children, both sons and daughters, in it. Second-generation men and women, then, were brought up in the faith even as their parents, or more particularly their mothers, were learning it. Evidence from Worcester supports Clarke's argument. Devotional societies, particularly women's sodalities, appeared in St. John's and St. Anne's parishes in Worcester as early as the 1850s. Local Irish Catholic newspapers and magazines throughout the period also consistently ascribed the role of religious educator and guide to mothers, not fathers.[54]

But second-generation Irish men and women did more than merely accept a religion passed on to them; they made it the center of the world they were creating in America. One reason they did so was precisely because Catholicism provided them with a tie, a link to their past, as Paula Kane has suggested, in the midst of "rapid social change" and a painful, almost violent, rupture in experience between themselves and their Irishborn parents and forebears. The practice of their faith, the highly institutionalized rituals and devotions, and even some of the values may have differed from the peasant folk Catholicism of their ancestors, but the thread of identification was never broken. In reality, the practices of peasant folk Catholicism would have been hard for these city born-and-bred factory workers and shop clerks to maintain, so the new devotions and refurbished rituals helped them to fill out and mark this old loyalty, these boundaries, with cultural stuff that was better suited to a modern world. The new devotionalism, though rooted in ancient beliefs and rituals of Catholicism, gave these second-generation Irish the necessary "invented traditions" to reinforce and embody—as Jay Dolan and Ann Taves have suggested—their sense of Catholic community and identity. There would be no holy wells or jumping through bonfires on the feast of St. John the Baptist in Worcester, but there would be pilgrimages to the shrine in nearby Leicester, giant Corpus Christi processions, and churches packed for novenas to St. Theresa of Lisieux.[55]

It is important to remember, however, that if this new devotional Catholicism gave substance to the Catholic identity and community of the second-generation Irish, it did not, by itself, determine what that identity would mean in relation to their non-Catholic neighbors. It did not determine whether they would think of that identity as a potentially alternative means of being American, acceptable to American Protestants, or an oppositional identity and community, self-consciously set apart and against Protestants and other non-Catholics. Devotional Catholicism dominated Worcester's Irish churches throughout the entire period of the late nineteenth and early twentieth centuries, but, as we shall see in later chapters, how second-generation and other Irish Catholics of Worcester understood their place in Worcester's society would change radically during that time from accommodation and interest in defining an alternative American Catholicism, to confrontation and commitment to a militant, oppositional American Catholicism. Rather than devotional Catholicism forcing a certain kind of relation with their neighbors, there is some evidence that changes in those relations affected the popularity and commitment to devotional Catholicism. When, for example, Worcester's Irish Catholics became more suspicious of their neighbors and more militant in asserting their religious interests in the early twentieth century, devotions and devotional societies—especially among men—seemed to multiply rapidly and become more broadly popular.

There were other reasons why the second-generation Irish made Catholicism such an important part of the culture they created. Many, like their immigrant parents and cousins, felt vulnerable in an often hostile urban industrial world, and Catholicism was a source of power or protection. Some second-generation Irish would labor in unskilled or semiskilled jobs that were as bad as or only slightly better than those of the immigrants, and they were thus exposed to the dangers of unemployment, injury, and disease that the Irish-born faced. Second-generation Irish, even the successful ones, appreciated and depended on the help of heavenly as well as earthly "friends" in an uncertain industrial world.[56]

Their experiences and hopes, however, differed in important ways from their parents', and Catholicism was also successful in Worcester because it was able to speak to those special hopes and experiences of the new generation. Unlike their parents, members of the new generation were born and grew up in the worst tenement slums of a grimy mill city, strictly governed by the rhythms of the industrial economy. As these members reached maturity, their city was being transformed by the wondrous displays of a rising consumerism and leisure culture, theaters and department stores, elaborate restaurants and amusement parks recreating Chicago's "White City." Like their non-Catholic neighbors they longed for the magical and the marvelous and found it not just in a commercial world but in the spectacles and mysteries of their faith.[57]

One source of the church's appeal to the new generation, then, was the grandeur, mystery, and beauty of its festival and rituals. "The marvelous is the great need today," Father John J. McCoy asserted in 1902, "as the material earth is a cold dead world." Religious festivals transformed that world. As the *School and Home Magazine* exclaimed in 1896: "He who does not feel, at Christmastime, a glimmering of the pure love of God must have, indeed, a calloused spiritual nature." Irish Catholics took great pride in introducing "sacred time"— saints' days and other holy days and sacred seasons—into New England. The *School and Home Magazine* berated the Yankees, "a gloomy crowd" of "barren imagination and narrow heart," in 1896 for their neglect of Christmas. McCoy argued in 1900: "Now New England knows Christmas with all its sweet symbolism and the children of Puritan descent watch for it, and listen for the story of the Christ Child and his mother as eagerly as do those who bear names like ours. The new life of the Easter time throbs joyously in the hearts of those who worship in Congregational, Baptist or Unitarian meeting houses . . . light has come into the face of gloomy congregationalism."[58]

It was not the festival days so much as the Catholic rituals and ceremonies practiced on those and other days that appealed to the American-born. These rituals were often painstakingly planned and executed to evoke the proper awe and reverence. Stephen Littleton delighted in the mix of choral and orchestral

music he heard at masses. Given the huge crowds attending such festival celebrations as the Corpus Christi processions, it seems likely that others found
the grandeur of this ritual impressive too. Prominent second-generation Irish
men in Massachusetts, such as Mayor John F. Fitzgerald of Boston, or William
Cardinal O'Connell, who grew up in Lowell, were much impressed by the
glory and spectacle of the church as young boys. Doris Kearns Goodwin suggests that the ceremonies and festivals of the church were "so deeply woven
into the fabric of [Fitzgerald's] life, that long after he had become thoroughly
acclimatized to the hurried style of city life he still responded deeply to all
manner of traditional pageantry and he still viewed the changing seasons
through the calendar of the Christian year."[59]

One did not have to be poor or even Catholic to appreciate such marvels.
McCoy pointed out smugly that thousands of Yankee Protestants desperate
for the marvelous in their own lives had turned to "quack" substitutes for the
true faith, like theosophy, Christian Science, and spiritualism. Increasingly
even mainstream Protestants disdained evangelical simplicity and became
fascinated with the Gothic and the baroque. Protestant churches built in
Worcester after the middle of the nineteenth century were great decorative
Gothic piles of stone and brick, little different from neighboring Catholic edi-
fices. During the same period, fraternal societies with elaborate rituals and
uniforms multiplied in Worcester, just as they did throughout the country.[60]

For young second-generation Irish Catholics, however, the pomp and majesty of their church had a special meaning. Born of an impoverished peasantry who boasted no high culture that Yankee Protestants deigned to respect,
the second-generation Irish found in the grand ceremonies and buildings of
their churches a visible link to an ancient and glorious tradition. Worcester's
Catholics often boasted of the grandeur of their churches and their ceremonies
and invariably saw them in the context of the worldwide church and its unique
heritage. Francis McKeon, in a poem celebrating Archbishop John J. William's
golden jubilee in 1895, wrote "Nor can thy people's eyes keep back their tears,
tears of joy to see this blessed day—the wilderness blossoms as the rose; the
humble church gives way to temple grand; the picket guard for serried ranks
make way." In 1900 Father John J. McCoy saw the growth of Catholicism in
western Massachusetts as only one more evidence of the triumph of the ancient faith: the "whole world hurrying back again to the knees of Christ's
vicar." American-born Irish Catholics in Worcester thus not only found
Catholicism's majesty awe-inspiring but symbolic of their inheritance of a
venerable, worldwide culture. They were not the poor slum children of be-
draggled peasants turned laborers and servants, but the heirs to Western
Europe's highest civilization and oldest tradition.[61]

For all of its attractions of mystery or earthly grandeur, the rigor of church discipline probably proved more attractive—or at least more necessary—to the American-born Irish. Irish Catholicism in turn of the century Worcester was still a demanding, sometimes harsh, faith. Many of the sermons or addresses of Worcester's Irish priests that have survived from that period were tirades against sins of intemperance, greed, slander, or lust, and painted the consequences of immorality in graphic terms. Mission priests focused heavily, indeed almost exclusively, on sin and God's judgment in their visits to parishes like St. John's or Sacred Heart. Six of the ten sermons preached by the Paulists at St. John's in 1889, for example, were entitled "Mortal Sin," "Lessons of Death," "General Judgment," "Occasions of Sin," "Duties," and "Hell." The Paulists were also very concerned about intemperance and lectured frequently at Worcester missions on its evils. After the mission at Sacred Heart in 1891, they reported that more than 600 men and women had taken the pledge to abstain from alcohol, half of them for life. Missions thus aimed less at invoking hidden magic in a gloomy world, than at defining the proper narrow path in a dangerous and tempting one.[62]

Devotions helped the righteous Catholic keep on that path. According to Catholic doctrine, devotions earned the supplicant the grace to resist evil; more prosaically, they instilled or hardened self-discipline by requiring prayers, personal sacrifices, or rituals, such as visiting churches or shrines, at the appropriate times. Worcester's Irish Catholics often talked about devotions in contractual economic terms of exchange: "the ready promises of all to perform some good work for the spiritual treasury" or "we go to the market" with God and the saints in a "bargaining spirit." To be successful, such practices taught, men and women must be disciplined, willing to forgo sinful pleasures and fulfill the terms of their bargain. The *Annals of St. Anthony's Shrine* preached in 1900 that sacrifice and self-denial were the keys to winning the saints' favor: "curb your self-will . . . repress your impatience." Turn of the century Irish Catholicism may have been grand and marvelous, but it was also a religion of moral rigor and discipline.[63]

Many second-generation Irish men and women found such virtues not only appealing but necessary to their adjustment to life in Worcester. In his study of Sacred Heart parish on New York's West Side at the turn of the century, Hugh McLeod concluded: "it seems fair to interpret the militant respectability of these Catholics as a means of protecting their families from aspects of local life that were unpleasantly prominent. Their Catholicism looks less like the famous opium than a stimulus to the sanctification of values that offered a basis for pride in a situation of suffering and humiliation and some defense against its effects." This seemed as true of the Worcester Irish as

McLeod's New York Irish. Many, perhaps most, of the second-generation Irish at the turn of the century in Worcester were the children of Famine immigrants. Their fathers and mothers bore memories of that catastrophe and the chaos of uprooting and the bewildering pain of settling in America. The church and its discipline seemed a means of enduring and perhaps escaping the anarchy and hardship that their parents remembered and they themselves experienced growing up in Worcester's Irish slums. The self-discipline the church preached, such as abstention from alcohol, was critical to men and women who were moving beyond the unskilled labor of their parents to the rigid work regimens of the factory worker or the starched respectability of the clerk. Yet it was perhaps even more important in helping them endure the frustrations of postponing marriage, for as we shall see second-generation men and women married very late, later than their parents and about as late as men and women in Ireland. They had good need of discipline, then.[64]

For all of its appeal to the American-born Irish, Catholicism might not have been so popular among them if church leaders had not worked so hard to harmonize it with American culture. Catholic leaders insisted relentlessly, as we have seen, on the compatibility of Catholic and American loyalties. In a land steeped in anti-Catholicism but nonetheless committed to religious freedom, it was easier to make that claim than the more tortured assertion that Irish Americans could be loyal to two countries, Ireland and America, at once. Catholic versions of respectability included many of the same virtues as Protestant ones: self-improvement, self-discipline, even temperance. Moreover, in some of the ways that Catholics differed from Protestants, they may have been more in line with the changes occurring in American popular culture than their Protestant rivals—or at least more in line than the more extreme evangelicals. While some evangelical churches in Worcester frowned on the growing mania for sports, for example, local Catholic churches embraced them with enthusiasm.[65]

There were limits to what church leaders could or would accept in American culture. Again, as we shall see, the church worried about men and women who took the American gospel of success too much to heart. Catholic priests in Worcester never threatened rights of private property and were implacable foes of socialism and communism, but they were also wary of the excessively ambitious and materialistic among their flocks, fearing the effects of ruthless individualism on their communities. They urged the goal of respectability on the new generation, but respectability within Catholic limits.[66]

The church also strongly resisted trends in the broader culture to permit women a greater public role or expanded freedoms. Church societies like the

Catholic Young Women's Lyceum and the Catholic Women's Club opened up new opportunities for self-education and entertainment for Irish women, but those societies were still tightly controlled by priests and limited in their public activities. The Lyceum was entirely Father Conaty's project; he issued invitations, and once women assembled, they recalled later, he "explained the aims and objects of a society as he wished ours to be." Similarly, the *Catholic Messenger* reported in 1907 that the women of the Catholic Women's Club followed the ideas of Father John J. McCoy, the club's founder, "to the letter." Clerical control meant among other things, that these clubs played little role in politics or agitation for public reforms. By contrast, the local Yankee-dominated Worcester Women's Club became a leader in local public health and educational reform. As discussed in detail later, the church also grew increasingly suspicious of emerging popular culture recreation sites such as dance halls, skating rinks, and movies that permitted women more recreational options or encouraged more sexual freedom.[67]

The church's embrace of American culture, then, was qualified and its mix of marvels and a moral code probably did not appeal to all members of the new American-born generation, but its accomplishment in engaging the new generation was, nonetheless, impressive. It did not preserve a peasant practice of the faith but rather invented or reinvented customs and rituals more suitable to the world of the American-born that, nonetheless, helped them to retain a crucial link of loyalty to the religious loyalties of their ancestors. It leavened their harsh world with mystery and pageantry, made them heirs to the West's richest cultural tradition, prescribed a convincing moral code for self-discipline, respectability, and self-improvement, and still permitted them to claim American nationality and participate avidly in many aspects of American popular culture. It did this and yet let them remain true to the central element of their Irish past, their Catholic faith. It was a faith and religious practice at once flexible and rigorous and, in the end, serviceable for them, and they made it their own.

"Halfway up the Ladder": Second-Generation Irish Men in the Economy

John F. O'Connor, the same American-born schoolteacher who committed his faith to verse in the 1890s, complained to his fellow second-generation Irish in 1899 that "the condition of the Irish race in this country is not what it should be or what it shall be. We are still three or four generations behind . . . we are only halfway up the ladder." Many in Worcester's Irish community at the turn of the century shared O'Connor's disappointment. Articles in the *Messenger* and *Catholic Messenger* in 1905, 1911, and 1913 echoed his frustration. The proportion of Yankees in the professional or high managerial classes in 1900 was more than double the proportion of second-generation Irish in those occupations that year, and while just over 16.5 percent of the native stock were semi-skilled or unskilled workers in 1900, over 34.8 percent of the second-generation Irish were semi-skilled or unskilled.[68]

The Yankees, however were not the only rivals for the Irish in Worcester's economic competition, and over the course of the turn of the century the Irish increasingly nervously eyed the competition of newer immigrants and ethnics. Irish immigrants, as noted, suffered directly from the influx of Swedes and French Canadians into Worcester, but spokesmen from the Irish community suggested ominously that members of the newer groups like the Jews or Italians threatened to surpass the American-born Irish as well. O'Connor, speaking in 1899, was convinced that the Irish "were already three or four generations behind where the Swedes and Germans are today." The *Catholic Messenger* was more circumspect in 1911 but anxious nonetheless: "If we are not careful, some of the new coming races will surpass us."[69]

Such gloomy prophecies may have reflected a sincere sense of frustration in Worcester's Irish community, but they also understated the real achievements of its American-born members. The occupational advance of American-born men and women over the immigrant generation was indisputable. Even in 1880, when most of the American-born men were but a step away from the schoolyard, a far larger proportion of them than of the immigrants were white-collar workers or skilled workers. In the next twenty years, as the new generation matured, the disparity between generations of men grew far more substantial. Nearly a quarter of the American-born men had gained white-collar positions by 1900, two and a half times the proportion of immigrant men, and one-third of the American-born men were skilled workers compared to one-fifth of the immigrant men.[70]

American-born Irish men had advanced not only beyond their own immigrant parents and cousins by 1900 but ahead of most other groups in Worcester as well. O'Connor was wrong. It is true that the proportion of French Canadian and Swedish foreign-stock men in the skilled trades was as high as or higher than the percentage of skilled workers even among American-born Irishmen, but very few French Canadian males had broken into white-collar work by 1900, proportionally far fewer than the American-born Irish. And though the Swedes were making rapid strides in Worcester, they held no advantage over the American-born Irish in white-collar jobs in the early twentieth century.[71]

If the occupational adjustment of American-born Irish men was paradoxical—progress but disappointingly slow—it reflected the complicated influences that shaped it. Examination of the opportunities available to the American-born Irish in Worcester, the skills or training that they could call upon in the competition for jobs, and the attitudes they brought to the marketplace, reveal some of the cross-pressures and conflicts—growing numbers of jobs, but persistent discrimination, for example, or desires for self-improvement but Catholic limits on ambition—that produced their ambiguous achievement.

Writers addressing the younger Irish generation in Worcester, and members of that generation themselves, often spoke glowingly of America's wealth and opportunities. Major John Byrne addressing "Catholic Young Men" in the *Catholic School and Home Magazine* in 1897 argued that America's bounty, democracy, and capitalism offered his readers a unique chance: "In no country on the face of the earth do the same conditions exist. These conditions assure to every man possessed of the character and qualifications an opportunity to win success in any legitimate field to which his ambition aspires." The *Catholic Messenger* concurred in 1913, arguing that there "is nothing to stop our young people from rising except themselves."[72]

The American-born Irish were well aware, however, that the reality of opportunity in Worcester did not always match the rhetoric of bounty proclaimed by more enthusiastic members of their community. Some had a sense that the possibilities for advancement were better in western cities than in their own New England. In 1884, the St. John's Temperance and Literary Guild debated the proposition whether the "west" offered better opportunities for "honorable success in life" than the east. The second-generation temperance men just embarking on their careers did not believe so then, but twenty-six years later the *Catholic Messenger* was convinced: "In the Far West the Irish own the banks, the mines, the live stock, ranches. . . . Here we reverse the scale and the Irish suffer for it in a thousand ways in Massachusetts." Statistical evidence from San Francisco and other California cities confirms the judgment of the *Messenger*. Second-generation Irish men could not match the occupational achievements of California's American-born Irish in climbing into white-collar work or even in securing skilled labor.

These discrepancies resulted, in part, from both the slower growth of Worcester's economy and the persistent discrimination which favored the city's Yankees or their Protestant allies. Second-generation men, just like the immigrants, suffered from the slow contraction of the boot and shoe industry, for example, for an even larger proportion of them than the Irish-born worked in the boot and shoe shops before the industry's slow decline. The young American-born may have made an easier transition to newer jobs than the older immigrants, but the boot and shoe trade's collapse was still a problem for them. American-born Irish men in the mills or machine shops also suffered from the favoritism Yankee manufacturers displayed towards rival Swedish workers.[73]

Prejudice and discrimination only got worse for American-born Irish as they ascended the city's economic ladder. "The banks," John F. O'Connor noted sourly in 1899, are "in the hands of others than the Irish, the great business of the country is also in other hands." For the second-generation Irish, Yankee control meant exclusion from networks of connections that might have aided their climb upward in places like the Washburn Moen Wire Company. In other cases, Yankee control meant outright discrimination against Irish men of any generation. In 1895, Richard O'Flynn reported that no Yankee-owned bank in the city of Worcester would hire an Irish Catholic, a charge echoed by other Irish men in the city over twenty years later.[74]

American-born Irish men seeking to advance by founding their own businesses also discovered their progress hindered by discrimination. F. H. Miller testified at a hearing on the charter of a new Worcester bank in 1895 that a small, tightly knit elite controlled the city's existing banks, an elite which often refused loans to men seeking to start new businesses. Even once started, Irish-owned businesses often experienced difficulty in attracting trade outside their own group. This was as true of large second-generation-owned construction firms like McDermott Brothers Contractors as it was of small immigrant-owned shops and stores. McDermott Brothers built over 250 houses, apartment buildings, meeting halls, and schools from the 1880s through 1915, but almost all of them were built for Irish Americans or for the Catholic church. Not until 1916 did McDermott Brothers receive a major contract from a non-Catholic business, U.S. Steel, which had absorbed the old Washburn Moen Wire Works. Even then McDermott Brothers may have won the contract because U.S. Steel had recently appointed an Irish-American, John F. Tinsley, to head the Worcester wire works. In 1915, the Knights of Columbus intimated darkly that non-Catholics often deliberately refused to patronize Catholic-owned stores and businesses.[75]

Such restrictions on their markets or clients hurt even American-born Irish professionals. John O'Connor was trained as a lawyer, but he turned to teaching in the public schools instead. He explained in 1899: "Where if I am a lawyer must I get my clientage? In the police court? One doesn't get rich there . . . the young American steps out of college and is looked after. He has friends and connections to look after him and perhaps at the outset steps into a position of $3,000 a year while our Irish young men have to give themselves to menial work." Perhaps because of these conditions, Irish newspapers and magazines throughout the turn of the century era felt that the small number of Irish professionals, almost all of them second-generation, was still far too large. In the *Alumna* in 1887 and the *Catholic Messenger* in 1912 and 1913, writers referred with alarm to the "overcrowding" of professional ranks among the Irish in Worcester. "Everybody knows" the professions are "overcrowded," the paper claimed in 1914, and most professionals endured a difficult initial "starving time," and even after that earned only a "fair living."[76]

To this complicated structure of opportunity, the American-born Irish brought a mixed bag of skills and educational resources. Conscious of the immigrant generation's poverty of crafts or trade skills, perhaps, spokesmen in the Irish community repeatedly warned parents to teach their boys and girls a skill. Nevertheless, few of the immigrants, even after many years of life in America, ever learned a craft themselves and thus few could pass trade skills on to their children. In 1900, only 15 percent of the Irish sons living at home with their parents were employed in the same industry as their fathers.[77]

The American-born Irish might have also learned the means of moving up Worcester's occupational ladder in school. Since Worcester had few parochial schools until the twentieth century, that meant public school for the vast majority of American-born Irish. Historians have offered conflicting testimony about the willingness of the Irish immigrant parents to provide education for their children. Years ago, Stephan Thernstrom suggested that Irish parents seemed indifferent to the education of their young and displayed no qualms about sacrificing their schooling for the child wages that might help the family to buy a home. More recently, others, like Joel Perlman, have suggested a more complicated picture, pointing to a disproportionately large number of American-born Irish graduating from high school or even attending college as early as the 1910s.[78]

Statistics measuring school attendance among the American-born Irish in nineteenth-century Worcester suggest that greater and greater numbers of second-generation children were delaying their departure from school as the century wore on. In 1899 the *Messenger* boasted that there were more graduates of Irish descent from Classical and English high schools and the state teachers' normal school than all other nationalities combined. The paper exaggerated, but it was true that, by 1901, the proportion of American-born Irish in the high schools was as large as their percentage in the elementary schools. The census samples suggest the same trend. One hundred and fifteen Irish immigrant families in 1880 and 114 in 1900 had children between fourteen and eighteen years of age. In 1880, only 36.9 percent of those families had a child over age fourteen in school, but twenty years later the proportion had risen to nearly a half. The census samples also reveal that the number of second-generation Irish males between the ages of eighteen and twenty-one attending school rose from 7 percent to 13 percent between 1880 and 1900.[79]

Such changes were probably not so much changes in attitude as changes in the circumstances of Irish families over the course of the nineteenth century. The principal cost to Irish families in sending their children to college or even to high school, the *Catholic Messenger* argued in 1913, was the loss of their offspring's earnings. In 1887, the *Alumna's* counsel to parents reflected the family's dilemma: "send your child to school . . . their little earnings will not make you richer and later you will regret what you should have done." The rising number of families who kept teenagers in school reflected, perhaps more than anything else, the aging of immigrant families and the maturing of their children. By 1900, there was a larger proportion of immigrant families with more older children than there had been in 1880 who did not need "the little earnings" of their adolescent members and could thus permit younger sons or daughters to stay in school. Older children worked, therefore, so their younger siblings could go to school.[80]

American-born Irish children, or at least those for whom their parents could afford it, found increasing chances to extend their education, but what did they learn in Worcester's public schools that might help them move up the city's occupational ladder? Worcester's schools imparted few specific mechanical skills to the American-born Irish who attended them. Albert Marble was superintendent of the schools for a over a quarter century in the late nineteenth century as the bulk of the second-generation Irish grew up. Marble steadfastly opposed manual training or commercial courses that might distract schools from their main purpose of "literary and intellectual education." Worcester's schools, however, did attempt to inculcate ideals, values, customs, and habits into their small Celtic charges. On the one hand the schools stoked ambition. In 1867, Superintendent Chenoweth, Marble's predecessor, wrote: "Are we to teach our children—thus did your fathers, follow ye in their footsteps and be ye like them? No! No! No! . . . . here lies a vast continent with all its virgin wealth waiting to be tamed and appropriated." Yet to surpass their fathers and tame that continent students needed to learn the virtues that would permit them to compete. The aim of the school, Marble rhapsodized in 1873, was to "cultivate true manhood" and eliminate the "throng of idlers and barroom loungers." Such manhood resulted only from competition and the virtues of industry, temperance, frugality, and punctuality that competition bred.[81]

Another powerful influence in shaping the attitudes of the American-born Irish towards social mobility was their own Catholic church. At times Worcester's Irish Catholic clergymen eagerly painted exciting pictures of future success for the young people of their parishes and outlined the kind of disciplined virtues that would make that success come true. In 1891, Father Thomas J. Conaty of Sacred Heart parish leaned over the podium at a meeting of the Catholic Young Men's Lyceum and exclaimed "Boys, the future is with us. The future of the country is in our hands." To win this future or to secure success, Conaty asserted, was not dependent on luck: "Industry and a good life are keys to the bank which contains it and every man can enter and satisfy himself. Bread will go on a man's table, clothes on his back, money in his pocket, if he looks after the pennies that he earns by his daily toil."[82]

Yet Worcester's Irish clerics seemed to mix this praise of ambition and industry with bitter condemnations of excessive materialism. The antimaterialistic theme, Joseph Lee has argued, was prominent in the sermons of Catholic priests in Ireland throughout the late nineteenth and early twentieth century and it was a recurrent point in the preaching of Worcester's Irish-born, and even second-generation Irish priests as well. McCoy, for example, inveighed against "the vast material power of the age" which "brings war to the spirit," and Conaty too preached submission to God's will. In 1891, he included a short poem in his parish bulletin:

> Only to be what he made me
> Though I am nothing still
> Never a look beyond me
> Out of my little sphere
> If I could fill another
> God would not keep me here.[83]

Irish Catholic priests feared not only the threat of an abstract materialism to the religious spirit of their peoples, they were also worried that the allure of upward mobility might encourage apostasy in a society where Protestants controlled most of the routes to success. As McCoy ruefully admitted in 1900: "Because Protestants as a body were rich they [young Catholics] believed that simply to be one was to receive uplifting." It was not the poor, but the rich and ambitious, then, many Catholic spokesmen in Worcester agreed, who were most likely to abandon their faith. It was, the *Messenger* contended in 1902, the "fairly well to do" who broke church rules such as the prohibitions against eating meat on Fridays to mask their faith or curry favor with Protestants. It was also because of the "unblushingly expressed desire of social advancement," Rev. Campbell, S.J., told Worcester's Holy Cross alumni in 1898 that so many young Catholic "traitors" "deserted" Catholic colleges in favor of their "richly endowed competitors."[84]

One of the most important effects of this complicated mix of Irish cultural attitudes and overt or covert discrimination against them was to virtually exclude Irish men from the top positions in Worcester's manufacturing companies, the heart of the local economy. Second-generation Irish men seemed able to move beyond general labor into promising industrial occupations at the blue-collar level. In 1900, only about 7 percent of American-born Irish men worked as simple day laborers compared to 31.2 percent of their immigrant fathers or cousins that year. By contrast, 14 percent of the American-born found jobs in machinery manufacture in 1900 compared to only 8.6 percent of the immigrants. Yet no American-born Irish men owned or managed these machine tool factories. In 1919 only 7.2 percent of the 104 Irish listed in the biographical section of Nutt's *History of Worcester* owned a manufacturing business, and all but one of the firms those eight men owned or managed were small, marginal companies.[85]

Irish writers in Worcester found this failure shameful and frustrating. By the early twentieth century it seemed to them that this was the most galling result of their people's limited occupational advance, for they understood well that such a failure meant their group could never match the power of their Yankee rivals. In 1911, the *Catholic Messenger* lamented that "the lack of Catholic men engaged in solid business is counted heavily against us as a people." As the paper noted, "Anglo Saxons [have] almost exclusive control." Two years later, the paper acknowledged that many Catholics had achieved modest prosperity, lived in "good houses," and enjoyed secure jobs, but it wondered why "so few of them are the proprietors of large business houses; how seldom they are found in high places in our banks and manufactures?" The paper offered a number of its own answers for their failures, such as the laziness of the new generation, or the chronic Irish weakness for backbiting and envy, but the actual causes were more complicated.[86]

Worcester's industrial community and culture had its roots in the ferment of technological innovation that transformed New England at the end of the eighteenth and beginning of the nineteenth centuries. Though later exaggerated in a triumphant nostalgia, the energy and initiative of hosts of young men working as mechanics either part-time on farms, or full-time as craftsmen, apprentices, or owners of small mills was critical to the takeoff of industry in the region. As Worcester's industry grew, the city's manufacturers made concerted efforts to keep this tradition of technological innovation alive. The most important lasting effort was the establishment in 1865 of Worcester Polytechnic Institute, originally called the Worcester County Free Institute for Industrial Science. Liberally endowed by local manufacturers, the school was free until 1889 and reasonably priced thereafter so that it might attract the best of central Massachusetts' budding innovative tinkerers. WPI's curriculum was a self-conscious attempt to marry the practical training of the shop with the scientific education of the classroom in order to sustain Worcester's technological leadership. The institute quickly realized the hopes of its supporters. Between 1871 and 1917, 461 of its graduates worked in Worcester and many of the city's most successful companies were founded by WPI alumni or teachers. They included the Rockwood Sprinkler Company, Norton Company, Morgan Construction Company, and Wyman Gordon Company.[87]

Because they were culturally predisposed to value its classical education or because of communal pressure and the desire to be with their own, most of Worcester's ambitious Irish Catholics who went to college enrolled not in WPI but in Worcester's own Catholic Jesuit school, the College of the Holy Cross. As the number of Irish attending high school grew throughout the 1880s, Holy Cross emerged as the second leading choice of male public high school graduates. In June of 1886, the *Academe,* the Worcester high school's paper, reported that eight senior boys with Irish names were going to college, six had chosen to go to Holy Cross, one to Boston University Law School, and one to West Point. Thirty years later the pattern had not changed; indeed it seemed to have become even more fixed. Of the ten Irish males from public Classical High's class of 1925 who listed their college preferences, eight planned to go to Holy Cross, one to Boston University Law School, and one to WPI. Throughout the turn of the century period, nearly one-fifth of Holy Cross's overwhelmingly Irish student body came from Worcester: 49 of 252 students in 1895; 110 of 597 in 1915.[88]

Few local Irish, it appears, immigrant or American-born, chose to attend WPI. Within a decade after its founding, WPI was already accepting students from around the world. In 1876 two young Japanese men attended the institute, and shortly thereafter students came from Chile, China, and Brazil. Yet, ironically, the distance between local Irish Catholics and Yankees may have become greater. Of 184 men who graduated from WPI between 1885 and 1890 listed in the institute's *Journal,* only eleven had Irish names, and but two of those had settled in Worcester. Thirty years later the proportion of Irish was about the same.[89]

This choice of Holy Cross over "Tech" had an important effect on the later career prospects of most of the graduates. The vast majority of the Holy Cross graduates went on to the priesthood or entered the professions of law, medicine, or teaching. Between 1870 and 1916, only 17.8 percent of Holy Cross graduates went into business. A full 46 percent became lawyers, doctors, or teachers (16 percent, 17.7 percent, and 13.1 percent respectively) and, as noted earlier, over one-third became priests.[90]

Second-generation Irish boys may have foresworn WPI because their community leaders were, at best, ambivalent about technical or business education. In 1911 and 1913, the *Catholic Messenger* urged parents to consider their sons' future; "if your boy is good at math," he should be sent to technical or scientific schools, but the paper also questioned the very notion that education should be judged by its practicality or tied to career advancement. Such questioning seemed prompted by the fact that Catholic schools, elementary, secondary, and college, put less emphasis on technical and scientific subjects than on traditional subjects of the classical curriculum and religious and moral training. Irish Catholic spokesmen, as we shall see, were also sensitive to charges that parochial schools were inferior to public schools and thus could potentially hinder a young man or woman's career. In the same year that it endorsed technical education, 1913, the *Catholic Messenger* rose to the defense of the classics and bitterly denounced attempts to measure education by the "almighty dollar," "by the ability to make a living," or "by the test of material value and usefulness." Shortly thereafter, in 1918, the Irish weekly again defended the classics and decried the effort to reduce education to the "materialistic" and the "utilitarian."[91]

It is also possible that young Irish Americans chose Holy Cross precisely because they wanted to become professionals as well as for the reasons of community loyalty or esteem for classical education previously noted. Irish Catholic tradition placed great value on the professional vocations. In Ireland, Joseph Lee has pointed out, "the temptation [of Catholic businessmen] to extract capital from firms to educate children into the professions was very great." Editorials and articles in the *Catholic Messenger* reveal that Irish Americans in Worcester were also very conscious of this traditional Irish penchant for the professions, with the paper complaining in 1911 about second-generation Irishmen's "mad rush to become professional men at all hazards without regard to the consequences." The paper exaggerated: the small proportion of second-generation Irish in the professions in 1900 hardly constituted a "mad rush" or even a small crowd. Nevertheless, despite alleged potential hazards, the American-born Irish did show a decided preference for the professions over manufacturing. Of the 104 Irish listed in the biographical section of Nutt's *History of Worcester*, 37 percent were professionals (15.3 percent lawyers, 10.5 percent doctors, 4.9 percent teachers, 3.8 percent clergymen, 2.8 percent judges). Interestingly, by contrast, only 7 percent of the 36 Swedes listed in Nutt pursued professional vocations, but over three quarters owned or managed manufacturing companies.[92]

Choosing to go to Holy Cross, and perhaps the professions, meant, however, that young American-born Irish men forfeited an alternative opportunity to launch a career in local business through Worcester Polytechnic Institute. This was not just because of the education students might receive but also through the friends and contacts they might make there. H. Winfield Wyman and Lyman Gordon, who founded what would prove to be one of the city's largest companies, attended Tech together in the early 1880s, and Milton Higgins and George Alden, who would establish an even bigger firm, the Norton Company, taught there at the same time. Indeed, WPI seemed such an important conduit to success that an ambitious young Scottish immigrant, James Logan, made a special effort to hang about the school and make friends with Tech men even though he was not enrolled there. He cultivated them so sedulously, in fact, that they made him an honorary member of the class of 1876 (the first honorary member of a class in the school's history). More important, he eventually parlayed his Tech connections into leadership of Worcester's largest envelope manufacturing company and a successful political career in the Republican party.[93]

Yet Irish Catholics who attended Worcester Tech did not find it as easy to strike up such richly remunerative friendships as these Protestants, Alden, Wyman, or even the nonstudent, Logan, did. While many Yankee or other Protestant Tech men enjoyed fabulous success in Worcester after leaving school, the achievements of almost all of the few Irish Americans who attended WPI and remained in Worcester were much more modest. The classes of 1885 to 1890, for example, produced sixteen Yankee men who settled in Worcester. Of those sixteen, eight became owners or executives in Worcester companies, including major firms such as Morgan Construction, Rockwood Sprinkler, and the Graton and Knight Company. Of the few Irish Americans who attended Tech in the late 1880s and also settled in the city, on the other hand, none became owners or executives: two ended up as middle-level engineering employees at Morgan Construction and the others worked in modest white-collar jobs outside of manufacturing. Unlike Wyman, or Higgins, or even Logan, who were all Protestants, these Irish-American students at Tech would not find the friends or make the connections that would help them later, nor would they be recognized by a Yankee-dominated business elite after they graduated. Those Irish who did not go to the school and chose Holy Cross or another college instead of WPI may have understood all of this beforehand and that is why they never sought entry to the engineering institute. They may have understood that Tech was not "their school" (though there is no evidence of official discrimination against them) and that it would not work for them as well as it did for Yankee or even Protestant immigrant boys. In any case, whether Worcester's Irish Americans did not go to Tech because they preferred Holy Cross, or because they understood that WPI would not help them as it did Protestants, few Worcester Irish followed the path to local economic success well worn by the region's Yankees through Worcester Tech.

Not finding a path through WPI to such success, local Irish Americans never discovered another means of entry into the local business elite. As we shall see, that local elite became more—not less—cohesive, exclusive, and dominant in the Worcester economy in the early twentieth century despite a revolutionary transformation of Worcester industry by market expansion and technological innovation at that time. Thus, even though Irish American men became better educated and more savvy about American culture in the twentieth century, the boundaries of the local economic elite remained as impervious to their penetration as ever before.[94]

The career of the only Irish American to make his way to the top of the local economic hierarchy is instructive in this regard—the exception that proves the rule. John F. Tinsley became superintendent of the South Works of U.S. Steel and Wire Plants in Worcester in 1911. A few years later he became general manager, and then president of the giant Crompton Knowles Loom Manufacturing Company in Worcester. Tinsley was an Irish Catholic, but he had been born in New Jersey, educated at Rutgers, and came to Worcester after he was appointed by U.S. Steel to run its local plant. He did not move up through the ranks of Worcester industry but penetrated it from outside after already reaching a high level. He thus became part of a just-then emerging class of floating executives for national corporations. As we shall see, as Worcester industry evolved, it remained largely homegrown and dominated by local Yankees, so there would be few branch plants in Worcester offering routes of entry into the city's elite for men like Tinsley. In other cities, where branch plants of national corporations dominated, local elites may have been more fluid and porous than in Worcester, where industry remained locally controlled.[95]

Many second-generation Irish men, like the first, continued to look to the political arena to carve out their own network of jobs and economic favors. By the early twentieth century, Irish interest in and success in politics had gone on so long and passed from one generation to the next that the editors of the *Messenger* considered it to be almost a racial trait: "born organizers" the paper called the Irish in 1905; "naturally cut out for politicians," it stated five years later. The rewards of government seemed very important to the second generation as they had to the first. The Knights of Columbus noted in its adult education circular of 1915 that government provided "higher salary and better working conditions than any other employer can offer." The government employed a full one-sixth of the second-generation clerical workers in 1900, but even that figure may underestimate the American-born generation's dependence on politics for upward mobility. The Irish first elected a mayor of Worcester in 1901, and they would not secure full control of the city's politics until the 1920s. By the second decade of the twentieth century politics had certainly become critical to the city's elite. Of the Irish Catholics listed in Nutt's *History of Worcester* in 1919, 42.3 percent held government or political party posts at some point in their lifetimes. The infield from the locally legendary Sacred Heart Young Men's Lyceum baseball nine of the 1890s neatly symbolized the importance of public employment for the Irish: Tom O'Reilly, first base, later a clerk in the Post Office; William Foran, second base, later a priest; John Gannon, shortstop, later superintendent of schools; and Ed Ryan, third base, later a fire department captain.[96]

In 1910, reflecting the persistent concerns of Worcester's Irish with their community's failure to produce enough successful businessmen, the *Catholic Messenger* charged that government and politics enticed young Irish men who might have succeeded better in commercial pursuits. It is possible that Irish men who became politicians, like Irish moving into the professions, missed opportunities in business, but it seems just as likely that the young American-born Irish man found it easier to follow the path that political power provided to status and security than to break into businesses dominated by the city's Yankees.[97]

"Young Women Were Out in the World . . . Earning Their Daily Bread"

The efforts of American-born Irish women to grapple with Worcester's economy had much in common with those of their second-generation Irish brothers. Like the men, they made substantial progress beyond the occupational status of the immigrant Irish. Second-generation women all but abandoned domestic service and many broke into the ranks of white-collar workers. Indeed, second-generation women matched up better against ethnic competitors such as the Yankees, Swedes, and French Canadians, than their Irish-American brothers did. Unlike for Irish men, community concerns about women's work focused less on competition with other groups or the threats of ambition and success, than on basic issues, such as whether women should work outside the home at all, and if so for what purposes. Within the framework defined by the responses to those questions, American-born Irish women found new opportunities for themselves but remained limited by the norms of their community.

Immigrant women might bite their tongues and keep their places long enough to reap the advantages of domestic service, but for second-generation women such sacrifices were both unacceptable and unnecessary. They had homes: between 69 percent and 86 percent of the industrial and white-collar women workers in 1880 and 1900 lived with their families; born in America, they profited little from their mistresses' course in American culture. Finally and perhaps most important in industrial or white-collar employment second-generation women had access to better-paying and/or more prestigious jobs than domestic service.[98]

What alternative sources of employment did second-generation single women find? Most of them worked in semi-skilled jobs such as boot and shoe or envelope mills, but, by 1900, 14 percent, or one in seven, second-generation women were skilled workers. The success of the American-born women in exploiting the explosion of opportunities in white-collar work was especially notable. Between 1880 and 1900 the number of female white-collar jobs, such as bookkeepers, clerks, and stenographers, rose almost 1,000 percent in Worcester. Second-generation Irish women took full advantage of these opportunities. The proportion of American-born Irish single women in white-collar occupations rose from a tenth to nearly a quarter between 1880 and 1900. In those two decades, for example, when the number of female schoolteachers in Worcester rose over 400 percent, the proportion of second-generation Irish women who were teachers rose from 5.7 percent of unmarried American-born Irish women to 8.3 percent in 1900. By 1910, over half the teachers in the Worcester public schools were second-generation Irish women, one of the highest percentages for any school system in the country. Interestingly, the proportion of second-generation Irish single women in white-collar jobs not only far surpassed the percentage of immigrant Irish women in such occupations by 1900, it also slightly exceeded the white-collar proportion of their American-born brothers: 24.1 percent of the second-generation unmarried women were white-collar workers that year compared to 23.9 percent of the American-born males.[99]

For a few American-born women, such success merely whetted their appetite for further accomplishments. Mary Agnes McGillicuddy graduated from the state normal school in 1880 and began teaching in the Worcester schools. She remained in the school department for more than thirty years, serving as principal of two Worcester schools in that time. Mary V. O'Callaghan also graduated from the normal school and taught second graders for ten years. Yet she abruptly left her teaching post to enter medical school and begin a long and prominent career as a doctor in Worcester. O'Callaghan's success inspired her niece, Clara Fitzgerald, in turn, to seek a medical degree and become a physician.[100]

That upward mobility appeared easier for American-born Irish women than for their second-generation brothers did not go unnoticed among contemporaries. Observers of the Irish community frequently noted that second-generation Irish women seemed more accomplished than second-generation Irish men. During the retreat for young people they conducted at St. John's in 1884, for example, the Paulists observed: "We find the women more cultivated than the men."[101]

Irish-stock women also seemed to fare as well or better against working women from other ethnic groups as Irish men did against their male competitors from other nationalities. Irish foreign-stock women still trailed Yankee women badly in the competition for white-collar posts, but the difference, especially in clerical posts, was less than the disparity between Irish and Yankee men. The census report on occupations in Worcester for 1900 recorded that 17.3 percent of Yankee men were clerical workers, a figure nearly three times as large as the 6.8 percent for Irish foreign-stock men. The proportion of Yankee female clerks, however, was less than twice as large as the percentage of Irish women in clerical occupations: 31.9 percent to 16.7 percent. French Canadian women outdistanced Irish foreign-stock women in the skilled trades, but Swedish women did not, and the proportion of Irish women who were white-collar workers was far larger than the white-collar percentages of either Swedish or French Canadian women.[102]

Second-generation women suffered from some of the same hindrances in their competition for better jobs that afflicted Irish men. They, too, gained little from the impoverished economic experience of their Irish inheritance. Immigrant women brought few skills to Worcester and added little in domestic service after they arrived; former maids passed down to their daughters only a knowledge of household tasks and, perhaps, an acquaintance with genteel American society. American-born Irish women also suffered employment discrimination, just as their mothers, fathers, and brothers did. In the early 1890s, a substantial Yankee protest movement attempted to limit the number of Irish women teaching in the public schools. Yankees also sought to limit Irish opportunities in other white-collar posts. In 1903 a woman who applied for an office job in one of Worcester's factories claimed she was turned away with an abrupt "We want no micks here." Two years later in 1905, John F. O'Connor raised the case of Elizabeth O'Malley before the trustees of the public library as a typical example of a qualified young Irish woman passed over for a new appointment because of her race and religion: "I believe that the exam paper of Miss Elizabeth O'Malley were [sic] jockeyed with and undermarked simply because she is an Irish Catholic girl." [103]

Irish women, however, also possessed some advantages in their search for better jobs. On the few occasions when Worcester Irish men spoke out on the education of women, they heartily endorsed women's access to secondary schools and college. In 1898 the *Messenger* praised the establishment of Trinity College, a Catholic girls school in Washington, for opening "a grand avenue to the higher education of Catholic women in this country." In both 1880 and 1900, the proportion of second-generation Irish women in school over age eighteen was larger than the proportion of American-born Irish males of a similar age. [104]

The Irish in Worcester also consistently praised working women. In 1894, "Anna" writing in the *Catholic School and Home Magazine* lauded "the nobility of the working girl" and attacked charges that working detracted from a woman's femininity. Nearly twenty years later, in 1913, the *Catholic Messenger* responded hotly to claims that employment outside the home somehow made women easy prey for procurers. The newspaper countered, "the young woman is good and true and to throw the onus of the evil of modern times upon her is a rank injustice." [105]

Despite their defenses, even praise, for working women, Irish writers and speakers never explicitly endorsed the right of women to work. Inevitably, they justified women's employment outside the home by referring to its necessity, caused by the "need to be helpful to their people" or "the forces of circumstances." This defense seems puzzling, since the circumstances of a large proportion of second-generation women were far from dire. The vast majority of American-born women employed in white-collar and industrial occupations for both census years (1880 and 1900) came from blue-collar families. Yet in both 1880 and 1900, the families of between 38 percent and 55 percent of these second-generation working women lived "comfortably," which meant that they derived income not only from a working daughter but also from either a skilled father and two working children or a semiskilled and or unskilled father and two working sons. An even larger proportion, a substantial majority of American-born working women, lived with at least one other employed sibling. No doubt second-generation Irish women did work "to be help-ful to their people," but often it was to help them achieve a taste of prosperity, not rescue them from poverty.[106]

Furthermore, there is evidence that Irish women did not work simply be-cause they had to, but because they wanted to, and that employment outside the home enhanced their self-esteem and sense of freedom. Comments in the *Messenger* as early as 1888 and as late as 1915 grudgingly admitted that women worked for themselves as well as for their families. Such work, the *Messenger*'s editorial in 1888 noted, undermined the former "slavery" of sisters to their brothers' wishes in Irish families. The 1894 article by "Anna" on the "nobility of the working girl" also suggested the beneficial effect of work on the con-fidence of women, describing the working girl as one "who dares to be in-dependent and earn an honest living."[107]

Many community leaders were not happy with such independence and continually tried to reinforce the boundaries of a restricted women's sphere. Frequent articles in the *Messenger,* the *Alumna,* and the *Catholic School and Home Magazine* counseled young Irish girls to learn household chores from their mothers, the better to prepare them for their future roles as wives and mothers. In 1886 the *Alumna* applauded the training of a young woman that would make "her . . . the light of the hearth and home." Nearly thirty years later, in 1915, the *Catholic Messenger* criticized young women for loitering about downtown after work, instead of rushing home to help their mothers care for the house-hold. Furthermore, despite the tradition of permanent celibacy in Ireland and evidence of its reappearance in Worcester, the *Catholic Messenger* in 1913 in-sisted that marriage was the normal, ultimate future for lay men and women.[108]

Yet there was noticeable evidence of growing self-confidence and rising as-pirations that, ironically, also drew on the cultural values of the community. Stout Irish Catholic defenses of young women out in the world earning their daily bread helped nourish such sentiments even with the attendant dis-claimers justifying such work as family obligations. Support for education did as well, and in a way that was never fully articulated the example of religious women, who also followed careers and proved the ability of women to manage institutions and organizations, must have encouraged Worcester's young American-born Irish women. These defenses of work education and the ex-ample of religious women combined with the changing female occupational structure in Worcester's economy and economic needs of Worcester's working-class families to give Irish women new opportunities for satisfying work and, indeed, greater personal autonomy and power. Immigrants were not prepared or equipped to take advantage of these opportunities; second-generation women were, and they did. Even though most of them married, most of them postponed marriage, and some, a proportion far larger than among immigrant women, never did marry. Among these single women emerged the vanguard of an entirely new phenomenon in Worcester: Irish professional women like Doctors Mary O'Callaghan and Anna Murphy. Such trends belied the frequent proclamations of church and ethnic leaders that Worcester's Irish community believed marriage and motherhood was the only worthwhile role for women. Change was in the air.

Abigail L. O'Hara, born in Worcester of Irish immigrant parents in 1866, both epitomized these trends and gave voice to the aspirations they reflected. O'Hara attended St. John's parish schools and the normal school before becoming a teacher in Worcester in 1887. She would remain a teacher for forty-eight years. One sister became a factory worker before marrying, another a nurse; O'Hara as a teacher, of course, remained single. She wrote often for Father Thomas J. Conaty's *School and Home Magazine,* and in 1894 she mused about "woman in the twentieth century" in an essay for the magazine. She shied from foreseeing a political role for women in the new century in that essay, but she was sure that woman "will do the intellectual work of the world...upon the same plane with man," would know no bounds to her "physical development" and would "lend her hand to every worthy cause." And a woman will not be afraid or ashamed of "single blessedness," she said. Marriage might still be "good and desirable for the greater number of women in the new century," O'Hara argued, "but the old maid will be such from vocation and she will have her compensations."[109]

The Mayor Lives at Home with His Parents

In 1901, Philip J. O'Connell was elected mayor of Worcester. A second-generation Irishman, he was the first mayor of Irish descent in the city's history. When elected he was thirty years old, unmarried, and living at home with his parents.[110]

O'Connell was typical of members of his generation in this respect. The second-generation Irish married late, men somewhat later than women, but both later than native-stock Yankees in Worcester and, as noted, later than Irish immigrants. In 1900 over half the American-born Irish males aged 30 to 34, O'Connell's age group, were unmarried; nearly two fifths in the age group 35 to 44 were unwed. This compared to only 40 percent and 15 percent, respectively, for Irish immigrant men that year, and 27 percent and 15 percent of native-stock Yankee males in those age groups. Average ages of marriage further substantiate the differences. In 1900 American-born Irish men married peasants demonstrated little such antipathy as late as the first few decades of the nineteenth century. Indeed, Ireland's population nearly tripled between 1750 and 1840, in part because the vast majority of Ireland's poorest peasants married young, and had large families. As one cottier told a British investigating committee in the 1830s: "[If] I had a blanket to cover her I would marry the woman I like and could get potatoes enough to put in my children's mouths I would be happy and content as any man." That attitude disappeared over the course of the nineteenth century as the economic conditions that permitted early marriage disappeared. In the transition from tillage to pasture, and from partible to impartible inheritance in Irish agriculture through the middle years of the nineteenth century, only one son, the heir, and usually at most one daughter, the recipient of the family dowry, could marry. All others had to emigrate or remain celibate and even the heirs had to wait until their parents were willing to give up their farms. Some sons remained "boys" well into their late thirties or early forties, waiting to marry.[85]

The influence of these customs and norms on how Irish immigrants in Worcester made decisions about marriage and family was clearly evident. Irish immigrant men in Worcester, for example, tended to marry later than native-stock Yankee men in the city. More Irish immigrant women remained unmarried into their late twenties than did Yankee women. Even more dramatic were the differences in fertility between the Yankees and the Irish immigrants. In 1900, 23.3 percent of Worcester's Yankee women, aged 45 and over and married ten to twenty years, had no children and only 34 percent had more than two. By contrast, only 8.3 percent of Irish immigrant women of the same age and married an equal number of years had no children, and 83.5 percent had more than two.[86]

Yet if the marriage and family practice of Worcester's Irish immigrants differed from that of the city's native-stock Yankees, this behavior was no mere imitation of old country customs and norms. If Irish immigrants in Worcester delayed their marriages, almost all of them did marry, nonetheless. Such was not the case in Ireland. In 1901 24 percent of the men and 20 percent of the women in Ireland, age 45 to 54, were unmarried. A year earlier, in 1900, only 7.8 percent of the Irish-born males in Worcester and 7.2 percent of the Irish-born women between the ages of 45 and 54 were still unwed. Indeed, a smaller proportion of Irish immigrants than Yankees remained unmarried after age 34 in 1900. Furthermore, Irish immigrants in Worcester may have delayed their marriages but they did not postpone them as long as the people they left behind in the old country did. In 1901 72 percent of the men and 53 percent of the women between the ages of 25 and 34 were single in Ireland, while only

52 percent of the Irish-born men and 35 percent of the Irish immigrant women in Worcester were unwed the year before.[87]

These discrepancies were not insignificant or mere aberrations in Worcester. Other historians have also noted the lower age of marriage among Irish immigrants in North America than among the Irish in Ireland. Some have speculated that the immigrants may have included a large number of "rebels" fleeing the agricultural system that would not permit them to marry or at least to marry when they wished. There is evidence in Worcester to support this hypothesis. John F. Coakley, a brewer, and his wife grew up on adjacent farms in Kerry, but they had to leave Ireland in order to achieve their desire to be wed. Other historians have argued that the new agricultural system and the change in marriage norms it inevitably created spread only slowly throughout Ireland. In large areas, particularly in the west, early marriage remained the custom because the market and the resulting changes to pasture and to impartible inheritance had not yet fully taken hold there. Presumably the marriage ages of immigrant men and women would rise over the course of the century in America as the new economic system spread over Ireland. That did happen in Worcester in the twenty years between 1880 and 1900. In 1880, only 22 percent of Irish immigrant males and 17.6 percent of the women, aged 30 to 34, remained unmarried; by 1900, 40 percent of the men that age and 24 percent of the women were still single.[88]

It was conditions in America, not in Ireland, however, that best account for the differences between the native Irish and Irish-immigrant patterns. As noted earlier, most immigrant men lived with siblings or, more often, boarded out with fellow Irish families after they arrived in America. These appear to have been purposely temporary accommodations until marriage. If an immigrant man did not marry by his late twenties or early thirties, his living arrangements began to change. Most unmarried Irish immigrant men by that age had moved out of their lodgings with an Irish family to live in large boardinghouses containing a number of lodgers of various nationalities. If an Irish immigrant man delayed marriage, then, he suffered the costs of drifting into an impersonal living situation and becoming alienated from his ethnic community.[89]

As domestic servants, most single Irish-born women enjoyed many comforts, but service had many drawbacks that made it, too, at best a temporary stopgap. Service required long hours of work for low pay. Yet it was the humiliation that was the greatest drawback. In 1902, a survey by the State Labor Bureau revealed that the vast majority of female retail clerks or even factory workers refused to consider working as domestic servants, principally because they found being subject to the whims and rigorous discipline of a master or a mistress distasteful. Most shop girls, for example, complained of the stigma of service, lost "social pride," or "loss of caste." The factory worker, the Labor Bureau concluded, is considered "socially superior" to the servant. In 1898, and again in 1904, Worcester's servants attempted to organize unions in the city. The Irish-owned *Worcester Evening Post* claimed in 1904: "Her particular grievance is that she is called a servant. That is more than she can bear, so objectionable is the designation that the girls are looking about for other employment." For these reasons Irish immigrant women did not persist long in service. In 1880, 76 percent of Worcester's unmarried Irish domestics were less than 29 years old; by 1900, the proportion had risen to 80 percent.[90]

For immigrant men and women, then, the alternatives to marriage were not residence in the homes of their parents, as in Ireland, but continuing to live as boarders or domestics, the former a makeshift arrangement not meant to sustain them indefinitely, and the latter an increasingly burdensome limit to their freedom.

There were risks in entering marriage, however, particularly for women. As desperate as they may have been to escape service, women quite literally recrossed the border from pleasant, sometimes luxurious surroundings into an impoverished, unhealthy, and crude world when they married. Their new husbands worked at the worst jobs in the city, vulnerable to every disease and injury that their harsh working conditions could inflict. Husbands thus most often died before their wives did. In 1900, 17 percent of all Irish-born women were widows, compared to only 8 percent of the men who were widowers. The plight of younger widows was particularly difficult, and for many there was no alternative but to seek charity. An Immigration Commission survey of Worcester's poor-relief applicants in 1910 found that 23 of the 48 Irish-born applicants were widows, 11 of them with five children or more. And if their Irish immigrant husbands did not die, then they might be overwhelmed by their burdens, become addicted to alcohol, and grow violent. In 1897, for example, Jerry Sullivan got drunk and hit his wife. She fought back, and in their struggle they knocked over a lamp that started a fire and destroyed their home. Richard O'Flynn also spoke of the wife of an alcoholic immigrant from Clare in the 1880s: "seldom was she without blackened eyes." Irish temperance reformers in Worcester constantly lamented the effects of drink on the home life of their people.[91]

Yet if marriage had risks for Irish immigrants, especially women, it also promised potential long-term advantages. Although there is some evidence which suggests that delaying marriage helped some Irish immigrant men accumulate property, for the vast majority of Irish immigrant men and women postponing marriage would do little to help them advance their careers or increase their incomes. Only a handful would escape unskilled or semiskilled labor in twenty years' time, let alone five or ten. Yet as Monsignor Byrne of Boston said in Worcester's Irish weekly, the *Messenger,* in 1901, if a man married early enough he could "rear a family which long before he lost his own usefulness has developed earning capacity." The earning capacity of these children, in fact, permitted some Irish immigrant families to even enjoy mild prosperity. In one Irish immigrant family interviewed by the Massachusetts Bureau of Labor Statistics in 1875, the father, a laborer, earned a little over $400 but two sons, aged 16 and 14, together earned over $500 more. Thus the family could afford a "well situated" and "well furnished" tenement with a "carpeted parlor" and have enough to dress well. The "earning capacity" of children was also critical to Irish immigrants bent on owning their homes. While 24 percent of Irish immigrant renters could draw on the wages of three or more working family members in 1900, 39 percent of Irish families with mortgages could rely on three or more incomes. For all of its potential hazards, then, Irish immigrant men and women knew that marriage was still their best option for fulfillment, perhaps even survival. In 1900, women of the immigrant-dominated AOH Ladies Auxiliary held a debate on the benefits of marriage and voted overwhelmingly in its favor. The two women arguing the affirmative even offered to marry immediately as proof of their convictions.[92]

Children, of course, incurred costs without producing income in their early years, but there were other ways for families to raise money. Occasionally wives worked outside the home although this was exceedingly rare in Worcester's Irish community. Norms inherited from the old country proscribed this practice, and it appeared that even fewer Irish wives worked outside the home than married women from other ethnic groups. More acceptable and more common was the practice of taking in boarders. Families with young children or no children were the most likely to take in boarders or sibling relations who presumably would pay their keep. In 1880 nearly 35 percent of the Irish immigrant families with no children took in boarders or siblings, and in 1900 nearly 30 percent of Irish households with children under seven added boarders or relatives. The percentages fell as parents and children grew older through middle age and rose again when the parents reached old age, but at virtually every stage of the life cycle at least some Irish immigrants took in boarders or kin. In 1900, for example, Mary McGrath, the fifty-year-old wife of a laborer and mother of a twenty-three-year old working son, took in a boarder. Just as the new immigrant needed a place to live, the immigrant family needed him; practical interests thus again reinforced the ties of reciprocity that flowed from the Irish communal ethos.[93]

Perhaps as important as a means of raising income, marriage and children were critical to immigrants as a hedge against the perils of the industrial system. The multiple incomes provided by children were especially useful during seasonal layoffs or even depressions. John Foley, a fifty-two-year old carpenter had a nineteen-year-old working daughter and two working sons of twenty-four and seventeen years of age in 1900. In Worcester's economy of varied industries, the chances that all four would be unemployed at the same time were slim. Foley's family was typical of Irish households headed by men his age. In both 1880 and 1900 over half of Worcester's Irish immigrant house-holds headed by men in their early fifties had at least two working children.[94]

As fearful for an Irish immigrant as unemployment or accident and disease was the prospect of a lonely and impoverished old age. Such a fear was justified. In 1892 over thirty of Worcester's Irish immigrants aged sixty-five or older spent their last days at the poor farm. Faithful children were the best defense against such a dire prospect. Old-country and religious norms required that children support their parents in old age. Indeed, Father Richard S. J. Burke even op-posed a Catholic old-age home in 1890, preferring to prick the consciences of the "sons and daughters who do not think enough of their father and mother to give them a home in old age." The vast majority of children apparently needed little reminding. In 1880 and 1900, over 80 percent of Worcester's married or widowed Irish-born women over age seventy lived with married children or headed their own households of adult working sons and daughters.[95]

Irish immigrants in America thus had good reason to deviate from the marriage norms and customs of the old country, but this deviation did not signal their acculturation to American individualism. Quite the contrary, working-class life in industrial America reinforced rather than weakened the Irish immigrant man or woman's dependence on family and thus reinforced their communal values and familism. In Ireland men and women who delayed their marriage or never married simply remained in their parents' house-holds. That option had been lost for Irish immigrants in Worcester when they crossed the ocean. Moreover, delaying marriage for Irish immigrant women in Worcester meant perpetuating the oppressive restrictions of life as a do-mestic, and for men it meant drifting away from the tight but fragile networks of friends and kin to impersonal and potentially lonely living arrangements. Furthermore, while early marriage without land meant a drastic drop in the standard of living and status of men or women in Ireland, it had no such effect on the lives of Irish immigrants in Worcester, or at least no such permanent effect. While the family might struggle when the children were young, the couple had a chance of achieving mild prosperity if they could make it to middle age. Indeed, working children were virtually the only means most

Irish immigrants had of improving their standard of living and providing a hedge against the insecurities of the economic system. For Irish immigrants in Worcester, the formula for survival was not an individual but a communal, and especially a family, strategy.

When Irish immigrants looked for marriage partners to produce these children and a family, inevitably they looked to fellow immigrants from the old country, thus reinforcing the sense of group solidarity and reciprocal obligation. There was some variation by class and occupation: almost all of the laborers, the poorest of the poor, married other Irish immigrants; one-fifth of the few upwardly mobile machinists wed second-generation Irish or non-Irish women. Yet since there were so few Irish-born at higher class levels, such distinctions had little effect on the overall rate of in-marriage among the immigrants, which was over 90 percent. Class, religion, and affinity for fellow exiles combined to limit Irish choices. Perhaps the only non-Irish group of substantial size to share their Catholic faith, communal values, and working-class status were the French Canadians, and the barrier of language was a powerful impediment to those unions. Since Irish families almost always took in Irish boarders when they added non-kin to the family as well, then over 90 percent of Worcester's Irish immigrant households were purely Celtic.[96]

An Irish Worcester: Irish Settlement in Worcester

Once married, Irish immigrant families invariably settled in or near one of the Irish neighborhoods on the east side of Worcester. Over the course of the nineteenth century Worcester's Irish settlements expanded from the tiny camp of the city's Irish canal-workers to a crescent of four large neighborhoods. Yet the expansion of Irish settlement did not signal an advance or improvement in the quality of their living conditions, for the continuing poor wages of Irish immigrants translated into equally mean homes and lodgings. Living in Worcester's east-side Irish neighborhoods meant eking out a hardscrabble existence in overcrowded tenements, set amid sprawling factories, poorly kept streets, and inadequate sewer drainage.

When Irish laborers on the Blackstone Canal first arrived in Worcester in 1826, local leaders shunted them off to a dreary pine meadow on the far east side of the village. Irishmen could not enter the town proper without a pass. They could not even bury their dead in Worcester; they were forced to carry them down the canal to Rhode Island. Edward Lincoln expressed the secret hopes of most of his fellow townsmen when he told them: "The Irish have come to build the canal, not to live among us."[97]

Of course the Irish did not leave Worcester, but neither did the vast majority "live among" the town's Yankee Protestants. In succeeding years, as the Irish immigrant population swelled, the site of the canal-workers' camp turned into Worcester's first Irish—or for that matter—first ethnic neighborhood, the Meadows. By the 1840s a second settlement, sometimes called Scalpintown, had emerged across the canal to the east. There, the Irish built their first church, St. John's. There, too, some of the richer Irish contractors like Tobias Boland lived, giving the area a slightly more prosperous air than the neighboring Meadows.[98]

By 1880, Irish settlement had spread out from these two small ethnic villages into a great arc of four Irish-dominated districts running along the inner rim of the city's east side. The first two Irish neighborhoods to grow out of the initial colonies in the Meadows and Scalpintown were East Worcester and the Island. They were not only the oldest of the Irish Worcester neighborhoods in 1880, but also the largest in that year; together they were home to over 52 percent of Worcester's Irish immigrants. East Worcester was an extension of the Meadows, spreading west from a mix of workingmen's cottages, two- and three-family homes, and factories near the railroad yards into the city's downtown and around its initial industrial district near the head of the Blackstone Canal. Bordering East Worcester to the south on the other side of the railroad tracks leading to Boston was the Island. The Island was an outgrowth of the old Scalpintown colony. The neighborhood was called the Island because the canal intersected with some narrow streams to separate the area from the rest of the city. For many of the city's inhabitants, the Island seemed to epitomize the city's working-class districts: a mixture of factories and rough housing on land virtually bare of trees and grass. Just south of the Island, but dominating its landscape were the city's gasworks producing "unseen sulfur dioxide fumes [which] hung continuously over the Island district."[99]

In the middle of the nineteenth century, two new Irish neighborhoods developed on the north and south sides of the city. The northern neighborhood was called variously Messenger Hill, Fairmount Hill, or, most often, just the North End. Dominated by the massive red brick complex of the Washburn Moen Wire Company's North Works and cut off from the rest of the city by a railroad on the east and a pond and park to the west, the North End seemed like an isolated mill village. South Worcester, by contrast, was more like a mere extension south of the Island and its mix of factories, cottages, and two- and three-family tenements. South Worcester, however, had much in common with the North End, for the Washburn Moen Company had located its other great plant just south of the neighborhood. In 1880, more Irish immigrants worked in the wire mills than in any other factories, and over 40 percent of the Irish wireworkers lived in either the North End or South Worcester.[100]

Irish first- or second-generation-headed households made up over half of all the families in each of the four Irish districts in 1880 (ranging from 53 percent in the North End to 59 percent in South Worcester). In the same year the four neighborhoods also contained nearly three-fifths of all Irish-born heads of households, two-thirds of all Irish immigrant boarders, and nearly two-thirds of all Irish immigrant adults in the city. Even most of the Irish-born who lived outside these neighborhoods still lived in one or another of the city's east side districts. The only substantial segment of Irish immigrant society to live on the west side were the servant girls, because their work demanded it. Since most Yankees lived on the north and west sides of the city, Worcester was clearly divided. As second-generation Irishman Dr. John T. Duggan lamented in 1893, the city seemed broken into two parts: "the east and west sides . . . the Irish and the Americans, the Catholics and the Protestants."[101]

The east side was by no means a large, undifferentiated slum; it contained a number of distinct neighborhoods of varying quality. There were hills on the east side too, Vernon, Union, and St. Anne's among the most notable, and the housing on those eastern hills, at least in the late nineteenth century, was often sturdy and the environments clean and healthy. There was also a fancy residential neighborhood straddling the Main Street border between the east and west sides in the southern part of Worcester. The eastern hills and Main South would be the first stops of the Irish out of their old neighborhoods as they inched their way up the economic ladder. But few Irish-born lived on the eastern hills or along Main South in the late nineteenth century; the two- or three-hundred-foot trek up to the top of the eastern hills or into Main South from the Island would take most Irish families a generation to accomplish.[102]

The vast majority of Irish immigrants landed and settled in the poorer flatlands of the east side where they endured the worst homes and physical environments in Worcester. The most visible evidence of the Irish east side's lower-class character was its housing. Statistics published by the Massachusetts State Census in 1895 and the United States Census in 1930 clearly demonstrate the superiority of housing on the west side over that in the east. Houses and apartments on the east side in those census years were cheaper and more likely to be dilapidated and overcrowded than west side homes. Worcester had few large tenement apartments; almost all east siders lived in one-, two-, or three-family homes. A study by the Associated Charities in 1905 found that about one-third of the 500 poor east-side families that the agency surveyed lived in single-family homes. Most of them were small and plain, with narrow fronts set flush against the street. No type of housing sheltered more east-side families, however, than the three-family tenements, known as "three-deckers." From the 1880s until about 1910 about half of all the residential units built in Worcester were three-deckers. In the 1890s most three-deckers had dirt cellar floors, separate stoves for heating on all three floors, and front porches on the first floor. Later improvements added steam boilers and porches on all three floors. Some three-deckers were handsome, almost elegant, but many were plain, boxlike structures, built on lots as small as 2,000 to 3,000 square feet. The worst of these, according to a survey made by a Worcester charity worker in 1905, were so ridden with rat holes or were so flimsily constructed that they provided little protection against the winter wind. Basement apartments in hillside three-deckers, like the worst tenement apartments in New York, offered their occupants neither air nor light.[103]

Outside their houses Irishmen found an east-side environment that was just as harsh and difficult. The crush of tenements and factories left them little open space for play or leisure. Even after the city provided the east side with parks, they were often too small and poorly maintained to meet the needs of nearby residents. Inadequate sewage disposal was also a longtime problem on the east side. From the beginning of the sewer system in 1868, Worcester's sewer lines flowed into the existing Mill Brook, which cut through the heart of the east side. Not until 1894 did the city finally cover the entire length of Mill Brook, but long before that date the water had become foul and dangerous. One east-side Irishman even attempted suicide in 1878 merely by jumping into the shallow but poisonous stream. Even after city officials covered Mill Brook, sewage often "flowed back and inundated the cellars of poor people" on the east side after heavy rains. In the 1930s, a resident of the Island complained: "Sometimes during a storm the brook gets sick and throws up into the Island area . . . a garbage lake is formed . . . an oversized, overflowing toilet."[104]

The east side's poor and overcrowded housing, lack of fresh air and play space, and poor sewage disposal combined with poverty and ignorance to make the area a breeding ground for disease. Throughout the 1880 to 1920 period, death rates in the east side wards, three, four, and five, consistently exceeded those of the west side wards, seven and eight. Smallpox epidemics, which ravaged the city as late as 1880, "obstinately remained" in crowded east-side neighborhoods, and tuberculosis continued to plague the people of Worcester, particularly "apparently healthy Irish immigrants," until well into the twentieth century. The report of a charity worker from St. John's parish in 1884 summed up well the suffering endured by the poorest on Worcester's east side: "Miss Riley called on this Kerr woman last night and found the baby dying of dysentery and Mrs. Kerr down with congestion of the lungs. The doctor says the baby will die and he has fears for the woman's life also. . . . I went down this AM and never found a more pitiful case in my life. All was cold, damp, dirty and as the doctor said they would all die from the bad air."[105]

Crime flourished on the east side as well. The Irish-born were disproportionately represented among arrests in Worcester into the twentieth century. In 1900 Irish immigrants made up a tenth of the city's population, but furnished a quarter of the men and women arrested by Worcester's police. Violent incidents occurred frequently in Irish neighborhoods. On May 19 in 1890 the *Worcester Telegram* reported an "incipient riot" on "Dungarvan" hill (more often called Oak Hill) that pitted Irishmen against French Canadian immigrants who had recently moved into the Irish neighborhood. It was the fifth "fracas" on the hill in recent months, the paper reported. Gangs roamed the streets of the Island and Washington Square in the 1890s, while the "Forty Thieves" and their "mollies" preyed on the people of the Summer Shrewsbury Street district in the 1910s. In 1916 the *Worcester Magazine* noted that for years the Island had been considered beyond the "dead line," a freewheeling district known for the "rugged nature" of its "proletariat."[106]

Although for many economics strictly limited their choice of residence to these east-side areas, support in times of crisis and opportunities for comradeship were also readily available there. Neighbors, for example, were not only the most proximate sources of fellowship but the most accessible sources of aid outside the family. The simple plea of a woman to a Catholic charitable organization in 1882 testified to the critical importance of neighborly charity: "she did not have anything to live on except what the neighbors give her." In 1880, over two-thirds of the Irish living in tenements of two or more apartments had only Irish neighbors, and in some neighborhoods like the North End or Washington Square the proportions were greater, three-quarters or four-fifths. The importance of easy access to friends even led some Irishmen from the same parts of Ireland to settle together in small clusters in Worcester. In the 1880s many migrants from Achonry in Sligo lived near each other in a section of East Worcester.[107]

Irish immigrants also found meeting places, friendly businesses or institutions, on the east side. In 1899 31 of the city's 35 Irish saloons listed in the city directory were located in the four Irish neighborhoods. The small retail shops of the neighborhood were also important to Irish immigrants. Not only saloons but grocery stores, drugstores, newsstands, and tobacco stores often served important functions as neighborhood social centers. Stephen Littleton, a young Irish Catholic man from South Worcester, noted in his diary the many days he spent talking over the issues of the day in Spillane's drugstore in South Worcester in the early 1890s. Grocery stores were perhaps most important, however, not for their social functions so much but because grocers could sustain a family through hard times with liberal extensions of credit. The loans or credit the unemployed received from local grocers, Alexander Keysar notes in his study of unemployment in Massachusetts, were "something other than purely social transactions; they were expressions of social bonds and conventions, of a culture that valued mutual aid and mutual obligation." Fifty-two of the seventy-nine Irish-owned grocery stores in the city were located in the four Irish neighborhoods.[108]

Finally, Irish immigrant families settling in the east-side neighborhoods could find Catholic churches easily accessible. Separate Catholic parishes served all four Irish Worcester districts: Immaculate Conception in the North End; St. Anne's in East Worcester; St. John's in the Island; and Sacred Heart in South Worcester. In 1880, small wooden structures still housed the parishioners of St. Anne's and Immaculate Conception, and the pastor of Sacred Heart said mass in a converted tenement. Yet the Irish with proud fervor would soon create more imposing houses of worship. In 1882, thousands of Irishmen led by blaring bands and gaudily uniformed militia companies marched through the streets of East Worcester to cheer the bishop when he laid the cornerstone for a new St. Anne's. Two years later Irish paraders again filled the streets, this time in South Worcester to celebrate the dedication of Sacred Heart, a sturdy brick church which still serves the parish today.[109]

Worcester's Irish Catholic churches offered the Irish-born natives in their congregations a raft of services. These were first and foremost religious institutions. In a sacramental religion like Catholicism, they were the sacred sites of many of the faith's most important rituals: baptisms, confessions, and especially the mass. Worcester's Catholic churches, as noted earlier, were also centers of many devotions, celebrations, and services that extended far beyond the basic rituals of the Faith.[110]

Churches offered parishioners material help in time of distress as well as spiritual succor. Father John Power established a small hospital at St. Anne's parish in the 1860s because the impoverished sick members of his parish had nowhere else to go. The Sisters of Mercy who staffed that hospital later opened an orphanage in St. Paul's parish after people kept sending homeless children to them. By 1900, the sisters were caring for over eighty orphans. Priests at St. John's church attempted to find places for orphaned children through announcements like the following at mass on Sundays: "There is an orphan boy about 11 years old who will be given into some family for adoption if any can be found to take him. If not he will be allowed to go for the summer for his board and clothing to any who wants his labor."[111]

The principal sources of day-to-day charity in the parishes, however, were the local conferences of the St. Vincent de Paul Society, which had been founded by Frederick Ozanam in Europe in the 1830s. The first parish conference of the society appeared in Worcester in 1851. By 1898 two more conferences had appeared. Most of the funds for the conferences were raised at parties, picnics, and other church entertainments, and they were meager. There was a reluctance among members of the society to help poor people who should have looked first to their families or "[to] indulge drunkards by giving them relief." Despite the small size of their treasuries and their caution, the men of the conferences understood only too well the enormity of the need in their parishes and struggled to meet it. In the week of July 4, 1882, the St. John's conference gave four women $1 in groceries, another woman a quarter-ton of coal and a man and a woman $3.50 in cash. In all, in 1882, the conference gave out $316 in groceries, $116 in coal; in 1883, $335.88 in groceries, $191.70 in cash. In the latter year they paid 700 visits to homes, interceded with the Overseers of the Poor to find relief and also used their own connections to force relatives to do their duty or to find jobs for the unemployed. Moreover, though miffed by the pleas of drunkards or the irresponsibility of ungrateful children, they understood their role was to offer help to the poor "without exposure or humiliation." Their pastor reminded them that these poor "are your equals," and they knew well that almost any one of them could easily become a petitioner some day.[112]

Churches were important social as well as religious centers. Parish fairs were often grand events extending over several days and attracting hundreds, sometimes thousands of people to church halls and basements where they danced, took chances on gifts ranging from a picture of the bishop to a ton of coal, caught a glimpse of elaborately costumed "living tableaux," and cast their votes in special elections for the most popular wire-mill foreman, the best woman retail clerk downtown, or the most popular saloonkeeper. (Even in parish fairs elections were serious business to Irish immigrants. One saloonkeeper in St. Anne's parish sought to assure his daughter's victory as the most popular girl in the parish by trading beers for votes.) Though some complained that priests saw fairs simply as fundraisers rather than entertainments and thus put too much pressure on parishioners to attend, the fairs nonetheless seemed very popular. Receipts of $18,000 from two Sacred Heart fairs in the early 1880s and $8,000 for a St. Anne's fair later that decade suggest that they seemed to meet both the pastors' and the parishioners' needs. Parish picnics were also major social and recreational events for Irish immigrant families. In July of 1886 2,500 members of St. Anne's parish packed a park on the shores of Lake Quinsigamond on Worcester's eastern border, where they ate, danced, watched track and crew races and baseball games, and rowed and sailed boats. Just one month later, St. Anne's filled twenty-two railroad cars for a parish excursion to Nantasket beach, and a later Sacred Heart picnic was so popular it shut down the South Worcester wire mills. Besides fairs and picnics, parishes staged concerts, plays, lectures, travelogues, stereopticon shows, and a host of other "times" for the members of their congregations.[113]

Conclusion

By the late nineteenth century Irish immigrants had become a commonplace in Worcester, understood as inevitable a part of the city as the factories they worked in or the tenement apartments they called home. They were no longer visibly alien figures to be gawked at; indeed, even to most longtime Worcester residents new Irish immigrants hardly seemed noticeable. That was, in part, because new people from more exotic lands wearing seemingly strange clothes and speaking unfamiliar, odd languages were pouring into the city. Yet it was also because Irish immigrants were different than their Famine-era predecessors. Ireland had changed; it was no longer the raucous, rural slum of the early nineteenth century. It was a more ordered, disciplined place by the beginning of the twentieth century. And because it had changed, the immigrants who came from Ireland in the late nineteenth century were better clothed, better educated, more disciplined, and more knowledgeable about the kind of society they were entering.

And yet if they did not seem like aliens to others, they felt like aliens. They were exiles, they felt, forced from the land they loved, still looking back over their shoulders and across the water to it—or to an increasingly idealized image of it. It was not affection for a childhood landscape alone that gave them a sense of being separate; they still had a distinct culture. Not all the older customs had been erased in Ireland's transformation and they had also created some new ones that they felt marked them as distinctly Irish. If they could not hit "the side of a mountain" with a hurley ball, they would learn the game if it was to become their sport. They also nursed a sense of oppression from the old country, of ancient rights lost, of old heroes and battles.

What nourished their sense of separation most, perhaps, was their continuing need for each other. They might not have looked very different from Americans, but they thought differently than most Yankees. The vast majority were not individuals pursuing an American dream of riches; they were members of families, networks, and communities dependent on each other for survival. That was still the lesson they brought from southern Ireland, which for all its changes was still an agricultural economy of small producers, a land of peasants. Yet it was also a lesson reinforced by conditions of poverty, prejudice, and economic insecurity in this city of Worcester. So Irish men and women in Worcester, whether fresh from the boat or old hands in America, still gathered with their friends in saloons and pubs and both men and women invoked the help of powerful "friends" among the saints of their church. And both even did things that seemed very un-Irish, like all marrying and marrying early, or eschewing rural America for tenement apartments in smoky, crowded east-side city neighborhoods, because that is what a communal or familial strategy dictated in the new conditions of this part of America.

For them, solidarity, loyalty, and this consciousness of the boundaries of who was "us" and who was "them" would be important for them principally as the best hope for survival, but it also was the only means most of them could see for improvement. If they were going to move up in American society, it would not be as individuals but as members of families, neighborhoods, or a whole ethnic community. In the end they did little such moving up. There were many reasons for this slow economic progress, such as lack of skills and prejudice, but, ironically, the very communalism that may, indeed, have helped them survive may also have held them back from exploiting the opportunities of Worcester's economy.

They may not have looked so distinct or different to Worcester's Yankees or other observers, but locked together in webs of friendship for survival, dreaming of a rural idyll at home, and nursing resentment here, they understood themselves as different—they understood themselves as Irish.

Two

The Second-Generation Irish

He entitled the piece "A Yankee in Ireland," and the title seemed to aptly capture his sense of alienation from that country. William J. Larkin wrote the article in 1926, to recount a recent trip he had made "back" to Ireland. His prose, though polite, even generous, was still distant; he was clearly describing a country foreign to him. Though he was the child of Irish immigrants, William Larkin and Honora Dunleavy, Larkin had been born in the United States, and America, or more specifically Worcester, not Ireland, was his home. Indeed, ten years later, Larkin would achieve a considerable local reputation for his nostalgic reminiscences of "Old Time Worcester" in a weekly column for the *Worcester Post*. Unlike immigrant exiles like O'Flynn or Thomas Kiely, who dreamed of crossroad dances in Waterford or pipers in Kerry, Larkin and many of his American-born Irish contemporaries would look back to dips in Worcester's North Pond, vaudeville shows at local theaters, or boat races on Lake Quinsigamond for the concrete stuff of their memories and nostalgia. The city streets, three-deckers, factories, saloons, ballfields, and the great churches of East Worcester or the Island, not the cottages and fields of Tipperary's Golden Vale, the villages and mountains of Dingle, or the curraghs and rocky cliffs of Connemara, filled the landscape of "home" for them.

Yet though Larkin described himself thus he was definitely not a "Yankee." Ireland may have been foreign to him in 1926, but it still meant a great deal more to him than France, Italy, or any other old world country. He recounted lovingly in his article the scores of lectures, stereopticon shows in church basements, and speeches at nationalist meetings he had heard that described his parents' home and prophesied her future glory. Doubtless too he had heard countless stories around the kitchen table and songs and poems he could recite by heart. He boasted proudly how he had taken his place in line on a cold, snowy February day in 1920 when Eamon de Valera came to Worcester and thousands of Irish American nationalists marched behind the Irish leader up Main Street. If he was diffident now in his tour, it may have masked some disappointment in the country he had come to believe was an idyllic paradise.[1]

The culture, loyalties, and very identity of American-born Irish men and women like William Larkin in turn of the century Worcester were then, and are now, very difficult to define. James Mellen, Larkin's old boss at the *Worcester Daily Times,* was convinced he knew where the fundamental loyalties of the new generation lay. In November of 1881 he wrote boldly that the "patriotism" of the new generation was "essentially American." There was plenty of evidence to support Mellen's assertion: the second-generation Irish in Worcester did in fact frequently express their enthusiastic allegiance to their native America in the turn of the century era. Second-generation Irishman Thomas Bonaventure Lawler hailed the American flag at a Knights of Columbus banquet in 1895: "the emblem of the mightiest aspirations of freedom the human heart ever conceived." Father Thomas J. Conaty, who was born in Ireland but brought to America as an infant, claimed in the same year that the leaders of the American Revolution were "our fathers because we are the inheritors of their deeds and they our fathers in liberty."[2]

Mellen believed, however, that the second-generation not only loved its native land, but had an "aversion to all things Irish." Young Irish Americans, he argued, "strive to tear themselves away from their Irish connections and under the cloak of their American nativity" renounce all obligations to Ireland and "stifle" in their hearts all "Irish feelings." Mellen offered no conclusive explanation for the American-born Irishmen's rejection of their past, but he wondered whether "the Irish youth expects to win respect and confidence from his American brethren" by turning away from Ireland and things Irish to demonstrate his deep devotion to the United States.[3]

For men like Richard O'Flynn, the immigrant from Waterford who also lamented the sad decline of Irish loyalties in Worcester, the very names of the new generation seemed proof of the loss of their "Irish connection." O'Flynn noted in 1879 that it seemed that "fewer children are being named after the Irish saints (Patrick and Bridget) by the Irish in America." Twenty years later, in 1901, a pamphlet published by the United Divisions of Worcester's Ancient Order of Hibernians grumbled that Irish parents in America were naming their children after every "bush and bramble" but ignoring the names of Ireland's patron saints.[4]

Such observations were accurate. In 1880 and 1900, about 10 percent of Irish immigrant women in Worcester were named Bridget, and 15 percent of Irish-born men were named Patrick. In the second generation the number of Patricks and Bridgets declined precipitously to about 3 percent of American-born Irish women in 1900 called Bridget and 4 percent of the second-generation males bearing the name of Ireland's legendary patron, Patrick. The statistics did not bode well for the future of the two names among the Irish in Worcester. Only 4 percent of the second-generation Irish families had a son named Patrick or a daughter named Bridget, or both.[5]

Nationalist spokesmen in the AOH and other organizations saw a cowardly denial of heritage in this sorry trend. The AOH noted in 1901 that such names had proved a handicap in the struggle for social and economic progress, since Yankee Protestants controlled most of the major corporations, prestigious law firms, elite social clubs, and well-regarded universities. An AOH speaker pointed out in 1914 that "so called humorists" commonly used the names Patrick and Bridget in Irish stereotypes ("Paddy and Biddy") that ridiculed the foibles and weaknesses of Irish peasants in the old country as well as Irish immigrants in America.[6]

But O'Flynn and the Hibernians may have read too much into the disappearance of Partricks and Bridgets among the American-born Irish and overestimated the new generation's abandonment of its Irish roots. Some members of the second-generation might have had an "aversion" to all things Irish and many naturally found their own native American culture more amenable, as Mellen and others asserted, but most American-born Irish still respected the land of their parents even if they did not call it home, and they were eager to reconcile their feelings for the old country with their American loyalties. Mellen himself was an American-born Irishman, and there were hosts of second-generation Irishmen in turn of the century Worcester who, like him, were fervent nationalists. Many American-born Irish in Worcester knew well and often repeated the litanies of the old country's ancient glories. Indeed, by the 1880s and early 1900s the featured speakers at the city's annual St. Patrick's Day celebrations were almost always second-generation, not immigrant, Irishmen, and in 1914 when the local AOH commissioned a series of public lectures on Irish history, most of the speakers were American-born Irishmen. Father John J. McCoy, a Connecticut native, summed up the sentiments of these American-born Irish in an 1897 speech in Worcester: "We are Americans of the Americans and loyal to the core. We have no land but this land yet a holy heritage is ours in the glory of our fathers' land."[7]

Reconciling that heritage or allegiance with American patriotism, however, was not easy. The second-generation Irish were well aware of their ambiguous and indeterminate position in American life. Mellen noted in 1881 that for most people the "sepulchers" of their ancestors lie in their own country, but "with the Irish American it is different for while he can partake of the joys of liberty in this land of freedom and equality, when he looks back he finds that the builders of this great asylum of freedom are not his ancestors and that he is here only by the generosity and liberality of this great republic. Ah no! his ancestors, his traditions are found in another land." On the other hand the American-born Irish were fully conscious of American nativist charges that they could have but one loyalty: America. Judge Edward Corcoran acknowledged in Worcester on March 17 in 1892: "In this land we hear that we are Americans alone."

Some American-born Irishmen went to extraordinary rhetorical lengths to try to resolve the paradox of their allegiances only to become lost in thickets of complex metaphors embodying contradictory hopes. In 1909 Judge Thomas Dowd told a St. Patrick's Day gathering in Worcester that America was creating a new "American nationality" through a "process of amalgamation." Dowd began his speech enthusiastically endorsing this trend, but by the end of his long oration somehow wound up urging Irishmen to "hold fast" to their Irish traditions "lest in the process of assimilation the traits of a great race" became lost.[8]

Most second-generation Irish orators resolved the dilemma of their dual loyalties by pointing to the contributions Irish men had made to America's greatness. Irish orators in Worcester developed a litany of Irish American heroes which they repeated faithfully at virtually every ethnic celebration. The list usually included such notables as John Barry, Philip Kearny, Philip Sheridan, and local Civil War heroes, such as Sergeant Plunkett or Captain Thomas O'Neill. These incantations of dead heroes were often gruesome, dwelling on the details of Sergeant Plunkett's wounds as he lost both arms at Fredericksburg or on the death of Captain O'Neill shot down at Cold Harbor. Such ritual bathing in the blood of ancestors served a number of purposes, however. Most obviously, the sacrifices of Irish soldiers in America proved Celtic loyalty to America and demonstrated critical Irish contributions to its preservation. Yet, the litanies, which often stretched back to Revolutionary times, also provided the Irish with their own line of descent back to the founders of the nation. As Vladimir Nahirny and Joshua Fishman have pointed out, such tracings of "bilateral" descent have been common among second-generation ethnics: members of the group need not feel alien in America if their people had been here from the beginning. This form of argument could be taken to ludicrous extremes, as John T. Duggan, second-generation

Irish mayor of Worcester, demonstrated in 1914. Duggan claimed irrefutable evidence (including the eight-volume researches of N. Ludlow Beamish and the opinions of Professor Rafu of Copenhagen) to prove that "centuries before the Spaniards, the Irish landed . . . in North America and introduced a civilization the traces of which still remain." If native Americans were really Irish, then it was the Yankees, not the later Irish, who were truly foreigners or aliens in the United States.[9]

There have been second-generation Irish in Worcester all through the history of Irish people there, but only at the end of the nineteenth century and opening of the twentieth did they constitute a majority of the local Irish community and create a culture, a pattern of everyday life, that came to dominate Worcester's Irish community. It was a complicated culture, made first out of their American experience and pride in being Americans. They dominated Worcester's baseball diamonds, for example, flocked to seashore boardinghouses and hotels, and filled vaudeville audiences. Yet they were Catholics, too, and not simply because their parents were, but because a new Catholic devotionalism met their own deeply felt needs for identity, wonder, and moral rigor. They were, then, as likely to crowd their churches as popular theaters, or march in pilgrimages to a local shrine as stroll the boardwalks at beaches.

What they did is forge a culture that mixed an avid embrace of emerging American popular culture and the new institutionalized, devotional Catholicism with practical adjustments to the opportunities and constraints they confronted in an industrial city dominated by Protestants. They created a Catholic version of American loyalties and culture, respectability and community, that nourished their efforts for self-improvement but set limits to how far that self-improvement would carry them. Most men moved up to better jobs than their immigrant fathers had or than the new immigrant men arriving from Ireland found, but anti-Catholic prejudice and their own culture's ambivalence about success prevented the men of the new generation from entering the highest circles of Worcester's industrial hierarchy. Prejudice and Catholic attitudes not only about success but about women's roles bounded the ambitions of second-generation women too, but competing Catholic values, practical working-class necessities, weaker competition from Yankee women, and a vast expansion of women's white-collar jobs opened up opportunities to second-generation women for meaningful work and autonomy. Perhaps the most curious aspect of the life the second-generation Irish created out of this complex interaction of American aspirations, Catholic values, and economic necessities was their marital behavior. In part because they did not want to risk the costs of marriage either to their own ambitions or to their parents' modest prosperity, and in part because Catholicism's moral rigor helped them postpone it, the men and women of the second generation were very reluctant to marry. Indeed, the second generation married later than the immigrant Irish and about as late as the Irish in the old country, and the proportions of second-generation Irish men and women who never married was far larger than the proportions of permanently celibate immigrants and, again, similar to the percentages of celibate men and women in Ireland. Though their marital behavior seemed, oddly, more Irish than that of the Irish-born, members of the new generation were, nonetheless, far more willing to marry outside the ethnic group, take in non-Irish boarders, and move out of the old neighborhoods than the immigrants were. Taking advantage of their better incomes and the opening of new neighborhoods through a vast expansion of the city, the second-generation Irish left the Island and East Worcester for better homes, but when they moved most did not move very far or very fast, and their movement did not dilute their Catholic loyalties or sap their intent to forge new Catholic communities in the new neighborhoods where they settled. The life the new generation made for itself, therefore, was complicated, reflecting the complex combination of practical constraints and opportunities with American hopes and allegiances and Catholic loyalties and values that shaped it.

Ironically, perhaps the names they received as children, in the end, suggested something of the paths their lives were going to take. For if those names hinted that their experience was going to be different than that of their Irish-immigrant parents, then those names also revealed the distance of the new generation from its Yankee Protestant neighbors. Few of the American-born might have borne the proud Irish names of Bridget or Patrick, but almost none answered to the names of "every bush and bramble" as the nationalists charged, or to the biblical or classical names so prominent among their Yankee neighbors: Piley, Homer, Ichabod, Augusta, Ida, or Mabel. The vast majority of second-generation Irish in Worcester carried names such as John, Mary, James, Katherine, or Margaret (18.9 percent were named John in 1880 and 20.3 percent in 1900; 29.1 percent were called Mary in 1880 and 24.6 percent in 1900; 7.3 percent James in 1880 and 13.5 percent in 1900; 6.6 percent Katherine in 1880 and 10.6 percent in 1900; 10.2 percent Margaret in 1880 and 7.7 percent in 1900). Such names might not have been so obviously Irish as Patrick or Bridget, but they were clearly sound Catholic names, names of the church's most hallowed saints, and appropriately emblematic of the kind of culture these second-generation Irish would create for themselves in Worcester.

An American-born Generation of Irish Men and Women

The American-born Irish appeared in Worcester almost as early as the immigrants. In 1828, less than two years after the canal workers settled in the town, a Reverend Robert Woodley was recording the baptism of Daniel, son of William and Bridget McCormick, and John, son of Richard and Mary Ryan. It was not until the Famine era and its aftermath, however, that the numbers of second-generation children really began to rise. By 1885 the state census revealed that there were more native-born Americans of Irish parents than Irish immigrants living in Worcester; by 1900, fifteen years later, the second-generation Irish outnumbered the immigrant Irish by almost two to one.[10]

Though published census statistics accurately recorded the numbers of second-generation Irish, they did not reveal their ages. In 1880, five years before the state census counted over 12,000 second-generation Irish in Worcester, there were only about 3,700 second-generation Irish in the city over the age of eighteen, and less than half of those were over the age of twenty-five. By 1900, the number of second-generation Irish adults (over age eighteen) had grown substantially larger, to over 9,000. Yet even then only a little more than half, or 57.7 percent, of the generation was over age eighteen and but 40 percent over age twenty-five.[11]

The youth of the second-generation Irish at the turn of the century raises questions about when the American-born Irish began to exert a powerful influence within Worcester's Irish community. Some historians of Irish America have suggested that the second generation might have surpassed the immigrants as the significant and determining force in Irish communities as early as the Civil War. That clearly was not the case in Worcester. Immigrant adults, in fact, outnumbered the American-born Irish by about three to one in 1880, and even in 1900 by a few thousand. If Worcester was typical, the second-generation Irish rise to numerical predominance (and, conversely, the immigrant Celts' decline) among the adults in Irish America took place very slowly and was not fully achieved until the twentieth century.[12]

Casey at the Bat: Second-Generation Irish and the New American Leisure Culture

As the second generation grew to maturity, a broad revolution was transforming the leisure culture of their native America. Indeed, the whole concept of "leisure" was a product of the twin trends of urbanization and industrialization that swept America in the late nineteenth century. New concepts of time, new regimentation and routines in work, the concentration of people in cities, rising disposable income and gradually declining working hours spawned a new urban leisure culture of organized sports, summer vacations, vaudeville and movies to replace the familial pastimes and agricultural rituals of a bygone age. Baseball emerged as a mass sport through the middle decades of the nineteenth century. Worcester boasted a "major league" professional team and a legion of amateur clubs by the 1880s. Worcester tourists and vacationers began travelling to seashore or mountain as soon as the railroads and steamboats made it possible. The theater, of course, was an ancient form of entertainment, but it, too, was dramatically transformed in the late nineteenth century as a cleaned-up vaudeville organized in national touring circuits expanded throughout the nation. Theaters did not open in Worcester—still steeped in Puritan tradition—until the 1850s, and vaudeville provoked suspicions in some quarters through the late nineteenth century. By the early twentieth century, if not earlier, however, even eminent Worcester citizens agreed that vaudeville and the theater had "won the hearty approval of the [city's] public."[13]

Worcester's second-generation Irish were not mere passive participants in this new culture, not converts to popular pastimes created by "real" Americans and then passed on to immigrants or the children of immigrants; the second-generation Irish themselves helped shape and create the new culture. It was as much theirs—perhaps, even more theirs—as any Yankee farm boy's or girl's. It was no accident, then, that when a young Worcester schoolteacher, Ernest Thayer, wrote the poem in the 1880s that would symbolize baseball forever, he chose a Casey (rumored to be modeled on an Irish contemporary of Thayer's), not a Saltonstall, Lowell, Thayer, Winslow, or even a Smith or a Jones, to be "at the bat."[14]

Worcester's American-born Irish participated in a full range of sports and games in the late nineteenth and early twentieth century. Both St. John's and Sacred Heart parishes fitted up parts of their church halls as gymnasia in the 1880s and clubs from both churches staged gymnastic exhibitions in that decade and the next one. Tennis was slower to become widely popular among the Irish in Worcester, but the Irish women of Sacred Heart's Catholic Young Women's Lyceum were sponsoring tennis tournaments as early as 1886. Crew racing aroused far broader and excited interest among the Worcester Irish from at least the 1880s on. Worcester's Irish churches often put on their own parish picnics at nearby Lake Quinsigamond in the 1880s and those outings almost invariably featured crew races. The most important contribution of the Worcester Irish to local rowing, however, was the Wachusett Boat Club. Founded in 1887, the Wachusetts were not exclusively Irish, but Irish Catholics often claimed it as "our" club and a number of young American-born Irish served as its officers and were prominent among its oarsmen in the 1890s and early 1900s. The half-Irish legendary Edward Hanlan Ten Eyck of the Wachusetts was the first American to win the Diamond Sculls at the Henley Regatta in England.[15]

It was the American trinity of so-called major sports, football, basketball, and baseball, that most fascinated the Worcester Irish and it was in those sports that they became most prominent. Parish societies and St. John's High School, made up largely of American-born Irish men or boys, sponsored football teams as early as the 1890s, and Irish names like Fitzgerald and Canavan also dominated the roster of the "Worcesters" who represented the city in matches against New Bedford, Lowell, and other city squads in the same decade. By the 1920s Holy Cross football had become a virtual citywide mania for local Catholics. In a 1928 editorial entitled "Athletic Mysticism," the *Catholic Messenger* hailed football: "in no other sport is sacrifice of self for good of the whole so emphasized." No wonder, the paper stated, so many Catholic schools have embraced the sport. Basketball caught on almost instantaneously in the Irish community after its invention in nearby Springfield in 1891. The second-generation-dominated parish temperance societies formed their own league, the Emmet Guards sponsored a crack team by the late nineties, and the Knights of Columbus organized several popular teams in the following decades.

Baseball, however, was the premier sport of the Worcester Irish as well as the nation. John B. Whalon, an Irishman, established the "first organized club in the city," the Excelsiors, in 1868. Almost all of Whalon's first starting nine were immigrant or American-born Irish. Throughout the 1880s and 1890s American-born Irish men continued to dominate many of the better local clubs while many purely Irish Catholic clubs formed their own strong teams. The exploits of the Catholic Young Men's Lyceum baseball teams merited front-page stories even in the Yankee-owned daily papers of the 1890s, and they eventually became local legends. In 1926, the *Worcester Post* contended that a quarter century earlier you "could count on one hand the athletically inclined readers of Worcester who did not know of the Lyceum baseball nine." The American-born Irish who made up the Lyceum club, the paper recalled, "swept" the local leagues regularly "for years." Irishmen played an important role in the promotion as well as the playing of baseball in Worcester. Martin Flaherty ran the city's first professional club in the International Association in 1879, and J. Joseph Kennedy and Connie Murphy, "an ex-ballplayer," owned pro clubs representing the city in the 1880s and 1890s.[16]

Irish-American women played a much smaller part in Worcester's sports revolution than their brothers, but they also took up some of the customs of America's emerging modern leisure culture, such as summer vacations, with equal enthusiasm. In the 1870s and 1880s railroads and steamship lines linked Worcester to a host of resorts, from the mountains of New Hampshire to the seacoast of Rhode Island. By 1888, Worcester's Irish weekly, the *Messenger,* stated that "most everyone knows" Block Island, an island resort off the Rhode Island coast, and listed twenty-five readers of the paper who were vacationing there. In 1886, the *Alumna,* monthly magazine for the graduates of St. John's girls school, suggested that "everybody that is anybody takes a vacation."[17]

Some Irish families were wealthy enough or had enough time to vacation together as a group. Police Sergeant William Hickey and his son (the future Catholic bishop of Providence, Rhode Island) traveled to Block Island in the late 1880s; and Mrs. Dennis Meagher and her daughter spent a week in Newport in 1888. Generally, however, husbands in late nineteenth-century Worcester seemed to have difficulty finding the time to go away, and Irish wives—at least those mindful of traditional family norms—were reluctant to travel without their spouses.

Single people, even single women, were bound by no such traditional restrictions, and they—it appears from the personal columns of the *Messenger*—made up the bulk of Worcester's Irish vacationers. In August of 1898 53 of the 74 vacationers listed in the *Messenger* were single women. Fifteen years later, 26 of the 34 vacationers listed were single women. On August 6, 1898, the paper reported that Misses Katherine and Margaret Walsh had gone to Block Island; Misses Julia and Hannah McDowell and Josie Joyce to Newport, Rhode Island; and Katherine Whalen to Old Orchard Beach in Maine. Though the birthplaces of these women are unknown, their white-collar or skilled blue-collar occupations suggest that most of them were American-born. Of the 22 who could be traced in 1898 17 were white-collar workers and 4 were skilled blue-collar workers. Similarly of the 17 traced in 1913, 7 were white-collar workers and 6 were skilled blue-collar workers. Very few immigrant women held such fortunate positions in Worcester in 1880 or 1900.[18]

Second-generation Irish men swept up in the American sports revolution, and their female counterparts in trips to the seashore or mountains, shared a common enthusiasm for American music. The tastes of the new generation of Irish Americans ranged remarkably. Many young Irish Americans took piano lessons or attended music schools, and throughout the 1880s and 1890s, parish societies of both men and women encouraged their members to take up the piano or violin and members' recitals became a routine part of most clubs' regular meetings. Young Irish Americans also had a taste for less "refined" music. Minstrel shows were popular in the Irish community through the early twentieth century. The St. Paul's Lyceum, St. Stephen's and St. John's parish dramatic or temperance clubs, largely second-generation in their memberships, frequently staged minstrel shows, and the Washington Club, like those parish societies made up largely of second-generation Irishmen, was famous for its annual vaudeville and minstrel shows in the 1890s and early 1900s. As tastes in popular music changed, young Irish Americans kept pace. In 1915 a Knights of Columbus cabaret featured songs like "Turkey in the Straw," "Bombay Boy," "Way Down Yonder in the Cornfield," and "Back Home to Tennessee." By that time, too, Americanized "Tin Pan Alley" versions of Irishness ("Mother Machree," "When Irish Eyes Are Smiling") had become staples of St. Patrick's Day and other Irish community celebrations.[19]

The new generation embraced American dance as well as music. In the 1880s, a group of local social clubs, made up largely of young Irish Americans, sponsored dances and balls every winter season so lavish and "dressy" that they were remembered for decades after. Men wore formal evening wear and women elaborate gowns. At a Highland Associates affair in 1887, Miss Nellie Collins arrived in "electric blue satin en train, elaborately trimmed with deep ecru lace drawn across the front and caught up with flowers." Miss Collins also wore "long tan colored kid gloves" and carried "a petite corsage bouquet." The societies made sure that the ballrooms and the accoutrements of the dance were as dressy as the guests. At a ball again in 1887, the Carrolltons (named after Charles Carroll of Carrollton, the only Catholic signer of the Declaration of Independence) gave each woman guest a twelve-page souvenir book, each page bordered in gold and bronze, and at a Washington Club ball in 1886 the members placed canaries in gilt cages around the room and hung "Turkish" rugs on the walls. Virtually all these dances or balls also featured grand marches, midnight banquets, and dancing until the "wee small hours" to the music of a fashionable band, most often Putnam and Babcock's Orchestra. Though formal affairs were held by Irish clubs in Worcester in ensuing decades, none, James T. McDermott contended in 1915, could match the splendor of the great balls of the 1880s. Nevertheless, Irish-American interest in American dances did not abate. By the early twentieth century, the *Catholic Messenger* reported, new Irish generations had become avid enthusiasts of the "Turkey Trot," and other new popular dances.[20]

The theater tastes of the American-born Irish also reflected their American predispositions. Parish drama societies in the 1880s and 1890s had often featured Dion Boucicault's plays or other dramas and comedies set in Ireland, but by the 1900s and 1910s American plays, such as the *College Freshman*, or *The Man From Broadway*, had become their common fare. The latter, put on by the St. John's Dramatic Club in 1916, included songs such as "Baseball Rag," "America I Love You," and "We All Go to the Movies."[21]

Commercial theaters in Worcester reflected these changing Irish tastes as well. Through the latter half of the nineteenth century, Irish comedians, replete with Connemara whiskers and ragged swallowtail coats, appeared frequently in broad farces and other comedies on the stages of Worcester's theaters. Plays continued to appear in Worcester celebrating the "Irish wit" or "Irish nature" of their characters in the 1900s and 1910s, but it was Irish Americans, not men or women in Ireland, who were depicted most frequently on Worcester's stages: "slum toughs" like Owen Kildare, fighting his way out of poverty with the help of a charity worker in *Regeneration*; or the rugged but kindly Catholic pastor of a mining town—"full of Irish nature, yet American to the backbone"—in the *Parish Priest*.[22]

The rising popularity of such plays among the Worcester Irish suggested that as the American-born generation matured and grew to dominate Worcester's Irish community, they began to demand plays that reflected their own experience in America, not their parents' or ancestors' in a distant and long-ago Ireland. Like the new Tin Pan Alley Irish tunes, "Mother Machree" and "When Irish Eyes Are Smiling," such plays also pointed to the emergence of a newly invented, commercialized Irish American popular culture that would flourish for the next fifty years. Irish slum toughs and parish priests would become central figures in American movies as the success of James Cagney, Bing Crosby, Pat O'Brien, and Spencer Tracy attested. Such plays and songs also suggested that, as in baseball or other sports, the American-born Irish did not simply take up the customs of an existing American popular culture but participated in the making or shaping of a new one. But whether they helped invent them or merely adopted them from others, Worcester's young Irish Americans clearly made the games, sports, plays, and songs of the new American urban leisure culture their own.

"Enthusiasm Never Flagged for an Instant:" Catholic Devotionalism and the Second Generation

If the American-born Irish shared with their Yankees counterparts the new American popular culture (or even led them in shaping it), they nonetheless remained very different from their Yankee neighbors. There were many aspects of their lives that defined the difference, but one integral part of their cultural inheritance that marked them as distinctly and visibly different was their faith. To suggest that Catholicism was part of their inheritance, however, is not to imply that it was fully formed in the Ireland of their parents and simply passed on to the new American-born generation as their parents had learned it. Though their parents may have passed on a loyalty to Catholicism, the faith the second-generation practiced was not necessarily the one that their immigrant parents had been raised in as children. Most immigrant parents of Worcester's second-generation had grown up in Ireland during the pre-Famine or Famine eras, when Catholicism was still a tribal folk religion and churches and priests were scarce in most parts of the country, particularly in the west, where many Worcester Irish hailed from. Some, but probably only a minority, might have caught hints of a new, disciplined, institutionalized faith ushered in by the devotional revolution in Ireland, but those changes would have been very recent by the time they left in the 1850s and 1860s. Yet the devotional revolution of the nineteenth century occurred not only in Ireland but in other countries as well, including America. Immigrants who did not know the new devotionalism in Ireland, or had only begun to encounter it there, would find it and slowly become accustomed to it in America. More important, however, most second-generation Irish in places like Worcester would be the first in their families to grow up in this new Catholicism of elaborate institutional rituals, mission revivals, abundant and varied devotions, and numerous organizations. Among both the men and women of this American-born generation, it would take root and flourish as it met their needs both for an identity linking them to their past and a grandeur and a discipline promising them a better future.

The devotional revolution that transformed Catholicism in Ireland after midcentury was but part of a broad Catholic revival that swept through the church in France, Germany, and even America, as well as Ireland. All across Europe and America, older public rituals like the mass or feast-day celebrations became more self-consciously elaborate, and older private devotions were revitalized. Through parish missions, Catholic revivals, the revolution also spawned new devotions and hosts of new church organizations. Though Catholics in turn of the century Worcester as throughout the world loved to emphasize the unchanging continuity of their faith, they were, nonetheless, very aware of recent changes in their church and its effect on their mode of worship. Indeed, in 1921, the local *Catholic Messenger* acknowledged matter-of-factly that Pius IX, pope during the middle and late nineteenth century, had been the "founder" of most of the devotions that had become popular among Catholics in the city.[23]

There were many causes of this devotional revolution. In part, it represented a conscious effort by Rome or Catholic elites to reclaim ground lost to the liberal political revolutions of the eighteenth and nineteenth centuries. Faced with diminishing temporal power, the Vatican asserted even more strongly its religious authority and revitalized devotional practice to help secure assent to that assertion. The devotion to St. Anthony that became so popular in Worcester, as well as in other parts of America, reflected such ultramontane purposes quite clearly: urging members to pray with the pope at certain times of the day; looking to the triumph of the church over its enemies; and encouraging hopes for a union in the one, true faith under the pope of all "princes and peoples." The devotional revolution was not simply the product of papal fiat, however. Conditions throughout the Western world nourished and encouraged this Catholic revival. Those conditions varied from country to country: in parts of Germany, as in Ireland, the new religious devotionalism was part of the response to new demands for sexual or other kinds of discipline required by economic changes. Nineteenth-century economic and cultural trends not only motivated lay Catholics to participate in the revival, they also made it possible through new communication technologies. The "print revolution" and innovations in the production of lithographs and pictures that did so much to encourage nationalist movements in that era also facilitated the rapid and broad spread of Catholic devotionalism as well. Catholic serials in the United States doubled in the 1860s, and again in the 1870s, and from 1850 to 1890 over a hundred different devotional guides were published in the United States. "Praying," as Joseph Chinnici has said, "entered the mass market."[24]

This worldwide Catholic religious revival had a profound impact on the Worcester Irish. Fundamental liturgies, like the mass, became almost operatically elaborate, and feast-day processions attracted hundreds, sometimes thousands, of participants. Parish missions, carefully planned religious revivals, stoked the fires of this religiosity, and sodalities and confraternities made sure that the mission fires kept burning. There were variations among the city's parishes in their response to the new devotionalism. Jay Dolan has noted that this devotional revolution not only transformed the immigrant's imported peasant faith in the United States but also overwhelmed a recently born, American "plain" style of Catholic piety, almost Protestant in its simplicity. In Worcester vestiges of the plain style or its spirit persisted in some of the city's parishes, most notably in Father John J. Power's St. Paul's Church. On the other hand, Sacred Heart and St. John's parishes, in particular, were alive with devotional rituals, liturgical pageantry, mission revivals, and the meetings of religious societies. In the end, all of the city's parishes, even St. Paul's, eventually embraced the new devotionalism as it swept through Worcester's Irish community.[25]

In the late eighteenth and early nineteenth century there were so few priests and churches in Ireland that many Irish, particularly in the west, enjoyed a limited liturgical life and, indeed, rarely attended mass, the church's central liturgy. When mass was accessible, the services might well be in rude huts or even outside in the open air on makeshift altars. When the poor Irish fleeing the Famine came to Worcester, they had little experience with, or interest in, extravagant services and fought bitterly with Father Matthew Gibson over Gibson's expenditures on priest's vestments, chalices, and altar cloths for the new St. John's church.[26]

Even as Irish churches became better established in Worcester and in cities across the nation, many historians contend, Irish Catholic ritual remained simple, even austere, especially when compared to richly baroque German, Polish, or French liturgies. Most masses in Worcester's Irish churches in the late nineteenth century were, in fact, simple and unadorned, but such churches also staged self-conscious spectacles of high masses, festivals, and special cele- brations that call into question characterizations of Irish ritual as plain and puritan. Trained choirs, complemented by organ, violins, trumpets, and even small orchestras were employed regularly to provide music in Worcester's Irish churches. Violins, an organ, and a choir moved smartly through selec- tions from Wagner's *Tannhaüser,* Haydn, and Neidermeyer for a typical 10:30 solemn high mass at Sacred Heart Church in 1895. St. Peter's church may have had the best musicians and the most elaborate musical programs of any Catholic church in the city. On one normal Sunday at St. Peter's in February of 1901, the parish's singers offered "three renditions by a vocal chorus, one rendition by a semi-chorus, one organ solo, three numbers by combined organ and violin, four vocal solos, a violin solo, a vocal duet, quartet, trio and two vocal solos with chorus" merely as a prelude to an evening vespers service. Though virtually all churches in Worcester complemented their liturgies with such elaborate music by the late nineteenth century, some pastors feared that it had become too much of a distraction. The pastor of St. Stephen's parish felt compelled to warn his parishioners not "to go to High Mass to listen to the music as one would go to the opera." In the twentieth century reforms of the liturgy would reduce choral and orchestral musical presentations at Catholic masses, but through most of the turn of the century period music in Worcester's churches was rich and elaborate.[27]

Music was only part of the grandeur of Worcester's late nineteenth-century Irish American Catholicism. Worcester's Irish churches regularly marked feasts or special events with the pageantry of processions. On Corpus Christi, a feast in June celebrating Christ's presence in the communion host, processions were especially elaborate. On Corpus Christi at St. John's parish in 1887 the grounds around the church were "very nicely decorated with red, white and blue bunting, the Irish, American and papal flags, evergreen and potted plants . . . and banners bearing such legends as 'Lauda Sion Salvatorem,' 'Domine Meus et Deus Meus,' 'O Salutaris Hostia,' and many others." The day began with the St. John's cadets, Emmet Guards, and St. John's drum corps marching from the Island east up Vernon Hill, where the main body of the procession had assembled. It included fifty little boys in blue bearing blue banners representing the five joyful mysteries of the rosary and fifty little girls in pink and fifty more in white for the sorrowful and glorious mysteries. The Children of Mary, St. Aloysius Boys' Society, young ladies, and men's sodalities made up the bulk of the parade. Scattered throughout were boys or girls dressed as guardian angels or shepherds bearing symbols of the virtues of faith, hope, and charity. Five priests, all vested, standing under a canopy carried by four senior members of the church and flanked by a bevy of altar-boys and censer bearers, joined the procession when it entered the church. There a choir of 114 voices and the City Band greeted the marchers with triumphant hymns. At the benediction, the Emmet Guards fired three salutes. In all, perhaps 5,000 to 6,000 people marched, attended the services, or watched the event. Such processions took place every year at St. John's through the 1880s and 1890s. May processions, part of a devotion to Mary, the Mother of Jesus, had also become an integral part of life in most Irish parishes by the late nineteenth century. The churches did not sponsor processions only for strictly liturgical events. Even the opening of the parish fair was important enough to prompt a procession. In October of 1887, two hundred little girls all dressed in white marched to the beat of "martial music" down Worcester's Main Street to open the St. Anne's parish fair at Mechanics Hall.[28]

Beyond the mass and these special feasts, Worcester's late nineteenth-century Catholics participated in a host of other devotional rituals that flooded the liturgical calendars of the churches. Catholics were not required to attend vespers on Sunday nights but the *Alumna* argued that "he who habitually failed to attend would be guilty of a venial sin at least." Vespers, in fact, seemed to be a regular and well-attended service in most of the city's Irish parishes through the late nineteenth century, until it was supplanted by other liturgies in the twentieth century. Novenas were common around important days such as the feast of the Sacred Heart in June or of the Immaculate Conception in December. Father Thomas J. Conaty of Sacred Heart and Monsignor Thomas Griffin of St. John's minced no words in urging, even demanding, attendance at the novena of the Sacred Heart in June of 1885 or the feast of the Immaculate Conception in December of the following year. During Lent, the stations of the cross, marking Christ's passion, were said in most Irish Catholic churches every Friday. Most churches also urged their parishioners to observe such practices as hearing mass on nine consecutive first Fridays and most also exposed the consecrated host (that Catholics believe to be Christ's body) during the Forty Hours devotion.[29]

Irish churches mixed this pageantry and ritual and its ancient connotations with a Catholic form of revivalism. The principal instrument of this revivalism was the parish mission. As Jay Dolan has pointed out, parish missions first took place in America at the end of the eighteenth century and had become an "accepted feature of Catholic evangelization" by the 1830s. At the end of the nineteenth century, religious-order priests, particularly the Redemptorists, Jesuits, Passionists, and Paulists, were conducting missions in parishes all over the United States. These missions were, as Dolan suggests, the Catholic equivalent of Protestant religious revivals. Worcester's Irish weekly, the *Messenger*, explained that "a mission consists in a series of sermons and religious exercises directed by missionary priests . . . its general aim is to excite penitential feeling by treating of man's destiny of free will, of the need for grace, of divine justice and the necessity of conversion." At Sacred Heart Church in 1891 this meant two weeks of extra masses in the morning and nightly instructions and benediction. At Sacred Heart and other Worcester parishes, the two weeks were often divided between women and men, a week apiece. Members of Sacred Heart who attended a mission conducted by the Jesuits in 1894 signed a pledge at the conclusion of the two weeks promising to never miss Sunday mass and to say their prayers every morning.[30]

Most of the city's Irish churches ran missions regularly every few years even though the religious orders running them could charge up to $800 or $900 for each mission. It is easy to see why pastors made the investment. Missionaries did not aim merely to instruct; they sought to inspire renewed emotional commitment to the faith from parishioners. After a mission in his St. John's parish in 1886, Monsignor Thomas Griffin noted in his diary: "Women's mission closed at 3. The church was packed. Men's mission opened. A still larger attendance at the men's opening. It was grand." He later counted 822 people who made their confessions during the mission and another nearly 200 who came forward to receive the church's sacrament of confirmation. Six years later at St. John's "every foot of space in the church and sacristy was packed with great crowds" for a Paulist mission at the same church. "Enthusiasm never flagged for an instant," the delighted, if exhausted, Paulists reported, noting that a whopping 3,680 women and 3,520 men went to confession. At Sacred Heart in 1888, the Paulists heard confessions from over 2,500 men and women though there were only 2,000 people in the parish at the time. Pastor Thomas Conaty, the Paulists reported, "knows his people well and could mention only a few who could not make the mission."[31]

Missions were the Irish parish's principal means of reviving devotional sentiment; sodalities and confraternities were the church's primary means of sustaining religious enthusiasm. Sodalities appeared in Worcester's Irish churches at least as early as the late 1850s. In 1860 for example, St. Anne's church boasted a Rosary and a Scapular and a Sacred Heart society and St. John's church, a Rosary and a Scapular society. As Jay Dolan has noted, however, devotional confraternities or sodalities did not seem to catch on in American churches until after 1860. By the 1880s sodalities were multiplying all over the United States and had become very popular in Worcester. By 1891, Worcester's Sacred Heart parish, for example, had seven sodalities: a Young Ladies Sodality of the Sacred Heart, Married Ladies Sodality, Children of Mary (two divisions), League of the Sacred Heart, Boys of St. Aloysius (three sections), Rosary Society, and Men's League of the Sacred Heart. Two years earlier a local observer estimated that as many as 900 of the parish's 2,000 members were enrolled in one or another of these organizations. Paulist missionaries also marveled at the many "large and flourishing sodalities" at St. John's parish, particularly young people's organizations.[32]

Sodalities, like other clubs, met certain social needs of their members and this accounts in part for their popularity, but they were first and foremost religious organizations and their rising strength is a clear reflection of Catholic devotionalism's powerful hold on the Worcester Irish. The principal activities of these organizations were the communal performances of Catholic rituals. At Sacred Heart parish, members of sodalities made annual retreats which included attending mass and hearing special instructions before and after work every day for a week. Sodalities at Sacred Heart also went to confession on certain prescribed days and received communion together on special Sundays. The Ladies Sodalities at St. John's made a novena nine days before the feast of the Immaculate Conception: "The novena is ended by a general communion on the morning of the feast and a 'reception' in the evening. At the reception the sodalists renew their promises of love and loyalty to their Queen [Mary, Mother of Christ] and new members are admitted to share in the spiritual blessings granted to those who seek in sodalities the special protection of the Blessed Virgin." Beyond these special liturgical events, members of sodalities met every two weeks or monthly to pray and ponder the special focus of their

at an average age of 31 and women at an age of 29; immigrant males wed an average of two years earlier and Irish-born women married an average of three years earlier.[111]

It was the marriage pattern of the American-born generation, then, and not that of the immigrants which most resembled the trend of late marriage and high celibacy that had come to dominate Ireland. Indeed, the statistical measures of marriage among Worcester's second generation and the Irish in Ireland at the turn of the century were almost eerily similar. Among the American-born Irish in Worcester in 1900, 71 percent of the men and 57 percent of the women between the ages of 25 and 34 and 25 percent of the men and 11.1 percent of the women between the ages of 45 and 54 were single; the proportions of single men and women in similar age categories among the Irish in Ireland in 1901 were 72 percent of the men and 53 percent of the women aged 25 to 34 and 24 percent of the men and 20 percent of the women aged 45 to 54. Only the last statistic, the percentage of "celibate" women, unmarried women aged 45 to 54, indicated anything but a slight divergence between the second-generation Irish marriage pattern in Worcester and that of the Irish in Ireland.[112]

Did this mean that the second-generation Irish were more "Irish" than their immigrant parents, or more than their recently arrived Irish-born cousins? It does seem to indicate that Irish norms and Irish perspectives on marriage were filtering through to the American-born generation from their parents. The immigrant Irish, it should be remembered, also married later than native-stock Yankees in Worcester, suggesting that inherited cultural values played an important role in the marriage behavior of both Irish generations. The key question here, however, is why the second-generation not only married later than the native-stock Yankees but even later than the immigrants. The answers to that question lie in the second-generation's prospects or aspirations for upward mobility and their life in the households of their immigrant parents.

Unlike the immigrants, second-generation Irish men and women may have feared that early marriage threatened their present or future occupational status. In 1915, the *Catholic Messenger* grumbled that young men seemed to be waiting to "get rich" before they married. Men hoping for bright futures may have been hindered by the burden of establishing a new household. For successful women the costs may have been even greater, especially if they valued their work, since marriage effectively ended an Irish woman's career. For second-generation women, unlike Irish-born females, this could mean abandoning high-status jobs such as teaching that had required heavy educational investments.[113]

There were numerous examples in Worcester of ambitious and successful second-generation men and women who married late in life or did not marry at all. Mayor Philip O'Connell, cited above, attended college and law school and served as an alderman and as mayor before marrying at age 34. James A. McDermott never advanced beyond grammar school, but he established a thriving contracting business before he wed at age 44. Successful women also often delayed marriage or avoided it altogether. Ellen T. McGillicuddy was a teacher and a principal before marrying a second-generation doctor, Michael Halloran. McGillicuddy's sister, Mary Agnes, also became a schoolteacher, but, as noted above, she never married. (One of the McGillicuddy brothers became a priest, the others a lawyer and a doctor, both married at age 33.) As noted earlier, Worcester's second-generation Irish women doctors, such as Doctor Mary V. O'Callaghan or her niece Doctor Clara Fitzgerald or Doctor Anna Murphy also did not marry.[114]

It is important not to overestimate the rising status or aspirations of the second-generation Irish in explaining their postponement of marriage. In 1900, not only were most of the white-collar workers in their early thirties unmarried, but so too were the majority of skilled and semiskilled or unskilled blue-collar workers. Indeed, the percentages were strikingly similar at all class levels.[115]

If second-generation Irish men and women did not postpone weddings solely because of what they hoped to gain, they may have shied from marriage because of what they were afraid to lose. Immigrant men and women had no families in Worcester; they had long since left their parents far behind in Ireland by the time they contemplated marriage. Their decisions to marry did not first require a decision to leave home; that choice had already been made. The American-born Irish, however, remained in their parents' households until they married. Unlike Irish immigrants (or even young Yankees) very few second-generation Irish in any age cohort ever became boarders. For second-generation Irish men and women to choose marriage, then, meant also to decide to leave home.[116]

For the American-born Irish, the difficulty or pain of this decision was an important obstacle to marriage. Many of Worcester's second-generation Irish enjoyed a relatively comfortable, unburdened, and socially active life as adult children in their parents' household. To choose marriage was to give up these comforts and benefits. In 1913, the *Catholic Messenger* claimed "young people in these days won't marry unless they can have all the luxuries they have been accustomed to in their parents' home." "Luxury" seems a surprising word to describe households usually headed by unskilled laborers, semiskilled factory

operatives, or aging widows. Some Irish households did achieve modest prosperity because a number of adult children living at home provided multiple
sources of income. In 1880, Dennis Briden's family enjoyed some security, despite the death of Dennis's father, because twenty-six-year-old Dennis and
three of his brothers, all over twenty, worked. In 1900, twenty-nine-year-old
Margaret Hormly lived in a home made prosperous by her own earnings as
a schoolteacher, her father's income as a carpenter, and the wages of two
brothers and three sisters.[117]

The circumstances of Dennis and Margaret were not the unique good fortune of a small minority of the American-born Irish. Over 75 percent of the
sons and daughters aged 25 to 34 living at home in 1880 had at least one working sibling. In 1900, over 80 percent had a gainfully employed brother or sister.
Furthermore, over 50 percent of the men and over 60 percent of the women
in both census years had at least two working siblings. Such multiple-income
families, while hardly enjoying luxury, no doubt provided some comfort for
many second-generation sons and daughters.[118]

Obligations to parents who were aged, infirm, or wished to reap the benefits of their children's wages, also forced a number of American-born Irish
men and women to postpone marriage. The *Messenger* frequently noted how
desperately parents tried to prevent their adult children from leaving the
household. In 1896, the *Messenger* scolded parents for not letting their sons
have steady girlfriends. In 1913, the paper charged: "Young people would
marry . . . if parents did not interfere."[119]

Why did Irish parents seem to promote delayed marriage among their children? Affection motivated some. In 1903, the *Messenger* argued that mothers
were particularly devoted to their sons, frequently ignoring faults such as
drinking and gambling in order to keep them home. Dreams that their children might achieve the wealth and status that had been beyond their own
reach moved other immigrant parents. The *Messenger* hinted frequently at
this motive for parental interference throughout the period, before openly
charging in 1913: "It is the foolish parents who usually object to marriage
unless the young people are in a position of influence."[120]

Parents, however, had self-interested reasons for delaying their children's
marriage. Immigrant parents, like their American-born children, also benefited when the family had multiple sources of income. As noted in the last
chapter, immigrant parents, too, enjoyed the comforts that working sons and
daughters could help provide and, as they grew older and less sure of being
able to support themselves, children also seemed their best potential insurance against an impoverished and desperate old age. About 40 percent of the

men and women aged 25 to 34 living at home resided with widows who had no occupation or with retired fathers. For older second-generation men and women, those between 35 and 44, the proportions were even greater, over 50 percent. For a substantial proportion of unmarried men and women living at home, the economic helplessness of parents may have been one more tie to the household, and therefore one more obstacle to marriage.[121]

The second-generation Irish postponed marriage not just because of the comforts or ties that held them to their old families but because of the costs of establishing a new one. In 1884, *Donahoe's* magazine of Boston stated: "ask a young man why he does not get married and he will probably say he cannot afford it." For the American-born Irish, like their immigrant parents or cousins, there were virtually no marriages where children did not follow quickly and in large numbers. The bulletin of St Paul's parish stated the consensus of community leaders clearly in 1918: "God has not blessed all married persons with these proofs of his love, but they who have refused this evidence of divine favor stand forth as objects of scorn before God and Man."[122]

Statistics confirm the American-born generation's strict adherence to their church's views on childbearing. An even higher proportion of American-born Irish women aged 45 years or older and married ten years had at least one child than immigrant wives in the same category, and nearly as many second-generation spouses had two or more children. More sophisticated statistical analysis using regression techniques confirms that the American-born generation had children at virtually the same rate in 1900 as immigrants when age and number of years married are controlled. The American-born Irish, like the immigrants, thus differed sharply from native-stock Yankees in the number of children they bore. If the American-born Irish sought to avoid the costs of children in marriage, they could not, or at least did not, avoid them as their Yankee neighbors did—by limiting fertility after marriage. They avoided those costs, or at least postponed them, by postponing marriage itself.[123]

A substantial proportion of American-born Irish postponed them entirely and never married. Historians such as Hasia Diner have focused on the reluctance of Irish women in America to marry because conflicts between men and women, exacerbated by alcoholism and sometimes escalating to wife abuse, made such marriages unhappy. American-born Irish women like Irish-born women in Worcester did marry later than native-stock Yankees, but a higher proportion of women of *both* the first and second Irish generations eventually married than did Yankee women. It was American-born Irish *men* who were the most extraordinary deviant case. They, not first- or second-generation

Irish women were less likely to marry at all than the Yankees or Irish immi-grants.[124]

Worcester's Irish press and spokesmen provided no ready explanation for this. It may be that American-born men were more likely to postpone marriage or forgo it altogether in order to pursue careers or accumulate property. Family obligations, either care of older widowed parents or responsibilities for younger siblings, may have pressed more heavily on second-generation men than American-born women, since the men were likely to be earning higher salaries. On the other hand, there was, perhaps, less pressure on males than females to marry. There is little evidence that the Worcester Irish deemed men failures or incomplete if they did not marry. Suggestively, in 1884, when the young second-generation Irish men of the St. John's Temperance and Literary Guild debated the question of whether "the married state is more productive of happiness than the single state," "the merits of the debate were not de-cided" by the assembled members.[125]

By contrast, as noted earlier, the Worcester Irish, at least officially, regarded permanent celibacy for women, outside of the religious life, as inappropriate. As Abigail L. O'Hara, ruminating in 1894, suggested, the Irish community had not yet accepted the "single blessedness" of the professional woman as a status equal to that of the married woman. Furthermore, it appeared that it was not only more important for women than men to marry, but for women to marry earlier than men. Second-generation Irish women in 1900 who had married in their late twenties were more likely to marry white-collar workers and less likely to marry immigrants than women marrying after age thirty. Women who postponed marriage too long, therefore, might run the risk of losing their appeal to prospective suitors: the culturally refined teacher in her late twenties could too easily became the "old maid schoolmarm" in her thirties.[126]

Postponing marriage could impose psychological costs on both men and women as well. It is likely that some of the conflict between immigrants and their children attributed to cultural differences may have simply reflected the tensions of men and women prolonging their adolescence into their thirties or forties. Sometimes the frustration of this interminable childhood produced severe tensions in households. Even the religiously devout Stephen Littleton argued constantly with his mother about staying out late, and was clearly frus-trated by his "usual midnight conversations . . . explaining to her where I had been." In 1903 and 1915, the *Messenger* reported with alarm evidence of adult children rebelling against parental authority and attempting to challenge their fathers as rulers of the household. Most Irish observers, however, felt the sexual frustrations built up over years of postponed marriage were even more difficult and dangerous than chafings against parental authority. No sexual activity outside marriage won religious sanction or community approval. [127]

The energetic, almost frantic, social life that the American-born Irish created for themselves may have been one means of dealing with these frustrations. To some the second-generation sons and daughters seemed overly eager to escape their crowded family apartments for vaudeville shows, local clubs, saloons, or even the street. Father John J. McCoy reported in 1900 that "the tendency of the young people in the parish [St. John's] towards societies and club life is marked to an inordinate degree and is bewailed by the pastor of weakening the foundation of stable family life." In 1881, the Irish owned *Daily Times* complained of the large numbers of young people who simply congregated downtown at night "and parade up and down Main Street."[128]

Escape to the clubs, theaters, or even the streets may have been one means of coping with prolonged adolescence, but religion and its strict moral code were probably more effective. Indeed, the theater and the streets might simply raise unacceptable temptations for sexual indulgence that only religion could counter. K. H. Connell has argued that in Ireland Catholicism was not the cause of late marriage and celibacy, but rather "the most persuasive of the agencies reconciling the young" to a "curious" marriage pattern imposed on them by economic exigencies. On the other hand, Nancy Landale and Stewart Tolnay have found that while second-generation members of all ethnic groups in America married later than their immigrant parents or cousins—perhaps the result of household economic influences on their marriage behavior—second-generation Irish Americans married much later than most other American-born children of immigrants. Such differences suggest the independent importance of cultural factors, such as Catholicism on the second-generation Irish. Without the supporting moral or ideological force of Catholicism and its sexual code, the strategy of postponing marriage to reap economic advantages or to avoid economic costs may have been too hard to endure.[129]

It is important, however, not to overstate Catholicism's independent influence on the second generation's marriage behavior. Irish immigrants were Catholics too, but Catholic sexual discipline did not make Irish immigrants marry as late as the second generation or forgo marriage as often. Catholicism's role should be seen less as the single overriding cause and more as a force combining with household economic circumstances to help shape the family strategies of the American-born. Indeed, by deciding to delay marriage and avoid the unacceptable economic costs that it threatened, second-generation Irish Catholics only increased their dependence on their religion to justify their decision and steel them in the face of temptation. Practical judgments about the advantages of delayed marriage and adherence to Catholic norms were mutually reinforcing. The fact that men of the new generation postponed marriage longer than women may also at least partially explain the apparent surge of religious devotion among them in the late nineteenth and early twentieth centuries.

Religious loyalty may also help to explain why such a relatively high proportion of American-born Irish married within the group rather than seek higher status through nuptials with the Yankees or members of other groups. Many more American Irish-born men and women, roughly a quarter of the men and a few percentage points more of the women in 1900, married outside the group than did the immigrant Irish. The Paulist fathers, conducting a retreat for young people at St. John's in 1884, thought that the cultured and ambitious women of the parish, in particular, were prone to marry outside the faith because of a lack of men with equal aspiration and refinement, and the *Messenger* later agreed, decrying the "young maidens," who "yearn for the companionship of better dressed men." Nevertheless, marriages across ethnic lines were not always cases of the second-generation Irish marrying up; a higher proportion of second-generation Irish women marrying unskilled workers found partners outside the group than American-born Irish women marrying white-collar workers. More important, despite this trend towards out-marriage, the substantial majority (over 70 percent) of second-generation Irish men and women continued to wed members of their own ethnic group, a smaller proportion than among the immigrants but certainly large enough to suggest a continued pervasive consciousness of group identity and solidarity among members of the new generation.[130]

Second Settlements and "Zones of Emergence": The First Second-Generation Move Out of Irish Worcester

Second-generation Irish residential patterns reflected the same mix of tentative independence and persistent group consciousness as second-generation Irish families. In 1900, the second-generation Irish were less segregated from the rest of Worcester's people than the immigrants. Yet the differences between the American-born and Irish-born Irish in this regard were not dramatic. The indices measuring second-generation segregation from the rest of the population were 41 in 1880 and 36 in 1990; for immigrants they were 46 and 41 in the same years.[131]

As such measures suggest, the American-born Irish were moving away from the old Irish districts on the east side, but only gradually. In 1900, nearly a majority of the second-generation Irish (49 percent) still lived in Worcester's four old Irish neighborhoods, the North End, East Worcester, the Island, and South Worcester. Many of these American-born Irish, of course, lived there not by their own choice but by their parents' decisions. They were the sons and daughters who remained at home, postponing their departure until they reached their thirties or even forties. Many second-generation heads of households and a smaller but still large proportion of the few American-born Irish boarders and servants also lived in Irish Worcester.[132]

Though many still lived in the old Irish neighborhoods, substantial numbers of the American-born Irish began to move away from the old districts in the late nineteenth century. More important, over half of the households headed by American-born Irish men or women resided outside Irish Worcester. Some, both of the boarders and the household heads, had merely found living quarters in nearby inner-city east side districts, Summer or Salem streets or Oak Hill, which bordered on the older Irish neighborhoods. These areas were virtually identical to the older Celtic neighborhoods, like the Island or East Worcester, in their east side location, housing, and gritty appearance but were simply not as thoroughly Irish. Thirty-four percent of the second-generation households, as compared to only 17 percent of the immigrants, however, settled outside the inner-city east side altogether, beyond both the Irish district and its adjacent neighborhoods. Some of these American-born Irish had crossed the city's magical boundary of Main Street into the west side, but the number of Irish west siders would remain small until the second decade of the twentieth century. Most of the second-generation families looking for better homes outside Irish Worcester remained within the east side but moved to second settlements or "zones of emergence" up onto the Vernon or Union Hills to the east and to the Main South neighborhood to the south and west.[133]

In 1900 Main South was in the middle of a transformation that had begun in the 1890s and would continue into the early twentieth century. In the 1870s, it had been largely a middle- and upper-class neighborhood, its streets lined with the large estates of "Shirtsleeves Joe" Walker, Worcester congressman, or Dr. Joseph Sargent, a prominent local physician, as well as more modest, but still stylish, well-kept, one- and two-family homes. In the 1880s and the early 1890s, trolley cars, especially after electrification in 1893, began to extend down Main Street all the way to Worcester's border with neighboring Leicester, and at the same time manufacturers began building plants at the southern junction of the Boston and Albany Railroad in the neighborhood. The largest of these factories was the Crompton and Knowles Loom Works. Spread out over 200,000 square feet and rising six stories over Beaver Street in Main South, this giant plant employed over 2,500 machinists and other workers.[134]

The Main South district's new factories attracted many Irish families to the area in the late nineteenth century, but these families were no mere overflow from the old inner-city districts. Nearly half of the neighborhood's Celtic families in the neighborhood were headed by American-born Irishmen in 1900, the largest proportion of second-generation families in the Irish population of any neighborhood in the city. One-seventh of all the city's second-generation Irish families lived in Main South in 1900. That figure included over one-third of all families in the city headed by skilled blue-collar American-born Irish workers. Many of these skilled workers were drawn to Main South's burgeoning cluster of machine shops and tool-making companies: more second-generation Irish machinists lived in Main South than any one district in Worcester. The extensions of the streetcars also helped to carry more prosperous Irish men there as well. The Paulist fathers reported after a mission in the neighborhood in 1885 that "people [in the area] for the most part formerly lived downtown but with the advent of trolley cars moved further out and purchased their own homes." "As a class," the Paulists concluded, the people of the neighborhood "compare favorably with Catholics in any part of New England." Perhaps because of this prosperity and the kind of houses available in the district, over half the Irish foreign-stock households in the Main South neighborhood lived in one- or two-family homes.[135]

The rapidly growing Irish population in Main South had begun to make its presence visible long before 1900. A few Irish saloons appeared along Main Street, just south of downtown as early as 1882. More important, Bishop O'Reilly carved a new parish, St. Peter's, out of St. Paul's, Sacred Heart, and St. John's, to serve the Main South area in 1884. Almost immediately, the pastor of the new parish, D. H. O'Neill, a second-generation Irishman, broke ground for a grand brick church to be built on Main Street across from Clark University. At that time the church had about 1,100 parishoners. By the time the church was completed in 1893, the parish boasted 2,400 members. As elsewhere among the Irish in Worcester, the church was a social center as well as a religious one. The parish sponsored excursions to local lakes in the summer and elaborate fairs and bazaars in the fall and winter, including a Harvest Festival in 1888 when "nearly every seat in the house was taken" for the Harvest suppers, the Farmer boys drill, and the crowning of the "Harvest Queen."[136]

Though the Irish presence was noticeable in Main South by the late nineteenth century, the Irish by no means dominated the district in that era. In 1900, the Irish were but another minority in a neighborhood filled with ethnic minorities. Many Yankee and British upper- and middle-class residents still clung stubbornly to the neighborhood in the face of the invasion by blue-collar ethnics. French Canadians had also migrated into Main South in large numbers in the 1880s and 1890s, and in 1893 the French established their own church, Holy Name of Jesus, along the district's border with South Worcester. Thus while the number of first- and second-generation Irish households in the Main South district grew by 680 percent between 1880 and 1900, they still constituted but 22 percent of the neighborhood's families in 1900. Furthermore, nearly 70 percent of the Irish families living in tenement apartments shared those tenements with non-Irish households.[137]

Vernon and Union Hills lay east of Main South, flanking the Island to the east, as Main South flanked that district to the west. Though located deep inside the east side, the Vernon and Union Hills were not slums. The steep slopes of the hills had deflected the tide of factories, tenements, and warehouses that had overrun the Island, East Worcester, and most other east side neighborhoods, leaving the hilltops almost exclusively residential in 1900. Indeed, some of the houses built on Vernon Hill in the late nineteenth century, such as George Crompton's "Mariemont," rivalled the mansions of Worcester's west side. Most of the homes on the slopes and summits of Vernon and Union Hills, however, were simple if neat cottages, substantial two-family homes, or sturdy, ample, and almost elegant three-deckers. If the eastern hills were not an exclusively wealthy area, they were, nonetheless, one of the most comfortable places in Worcester to live and certainly one of the most attractive on the east side.[138]

The eastern hills thus attracted different types of Irishmen than the Island below or even Main South further west. As in Main South, second-generation Irish men or women headed a large proportion (40.1 percent) of the Hilltops' Irish families in 1900. Yet while Main South had a largely skilled blue-collar Irish population, the Hilltops seemed to be especially attractive to Worcester's slowly expanding Irish white-collar class. Over two-fifths of the Irish foreign-stock families on the hills were headed by white-collar workers. Furthermore, an even larger proportion of the Irish on the hills than in Main South lived in one- or two-family homes.[139]

As the number of white-collar Irishmen in Worcester increased, the number of Irish families creeping to the top of the eastern hills also rose. In 1900, the Irish made up only 11 percent of the people living on the eastern hills, but the Celtic population there was growing quickly. Between 1880 and 1900 the Irish population on the Hilltops had risen by 332 percent, and in the first few years of the twentieth century some streets and blocks on Vernon and Union Hills became thoroughly Irish. Worcester's 1904 *House Directory,* for example, listed an almost unbroken row of Grogans, McHughs, Cahills, and McKennys on

Union Avenue from Vernon Street up the slopes of Vernon Hill to Arlington Street. Parts of Mott Street, South Street, and Penn Avenue had also become almost exclusively Irish by that year.[140]

Visible signs of the Irish presence had also begun to appear on the Hilltops in the last few decades of the nineteenth century. In 1872 Monsignor Thomas Griffin built a school for girls on Vernon Street about half way up Vernon Hill and in 1899 constructed a convent nearby. In 1893, the monsignor and the Sisters of Providence also opened St. Vincent's Hospital on the very top of the hill. In 1887, in recognition of Irish movement east out of the Island and East Worcester the diocese had created St. Stephen's parish up Grafton Street about a quarter mile east of St. John's. St. Stephen's, however, lay north of the hilltops, and its territory included only part of the northern slopes of Union Hill and none of Vernon Hill. Most of the Irish on the hills thus continued to belong to St. John's parish below them on the Island plain. By the early 1900s many of them began attending mass in the convent chapel rather than walk down the hill to the parish church on Temple Street. In 1911, despite complaints by Father Thomas Donohue of St. John's, that it would slice off some of the wealthiest members of his parish, the diocese created Ascension parish for the people of the Hilltops. Over the next two decades the new parish flourished with a full and diverse array of societies and sodalities and an active associational life.[141]

"Quiet Homes" and "Catholic Spires": The American-born Move to the City's Periphery

In 1866, Father John J. Power, the second-generation pastor of St. Anne's, began construction of a new Catholic church, St. Paul's, on High Street, just west of Worcester's downtown. Power knew a new Catholic diocese encompassing Worcester County and all of western Massachusetts would soon be carved out of the diocese of Boston. The ambitious Power fancied himself a bishop and his new church in Worcester as his cathedral. Before Power finished his church it would cost over $200,000. John J. Power never became a bishop, nor did his church become a cathedral until 1950. Before he died in 1902, however, Power had added a rectory, orphanage, and home for working women to his Catholic complex on Worcester's west side. [142]

Only John J. Power's ambition could account for the construction of St. Paul's on Worcester's west side in the 1860s, for there was little other reason for building a Catholic church there. There were few Irish-born or second-generation Irish living on the west side even fourteen years later in 1880. Extension of streetcar lines after electrification of the system in 1893 accelerated interest in west side development enormously, and by 1901 the Worcester real estate index listed seventeen new residential parks on Worcester's west side or in its northeast corner. Nevertheless, a year earlier in 1900, while 31 percent of all Worcester's families lived on the west side, only 14.4 percent of the American-born Irish households lived there or in the other newly developing peripheral areas such as the northeast corner. This was nearly double the proportion of Irish immigrants living in those districts, but hardly reflected a major invasion by the American-born Irish of the Yankees' west side stronghold.[143]

Such an invasion never occurred, in part because the Yankees resisted Irish entry. Residents of the elite Elm Park district of the west side were particularly fierce in their determination to keep the Irish and other ethnics out. In 1888, Philip Moen of the Washburn Moen Wire Company bought and leveled a three-decker in the Elm Park neighborhood, because he and his Yankee neighbors judged the French Canadians who liked to smoke their clay pipes on the tenement's stoop to be "eyesores." Later in the 1890s six homeowners on Cedar Street in the same neighborhood banded together in a covenant association to prevent "inappropriate" families from buying property on their street. Further south, on the west side in less wealthy but comfortably middle-class Yankee districts, Protestant ministers leapt to the leadership of the anti-Catholic American Protective Association in the 1890s, and precincts there became the strongest nativist political strongholds in the city.[144]

Yet for the American-born Irish, like their immigrant fathers and cousins, it was not Yankee prejudice so much but the constraints imposed by their work and income which slowed their migration to the west. The vast majority of even the American-born Irish were blue-collar workers who could afford only relatively cheap housing. There were far fewer tenements on the west side than on the east, and apartments and houses were more expensive in the western districts. More important, most second-generation workers, like their immigrant parents and cousins, needed to be close to places of employment, and most of the west with its steep ridges and absence of railroads had no factories or mills. Thus while a little over one-fifth of the second-generation Irish families headed by white-collar workers had moved to the west side by 1900, only about one-eighth of that generation's skilled blue-collar workers had moved west across Main Street by then.[145]

In the first two decades of the twentieth century, Irish population on the west side and in other peripheral areas like Lincoln and Burncoat streets in the northeast corner grew substantially. In part, the Irish were being pushed out of the east side as Italian, Polish, or Lithuanian immigrants expanded their small colonies to extensive ethnic villages. Yet the Irish population on the west side also increased because the further development of western districts opened up vast new areas there to settlement. Between 1900 and 1912, the miles of track operated by the Worcester Consolidated Street Railway rose from 46 to 251, and the number of passengers increased from 14 million to 59 million. The extension of lines and improvement of service meant that west side residential parks like Montvale and Franconia, which had only just appeared on the real estate market in 1900, became fully developed by 1913. By 1920, 41 percent of the people of Worcester lived west of Main Street or in the Northeast Corner.[146]

As the American-born Irish grew to maturity, many of them took advantage of these new opportunities to move west. In 1911, the *Catholic Messenger* reported with pleasure that "a surprisingly large number of Catholics have located in the western outskirts of the city . . . where formerly a Catholic resident was unknown." Some Irishmen, such as the American-born contractor James A. McDermott, became so wealthy in the early twentieth century that they could afford to move into the west side elite district near Elm Park. McDermott moved to Cedar Street in that neighborhood in 1906, and despite the mixed reception that he and his brood of rambunctious children received from Worcester's proper Yankee west siders, his family remained there until 1932. In all, 62 percent of the Irishmen prominent enough to be listed in the biographical section of Nutt's *History of Worcester* in 1919 lived on the west side or in the northeast corner. Not all the Irish who moved to the west side were so prominent, of course, but most of the families who moved to the western and southwestern sections of the city had at least one skilled blue-collar or white-collar family member. In 1912, 44 percent of the Irish families living near the new Blessed Sacrament church on the west side had at least one member who was a white-collar worker, while another 36 percent had at least one skilled blue-collar family member. In the same year, 58 percent of the Irish families who had settled near the site of the soon to be established Our Lady of the Angels church in the southwest had at least one white-collar member. The *Catholic Messenger* summed up the critical importance of rising Irish affluence to the Irish westward migration in 1911, when it proclaimed: "As fortune favors us and better things which others have enjoyed come within our reach, we seek to secure them. Among these are quiet homes, far removed from the turmoil, the dirt and the smoke of the busy center and such homes as these the Catholic people are seeking."[147]

The meaning of this migration should not be misunderstood. Irish Catholics still confronted prejudice and discrimination there or in the northeast corner. Yankee families in the southern part of the west side continued to complain about the Catholic invasion of their neighborhoods, and inhabitants of the elite district organized to prevent Catholics from buying Park Street church in their neighborhood in 1910. When the diocese finally purchased land for the new Blessed Sacrament church on the west side, local priests were very worried that announcement of the church's intentions would provoke harsh protests. Many third-generation Irish Americans remember having non-Catholic friends when they grew up on the west side, but they also remember incidents of prejudice and name-calling.[148]

Perhaps as important, they also remember the critical importance the church played in their lives. When the *Messenger* took note of Irish migration to the west side, it assumed that Catholicism would remain central to the lives of the migrants. The paper talked in terms of conquest, not assimilation, when it predicted that "Catholic spires" would "soon" be as numerous on the west side as on the east. Beginning the very next year, the *Catholic Messenger's* dream began to be realized, as the diocese created Blessed Sacrament parish on the west side and Holy Rosary parish in the northeast corner. Within five years, the diocese would form two new parishes in those districts, Our Lady of the Angels in the southwest, and St. Bernard's in the northeast. By 1916, all these new parishes together boasted over 8,000 members, and by the 1920s Holy Rosary and Blessed Sacrament each served over 2,500 Catholics. These parishes performed much the same functions as spiritual and social centers that older parishes like St. John's or Sacred Heart did in Irish Worcester neighborhoods—though sometimes with upscale twists: Blessed Sacrament, for example, quickly became famous for its "lawn parties." The parish, however, also boasted a full range of societies and clubs and by the 1920s had opened an elementary school. In the same decade, Blessed Sacrament, which at its founding had held its services in a storefront, also built a huge Gothic church, one of the largest churches in the city, making a symbolic statement of the continuing significance of Catholicism in the life of its members, even as they moved into the better part of town and settled among non-Catholics. In Worcester, then, as Ellen Skerret has pointed out for Chicago, Irish movement to suburban or peripheral areas did not mean an abandonment of the Catholic community.[149]

Moreover, despite this dispersal of the American-born Irish to the west and north, the bulk of Worcester's Irish, immigrant and American-born, remained in or near the east side and community spokesmen continued to identify that area as the heart of Irish Worcester. In 1913, for example, the *Catholic Messenger* launched a bitter attack against the snobs and hypocrites of the west side who dared to impugn the moral character of east side boys. The

Irish in Worcester would consider the east side and the old Irish districts home until well into the twentieth century.[150]

Conclusion

Through the end of the nineteenth and first decade of the twentieth centuries a new generation of Irish grew to maturity and began to dominate the local Irish community. It was an American-born generation; its members were proud of their native land and were eager participants, even makers, of its popular culture. But it was a generation of both men and women who were also loyal Catholics. Catholicism helped link them to their parents, but the Catholicism the members of the new generation practiced—the Catholicism that they, in fact helped to create—was not the religion most of their parents had known in rural Ireland in the early or mid-nineteenth century. It was an institutionalized Catholicism, rich with ceremony and music, thick with various devotions and highly organized, with societies, clubs, and sodalities. It was a Catholicism that did not just help them identify with the past, but helped them meet the needs of their present for cultural and social respectability, for grandeur and discipline.

American and Catholic loyalties, values, and customs shaped the lives that the second-generation Irish created for themselves in turn of the century Worcester, but they were not the only influences molding those lives. The changing local economy, persistent prejudice, and the physical evolution of the city confronted the new generation with a concrete field of opportunities and constraints as they sought to work out Catholic and American loyalties, values, and customs in their everyday lives. Those lives were complex, reflecting the interaction of many influences: second-generation Irish men moved up the city's economic ladder, but never reached the top; second-generation women found opportunities for mobility and autonomy despite their community's repeated affirmations of strict limits on the role of women; both men and women married late, later even than the immigrants and as late as the Irish in Ireland; and Irish men and women moved out of their old neighborhoods, but slowly, and created new Catholic communities in new localities. The new generation was creating a new life, and it was a messy process. If they knew that they wanted to be American and Catholic, the opportunities and constraints of their environment shaped what that meant in concrete terms.

Yet the Irish in Worcester were not just individuals unconsciously forging a new culture as they made their way in the everyday world. They were also

members of a community self-consciously struggling to define a group identity and group boundaries and determine a community strategy for relating to
their neighbors. Would the Catholic Americanism of the second-generation
Irish, for example, be an alternative variation on being American, acceptable
to their Yankee neighbors, or a new version of American loyalties and culture
set in opposition to a native-stock Protestant mainstream? Would it also be a
Catholic Americanism that would include other Catholic ethnics or one that
would be confined to Irish descendants only? Would the boundary between
the Irish and non-Catholics, or between the Irish and other Catholic ethnics,
like the French Canadians or Italians, be scarcely visible and hardly defended,
or obviously drawn and heavily fortified? The answers to those questions would
change over the course of the turn of the century, not only as members of the
new generation grew older and more experienced, but as new groups moved
into Worcester and old ones changed, the balance of power in local politics
shifted, and movements rose and fell or policies emerged and faded in places
as far away as the Vatican or Ireland. In the next four chapters, we turn to how
the immigrant and second-generation Irish of Worcester negotiated their definitions of group identity and boundaries and crafted strategies of group relations through the events and trends of the turbulent turn of the century era.

Three

The Search for Accommodation

The 1880s and Early 1890s

"The YMCA . . . is an institution of which much can justly be said in praise . . . a power for good in the community." So wrote Joshua O'Leary, the second-generation editor of Worcester's Irish weekly *Messenger,* in 1893. The endorsement is surprising, perhaps even shocking in an age when the "Y" was still an active agency of Protestant evangelization. The organization was anathema to the official Catholic church and most Catholics. In a few more years it would become anathema to most Worcester Catholics as well and even to O'Leary's successors as editors of the *Messenger.* That an Irish Catholic paper—especially an Irish Catholic paper in a New England city, where Irish attitudes towards their Protestant neighbors have long been characterized as unrelievedly suspicious, acrimonious, and even "paranoid"—should praise a Protestant evangelist organization seems inexplicable.[1]

What is more important, however, is that in the 1880s and early 1890s, O'Leary's praise for Protestant organizations did not seem shocking to Irish Catholics in Worcester, nor did his grander dream of reconciling Catholic Celt and Yankee Protestant seem distant or deluded. Not all, indeed perhaps few, pursued that goal with such confidence or determination as O'Leary. Nevertheless, an enthusiasm for American popular culture, an insistent emphasis on American identity and the search for a peaceable accommodation with the local Yankees dominated Worcester's Irish community in that period. In the 1880s and 1890s the Worcester Irish deliberately refrained from building Catholic schools (and in the process defied a mandate of American Catholic bishops), sought out Protestant cooperation in building a Catholic hospital, flocked to the cause of temperance in heretofore unseen numbers, mounted a campaign for home rule in Ireland self-consciously crafted to attract Yankee Protestant support, and—as noted in the opening of this book—stayed home about as often as they marched on St. Patrick's Day.

There were, of course, discordant notes, deviations from the trend to accommodation. Ethnic militants and a varied band of nationalists clung to old country ways, struggled to stoke the fires of ethnic pride, and sought to rouse Worcester's Irish community to back radical transformation of the old country's politics and economy. The Ancient Order of Hibernians fought hard for the St. Patrick's Day parades as a means of demonstrating Irish power, and an unlikely coalition of male factory workers and female teachers, clerks, and milliners backed the radical nationalism of Michael Davitt and Patrick Ford and challenged the stranglehold of conservative priests and politicians on the local Land League. Yet neither the Hibernians nor the nationalist radicals were very successful; radicalism and ethnic militancy remained minor themes in the history of Worcester Irish of the 1880s.

The second generation was far more attracted than the first to the temperance societies and the middle class of both generations formed the core of the conservative nationalist movement, but the trend to accommodation in the Irish community of the 1880s can hardly be explained by the "emergence" of the new American-born generation or the rise of an Irish middle class. The new generation's cultural perspective was too complicated to suggest that they were rebels against every element of their past, eager at every opportunity to "out-Yankee the Yankees." More important, even had the American-born or the middle-class Irish been unanimously predisposed to accommodation and American culture, both groups were but a small minority in Worcester's Irish community. Though the second-generation Irish outnumbered Irish immigrants as early as 1885, the vast majority of the American-born Irish were still very young in the 1880s. Furthermore, only a little over 5 percent of the Irish foreign stock were white-collar workers in the 1880s. It is difficult to attribute the trends of the 1880s to the emergence of the new generation or the Irish middle class, simply because it is impossible to say that either "emerged" in that decade.[2]

It was not changes within the Irish community therefore, or at least not those changes alone, that explain the trends to assimilation and acculturation; it was changes in the environment of the Worcester Irish, in the economy and the politics of the city, that combined with changes within the group to produce these trends. Historians have long depicted the environments of New England cities like Worcester as harsh and unyielding for Irish exiles and their children. Slowly growing economies and, more important, viciously hostile, powerful, and well-entrenched Yankee neighbors hardly fostered dreams of peaceful accommodation or eager yearnings for acculturation. Worcester had its maturing economy, its Yankees, and its traditions of puritan suspicion of Catholics, and, indeed, its Know-Nothings in the 1850s, as other New England cities did, but the Worcester environment of the Irish was much more complicated than such a depiction suggests and, as important, it was dynamic, changing. By the 1880s the political, social, and economic life of Worcester had evolved into an atmosphere favorable to Irish hopes of finding a peaceful place for themselves as Americans in the city's society. Memories of shared sacrifice during the Civil War were in full flood by the 1880s, blotting out the Know-Nothing conflict that had divided Irish and Yankee before the war. More important, divisions over culture and economic interest split the Yankee community, opening up opportunities for political alliances between the Irish and Yankee factions, and, temporarily at least, muffling overt nativism. Irish Americans had no strategic alternative to such alliances in local politics for they were too weak to have any say in city government without allies and there were no other groups in the city but the Yankees who were powerful enough to help them. They also could not follow a strategy of class mobilization or class politics because the city's working class was too deeply divided to permit such a strategy to be successful. The Irish, therefore, needed powerful Yankee friends as much as those Yankees needed Irish votes. This political alliance across ethnic lines, in turn, made alternatives to social and cultural accommodation impractical. Aggressive ethnocentrism and resistance to acculturation, for example, would endanger Yankee-Irish friendships without promise of any concrete returns. Necessity thus nourished conviction in the Irish search for accommodation in Worcester in the 1880s.

There were other trends taking place far from Worcester that helped encourage this Irish embrace of accommodation. In Ireland, Charles Stewart Parnell, charismatic, powerful, but ultimately conservative, dominated the revived Irish nationalist movement, fending off militants and radicals there and making it harder for them to mobilize in America. Led by Archbishop John Ireland in Minnesota and James Cardinal Gibbons in Baltimore, a group of liberals also emerged among the Catholic hierarchy, argued strenuously for the embrace of American culture and openness to American non-Catholics, and for a time won the approbation of the Vatican.

Convinced that they had friends in the Yankee community and hoping that the tentative ethnic peace of the 1880s would endure, Worcester's Irish Americans thus heeded Parnell and not his militant critics, and Gibbons and Ireland, not their conservative antagonists, and sought an accommodation with their neighbors. Incidents at the very end of the 1880s and beginning of the 1890s would signal the end of that peace, but those incidents would seem small and isolated until the mid-1890s. Until then, looking back on a long period of relative ethnic peace and harmony, some in the Irish community would think they had entered a new, more hopeful era in their history.

Yankee and Irish: The Early Years

When the first Catholic Celt arrived in 1826, fear of papists and hostility to immigrants were deeply rooted traditions. As late as 1820 there were but 19 immigrants in a town of 3,000 people, and anti-Catholic maxims and stories were staple features of local schoolbooks, as Worcester's children quite literally learned suspicion of Rome with their alphabet. It was not surprising then that Worcester's first Irish Catholics terrified the town's Yankee Protestants.[3]

Nevertheless, not all Yankees were hostile to the Irish in those early years. The owners of the Blackstone Canal came to appreciate the Irish Catholic navvies who built it and helped many of them find jobs in the canal company or in nearby warehouses after the waterway was completed. William Lincoln of the Canal Company, descended from the great Levi Lincoln, attorney general in Jefferson's cabinet, helped bring the Irish into the local Democratic party. A number of Yankees also helped the Irish buy the land for their first church.[4]

With the help of these friends, the Irish were able to coexist with their Yankee neighbors in relative peace through the first quarter-century of their settlement, but in the early 1850s they became the target of the local Know-Nothing crusade. Over ten months in 1854 the membership of this fiercely anti-Catholic and anti-immigrant secret society skyrocketed from 106 to 1,120 men (5 percent of Worcester's entire native-stock population of men, women, and children in 1855). By December of 1854 the Know-Nothings were strong enough to elect George Richardson mayor of the city by a five-to-one margin, as well as four of the city's eight aldermen and thirteen of its twenty-four common councilmen. In the state elections that year Henry Wilson, the Know-Nothing candidate for governor, carried Worcester with 62 percent of the vote and the nativists captured all five of Worcester's seats in the state's House of Representatives.[5]

Political and economic frustrations shaped the character of the Know-Nothing movement in Worcester. The rhetoric and ideology of the nativists was strongly reformist as the Know-Nothing *Worcester Daily Evening Journal* incessantly hammered home the virtues of temperance, antislavery, and other reform causes in its columns, and the new Know-Nothing American Party drew particularly well from former Free-Soilers. The *Journal* also frequently backed working-class causes like the ten-hour day and attacked "what are termed the first circles of society," the rich and well born, who, the paper alleged, indulged in drink and hindered "the progress of temperance and virtue."[6]

The reformist and working- and middle-class nature of Worcester's Know-Nothings suggested some important clues about the future course of relations between Irish and Yankees in the city. It suggested the kind of cultural issues which divided Irish and Yankees and would continue to be critical questions for their relations in the future. Though slavery would be abolished, other moral reform issues, particularly temperance, would continue to be at the center of Yankee-Irish relations for another three-quarters of a century. More important perhaps, the Know-Nothing crusade's attack on members of its own Yankee elite as well as Catholic immigrants revealed that there were important differences among Worcester's Yankees about how to deal with their new Irish neighbors.

The Know-Nothing movement declined almost as quickly as it had arisen, and in a little over half a decade Irish and Yankees in Worcester would share a common ordeal which would help them unite in spite of their differences. The crisis of the Civil War did not merely postpone the local conflict between Irish and Yankee, it gave the Irish an opportunity to prove their loyalty to the Republic and lay the foundation for future cooperation between the two groups. Though the Irish made up about 30 percent of Worcester's population in 1860, they contributed about 40 percent of the city's soldiers during the war (1,109 of 2,836 total enlistments), and suffered over half the city's casualties (166 of 304). Two local Irishmen, Sergeant William Plunkett and Captain Thomas O'Neill won the Congressional Medal of Honor. Plunkett lost both arms saving his regiment's colors in the futile Union charges at Fredericksburg but somehow survived. O'Neill was shot down in the slaughter at Cold Harbor. Later reports said the dying O'Neill asked to be turned towards the enemy and wrapped in the American flag. "Write to my dear mother," he supposedly told a colleague, "and tell her I die for my country." Whether the dying captain said those words or Worcester's chroniclers of the war merely wished that he had, the sentiments were heartily appreciated by Yankee and Irish alike. His funeral back in Worcester was a major civic occasion. Members of the city government, the city's Irish societies, a band, and a detachment of militia marched behind the hearse along streets crowded with mourners from St. John's church to the Catholic cemetery in South Worcester.[7]

The goodwill won by the sacrifices of Worcester's Irish soldiers created a favorable atmosphere for the settlement of some of the lingering disputes between Irish Catholics and their native-stock Protestant neighbors. In 1862, Father John J. Power, then of St. Anne's church, with the backing of a number of "prominent citizens of that city," including the mayor and superintendent of schools, petitioned the legislature to change the state's law on the reading of the Bible in the schools so "that no scholar [would] be compelled to read any particular version of the Bible against the wishes of his parents." After much debate, Power's bill became law, a tribute to "the loyalty displayed by the adopted citizens in this hour of national trial."[8]

Memories of the war and the shared sacrifice of Irish and Yankee seemed to grow stronger, not weaker, in Worcester with the passage of time. Lectures on the war and sentimental plays evoking its experience like the *Little Drummer Boy* became increasingly popular in the city through the late 1870s and 1880s as the war's horrors faded into the haze of a romantic crusade. O'Neill was dead, but Sergeant Plunkett lived on through the late nineteenth century, a striking living symbol of Irish valor and commitment to the cause of the Union. Yankee speakers at memorial services or the dedications of local monuments often invoked the Celtic contribution to the war effort. In 1884 U.S. Senator George F. Hoar lauded Worcester's Celtic soldiers at the anniversary celebration of Worcester's first settlement. Worcester's Irish gushed their thanks in return. John J. Riordan wrote to the senator "as the son of an Irishman," stating his "profound gratitude for your unprejudiced" speech. "Our greatest prosperity," Riordan concluded, "will only be attained by the total destruction of class feeling."[9]

"Each to His Pleasure" or "A Concerted Attack against All that Is Bad": Cultural Divisions in the Yankee Community

Ironically, it was not the civic harmony induced by the war that had the most significant impact on Yankee-Irish relations, but the divisiveness within the Yankee community itself. As Worcester grew and transformed into an urban industrial city, its Yankee population also changed and the stresses of those changes opened severe rifts within the Yankee community over issues ranging from music to municipal improvements.

Yankee culture in Worcester became increasingly complex and diverse in the nineteenth century. The religious monopoly of Congregationalism had long since passed by the 1870s and 1880s, and the steady growth of newer denominations in that era was notable. The Episcopalians were small in number but well established. Their main church, built in 1843, thrived in the late nine-teenth century and Episcopalians began to plant smaller parishes in the four corners of the city by the 1880s. Even among the churches of the old ortho-doxy, Congregationalism, new men with new ideas were making a significant impact. Most noteworthy was Daniel Merriman, who reigned at Central Con-gregational for more than two decades at the end of the nineteenth century. Known in Worcester for his learned sermons, cultivated taste for art, and im-peccable social graces (he was reputed to be the first man in Worcester to own his own evening clothes), Merriman was a critical figure in the expansion of Worcester's cultural horizons. He led efforts to found an art museum in 1896 and served as its first president.

Stephen Salisbury III who supplied much of the money for that venture, typified the broadening cultural horizons of many Yankees at the end of the nineteenth century. Salisbury was the richest man in Worcester and a man of broad and diverse cultural interests. He was a devoted amateur archaeologist, most noted for his study of pre-Columbian Mexican cultures. Salisbury's funds were critical not only to the art museum but to virtually every other significant cultural institution in late nineteenth-century Worcester. Funds from Salisbury and a host of others in Worcester helped support the Worcester Music festival, for example. Begun as a choral competition, the festival developed into a rich presentation of serious and sophisticated classical music in the 1880s and 1890s. In addition to these institutions, Worcester Yankees created a host of new clubs and associations that reflected expanding cultural interests: the Art Society, the Bohemian Club, and other drama and literature clubs.[10]

The changes in Yankee culture included a new appreciation of leisure as well as a broadening cultural vision. Theatrical performances had been banned in the city until the middle of the nineteenth century, but by the end of the cen-tury Worcester boasted three large theaters regularly offering hundreds of patrons a rich theatrical fare. Two of them, the Front Street and Lothrop Opera Houses, served the tastes of the city's Irish or other ethnics for vaudeville and broad melodrama, but at least one, the Worcester Theater, served a tonier pa-tronage of wealthier Yankees. Founded in 1869, the original Worcester Theater burned in the late 1880s. *Light*, a weekly devoted to the social life of Worcester's Yankee community, reported that "everyone" attended the opening of the re-built theater in 1890. The "dazzling row of white shirt fronts," the paper re-ported, included such Yankee swells as the young financier Harry Worcester Smith, and Rockwood Hoar, the son of Senator George Frisbie Hoar. Balls fea-turing men in evening dress and women in elegant gowns dancing amidst banks of flowers and richly decorated tapestries were also popular in some Yankee circles in the eighties and nineties, and social clubs sponsoring sumptuous dinners and elaborate entertainments multiplied in that era. The Worcester Club, an elite men's club founded in 1886, was the most prominent of them, but there were many others. Some young men sought more active amusements than spirited discussions over cigars in the paneled rooms of men's clubs. In 1895, a group of local sports, taking the English gentry as their models, founded the Grafton Country Club. The club's motto, "Each to His Pleasure," aptly summed up the club's rounds of elaborate dinners, reckless horse races, and wild fox hunts. More plebeian sports such as tennis, bicycling, baseball, and football also gained favor in the Yankee community in the late nineteenth century. In 1890 *Light* predicted "the chances are that inside of another decade the number of people in the moral and intellectual classes, if they may be so styled, who openly favor athletic sport will have doubled."

Like their Irish counterparts, many Yankees also rushed to take advantage of the new improvements in transportation that opened up the mountains and the seashore to summer visitors. Names of vacationers to Cape Cod, the White Mountains, Saratoga, and Block Island filled *Light*'s columns in the summers of the 1890s. Some people ventured farther afield. Mr. and Mrs. E. D. Buffington went on an Egyptian tour in the 1890s. Stephen Salisbury preferred Mexico. He was thrilled by the "animated dances," the "pretty people," and champagne breakfasts (it was rumored he fell in love there). "I danced all day," he confessed to his diary on a trip south of the border in March of 1886.[11]

For most Worcester Yankees, however, such indulgences were neither pleasurable nor enlightening but ominous signs of incipient degeneration. Most local Yankees grew to appreciate the music festival but only grudgingly. Robert M. Washburn, descendant of one of Worcester's first families, remembered: "A people which had hitherto unrestrainedly found delight in 'The Old Oaken Bucket'" had to "loyally simulate pleasure with some effort at a seventy-two bar fugue in B minor by Bach." Clark University, founded in 1889, provoked more skepticism. Just a year after its establishment, Yankee traditionalists assailed anthropologist Franz Boas and his fellows at Clark as "the scum of German Universities," for their investigations of physical growth and development in Worcester schoolchildren. Such charges seemed grounded in deeper fears of the university's relentless scientific assault on old pieties.

The new leisure activities were, perhaps, even more troubling to many Worcester Yankees than these cultural innovations. As Albert Roe sternly warned in the *Worcester Methodist* in April of 1888: "If Methodism means any one thing more than another . . . it means first, last and always a concerted attack against all we deem bad." "All" included: drinking, an "unmitigated curse"; smoking; gambling; and the theater. Traditionalists pilloried the new Worcester Club for seeking a liquor license, charging that the elite club would transform Worcester's leaders into degenerate sots, destroying them and the community they led in the process. Reactions to the growing popularity of sports were less hysterical but still suspicious. In 1888 the *Worcester Methodist* warned young readers: "Over-exertion in ball playing will incapacitate you . . . who cares for a strong arm or leg?" On Sunday, of course, standards of proper behavior were even higher. "On Sunday," Olive Prouty, daughter of aspiring manufacturer Milton Higgins, remembered, "there were no games allowed . . . no exercise except walking, no driving except to church, no lessons for school the next day. . . . One of my favorite diversions was Doré's volume of Bible pictures. I'd pore over them for hours."[12]

Such sentiments testified to the continuing power of older, staunchly evangelical Yankee perspectives in Worcester. Though Episcopalianism was growing in the 1880s, it was not growing any faster than churches rooted in Worcester's evangelical tradition. Even as late as 1900, one-third of Worcester's churched Protestants were Congregationalists, and another quarter Baptists and Presbyterians. Together those three sects built no less than eighteen new churches in the last three decades of the nineteenth century. The typical minister of these new churches was not the liberal Merriman but the fiery fundamentalist, David O. Mears, pastor of the Piedmont Congregational church located in the heart of the Main South and Chandler May districts. As Merriman was the architect of liberal cultural innovation, Mears was the champion of the old evangelical orthodoxy. Within a few years of his appointment he paid off the huge debt on his new Piedmont church with a mixture of energetic arm-twisting, inspiring invocations, and vague hints that the "Romanists" might buy the church if the congregation did not save it. He was responsible for the establishment of a YWCA in Worcester, claimed to have started the first antisaloon league branch in America, invited Anthony Comstock to speak at his church, and counted John Gough, the famed temperance crusader, as a close friend and comrade in the fight against the liquor traffic. While Mears was the most prominent, there were other ministers of like conviction—Lansing of Salem Street Congregational, or Southgate of Pilgrim Congregational—who found fertile fields in Worcester.[13]

Evangelical orthodoxy and traditional morality found broad-based support in Worcester's Yankee community in the late nineteenth century. The occupational backgrounds of Mears's congregation testified to the evangelicals' continuing appeal to middle- and working-class Yankees. In 1883 nearly half of the members of Mears's church were skilled blue-collar workers and another third or more were clerks or small shopkeepers. The rich, well-born, and power-ful, on the other hand, were far more likely to be Episcopalians or Unitarians than was the Yankee population at large. As the "dazzling shirt fronts" at the Worcester Theater, the fox hunts at the Grafton Country Club, and the men gathered at the Worcester Club bar suggested, the wealthy and socially promi-nent were more likely, too, to partake of long-forbidden or newly fashionable leisure activities. Nevertheless, the evangelicals found support among segments of the elite as well. Manufacturers, like the upwardly mobile Milton Higgins or even the established Philip Moen, head of the city's largest company, often remained devoted to a stern Calvinism and a strict morality. None of Mears's church members in 1883 were lawyers or bankers, only three were doctors, but no less than twelve were manufacturers.[14]

One reason for the enduring vitality of the evangelical orthodoxy among Worcester's Yankees was the continued transfusion of "new blood" from rural New England into the city's Yankee community. In 1900, nearly 40 percent of the Yankee heads of households had been born outside Massachusetts and 47 percent had parents born outside the state. Many of these migrants, like Milton Higgins, came from the rapidly depopulating New England country-side. In 1885, 30 percent of the native-stock population in the city had been born in other New England states or their parents had been born there, most of them migrants from northern New England: Vermont, Maine, and New Hampshire. Even in 1900 nearly one-third of the city's Yankee adults came from other New England states, one-fifth from northern New England.[15]

Like immigrants from overseas or French Canada, many of these Yankee mi-grants pined for their native land. They formed clubs, the Sons and Daughters of Vermont, Maine, or New Hampshire, and consciously labored to preserve the symbols, customs, and values of their rural upcountry homes. Vermont re-unions in 1876 and 1884 featured "viands" of an "old-fashioned country variety," doughnuts, brown bread, Vermont pork and beans, applesauce, and baked Indian pudding, and in 1880s members enjoyed "old-fashioned dancing." Recreated scenes of an "upcountry kitchen" with "antique furniture," spinning wheels and farm implements and living tableaux were also popular at such gatherings. Usually the reunions included poetry readings, songs, and speeches by prominent local migrants as well. Clark Jillson and Samuel Hildreth, native Vermonters and prominent conservative Republicans, spoke often at gather-ings of the Vermont association. Such speeches, poems, and dramatic scenes reeked of nostalgia for "berry picking in the hills and valleys," the old school-house on the hill, and the "song of the spinning wheel." Speakers also invari-ably pointed out that the simple rugged northern New England states were not known for their "high culture" or "polish" but built moral "character" and religious devotion.[16]

A theme of guilt, a sense that emigration was "necessary" to find "opportunities" but lamentable because it meant the abandonment of home, loved ones, and possibly virtue, pervaded many of these recollections. A living tableau, depicting first a scene of "Ma," "Pa," and "Sis" pleading with a young boy not to migrate followed by a portrait of the emigrant's return "in rags" to a joyous welcome, was immensely popular among Worcester's Vermonters in 1878.[17]

Worcester's Economy and the Prospects of Class Solidarity

In less than half a century, Worcester was transformed from a tiny agricultural market village and sleepy shire town of the 1820s to a modern industrial city. This economic revolution might have caused Worcester to divide along class lines: a controlling economic elite pitted against an aroused working class. Yet divided by both culture and interest, neither the overwhelmingly Yankee economic elite nor the multiethnic working class could, or would, act cohesively in the 1880s. Indeed, the fragmentation of both permitted the cross-class alliances that would dominate Worcester's politics throughout the decade.

Economic interest as well as culture divided the Yankee elite. The city's economic and population rise fueled the rapid growth of its banks, insurance companies, large utilities, and big downtown retailers. Between 1873 and 1890, for example, deposits in the city's largest savings banks rose from 11 million dollars to 25 million and mortgage loans from 5 million to 11 million. Bankers, utility magnates, and downtown merchants were very interested in fostering the expansion of the city's neighborhoods and the development of the downtown.

The heart of the city's economy, however, was manufacturing, and through the 1880s Worcester's manufacturing, was carried on by numerous small shops. Companies in the city employed an average of 22 workers in 1875 and carried on business with a lean capitalization of $22,374. By comparison, factories in Fall River in 1875 averaged 152 workers and capitalization of over $210,612. Owners of such small companies operated on a shoestring and worried about the costs of taxes and rates for water use and other city services. They also had an ambivalent, complicated relationship with local capitalists like Stephen Salisbury. On the one hand they depended on men like Salisbury to provide space and power for their fledgling companies in one of the many factory buildings he built and equipped with power for that very purpose. On the other hand they resented such dependence on a "parasitic non-producer." Many of these small manufacturers were newcomers in Worcester, had only small amounts of capital invested there that they might easily uproot, and competed with one another in local or regional markets as much as with manufacturers in other cities in national ones. They were, then, less likely to identify themselves as part of a local economic elite whose fortunes were tied to the city of Worcester, and thus were less susceptible to the boosterism that animated most drives for municipal improvement. Although there was extensive intermingling of the manufacturing, financial, and big retail elites in Worcester, these groups, nonetheless, also often divided over critical issues of urban development and revenue.[18]

In 1874, local businessmen, important manufacturers like Philip L. Moen and Lucius J. Knowles and prosperous merchants like Lewis Barnard among them, founded a Board of Trade. The purpose of the organization was "To promote the business interests of Worcester and its vicinity and to secure the advantages which the city offers to trade and manufacturers as well as to cultivate a more intimate and friendly acquaintance among the business men of the city." Over the next five years the board considered such issues as improved water supply for the city, a municipal board of works, and an extension of the city's street railways. By 1880, however, the board had fallen on hard times, and for the entire decade of the 1880s it was "inactive," maintaining only a "nominal existence," a sterile monument to the Worcester business community's inability to find common ground.[19]

The divisions among Worcester's businessmen should have opened opportunities for the city's workers to assert their own interests. Yet, themselves divided by culture and interest like the business elite, they could not. Thus, though members of Worcester's working class made several efforts to organize and wring changes from their bosses in the 1870s and 1880s, they had little or no enduring success.

Labor fought and won few battles in Worcester in the 1880s. Between 1881 and 1884, the U.S. Bureau of Labor Statistics recorded but one strike in Worcester, a nonunion walkout by 250 metalworkers in 1881. In the same period, the bureau reported over 70 strikes in Fall River that involved over 8,000 workers, 6 strikes in Lynn of 2,500 workers and major strikes in Lawrence, New Bedford, and Lowell.

In 1885, however, Worcester's economy plunged into a severe, if brief, recession. In all, nearly 30 percent of Worcester's workers were idle for an average of four months. Such conditions gave Worcester's enfeebled labor movement new life. Four Knights of Labor locals had already been founded in the city before 1885 and three still survived to that year. Four more appeared in 1885–86 and two in 1887. Worcester's workers were not only better organized but more militant after the recession. Nearly two thousand boot and shoe workers struck and stayed out for over twelve months. In addition to the shoe workers, the masons, sheet workers, compositors, and woolen workers all struck in 1886 or 1887. Egging on all of them was the second-generation Irishman, James Mellen, and his *Daily Times*, with sharp-edged republican rhetoric assailing "mill aristocrats" and invoking the principles of the American Revolution's Declaration of Independence for the rights of workers.[20]

The new unions and even the rising number of strikes hardly signaled a revolution in Worcester's labor history. As *The Daily Times* confessed sadly in 1885, "in every city in New England this order [the Knights of Labor] is far in advance of the organization in this city, although there are not so many workmen comparatively." The increasing strike activity in the city was also misleading. The bootmakers' strike was less the opening battle in a class revolution than the desperate and pathetic death struggle of a dying trade. Strikers were so careful not to offend their "very Christian" bosses, the bootshop owners, that their rhetoric occasionally passed from conciliatory to cloying. Late in January of 1887 a strike spokesman claimed: "I do not believe that businessmen intend to be mean. They have some fine feelings; and if they took seats in our meeting they would admit that we have taken a just course in this matter." Furthermore, the Bureau of Labor Statistics reports reveal all of the strikes in the city steel and wire mills in 1887 lasted fewer than five days. As P. J. Maguire, the great founder of the Carpenters Union, contended in 1889, Worcester remained "one of the scab holes of the state."[21]

The causes of labor's weakness in Worcester were complex. The very fragmentation and diversity of Worcester's manufacturers, split into a number of industries and small shops, may have worked to their advantage in confronting labor. A complicated mix of metal trades, machinery manufacture, boot and shoe making, textiles, and a host of other industries distinguished the city sharply from most Massachusetts cities where shoes or textiles dominated. Worcester's workers were not only divided by trade, but within each industry divided into small factories and shops. A powerful labor movement could only have emerged piecemeal in Worcester, organizing trade by trade, and shop by shop, workers who had little in common.

Surprisingly, even the larger split in the business community between manufacturers and retailers, bankers, merchants, and others did not help Worcester's workers, but, indeed, helped to further divide them. Though Yankee and Irish workers sometimes banded together as in the bootworkers' strike they were more often divided by culture and political interest. Many Yankee workers appeared to believe that their common interests were with their manufacturing employers. They had abundant examples of men who began on the shop floor like themselves and rose through technical innovation or sharp bargaining to run their own companies. Ichabod Washburn, Loring Coes, and Samuel Hildreth were only the most prominent of the driven mechanical tinkerers who worked their way up to own their own businesses. Whether lured by visions of success or not, Yankee workers, particularly in the machine shops, seemed to share their employers' commitment to temperance, evangelical religion, and loyalty to Republican party orthodoxy. Irish workers, of course, had a different religion and less reason to expect that hard work and temperance would catapult them up the city's economic ladder. Local political conditions, as we shall see, also conspired to draw the Irish away from common interests with fellow workers and into their own alliance with a different segment of the Yankee elite, bankers, real estate dealers, and large merchants, whose cultural predispositions and economic interests caused them to defect from the Republican party. Each group of workers, Yankees and Irish, looked to different factions within the elite for political allies rather than to one another.[22]

Yankees and Irish: The Forging of an Alliance

The cross-class alliances that doomed Worcester's labor movement also structured the city's municipal politics for much of the late nineteenth century. This peculiar configuration of coalitions that crossed not only class lines but ethnic, religious, and partisan ones as well, was rooted in the factionalism of the Yankee community and the political weakness of the Irish one. A small group of Yankee Republican independents, disdainful of evangelical Protestant culture and eager to exploit the riches promised by Worcester's rapid growth, confronted a much more numerous, culturally orthodox, and economically cautious group of fellow Yankees who dominated the Republican party. To get their way in municipal politics, the independents had to bolt the party in local elections and find allies who would help them overpower the Republican loyalists who dominated the Republican party. They found willing partners in the Irish, who had too few votes to challenge for control of the city by themselves and could find no allies among other immigrant groups to help them. Pitching in together under the banner of an informal party called the Citizens' slates, the alliance of independent Yankee Republicans and Irish Democrats grew so powerful by the early 1880s that it eclipsed the two regular parties, the

Republicans and the Democrats, in municipal politics. Even after the coalition's decline in the latter half of that decade, partisanship in municipal elections remained subdued and ethnic antagonism was muffled.

The vast majority of Yankees remained loyal to the Republicans and never even considered bolting the GOP for the Citizens' slates. The Yankee middle- and working-classes were especially unyielding in their Republican partisanship and gave the loyalist faction a mass base that allowed it to dominate the party. In 1883, for example, 71.8 percent of the petition signers for Samuel Hildreth, loyalist candidate for mayor, were low white-collar or blue-collar workers. Moreover, middle-class voting districts like Ward Seven on the southwest side were the most consistently Republican wards and precincts in the city. Loyalists were less well represented among the Yankee elite, but they could count on a share of Yankee cultural and economic leaders. Evangelical ministers were perhaps their most prominent spokesmen, but manufacturers also sometimes played an important role in loyalist efforts. The same Hildreth petition reads like a who's who of Worcester's manufacturers, particularly its metal and machinery makers. The wealthier and best established manufacturers such as Philip Moen of the Washburn Moen Wire Manufacturing Company moved back and forth between the two Republican factions, independent and loyalist, underscoring the fluidity of distinctions between the two GOP groups.[23]

Republican independent voters were a much smaller group, always a minority within the Yankee and nominally Republican population. In 1876 the *Worcester Evening Gazette* suggested that the differences between Republican independents and loyalists were generational: younger men growing to maturity after the Civil War were more likely to be independents. In local politics, however, occupation or economic interest and cultural outlook seemed the critical determinants. Real estate investors, downtown businessmen, bankers, and insurance lenders eager for urban improvements and development were key members of the Citizens' coalition. Liquor wholesalers and their clients, grocers or provisions dealers, fearful of prohibition or strict regulation of the liquor traffic were another. Of the thirty-nine names on a petition for Elijah B. Stoddard, Hildreth's Citizens' slate opponent in 1882, nine were bankers or downtown merchants and ten were lawyers. Only one was a manufacturer. The independents had a less reliable voting base than the loyalists, but they seemed to draw best in the northern part of the city, particularly the wealthy west side Ward Eight and the north side Ward One.[24]

The independents usually had a raft of wealthy and socially prominent leaders, abundant money, numerous campaign workers recruited from the liquor dealers, the support of the city's two most prestigious newspapers, the *Evening Gazette* and the venerable *Daily Spy*, and a program of municipal improvements that was widely popular, but those assets did not translate easily into political power. The more numerous loyalists blocked their efforts to control the Republican party caucuses, and unless mutually beneficial deals could be struck the independents could not find a path to power within the GOP. They thus often looked outside the party to Irish Democrats for the precious element that their faction lacked, a mass base of voters, and created the ad hoc alliances that were known as the Citizens' tickets.

Worcester's Irishmen needed that alliance as much as the Yankee independents did. In 1881, the *Worcester Daily Times* estimated the number of Irish voters at about only 3,000 out of a total electorate of about 10,000 to 11,000. State census statistics and the census samples suggest that the *Times* estimates were essentially correct. Worcester's Irish, therefore, could not elect one of their own or an ally mayor with only their own votes, and because of Worcester's charter they could not even elect aldermen, members of the bicameral city council's upper chamber, from their own wards. According to that peculiar charter, aldermen were nominated for each ward but elected citywide. The Irish desperately needed allies then, not just to help place friends in the mayor's chair, but to elect aldermen from their own wards. They could not find those allies in other immigrant groups simply because there were no other groups in the city with enough votes to help them. In 1882 and 1883, the *Times* scolded Irish Democrats for not cultivating support among the city's French Canadians. Yet in 1885, there were only 284 French Canadian voters in Worcester (and contrary to the *Times* contention, most of Worcester's *Canadiens* voted for the Democrats in 1880s). The Irish thus could look for political allies only among Worcester's native-stock Yankee Republicans.[25]

Born of desperation, this seemingly incongruous coalition of wealthy Yankee bankers and businessmen and poor Irish workers proved amazingly durable and successful. Though there were hints of the coalition at work in earlier elections, the Citizens' alliances did not emerge as a persistent force in Worcester until the late 1870s. In 1876, a genial wisecracking Yankee Democrat named Charles Pratt had upset a Republican party sharply divided between its loyalist and independent factions and saddled with an image of stinginess in a deepening depression. Pratt may have been a Democrat but he was well connected to the Yankee commercial and banking elite. He quickly struck a deal with the Republican independents in his first term and rode to easy victories in the next two elections as a Citizens' candidate. Indeed, so powerful was the Citizens' coalition in those elections that neither of the major parties nominated candidates for mayor to oppose Pratt. Between 1876, Pratt's first election, and 1884, Citizens' candidates triumphed in seven of the nine contests for mayor. In only a little over half of those elections did either the Democrats or Republicans even bother to nominate a candidate for the post. As the *Evening Gazette* and the *Daily Spy*, the principal organs of the Yankee elite, and the *Worcester Daily Times*, the Irish newspaper, all acknowledged, partisanship seemed to almost disappear from Worcester's local politics in the late 1870s and early 1880s. The Citizens' coalition, the formal representatives of the alliance between the Irish and Yankee independents, reigned supreme.[26]

Irish contributions to these victories were vital. The normal strategy for a Citizens' candidate for mayor was to sweep the Irish wards and hope to steal enough votes in Republican precincts to win the election. In only one of the Citizens' victories between 1877 and 1884 did the Citizens' candidate for mayor lose in the Irish Democratic east side Wards Three, Four and Five. In the two most hotly contested Citizens' wins in 1883 and 1884, the Citizens' standard-bearer, Charles Reed, ran up majorities of nearly three to one in the Irish Democratic wards permitting him to win a narrow victory after taking a smaller but critical 40 percent of the vote in the Republican wards.[27]

After the elections, as Robert Kolesar has shown, Irish Catholic aldermen and common councilors remained steadfastly loyal to their wealthier allies. They enthusiastically backed expansion of city services. Perhaps more surprisingly, they also loyally supported utilities seeking to maintain or raise rates and even blocked middle-class Republican aldermen from prying into special favors bestowed by city government on wealthy and well-connected Republican independents. In 1886, for example, all of the Irish Democratic common councilors from Worcester's impoverished east side voted to prevent open hearings investigating the low property-tax assessments of Worcester's wealthiest citizen, Stephen Salisbury.[28]

The Irish received considerable benefits in return for their loyal support of the Citizens' coalitions. The first Irish alderman in Worcester's history, John L. Murphy, won his office as a Citizens' nominee in 1878, and in the next six years of the Citizens' era, three more Irish were elected aldermen. In 1884, after some hard bargaining, Worcester's Irish Democrats were able to wring two nominations for alderman from their independent Yankee allies.[29]

The Irish rank and file as well as their leaders prospered under Citizens' administrations. Between 1876 and 1884, the number of Irishmen on the police force rose from eleven to thirty-eight. By the end of the 1880s, immigrants, most of them Irish, made up over two-thirds of the laborers employed by the city sewer department. As early as 1881, forty-one of Worcester's schoolteachers were Catholics and that number increased steadily throughout the decade. Irish contractors also prospered under Citizens' administrations. Jeremiah Murphy, an immigrant from Cork, built the police headquarters, a firehouse, and other public buildings. *The Worcester Telegram,* the principal organ of middle-class Republicans in Worcester, noted slyly of Murphy that he "got all the City Hall work" because he always bid just under the competition; the paper wondered if he had a "mascot" at City Hall. It was not simply the Citizens' administrations' recognition or patronage that made them attractive to Worcester's Irish. The policy of development, of improved city services pursued by Citizens' mayors helped east side Irish neighborhoods as well as wealthy landholders. In 1877, Charles Pratt began extension of the city's sewer system into the Island neighborhood, where sewers were badly needed. Later, Citizens' administrations worked vigorously to improve or extend sewer systems in East Worcester and South Worcester. Policy, therefore, as well as patronage made the Irish steadfast supporters of the Citizens' Coalition.[30]

In the middle and the late 1880s, the Citizens' coalition began to fray as pressure built in both parties for stricter party loyalty. Republicans began to worry whether defections in municipal elections might be weakening the party's hold on its voters in state and local elections. In 1884, 1888, and 1892, the vote for Grover Cleveland, the Democratic nominee for president rose from scarcely more than 2,000 to 5,000 and then to nearly 7,000. A new newspaper, the *Telegram,* appearing as a weekly in 1884 and a daily in 1886, became the voice of a new intensified Republican partisanship. Rock-ribbed Republican, caustically anti-elitist, and broadly popular, the *Telegram* hammered and slashed at the "November Republicans" who weakened the GOP by their partisan treachery in December municipal elections.[31]

The reemergence of the temperance issue also seemed to have a profound effect on the Republican party in local elections. Temperance had been of little importance in city elections in the 1870s when the state imposed its own solutions to the liquor problem, first prohibiting and then licensing sellers of liquor. In 1881 the state abdicated responsibility for regulating the liquor trade to the voters of the cities and towns, permitting them to choose between prohibition of the sale of liquor by refusing to license sellers, called "no license," or permitting its sale by authorized sellers, called "license." In Worcester these local option elections provoked a temperance political movement which sought to carry the city for no license and seize control of the Republican party.[32]

As Republicans tightened discipline in their party, some Democrats grew restive about the deals that they had struck with independent Republicans to form the Citizens' Alliance. In 1884, many local Irish Democrats revolted against their party's national ticket and threw support behind Benjamin Butler for president of the United States. In that election, Butler nearly beat

Cleveland in Ward Three and did edge him out in Wards Four and Five on the Irish east side. In addition, two Butler men were elected state representatives in Wards Three and Four and another ran ahead of the Democrats in Ward Five. The next year, 1885, inspired by Butler's strong showing and fiery rhetoric, Democratic insurgents urged the party to throw off the yoke of the Citizens' alliance imposed by wealthy Republicans and the liquor dealers and send a rejuvenated Democratic party into the local election to fight the Republicans. John R. Thayer, prosperous lawyer and famed foxhunter, was the unlikely leader of the rebels. (When Thayer ran for Congress years later, Republican Senator George F. Hoar asked a crowd if they would rather have a hard-riding, foxhunting rake or an intelligent and respected leader for their representative in Washington. Thayer replied at his own Democratic rally that the people would rather have both than neither.) He and his supporters managed to commit the Democrats to a partisan contest, but their attempt to win the mayoral nomination provoked a bitter and wrenching fight within the party. Screaming debates and fistfights broke out in the meetings in Wards Three and Five, but conservative Democrats like the Irish-born Andrew Athy kept their heads and coolly rammed through the nomination of Charles Pratt, the original Citizens' candidate. Pratt, however, was the hopeless partisan nominee of a minority Democratic party that had quite deliberately repudiated its former Republican allies.[33]

Shunned by the Democrats and under increasing pressure to remain loyal to their own party, most independent Republicans turned back to the GOP to make the best deal they could with Republican loyalists. They succeeded in tempering the loyalist surge by helping to nominate Samuel Winslow, a small manufacturer and temperance advocate, but a moderate, for mayor. Over the next ten years independent Republicans would again seek and secure Citizens' alliances with the Democrats, but many seemed as willing to pursue their ends within their own party, or at least they were more fearful of bolting it than they had been in the early 1880s. Whether because of this new reluctance of the independents to defect or the growing strength of loyalists reinvigorated by temperance, the GOP would dominate municipal politics in Worcester through the late 1880s and early 1890s.[34]

Winslow's victories ended the Citizens' coalition's dominance of local politics, but it did not break the city into warring ethnic camps or even permanently disrupt the Irish-Yankee alliance. Winslow's principal supporters were the loyalist Yankee temperance reformers, but he was no fanatic and he was shrewd enough to placate both factions in his party; and though not particularly friendly to the Irish, his administration was no nativist crusade. Indeed, patronage continued to flow to the Irish. Over the five years from 1885 to 1890, for example, Irish women received fully one-quarter of the teaching appointments in the public schools. Political tensions between ethnic groups were increasing in Worcester during the late 1880s but they did not explode into open ethnic warfare.

This was true even in 1887 when Andrew Athy, an immigrant from Galway, became the first Irish Catholic to run for mayor in the city's history. What is most remarkable about Athy's candidacy is that it was unremarkable. Athy was a last-minute choice nominated only after the Democrats had exhausted all other possibilities. They had nominated Charles Pratt, but he had refused. They then offered the nomination to Joseph Walker, a Republican, and had been turned down. Just days before the election they put up Athy. The *Spy,* often a voice for Republican independents in city politics, noted quietly, "Of Alderman Athy we do not wish to speak disrespectfully. He is honest, sensible and familiar with city affairs [but] he must rely solely on the Democratic vote and there are not enough Democrats in Worcester to elect him mayor if they should all vote for him." The *Spy*'s assessments both of Athy's character and his chances were accurate. He was a safe man, not a rabble-rouser, and he went down to an inevitable but respectable defeat. His vote was very similar to that given to the Yankee Democrat John R. Thayer the year before; Athy polled only slightly higher in Irish precincts and slightly lower in Yankee ones than Thayer had. In any case, it was a mark of the times in Worcester that the first direct Irish-Yankee contest for the mayor's chair produced scarcely a ripple of ethnic feeling on either side.[35]

The weakening of the alliance between the Irish and the Yankee elite in the late 1880s should not obscure the remarkable environment the Worcester Irish enjoyed in the thirty years after the Civil War. Instead of the frequently depicted inevitable, unyielding, and bitter hostility between monolithic blocs of Irish and Yankees, relations between the two groups were relatively peaceful, and between the Irish and independent Yankees almost cozy. The legacy of the Civil War, the absence of class conflict, and more important the pragmatic political partnership between Irish and the Yankee independents made them so. The watchwords of the era seemed accommodation and compromise.

Leaders of Accommodation: The Power of the Priests

Though local ethnic harmony provided a nourishing environment for the pursuit of accommodation by the Worcester Irish, leaders of the local Celtic community gave that policy a concrete shape. Politicians like Athy and Matthew McCafferty played a role in this effort but they had limited influence over the community's institutions and associations. Joshua O'Leary was a more important figure if only because he emerged as the clearest and most forceful spokesman for accommodation through his newspaper, the *Messenger*. Yet he too had little control over the organizations of the Irish subcommunity in Worcester. Ultimately, it was the priests—powerful, energetic, and inspired by fresh trends in their church—who played the most significant role in shaping the response of Worcester's Irish community to its hopeful environment of powerful Yankee friends and fragile ethnic peace.

The *Messenger* was owned by James Doyle, the American-born son of Irish immigrants to Worcester, but the second-generation, New Hampshire-born O'Leary, not Doyle, gave the paper its special character in the 1880s and 1890s. Throughout that period, O'Leary persistently hammered home the themes of accommodation, respectability, and embrace of American culture. O'Leary was a strong backer of the Citizens' coalitions and friendly elite Republicans, but he carried efforts at accommodation beyond politics as well, praising, as noted earlier, Protestant institutions and societies. His paper also ceaselessly encouraged young Irish men and women in their efforts to become respectable Americans. The personal columns were filled with encomiums for young men and women who were bettering themselves. O'Leary took particular pride in Irish graduates of Ivy League schools. Proclaiming that "the way to Catholicize America is to Americanize Catholicity," O'Leary regularly praised public education, spoke favorably about temperance, and repeatedly denounced French Canadian, German, Polish, and other Catholic "malcontents" for indulging in "inexpedient . . . sentimental foreignism." "In time," he contended, "all such distinctions of churches as Polish or German or anything else must give way."[36]

O'Leary certainly voiced the dominant mood of the Irish community in the 1880s and 1890s and even perhaps helped foster it, but the predominant influence in the Irish community in that era were Worcester's Irish Catholic priests. The priests had important resources that neither the politicians nor the journalists could match. They not only had substantial power over their flocks but, in the late nineteenth century, a significant degree of autonomy in the church as well. As a number of historians have demonstrated, Catholic dioceses in the late nineteenth and even early twentieth centuries were rarely the rigidly centralized and hierarchical organizations they were reputed to be. They more often resembled feudal states than modern autocracies, with the pastors in their parishes acting as independent feudal lords. Pastors, not bishops, had control of most of the funds they collected in their parishes. They could raise and spend money with little control from the bishop. They often used this money to build up their parishes, but it also made them wealthy: John Power of St. Paul's, for example, left a substantial estate at his death. The priests' relative security from displacement augmented their financial autonomy. The canonical procedures bishops had to use to remove them were cumbersome and time-consuming. Worcester's Irish pastors thus had long tenures at the turn of the century. Those who were or became pastors of Irish churches in the 1880s would serve an average of twenty-eight years in their positions. All either died in their posts or were promoted to more important or lucrative positions. In the 1880s and early 1890s Worcester's Irish priests employed this power to exploit the sentiment for accommodation among their people and organize it for their own purposes. In part this was because the rise of Catholic Liberalism in that era gave them concrete ideas and inspiration to pursue such a course. In part, it was simply because of the force of personalities of new clerics appearing in the 1880s, or older ones coming into their own. In any case, ultimately it was the priests, not the politicians or journalists, who had the greatest influence on the Worcester Irish.[37]

If the older interpretations of authority and power in the church seem oversimplified, so too do older conceptions of the attitudes and ideas of its Irish priests. Older historians of Catholicism depicted a church led by conservative Irish priests steeped in suspicion of Protestants by oppression in Ireland and nativism in America and committed to separating their people from mainstream society. Analyses in the last two decades suggest a much more complicated interpretation of both the church and its priests. Donna Merwick, for example, detailed a broad range of origins and opinions among Irish priests in Boston. She, Robert Sullivan, and others have shown that the Catholic clergy were neither overwhelmingly immigrant nor unanimously committed to jealously separating their people from the American mainstream. Merwick's interpretations seem to aptly characterize Worcester's small group of Irish clerics as well. The vast majority of Worcester's Celtic priests, for example, were second-generation Irishmen and had been educated in public, not parochial, schools. They were at home in American culture and ambivalent about walling off their flocks from other Americans in separate institutions.[38]

Also significant in its impact on Worcester's church and its priests was the movement called Catholic Liberalism emerging in the American church in the 1880s. Broadly speaking, this Liberalism was an attempt by some Catholics to adapt their church to the modern age and in particular to the culture of what they believed was the age's most progressive nation, the United States. Worcester's priests did not call themselves Liberals, but their support for positions characteristic of the Liberal cause, interfaith cooperation, indifference to parochial schools, and support for temperance, suggests Liberalism's influence upon them. Moreover, Liberal leaders like Issac Hecker, Edward McGlynn, Walter Elliott, and John Keane appeared often in Worcester. As noted earlier, the Paulists—Hecker and Elliot's religious order and the vanguard of Catholic Liberalism—also gave several missions in Worcester at Sacred Heart and St. John's that were very well received.[39]

Whether the priests were Liberals or not, ultimately the extent of their impact on Worcester's Irish community depended on their intelligence, energy, charisma, and political savvy. As might be expected, these gifts were not equally distributed among Worcester's Irish clerics. Of the priests who sought a public role none was more effective than Monsignor Thomas Griffin, pastor of St. John's parish. Indeed, in 1905 the *Boston Herald* would liken the shrewd and indomitable Griffin to a captain of industry, reciting a long litany of his land deals and construction projects. The bullheaded, square-jawed Griffin, a native of Cork in Ireland, was the consummate brick and mortar priest. Despite his prominence it is difficult to determine Griffin's ideology. He was a strong supporter of parochial schools, often a conservative position, but he also boosted temperance, a cause often favored by the liberals.[40]

Griffin's rival in Worcester, Father John J. Power, was a very different sort of man than the St. John's pastor: "bright and learned, studious . . . dignified and distant," frail and ascetic. Nevertheless, despite his sickly constitution he was a pastor in Worcester for nearly fifty years and as much a power in the city for most of that time as his rival, Griffin, across town. Power was born to Irish immigrant parents in Charlestown, Massachusetts, in 1828. He attended public schools, the town academy, and Holy Cross before entering the seminary at Montreal. In 1856 he returned to Massachusetts where he was first pastor of St. Anne's, and ten years later began construction of St. Paul's on the city's west side. He would remain the pastor of St. Paul's for the next thirty-six years.[41]

Power's reluctance, even refusal, to build a parish school at St. Paul's was indicative of his stand in the controversy of opinions dividing his church in America. Power believed strongly that his people should reconcile their differences with American Protestants and learn the ways of American culture. He was a member of the exclusive St. Wulstan's society which boasted George F. Hoar and G. Stanley Hall among its select members, and his best friend was Dr. John Green, a prominent Mason of distinguished Yankee lineage. There is no direct evidence, but it seems likely that Power favored the alliance between Yankee independents and Irish Catholics. Indeed, in the 1890s Republican nativists suspected him of a dark conspiratorial role in promoting that alliance through the columns of the *Worcester Evening Spy.* Power did play an open and direct role in the politics of education. He not only nursed a bill addressing Catholic complaints against Bible reading through the legislature, he also served on the public school committee in Worcester. He was a strong supporter of public education and indifferent, perhaps even hostile, to parochial schools.[42]

Ironically, though the power and authority of Griffin and Power were undeniable, it was two younger men, one a fledgling pastor and the other a mere curate who would emerge as the most influential of Worcester's priests in the 1880s. These two were John J. McCoy and Thomas J. Conaty. They had much in common. Both were American-bred if not American-born. McCoy was born in Connecticut in 1853 but grew up in Holyoke, Massachusetts. Conaty was born in Ireland in 1847 but was brought to America almost immediately after his birth. Both Conaty and McCoy attended public schools and Holy Cross and the Grand Seminary in Montreal. Perhaps most important, both men were committed to a kind of moderate Catholic Liberalism. Conaty's parish was a model of devotional fervor and McCoy eagerly promoted devotional practices as a curate at St. John's; but though neither mixed socially with Yankees like Power, they were not implacable enemies of Protestants. Conaty, in fact, spoke frequently to Protestant audiences. Moreover, neither man seemed to be a strong advocate of parochial schools in the 1880s, though they were careful not to broach their opposition publicly. Both were also leaders in the temperance crusade. Conaty was twice president of the National Catholic Total Abstinence Union and McCoy was the founder and president of the local Diocesan Temperance Union. Indeed, Conaty was already steps ahead of McCoy by the 1880s in a drive for national prominence that would catapult him into the rectorship of Catholic University and then the head of the diocese of Los Angeles. Nevertheless, the appearance of both men in the city in the late 1870s and early 1880s was an important element in moving Worcester's Irish community to pursue accommodation with their neighbors and adoption of American ways.[43]

"Not Limited to Any Creed or Race": Building an Irish Institutional Network in an Era of Accommodation

The priests' influence in fostering the trend to accommodation was, perhaps, most evident in their decisions about building up the Catholic institutional network in Worcester. In the 1880s the new American-born generation was still young and the middle class still small, but sheer growth of numbers and, in particular, increase in the number of multiple-income families had substantially augmented the Irish community's financial resources. There was money available—painfully earned and thus grudgingly given—but nonetheless still available for the construction and support of new church institutions in the 1880s and 1890s. Moreover, there were also more abundant resources of religious personnel in the late nineteenth century than in the church's earlier years. During the nineteenth-century devotional revolution the number of priests in Ireland increased enormously and vast numbers of men and women in America also sought out the religious life in the same era. Worcester's Irish thus had the means to build and staff new institutions, but what institutions would they build? Parishes would be added: St. Peter's in 1885 and St. Stephen's in 1887. Yet the construction of those churches reflected less philosophical choices about how Catholics should adapt to the Worcester environment than simple practical recognition of the growth of the Irish population and its geographic shifts. The decision to build a nonsectarian hospital, however, in 1893, and more importantly the failure or refusal to build parochial schools throughout the 1880s and 1890s did, indeed, reflect such choices.[44]

Irish efforts to provide medical care for their people in Worcester stretched back to the earliest years of the city's Catholic community. In the 1830s, only a few years after the first Irish arrived in Worcester, they established a small medical facility near the infant St. John's church (or Christ Church as it was known then). In the 1860s John J. Power, then pastor of St. Anne's, created a more formal medical institution in East Worcester which he named St. Elizabeth's. St. Elizabeth's served as Worcester's only hospital until 1872 when the city government opened a hospital. Power, a strong supporter of public institutions and steadfastly opposed to sectarianism, immediately closed St. Elizabeth's after the new city hospital opened, proclaiming that the new, welcome city hospital made a Catholic hospital unnecessary.[45]

In the 1890s, the Irish would build a new hospital in Worcester, first named the House of Providence, later St. Vincent's. The new hospital was clearly an Irish Catholic institution: the bishop of Springfield chaired the board of trustees, and three-quarters of those trustees were Irish Catholics; the Sisters of Providence made up the core of the nursing staff; half of the hospital's doctors were Irish Catholic men and women; and thirteen middle-class Irish Catholic sponsors gave the hospital its first $1,335 in contributions. It is undoubtedly true that St. Vincent's would not have been possible without substantial growth in the resources of the Irish community.[46]

Nevertheless, Yankees played a vital role in the institution from its inception. Stephen Salisbury was elected vice chairman of the board of trustees. Elijah Stoddard, a former Citizens' party mayor, and Charles Chase, a banker and prominent Citizens' backer, were trustees, and Doctors Homer Gage and Leonard Wheeler served on the medical staff almost from the beginning. Worcester's wealthy Yankees were also a principal source of financial support for the fledgling institution. Stephen Salisbury gave $1,000 in 1894 and over $1,000 in 1898. A number of other prominent Yankees also made substantial contributions to St. Vincent's. Indeed, a Sister of Providence would later rue-fully recall that the city's Yankees seemed far more enthusiastic about the new hospital in its infancy than the stingy Worcester Irish. The principal reason for Yankee generosity was probably their recognition that the city desperately needed a new medical facility. In the 1880s the number of hospital beds in Worcester increased 1000 percent and yet the city hospital was turning patients away in the early 1890s. The recognition by Irishmen and Yankees that Worcester needed a hospital, however, did not mean that they had to join together to build one. That cooperation seemed possible because of the harmonious relations already established between the Irish and their Yankee allies in municipal politics.[47]

Founded and supported by Yankees and Irish, St. Vincent's quickly won a reputation in Worcester for evenhandedness and tolerance. The *Messenger* reported in June of 1894 that "this is a point which the sisters wish to emphasize. The administration is based upon broad and liberal principles . . . the matter of religion is not considered there when there is a question of admitting a patient." Yankee dailies picked up on St. Vincent's nonsectarian character as well. The *Spy* noted the "very noticeable . . . warmth of greeting" for Stephen Salisbury when he spoke at the opening of the new hospital building in 1895. The paper continued by recounting Thomas Conaty's promise that the hospital "has not been limited by any religious feeling, neither is [it] limited to any creed or race." Virtually every account of the hospital in the press or its own publications in the 1890s stressed its nonsectarian character.[48]

St. Vincent's was a concrete and powerful symbol of Yankee-Irish cooperation, but the refusal of the Worcester Irish to build parochial schools was an even more telling indication of their search for a peaceful accommodation to their Worcester environment and, in the broader sense, to American culture and society. In 1884, America's Catholic bishops gathering in Baltimore ordered every Catholic parish in America to build a parochial school within two years of the close of their meeting. In 1884 there were five Irish Catholic parishes in Worcester. Only one, St. John's, had a school or, more accurately, two schools: one served boys and girls through the lower elementary grades, and another educated girls through secondary school. By 1893, there were seven Catholic parishes, but still only St. John's had a school. Actually the parish by then had three, having added a boys' high school to its elementary school and girls' secondary school. None of the other parishes had begun to build a school or even to raise money for one.[49]

Some historians have suggested that the Massachusetts Irish were simply too poor to afford parochial education. Irish upward mobility was, indeed, slow in Worcester and many of the Irish churches in the city suffered from the continuing poverty of their parishioners. Nevertheless, even in the twenty years between 1880 and 1900 the number of white-collar Irish workers in Worcester increased by 91 percent; the number of skilled blue-collar workers by 31 percent; and the number of multiple-income families by 80 percent. Moreover, while some Irish parishes struggled, others thrived. Immaculate Conception, despite its humble congregation, cleared its debts in the early 1890s; St. Peter's and St. Paul's erased theirs soon after. St. Paul's also maintained an orphanage and built a new home for single working women in the mid-1890s, and Sacred Heart added clubhouses and meeting halls to its parish complex throughout the 1880s. Neither of these parishes nor Immaculate Conception built a school.[50]

It was not their lack of resources but their lack of will or even interest that kept Irish priests and congregations from building schools. In the wake of the Baltimore Council mandate, few of Worcester's Irish pastors openly stated their opposition to parochial schools. John J. Power was an exception. While participating in the dedication of a public school in East Worcester, he praised the "necessity of our public schools and their ennobling influence." To a friend he confessed that he did not believe that parochial schools could "compete" with public ones, and one of his Yankee intimates, Samuel Swett Green, claimed: "He [Power] always favored, I believe, the sending of foreign born residents to the public schools." Green added suggestively that "this position pleased his fellow Protestant citizens." None of Power's Catholic colleagues were as forthright in their questioning of parochial education. Thomas Conaty, in fact, leaped to defend the right of Catholics to build their own schools when local Protestant ministers like David Mears attacked parochial education in the late 1880s and early 1890s. Conaty, however, like Power and Dennis Scannell of St. Anne's, served on the city's public-school committee. Conaty also praised the public-school teachers of his parish, listing them just after parishioners who became priests and nuns, in the honor roll of success published in the parish bulletin. Most important, though he promised to build a school at least three times in the 1880s, Conaty never even began raising funds for it. Walsh of Immaculate Conception also promised a school but never built one.[51]

Worcester's Irish priests might have built schools if their own parishioners had demanded parochial schools. The Irish laity in Worcester, however, seemed as enthusiastic about public education and as skeptical about parochial schools as their priests. One reason why Worcester's Irish laity opposed parochial schools was their sense that Catholic education simply was not very good. This opinion grew in part out of the disastrous early history of parochial schools in Worcester. Even sympathizers of parochial education remembered that the church schools established in Worcester in the 1850s were terrible. As late as 1887, graduates of St. John's school, who were strong supporters of parochial education, confessed in their monthly, the *Alumna*: "Those schools were never a great success and their failure has been a cause of discouragement with some people ever since . . . we even now sometimes feel the effect of that old time failure." Worcester's Irish Catholics in the late nineteenth century were skeptical of contemporary parochial schools as well. In 1886, the *Alumna* reported a number of complaints against Catholic girls' schools, particularly against their emphasis on "purely mechanical recitations" or undue attention to unnecessary skills such as fine needlework or etiquette. Eight years later the *Messenger* suggested that "an idea prevails even among some Catholics" that parochial schools also devoted too much time to training in religion. In 1891, the *Messenger* applauded action taken by school authorities in nearby Fitchburg, Massachusetts, to close down French Catholic schools in that town. The paper claimed that the French schools were not providing a good education for their students and that there could be "no lowering [of] the test of efficiency" to maintain parochial schools.[52]

Implicit in these criticisms was a comparison of Catholic schools with public schools, a comparison which most of Worcester's Irish Catholics believed left parochial schools wanting. Irish Catholics in Worcester regularly praised the city's public schools. Joshua O'Leary's *Messenger* lauded the "grand work" of public schools in the 1890s and hinted broadly in 1892 that parochial schools could not match the high standards set by their public counterparts. John F. O'Connor, a student then at Worcester's English High School, told a cheering Irish crowd in 1891 that "he was pleased to see so many Irish children educated in the public schools and he only regretted that the number was not larger." Even the *Alumna* conceded in 1886: "Of course, if a Catholic had eyes which could see nothing in life more beautiful than a dollar, a heart that had no hope beyond a good position be it political or commercial then all the shiny chatter about the grand privileges of our public schools would be music in their ears."[53]

In this praise, Worcester's Irish Catholics, both priests and laity, not only recognized the quality of instruction in Worcester's public schools but revealed their conviction that those schools were no threat to the religious beliefs of their children. Perhaps in no other aspect did the political alliance between Yankees and the Irish work more to the benefit of the latter than in school patronage. Albert P. Marble proved to be a firm and fast friend of the Worcester Irish throughout the nearly three decades he served as superintendent of the Worcester schools. "People prefer to choose their own church," Marble proclaimed and, as Robert Kolesar has pointed out, Marble consistently pursued policies accommodating the Irish community. His links to the Catholic community were so strong that Yankee nativists regularly singled him out for attack in their campaigns against the Citizens' coalitions. This cozy relationship meant that Catholics had little fear that the schools would force Protestant-inspired Bible readings or prayers on their children. Perhaps even more important, it meant that the proportion of Catholic teachers in Worcester's system rose steadily to almost 40 percent by the late 1880s. Local Irish Catholics thus scoffed at critics who suggested that they should fear Protestant proselytizing in their public schools. In the 1890s Stephen Littleton reported his friends' vehement denunciation of a local French priest who had charged that Protestant heresy was rampant in the public schools. Even the *Alumna* dismissed fears of Protestant proselytizing in the public schools as "ridiculous," given that so many of the teachers were Catholics.[54]

While local conditions convinced most of the Worcester Irish to support public education and forgo building parochial schools, national Catholic Liberal leaders and their ideas helped the city's Irish justify their position. Father Edward McGlynn, a well-known radical from New York and fiery opponent of parochial education, remained popular in Worcester even after his superior, Archbishop Corrigan, excommunicated him in 1887. In 1891 800 to 1,000 people flocked to a Worcester hall to hear McGlynn, then under interdict from Rome, launch a vociferous assault on parochial schools.[55]

Joshua O'Leary of Worcester's Irish weekly, the *Messenger,* was perhaps the most prominent and persistent local lay champion of the Liberal cause against parochial education. O'Leary stressed the contingency of the Baltimore Council's edict, underlining what he believed to be the bishops' intention that their command to build parochial schools applied only "wherever practicable." Like many Catholic Liberals in the early 1890s, he also looked with favor on cooperative arrangements between Catholic parishes and public schools to provide time for religious instruction in public schools. School boards had worked out variations on such plans in a number of towns around the nation, most notably at Stillwater and Faribault, Minnesota, in the archdiocese of the Liberal leader, Archbishop John Ireland. It was the prospect of working out similar arrangements in all cities and towns throughout the country, O'Leary believed, which offered the best "glimmer of hope" for a resolution of the school question.[56]

"More American than the Americans Themselves": The Rise of Temperance and Respectable Irish Clubs

The clubs and societies of the Worcester Irish in the 1880s also clearly reflected their interest in accommodation and enthusiasm for American culture. Temperance societies flourished in Worcester's Irish community in that decade. Clubs of American-born Irishmen who were not willing to abandon drink, but were as much or more devoted to American popular culture as the temperance men, also boomed in the 1880s. Meanwhile, more militant, ethnocentric societies like the Ancient Order of Hibernians, which drew their members largely from the immigrant working-class population, languished and barely survived in the optimistic atmosphere of the 1880s.

The persistent importance of drink in Irish culture has often been discussed; less well known are the efforts of Irishmen to avoid whiskey and beer. As early as the sixteenth century Irish bishops attempted to outlaw excessive drinking at certain celebrations. More successful, at least in the short run, was Father Theobald Mathew, a nineteenth-century Capuchin priest from Cork. Mathew became the charismatic leader of a great temperance crusade which swept Ireland throughout the 1830s and 1840s. Perhaps as many as a million Irish took the pledge to abstain from liquor at the height of Mathew's temperance revival. The Mathew crusade fizzled out almost as quickly as it had arisen, leaving little permanent result. Temperance crusades would again rise in Ireland, most notably the Pioneer movement, but only after Irish temperance took root and began to grow in America. By 1872 there were scores of parish temperance organizations scattered throughout the United States and an umbrella organization, the National Catholic Total Abstinence Union of America, was formed to represent them. In 1885 there were at least 40,000 Irish Catholic temperance men in America and total abstinence had become an important part of the Liberal Catholic agenda. Archbishop John Ireland was a particularly strong temperance advocate. By the 1880s the Irish-American total abstinence movement was far larger than the temperance crusade in Ireland.[57]

Temperance had a long history among the Irish in Worcester. In 1840 Father James Fitton organized the first Catholic total abstinence society in the city, but the real beginning of Worcester's Irish temperance crusade was in 1849 when Father Theobald Mathew himself visited the city on his tour through the United States. With the strong support of local Yankees, Mathew held a meeting at City Hall. Illness prevented Mathew from making a speech but he did administer the total abstinence pledge to some four hundred Irish men. A few weeks later some of these men met to form the Father Mathew Total Abstinence Association and secure the conversions made during its namesake's mission.[58]

Over the next thirty years the temperance cause endured but hardly thrived among the Irish in Worcester. The Father Mathew Society became one of the most important associations in Worcester's Irish community, figuring prominently in virtually every community celebration or event. Every attempt to found new temperance societies failed, however. In 1874, laymen organized the St. Patrick's Temperance Society but within two years members of that group had merged into the Father Mathew Society. Later in that decade priests at St. John's tried several times to establish a parish temperance society but with no success.[59]

In the 1880s, however, Worcester's Irish temperance movement flourished. In 1881 the Father Mathew Society with 180 members was the only Irish temperance organization in the city. By 1888 there were nine Irish temperance clubs or societies in Worcester, boasting over 1,200 members. Some of the new organizations were affiliates of the Father Mathew Society, such as the Father Mathew Cadets or the Knights of Father Mathew. Most of the societies, however, were connected to parishes. They included the St. John's Temperance and Literary Guild, the St. Anne's Total Abstinence Society, the Catholic Young Men's Lyceum of Sacred Heart parish, and the St. Paul's Lyceum. The St. Anne's Total Abstinence Society and the Catholic Young Men's Lyceum both had clubhouses at one time or another in the 1880s and 1890s, and in 1888, as if to give physical embodiment to the entire temperance revival, the Father Mathew Society built a grand new meeting hall on Green Street in the Island.[60]

The close affiliation of most of the new temperance societies with the city's Irish parishes suggests the critical role played by Worcester's priests in the Celtic temperance revival. Pastors or curates organized all of the parish temperance societies, freely intervened in their policy debates, and provided them with meeting places. The last power was important, since it meant that priests could toss their temperance societies out of their halls if the teetotalers did not submit to clerical guidance. In the 1880s, at least two Worcester pastors used this power to discipline their parish societies. Clerical leadership of the temperance movement relied much less on naked power, however, than on priestly energy and initiative. In 1899, for example, a retrospective published by the St. Paul's Lyceum attributed all of the organization's success to the "wise counsel and constant unselfish labors" of its founder, Father Thomas Hanrahan. Even after Hanrahan's transfer to another church, the history recounted, "no affair conducted by the Lyceum is ever considered complete until a detailed account of the same is sent to reverend Father."[61]

Though virtually all of Worcester's priests supported the temperance movement, John J. McCoy and Thomas J. Conaty were its moving forces in the 1880s. It would not be an exaggeration to suggest that the emergence of these two clerics in the early 1880s was one of the principal causes of the temperance revival among the Worcester Irish in that decade. McCoy, for example, succeeded where many before him had failed, by organizing the St. John's Temperance and Literary Guild in 1883. He also formed two temperance militia groups for younger men, the St. John's Temperance Cadets and the Father Mathew Cadets in the mid-1880s. Conaty, meanwhile, was making his Sacred Heart parish a temperance stronghold. In addition to the Catholic Young Men's Lyceum, Conaty organized temperance societies for single women, young boys, and older married men. Conaty and McCoy also boomed the temperance message from their pulpits and Conaty pushed the temperance cause through the columns of the *Catholic School and Home Magazine*, which he founded in 1892.[62]

McCoy and Conaty were able and active men, but the explosion of interest in temperance among the Worcester Irish in the 1880s was not simply the result of their work alone. One trend which sustained, if not inspired, the Irish temperance movement in the 1880s was the rise of Liberal Catholicism in that decade. Worcester's Irish temperance men were well aware of Archbishop John Ireland's passionate commitment to the temperance cause. Members of the St. John's Temperance and Literary Guild regarded Ireland as a hero and praised him often. Catholic temperance publications in Worcester also praised or quoted other Catholic Liberal leaders throughout the late 1880s and early 1890s.[63]

The revival of the temperance question as a focal point in local political controversies, however, undoubtedly had a more powerful effect on the Catholic temperance crusade in Worcester. The annual referendums over liquor licenses were bitterly fought contests. On occasion, such as in 1885 and again in 1889 or 1891, the no-license forces triumphed and made Worcester a "dry" city. In those elections resentment of the power of the liquor interests in local politics drove even some normal "wets" to vote for closing the saloons. Even when license won—the usual outcome—the temperance forces mounted emotional, well-publicized campaigns which riveted attention on the drinking issue nearly every year.

The repoliticization of the temperance issue cast in bold relief significant differences between Irishmen and Yankees over drinking. No custom seemed to distinguish the two groups more clearly; no issue separating them seemed more charged with emotion and heat. Almost from the time the Irish arrived in Worcester in the 1820s, Yankees had condemned them as drunkards. In the late nineteenth century Yankee loyalist newspapers and evangelical spokesmen continued to regularly castigate Irish drinkers and Irish saloonkeepers, as well as Irish voters, for voting in license. The stereotype of the drunken Irishman and the association of drunkenness and crime with the Irish community also appeared almost every day in the *Spy*, the newspaper of the liberal Republican independents. All Yankees, moral reformers and cultural liberals alike, seemed to agree that the Irish drank too much for their own, and the community's, good.[64]

Some Worcester Irishmen seemed to agree or, at least, acknowledge and regret their people's peculiar weakness for alcohol. Shame over this vice and a wish to rid their people of it runs through the rhetoric of Worcester's Irish temperance leaders. In 1889, Stephen Littleton attended a temperance meeting at St. Paul's where John J. Power spoke at length on alcoholic indulgence, "the weakness of the Irish race." Thomas J. Conaty confessed in 1887 that "intemperance was the only charge that could be fairly lodged against the modern Irishmen." That same year, Thomas Griffin toured his parish and found that the "percent of drunkenness is really appalling." "The use and abuse of alcohol among us is a shame and a scandal to our people," he moaned. "If a Protestant were to make this tour he would ask are these the people of God? are these the members of the true church?" Father James Cleary noted in Conaty's *Catholic School and Home Magazine* that the tradition of drinking was Irish, not American, and "we are not to be ruled by the customs of other lands; the sound judgement of the American public is competent to regulate its own customs in accordance with the best interests of our common country."[65]

Drinking was shameful these Irish felt because it seemed to guarantee economic failure and the plunge into moral degradation. Like native-stock temperance spokesmen, Irish total abstinence leaders saw drinking as the root of a wide array of vices and evils. Thomas J. Conaty's blistering, all-encompassing attack summed up their sentiments: "Estimate if you can the ravages of intemperance. It gives loose run to appetites, corrupts hearts, ruins homes, deforms the mould in which character is formed and poisons our public life." Perhaps the most frequently expressed theme by Conaty and others was drink's relation to poverty. Conaty charged again in 1895: "it is largely responsible for the rags of the beggar, the idleness of the loafer, the ignorance of children, and the misery of pauperism."[66]

While indulgence in drink condemned Irishmen to poverty and alienation from American life, Worcester's Irish priests argued, participation in the temperance movement offered them self-improvement, respectability, and wholesome involvement in American culture. Through it they could overcome the stereotype and prove that they could be good Americans. The Catholic Young Men's Lyceum proclaimed that once a young man took the pledge and entered a total abstinence society, he discovered an association that stood "not only for temperance but everything that tends towards the advancement of its members . . . it creates in him a desire to improve his condition in life. It offers encouragement to his honest ambition and fills him with the thought that, although deprived, perhaps, of an early education, there still remain opportunities which if taken by a firm and timely grasp may enable him to fulfill the duties of any position in life with credit to himself and associates." The desire for self-improvement and yearning for respectability pervaded virtually every gathering of the temperance men, as their monthly or bimonthly violin or piano recitals, declamation contests and debates attested. Temperance societies like the St. John's Temperance and Literary Guild or the CYML also helped their members to improve themselves with courses in bookkeeping or crafts and trades.[67]

Worcester's Irish temperance men may have sounded like Protestant prohibitionists, but they remained very different from Protestant teetotallers in important ways. Worcester's Irish temperance societies were first and foremost "Catholic societies." They were not only organized and governed by priests and met in church halls but practiced Catholic religious devotions such as receiving communion in a group as routine activities. There were other differences between the Yankee temperance men and the Irish total abstainers as well. Women played a critical role in the Protestant crusade, but the Irish temperance movement was overwhelmingly male. In 1886 Father Thomas J. Conaty founded the Catholic Young Women's Lyceum, a temperance society and the first permanent, formal organization for Irish women in Worcester beyond parish sodalities and altar societies. Nevertheless, the CYWL was the only women's organization among the seven or more parish temperance clubs in Worcester, and it remained tightly controlled by its priest-founder.[68]

The Irish movement was not only overwhelmingly male, there was, as Roy Rosenzweig has suggested, a rough-and-ready masculine character to Irish temperance societies which distinguished them from associations of Yankee teetotallers. Celtic total abstinence leaders in Worcester recognized the effete and unmanly image that temperance suggested. To offset that image they vigorously promoted sports and military drill in their societies. John J. McCoy renovated some basement rooms in the St. John's Institute as a gymnasium for the members of his temperance guild and outfitted the St. John's and Father Mathew Cadets he led in natty uniforms and rifles for their frequent drills and parades. Parish temperance baseball, football, and track teams were prominent throughout western Massachusetts. Victory in sports and games became so critical to members of the societies that they sometimes broke into brawls around their clubhouse pool tables or recruited "ringers," talented athletes of dubious commitment to the total abstinence cause, to bolster their baseball or football squads.[69]

Importantly, however, it was not Irish games of hurling or Irish football but the newly minted sports of American popular culture, such as baseball and football, that Irish temperance men played, and the distinction was very important to them. They may have been different than Protestant teetotallers but they were very proud of being American. One temperance association, the Father Mathew Society, remained fiercely committed to the preservation of the old country's games and sports, but the vast majority of Worcester's Celtic temperance men in the parish societies were intent on forging a new Irish image in Worcester, that of the clean-living and hard-playing all-American, not the besotted, unruly, and foreign drunk.

For Celtic temperance men participation in American sports was but a part of a broader passionate identification with America and its opportunities. On March 17, 1887, members of the Catholic Young Men's Lyceum applauded John Boyle O'Reilly when he confessed that the Irish reputation for "improvidence" might have been well earned in the old country but not in America. O'Reilly stated "that on leaving the old country the Irishmen dropped most of [their] bad traits to become the strongest and most athletic race in the world." The Irish in America, O'Reilly claimed, had a "mission to fulfill in furnishing bookkeepers, cashiers and bank presidents who could be trusted." Richard H. Mooney, a member of the Lyceum and principal of a local grammar school, also spoke that night and "called attention to the growth of his people in this city in respect to property and emphatically denied that they were improvident and reckless." He quoted United States Senator George F. Hoar's praise of Worcester's Irish "and added that the Irish had the faculty of becoming more American than the Americans themselves."[70]

Given these sentiments it is not surprising that most members of the city's Irish temperance clubs were young, upwardly mobile, and American-born. Observers of the temperance men almost always described them as "young," as "Irish Americans" (not Irishmen) or American-born. Mooney, himself was born in Worcester of immigrant parents. Two-thirds of the men who joined the St. John's Temperance and Literary Guild in the 1880s and could be traced into the 1880s census were second-generation Irish. An even larger proportion of delegates from parish temperance societies to the citywide United Irish Societies Convention in the 1880s were also American-born. Like the rest of their generation, members of the parish temperance societies had also begun to break into skilled blue-collar trades and even white-collar positions. Of the St. John's men in the 1880s 11 percent held white-collar jobs. The proportions were even greater among the temperance delegates to the United Irish Societies Convention. Of those 114 men, 42 percent were white-collar workers, 32.4 percent were in skilled blue-collar trades. Members of the Father Mathew Society, the single society among the temperance men to cling so steadfastly to Irish culture, had, as might be expected, different social backgrounds than the members of the parish total abstinence societies. The Father Mathew men were older, less upwardly mobile, and, most importantly, overwhelmingly immigrant, though few were recent immigrants and most had been settled in Worcester for many years by the 1880s. The Father Mathew Society, however, was an anomaly among Worcester's Celtic temperance associations in the 1880s. In that decade it was members of the younger American-born generation who flocked to the total abstinence standard and fueled Worcester's Celtic temperance revival.[71]

The yearnings for respectability, the commitment to self-improvement, and the passion for American popular culture that inspired the temperance men also excited some of their fellows for whom drinking was not the central issue. Literary or educational clubs blossomed in the parishes, particularly at St. Peter's and St. Paul's churches. The Chatham Club at St. Paul's and the St. Peter's Mutual Advancement Society were typical. The Chatham Club, the *Messenger* reported in 1895, "is composed of a number of intelligent and earnest young men with the object of increasing their store of useful knowledge by the systematic improvement of spare hours." The St. Peter's Mutual Advancement was equally high-minded, committed to "solid study" and "literary work along lines of culture and mutual advancement." Similar clubs composed of Irish women also emerged in the 1880s and 1890s; the Lady Fullerton Circle, for example, complemented the Chatham Club at St. Paul's.[72]

Not all members of Worcester's young Celtic generation were so serious in their purpose. Paralleling the rise of the temperance associations and the improvement clubs in the 1880s and early 1890s was the emergence of a group of clubs devoted to pleasure, games, and "social diversions." The principal societies of this group were the Highland Associates, the Carrolltons, Crescents, and the most important and enduring of all, the Washington Club. These clubs displayed no interest in total abstinence and their purposes were purely recreational. One old member of the Washington Club would recall fondly that the Washingtons were the "relaxingest" club he ever knew. The club men may have been singlemindedly devoted to pleasure, but like the Irish tee-totalers they chose American, not Irish, amusements for their entertainment, and more subtly perhaps, sought in their leisure activities their own versions of American respectability. Most important to all the men of the social clubs were their entertainments, banquets, and balls. The Washingtons, for example, were famous for their vaudeville and minstrel shows. They boasted more than a "score" of good speakers, actors, and singers among their members and their "minstrel performances . . . were the social events of Worcester." All of the clubs sponsored elaborate balls during the winter social season.[73]

There were strong suggestions beyond their embrace of American popular culture that the Washingtons and members of the other social clubs were passionate about their American loyalties. The names of the clubs, the Carrolltons after Charles Carroll, Catholic signer of the Declaration of Independence, and, more obviously, the Washington Club, suggested something of the perspectives of club members on their identities. Appropriately enough the Washington Club marked the first president's birthday with a major banquet and rhetoric effusively praising the promise of America. In 1892, the *Messenger* described the members of the Washington Club as largely Irish, all-Catholic, and without exception "loyal to the United States and its institutions." Proclaiming their American loyalties clearly, the social clubs seemed noticeably cautious about collaborating with other Irish societies in ethnic community celebrations. Only the members of the Washington Club were invited to meetings of the United Irish Societies Convention to plan St. Patrick's Day parades, but even they rarely sent delegates and when they did they voted against the parade.[74]

Given such sentiments it should not be surprising that the social clubs like the temperance societies were most attractive to the socially mobile and the new American-born generation. Descriptions of the Washington Club and other social clubs almost invariably described the members as "young" and "Irish Americans." The rules of the Washington Club, like those for many of the parish temperance associations, limited members to young men between the ages of twenty-one and forty-five. Over 50 percent of the Carrolltons drawn from a sample of the club's members in 1886 were white-collar or skilled blue-collar workers, and the same year over 80 percent of the Washingtons were white-collar workers. The Washingtons were already well on their way at that point to being the "leading Catholic society among the young men of the city."[75]

The Washingtons and their fellows in the social clubs or temperance societies were no mere mimics of the Yankees, but they were, nevertheless, passionate devotees of American popular culture and proudly loyal Americans. That
such sentiments flourished in the 1880s seems again clear evidence of a cultural and political environment that nourished Irish accommodation. The revival of the temperance issue in local politics, of itself, need not have provoked
a temperance revival among the Worcester Irish, for example. Indeed, if it
had become—as many Irish and independent Yankee Republicans feared—
the spearhead of a new nativist crusade, it might have just as likely sparked a
resurgence of ethnocentrism among Worcester's Irish as a temperance revival. The temperance issue, however, achieved significance without destroying the delicate balance of the city's politics and the ethnic peace that balance
sustained. The revitalization of the issue, combined with the inspiration of
Catholic Liberalism, prompted the local Irish to openly confess the tendency
to alcoholic indulgence among their people and to pledge themselves to overcome it and prove themselves good Americans. Moreover, though traditional
Catholic doctrine and their own leaders condemned prohibition as government coercion, some Irish temperance men undoubtedly went further and
backed the no-license cause on at least a few occasions. Though instances of
formal Irish-Yankee cooperation in the temperance movement were rare, the
votes of Irish teetotallers may have been critical to the two no-license triumphs
of the decade, in 1885 and 1889. Nevertheless, just as important, there is little or
no evidence of suspicion or hatred of Protestants among the temperance men
or "club men." The Washington Club's famous variety and minstrel shows attracted a number of prominent Yankees, and in an extraordinary act of interreligious cooperation the club donated a table to the Knights Templars in 1893.
In thanks, the Templars threw a banquet for the Washingtons which opened
with a procession of the members of the two societies marching into the room
arm in arm.[76]

While temperance and other clubs seeking accommodation thrived in the
1880s, militant ethnocentric societies suffered. The Ancient Order of Hibernians was the principal such organization in Worcester throughout the turn
of the century era. An outgrowth of the old "Ribbonmen" secret societies in
Ireland, the AOH established its first American branches in the 1830s. Thirty
years later a state organizer came to Worcester to found the city's first local
division. Over the course of the next half century or more the AOH stood for
the preservation of Irish culture and the aggressive, almost belligerent, assertion of Irish interests in Worcester. It also appeared to draw most of its
members over that period from semiskilled and unskilled Irish immigrant

workers. Between 1884 and 1896, for example, 81 percent of the delegates to Worcester's United Irish Societies Convention were Irish-born and nearly half of these men, presumably leaders in their societies, were semiskilled or unskilled workers.[77]

The Hibernians thus advocated ideas and represented segments of Worcester's Irish population which were very different from those of the temperance men, and it is perhaps not surprising that the AOH floundered in the environment that nourished the temperance organizations. The Hibernians grew quickly in the early and middle 1870s, but between 1876 and the late 1890s, in the words of the Hibernians' official historian, "matters seem to have been running very slowly for the order." After three local divisions of the Hibernians were founded in the early 1870s, no new divisions appeared in Worcester until 1896. From the number of men the Hibernians turned out for important ceremonial occasions, it does not appear that they counted many more than five or six hundred members in the late 1880s, or about half the number of Catholic Total Abstinence men in the city at that time.[78]

In part, the AOH suffered from the local church's continuing suspicion of its purposes. The church had never been comfortable with the order's secrecy or its alleged ties to secret societies in rural Ireland like the Whiteboys and Ribbonmen. Remembering the havoc such transplanted groups had wreaked in Irish colonies like Worcester in the 1840s and reflecting the church's longtime suspicion of secret orders, Bishop John Fitzpatrick of Boston condemned the AOH in the 1850s (Worcester was still a part of the Boston diocese then). When the Worcester division first organized, therefore, it met secretly in a house near Green Street in the Island "until the time came [that] they could overcome public prejudice and meet in a public place." Patrick T. O'Reilly, the Irish-born pastor of St. John's and later bishop of the new Springfield diocese, was more sympathetic to the Hibernians. He approved their constitution and even permitted the AOH to meet at St. John's church. O'Reilly's favor helped the AOH grow, but the order's troubles with local church officials were not over. In 1878, Father Cuddihy in nearby Milford, Massachusetts, condemned the Hibernians, citing their implication in the Molly Maguire violence in the Pennsylvania coal fields. Cuddihy refused to give members of the order communion in his church. Priests in Worcester, most notably John J. Power, disputed Cuddihy's condemnation and continued to give the organization their support, but damage had, again, been done.[79]

The Hibernians may have also suffered from the revival of the temperance issue in local politics. Richard O'Flynn noted acidly in 1880 "there was not a rumseller, however low, [who] was not a member of the organization in its palmy days." Picnics run by the AOH to celebrate the Fourth of July or other holidays often degenerated into drunken, rowdy sprees in the 1880s. In 1885 Worcester's Yankee and Irish papers alike complained that many who attended a Hibernian Fourth of July picnic arrived "intoxicated," and continued to drink heavily, swagger, and fight—to be "on the muscle" in the *Telegram*'s words— throughout the day. Two years later the *Telegram* charged that "heavy drinking" and a "scrap every fifteen minutes" marked the AOH's annual Independence Day affair. In the new era of sensitivity to the temperance issue during the 1880s the close connection of the order to the saloon trade and to such antics seemed to confirm Yankee stereotypes and embarrassed many Worcester Irish, particularly the Catholic clergy.[80]

Perhaps the most important reason for the Hibernians' weakness in the 1880s, however, was that they stridently advocated Irish ethnic interests and the preservation of Irish culture; both positions were out of step with the times. The same political environment that nurtured accommodation and the embrace of American culture, as evidenced in Irish opposition to parochial schools or the Celtic temperance movement, made the AOH's ethnic militancy seem irrelevant or out of place. Angry assertion of Irish interests made little sense when the Irish did not have enough votes to act independently. Those interests seemed best served in the 1880s by the alliance with the Yankee independents, and maintenance of that fragile coalition appeared to proscribe revivals of ethnic wrangling. The most prominent of the Hibernians, Andrew Athy and Matthew McCafferty, and other politicians understood this well. Tied tightly into existing political arrangements, they could hardly be expected to encourage, much less lead, the Hibernians in a revival of ethnocentrism. In an age of compromise and accommodation, the AOH's belligerence simply did not fit.

"St. Patrick's Day Will Become an American Day": Celebrating the National Holiday

The environment and their relative weakness notwithstanding, the Hibernians persistently sought to advance their brands of Irish ethnocentrism throughout the 1880s. This brought them into conflict with the temperance societies on at least one issue: the Irish community's sponsorship of parades on St. Patrick's Day. The annual controversies and debates ignited by that issue provide a uniquely revealing record of the conflicting perspectives of the two groups on Irish adjustment in Worcester.

From its inception in 1847, the St. Patrick's Day parade figured prominently in the internal conflicts of Worcester's small Irish community. At that first parade, the long-brewing division between immigrants from eastern and western Ireland came to a head as societies representing both groups marched in a stormy procession from St. John's church to the new campus of Holy Cross College about a mile to south. The bitter exchange of insults between the rival societies touched off the round of battles that plunged Worcester's Irish community into anarchy for the next few years. By the middle of the 1850s many of these conflicts had dissolved as the Worcester Irish gathered to face a threat from outside the community, the Know-Nothings. In 1855, at the height of the Know-Nothing hysteria, the St. Patrick's Day parade became an important symbol of Irish solidarity and resolution. The Father Mathew men who had marched annually since the early 1850s demanded and received assurances from the newly elected Know-Nothing mayor that year that they would be protected from nativist assaults in their march on St. Patrick's Day. The vast majority of Father Mathew members then proceeded to march not once but twice that day in an atmosphere "where every opportunity was taken to outrage and insult the Irish Catholic citizens of Worcester." Some Irishmen, however, refused to march with their fellows on St. Patrick's Day. Dr. Edward Fitzgerald, a graduate of Trinity College in Dublin, would not join the march because he felt that "there were no cultivated members of his race participating and that it was beneath his dignity to parade with his humbler brethren."[81]

In the next quarter century the St. Patrick's Day parade became an established annual event among the Irish in Worcester. The American Civil War, the need to raise money for the Fenian nationalist conspiracy after the war, and the depression of the 1870s occasionally reduced the size of the processions but did not alter the custom. More often, the parades were large and lively processions heartily applauded by community members. In 1861, for example, Irish workingmen wound their way through Worcester's downtown streets in a giant torchlight procession, and in 1873 over 850 Irishmen from a number of the city's different Celtic societies paraded.[82]

Through the 1880s the parades grew larger and even more impressive. In that decade there were often over 1,000 men in line winding their way through the east side tenement districts before emerging onto Main Street to parade proudly through the center of the city. The colors of the processions were as striking as their size. They included militia companies like the St. Anne's Cadets dressed as Zouaves in red pantaloons, green jackets, and Turkish fezes; their rivals, the St. John's Cadets, in trim gray jackets and kepis; and Hibernian riflemen in green uniforms and plumed helmets. There was even, on occasion, an Irish cavalry contingent, the Knights of St. Patrick, armed, uniformed, and mounted upon "splendid steeds" prancing down Worcester's streets. Civilians from the AOH or other societies marched in the parade as well, wearing their "Sunday Best" and the regalia or badges of their orders. A platoon of police, a number of bands, and a long trail of carriages carrying the city's Irish priests filled out the line of march. The most impressive, or perhaps simply the oddest, group in the parade every year were the Knights of Father Mathew, who patterned their uniforms of steel helmets, cuirasses, and battleaxes after the famed Irish "gallowglasses," or heavy infantry, who fought for the O'Neills and O'Donnells against the armies of Queen Elizabeth three hundred years before.[83]

Though the parade appeared well established by the 1880s, Worcester's Irish marched on only about half of the St. Patrick's Days between 1881 and 1896. Some of the parades were canceled because their cost, an average of about $450, could not be justified in the face of other more critical demands for funds made upon the Worcester Irish. In 1881 Irishmen in Worcester and across America agreed to forgo their parades and send the money raised by St. Patrick's Day lectures to support the "Land War" in Ireland. In other years such as 1885 or 1894, economic hard times forced cancellation of the parade. Some Worcester Irishmen felt that it was "little short of criminal" to spend money on a parade when so many of their countrymen were unemployed.[84]

These special circumstances, however, did not fully account for the failure of the Worcester Irish to parade every St. Patrick's Day, or, perhaps more important, explain the divisiveness the parade provoked among the city's Irish. It was the growing strength of the temperance movement, more specifically, the parish temperance societies, that made the parade uncertain every year and excited so much controversy over the march in the Irish community. As the temperance societies increased in number, they became a powerful force in the Convention of United Irish Societies, a temporary federation which met every year for the sole purpose of planning the parade. Between 1884 and the early 1890s, the number of total abstinence societies in the convention rose from three to seven or more. The temperance men were not only powerful; they were also contentious. They consistently opposed the parade, arguing that it encouraged excessive drinking and fighting and absorbed money and resources which could be better used for more constructive and long-lasting projects. Of the 33 votes cast by temperance societies in the convention between 1885 and 1895, 20 were against the parade, 3 for it, and 10 were abstentions. A delegation from the Washington Club appeared at only three conventions and voted against the parade all three times.[85]

Irish temperance men were very sensitive to the excessive drinking that seemed to mar every St. Patrick's Day. In 1890, Richard O'Flynn dismissed a lurid report of Irish drunkenness and violence in a local prohibition paper as obviously biased, but O'Flynn still acknowledged "Oh! to see ourselves as others see us . . . a small faction of the immense crowd and yet it is too true, there are many who felt that it must be necessary to fill up with rat poison in order to properly celebrate." Because of their concern about drunkenness on this national holiday, the temperance men and their allies took steps to eliminate drunken carousing on St. Patrick's Day. The clergy frequently implored their flocks to refrain from drink and, along with temperance laymen, beseeched Irish saloonkeepers to close down for the day. In some years, temperance men also urged the convention to schedule the parade for the morning just after mass, before workingmen had a chance to drop by their favorite saloons.[86]

For the temperance men and other parade opponents, the procession not only threatened to confirm stereotypes of their people, it wasted funds which their community sorely needed for more worthwhile projects. The temperance men, in particular, were interested in building halls and clubhouses for young men, facilities for lectures and night classes and wholesome recreational amusements. Richard O'Flynn, seeking help for the Father Mathew Society in this effort, argued the society's cause in the convention: "Whilst every other nationality [is] progressing, it should not be said ours was regressing [We should have] a building creditable in every respect of which coming generations will feel proud . . . and we hope [it] will be a great factor for good in our beautiful city raising men and women to a higher plane in the social scale . . . teaching its members honesty and sobriety and thus letting them do God's work." By contrast as O'Flynn suggested "What are the results attained by the parade? Does it confer any lasting benefit? . . . it is a passing show, a shadow leaving after it nothing tangible or practical in return for the great labor and expense incidental thereto."[87]

Supporters of the parade denied or ignored these points. In 1884 they vehemently opposed the suggestion that the parade be held in the morning, to curtail drinking. Thomas McGourty of the AOH vigorously asserted that "we are not a set of inebriates as has been insinuated. If the workingmen can be accommodated by having the parade in the afternoon we should do so." Despite his vehemence, it is questionable whether McGourty and his fellow Hibernians really cared whether the parade encouraged drunkenness. The AOH's rowdy July Fourth picnics testified to their indifference to Yankee stereotypes of drunken Irishmen. Indeed, since saloonkeepers played such a prominent role in the AOH, at least some Hibernians might have invited increased tippling on St. Patrick's Day.[88]

The Hibernians, like the temperance men, were concerned about image, but unlike the temperance men, they believed that the parade enhanced rather than detracted from their people's reputation. Parade advocates worried less about proving the respectability of the Worcester Irish than about demonstrating their community's power and strength. As James Early and Thomas McGourty suggested in 1892, an ethnic group like the Irish "who are numerical in excess of all nationalities" would be "humiliated" if they did not take advantage of opportunities to parade. It was important, D. J. Courtney argued in 1890, to "command the respect of our enemies" through displays of solidarity.[89]

For the Hibernians, the parade was more than a means for Irish men to display their power; it was also an opportunity for them to reaffirm their loyalty to their own group and community. As William Regan said in a speech before the convention in 1884, support for the parade and marching in it were a test of how "Irish" the Irish people in Worcester really were. J. Frank Quinn expressed the same sentiments more colloquially a year later when he exclaimed: "Why should we care for a little trouble or a walk in the mud. Our people was crushed but they stood up for their manhood. . . . We love our race and nationality."[90]

Parade backers thus frequently excoriated their opponents for their lack of "patriotism." Richard O'Brien sounded a persistent theme in 1887 when he charged that the young parade opponents did not have the "spirit of their sires." In 1890, Richard O'Flynn claimed that the young teetotallers who were reluctant to parade were "too Americanized—the young men are a little vain—perhaps as they grow older some of the conceit and starch will be washed out." Even some of the parish temperance men themselves seemed to concede that their refusal to parade was a sign of their declining ethnic loyalty. On St. Patrick's Day in 1890, as noted in this book's introduction, Daniel Boyle exhorted his fellow members of the St. Paul's Lyceum "not to let their mothers and fathers come out on the street this afternoon and find them ashamed to call themselves Irishmen."[91]

Boyle's plea to his fellow temperance men reflected the ambivalent feelings many young second-generation Irish felt about the parade. It is important once again not to oversimplify the perspectives of the American-born Irish on their ethnic loyalties. In 1888, no less an advocate of American loyalties than Richard Mooney introduced the motion for the parade. Moreover, if the temperance societies voted consistently against the parades, they nonetheless just as consistently continued to attend the United Irish Societies Convention. More important perhaps, many of them marched in the parade even if they did not vote for it. Indeed, one or more of the parish temperance societies marched in the parade almost every year between 1882 and 1893. The American-born temperance men were not trying to abandon their group so much as to transform it into a people loyal to their old-country past and their faith but acceptably American. Mooney, the American-born leader of the Catholic Young Men's Lyceum seemed to inadvertently sum up the confusions of that effort when he expressed the hope that St. Patrick's Day would become "almost an American day."[92]

The Hibernians were unequivocal in their position on the parade, but their support for it was not a simple, stubborn effort to maintain an old-country tradition. Hibernian backing for the parade no doubt reflected the immigrant desire to hold on to cherished old-country festivities in the cold and dreary monotony of industrial Worcester. Raucous celebrations of St. Patrick's Day in the new environment were very similar to the drinking and carousing that were essential rituals of the country fairs of rural Ireland. Many Irish peasants witnessed or even participated in the political processions of Daniel O'Connell's Emancipation or Repeal campaigns in the early nineteenth century, and thus some Worcester immigrants may have brought a familiarity with these demonstrations with them from Ireland to America. Nevertheless, Irishmen marked St. Patrick's Day much differently in Ireland than in America. St. Patrick's Day was an important feast day but by no means a universal fair day in Ireland, where local customs or the agricultural calendar determined fair dates. Indeed, in most parts of Ireland, peasants marked St. Patrick's Day quietly in church services. Moreover, though there were some parades—or more accurately military reviews—on St. Patrick's Day in Dublin or other large cities, such elaborate military drills were obviously unknown in the small towns and villages where most of Worcester's Irish immigrants had lived. St. Patrick's Day celebrations in Worcester and throughout America were, therefore, at best, an amalgam of old-country customs and cultural borrowings, and the parades themselves owed as much or more to the new tradition of American popular parades as they did to Ireland's political processions or military reviews.[93]

The parade then was an invented tradition in America, but one that seemed to have a special meaning for Irish immigrants. The traditional communalism of these Irish immigrants, many of them recent newcomers, reinforced by their experiences as unskilled or semiskilled workers in America, helped shape their attitudes towards the parade. Given their poverty and poor chances for upward mobility as individuals, the solidarity of their community was vital to them. It offered them protection and, as it grew more powerful, perhaps even hope for advancement. For those men the parade became a vital symbol of their community's solidarity and power. Its size and splendor and its route of march were visible manifestations of Irish strength: hundreds of well-dressed and sometimes well-armed Irishmen marching through Worcester's east side to reaffirm Irish dominion there before emerging on to Main Street to demonstrate Irish power to the whole city. The failure to parade raised the specter that not only was the proper celebration of St. Patrick's Day fading away but that their community, the community they depended on so vitally, was itself dissolving. The immigrant Hibernians could not tolerate that prospect and thus voted almost unanimously to support the parade in convention votes from 1884 to 1895. Unfortunately for them, those votes were often not enough to ensure a parade in the 1880s and 1890s when accommodation held sway and the temperance movement was waxing strong.[94]

"America in 1776 Transplanted": Irish Nationalism in Worcester in the 1880s

Support for Irish freedom had a long history among Worcester's Irish, but conflicts over what freedom meant for Ireland and the best methods of attaining it had also divided the community for nearly as long. In the 1880s, fueled by a new agricultural crisis and inspired by the charismatic Charles Stewart Parnell, a nationalist movement arose in Ireland and America which dwarfed all previous agitations. Nearly all the Worcester Irish became involved in this new phase of activity, but internal conflicts persisted. Controversy erupted over whether freedom for Ireland meant limited autonomy, or home rule, within the British Empire, independence as a republic, or—a new possibility raised in the 1880s—a quasi socialist democracy where the state would own all of the new country's land and natural resources. Worcester's Irish also debated a variety of methods for winning this freedom—constitutional parliamentary agitation, economic boycotts and tenant strikes, or guerrilla warfare. Conflicts over those issues revealed even more graphically than debates over the St. Patrick's Day parade the deep political, economic, and, perhaps most notable, gender divisions within Worcester's Irish community. Yet it also demonstrated clearly how the power of the priests and the politicians of the Citizens' alliance stifled dissent and dominated Worcester's Irish community.

The participation of the Worcester Irish in the struggle to free Ireland extended back to the early years of the community. In the early 1840s, when Daniel O'Connell launched a mass movement to repeal the Act of Union binding England and Ireland, Worcester's Irish contributed substantial sums to the repeal cause. Later in that decade, the more prosperous, older, eastern Irish immigrants had turned from O'Connell to the Young Ireland movement, a band of middle-class romantic revolutionaries in 1846, to find hope for Ireland's freedom. In Ireland the Young Ireland revolt quickly passed with the exchange of a few volleys in a Tipperary cabbage patch, but within a decade veterans of the Young Ireland movement and Irish urban workers forged a new nationalist organization, the Fenians, dedicated to the overthrow of British rule and the creation of an independent Irish republic. Worcester Irishmen responded quickly to this opportunity. In June of 1859, only a year after the first Fenian societies organized in Dublin and New York City, twenty-two Irishmen gathered to form a Worcester circle of the Fenian brotherhood. By the Civil War's end in 1865, as many as 45,000 men had taken the Fenian oath in America and hundred of thousands more were sympathetic to the society. In Worcester, three hundred Fenian men, marching in a body "for the first time," joined the city's Fourth of July parade in 1865. That same year thousands of Irish packed a meeting at Mechanics Hall to cheer Fenian speeches and pledge money to the coming war to free Ireland.[95]

After the Civil War, Fenian fever continued in Worcester and the nation at large despite the organization's near comic-opera bungling in two quick, futile, and embarrassing invasions of Canada and a "rising" in Ireland hardly worthy of the name. Worcester's Irish supplied soldiers for the first Canadian invasion in 1866, gave $500 to finance it, and helped ship arms north to the Fenian army. Two years later, even after the invasion's failure and the botched "rising" in Ireland, Fenians could still draw a "large turnout" to Mechanics Hall to listen to heroes of the Brotherhood like O'Donovan Rossa and to pledge their few dollars to the future revolution. Many Yankees, infuriated at England for her help to the Confederacy in the Civil War and, perhaps eager to befriend Irish voters, also praised the Fenian cause. The *Gazette* in March of 1867 declared: "The Irish have our warmest sympathies in the struggle for national life." An Irish nationalist from New York who visited Worcester in the same year marveled at the "evident harmony existing in Worcester between the American and foreign citizens."[96]

Fenianism finally collapsed after one last bungled invasion of Canada in 1870, but Irish nationalist sentiment remained strong in Worcester and around the nation. In 1878, an intense, one-armed man came to Worcester to visit the remnants of the Fenian organization. Evicted with his family from their home in Mayo, robbed of his arm by the mill machines of Lancashire, and later imprisoned for running guns to his revolutionary comrades in Ireland, Michael Davitt was a living symbol of Ireland's travails and a full-blown Fenian hero. Touring America to reinvigorate the revolutionary cause, he and his colleagues, John Devoy and others, were also considering a new strategy for the liberation of Ireland. The new strategy would link the revolutionary descendants of the Fenians, the Clan na Gael in America and the Irish Republican Brotherhood in Ireland, to an aggressive faction of Ireland's Home Rule party in Parliament and would capitalize on a deepening agricultural depression in Ireland with a program of land reform. Davitt may have spoken of these developments in his speech at Worcester but there is no record of his talk. All that is known is that he felt he delivered his lecture well, was pleased with the warm reception, and pleased his listeners in turn by complimenting them on the absence of factionalism in the local nationalist movement.[97]

The following year Ireland's agricultural crisis worsened and the new strategy, "The New Departure" as it was called, was realized in the Land League. The League was both a land reform movement and a nationalist crusade, tapping for the first time in modern Irish history both the economic and political discontents of the Irish peasantry. The result was an enormous mass movement. The first branch was organized in the spring of 1879 and within a year hundreds of branches had sprung up all over Ireland.[98]

Davitt played a role in organizing the League, but the leader both in fact and in name was Charles Stewart Parnell, the emerging power in the Irish Home Rule party in Parliament. A Protestant landowner from Wicklow, just south of Dublin, Parnell was a curious figure to be leading masses of Irish peasants in an agitation for land reform and Irish freedom. He would in fact prove more conservative than men like Davitt and other significant leaders of the League. While they dreamed of an independent Irish republic and a radically restructured Irish economy, he sought the limited autonomy of a state or dominion in a federal empire, i.e., home rule, and cautious reform of the land system's abuses. Yet he understood that even to achieve those limited objectives he had to mobilize the potential power of the Irish masses. Charismatic, politically savvy, and often deliberately enigmatic, he skillfully rode the Land League in pursuit of those goals.

In the fall of 1879 Parnell embarked for the United States where he established an American Land League as a formal support organization for the League in Ireland. From January to March he traveled 16,000 miles throughout the United States, spoke in 62 cities as well as before the joint houses of Congress, and helped raise hundreds of thousands of dollars. On March 10, 1880, just before he returned to Ireland, he and Irish American supporters founded the American Land League and by May it had enough branches to warrant a general convention.[99]

Despite the general enthusiasm for Parnell and his message, the League in America, like the movement in Ireland, was made of disparate elements which quickly split into three broad factions. On the left were the radicals led by Patrick Ford, editor of the *Irish World*. Ford and his backers, like the Davitt wing in Ireland, thought the land question was the central issue in the crusade. Ford also believed that the war for land in Ireland was but a part of a more general fight by workers in America and England against economic oppression. Ford himself, though not all of his followers, became a devotee of the American social reformer Henry George and backed a radical scheme for land nationalization in Ireland. Impatient and ever suspicious of the British government, Ford and his supporters urged vigorous tactics—they were particularly fond of the rent strike—in the land agitation. Opposing Ford were two factions: a group of respectable conservatives led by Boston's John Boyle O'Reilly and Patrick Collins; and the bulk of the Clan na Gael, "physical force" nationalist heirs to the Fenians, led by John Devoy. The conservatives were Ford's ideological opposites. Ireland in a federal empire was their principal goal, not a revolution in the land system, and they were willing to consider reasonable compromises with the British government on the land issue and the question of Irish autonomy. They favored tactics that were equally circumspect, placing their hopes largely in peaceful political mobilization and parliamentary maneuver. The last faction, led by the Clan na Gael, sought Ireland's unqualified freedom as an independent republic, not home rule, as their goal. They were willing to go along with parliamentary maneuvering in the short run to prepare the country for the inevitable violent showdown with the British crown. Agitating the land issue was also important to them but largely as a tactic to help foster support for the nationalist cause. They viewed Ford's obsession with economic reform as a dangerous distraction from the primary goal of independence. Through much of the League agitation they thus allied with the conservatives, helping to elect Collins president of the American Land League and make O'Reilly's *Pilot* and Lawrence Walsh, a Catholic priest, the official channel for American donations to the Irish League. Ford sidestepped this attempt to shut out his faction by encouraging League branches sympathetic to his views to send their donations to him so that he could pass them on to the Land League in Ireland.[100]

The response of the Irish in Worcester to all these developments was very slow, and, even once made, their first efforts were tentative and conservative. On January 13, 1880, the United Irish Societies Convention met and concluded "that the people of this city should be called upon to express their sympathy with the suffering people of Ireland in some public and suitable manner." The convention then appointed a committee, dominated by politicians such as

Mathew McCafferty, Andrew Athy, Jeremiah Murphy, James Mellen, and Francis Plunkett, to carry out this nebulous charge. Meanwhile an "American Committee" composed largely of members of the city's Yankee elite had formed to raise money for humanitarian relief of the starving peasants in Ireland. The two committees met in the last week of January in 1880 to coordinate their relief efforts. Richard O'Flynn noted with chagrin that the American committee appeared in full at that meeting, but to their shame only three of the appointed Irish braved the biting winds and slippery ice of that wintry night. Nevertheless, the joint committees, such as they were, agreed on an appeal to the citizens of Worcester to "relieve the distress in Ireland" to be published in the *Daily Spy.* That appeal was couched in conservative terms to be sure to reach well beyond the city's Irish community. Citing authorities such as the duchess of Marlborough and the Dublin archbishop of the Protestant Church of Ireland, the appeal called for donations to Ireland's suffering poor and scheduled a mass meeting at Mechanics Hall to kick off the fundraising campaign. Stephen Salisbury, the wealthiest man in Worcester and the principal architect of the Citizens' Party coalitions, and George Verry, former Democratic mayor, signed for the Yankees; McCafferty, Mellen, and John O'Gorman, a member of the common council, for the Irish.[101]

The ensuing campaign for Irish relief continued to reflect not only successful cooperation between the Irish and the Yankees but the conservatism that cooperation seemed to make necessary. On February 7, 1880, the two committees staged their great mass meeting at Mechanics Hall. Seven Yankees spoke, including three present or future Citizens' Party candidates for mayor and three Protestant clergymen. These speeches were uniformly charitable, ecumenical, and safely nonpolitical. Most of the Yankees stressed, as Rev. Huntington, rector of the Episcopal All Saints church, did that "the cry is one that appeals to our ... humanity." Many also played upon the cooperation which the movement exemplified. Huntington contended: "We should know no Catholic, no Protestant, no Tory, no Whig; no Democrat nor Republican." W. S. B. Sprague (who would later be elected mayor as a Citizens' ticket nominee) invoked the shared sacrifice of the Civil War: "when the call was made a few years ago for men to defend the life of this nation the Irishmen rallied around the flag and gave their lives that the country might live. For that if no other reason ought Americans to give liberally to the relief of people in Ireland." Few Yankees dared venture into Ireland's political morass. Mayor Kelley, who presided over the meeting, politely but firmly dismissed "the remote causes" which caused the Famine because they do "not now concern us." The Irish speaking at the meeting raised the political question more directly but were no more challenging. Both Monsignor Griffin and Father Thomas J. Conaty praised Parnell and home rule. Yet both men also expressed their "shame" at "having to stand before the people of Worcester" and ask for help for their starving countrymen. As Thomas Brown has pointed out, such shame was a powerful motive in spurring many American Irish to work to free their homeland and raise its status and, thus, also their own, in American eyes. Conaty and Griffin also seemed, however, to be obliquely acknowledging the dependence of their people on Yankee wealth and goodwill. In any case this harmonious display was a useful first step in the relief campaign. Within a month the citizens of Worcester sent $1,000 to the *Boston Pilot* for Irish relief through the campaign's treasurer, Henry Marsh (Marsh would also later become mayor with Irish support). This was in addition to the $1,700 collected the same month in the city's Irish parishes.[102]

As substantial as these contributions may have been, they did little to advance the cause of Irish freedom, which continued to lag in Worcester. An early attempt to found a local Land League branch ended disastrously, but on November 10, 1880, "leading Irishmen" met to try again to establish the Land League in Worcester. Three days later they organized officially and elected officers. Politicians dominated the new branch: Andrew Athy, former state representative, soon to be alderman and candidate for mayor, was president; the sharp-tongued and well-connected contractor, Jeremiah Murphy, vice president; Eugene Moriarty, state representative, secretary; Patrick Quinn, a common councillor and future state representative, treasurer; and three common councillors on the executive board.[103]

The politicians would not prove as energetic, effective, or influential in the new nationalist agitation, however, as Worcester's priests. While the politicians were forming the Central Branch of the Land League, the young Conaty and McCoy were moving to create a branch of the Ladies Land League in Worcester. Parnell's sisters and Ellen Ford, sister of Patrick Ford, established the first Ladies Land league in New York in October of 1880 to broaden the League's pool of supporters and potential contributors. With McCoy presiding and Conaty serving as treasurer, Worcester's branch of the Ladies League organized on November 17. For the first few months at least the new branch appeared to prosper and perform the docile service that McCoy and Conaty expected. By February of 1881 the ladies branch had raised at least $700. By then priests in Worcester's other Irish parishes had also begun to mobilize support for the Land League under their conservative direction. On February 6, 1881, Dennis Scannell, pastor of St. Anne's, and his curate, John Drennan, organized an East Worcester branch of the League. Drennan was elected the first president and Scannell the treasurer. Later that year Father William Walsh, pastor of Immaculate Conception, formed a North End branch of the League.[104]

Throughout the later months of 1880 and most of 1881, Worcester's Irish priests tightly controlled Worcester's nationalist movement and directed it along conservative lines. The most important of the clerics was Thomas J. Conaty. He presided over or spoke at most League meetings, emerged as the principal League spokesman in local newspapers, arranged for national leaders to come to Worcester, and chaired Ladies Land League sessions. Conaty was more than a local leader, however. By January of 1881 he was a national power in the Irish American Nationalist movement, treasurer of the American Land League, and one of Patrick Collins's principal conservative allies.[105]

Worcester's lay Irish leaders and the Central Branch of the Land League they controlled aligned themselves with the priests and the conservative faction of the Irish Nationalist movement. By February of 1881 membership in the Central Branch had swelled to 225 men, and throughout 1881 and 1882, a small but constant stream of funds flowed from Worcester's Central Branch through O'Reilly's *Boston Pilot* to Ireland's nationalists. In 1881 it appeared that nationalism in Worcester would be respectable, conservative, and clerically controlled.[106]

Some Worcester Irish did not yield so readily to the priests and the politicians, however. These were the women of the Ladies League led by the redoubtable Maria Dougherty. Little is known about Dougherty before the Land League era except that she was an unmarried milliner who ran her own shop in Worcester (her name is even spelled differently, Dogherty, Docherty, and Doherty, in different sources). In November of 1880 she was elected president of the city's ladies branch and by January of 1881 had become Worcester's most outspoken critic of conservative nationalism. At a meeting of the Ladies League on January 5, 1881, while both Conaty and McCoy looked on, she roasted John Boyle O'Reilly for lecturing around the country "for a large fee" while ignoring the land agitation, and she assailed Collins for failing to rebut newspaper attacks on the League. A week later she followed a cautious speech by a curate from St. Anne's with another ringing attack, this time labeling Worcester's own nationalist leaders timid and lazy. The Irish people of Worcester "should stop idolizing people who don't deserve it," Dougherty contended. Mellen in the *Times* decried Dougherty's attack on two "sterling Irishmen" as the "acme of folly" and tauntingly asked if the "daughter of Rebecca" was married.[107]

This sniping did not deter Dougherty or dampen the enthusiasm of other female nationalists. Membership in the ladies branch rocketed from 160 in early December of 1880 to 400 by late February in 1881. Dougherty openly proclaimed her support for Patrick Ford and Michael Davitt's radicals and moved to align the Worcester ladies branch with that faction. In February she thundered that the people of Ireland could not be "timid" and hinted that the League in Ireland should organize a rent strike among the peasants, the favored strategy of the radicals. She and members of the ladies branch also praised Ford often and began sending most of the money they raised to him or directly to Anna Parnell in Ireland rather than through the conservatives' treasury at the *Pilot*. These were substantial sums, totaling about $3,100, far more than the funds raised by the conservative men of the Central Branch. Little wonder that Patrick Ford himself lauded the ladies branch as "the life of the Land League movement" in Worcester, and effusively praised its leader, Dougherty.[108]

The emergence of Dougherty and the Ladies Land League at the forefront of radical opposition to Worcester's conservative nationalist leadership is difficult to explain. Indeed, the branch was truly a surprising phenomenon in Worcester no matter what its political stance. Aside from parish sodalities there were no Irish women's organizations in Worcester in the early 1880s. It would not be until the late 1880s or early 1890s that the Catholic Young Women's Lyceum and the Ladies Auxiliary of the AOH would appear in Worcester. Puzzling too were the class and generation of women leading this radical organization. No lists of the branch's members remain, but various sources suggest that second-generation teachers and professional women played critical roles in the branch. Recalling the Land League in a newspaper interview in 1906, Dougherty identified American-born Dr. Mary V. O'Callaghan, a medical doctor, and Margaret Geary and Annie Athy, both schoolteachers, as her principal assistants in the branch. The program from a major Ladies League event listed Mary Eagan and Katie McCarthy, both schoolteachers, as well as Geary, Athy, and O'Callaghan as the branch's leaders.[109]

Why would these upwardly mobile, eminently proper American-born women join a nationalist faction supported largely by immigrant workers and pursuing a radical program in Ireland and America? Perhaps they were simply following the lead of their national leaders. Davitt after all had helped found the Ladies League. Parnell's sisters, cofounders of the American Ladies League and leaders of the Irish Ladies League, were not as conservative as their brother, and they had enthusiastically backed the radicals from the beginning of the land agitation. Patrick Ford's sister, Ellen, also played an important role in the Ladies League, serving as its first vice president. Ladies Leagues throughout America thus aligned with Ford's faction just as Worcester's branch did. In her reminiscences twenty-five years after the land agitation, Maria Dougherty remembered "how Worcester women became interested in forming a land league because of the articles about the movement in Patrick Ford's *Irish World* which they read diligently."[110]

Yet women who responded with such energy and enthusiasm and who braved the opposition of the church and political leaders of their community were inspired and moved by more than the simple desire to follow distant national leaders. The branch's furious activity and heated rhetoric suggested deeper causes. Descriptions of the Ladies Land League branch's meetings are sketchy, but evidence of group songs, recitations from Irish poems and history, and fiery speeches suggests that the Ladies League offered a unique opportunity for Irish women to achieve a sense of gender solidarity. Perhaps, more importantly, the League provided women with a chance to assert themselves in a public cause. It allowed them to prove their competence as well as challenge the male leaders of their community. Still flushed with pride, Dougherty remembered a quarter of a century later how much she and her fellow members of the Ladies League had accomplished by themselves: traveling to New York to contract speakers, arranging for halls, and planning fundraisers. White-collar, upwardly mobile women like Margaret Geary or Mary O'Callaghan who were Dougherty's principal aides may have felt this need even more. In Worcester's Irish community second-generation women were at least as well educated, and perhaps even more occupationally successful, than Irish men of either generation and yet they played almost no role in the social, cultural, or political leadership of their community. Teachers like Geary or Eagan often participated in American political campaigns but always behind the scenes, stuffing envelopes or checking lists at party headquarters. In the Ladies Land League they were able to move to the front of the political stage.

It is important not to overestimate the rebelliousness of these women. The Ladies Land League would prove virtually the only forceful demonstration of women's independence among the Worcester Irish in the late nineteenth century. Indeed, in her study of Irish women in America, Hasia Diner has suggested that both Celtic men and women in nineteenth-century America agreed that women should limit their ambitions to the economic sphere and leave politics and public life to men. Irish women, Diner argued, "felt no need for politics. . . . that turf belonged to men." Yet Diner ignored the Ladies Land League, which was a powerful force in many American cities, not just in Worcester, and thus underestimated the interest of nineteenth-century Irish women in a public role. The Land League agitation provided talented and skilled American-born women in Worcester an opportunity—perhaps their only opportunity—for a role that they clearly desired and eagerly embraced.[111]

That agitation grew increasingly bitter over the course of 1881, moving the nationalists on both sides of the Atlantic towards crisis. Parnell, though privately amenable to a new land law passed by Parliament, attacked it because it and other British measures were unpopular with the Land League's rank and file. Parnell assailed it so strongly that he was thrown into jail in October of 1881. He immediately issued a "No Rent Manifesto," calling upon tenants to refuse to pay their rents, and the British government in turn suppressed the Land League. Anna Parnell's Ladies Land League filled the breach and served as the organizational vehicle for continuation of the agitation in Ireland. Yet after Parnell's imprisonment, the Land League's campaign seemed less a peaceful protest crusade than a guerrilla war, as agrarian violence steadily increased.[112]

Parnell's arrest, the suppression of the Land League in Ireland, and the issue of the No Rent Manifesto touched off an explosion of nationalist activity in Worcester. As the nationalist movement in Ireland and its Celtic supporters in Worcester became more radical, Worcester's Yankees began to shy away from the crusade. On October 16 Irishmen packed the Worcester Rink for a special "indignation meeting" to protest Parnell's arrest. The organizers of the meeting, most likely Conaty, McCafferty, and Father John J. McCoy, asked Mayor Kelley (born in New Hampshire of a very old Scotch-Irish Protestant family) to preside but he refused, arguing that he "might compromise somebody's view." George Verry, a former Democratic mayor and a candidate for the state senate, was the "only American representative" to speak.

At the meeting, Conaty, McCafferty, and a number of others continued to seek Yankee help by justifying the movement in American terms, but these desperate efforts to obscure the growing radicalism of the city's nationalist movement rang hollow at the rink. Conaty's colleague, Father John J. McCoy, reflected far better the now angry sentiments of the Worcester Irish. The hardened former athlete, McCoy, saw no further need for appeasing Yankee conservatives:

These so called Americans par excellence care more for the crocodile tears which that raiser of hogs, human and otherwise, Queen Victoria shed over the bier of Garfield than they do for the red hot torrents of your heart's best blood which your people have been shedding from the beginning. It is well to get the lesson. It is well to know one's friends, it is well to remember your enemies too in November. A Paddy's vote then counts like that of the biggest of them.

McCoy went on to argue that, just as a man can save himself only by his own efforts, so Ireland could be saved only by Irishmen in Ireland and America: "It is to be the work of Irishmen and theirs exclusively."[113]

While the leftward turn of the nationalist movement in Ireland shook the conservative Irish in Worcester and scared away local Yankees, it, conversely, boosted the power and spirits of the local leaders of the radical faction: the women of the Ladies Land League. Indeed, because the Ladies Land League in Ireland had become the principal organization there for sustaining the land war, the women in Worcester's Ladies Land League seemed to grow in confidence. On November 5, 1881, they sent a fresh $500 to Mrs. Delia Parnell, Parnell's mother, for the Ladies Land League in Ireland. Two weeks later the feisty Maria Dougherty congratulated Patrick Ford on his acerbic "Open Letter to Gladstone" which revealed "the criminal history of the British empire." She enclosed $5.00 to send 100 copies of "that greatest of all pronouncements— the No Rent Manifesto" to Ireland "or, if you like, benighted England."[114]

The most powerful impact of the events of October was not on the Yankees, the priests, or Irish women of Worcester, however, but on the city's great silent mass of Irish immigrant workingmen. Throughout most of the Land League agitation they had remained inert or invisible as the priests and politicians on one side and the women on the other dominated the movement. Yet the No Rent Manifesto roused the workers. In late December of 1881 Irishmen from the Quinsigamond Wire Works of South Worcester forwarded $50 to the *Irish World*. It was the first time a group from Worcester identifying itself as a workingmen's organization had made a donation to the Land League cause. The letter explained that it was "contributed by workingmen in appreciation of the No Rent Manifesto . . . we regret our inability to forward a more vigorous protest against the Coercion Bill." We look forward, the letter added, to "the death knell of landlordism." A week later a South Worcester branch of the Land League sent $45 to Ford's *World*. In their letter to the paper the leaders of the branch proclaimed: "We the undersigned all readers of the *Irish World* and sound believers in its doctrines seeing your appeal for the No Rent Manifesto we started out among our friends and lovers of old Ireland. All our subscribers are no rent men. Float the no rent banner high. . . . Down with the land thieves they must go. But they certainly will not be let to go to Connaught. [A play on Cromwell's famous cry in his conquest of Ireland: "To hell or Connaught"]." The letter was signed by James Ronan, a spinner, Michael Cody, a machinist, and Michael O'Hara, a laborer. The North End also rallied to the cause. James Butler of the North End branch sent $20 to Ford's *Irish World* claiming "our organization consists of 125 members," and promising "you may hear from us soon with a larger amount to help the cause of putting down landlordism in Ireland." Butler and the fellow members of his branch were true to their word. Within a month they sent an additional $334.92 to Ford and the *World* to be forwarded to the No Rent campaign in Ireland.[115]

Worcester's Irish immigrant workers, so long dormant, had rallied to the radical cause. That they provided most of the new support for the radical nationalists seems evident from a number of sources. The Quinsigamond Wire Works donors were, of course, largely blue-collar workers, but so were the vast majority of contributors from the South Worcester and the North End branches who can be traced in city directories. Indeed, of those traced from the two branches, 16.8 percent were skilled and 78 percent semiskilled or unskilled blue-collar workers. The generation of the new contributors is harder to determine, but of the few men who can be traced in the census of 1880, 90 percent (19 of 21) were born in Ireland.[116]

Despite this new radical surge from below, local conservatives gave ground grudgingly to their newly powerful opponents. Conaty clearly was not comfortable with the No Rent Manifesto's implications but he had recently endorsed it at the national meeting of the Land League in Chicago. He could not back away from it but he did not wish enthusiasm for the tactic to sweep away conservative control of the movement in Worcester. He thus called a meeting of local nationalists on January 12, 1882, to ratify the Chicago convention's support of the manifesto and of Parnell's policy but made sure that the conservatives retained full control of the gathering. He enlisted the newly elected Yankee Citizens' mayor, Elijah B. Stoddard, to preside over the meeting. Stoddard gave a brief address endorsing home rule and "fair rent." John Boyle O'Reilly, however, was the featured speaker of the evening. O'Reilly, it appears, had become the Worcester conservatives' choice as a counterweight to Ford, for they praised the Boston editor at every opportunity. At the Worcester meeting, O'Reilly spoke little about land reform but instead stressed the need for Irish Americans to be respectable as well as potent in the fight for home rule. Conaty capped the meeting by arguing that the nationalist movement should "strive for what is attainable," not grand schemes of social reconstruction. Moreover, Conaty argued, the movement should "enlist all classes," including the priests. In what seemed to be a direct reference to Ford, Conaty asked the nationalists in the audience to "frown down that man or newspaper that tries to disseminate disunion or introduce wrong means" to the movement. The priest concluded by solemnly warning that the "national question" was of greater importance than land reform.[117]

These efforts did not check the increasing power of Worcester's radical nationalists. Indeed, in the middle of February the radicals scored their biggest success. Between February 12 and 16 they staged a bazaar at Mechanics Hall that raised nearly $5,000 for the Ford faction. As that sum suggests, the bazaar drew "immense" crowds to hear speeches and music, indulge in ice cream, candy, pies, and oyster treats and bid on an odd collection of prizes including silver spoons, bedspreads, chromolithographs of the Sacred Heart, pictures of Parnell and Michael Davitt, and a "Land League cushion." On the last night the hall was packed to overflowing as Land Leaguers from towns all around Worcester County chartered special trains to join their fellow radical sympathizers from the city in a celebration of the No Rent cause.[118]

The bazaar drew support from a number of sources, but the principal organizers of the event were the long-time leaders of the radicals in Worcester, the women of the Ladies Land League. The *Irish World* hailed Dougherty, who "worked incessantly for the success attained." The *Spy* also pointed to Maria Dougherty as the "prime mover in this work" and contended "to her indefatigable efforts is the success of the bazaar principally due."[119]

The priests and many of the politicians, meanwhile, remained noticeably aloof. Even the Yankee papers could not help but notice that "With perhaps one or two exceptions not a Catholic clergymen has been in the hall since the fair was opened." The *Spy* noted that some radicals believed the priests resented the bazaar because it cut into their fair business, a prime source of revenue for parishes, but the paper more accurately attributed the priests' absence to ideological differences with the bazaar's organizers. As the Yankee daily suggested:

> The Emerald Bazaar has been a success notwithstanding the fact that it was arranged against the wishes of the local Catholic clergy and especially those who have been most active in the Land League cause since the present agitation began. The friends of the cause have been divided since the Chicago [Land League] Convention, the clergy and their friends having taken grounds against the No Rent Manifesto relying mainly on Home Rule as a basis for discussion. The more enthusiastic Land Leaguers under the lead of Miss Maria Dougherty, president of the Ladies Branch of the Land League still adhere to the favorite measure of Parnell and Davitt and the bazaar has received its support from this class.[120]

The *Times* would later rightfully dispute the *Spy*'s oversimplification of the conflict, and particularly its misrepresentation of Conaty's complicated position on the manifesto, but the *Spy*'s characterization was basically accurate. Even the organizers of the bazaar conceded that their event had brought the movement's ideological conflicts to a head. The women of the Ladies League noted: "it is unfortunate that worthy as is the object of the bazaar there are some who look upon it with anything but favor . . . we at least expected that those of our people who were not with us would not openly and avowedly place themselves against us. . . . if the Land League has violated the eternal principles of truth, if religion and morality are in danger of being subverted then gladly would we sever our connection with the Land League and disown our relationship with such a barbarous people as the Irish."[121]

If the women of the Ladies Land League sounded smug, they had won that right, for they and their faction had grown so powerful in Worcester by the winter of 1882 that they began to drag the priests and other conservative nationalists further and further left over the rest of that season. On St. Patrick's Day, Father John J. McCoy published a poem celebrating Michael Davitt, raising the Irish radical into a pantheon of Irish heroes that included Brian Boru, Ireland's last high king, and other legendary figures from Ireland's ancient past. "Then God chose the dreamer to lift up poor Erin" the priest wrote, "the land said the angel belongs to the people . . . the priest will give blessing . . . God will be with thee." Conaty too seemed to be drifting left in March. On St. Patrick's Day he launched into a bitter attack on "landlordism" in Ireland and quoted a John Stuart Mill dictum that had become the credo of the Land League: "The land of any country belongs to the people of that country."[122]

The Central and East Worcester branches, conservative strongholds to date, also began to crack under the radical onslaught through the spring of 1882. In late April the East Worcester branch of the Land League reorganized and elected a new slate of officers. Long dominated by Father Dennis Scannell of St. Anne's or his curates, branch members now voted laymen into all the important offices. The Central Branch, the conservative bastion, also seemed ripe for change. In late April and early May the *Times* printed long letters severely criticizing the conservative Boston "whigs" who ran the branch. One letter signed merely "Clan na Gael" proclaimed "Patrick Ford is the man and to his noble paper and not to Boston whiggery is due the success of the Land League in America." Another letter signed "Celt" stated that "there is a certain influence brought to bear upon the branch which may be called whiggism or conservatism which has proved a wet blanket on the success of the branch." Whether these dissenters contested the branch's elections in early May is not known, but if they did, their challenge was beaten back as all the old officers retained their posts. Nevertheless, the momentum of the radicals still seemed only momentarily checked, not halted.[123]

The very day after the Central branch's elections on May 4, 1882, the course of the nationalist movement in Ireland changed abruptly causing in turn a dramatic shift in the tides of sentiment in Worcester as well. On that day, May 5, Parnell emerged from jail having struck a deal with the British government that became known as the "Kilmainham Treaty." Parnell agreed to the elimination

of the Land League and the end of the land agitation in return for new legislation making necessary adjustments in the land law. Immediately after leaving prison he disbanded Ireland's Ladies Land League, which had carried on
the protest after the Land League itself had been suppressed. In sum, Parnell
left prison to redirect the movement along conservative lines: to seek Home
Rule by parliamentary methods; and to relegate the quest for land reform to
secondary importance.[124]

Not all Irish nationalists agreed with the efforts of their newly freed leader
to set the movement on a conservative course. Parnell's sisters, who were the
leaders of the Ladies Land League, were outraged but powerless to contest
their brother's decision. More ominous was Michael Davitt's opposition to the
Kilmainham treaty. Davitt now broke openly with Parnell and moved, at least
temporarily, to embrace Henry George's scheme of land nationalization.[125]

Parnell was no less a hero in Worcester for his compromise, however, and
the conservatives moved swiftly to capitalize on his popularity. Tacking back to
the right again, the *Times* dismissed the No Rent campaign as a mere tactic that
might have degenerated into communist revolution if Parnell had not wisely
chosen to compromise. "It [the No Rent campaign] may now be safely laid
aside," the paper claimed, "without any reproach to the Irish leaders." The
Times now led an assault on Ford and the radicals, roundly criticizing Davitt
as well for his new commitment to land nationalization. Reflecting what appeared to be the new strategy of the conservatives, the paper consistently
praised Parnell, the "safe leader of the Irish people," for his "prudent counsel"
and assured leadership. They also branded opposition to Parnell or persistence in radical ideological schemes as disloyalty or "rebellion" against the movement. Parnell, more than ever before, had become the indispensable man for
the conservatives, almost a totem, and identifying him with their movement
they were able to turn the tables on the radicals who had so long chided them
for lack of zeal in the cause.[126]

The local radicals were perplexed by the turnabout in Ireland, but Parnell's
deal did not break them. Undaunted, Dougherty traveled to New York where
she arranged for Michael Davitt and the radical priest Father Edward McGlynn
to speak in Worcester in early July. Davitt had just begun a tour of the United
States, hoping to rally the radical faction, and he and McGlynn agreed to add
Worcester to their schedule.[127]

Davitt, however, could not and would not save Worcester's radical Irish nationalists. The Davitt who appeared in Worcester on July 2, 1882, was a different man than the Davitt who had broken with Parnell in May. Even before he
arrived in Worcester he had begun to back down from his radical positions

and loudly protest his loyalty to Parnell. By the time he reached Worcester he seemed a broken man. Sick and hoarse (he wore an overcoat during his speech despite the July heat) he spoke only long enough to dismiss rumors and slanders that he differed from Parnell and to thank the people of Worcester for the kindness that they had shown him four years before. By the fall the League would be practically if not formally extinct in Worcester.[128]

The end of the Land League meant the end of the radical nationalists in Worcester as well, but before dismissing them it is useful to further probe their motives, the motives of their opponents, and the causes of their rise and fall. The fortunes of the radicals, like those of Irish American nationalism generally, clearly rode on the course of events in Ireland, but if events in Ireland dictated the radicals' success or failure, deeper motives were the wellsprings of their protest. Thomas Brown has suggested that a passion for respectability and acceptance drove the Irish nationalist movement in America. Specifically, Brown argued that Irish-American nationalists felt the need to lift Ireland up from its backward slavery in order to raise their own status in America. Brown's analysis seems to explain Worcester's conservative Irish nationalists, who seemed motivated by this concern for respectability and invoked it often in a plea to their own supporters. In a long editorial in late 1881, for example, the *Times* accused the American-born Irishman of being too interested in winning "respect and confidence from his American brethren" and warned "let them reflect . . . remember . . . that as the Irish are exalted they are exalted also and as their race is crushed and defeated they are humiliated." John Boyle O'Reilly expressed similar sentiments when he came to Worcester to address a large nationalist meeting in January of 1882. O'Reilly asserted that the Irish came to America "to build ourselves into the republican walls of this land and make ourselves a potent factor in this country. . . . We must make our element respectable and potent." To do that, he thundered, the American Irish must free Ireland. Indeed, he contended that the Irish in America would gain more from home rule than the Irish in Ireland would, implying that their status was dependent on Ireland's fate. Brown was not wrong in arguing that a concern for respectability motivated Irish American nationalists but it was the conservative nationalists, not the radicals, who were moved most by this passion.[129]

For supporters of radical nationalism, interest in Ireland's cause was not an attempt to prove their Americanism or gain respect from the natives of their new country. It was a visceral and direct response to the concrete injustices of an oppressed Ireland epitomized in the hated landlordism. Most of the Worcester workingmen who contributed to Ford's *World*, it appears, were immigrants, and their bitter denunciations of the landlords were inspired, at least in part, by their firsthand experiences on the land in Ireland. A number of men asked Ford to send copies of his paper to their home villages and towns in Ireland in order to spur the battle against the landlords. John Murren, James Henry, Paul Henry, and nine others wrote to Ford in March of 1882: "The donors of this small contribution formerly belonged to Achonry [a small village in County Sligo] so they are most anxious to have . . . money sent there to be conducted for the destruction of landlordism. Landlordism is a blasphemy against the creator. Until landlordism goes only then will Ireland become happy and prosperous." Other Worcester Irishmen asked Ford to send his paper to Cahirceveen in west Kerry or towns in County Clare.[130]

That this support for the radicals reflected not merely an identification with their Irish cousins but a crude kind of class antagonism also seems clear. If the supporters of radicalism had merely wished to free Ireland or even free it by violent means, they had other options: the "Boston whiggery" of the *Pilot* and their own leaders or John Devoy's Clan na Gael. As "old" readers of the *World* they were aware that Ford wished a transformation of Ireland's economy. Moreover, the vast majority of Worcester's radicals, aside from members of the Ladies Land League, were unskilled or semiskilled workers, and their rhetoric reflected fierce class resentments that seemed fueled by some of their own experiences and frustrations in America. In a vague, but nonetheless telling way, Worcester's Irish workers saw the cause of all the world's poor in the Irish peasants' battle with the landlords. Men from the Quinsigamond Wire Works sent their money to Ford "to rescue toiling humanity from the slough of misery and degradation in which it has been placed and kept for centuries by land thiefism and its concomitant evils." Other contributors also denounced "the land thieves" who "crucified" the poor. That organizers sometimes collected their Land League donations on the factory floor is particularly suggestive of the implicit if not explicit links Worcester's Irish immigrant workers must have seen between their American industrial experience and the plight of Irish tenants.[131]

In other cities Land League branches of workers often gave birth to Knights of Labor assemblies or union locals, but for Worcester's Irish worker radicals and for their female allies, mobilization, expressions of anger, and protest began and ended with the Land League and the Land War. As noted earlier, Worcester's workers were too divided by different industries, occupations, and a complicated politics that aligned many Yankee and Irish workers with opposing middle-class or elite factions to come together in a powerful labor movement. In the wire mills, where the radical Land Leaguers were strongest, prospects for unionization worsened rather than improved through the 1880s as Swedes, favored by management, trickled into the workrooms and further fragmented the workforce on ethnic lines. There would be little chance of successful organization there.

For Irish women there would be even fewer opportunities for protest after the collapse of the Ladies Land League. Future women's organizations within the community, like the Catholic Young Women's Lyceum, would be tightly controlled by the priests, and the women's movement outside their ethnic community had little room for them.[132]

For both these groups of outsiders, women and the immigrant "men of the workshops," the nationalist movement, and in particular the Land League, appeared to give them an opportunity and even a language or set of symbols for seizing a public role and expressing frustrations that they could not assert in the normal course of the city's politics or labor relations. Invoking unselfish devotion to the old country's cause and its past struggles, the workers, and particularly the women, were able to claim the high moral ground of nationalism, justify their deviance from normal roles in the case of women or long-time quiescence in the case of workers, and challenge the leaders of their community, the priests as well as the politicians. Events in Ireland were critical to them, for those events inspired and sustained their claims that they were the purest of nationalists and the most fit to direct the local movement. Yet if events in Ireland like the No Rent Manifesto legitimized and sustained them, those events could as easily bring them down. Parnell was critical to them; as long as he equivocated or even appeared to lean to the radicals they could continue to flourish, but when he turned openly and decisively to the right in the Kilmainham treaty, the radicals—the women and workers—were finished. Without Parnell in Ireland, Worcester's environment and Irish community, which boasted no labor movement or prospects for one, and was dominated by the politics of accommodation between Yankees and Irish, would not, could not, sustain these outsiders. As it turned out, they were done not only in the nationalist movement but after it as well, for that environment and community could not sustain them outside the nationalist arena either.

Though their radical opponents had disappeared by the fall of 1882, the conservative nationalists still faced opposition over the next few years from the militant "physical force" men. In 1885 the *Times* reported that a "famous Irish dynamiter" (the paper gave only a last name of Byrne) had arrived in Worcester probably to organize a club supporting a bombing campaign waged by Irish nationalists in England. O'Donovan Rossa had inspired that campaign, and his ledger also reveals that in 1885–86 at least thirty-nine Irishmen in Worcester subscribed to his paper, the *United Irishmen*. The subscribers included a few grocers and saloonkeepers but most were laborers, or other unskilled or semiskilled workers. Byrne's visit, a resolution endorsing the dynamite campaign offered on the floor of the Convention of the United Irish Societies in 1885, and some loose talk in the *Times* applauding leaders of the Clan na Gael or praising the nationalists who had killed the British government's chief secretary for Ireland in Dublin's Phoenix Park in 1882, suggest a restiveness, perhaps, a grumbling impatience with the limited goals and decorous methods of nationalism in Worcester's Irish community.[133]

Such restiveness would, however, remain muted and hesitant in Worcester and throughout much of America in the middle 1880s as Charles Stewart Parnell and his Home Rule Party rose to the zenith of their power. Like most Irish Americans, the bulk of Worcester's Irish enthusiastically enrolled in Parnell's triumphant crusade for home rule. In February of 1886 the Convention of the Union of Irish Societies unanimously passed a resolution offered by John Burns of the AOH. The resolution hailed the sweeping victory of Parnell's party in the 1885 parliamentary election as a "glorious victory" offering Irishmen "the opportunity which they have long desired to strike a blow for their motherland with the best advantage to themselves and their kindred at home." The resolution pledged unqualified support "to the chosen leader of the Irish people, Charles Stewart Parnell," not only moral support but "all the material and financial aid required for the sustainment [sic] of the national movement in Ireland." A little over two weeks later Thomas J. Conaty organized a meeting in Mechanics Hall to kick off the collection of donations for the Irish parliamentary party fund. The Hall was filled "to utmost capacity" according to the *Spy* as hundreds of Worcester Irish sang songs and cheered speeches by John Boyle O'Reilly and Conaty.[134]

The clergy, politicians, and the Irish middle class in Worcester dominated this effort to back the parliamentary party. Conaty's role was again central. He organized the fund-raising campaign and spoke at all the important meetings. Irish politicians were also prominent. Of the eighteen men elected at the Mechanics Hall meeting to collect donations, more than half had or would serve in city government posts. Many of the others were prominent Irish businessmen. Thus though most of the men were Irish-born, they were hardly typical of the Irish immigrant population in Worcester. This might be expected of the leadership, but less likely was the notably high status of the Irish men and women who actually contributed to the parliamentary fund; 41.4 percent were white-collar workers and 40.4 percent were skilled artisans or craftsmen. This clearly was a very different group of Irishmen than the men from the forges and furnaces in the wire mills who had poured out their pennies for the Land League radicals five years before.[135]

As important, however, was the return of the Yankees to the Irish national-ist movement. Yankee notables packed the stage at the meeting to launch the parliamentary fund subscription and to hear O'Reilly and Conaty praise Par-nell's moderate goals and methods. Well-known Yankee Democrats and Citizens' coalition candidates and political brokers, including former Citizens' mayors Pratt and Reed and future Citizens' mayor A. B. R. Sprague, were particularly well represented. Within the next week Charles Chase, Joseph Walker, A. G. Bullock, Henry Marsh, and a host of prominent Yankees issued a call for a meeting of businessmen "to consider claims and needs of the Irish Parlia-mentary Party and the aims of the Irish National League." Conaty chaired the meeting, which included many of Worcester's wealthiest Yankees, and he gave the principal speech. The priest blamed Irish poverty on England's restrictive legislation and argued that it was British oppression that bred frustrations and ultimately agrarian violence. An Irish committee composed of Athy, Jeremiah Murphy, John F. H. Mooney, and common councillor James C. Coffey also made an appeal to the Yankee businessmen, couching their request in terms of the ideals of the American Revolution. The business leaders in turn voted a resolution that spoke of "our hearty sympathy to the people of Ireland in their efforts by peaceable methods to secure a system of Home Rule" much like that autonomy that other British colonies enjoy. Individual Yankees echoed the resolution's emphasis on "peaceable methods." Adin Thayer praised the work "by such conservative and eminently proper methods . . . tempered with thoughtfulness and moderation." Frank Goulding recalled the "wild and fierce outbreaks of misdirected violence" which alienated sympathy in past years, but he heartily approved the new effort. Other Yankees like J. O. Marble in-voked the experience of their forefathers in the Revolution in obtaining free-dom from a cruel oppressor in justifying their contributions to the Home Rule party. Many men pledged large donations to the meeting while others joined the subscription later. When the accounts of the collections were finally closed, Yankees had given over $922 or nearly 40 percent of all the money raised in Worcester for the parliamentary fund.[136]

The defeat of the Home Rule Bill in June of 1886 discouraged neither Irish nor American support for the Home Rule party. The close margin of the vote, the commitment of Gladstone and his Liberal party to home rule, and the recognition, by a substantial proportion of the British Parliament, of Irish claims to some form of autonomy for Ireland buoyed the hopes of the Irish and Irish Americans both in Ireland and America. There was "never a time when the prospect for home rule seemed to be so promising," the state National League organizer announced at the annual election of Worcester's local branch in November of 1887. Parnell, of course, had long since become a hero to the Worcester Irish, but Gladstone now won their accolades as well. The *Alumna*, for example, wrote: "A great English party is irrevocably committed to Home Rule . . . the greatest English commoner that ever led a party is at its head." Gladstone had become so popular among the Worcester Irish in this era that a local Celtic contractor named one of his apartment buildings after the English prime minister. It still stands today.[137]

On November 13, 1890, the excitement in Worcester was palpable. Thomas Power O'Connor and William O'Brien, two leaders of the Irish Nationalist party in the British Parliament, arrived at Worcester's Union Station at 3:40 in the afternoon. As most of Worcester's men were still at work, a crowd of "mostly women" greeted the two men. By the time their train pulled into the station, nearly 2,000 Irish and their sympathizers were there to greet them. They rushed at the Irish MPs, grabbing for their hands and touching their clothes as the committee escort bundled them and O'Brien's wife off to St. John's church a few blocks away. O'Brien barely had time to shout over his shoulder to the reporters as he was whisked away, but he was buoyant and confident. The next elections, in two years, would bring a great Irish victory. There was "no possible doubt of the result being in favor of home rule." That night Mechanics Hall was "crammed," packed "as thick with people as sardines in a box," to hear the two men speak. Nearly $2,000 was collected in receipts and donations in that one night. Father Conaty led off the evening by pounding away at the theme that had become the hallmark of his every nationalist oration, that Ireland's home rule fight was a mere replication of America's struggle for independence more than a hundred years before. United States Senator George Frisbie Hoar, escorted to the hall by Andrew Athy, then rose to make his address. He touched off wild cheering with his opening "Fellow citizens, brethren Americans." He then lauded the "great and noble cause" of home rule: "it is the cause of our own revolutionary fathers." O'Brien followed Hoar and was greeted by a standing ovation. O'Brien appealed not only to Irish Americans "but to all citizens of this free and glorious land." He was richly generous in his praise of Gladstone, and applause echoed through the hall each time O'Brien invoked the great English Liberal's name. T. P. O'Connor was the final speaker. The genial red-faced Irishman had spoken in Worcester before, back in 1881 just days after the British government had slapped Parnell into jail. Perhaps recalling that day and the course of events since, he was "quieter," "less fervid" than his colleague, almost wistful. "There is something bewildering and dazzling," he closed, "in the thought that the fight of seven hundred years is about to come to an end."[138]

Conclusion

Buried by the half century of religious and ethnic acrimony that followed it, the trend to accommodation among the Irish in Worcester in the 1880s and early 1890s is difficult to recapture and assess. It is difficult because there was no single movement of accommodation or a widely shared and publicly articulated vision of where it might lead. Aside from Joshua O'Leary, perhaps, few Irishmen in the Worcester of the 1880s said much about what their place in Worcester and America should be or how the city's or the country's culture or political and social structures could be altered to permit them to assume that place. Rather than a single, broad, self-conscious movement, the trend to accommodation in the 1880s and 1890s seemed a sum of many accommodations. It was rooted in the first accommodation, a political one, made necessary by the limits of Irish power and made possible by the divisions within the Yankee community. That accommodation tied Irishmen and some Yankees together in local politics and led to further cooperation outside the narrow realm of municipal government in ventures as disparate as building a hospital or raising money to free Ireland. The political ramifications of the alliance also encouraged Worcester's Irish to participate in important aspects of a common Worcester community life with their Yankee neighbors, most notably in sending their children to the city's public schools. Moreover, in this atmosphere of fragile ethnic peace and tacit harmony it was easy for young American-born and upwardly mobile Irish Americans to embrace the culture of their American home and deliberately shed ancestral customs like drinking that marked them as aliens. National or overseas movements like Catholic Liberalism or Parnell's moderate home rule nationalism were critical to these efforts. Those broad movements provided the city's Irish with the language and authority to understand, explain, and defend their accommodationist goals and actions. Nevertheless, the trend to accommodation among the Worcester Irish in the 1880s and early 1890s was no mere reflection of national or international movements. The languages of Catholic Liberalism or home rule nationalism were not fixed and Worcester's Irish often interpreted them for their own ends. The city's Irish women, for example, exploited the ambiguities of Parnell's rhetoric and actions to challenge dominance of the local nationalist movement by priests and politicians who claimed to be Parnell's representatives. Moreover, there were other broad and powerful movements in late nineteenth-century Ireland and America that had little impact on the Worcester Irish. Conservative Catholics, the Clan na Gael, and the Knights of Labor all suggested courses that Irishmen in other cities took, but Worcester's

!rish did not. National trends or movements in America or in Ireland limited how the Worcester Irish could respond to their environment, but ultimately local circumstances, particularly the structure of power relations in Worcester, determined the responses the city's Irish chose.

It is important not to overestimate the trend to accommodation among the Irish in Worcester. Few even of the young Irish temperance men who sacrificed the time-honored custom of the communal glass were willing to disavow their ancestry entire, and certainly neither they nor other Irish Americans in Worcester thought of abandoning their distinctive faith. Ethnic boundaries in Worcester in the 1880s and 1890s were blurred or deemphasized but they still existed. Perhaps if the trend to accommodation had continued, they might have eventually been rendered meaningless, but such a prospect was still distant from the Worcester of the late nineteenth century. There was a heavy burden of past antagonism between Irish and Yankee, Protestant and Catholic, and the memories of religious and ethnic warfare were still very fresh.

In the 1880s and early 1890s it thus appeared that either consciously or unconsciously many of Worcester's Irish Americans sought not so much to merge into Yankee society and culture as to create an ancestrally Irish and Catholic version of being American that would prove acceptable to their neighbors. To borrow terminology from a different context, they were groping for an *alternative* Catholic Americanism, not an *oppositional* one. The boundaries that divided them from Yankee Protestants remained, but the Irish—and many Yankees—struggled to keep them from becoming battlefields. That was changing, however, even as O'Connor spun out his dream of an independent Ireland in Worcester's Mechanics Hall on a happy evening in the autumn of 1890.

Four

Ethnic Revival

The 1890s and Early 1900s

Emboldened by a little whiskey and the delirium of a great victory, Push Brown "well known character of Southbridge Street" climbed up on a hitching post in front of the *Telegram* offices and began to address the crowd before him. It was February 19, 1901. "Wait until McKinley comes to Worcester. He ought to come and visit Senator Hoar on the 17th of March and then Mayor O'Connell could introduce him to the crowd from City Hall steps. Mayor O'Connell will close the schools on the 17th of March and St. Patrick will get some recognition from the Democracy of Worcester." The good-natured crowd jeered and hooted. Push responded by challenging to fight any one of them for five dollars. His challenge only encouraged more laughter and jeers, and the disgruntled Push finally lowered himself from his perch and limped to a park bench to rest his head still ringing from jubilation and drink. Tomorrow, the crowds would be gone and the Common would be his again: shuffling from bench to bench and haranguing startled passersby who intruded into his domain. Yet tomorrow, Philip J. O'Connell, the son of an Irish Catholic immigrant would be mayor of Worcester, the first Irish Catholic ever to hold that office. Push Brown exaggerated, but only a little; Worcester would be a different city.[1]

O'Connell's election was important not only for what would follow it, but for what preceded it as well. Few Irishmen in Worcester would have chosen Push Brown as a spokesman, but his belligerent ethnic pride aptly reflected the new attitude of his people in the 1890s and early 1900s. In those years, the temperance societies collapsed, moderate Irish nationalism disappeared, and Joshua O'Leary's Liberal Catholic newspaper, the *Messenger*, folded. Accommodation was dead, killed by a brutal depression, the influx of hostile new immigrant groups, the revival of nativism, and the end of the cross-ethnic Citizens' alliances. In the economic turbulence of the nineties, there were some hints that Irish workers might join with their working-class fellows in other groups to form aggressive unions or class parties in Worcester, but those small hints faded quickly. Ultimately, in accommodation's place a new Irish ethnic assertiveness, even belligerence, reigned, accompanied by a self-conscious revival of interest in Irish culture. Provoked by the new nativism and ethnic rivalry but also inspired by O'Connell's triumph, the Ancient Order of Hibernians, the Clan na Gael, and other like-minded Irish clubs and organizations led this new assertion of group interests and this cultural revival. Weak and ineffectual in the 1880s, the Hibernians and others flourished in a new atmosphere thick with group tension and hostility. Like Push Brown, the Worcester Irish in the 1890s and early 1900s would be quick to proclaim their pride in being Irish and even quicker to challenge suspected enemies.

The End of Accommodation

Signs of faltering in the old efforts of accommodation appeared very early in the decade of the 1890s. The conservative Nationalist movement was one of the first to suffer. Even as the Nationalist M.P.s William O'Brien and T. P. O'Connor rose to address the cheering crowds in Worcester's Mechanics Hall in November of 1890, their Home Rule party was on the verge of disintegration in Ireland. Four days after their appearance in Worcester, Captain O'Shea filed a divorce suit against his wife, Katherine "Kitty" O'Shea, exposing Charles Stewart Parnell as her paramour. William Gladstone, under pressure from England's dissenting Protestants, proclaimed that he could no longer cooperate with an Irish party headed by a public adulterer, and in the first week of December, a little over a fortnight after O'Brien and O'Connor had spoken in Worcester, the members of the Home Rule party, under pressure from Gladstone, met to vote on Parnell's leadership. Fearful of losing their chances for home rule, the majority of the party voted to depose Parnell from his post as leader. Gladstone's condemnation and the vote of the Irish party then spurred the Catholic church to repudiate Parnell as well. Ireland's "uncrowned king" refused to give in and took to the country to defend himself and regain his leadership. The Irish nationalist movement was torn apart in the ensuing year as the party and its voters broke into brawling factions. Even Parnell's death on October 6, 1891, did not heal the divisions and the Irish parliamentary party remained fractured for the rest of the decade.[2]

Worcester's Irish nationalist sympathizers were dismayed and confused by the Home Rule party's breakup. Some of the Yankees who had played such a critical role in the conservative nationalist movement were quick to condemn him as "selfish" for trying to retain his post after Gladstone had denounced him. Local Irishmen, on the other hand, were more cautious. As late as February of 1891 the *Messenger* was urging the Worcester Irish to wait and see how the divisions in the nationalist movement would be resolved, but the paper soon began despairing that the wretched Irish quarrel would never end and criticized Irish-American nationalists for trying to revive the movement in the United States while it remained splintered in Ireland.[3]

Despite the factions both at home and abroad, partisans of home rule would mount one last campaign for their goal before the issue was buried by the British Parliament. In 1892, British Liberals, allied with both factions of Irish nationalist MPs, once again gained control of the House of Commons. Both the Parnellites and the anti-Parnellite Irish party members had created organizations to raise funds and manage their agitations: The Parnellites formed the National League, and the anti-Parnellites the Irish National Federation. Despite their hatred of each other, and further squabbles within the anti-Parnellite wing, both factions unanimously backed Gladstone's new Home Rule bill in 1893.[4]

In March of 1893 while the bill was making its way slowly through Parliament the Irish in Worcester began to mobilize in support of it. C. O'Connell Galvin, a young Irish-born reporter for the *Spy*, initiated the effort upon the request of the leaders of the Irish National Federation in Boston. At a meeting of the Catholic Institute in St. John's parish, "representative" Irish Americans voted to create a branch of the federation in Worcester. The leaders were the same men who had guided the conservative nationalist movement in Parnell's heyday: Andrew Athy, the alderman, was president and Father Thomas J. Conaty was treasurer. The infant organization issued an appeal for funds to back this "final struggle for Irish national autonomy which under Mr. Gladstone's superb advocacy is now almost on the threshold of victory," and held a general meeting on April 3, 1893, that brought out about 1,500 people including a number of sympathetic Yankees. Conaty gave the principal speech. Five hundred dollars was raised largely from the same groups, Yankees and white-collar and skilled blue-collar Irishmen, who had supported Parnell's Irish Parliamentary party in 1886. Indeed, the entire movement was a revival of the conservative nationalists of the 1880s.[5]

It would not last, however. The House of Commons passed the new Home Rule bill by a small margin but the Lords defeated it overwhelmingly, and the

Liberals refused to give up their control of Parliament over the issue. Gladstone retired and home rule was dead for nearly another twenty years. After the defeat of the Home Rule bill and the local social and political revolutions which fundamentally transformed Worcester's Irish community in the middle and late 1890s, moderate or conservative home rule nationalism would not reappear in Worcester until the early twentieth century. Even then it would never regain the strength it had had among the Worcester Irish in the 1880s.

Moderate nationalism, embodied in the home rule movement was but one of the efforts of accommodation in the 1880s that fell victim to the tumult and passions of the 1890s. Worcester's Irish temperance movement also collapsed in those years. In 1894, the secretary of the Springfield Diocesan Catholic Total Abstinence Union (Worcester's temperance associations were affiliated with the union) lamented that "perhaps at no time in our history has the union suffered as it has during the past ten months." By the following year, three of Worcester's most prominent Irish temperance societies had disappeared, including the largest one, the St. John's Temperance and Literary Guild.[6]

Joshua O'Leary's *Messenger,* the tribune of Catholic Liberalism in Worcester and the leading advocate of accommodation among the city's Irish, became another accommodationist casualty of the nineties, when it folded in 1896. O'Leary began a new newspaper in March of 1898 dedicated even more explicitly to his old causes. In the first issue of his new paper he argued that "the good sense and enlightened conscience of our non-Catholic fellow citizens have rendered futile all attempts to seriously disturb the amicable relations that have so long existed between the Catholic and non-Catholic peoples of Worcester." He thus called his new paper the *Recorder* because Worcester's Catholics needed no "defender of a cause" but merely "a recorder of events." O'Leary pledged to "cordially" cooperate with all other religious denominations. Eighteen ninety-eight was not 1888, however, nor even 1892, and after barely limping into 1899 the *Recorder* ceased publication. There would be little room in the ethnically and religiously charged 1890s for a happy recorder of amicable relations between Catholics and Protestants in Worcester.[7]

Catholic Liberalism, like conservative nationalism, was a victim—at least in part—of political struggles occurring far from home. While Ireland seethed with internecine conflict that doomed the conservative nationalist movement in America as well as at home, the Vatican began to move against the Liberal movement in the Catholic church. In 1892 Catholic Liberals had grown so powerful that it appeared that they might reverse the American church's commitment to the creation of a separate school system. By the middle of 1893, however, the pope, perhaps growing skeptical of America's usefulness to

Vatican political aims or disappointed by the revival of Protestant hostility to the church in the United States, or simply fearful that the Liberals had become too bold and powerful in Europe as well as America, began to rein them in. Over the next two years the Vatican reaffirmed the Baltimore Council's mandate to establish a separate Catholic school system, issued a decree prohibiting Catholic membership in non-Catholic fraternal orders—the Odd Fellows, Sons of Temperance, and Knights of Pythias—and criticized Catholic participation in multi-faith conferences such as the World Parliament of Religions held in 1893 at the Columbian Exposition in Chicago. At the end of the decade in 1899, Leo XIII issued an encyclical which condemned an "Americanist" heresy. While vaguely worded, the encyclical seemed a clear warning to the Liberals of America to return to Catholic orthodoxy and refrain from further efforts to mold their church to American culture or to reconcile their differences with the American Protestant majority.[8]

The Worcester Irish were fully aware of the Vatican's crackdown on the Liberals. Joshua O'Leary's *Messenger* expressed bitter disappointment when the Vatican reaffirmed its insistence on the Baltimore Council's decree of separate schools. In 1895, Worcester's priests read out from their altars the Vatican's prohibition of membership in the Knights of Pythias, Sons of Temperance, and Odd Fellows. That decree was republished several times in local Irish newspapers over the next ten years. Little mention was made in any Worcester newspaper of the pope's condemnation of Americanism in 1899. Joshua O'Leary had stubbornly defended Liberalism in his new weekly, the *Recorder*; in 1898, he branded the attack on Liberalism an assault on the "American spirit" and its grand achievements. Yet by the time the encyclical was issued the next year, the *Recorder* was defunct and Liberalism or Americanism could find no open defenders among the Worcester Irish in the face of the pope's decree. Over the next few years the term "Liberal Catholic" emerged as an epithet among the Worcester Irish. It came to stand for men or women so eager to curry social standing or favor from Protestants that they were willing to compromise the essentials of their faith. By 1905, the *Messenger* claimed that Worcester's Irish had abandoned any interest in reaching out to their non-Catholic neighbors. Indeed, the paper claimed that the city's Irish feared "the openly avowed enemy of our faith far less than he who masks his purposes under pretended liberality and friendship."[9]

The decline of interest in accommodation and acculturation clearly owed much to international events and trends such as Parnell's fall and the Vatican's crackdown on Catholic Liberalism, but there were more immediate and more important causes of that decline closer to home. One was a change in local leadership. The old leaders of the Citizens' alliance, the Catholic temperance movement, Liberal Catholicism, and the conservative nationalists moved out of the city, retired to private life, or passed away. After the *Recorder* folded, Joshua O'Leary left journalism and all but disappeared from public life. More important, the clerical leaders of temperance and Liberalism either won higher posts outside the city or faded into old age. John J. McCoy left the city as early as 1886 to become a pastor in a rural Worcester County parish. He would return, but not until 1905. Conaty left in 1896 to become rector of the Catholic University of America, toasted in his farewell by both Protestants and Catholics alike. John Power, always frail, declined in vigor in the late 1890s and died in 1902. The Irish leaders of the Citizens' coalition also passed away. Major McCafferty died in 1885. Andrew Athy lived on until 1898. His funeral that year testified to his power and popularity. It was a major public event as thousands of mourners trailed the cortege winding its way through the city.[10]

It was not so much the passing of these men, however, as the passing of the circumstances and conditions that had encouraged them to pursue accommodation that made the 1890s so different from the 1880s for the Irish in Worcester. One of those conditions was the catastrophic downturn in the city's and the nation's economy in 1893 that broke the uneven but resilient prosperity the local economy had enjoyed since the early 1880s. The depression might have catalyzed class conflict in Worcester as it did in many other cities. Yet despite dramatic change in the organization of both Worcester's business community and labor movement in the 1890s, such class divisions did not emerge in the city. Rather the depression seemed to merely exacerbate ethnic tensions in Worcester that were already on the rise. One reason the city's climate of ethnic relations worsened for the Irish in the 1890s was the emergence of new immigrant groups, the French Canadians, the Swedes, and the British, as significant elements in Worcester's social, economic, and political life. As the three groups sought to secure housing, jobs, cultural autonomy, and political power, they all came into conflict with their Irish neighbors. Yet more important for the Irish were the changes that occurred in their relations with their Yankee neighbors. Resentments of the Irish and their independent Yankee allies reached a fever pitch among Yankee loyalists in 1893 and then exploded in the emergence of the American Protective Association (APA), the first revival of open nativism in the city since the Know-Nothings. It was not just the revival of nativism among the loyalists, however, but also the breakup of the Irish political alliance with the Yankee Republican independents in the Citizens' slates that followed the nativist crusade, and the decision of the Irish to contest for power on their own, that fundamentally

altered the nature of Yankee-Irish relations in Worcester. It was these changes—
the collapse of old arrangements that had smothered ethnic tension and
blurred ethnic boundaries and linked the Irish to members of the Yankee
elite, and the eruption of seething, turbulent ethnic rivalry and competition—that doomed the old accommodation. And it was these changes, too,
that spurred an ethnocentric revival among the Irish: the rebirth of the AOH,
Irish county organizations, physical-force nationalist societies like the Clan
na Gael, and other clubs all committed to the encouragement of group solidarity, aggressive assertion of ethnic interests, and self-conscious preservation of old country ways.

Depression and a New Economy for Businessmen and Workers

Throughout the late nineteenth century many of Worcester's industries rode
their own cycles of boom and bust, but in 1893 the depression brought nearly
all of them down. Even Worcester's most promising and resilient industries
such as machinery manufacture or wire-making were leveled by this economic
disaster. On one day in August of 1893, for example, three of the city's strongest
metalworking and machinery companies shut down their machines and barred
their doors: Prentice Brothers, makers of heavy drills; the Curtis Machine
Shop; and the Harrington and Richardson firearms manufacturer. The great
Washburn Moen wire manufacturing plants also closed that summer. By the
end of August, the *Telegram* estimated that Worcester's "great army of unemployed" had swelled to 10,000 workers. The State Bureau of Labor Statistics fixed the number of unemployed in Worcester at 9,000, or an astounding
41 percent of the city's work force by January of 1894.[11]

The human costs of this catastrophe were, of course, enormous. In the initial shock following the first mill closings and layoffs in the summer of 1893,
men drifted aimlessly. Hundreds gathered on the city Common in the very
center of Worcester because they had no place else to go. "Droves" of wireworkers, lunchpails in hand, appeared before the locked gates of the Washburn Moen Wire Company plants, hoping that the gates would miraculously
open so that they could work again. As forlorn as it seemed, that was, perhaps, still their best hope, for there was little help available for them and their
families from government relief and private charities. In August of 1893, the
Worcester Telegram reported a "flood of applications" for relief pouring into
the city clerk's office, but the office distributed only a few dollars in aid. Local
charitable organizations attempted to fill the new need, but in the end their
contributions too were meager. In the midst of the crisis, a "Committee of

Nine," formed from among the city's most prominent citizens, including Rev. Thomas J. Conaty, initiated a major fund-raising drive for local charity. The committee, however, raised and distributed only $8,000, or less than one dollar for every unemployed worker in the city.[12]

The depression would have important effects on life in Worcester, but it was a symptom of change as well as a cause. It reflected a transformation of Worcester's economic life, specifically the further integration of local industry into the national economy. More and more manufacturers in Worcester were making goods for a broad national or even international market and were reorganizing their structures, expanding their plants, and joining together with other companies to gain a competitive edge in this vastly expanded field of competition. Worcester's labor movement was transformed in this new environment too. The feeble Knights of Labor were swept away and more durable, feistier trade locals took their place. Socialist and workingmen's political organizations were spawned by the depression's havoc as well. But despite the depression and all these fundamental changes, the unions and the socialists would remain weak in Worcester; competition and conflict would be fought out on ethnic and religious, not class, lines in the city during this tumultuous decade.

In the 1880s and early 1890s there was a noticeable trend towards restructuring and plant expansion among Worcester's manufacturers. Most Worcester firms remained small through the 1890s, but Worcester industry began to "shake out" in the 1880s and 1890s; the average number of workers and capitalization in machinery companies nearly doubled between 1875 and 1895. Companies began to break out from the pack, incorporate, expand their operations, buy new equipment, and move out of cramped quarters in the city's downtown to build new modern factories in open spaces with easy, often direct, access to railroads two or three miles north or south of the city center.[13]

The principal cause of this plant expansion and relocation was the accelerating integration of Worcester's industry into national or even international markets. Some Worcester firms like Washburn Moen Wire Manufacturers had already been involved in national and international networks for years. But smaller companies becoming big, or hoping to become big, began to participate in the late 1880s and 1890s. Graton and Knight beltmakers, for example, opened their first branch store in Chicago in 1893 and over the next three years started four other stores in different parts of the country. To keep up with this expanding demand, the company built a new factory in 1893. The trend to integration of the economy had an especially powerful effect on the machinery manufacturing industry in Worcester. In 1890, for example,

Prentice Brothers and F. E. Reed, machinery makers, both began to develop "a large foreign business" that "materially aided both concerns." Prentice Brothers built a new factory with new equipment in 1895; F. E. Reed enlarged their works in 1888, 1889, and 1890.[14]

These changes not only provoked expansion of individual firms in Worcester they also spurred increased collaboration among all of the city's businesses. In the 1880s, the business community had been split, so split, in fact, that no organization spoke for the political interests of business in the 1880s. The Board of Trade had been chartered in 1875 and prospered for a few years, but it lapsed into inactivity after 1879. In the summer of 1891, a group of businessmen, eager to create a new business organization, were surprised to discover that the charter of the old one was "still extant," and revived the board.[15]

Manufacturers, especially the larger ones engaged in national or even international trade, played an important role in the revived board. C. Henry Hutchins, president of the Knowles Loom Manufacturing Company was the board's first president, and Philip Moen of Washburn and Moen, and A. M. Stone, a major boot manufacturer, were vice presidents. In 1893, half the board of directors were manufacturers, including F. E. Reed and Edwin Curtis, both machinery manufacturers, and James Logan of Logan, Swift and Brigham Envelope Manufacturers. Manufacturers seemed to sense that they needed every possible advantage to compete in a broader market and began to see that competition as not simply firm against firm but city against city. The board thus lobbied for a whole series of services to improve foreign and national trade, like better railroad connections, lower freight rates, express free delivery, and 24-hour telegraph service for Worcester. The board was also interested in reforming city government and fostering municipal improvements. Manufacturers needed an extension of city services to new plants and looked to the city government to help lower some of their costs such as water rates. The board, however, also led the fight for a new charter in 1893 and more broad-based municipal improvements like repaved streets because its members believed a bigger, better Worcester would help its manufacturers to compete in the new national, even international economy.[16]

Retail or wholesale merchants, bankers, and land developers, for their part, began to better appreciate the need for united action as well. They had begun to recognize that in the rapidly consolidating economy of the late 1890s and early 1900s, local factories might be closed down or uprooted by distant absentee owners and devastate the local economy unless Worcester created a competitive environment. As the Board of Trade argued in 1897: "Worcester is bound to grow, but if the capitalists should become convinced that through encouraging manufacturing business they were enhancing the value of their own property," it would grow more quickly. The "capitalists," and merchants, however, also had their own reasons for concerted action in building up Worcester. The extension and electrification of the streetcar lines in the 1890s gave the city's downtown a new, modern look; new large department stores such as Sherer's, Denholm and McKay, and Barnard and Sumner and Putnam appeared on downtown city streets by the 1890s. Corporate headquarters and insurance companies began to locate or expand their offices downtown. In 1896, the State Mutual Company built the city's first modern office building on Main Street in the heart of downtown Worcester. Thus big downtown merchants along with other representatives of Worcester's growing downtown interests such as real estate developers and contractors, and leaders of the new utilities, such as the electric and telephone companies, joined with the manufacturers, filled out the board's leadership, and backed municipal improvements.[17]

These changes were just beginning in the 1890s. The local trend to business growth and consolidation would not really accelerate until the late 1890s or early 1900s and thus most local manufacturing firms would remain small through the early 1900s. Still the transformation of the local economy, the reorganization of companies, and the knitting together of the business community had begun, and when the transformation was completed Worcester, the town of farm-boy mechanics and small producers, would be gone forever.[18]

Workers, too, struggled to gain a foothold in the new economy, but though they were more successful in the 1890s and early 1900s than before, their efforts never crystallized into a potent, class-conscious movement. As in the country at large, the increase in labor's strength in Worcester was part and parcel of a radical transformation of the structure and ideology of the city's working-class organizations. The Knights of Labor, already feeble in Worcester, wasted away quickly in the late 1880s. Craft unions, either newly formed or suddenly revived, emerged to become the driving force of the labor movement in Worcester and throughout America.

Worcester's craft unions came into their own in the 1890s. Some had been founded long before and acquired checkered histories before finally stabilizing in the 1890s. Molders Local No. 5, for example, had been founded in 1862 but reorganized in 1890. Many of the other locals were younger, the steam and hot-water fitters and coremakers formed locals in 1891, the painters and decorators in 1887, and the street railway workers in 1893. The creation of a Central Labor Union in 1888 typified the surging strength of the trade unions in Worcester. Within a year, ten locals boasting over 1,400 members had become affiliates of the CLU. In this, the "heroic age" of the trade unions, locals in Worcester as elsewhere in America were active and aggressive. In the late 1890s the coremakers and the stonecutters both undertook important and successful strikes, and the bottlers combined a strike and a boycott of Bowler Brothers, one of the city's largest breweries, to win a closed shop.[19]

The carpenters' strike in 1890, however, was the largest and most fiercely contested effort made by the craft unions in this era, and it reflected both the new militancy and the persistent weakness of the labor movement in Worcester. After several false starts, over 800 of the city's 1,200 carpenters went out in late June. Over 200 pickets also set up lines at construction sites around the city, and they offered optimistic reports that the strike had virtually paralyzed building in Worcester.[20]

Nevertheless, there were ominous signs from the strike's very beginning that it was not proceeding as successfully as the carpenters had hoped. Despite their early militant rhetoric the carpenters had actually put off their strike several times before grudgingly agreeing to it, and as the strike unfolded they never made a clear statement of their goals. By the second week of the strike many of the union men had begun to filter back to work and together with scabs they provided contractors with more than enough workers. Officially the strike would linger on into August but it was clearly hopeless by the first week in July.[21]

There were several reasons for the carpenters' defeat, but internal ethnic and cultural conflicts were critical. In some respects the carpenters' strike seemed to reveal clearly the clash of class interests that divided middle- from working-class ethnics in Worcester. Many, perhaps most, of the contractors were Irish or French Canadian and among these were several special targets of the strikers, including McDermott Brothers, William Powers, Francis Gallagher, and George C. Reidy, as well as several French Canadians. James A. McDermott, self-educated and self-made second-generation son of a County Louth immigrant, made his feelings about unions very clear during the strike: "I shall sign no union agreement for I have nothing to do with any union as I run my business myself." Nevertheless, ethnic loyalties more often undermined the class allegiances that the strike depended on. Many of the carpenters had strong personal and ethnic links to their employers. William Powers claimed that many of his employees had worked with him for ten or twelve years and that he had helped them bring their families to America from the "old country." French Canadian workers also balked at walking off a job that was critical to their ethnic and religious community: the building of an orphanage for a band of French Canadian nuns. Finally, strikers bitterly resented scabbing by ethnic enemies. The Irish and the French, for example, were angry at the "PEI [Prince Edward Island] men and the Nova Scotians who are coming into the city to take the places vacated by the strikers."[22]

The carpenters' strike revealed that the new Worcester labor movement of the 1890s and early 1900s, if more firmly established and feistier than the labor organizations of the 1880s, was, nonetheless, still weak and limited. The carpenters were the only trade in the city willing to join the nationwide strike for the eight-hour day in the spring of 1890. Three years later when the economy plunged into depression and strikes reverberated throughout the nation, Worcester's quiet was punctuated by only a few halfhearted labor protests. Moreover, what victories the local labor movement won occurred largely on the periphery of the economy, in marginal industries like brewing or cigarmaking. The great wire mills, machine shops, and other factories at the heart of the city's industry remained unorganized or represented by unions too weak and timid to matter. In March, 1892, wiredrawers struck for the first time in two decades at the Washburn Moen North Works. But their strike was a spontaneous walkout by unorganized workers which was "amiably settled between the workmen and the corporation" within a week. Later in the decade when molders and machinists went on strike around the country, Worcester's molders and machinists remained at their jobs. In sum, labor in the 1890s had established a permanent but limited beachhead on the shore of Worcester's economy.[23]

Working-class political activity emerged somewhat later in Worcester than the new labor movement, but after the numbness from the shock of the depression wore off and yet memories of its bitter hardships remained fresh, Worcester's workers began to mobilize politically. In 1897 a delegation of the city's labor leaders, claiming to represent more than 3,000 voters, appeared at Democratic caucuses and demanded that the party nominate a labor man for alderman. They returned to the Democrats in 1903 with demands for more representation and gradually won aldermanic nominations for Jefferson Pierce, president of the state Federation of Labor, and others on the Democratic ticket. Such efforts helped make labor a political force in Worcester. It remained, however, a mere adjunct of the Democratic party and a weak one at that, for all of the Democrats' labor candidates failed to get elected.[24]

Meanwhile the Socialists had also entered Worcester's political arena. Socialists drew their new strength from two sources: recent immigrant groups like the Finns, Swedes, and British, who boasted radical traditions, and populists roused by the Bryan campaign. The *Worcester Evening Post* claimed in 1897: "In Worcester almost to a man the populists who some years ago maintained a party organization here are now identified with the . . . Socialists." That year the Socialists made a dramatic debut in Worcester's mayoral politics. Their candidate for mayor, Dr. Rostow Wood, polled 1,129 votes or nearly 12 percent of the total vote cast for mayor. As might be expected, Wood ran well on the east side in Wards Three, Four, and Five as well as some Swedish and Finnish precincts in Ward Two. Socialist candidates continued to run up substantial votes for mayor and other offices, such as alderman, over the next three years.[25]

In the early twentieth century, however, Socialist strength began to decline. Though the Socialists' vote remained strong in aldermanic elections as late as 1907, their tally for mayor began to fall off drastically in the first few years of the twentieth century.The Socialists failed in Worcester for many of the same reasons they failed in the country at large. There was no large German migration to Worcester in the mid-nineteenth century and only a small stream of Jews later, and so aside from a small group of Swedish Finns, there were few immigrants who brought radical traditions to Worcester. Union suspicions and hostility also posed a critical obstacle to Socialist growth. The Worcester labor movement had taken a decided turn to business unionism in the 1890s and, despite its ventures into politics, the limited concrete goals of business unionism remained its underlying principles. In 1899 the *Spy* thus reported that local "trade unionists and socialists have no love for each other," and in 1903 union leaders told the Democratic caucuses that they preferred to work through them, not the Socialists, who do not "mean well for the welfare of the country." Finally, the Socialists suffered from their own internal squabbles and strategic mistakes. As in the rest of the country there was not one but two Socialist parties contesting for votes in Worcester, each with a full slate of candidates. Socialists also had only themselves to blame when they nominated men for mayor such as Rostow Wood, an amiable septuagenarian who was a former prohibitionist and who, according to the *Telegram*, had a hard time deciding whether intemperance or capitalism was really at the root of workers' problems in America.[26]

It was ethnic divisions, however, as much as anything else that undermined working-class solidarity in Worcester and thus, ultimately, both the labor movement and working-class political organization in the city. Culture divided Worcester's workers: the evangelical Protestant Swedes from the Catholic Irish; the French-speaking Canadians from the English-speaking Irish or British. Yet it was not simply because of cultural difference, but because of the clash of ethnic economic and political interests that became so intense in the 1890s that working-class solidarity could never be achieved. The carpenters' strike may have revealed *intra*ethnic tension between classes but it demonstrated even more clearly the bitterness of *inter*ethnic competition that in the end helped undermine the carpenters' effort. The city's major groups of workers, the Swedes, French Canadians, Englishmen, Yankees, and Irish, all saw their interests—and potential allies for asserting or defending them—in very different ways during the 1890s. Pursuing those interests in the midst of the depression's scarcity touched off an ethnic war. This war aborted class solidarity even as it had killed liberal accommodation and compromise; aggressive advance of ethnic interests and goals became the norm in the nineties.

"The Irish Are the Worst Enemies of Our Race": The Emergence of French Canadian, Swedish, and British Rivals

Before 1880, and even through the early years of that decade, there were only two important groups in Worcester, the Irish and the Yankees. By the late 1880s, that was no longer the case, as the French Canadians and Swedes began to edge the Irish out of industries and overrun old Irish neighborhoods. In 1880 first- and second-generation Irish had been a majority in five of twenty-three enumeration districts in Worcester, but by 1900 they were a majority in only six of seventy-two districts. Similarly, the proportion of Irish foreign stock in all Irish tenement buildings (only Irish neighbors) was 70 percent in 1880, but fell to 56 percent by 1900. Still largely foreign-born and hampered by language difficulties, both the French Canadians and Swedes were slower to gain significant political power. Yet by the middle and late 1890s they, and to a lesser extent the British immigrants, had enough voters to begin to assert themselves in a local political arena heretofore dominated by Yankees and Irishmen. New immigrants might have proved a boon to the Worcester Irish (potential allies as the Irish sought to challenge Yankee power) but not in this case. All three of the new immigrant groups saw the Irish not as possible friends but as threatening enemies and acted accordingly.[27]

French Canadians may have entered Worcester as early as the eighteenth century as they and their native American allies repeatedly raided central and western Massachusetts, but the first French did not settle in the town until the 1820s and it was not until the 1840s that there were enough French in Worcester to warrant a demand for their own priest. In the 1860s, French Canadian migration to Worcester increased significantly, and a steady stream of Canadians flowed south for the next three decades. By 1900 the French Canadian population would peak at a little over 5,000. Meanwhile, a new generation of French Canadians, born in America, was growing up, and by 1910 there were over 14,000 first- and second-generation French Canadians in Worcester.[28]

This growing French Canadian presence in Worcester had significant economic consequences for the Irish. Canadians began competing with the Irish for jobs as early as the 1840s when Irish railroad contractors sought out French workers to replace their more rebellious and expensive fellow countrymen. Competition between the two groups grew far more fierce, however, as the French population increased and thousands of the former *habitants* found jobs in the skilled trades of the construction industry. In the 1880s and 1890s the French also made inroads in the leather and textile industries where they competed with Irish workers as well.[29]

Despite their relative success in finding skilled blue-collar employment, the French were, like the Irish, overwhelmingly working-class people, rooted by their needs for access to their jobs and for cheap housing to Worcester's east side. By the late 1880s there were three French Canadian neighborhoods in Worcester: one downtown west of the Island; one along the border between Main South and South Worcester in the southeastern part of Worcester; and the third up the slopes of Oak Hill, just west of the Island and south of East Worcester. By the middle of the 1890s French Canadians had built churches in two of these new neighborhoods, St. Joseph's on Oak Hill and Holy Name of Jesus near South Worcester.[30]

The French did not invade and overrun Irish districts so much as settle in the interstices between them, but the rapid growth of French neighborhoods in Worcester's tightly packed east side could not help but affect the Irish. The Irish in South Worcester felt the impact the most. There, French spillover across the neighborhood's borders helped reduce the Irish proportion of the district's population from over 50 percent to 20 percent between 1880 and 1900. In 1890 there were 60 families on Southgate Street in South Worcester, headed by men or women with Irish names, and 29 headed by French men or women; by 1904, the numbers were 56 French and 40 Irish. By the turn of the twentieth century, more than one in every eight Irish immigrant tenement households in the Island, South Worcester, East Worcester, or Main South, lived in buildings housing at least one French Canadian family. There was visible evidence of the French presence looming over Irish neighborhoods as well. All three French churches built or purchased before 1900 were almost literally within sight of an Irish church: Notre Dame across the railroad tracks from St. John's in the center of the city; St. Joseph's down the street from St. Stephen's (in the twentieth century the churches would be across the street from one another), and Holy Name a few hundred yards behind St. Peter's.[31]

These churches suggested more than the French presence on the east side; they symbolized the French commitment to maintain an ethnic culture and society separate from their coreligionists, the Irish. The three French parishes were but the most visible manifestations of a complex network of institutions, businesses, and associations that the French created to preserve their social and cultural autonomy. By the mid-1890s the French would boast three parochial schools, an orphanage, fraternal societies or clubs, and a biweekly newspaper, *L'Opinion Publique*, of not just local but regional significance.[32]

The motive behind the construction of this large subsociety was the French Canadian notion of *survivance*. Hammered out as a rough strategy for national survival in a century of life under British rule in Canada, exponents of *survivance* dictated that French Canadian culture and identity was rooted in the inextricable linkages of language, religion, and nationality. If French Canadians became so assimilated that they lost their language, then they would lose their faith as well. A curate from Worcester's French Canadian parish of St. Joseph's summarized the *survivance* doctrine in the early twentieth century: "Let us remain French if we wish to remain Catholic."[33]

Irish American bishops were often unsympathetic to French demands for separate churches and schools, and their opposition sparked battles with French Canadians in Millbury and Ware in Worcester County and in Danielson, Connecticut, just over the state line, throughout the 1880s and 1890s. Worcester's local French press just as stalwartly defended their fellow ethnics in their resistance to Irish-American assimilation. By the early 1890s many French in Worcester probably agreed with one of their leaders who declared "the Irish are the worst enemies of our race."[34]

A controversy near the end of that decade between the French in the nearby town of North Brookfield and the bishop of Springfield revealed just how intense those feelings of anti-Irish antagonism had become in Worcester's French Canadian community. The crisis began in 1896 when a group of French Canadians in North Brookfield sought to leave their old parish and form a new French-language church. When Bishop Thomas Beaven, an American native of English and Irish ancestry, refused to authorize a new parish (a refusal many French felt was couched in offensive terms) the French Canadians in North Brookfield founded their own parish and imported a priest from Canada to serve as pastor. Bishop Beaven then ordered the French to leave their new church and abjure their renegade priest. A stalemate ensued until 1900 when renewed efforts by the bishop to end the controversy prompted French Canadians in Worcester to respond. The newspaper *L'Opinion Publique* issued a call for a meeting in Worcester to discuss the North Brookfield controversy. The sympathies of those who attended the meeting were obvious from the start: "in the course of the discussion, the audience applauded and cheered each speaker who alluded to the perseverance of the North Brookfield Canadians." One of the speakers was L'Abbé Berger, pastor of the controversial French Canadian parish of North Brookfield, who revealed the underlying ethnic antagonisms which sparked the North Brookfield affair: "I count many good friends among the Irish clergy and this nation has its qualities but I say that between the Irish and the Canadians there is a natural antipathy. The characters of the two nations are irreconcilable."[35]

Religious controversies like North Brookfield both fed and fed off the growing political antagonism between the Irish and French Canadians in Worcester. Through the middle of the 1880s, the number of French Canadian voters was so small in the city that both parties could safely ignore them. By the early 1890s, however, the number of French Canadian voters had grown considerably and so had the Canadians' ambitions for political recognition. In 1893 Irish Democrats in Ward Three refused to back the French Canadian John Jandron for the Common Council. Jandron ran anyway as an independent Democrat and won by drawing votes from some French Canadian Republicans. Two years later Irish Democrats again refused to nominate Jandron for the Common Council post and alienated French Canadians not only in his ward but throughout the city. Over the next five years the Republicans nominated fifteen French Canadians for municipal offices while the Democrats put up only six. Mistreated by the Irish in local politics as well as in the church, the French thus began drifting away from the Celtic-dominated Democrats to the Yankee-led GOP over the latter half of the 1890s.[36]

While French Canadian migration to Worcester built up gradually to a climax in the 1880s, the Swedish influx to the city seemed to come almost all at once in the last two decades of the nineteenth century. The first Swede, Sven Pulson, came to Worcester in 1868, but only a handful of his countrymen followed in the economically depressed 1870s. Indeed, as late as 1880 there were only about 1,000 Swedish immigrants in the city. By 1890, however, the number had risen to 4,558 and by 1910 there were 14,347 first- and second-generation Swedes in Worcester.[37]

No other city in New England attracted so many Swedes as Worcester. Indeed, the city's Swedish population was double the size of the Swedish community in any other city in the region. Most Swedish immigrants to America passed beyond the East Coast to the rich farmlands and new cities opening in America's middle west and plains states. The anomaly of Swedish concentration in Worcester was a classic example of the importance of networks and niche-building in the immigration process. Worcester's largest company, the Washburn Moen Wire Works, had imported Swedish bar iron since its earliest years of operation, and several of its executives, including Philip L. and his son, Philip W. Moen, visited Sweden in the 1870s to negotiate sales or to study Swedish metallurgy. It does not appear that these men tried to recruit Swedish workers on these trips, but when some Swedish ironworkers drifted into Worcester after a stop in Michigan, the company eagerly snapped them up. Later it sent representatives to Castle Garden to lure more Swedish wireworkers to the city. Soon after, historians John McClymer and Charles Esthus note, "Word went out to Karlskog and Degefors [ironmaking districts in Sweden] that Washburn and Moen needed experienced iron workers and that Swedes were welcome . . . the floodgates were opened. . . . news about the city's metal industries spread into Varmland towns and villages through the network of American and Swedish congregations and their itinerant pastors. Hundreds of Swedish workers with families and friends came into the city."[38]

A second stream of Swedish migrants came from a very different part of Sweden: the pottery-making villages and towns in the region of Hoganas. This second stream had actually begun earlier than the Varmland migration— Sven Pulson was from Hoganas—but it grew more slowly. This migration, like the one drawn by the Washburn Moen Wire Works, was tied to an economic niche Swedes found in Worcester's economy. This niche was in the Norton Company, a manufacturer of vitrified abrasives, that came to rely on Swedish potters from Hoganas for its workers. As the company grew—slowly in the 1880s, more quickly in the 1890s and early 1900s—this stream of Swedish migrants became a river.[39]

Favored by Yankee millowners, Swedish workers quickly became formidable competitors for the Worcester Irish in the struggle for jobs in Worcester's factories. The Swedish flood into the wire mills was extraordinarily rapid. In 1880 there were only 762 Swedish workers in Worcester; by 1889, there were 900 Swedes in the Washburn Moen wire mills alone and the Swedish wireworkers already outnumbered the Irish working in the company's plants. Swedes did not compete with the Irish only in the wire mills, however. A number of Worcester's machinery manufacturers also sought out Swedish workers. Edgar Reed of F. E. Reed, makers of lathes, met Swedish immigrants as they arrived at Worcester's train station and signed them up on the spot for work in his shop. As the Swedes moved into Worcester's wire mills, machine shops, and foundries, Irish immigrants were crowded out. Between 1880 and 1900 the proportion of Irish immigrants in the metalworking industries actually declined from 17 percent to 12 percent. Even Irish women were not safe from the Swedish immigrant challenge. Swedish women took up domestic service positions in Worcester in far greater numbers than any other sizeable non-Irish group in the city. Like their male counterparts, they, too, often enjoyed the favor of Yankee employers over the Irish or other Catholics.[40]

The Worcester Irish chafed at the rapid economic progress of the Swedes. Some grudgingly acknowledged the superior skills of the Swedes but others contended that the Scandinavians owed their success less to their skills than to their Protestant religion and Republican politics. In 1886 James Mellen accused the Washburn Moen company of "systematically substituting Swedes for Irishmen" in its mills. Mellen suggested that the company believed the Swedes would be more docile, that the owners could "control [the Swedes] at will." Later that year the *Times* contended that "many people" in Worcester believed that the Washburn Moen company was trying to displace its Irish "papist" workers with "orthodox" Protestant employees.[41]

Favored though they might have been, Worcester's Swedes were still blue-collar workers who needed cheap housing and homes near their work, and that inevitably meant tenements in or near the city's east side. The high proportion of wireworkers among the Scandinavian newcomers virtually dictated that the first two Swedish neighborhoods would be within walking distance of the North and South Works of the Washburn Moen Wire Company. In the north, Swedish workers and their families settled along the slopes of Bell Hill in the Summer Shrewsbury Street neighborhood, set in between two heavily Irish districts, the North End and East Worcester. In the South the Scandinavians sought homes next to the sprawling South Works in a neighborhood that became known as Quinsigamond Village. This southern Scandinavian colony was a short distance south and west from the center of the Irish South Worcester neighborhood.[42]

Neither of the Swedish settlements supplanted an entire Irish neighborhood, but the influx of thousands of Scandinavian newcomers made some changes in Irish neighborhoods inevitable. Displacement of Irish families did occur on the fringes of the major Celtic neighborhoods. By 1888, streets like Thenius and Stebbins in Quinsigamond Village that once had many Irish families, were overrun by Swedes. Irishmen who remained in or near major areas of Swedish settlement began to share their tenements with the Scandinavian newcomers. In 1880 no Irish family in the census samples lived in a tenement house that included a Swedish household. By 1900, in the North End, Summer Shrewsbury Street, and South Worcester, 10 percent or more of all the Irish families lived in apartment buildings that had Swedish families above, below, or beside them. Such proximity did not encourage understanding. Turf fights by gangs of boys and young men of the two nationalities were common throughout the 1880s and early 1890s.[43]

Profound cultural differences aggravated the bitter competition between Swedes and Irish for jobs and housing. Many of Worcester's Swedes, particularly most of the families living in the southern neighborhood of Quinsigamond Village, were fervent evangelical Methodists, Baptists, or Congregationalists, who were strong supporters of prohibition and regularly voted against liquor licensing. Those sentiments clearly endeared the Swedes to Yankee manufacturers and middle-class Protestants and obviously divided the Swedes from the vast majority of their new Celtic neighbors. Indeed, Swedish newspapers in the late 1880s and early 1890s regularly reviled the Irish as "unscrupulous," "dangerous," "scoundrels," and "drunkards." Such sentiments were not confined to newspapermen. In 1907 two Swedes became so incensed by a fellow Swede who called them "Irishmen" that they killed him.[44]

Swedes and Irishmen fought in the political arena as well as through the newspapers or in the streets. The *Times* argued throughout the 1880s that the Yankee millowners were working the "religious racket" in trying to tie the newly arrived Swedes to the Republican party. The paper underestimated the political independence of the Swedes. As their political power grew through the middle of the 1890s and early 1900s the Swedes displayed a willingness to shift their votes as their ethnic interests demanded. Nevertheless, their religious sentiments and close economic relations with Worcester's Yankees drew the Swedes to the Republican party. The first Swedish Republican club appeared in 1884 and a number of others followed in the late 1880s and early 1890s. Swedes elected their first school committeeman in 1889 and first common councillor in 1893. Both were Republicans. In 1899 John G. Hagberg scored a stunning success for the Swedes by breaking the longtime Irish Democratic hold on the Ward Five, or South Worcester, seat in the state legislature.[45]

Fewer in number and less noticeable than the Swedes were immigrants from Britain and Scotland. Most Yankees, of course, were of English (if distant) origins and British immigrants had been coming to Worcester from the town's inception without causing a stir. Nevertheless, there was a noticeable increase in the British immigrant population in the 1880s. In 1885 there were but 1,703 British immigrants in the city. By 1895 their number had grown to 2,623. Many of these British newcomers were woolen workers who had come to Worcester to work in the carpet mill owned by their countryman, Matthew Whittal, in South Worcester. These workers also settled in that neighborhood, just north of the Irish settlement in that district, becoming one more group hemming in South Worcester's beleaguered Irish.[46]

Staunchly Protestant and steeped in loyalty to the Crown, the new British immigrants appear to have arrived in Worcester eager and ready to battle their hereditary Celtic enemies. British social clubs founded in the late 1880s such as the Sons of St. George gloried in Britain's worldwide triumphs. The *British American World*, a short-lived newspaper published in the 1880s, also lauded the success of Britain's imperial arms while vociferously condemning Irish efforts to dismember the Empire through home rule. Throughout the 1890s British Americans were also noticeably active in the various nativist anti-Catholic associations that rose and fell during that decade.[47]

It was not until 1898, however, that a controversy erupted that pitted Worcester's British and Irish against each other in open political conflict. The root of the controversy seemed innocuous enough: a British American proposal to donate a drinking fountain to the city to honor Queen Victoria on the occasion of her Jubilee. Irishmen in the city, however, considered the fountain nothing less than an insult to their race, a symbol of Worcester's official homage to an empire that still held their homeland in bondage. When a majority of the Worcester City Council's Committee on Streets tentatively accepted the British American Association's fountain in October of 1898, Worcester's Irish community exploded with frantic demonstrations and heated rhetoric. For the next two months the city's Irish-owned weeklies, the *Messenger* and the *Recorder*, repeatedly inveighed against the fountain, and a number of Irish associations flooded the city's Board of Aldermen and Common Council with petitions urging rejection of it.[48]

This outcry forced the city council to call a hearing on the question on November 8, 1898, a hearing the *Worcester Telegram* described as one of the "hottest" city council sessions "in a long time." A large crowd packed the council chambers to hear Edward J. McMahon, a second-generation Irish lawyer, and Rev. George W. Kent, a London-born Unitarian minister, trade ethnic insults in what was supposed to be a debate on the merits of the fountain. Kent ridiculed the "Hibernian logic" of his opponent, condemned the Irish for having made no substantial contributions of their own to the city, and sardonically alluded to Worcester's plethora of Irish saloonkeepers near the Common who dispensed less wholesome refreshments than the Fountain's innocent water. Kent's jabs were in vain, however. The aldermen, apparently fearful of the fountain controversy's effects on the December city elections, tabled the British Association's proposal. (One local political expert predicted that aldermen backing the fountain might lose as many as 1,000 votes in the east side wards.) After the election the city legislators appeared to conveniently forget about the fountain and it was never built. As late as 1906, however, the Irish newspapers in Worcester still spoke of the conflict over the fountain as a major battle in their war against their ethnic enemies.[49]

While the Irish won this battle over the fountain with the British, the controversy was revealing of how much their environment had changed from the 1880s to the 1890s. New ethnic groups had emerged in Worcester as significant economic competitors and political powers. The British were the most vocal of these groups but also the smallest and weakest; the French Canadians and Swedes were much larger and would prove more formidable rivals for the Irish in the long run. The fountain controversy also revealed that the emergence of these groups had considerably increased the level of ethnic tension in the city. The bitter shouting match in the council's chambers over the fountain was typical of a decade of sharp exchanges and conflict over ethnic issues. In this conflict, as the North Brookfield affair, the brawls with Swedish gangs, and the fountain controversy revealed, the Irish were becoming increasingly beleaguered and challenged in Worcester.[50]

"Fair Play . . . to the Descendants of the American Revolution": The Revival of Nativism in Worcester

The real key to growing Irish isolation, however, was not the rise of these new immigrants but the disruption of their relations with the city's Yankees. This was a complicated process that would develop over the entire decade, but it began with the growing power and increasing anger of the Yankee Republican loyalists leading to the revival of organized nativism and two bitterly fought city elections in 1893 and 1894.

The balance of Worcester politics had begun to turn as early as the middle of the 1880s. Yankee Republican loyalists had ridden the temperance issue to dominance of both the Republican party and the city over the latter half of the 1880s. Loyalist rule had been no *Kulturkampf*. Neither Samuel Winslow nor his successor, Francis Harrington, sought to persecute the Irish or make them the focus of a new nativist crusade. Nevertheless, their victories testified that the loyalists, bolstered by a Yankee middle class imbued with a strong spirit of evangelicalism, were aroused, well organized, and confident in the assertion of their power. Moreover, by the late 1880s and early 1890s, no-license sentiment had reached a fever pitch in Worcester. In 1889 the city voted for prohibition for only the second time in a decade, and after a razor-thin defeat in 1890 no-license swept the city again in 1891. The latter election was particularly ominous. Defections by east side Irish total abstinence men had been critical to temperance victories in 1885 and 1889, but there were no noticeable defections in east side precincts in 1891. The no-license forces won that battle by rousing the Republican wards to a prohibitionist frenzy and simply over-

whelming the east side pro-license forces. Finally, nativist suspicions of parochial education and fears for the purity of public education were rising throughout the nation and the state. The Massachusetts state legislature began a
bitter debate over those issues in 1888 and nearby Boston seethed with interethnic conflict over public and parochial schools in the late 1880s and early
1890s.[51]

Nativists in Worcester began to focus on the schools too in the late 1880s
and early 1890s and found a clear target for their mounting rage: Superintendent of Schools Albert Marble. Marble had been painfully solicitous of Irish
American interests and needs for much of his long tenure as school superintendent. In addition to affording Irish men and women a healthy share of
teaching appointments in the schools, Marble also tiptoed around culturally
sensitive issues that might offend the Irish and other Catholics. The state, for
example, ordered the public schools to teach "temperance physiology," but
Marble refused to put such a course in the schools' curriculum. He explained
in 1886: "Is the child of a saloonkeeper," he asked, "to be taught that his father
is no better than a robber or a murderer and not entitled to the respect of his
children?"[52]

Such sentiment and policies had enraged Republican loyalists for nearly a
decade but it was not until open conflict between Catholics and Protestants
emerged in Worcester's high school in 1889 that some loyalists finally took up
a crusade to depose Marble. Irish Catholics once had been virtually unknown
in the high school but by the late 1880s that was no longer true. In 1889, simmering mutual antagonism between Irish and Yankee students reached a
flash point when a contest for control of the "Eucleia," the school's debating
club, broke into public controversy. Alfred S. Roe, the principal of the school
and editor of the *Worcester Methodist*, decided that Protestant members of the
club could leave the increasingly Irish-infested Eucleia to form their own club,
the "Sumner." This did little to calm the school. In the spring a new controversy erupted when the school's seniors rejected an Irish Catholic who had
been elected editor of the school newspaper by the paper's staff. There were
other sources of tension as well. Irish Catholic students complained that the
school's teachers, mostly Protestant, offered special tutoring for Protestant
children but gave no such help to them.[53]

Marble blamed Roe for letting the controversies get out of hand and for
favoring the Protestant students. In the spring of 1889 he moved to take control of the school's extracurricular activities himself, and at the beginning of
the next school year he imposed severe restrictions on student newspapers
and clubs and issued orders barring teachers from tutoring students. Roe

was furious and submitted his resignation, effective in the next school year. The principal's resignation soon became a cause celebre prompting local temperance advocates and other Republican loyalists to rush to his support.[54]

As the Roe controversy raged, Dr. David O. Mears, the fierce evangelical pastor of Piedmont Congregational Church weighed in with his own attacks against Marble and Irish Catholic power in the local schools. In December of 1890, not long after Roe's resignation, Mears wrote a letter to the school board charging it and Superintendent Marble with discrimination against American Protestants in favor of Irish Catholics in the hiring and promotion of teachers. School teachers in Worcester had to take a rigorous standard examination to qualify for posts but then were appointed on the recommendations of individual school board members in consultation with Marble. Mears charged that one of "the brightest young ladies" in his congregation, an experienced teacher of good family, had been waiting for an appointment to the public schools for several years. He also claimed that in the last few months, fourteen women with "names not American" had been appointed while several Yankee women had been passed over.[55]

The pastor forced a series of hearings by the school committee which erupted into acrimonious debate between Charles Hildreth, former Republican loyalist mayor and a member of Mears's congregation, and Eugene Moriarty, an Irish immigrant and Democratic power on the east side. Moriarty objected to Mears and Hildreth's suggestions that some names were more American than others and that Catholic names were not American names. The committee eventually produced a careful report demonstrating the large number of Yankee women teaching in the public schools. Mears was not satisfied; he accused Marble of manipulating the committee and he scoffed at the statistics. Nevertheless, the conflict subsided in the winter of 1891.[56]

The high school controversy and Mears's harsh rhetoric reflected the increasingly strident and overt hostility creeping into the politics of Worcester's Republican loyalists. That hostility continued to build through the early 1890s. Beginning in 1890, middle-class Republicans started to mobilize support at the Republican ward caucuses to oust Marble. In that first year of their campaign the anti-Marble school committee candidates picked up over 2,600 votes. Over the next three years the anti-Marble sentiment grew steadily in the Republican party.[57]

In 1893, the assault on Marble came to a head. Still reeling from the summer's first brutal shocks of depression, Worcester became embroiled in a harsh political campaign rife with bitter invective and ethnic baiting. A new openly anti-Catholic newspaper, the *American*, spearheaded the nativist assault on Marble.

The critical issue, the paper argued, was who should control the schools: "Our schools are American, they are Protestant"; "papacy," the *American* stated, "is the avowed enemy of our school system." Throughout the city, Republicans fought in their caucuses over nominees for school board positions; the anti-Marble GOP loyalists were almost uniformly successful. Pro-Marble forces put up a number of independent candidates in the general election, but they too went down to defeat. The long crusade to oust the superintendent had come to a successful conclusion.[58]

Control of the schools was not the only ethnically divisive issue on the ballot in December of 1893; voters also passed on changes on the city charter which promised to drastically alter the balance of power in Worcester politics. Debate over municipal reform had been burning for several years, prompted, in part, by leaders of the newly revived Board of Trade. Mayor Marsh, a long-time friend of the Irish, with support from the city's only Irish alderman, Francis Plunkett, as well as the city's independent Republican, created a charter commission to suggest the necessary reforms. The commission recommended increasing the power of the mayor, reducing the powers of the board of aldermen, and changing the method of electing the aldermen. At the time, each ward nominated candidates for the board but the nominees were elected citywide. The new proposal would eliminate the nominations by ward but mandated that voters could vote for only six of the nine candidates, virtually insuring three seats on the board for the minority party. Democrats who had sometimes been able to elect only one or two aldermen under the old system were, of course, jubilant. Their independent Republican allies also stood to gain from the charter through the elimination of nominations by the troublesome ward caucuses that they had always had difficulty controlling. Republican loyalists, however, still held a majority in both the Board of Aldermen and Common Council and killed the charter commission's recommendations and the minority representation proposal. In March of 1893 charter reform seemed dead in Worcester.[59]

Charter reformers, however, had not given up. They bypassed the city government and petitioned the state legislature to place some of the charter reform measures on the ballot at the municipal election in December. Stephen Salisbury and Irish Democratic legislators were prominent in that effort. By June the legislature had agreed to force a referendum on the charter changes increasing the mayor's power and providing minority representation (a change in the school committee which neither the Irish nor the GOP loyalists wanted was dropped). The nativist *American* and the Republican partisan *Telegram* opposed the charter changes; the Republican independent *Spy* and the *Messenger* supported them. The *American* fulminated against the new method for electing aldermen: a "bare faced" effort to increase Irish power and give "undue representation and therefore control of our civic affairs to those decidedly and now openly opposed to institutions distinctly American." The city voted on the charter question in the December elections, and, despite virulent opposition, charter proponents won in a very tight vote.[60]

The nativists continued to wage bitter war on Worcester's Catholics and Liberal Republicans through 1895. In 1894, the nativists sharply contested the nominations of Henry Marsh for mayor and Stephen Salisbury for state senator and lost a second fight over the charter by a mere 29 votes. By 1895, the *American* had disappeared but religious and ethnic prejudice figured prominently in the campaign to win municipal suffrage for women that year. Senator Hoar, a firm and fast friend of the Irish and religious toleration, was also a stalwart supporter of suffrage, but the local suffrage movement in Worcester had a distinct nativist tinge. Both David Mears and Alfred S. Roe, the central figure in the high school controversy, played prominent roles in Worcester's branch of the Woman's Suffrage League. Indeed, when Roe went to the legislature in 1892 he became the leader of the woman's suffrage forces. The *American,* before its disappearance in 1884, also enthusiastically boomed woman's suffrage. During the effort to win a referendum on granting women the suffrage in municipal elections in 1895, the nativist influence on the suffrage movement grew so strong that Hoar was booed off the platform at one suffrage rally. The referendum failed in Worcester as well as statewide, but predictably the vote correlated closely with the votes against the new charter. One of the two precincts where the suffrage referendum carried, Ward Seven, precinct 3, had long been among the strongest nativist bastions in the city.[61]

The nativist campaigns were new battles in an old war between the Republican Yankee loyalists and the Irish and their independent Republican allies. Votes in the school board elections and the charter fight in 1893 followed the same pattern as the battles of the 1880s: the strongest opposition to Marble and the charter came from the southern wards—Wards Six and Seven—and parts of Wards One and Two in the northeast; strongest support for the superintendent and the charter came from the Irish-dominated east side wards—Wards Three, Four, and Five—and elite sections of Wards Eight and One. The business community appeared less divided in these battles, or, at least, in the struggle over the charter. The newly revived Board of Trade, representing many manufacturers, played a leading and vigorous role in behalf of charter reform. Some small manufacturers, like Charles Hildreth and David Hale Fanning, were prominent in the anti-Marble agitation, however. Finally, the *Telegram,* the voice of the loyalists since the mid-1880s, lined up with the

American against Marble and the charter, while the *Spy*, long-time tribune of the independents, and the Irish *Messenger* supported both.

Though the battles over Marble and charter changes were largely fought along old battle lines, they also opened a new chapter in Worcester's long history of organized nativism. One of the leading organizations of this phase in nativism's history was the American Protective Association, founded in Clinton, Iowa, in 1887, which pledged its members to never vote for a Catholic, hire one when a Protestant was available, or join one in a strike. The APA was such a shadowy organization that some recent historians have disputed its importance or even its existence in many American cities during the mid-1890s. In Worcester, too, the APA appeared to be very secretive, but all of the major newspapers in the city, those favoring nativism and those opposing it, agreed that a branch of the society existed in Worcester. References in the *American* suggested that there were about 800 members of the local APA branch in October of 1893. There were other, less secretive "patriotic" societies in Worcester, however, that were also closely aligned with the nativist movement. The most prominent were the branches of the Order of the United American Mechanics. The nativist weekly, the *American,* followed the OUAM's fortunes closely and in January of 1894 boasted that the OUAM's local affiliates counted over 1,500 male and female members.[62]

Most of these men and women were from the ranks of what the *American* called the "great middle class." Rosters from councils of the OUAM reveal that over 65 percent of their members were either low white-collar or skilled blue-collar workers. Frustrated for a quarter century or more by the indifference or hostility of the wealthy of their own religious and ethnic group they nursed a fiercely bitter resentment of the city's elite. Nativists were particularly angry at the "rich and *soi disant* educated" who sent their children to private schools and, therefore, were quite willing to satisfy Irish claims to the possible detriment of the only schools available to the "great" middle class. In opposing the renomination of Stephen Salisbury for the State Senate, the *American* argued: "There are questions that are embedded in the lives of the common people far deeper than any millionaire can fathom. The working people are the ones who are most in need and who is better qualified than one of their own men who has lived and labored among them?" Salisbury, the paper asserted, was a member of the "aristocratic class . . . his education and association have always kept him aloof from the working man."[63]

Yet, as such sentiments suggest, if the middle- and working-class nativists felt deserted by members of the elite, they also felt frighteningly vulnerable to being elbowed aside by immigrants and their children in the competition for jobs, status, and power. It was no coincidence that the opening skirmishes of the rising crusade focused not only on cultural issues of drinking, but on Irish threats to Yankee control of prestigious organizations in the high school and more nakedly on the hiring of Yankee women and men as teachers in the schools. The onset of the depression in 1893 only exacerbated these fears of competition for jobs or status. In 1894, a prominent local leader of the OUAM, whose membership included hundreds of blue-collar workers, cried out against the "debased foreign labor" which is "crowding the country." That same year the *American* called for the establishment of a trade school in Worcester that would be restricted to "native stock children" to preserve the precarious status of blue-collar Yankee craftsmen.[64]

Not only their workplaces but their neighborhoods, too, were increasingly vulnerable to foreign incursions. Middle-class Yankees living in Main South and Chandler May in Wards Six and Seven and the southern parts of Ward Eight witnessed slow but frightening ethnic transformations of their neighborhoods in the 1890s. Though the Irishmen who moved into Main South and Chandler May tended to be more prosperous than the Irish they left behind on the east side, identification in the nativist press of foreigners and Catholics with crime and drunkenness was so complete that frightened Yankees undoubtedly overlooked the eager respectability of the newly mobile Irish. Precincts in southwestern neighborhoods thus delivered the strongest votes against Marble. Neighborhood notables, including the principal of Chandler Street School and ministers David O. Mears, Dr. A. Z. Conrad, and Thomas Atkinson, were also among the most important leaders of the nativist agitation.[65]

That most of the nativists were Yankees should be no surprise, but the attempt to redefine and assert that identity was critical to the movement. In some respects, the new nativism of the 1890s was an attempt by some native-stock Protestants to forge a Yankee ethnic group to counter the seemingly well organized Catholic ethnics. In April of 1893, the *American* asked: "Why is it that Americans do not stand by each other? All can see the foreign element unite to attain some particular end and win, while Americans are always . . . divided into factions."[66]

To clearly work out the boundaries of this new group and provide it with a distinct cultural identity, the nativists revived or invented customs or symbols from a hallowed, rural Yankee past. Nativist organizations sponsored "New Hampshire and Vermont suppers" featuring staples of Yankee cuisine such as buckwheat pancakes and hulled corn, just as the clubs of northern New England migrants—the Sons of Maine, New Hampshire, and Vermont—had done in the 1870s and 1880s. Yet the celebration of Yankee culture by nativists in 1893 was no mere sentimental indulgence by recent emigrés; it was an explicit and self-conscious effort to forge the symbols of a new, urban, Yankee ethnicity. The *American* argued in 1894 that if the Irish should have their shamrocks and the French their fleur de lis, then why should not the Yankees proudly display the "buff and blue" of their revolutionary ancestors and "why should not the Yankee have his day, April 19th, as the Irishman, the Scotchman, Welshman and the French have theirs?"[67]

Yet despite the nativist movement's deliberate cultivation of Yankee ethnicity, it did approve of some of the newcomers arriving in Worcester from Europe or even Asia. Though the *American* seemed particularly enthusiastic about the Anglo-Saxon affinity of native-stock Americans and British immigrants, it also warmly complimented the Swedes and even the city's recently arrived Armenian immigrants.[68]

The key was that many of the Armenians and all of the Swedes were Protestants, and ultimately it was Catholics, not immigrants, whom the nativists feared. "Ecclesiastical tyranny" embodied in the Catholic church had become an increasingly dangerous threat in recent years, the *American* argued, because "Catholics vote as a unit under the direction of a foreign episcopate." "The time has come," the *American* asserted in October of 1893, "when Americans will have to do something besides suck their thumbs and let the Roman Catholics have their way." There were, then, clear and close links between the evangelical churches and the nativist crusade. Revivals held in several of the evangelical churches in nativism's Main South and Chandler May strongholds in Wards Six and Seven helped stiffen the religious resolve of the anti-Marble forces in the summer and fall of 1893. Many of the leaders of those churches, including Dr. A. Z. Conrad of Old South, were contributing editors to the *American* and were listed prominently on the masthead. The paper, not surprisingly, also devoted substantial attention to the activities of the city's evangelical churches. Indeed, the *American*'s coverage of religion was so comprehensive and enthusiastic that some of its own readers complained that it was too "churchy."[69]

There were many reasons for this revival of nativism in Worcester. Over the course of the late 1880s and early 1890s the Republican party in the state and the nation at large had reacted to growing Democratic strength by playing upon cultural issues such as schools in order to tighten party discipline and mobilize the party faithful. A state and national environment of partisan rivalry, ethnic tension, and cultural conflict thus helped nurture the new nativism.[70]

Whatever the broader environment, however, it was the local present and future threat of Irish and other Catholics to the largely middle- and working-class Yankee Republican loyalists that inspired the city's new nativist crusade.

The large and increasing numbers of Catholic immigrants and their children seemed to spell inevitable doom for Yankee control of the politics of their city. Not only nativist doomsayers, but Irish Catholics and their independent Republican allies expected the Catholic triumph to be inevitable. (Some Yankee independents argued for the charter changes giving the Democrats three seats on the Board of Aldermen as a generous concession that might be reciprocated *when*—not if—the Irish and the Democrats ruled Worcester.) Yet it was not the vaguely ominous, distant threat of Catholic power that provoked local Yankees so much as the more specific and immediate threat that a new American-born Irish and Catholic generation posed to strongholds of Yankee middle-class interests: the city's southern Yankee neighborhoods; skilled blue-collar and white-collar jobs, such as clerks, bookkeepers, and schoolteachers; and native-stock domination and control of Worcester's high school, the city's principal mechanism for gaining, holding, or improving economic and social status. That some members of the Yankee elite, themselves invulnerable by wealth from this threat, had betrayed their religious and ethnic fellows and abetted the Irish assault through favoritism in the city schools and manipulation of the city charter made the Celtic challenge all the more maddening to middle-class nativists. The frustrations of competition were thus growing throughout the late 1880s and 1890s. With the onset of the depression in 1893 they became even more intense and plunged the city into open ethnic warfare for nearly two years.[71]

Washed Away in a Heavy Rain: The End of the Citizens' Alliance

Even given its powerful and long-term effects on the Irish community, the reappearance of organized nativism was only one, and perhaps not even the most important, change in Worcester politics in the 1890s to affect the city or its Irish residents. During that tumultuous decade, the Citizens' Alliance revived, enjoyed brief, spectacular success, then disappeared forever from Worcester politics. The late 1890s thus became a watershed era in the city's politics. Several diverse trends in Worcester's economic and social life and its political institutions combined to destroy the Citizens' alliances and make this a turning point in the city's political history. Some were broad and subtle. The electrification of the street railways opened up the city's peripheral areas to settlement by the Yankee middle class. This made the heretofore staunch Republican loyalists among the native-stock middle class more sympathetic to municipal improvements and thus to the wooing of the GOP's independent faction. Some changes were more specific and distinct. Changes in state laws governing the scheduling and conduct of party caucuses, particularly the Luce law of 1903, made it more difficult for Worcester's political leaders to build last-minute alliances across party lines. The two most important changes reshaping Worcester's politics in the late 1890s, however, were the transformation of the local press, and the emergence of the new ethnic groups as "players" in the local political arena.[72]

One of the most important changes affecting Worcester's politics in the 1890s and early 1900s was the rise of the partisan press and the decline of the old independent sheets in the city. By the turn of the century no paper in the city could approach the popularity of the *Telegram,* the fiercely partisan voice of the Republican middle class. Through the middle 1890s the circulation of the *Telegram* increased by 1,500 to 2,000 a year, reaching 17,000 or 18,000 by 1898—at least double and perhaps four times as large as the *Spy*'s patronage in that year. This large readership and the sharpness of the *Telegram*'s attacks on both Democrats and tepid Republicans gave the paper a fearsome reputation. One observer claimed in 1898 that the "*Telegram* has probably knocked out more powerful politicians than any other paper in the Commonwealth."[73]

As important as the *Telegram* in contributing to this new partisan atmosphere was the emergence in the late nineties of a popular and financially stable Democratic party paper, the *Worcester Post.* In 1897, Eugene Moriarty, an Irish immigrant, with financial help from Peter Conlin, a second-generation Irish saloonkeeper, bought the paper from two printers, who had run it on a shoestring. Charging only a penny and liberally indulging the public's interest in murder and melodrama, Moriarty carved out a special clientele for the paper among the "masses of the Democracy" on the city's east side. It "reaches the Irish Americans particularly," an advertiser noted in 1898, and the next year Moriarty boasted a paid and proven circulation of over 13,000. Though perhaps less unrelenting, less consistent, and less clever than Graham Christy's *Telegram,* Moriarty's *Post* was unabashedly Democratic and added a new partisan edge to the city's municipal politics.[74]

While the new partisan papers flourished, the independent dailies like the *Spy* and the *Gazette* suffered in the 1890s. By the late 1890s, advertisers asked to comment on the local papers invariably dismissed the *Spy,* the principal mainstay of the independents and the Citizens' movement, as "old," stodgy, and "conservative" with a steadily diminishing circulation. By 1903, the *Spy* seemed on it last legs, when George F. Hoar, long a friend to the local independents, wrote to his son Rockwood:

> Thirty years ago there would have been no difficulty in getting from the leading Republicans in Worcester a sufficient sum to put the *Spy* on its feet and to secure a competent editor. I suppose as newspapers are conducted now, a much larger sum would be needed and what could have been done

for 30,000 or 40,000 dollars would now require 150 or 200 thousand and that the contributors would not be likely to have any income on that for some year or two. But we certainly need a decent Republican paper in Worcester and all our business and social and political interests will suffer, if we do not have one. Is it not possible to get a few of our leading men to take the matter up?

In his reply, Rockwood, a future congressman, warned his father off such an attempt: it would not be "'feasible' to get a combination of citizens to buy any newspaper which was not now self supporting." The *Spy* folded the next year after over a century and a quarter of publication.[75]

Perhaps as important as the changes in the city's newspapers was the emergence of the French Canadians and the Swedes as major players in Worcester's political arena. By 1899 the Swedes and the French each boasted an estimated 1,800 and 1,600 voters respectively, substantial potential power in a municipal electorate that averaged about 13,250 voters up to 1900. Through the late 1890s both groups tended to align with the Republicans: the French Canadians swinging over from the Democrats after 1895; the Swedes holding fast in their GOP loyalties almost from their arrival. Members of both groups, however, sought to maximize the power of their own ethnic communities and were willing to bargain sharply with leaders of both parties to achieve their goals. The effects of their emergence on Worcester politics were complicated. The new groups did not automatically supplant Irish Democrats as potential allies for the Republican independents, because it was not clear that they would align with the elite against the Republican loyalists. The Swedes had good connections with Worcester's businessmen who were often independent Republicans, but they were fervid evangelical Protestants and rabid temperance men, and that made them sympathetic to the GOP loyalists. French Canadians might find the independents' cultural policies more amenable, but loyalists nonetheless worked hard and successfully to cultivate French Canadian voters in the late 1890s. What the advent of these new groups (as well as some much smaller ones, such as the Jews, called the "Hebrews" by the Worcester press) did mean was that the range of strategic alternatives had widened and both Republican factions could forge a coalition broad enough to win mayoral elections within the GOP without crossing partisan lines and seeking Irish Democratic allies.[76]

The potential for all these changes to revolutionize Worcester's politics was not immediately apparent in the mid-1890s. If anything, in 1895 and 1896 the city seemed to turn the clock back on its politics to the banner days of the Citizens' alliances. In those two years, Citizens' nominee Augustus B. R. Sprague, a mustachioed, venerable veteran of the Civil War won solid victories over Republican opponents in races for mayor. Sprague was recruited by what Philip W. Moen of the Washburn Moen Wire Works called the "best elements" of the city, a team of businessmen led by A. W. Parmalee, wire manufacturer, Augustus Bullock, president of State Mutual Life Assurance Company, Stephen Salisbury, and several other wealthy manufacturers and merchants. Like Citizens' candidates before him, the new candidate was a strong supporter of municipal improvements to help Worcester maintain or improve its competitive position in the new national economy. That program, his long and close association with the city's business community, and his age appeared to make him the safer choice for mayor to businessmen and voters than the two young, inexperienced, and cost-cutting Republican candidates he faced, Rufus Dodge in 1895 and Samuel Winslow in 1896. As Charles Heywood, a shoe manufacturer, stated in 1895: "the city at this time needs a strong businessman" so that it can keep its "business position" and "exploit its advantages" against competing cities and regions. With the Democrats only too happy to go along with the Sprague boom and revive the Citizens' Alliance, the alliance rolled to victories behind Sprague in 1895 and 1896 with the same strategic formula that had proved so successful in the early 1880s: big majorities on the Democratic east side topped off by enough Republican votes in the elite districts of the north and west sides. Even in 1896, after McKinley's smashing victory over Bryan in Worcester, this coalition held. In each of the Republican-dominated wards the Citizens' candidate Sprague ran anywhere from two to three times to nearly four to six times better than Bryan, while his opponent, the Republican nominee, Samuel Winslow, polled only three-fifths of McKinley's vote in Republican Wards One, Seven, and Eight. As the *Gazette* remarked: "Several thousand Republicans take delight in the Citizens' movement for local elections. They are always ready to smash the party slates and even the prestige of a great national victory would not keep them in line."[77]

As formidable as Sprague appeared in 1896, the Citizens' movement was much weaker than it seemed. The Democrats were the foundation of the Citizens' Alliance. Yet the Democrats were in disarray in 1896. Yankee Democrats in the upscale wards, a minority but a growing one during Cleveland's reign, deserted the radical party of Bryan for McKinley in droves. The *Gazette* predicted that several of these "sound money men . . . will no doubt remain in their new home of the Republican party." Perhaps more ominously for Citizens' leaders, the Democratic base on the east side also eroded. Bryan's vote in Wards Three, Four, and Five in 1896 fell by one-fifth, or nearly 700 votes, from Cleveland's in 1892, as French Canadian defections and workingmen's flirtation with the Socialists undermined the old Democratic stronghold. As the *Gazette* suggested at the beginning of the 1896 mayoral campaign, most Democrats will probably support Sprague, "but how many Democrats Worcester has, it is not easy to learn."[78]

In 1897 problems in the Sprague administration and the clever campaign of a more mature Rufus Dodge exacerbated the weaknesses in the Citizens' coalition and brought Worcester's last Citizens' mayor down. The old Democratic leader, James H. Mellen, a long-time critic of the Citizens' Alliance, worked "quietly" to undermine the Citizens' ticket. The *Gazette* reported after the election, "probably a good many of them [the Democrats] knifed their party's nominee out of friendship for James H. Mellen." The Socialists also ran well for mayor in 1897, piling up a creditable vote on the east side, a "serious loss" to Sprague. Dodge, renominated by the GOP without opposition, capitalized on Sprague's Democratic troubles by reassuring east siders that he would make no changes in the license commission or police enforcement of liquor laws. He also worked hard to attract French Canadian support.[79]

Yet Sprague did not lose the election on the east side. Sprague's vote fell there, but Dodge's east side totals also declined from Samuel Winslow's of the year before. Sprague's real problem turned out to be the Republican voters in his coalition. Middle-class Yankees, who had been moving out to new neighborhoods after the electrification of the street railways in 1893, and had benefited from Sprague's commitment to expanding city services there, were still sensitive to the costs of their transportation and services. Sprague was hurt by an investigation of the Consolidated Street Railway that accused the company of watering its stock and subsequently overcharging its customers. Dodge, a long-time nemesis of the Consolidated, could make that case against the railway better than Winslow in the previous year, since Winslow's family was intimately involved with the company. Many prominent Republican businessmen active in Sprague's previous campaigns "kept in the background this year," the *Gazette* said: some voted for Dodge and others simply stayed home. The year before, in 1896, the paper noted, there had been "fine weather" on election day, but in 1897 rain fell in "torrents" in a "howling gale." There was, the *Gazette* noted "plain evidence of apathy [among] many who desired [Sprague's] election." The Citizens' Alliance thus fizzled out with a whimper in the rain. The Republican independents, who had made it possible for decades, now abandoned the alliance with a shrug; they would rather stay home and see it founder than risk getting wet to save it.[80]

During the 1897 campaign, Rufus Dodge had worked hard to change his image and he continued that transformation over the next three years as mayor. After taking office, Dodge eventually presided over an enormous increase in expenditures for sewers, water, roads, and other improvements. Dodge also moderated his cultural policies. Once in office he held to his campaign promises not to tinker with the liquor commission or the police department's enforcement of the liquor laws. By his third campaign in 1899, Rufus Dodge, still revered by most loyalists and newly appreciated by old independents, had made himself the Republican party's indispensable man.[81]

Dodge's power within the Republican party was so great that he not only easily beat back challenges within the party caucus, he also frightened away potential Citizens' nominees. Sprague, observers claimed, feared the wrath of the *Telegram* too much to run as a Citizens' candidate again, and other potential candidates worried that the Citizens' nomination would destroy their prospects for advancement within the Republican party. The new partisanship, then, hindered the search for a Citizens' candidate.[82]

The Citizens' coalitions were gone for good, though no one knew it then. They were gone because it became easier for Republicans, loyalists or independents, to patch together winning coalitions from within their own party from among the array of newly powerful ethnic groups, and because it became harder for Republican independents to cross partisan lines because of new rules like the Luce law or the threats of partisan newspapers like the *Telegram*.

The Republican party had changed, but the end of the Citizens' Alliance owed as much to the changes in the Democratic party as to those in the GOP. In the 1880s, Irish Democrats might have accepted Dodge's brand of reasonable Republicanism as fate and waited for independents to grow restive enough to initiate another cycle of the Citizens' Alliance, but by the late 1890s the Democrats had become an Irish party led by young men largely of the second generation who were hungry for political status and power and bridled at being junior partners in a Yankee-led coalition.

Without the help of the independent Republicans, the Democrats nominated their own candidates for mayor in 1898 and 1899: James K. Churchill, a Scotch-Irish Protestant, and John Alden Thayer, a Yankee of distinguished local lineage. Both were chosen to attract Republican independents, but the strategy failed miserably. The Democrats were slaughtered both years. Their mayoral vote actually fell below totals they had amassed fifteen or even twenty years before when they had last nominated their own candidates.

On December 9, 1899, just before the Democrats suffered their second successive embarrassing defeat in Worcester's mayoral elections, second-generation Irish lawyer and former chairman of the party, John E. Sullivan, issued a blistering indictment of his party in the local press, arguing that the city's Democrats were far worse off than they had ever been before because they had become an exclusive "Irish Party." Many political observers agreed with Sullivan, and Democratic choices for aldermen or party committee posts clearly substantiated his claim. All but one of the Democratic aldermen elected between 1895 and 1899 were Irish-born or the sons of Irish immigrant parents. Party committee posts revealed the same trend as well. In 1895 nineteen of the Democratic party's forty committeemen were Irish; by 1901 that number had risen to twenty-six. Sullivan's explanation for the greening of the Democrats was that "We squeezed out the other nationalities." Sullivan exaggerated the ability of Irish Democrats, heading a minority party with few national or local patronage resources, to gain or regain the loyalty of other groups, but a number of Democrats and Republicans alike agreed with him that Irish Democrats made few efforts, except at the head of their ticket, to reach out to other ethnics. Irish Democrats seemed little troubled in the late 1890s that their party had become an Irish party, or at least not sufficiently alarmed to change the party's course.[83]

Such a strategy appears inexplicable in view of the party's dire straits at the end of the 1890s, but there were good reasons for the indifference of Irish Democrats to other groups. As Sullivan suggested, the new charter provision insuring minority representation on the Board of Aldermen was one important reason. This new system took effect in 1895 and guaranteed the Democrats three aldermanic seats no matter how small their vote. Yet Irish Democrats had almost no chance to patch together a coalition large enough to challenge Republican control of the Board of Aldermen or the Common Council. Independent Republicans might be lured away from their party's official standard-bearer in municipal elections but only for mayor, not aldermen or common councillors. There was little incentive then to try to attract other groups to the party, and, indeed, for ambitious Irishmen hungry for seats on the Board of Aldermen, there were good reasons to exclude groups whose representatives might merely complicate the fight for the few sure positions. The fights for aldermanic nominations in the Democratic party, as Sullivan lamented, thus became exclusively Irish affairs, so narrowly restricted and ethnically isolated, in fact, that the contests sometimes devolved into struggles between factions representing different counties in Ireland. The county factional infighting became so intense that even the American-born were drawn into the melee. Just before the municipal election of 1898, for example, the *Post* noted warily that James Mellen seemed intent on the "annihilation" of his Kerry and Cork enemies: "gosh blank every gosh blank Kerryman in town" summed up his attitude, the paper claimed. Charter change thus permitted the Irish to claim the Democratic party for themselves and fight over its spoils with little fear of loss, if little hope for gain.[84]

The Irish excluded others from the party not only because they could do it, but because they believed they had a right to control the party and its spoils. That claim was based on their growing electoral strength. The Swedes and French Canadians may have emerged as significant powers in the 1890s but the Irish vote was increasing, due largely to the maturing of the American-born generation. In 1880 only about 3,700 second-generation Irish were age eighteen or over. By 1900, the number had risen to approximately 9,500. Since the number of immigrants eighteen or over had remained the same, or had grown even slightly larger, to about 11,000, in 1900, the Irish vote in Worcester had clearly expanded enormously by the end of the 1890s.[85]

By that time, too, a new generation of Irish political leaders had emerged to assert their people's claim to political recognition. Indeed, the number of new, young, American-born Irishmen breaking into the front ranks of the Democratic party at this time was striking. They included, of course, Philip O'Connell himself, only 24 years old when elected a common councillor and 30 when elected mayor. There were others, however: John H. Meagher, a lawyer, chairman of the Democratic City Committee at age 27 in 1898–99 and an alderman at 31; Dr. Thomas J. Barrett, a dentist, elected alderman in 1897 at age 32; James F. Carberry, state representative at the age of 30 in 1898 and an alderman in 1899 and 1900; John Ratigan, Harvard-trained lawyer, elected school committeeman at age 28 in 1887, alderman in 1903, and candidate for Congress in 1904; and John T. Duggan, a doctor and American-born son of an Irish immigrant policeman, first elected school committeeman in 1891 at age 36, and mayor in 1905. This new generation of Irish political leaders (with a few holdovers from an earlier era, like the immigrant David F. O'Connell), buoyed by the wave of their people's growing political power and hungry for the recognition they felt they and their people deserved, would dominate Worcester's Irish politics until well into the twentieth century.[86]

At the beginning of the century the future of such men seemed limited. Despite rumors of serious factional fights in the Republican party, no one seemed to think that Philip O'Connell had any real chance to win when he was nominated for mayor in 1900. In nominating O'Connell, James F. Carberry proclaimed bravely that "it was time for the Democratic party to stand on its own feet." The *Post* declared the nomination "party suicide" and reported that the Democratic city convention received the nomination with the "stillness of a graveyard." Even O'Connell himself seemed to have little hope. He claimed "he would be satisfied if he could reduce the Republican majority and pave the way for the election of a Democratic nominee in the future."[87]

Yet, of course, he won. More accurately he won the special election in February of 1901 after the initial election of December 1900, remarkably, ended in a dead heat. His victory was not simply a milestone in the life of the Irish community; it was the beginning of a new era in Worcester's municipal politics. The Democratic vote for mayor nearly doubled. Irish voters played a critical role in O'Connell's victory. Turnout was very high in Irish districts: in heavily Celtic precincts like Ward Three, precinct one, and Ward Four, precinct two, O'Connell had one-quarter to one-third more votes than Thayer had the year before. Moreover, O'Connell's vote increased noticeably in those same precincts from the December election to the special election in February, after his fellow Irish realized that one of their own had a real chance to become mayor.[88]

Still, the O'Connell vote increased virtually everywhere in the city over the totals of the two previous Democratic mayoral candidates and over Bryan's vote in the presidential election of November 1900. Newspapers at the time pointed to the unusually intense factionalism and backbiting plaguing the Republican party as the principal reason for O'Connell's success. Several observers, even former backers of the charter change, blamed the minority representation provision that limited the GOP to six aldermen. The *Spy*, originally a backer of the new charter's aldermanic election system, came to decry it as "an apple of discord" that had led to "tricks and trades" and "treachery" in the local Republican party. Dodge's popularity in the late 1890s had kept a lid on the boiling Republican pot, but it exploded when he retired. Swedes, Main South Yankees, and French Canadians all felt that they had been slighted at one time or another in the bargaining for the GOP's six aldermen nominations during Dodge's three years as the party standard-bearer. Old independents had also simply stayed away from local politics since Sprague's loss in 1897 rather than vote for Dodge or his two Democratic opponents.[89]

Though few seemed to understand it at the time, however, O'Connell's victory was not a temporary aberration. Most observers believed the old alignments had only been temporarily thrown out of kilter by Republican fratricide. The *Spy* even held out hopes that O'Connell would abandon the Democrats and run for reelection on a Citizens' ticket in 1901. When O'Connell refused even to consider such a course, the *Spy* seemed puzzled and huffily dismissed his impudence: "Were he without his party's nomination or were he a Citizens candidate, the Republicans might openly consent to give another term," but it would be "humiliating," the paper said, for GOP independents to back a Democrat. O'Connell lost his reelection bid as well as another try for reelection in 1902, and David O'Connell was also defeated twice, in 1903 and 1904. Yet all of these elections were close, and in all of them the votes for the two O'Connells were almost double the votes for Democratic candidates, Thayer and Churchill, in 1898 and 1899. The Democratic party seemed rejuvenated, but it was only so in municipal elections, not in state or presidential contests. Philip O'Connell ran at least 192 votes ahead of the Democratic gubernatorial candidate in every ward in Worcester in 1902; David O'Connell ran 167 votes ahead of the Democratic presidential candidate, Alton B. Parker, in all but one ward, and over 300 votes ahead of Parker in six of the eight wards, two years later in 1904.[90]

Philip O'Connell's victory and the subsequent Democratic revival in municipal politics was a paradox. Many within the Irish community saw his win as an Irish triumph, a historic coming of age of Irish power. No longer would the Catholics serve as foot-soldier fodder for a Republican-led Citizens' army. It was a time, as Carberry said, for the Democratic party, and he might have said for the Irish community of Worcester, "to stand on its own feet." O'Connell's victory thus helped nourish an ethnocentric revival in the Irish community. That became clearly evident the month after his win, when he convened Worcester's St. Patrick's Day celebration at Mechanics Hall. As Philip O'Connell rose to speak that night, applause and cheers rolled over the hall. Three times he quieted the crowd; three times the assembled Irish rose again to roar their pride. A little girl appeared and walking shyly down the center aisle amidst the tumult, handed the young mayor a bouquet, curtsied, and hurried away. And the applause rained down once again. This enthusiasm was "natural," the *Telegram* noted, for "never" before in the history of "their race" had an Irishman appeared at the St. Patrick's Day celebration as the city's chief executive. Incited by the tensions of the depression, the fights with Swedes, French, British, and other ethnics, the provocations of the APA, participants in the Irish ethnic revival found in O'Connell's victory proof that the Irish were now powerful enough to rule Worcester without Protestant help.[91]

But the irony was that Philip O'Connell did not win on the strength of Irish votes alone. He and David O'Connell relied heavily on large numbers of "municipal Democrats"—disaffected Republicans or apathetic Democrats and independents who voted for the GOP or did not vote at all in presidential or state elections but came out to vote Democratic in city contests. Some of these voters may have been Irish or Catholics who had simply found no reason to vote in local elections previously but were now drawn to the polls by the two Irish candidates. Yet their large numbers in virtually every ward and precinct of the city suggest that many were not. Persistent factionalism in the Republican party undoubtedly accounted for some of this vote. (Even business leaders stepped gingerly amid the bitter feuds within the GOP in the early 1900s.) In addition to disaffected Republicans, small homeowners in both parties responding to the two Irishmen's somewhat surprising enthusiasm for budget and tax cuts probably also voted for the Democrats in municipal elections. Whoever they were, disaffected Republicans, hidden Democrats, or property-owners seeking relief from Republican extravagance, the "municipal Democrats" were still not numerous enough to guarantee a Democratic victory; the Democrats won only once in the four elections from 1900 to 1904. Philip O'Connell and later Dr. John Duggan understood the ethnic diversity and fragility of these Democratic coalitions and soft-pedaled ethnic and partisan appeals in their campaigns. Indeed, Philip O'Connell self-consciously cultivated Republican voters so much that his vote fell—some saw "treachery"—in Irish districts in 1901 and 1902 because he did not seem partisan enough to his Irish critics. The ethnic partisans of the new Irish ethnic revival, on the other hand, could see only new Irish power revealed in his victory and David O'Connell's near misses; they could not see that it depended on non-Irish voters, a weakness and dependence that would ultimately undermine their own Irish ethnic renaissance.[92]

An Ethnic Revival, an Immigrant Rising:
The Ascendancy of the Ancient Order of Hibernians

The dramatic transformation of the political, social, and economic environment of the Worcester Irish in the 1890s and 1900s provoked an equally dramatic revolution within their own community. As changes in the environment had brought the accommodationists, the temperance men, and Catholic Liberals down, so they also lifted their old enemies, the Hibernians and other ethnic militants, up. This ethnic revival emerged first during the depths of the depression and the APA crusade in the mid-1890s, gained strength as the fountain controversy erupted in the late 1890s and reached full flower as Irish Catholics rose to challenge Yankee Republicans for control of the city in the early 1900s. Instead of embracing American culture, jettisoning their old world customs and tempering their voices to reach out to Protestants, the societies that dominated the Irish community in the decade straddling the turn of the century worked hard to revive or preserve their Irish cultural heritage, foster group solidarity and pride, and firmly, even belligerently, assert the rights and interests of their people. The societies at the heart of the ethnic revival of the 1890s were the Ancient Order of Hibernians, the Clan na Gael, the Irish National Foresters, the Gaelic League and Gaelic sports clubs, and

Irish county associations such as the Sligo Club or the Thomas Francis Meagher Club (for natives of County Waterford). The growth of these clubs offers the clearest demonstration of the strength of the ethnocentric revival among the Irish in that period. Their efforts to defend or advance Irish interests or preserve and promote Irish culture provide the best concrete definition of the revival's attitudes and ideals, and their memberships, largely immigrant and blue-collar, provide the best evidence of the social backgrounds of its supporters as well. Once on the margins of Irish community life, the working-class immigrants had now moved to its center; once silent, they had now found their voice.

In the late 1880s and early 1890s the three AOH divisions in Worcester could count about 500 members. In the mid-1890s, in the midst of the APA's nativist crusade and the depression, the order began to grow again. By 1901 there were over 2,500 members of the order in Worcester. Most of those new Hibernians were members of the seven new divisions of the order founded between 1894 and 1901, the first new AOH divisions established in Worcester since 1876. Over 500 of these new Hibernians were women, members of Worcester's first ladies auxiliary, founded in the middle 1890s.[93]

Capitalizing on its growing popularity, the AOH helped secure its leadership of Worcester's Irish community by gaining a newspaper voice for its policies. In 1898, Thomas J. Kiely, an immigrant and a member of the AOH and Clan na Gael, helped bring back Joshua O'Leary's old *Messenger* which had stopped publishing two years earlier. It is unclear whether the AOH officially contributed to the paper's revival or asserted formal control over its editorial policies. Kiely did claim that the *Messenger* was the official organ of the Hibernians in Worcester. More important, however, he made the weekly a consistent and fiery advocate of the policies of both the AOH and the Clan during his eight-year tenure as the *Messenger*'s editor.[94]

The Hibernians also won new prominence in the local Irish community by constructing their own grand meeting hall during this period. The Hibernians had talked of building their own hall since at least the 1880s but did not seriously begin to raise funds for it until 1895. By Easter of 1901 the building was complete. Costing over $40,000, it was three stories high and had several meeting rooms, a hall, a library, and a social room. Nearly 7,000 people turned out to tour this "monument" to Celtic progress and power on the day it opened.[95]

The AOH was the leader of the Irish revival, but old organizations, like the Clan na Gael, and new ones, such as the Irish National Foresters, also profited from the new popularity of Irish ethnocentrism in the 1890s. Though there is little explicit evidence, the Clan had probably existed in Worcester through the 1880s. Given the strength of moderate nationalism in the city in that decade, however, it was probably weak and its members fearful to publicly advocate their cause of violent revolution in Ireland. In 1893, however, as moderate nationalism embodied in the Home Rule bill failed and the APA revived overt anti-Irish, anti-Catholic antagonism in Worcester, the Clan came out into the open for the first time as the Knights of Robert Emmet. The *Messenger* did not report any specific number of members for the Knights of Emmet, but did note that it was one of the fastest growing Irish organizations in the city at the time. In 1896 another Clan circle emerged publicly as the O'Connell Associates.[96]

The Irish National Foresters appeared much later than the Clan na Gael's revival and was a much different organization. The principal purpose of the Foresters was to provide insurance for its members, not foment revolution in Ireland. Nevertheless, the INF did actively foster Irish culture and that commitment made it very appealing to the Worcester Irish during the ethnic revival. The first branch of the society, named for Charles Stewart Parnell, did not appear until 1902, after nativist tensions, the fountain controversy, and O'Connell's election had generated considerable momentum for the ethnic renaissance. Within only three years, four more branches were organized, including two for women. By 1907, the INF would boast more than 600 members in Worcester.[97]

In addition to these societies a host of smaller clubs and groups, all reflecting the new spirit of ethnocentrism, emerged in Worcester in the 1890s and early 1900s. Among them were a branch of the Gaelic League and many Gaelic football clubs. They also included county societies, most notably the Sligo Club, established in 1899, and the Thomas F. Meagher Club, for County Waterford natives, formed that same year. County rivalries had split Worcester's Irish community into bitter factions before the Civil War but there had been no formal county clubs in the city since at least the 1870s. It was the squabbling between different Irish factions in the Democratic party that gave the county clubs new life. They were formed to mobilize supporters of opposing sides in a fight for control of the party in the late 1890s. Their existence was thus a uniquely illuminating example of how politics and the contest of power shaped conceptions of group loyalties and boundaries and structured Irish social life. Though encouraging narrow county loyalties, the clubs were very much a part of the broader ethnic revival, for they focused their members' vision on the homeland, not on America, sought to preserve or revive Irish culture, and defended or asserted Irish ethnic interests, just as the Hibernians or the Clan did.[98]

The AOH, Clan na Gael, and other new associations claimed broad and diversified constituencies within Worcester's Irish community. Leaders of the

Clan boasted in 1893 that members from all "classes" could be found in its ranks, from the laborer fresh from Ireland to the professional Irish American, born and long established in Worcester. Spokesmen for the Hibernians also claimed to find the interest of the new American-born generations "gratifying" in 1900; indeed, virtually all of the second-generation Irish politicians of the late 1890s and early 1900s (including Philip O'Connell) were members of either the AOH or the Clan na Gael, or, most often, both.[99]

Nevertheless, the few membership rosters or lists of officers of the AOH and the Clan that survive from that period suggest that these organizations actually drew their support from a very distinct segment of Worcester's Irish community: the immigrant, lower-class Irish. Through the 1890s as in the 1880s, for example, the vast majority (81 percent) of the Hibernian delegates to the Convention of United Irish Societies had been born in Ireland. Even after the Convention's demise and the AOH's popularity began to rise, immigrants continued to dominate the order's leadership. In 1899 and 1902, 68 percent and 80 percent of the officers of the AOH divisions in Worcester were Irish immigrants. More revealing, perhaps, 70.9 percent of the men who joined the new AOH branch, Division 36, between its founding in 1897 and 1902 were Irish-born. These Hibernians were not just immigrants but recent newcomers to America. Over half of the Hibernian delegates to the Convention in the 1890s had come to America since 1880 and nearly nine-tenths of the new members of Division 36 had emigrated since that date. Given their immigrant origins it is not surprising that most of these Hibernians were also blue-collar workers. Over 90 percent of the men who joined Division 36 between 1897 and 1904 and just under 90 percent of the members of Division 35 in 1906 were manual workers, and half or more from both divisions were semiskilled or unskilled manual workers at the very bottom of the economic hierarchy. Even the vast majority of the AOH's delegates to the Convention in the 1890s were blue-collar workers and over half were unskilled or semiskilled laborers. In 1902, prompted by the occasion of a state convention of the AOH in Worcester, the *Messenger* described five of the most prominent Worcester Hibernians. The five included a liquor salesman, a saloonkeeper, a grocer and wholesale liquor dealer, an insurance agent, and a factory foreman. Local politicians may have been members of the Hibernians and the other new clubs, but the AOH was led largely by neighborhood men, almost as anonymous as the rank and file they led.[100]

It seems clear that while the tumultuous events of the 1890s had discouraged the American-born and upwardly mobile advocates of accommodation, they had, conversely, roused and inspired the previously quiescent, immigrant, lower-class backers of aggressive Irish ethnocentrism. It is not surprising that recent immigrant Irishmen should be receptive to appeals to Irish ethnic solidarity and the preservation of Irish culture. Despite the Irish community's deep roots in Worcester by the end of the century, most Irish immigrants arriving in the city in the 1880s and 1890s still felt themselves exiles in a strange land far from their true homes in Ireland. And despite the many economic and educational changes occurring in Ireland over the latter half of the nineteenth century, most Irish immigrants remained peasants still anchored in an ethos of communal reciprocity and solidarity. More specifically, many of the most recent immigrants were probably from western Ireland, where traditional Irish culture was only slowly receding and many, no doubt, knew of or participated in the Land War or, its later phase, the Plan of Campaign in the 1880s, and some, perhaps, in the Gaelic Athletic Association or the Gaelic League in the 1890s, before they left for Worcester.

Yet many of those same immigrants had remained quiet and immobilized through much of the 1880s. It was not their experiences in Ireland that awakened the immigrants in the 1890s but trends and events in America, more specifically in Worcester. It was the depression, the rise of the APA, the emergence of new immigrant rivals like the Swedes, the British, and even the French, and finally their own people's drive for political recognition in the early 1900s that roused them. Irish immigrants at the bottom of the city's economic hierarchy suffered most from the competition of new foreign-born groups like the Swedes in the wire mills or the French Canadians in construction. Rooted on the east side, they also lacked the means to escape invasions of their neighborhoods by the same groups. Finally, they had few prospects for economic advancement on their own; they would move up in status or income only if the community as a whole did. Thus, if Irish Democratic candidates were usually American-born, the immigrants, nonetheless, stood to profit as much or more from their group's drive for political power as the second generation did. Besides the large number of city-laborer jobs they could aspire to, they could also gain a new sense of status from their group's newly achieved political power over their new and old enemies, a sense of importance they had little chance to gain on their own.

"The Lowly and Unfortunate, Trampled, Bleeding and Unheeded": The Irish Militants and the Triumph of Ethnic over Class Solidarity

The triumph of ethnic militancy among Irish immigrants in the 1890s was not a foregone conclusion, however. Given their poverty and the ethos of communal solidarity, they might have become willing enlistees in a labor army devoted to assertion of class, not ethnic, interests. The Hibernians, their allies, were strongly committed to the rights of the workingmen and to labor organization. AOH Gaelic football teams played matches at union labor-day celebrations, and unions met at the AOH hall. More significantly, perhaps, the AOH brought the old radical priest Edward McGlynn to Worcester to speak in 1899. After this famous cleric died, the Hibernians, particularly the Ladies Auxiliary, and the Clan na Gael, were prominent participants in a local effort, led by the former Ladies Land Leaguer, Maria Dougherty, to raise funds for a memorial to him. As the *Messenger* eulogized him, McGlynn's appeal to these groups was his love for the "lowly and unfortunate, trampled, bleeding and unheeded." Thomas Kiely, Hibernian and Clan member, also gave strong support to labor causes and even radical reform in the reborn *Messenger* during the late 1890s. Kiely inveighed repeatedly against "the gilt-edged fashionables whose hands are soft and hearts are hard." He asked why, if factory owners could band together in trusts and monopolies, laborers could not do the same. "Modern methods of offense," he concluded succinctly, "must be met with weapons just as modern." In 1899 Kiely strongly backed efforts to secure an eight-hour day for city laborers; he pointed out that the question "has a special interest for all workingmen, for a precedent established in any department of labor cannot fail to have a general influence."[101]

The most remarkable instance of the *Messenger*'s support for radical reform, however, came in 1898 when the paper printed a series of articles by a local Irish worker backing Marxist socialism. David Doyle, a bottler from the Main South neighborhood, president of the Worcester Bottlers local, and frequent socialist candidate for municipal office, was the author of the articles. In the first article, appearing on April 9, 1898, Doyle led his readers through a long Marxist analysis of history, tracing the evils of the "exploiting class" from a period of "feudal slavery" to "industrial slavery." In subsequent articles, he refuted "absurd" objections to socialism. In November of 1898, he wrapped up the series with a concluding personal piece entitled "Why I am a Socialist," attacking the "criminal imbecility" of the present capitalist system and suggesting that America begin the march to collective ownership by demanding public control of the railroads, and the gas, electric, and other utilities.[102]

In the early 1900s the AOH and the Hibernian-backed *Messenger* continued to back labor and reform, but the paper by then had decidedly abandoned its brief flirtation with socialism. Beginning in the fall election campaign of 1903 and continuing through early 1904, Kiely began a powerful assault on the socialists. He attacked the radicals on several points but curiously not on economic issues. Instead he repeatedly denounced the socialists as "purely irreligious infidels . . . whose chief doctrine is antagonism to the Catholic church." "Atheism" was the keynote of socialism, a *Messenger* headline read, and this led the socialists to advocate "free love" and destruction of the "sacred institution of marriage." "The only safeguard of the people in this country against socialism is the Catholic church," the paper argued.[103]

The *Messenger*'s emphasis on the religious sources of its opposition to socialism may obscure the more practical reasons why it and other advocates of Irish ethnocentrism abandoned their flirtation with the socialists so quickly in the early 1900s. Clearly the church's position in 1903 was little different than it had been in 1898 and 1899 when Kiely printed Doyle's defenses of socialism. Indeed in 1899, just a few months after Doyle's last column, the *Messenger* itself printed the sermon of R. S. J. Burke, former pastor of St. Stephen's, denouncing socialism in much the same language Kiely himself would use some four years later.

The difference between 1898 and 1903 was the political situation in Worcester, and, more particularly, the prospects of the Democratic party, the Irish leaders of it, and the socialists in local elections. In 1898 the socialists were not an important threat to Irish political prospects because the Irish and their Democratic party seemed doomed to perpetual minority status anyway. In 1903 that was no longer the case. Irish Democrats had a chance to win the mayoral contest and control the city. The socialists, though too weak to win many elections, were, nonetheless, dangerous because they could attract voters away from the Democrats and threaten newly won Irish political power. The *Messenger* said as much after the 1903 state elections when it claimed to draw "encouragement from . . . [the elections] especially in the reduced vote of the Socialists, whose aim is to draw from Democratic strength. The Democracy can thank the readers of the *Messenger* for this result which means the overthrow of Socialism as an important factor in Worcester campaigns."[104]

The *Messenger*'s boasting made it clear that Kiely, his fellow Hibernians, and the other participants in the Irish revival were interested primarily in the advancement of Irish ethnic interests and only secondarily in substantive reforms on behalf of a broader, ethnically plural, working class. When the two clashed the sympathy for labor inevitably gave way. A practical but telling example was the AOH's decision to hire McDermott Brothers contractors to build their new hall in 1900. McDermott had been a staunch opponent of the carpenters' strike in 1890 and enraged the local building-trades locals by frequently employing nonunion labor. The Hibernians and Kiely were first and foremost Irishmen, and a bit of doggerel verse which appeared in the first edition of the revived *Messenger* made this point clearly:

We love the Yankee nation
We'll back it against creation
But Ireland free we want to see
We're Irish all the time.[105]

Power, Culture, and Manhood: The Irish Ethnic Militant Style

"Being Irish all the time" for the Hibernians and other organizations engaged in the ethnic revival meant more than simply identifying as Irish; it meant a new, aggressive, almost belligerent attitude. It meant a vigorous and pugnacious response to nativist attacks or alleged slights and an active, sharp assertion of Irish rights and interests. The Hibernians displayed little appreciation of the temperance men's faith in individual success through individual improvement. They believed in a strategy of group solidarity and assertion that was more appealing to their immigrant members and was perhaps a more realistic means for them to achieve some advancement. In the turmoil of the 1890s, then, the new chauvinists had left accommodation far behind; they were eager now for the fight. In 1903, the *Messenger* contended: "This thing about keeping quiet about race and religion when the other guy is using it for all it's worth against Catholics is about played out."[106]

The AOH's vigorous assertion of Irish rights and interests inevitably led them into local politics. The Hibernians wanted to mobilize a militant response to the APA but the order had only just begun to grow at the end of the APA's heyday in 1893 and 1894. By the time the controversy over the fountain commemorating Queen Victoria's Jubilee broke in 1898 the Hibernians were waxing strong and were now ready for battle. According to the *Messenger,* Irish sentiment against the fountain had been running high for many months in the fall of 1898 but no member of the Celtic community or Irish organization appeared willing to step forward and publicly oppose it. On October 16, however, "at the eleventh hour," representatives of all the city's AOH divisions met and plotted a campaign against the fountain. They began by circulating a petition against the monument which they presented to the City Council later that week. They also helped to pack the council chambers for the heated debate between British and Irish spokesmen on the issue. While the Hibernians and their allies employed a variety of arguments in this campaign, it seems clear that their own motives for opposing the memorial were rooted in their Irish loyalties. They viewed this "outrage," this "desecration," simply as an insult to the Irish race, a deliberately provocative reminder of the humiliating subordination that their countrymen still endured across the sea. The

Hibernians' successful opposition to the fountain was an important milestone in their rise to leadership of the city's Irish community. For years thereafter the order triumphantly advertised its leadership in defeating the fountain as evidence of its close attention to Irish interests as well as of its bold aggressiveness and formidable power.[107]

Even as the fountain controversy raged, the Hibernians and their newspaper, the *Messenger,* also became actively involved in asserting Irish interests in the traditional activities of politics: winning elections and securing patronage. Unlike O'Leary in the old *Messenger,* who had shrunk from partisanship and ethnic appeals, Kiely's *Messenger,* from its rebirth in 1898, was a frankly Democratic paper committed to the advancement of Irish Democratic interests. In 1900, the *Messenger* was the only paper in Worcester to endorse Philip O'Connell, standing by the young Irish American even when the Irish-owned and Democratic *Post* had given him up for lost. Kiely's editorials on behalf of O'Connell were characteristically blunt and assertive. He ridiculed Republicans who suggested that their votes for O'Connell would prove their highminded liberalism: "Hasn't the Catholic an equal right to the suffrages of his fellow citizens as anyone else? If he has where does this broadminded liberal spirit come from of which we hear so much boasting? To come to the point, isn't half the population of this city Catholics and what is there to wonder at in choosing a Catholic mayor even though it is the first time it has happened." During the election, rumors flew that O'Connell had enlisted the clandestine forces of the Clan na Gael as well as the AOH, a nominally nonpartisan organization, in his campaign. The *Messenger* denied these reports but such stories were suggestive of the Hibernians' interest in his candidacy.[108]

The *Messenger*'s enthusiasm for Democratic candidates was rooted in a desire for the concrete rewards of patronage as well as the symbolic satisfactions of seeing one of their own elected mayor. Kiely of the *Messenger* understood Philip O'Connell's victory like Push Brown did, as the opening of a new era in Worcester's politics. Now Irishmen no longer had to wait for the crumbs their Yankee allies might deign to give them; they had the power and votes to claim their fair share of the spoils of the city's politics. Shortly after David O'Connell's loss in the 1903 mayoral election, the *Messenger* began an assault on Yankee discrimination in patronage appointments, hoping to rouse the Irish and other ethnics to challenge Yankee power. The paper charged that "Irish Americans are almost entirely excluded from the offices secured from political effort and its adjuncts in Worcester," a situation, the paper claimed, "unparalleled in any other city of the United States where there is anything like a similar population." The paper continued its assault for several weeks in early 1904, urging the "ostracized" ethnics to band together under Irish leadership, seize control of the city, and gain the posts they deserved. "If [they] do not unite," after this "exposure" of discrimination, Kiely wrote, "and banish from office such a regime they are deserving of no sympathy."[109]

The AOH and its chauvinist allies sought public recognition of their national heritage and old-country culture from the government as well as the concrete rewards of patronage. Leaders of the AOH, for example, conducted an investigation into the holdings of the public library in 1905 to make sure that Irish literature and history were properly represented. They also launched a much more ambitious and enduring effort to include Irish history in public school curriculums. On February 24, 1907, about 200 members of the AOH and other Irish societies met to take the "first aggressive step toward the introduction of teaching Irish history in the public schools." During the meeting, the *Telegram* reported, "the writers of the present day histories and especially those of the United States came in for considerable unfavorable comment" on their neglect or distortion of the Celtic role in the building of America. The *Messenger* also began a series of editorials and articles backing the movement, darkly reminding the city's politicians that "those requesting it [Irish history in the public schools] represent the largest single element in the population of the city."[110]

The AOH fought for Irish interests outside of the political system as well as within it. It carried on a war against businessmen who were perpetuating demeaning stereotypes of the Irish. The Worcester Hibernian divisions created a committee to visit local shopkeepers who sold confections or souvenirs insulting the Irish on St. Patrick's Day. Implicit in these visits was the threat that the order might organize a boycott of unyielding merchants.[111]

Leaders of the order, however, seemed much more concerned about stereotypes of Irish men and women on the stage. Until the late 1890s Worcester's Irish seemed to find "Irish comedians" amusing, and few if any local Irish protested the theatrical lampooning of their people. Indeed, Irish church and other societies even put on their own productions that played upon such stereotypes. In the late 1890s and early 1900s, however, Irish attitudes began to change. Reflecting the new sensitivity to prejudice and the aggressive defense of ethnic interests that were characterisitic of the local Irish revival, and inspired by the national AOH convention's attacks on the stage Irishmen, the local AOH led a vigorous campaign against the Irish comedians' excesses in Worcester. In 1902, the Worcester county convention of the AOH condemned "all the so called impersonators of the Irish character that are disgusting and degrading in nature and an insult to the Irish race." A year later, Kiely's *Messenger* urged its readers to boycott plays with Irish comedians, or form "hissing brigades" or even to bombard the "unfortunate actors" from balconies. By 1906, the AOH's county convention reported substantial progress in "stamping out" stereotypical depictions of the Irish in Worcester theaters.[112]

A commitment to preserving or reviving Irish culture was another important element in the new ethnic militant style, and the Hibernians and their allies carried that commitment beyond promoting Irish history in the schools or library. The Gaelic revival in Ireland was a critical influence on their efforts. The organization of the Gaelic Athletic Association in Ireland in the 1880s to counter the spreading allure of English sports with a revival of the Irish games of hurling and Gaelic football, and the founding of the Gaelic League in 1893 to revive the Irish language, gave them an enormous boost. GAA teams and Gaelic League branches in Worcester drew inspiration, programs, and even personnel from their counterparts in Ireland. As important, perhaps, they reflected the same kind of self-conscious effort to give cultural substance to the Irish identity that animated the movements in Ireland.[113]

Efforts to revive Irish sports in Worcester had begun as early as the 1880s, but it was not until the middle of the 1890s, however, that Gaelic sports suddenly caught on and became established in Worcester. The influence of Ireland's GAA on this upsurge was clear and direct. Many of the best players on the new Irish football teams or hurling squads, as the *Messenger* explained, had only "lately arrived" from Ireland where "they have learned the latest wrinkles of the game." The new immigrants undoubtedly improved the quality of play locally but the rapid proliferation of clubs in the city suggests that Gaelic football had developed an appeal to far more than the fifty or so GAA veterans who formed the cores of the new teams. By 1900 there were at least three private clubs playing Gaelic football in Worcester and two of the AOH divisions had also formed their own teams. These teams sought out competition throughout Massachusetts and as far south as New York. In 1898, the *Messenger* expressed concern that the rapid multiplication of clubs in the city would dilute the talent on the city's teams and prevent any one of them from being strong enough to defeat squads from other towns. In 1902, however, the city's Young Irelands won the Gaelic football championship of America in the "prettiest exhibition of Gaelic football ever played in Worcester." The growing number of clubs, the general improving quality of play, and such successes moved the *Messenger* to boldly prophesy that Gaelic football would soon "surpass the brutish football played by American colleges on this side of the ocean." Hurling, it appears, never achieved the same popularity as Gaelic football in Worcester. Nevertheless, members of the AOH and its allies did help found the city's first enduring hurling clubs, such as the Sarsfield Hurlers, as well as sponsor frequent exhibitions of the sport in the late 1890s and early 1900s.[114]

The AOH and its allies played an even more direct and explicit role in the movement to promote the Gaelic language in Worcester. Here, as in the campaign against the stage Irishman and the effort to introduce Irish history into the schools, the Hibernians took inspiration from national efforts by the AOH. In 1890 the AOH convention agreed to endow a Gaelic language chair at the new Catholic University in Washington, and in 1902 the order endorsed the Gaelic League. The AOH divisions of Worcester County passed resolutions urging study of the language at nearly every one of their conventions in the early 1900s. More concretely, the Hibernians and the Clan na Gael, seeking to bring Worcester "in line with the chief cities of the country," formed a local branch of the League in April of 1899. The few adults involved in the branch's efforts appear to have been mostly immigrants who had been fluent Gaelic speakers in Ireland, but the Worcester League did enroll over 100 young Irish Americans in its classes by April of 1900, forcing the formation of six different classes of such young "scholars." Every year, through 1904 at least, the League also put on an annual Feis or festival permitting the youngsters to demonstrate their knowledge of their ancestors' tongue. Students also, apparently, proudly carried this knowledge of their ancient tongue into their own public schools. In February of 1900, the *Messenger* noted with pride, "little" Minnie McCarthy sang "The Star Spangled Banner" in Gaelic to her eighth grade class at the Gage Street School in East Worcester.[115]

The emergence of Gaelic sports and the Gaelic language in Worcester in the late 1890s was the result of self-conscious efforts to revive or reinvent old, forgotten customs, but the AOH and its allies also sought to preserve Irish pastimes that were fresher and more familiar to Worcester's Irish. Though the Hibernians and the Irish National Foresters, for example, staged American balls and cotillions, they also often hired pipers to play jigs and reels for their picnics or dances. More controversial, perhaps, was the Hibernians' strong defense of Irish rights to drink. Many prominent Hibernians were saloonkeepers: Hugh Flynn, vice president of Division 24, founder of the Sarsfield Hurling Club, owned a saloon on lower Grafton Street on the eastern border of the Island; John J. Rogers, county president, had a barroom on Front Street in the center of the city; and Michael Horan, captain of Company B of the Hibernian Rifles, ran a tavern on Mechanic Street between downtown and East Worcester. Little wonder then that the Hibernian-backed *Messenger* steadfastly boosted the pro-license cause during the late 1890s and early 1900s. In the defense of drinking, as in the promotion of Irish history in the public schools, Worcester's Hibernians and other participants in the ethnocentric resurgence were unwilling to trim even the controversial aspects of their culture to please their Yankee neighbors.[116]

As much as the customs they sought to revive or preserve, the Hibernians seemed also to stand for values and attitudes that distinguished them subtly but distinctly from the accommodationists of the 1880s. The aggressive assertiveness and pugnaciousness of the Hibernians and their allies seemed more than just a political tactic; it appeared rooted in the Hibernians' belligerent masculinity. Kiely's *Messenger* delighted in the "physical superiority" of the Irish—"none excel the sons of the Emerald Isle in brawn"; praised blue-collar laborers and conversely derided white-collar clerks as "counterjumpers"; and had little sympathy for its predecessor's, O'Leary's, fastidious antagonism to smoking, boxing, and other masculine pleasures. The Hibernians' rowdy picnics in the 1880s and their rugged, occasionally bloody, football and hurling matches in the 1890s were renowned throughout Worcester. Sometimes the raucous behavior that the Hibernians celebrated got out of hand. In 1895, Cornelius O'Sullivan, a member of the Hibernian Guards, knocked Harry Dolan "senseless to the floor" with a right cross when Dolan tried to cut into the coat line at an Hibernian dance. Dolan later died as a result of the blow.[117]

In short, the AOH appeared to be the organized expression of a form of Irish immigrant male culture, the rowdy masculinity of the "bhoys," described by Richard Stott and others. Irish temperance men, too, were hardy athletes and rough and ready in their own way, but their earnest pursuit of respectability set them apart from the Hibernians, and the teetotalers' renunciation of alcohol was a renunciation of the "bhoys" cultural hearth, the saloon. For their part, the Hibernians' identification with the saloon was not accidental or irrelevant; as several scholars have pointed out, the saloon was integral to their communalism and definitions of masculinity. The Hibernians thus stood for more than the conscious revival or preservation of Irish culture, they embodied a distinctive notion of what it meant to be a man.[118]

And because the definition of manhood was linked to definitions of womanhood, the AOH stood for distinctive notions about what it meant to be a woman, too. Few in the Irish community were very sympathetic to public roles for women, but the AOH seemed particularly adamant in its opposition. The *Messenger* under Kiely frequently condemned suffragettes, lampooning "the Amazons who flock annually to our state houses and cast kindly or withering glances at the legislative orators as they deal gently or otherwise with their pet hobby—woman's suffrage." Though the AOH formed ladies auxiliaries in the 1890s and early 1900s, male members tightly controlled them. When the first AOH auxiliary was formed in 1894, for example, men called and chaired the meeting and told the women what "was expected" of them in the new organization.[119]

It is important not to exaggerate or misinterpret the Hibernians' opinions about women. Hibernian men and women, like most Irish Americans, continued to strongly support women's right to work and even to earn a wage equal to that of men. They praised education for women, urging Irish women to consider seriously the benefits of college. It would also be a mistake to attribute the Hibernians' attitudes to the simple influence of traditional Irish culture. The roles of women were changing rapidly in Ireland throughout the nineteenth century, and in many areas they became much more restricted after the Famine than before. The tradition the Hibernians invoked thus may have extended little further back than their own, or that of their parents' generation. That they were so virulently opposed to women's public roles may also testify much to the close links between nativism and women's suffrage in Worcester. The blending of nativism and the suffrage movement could only have stiffened the resolve of Irish ethnic militants against extension of the franchise.[120]

Nevertheless, because of nativist domination of the women's rights movement on the one hand, and the hostility of the ascendant Hibernians to expansion of women's roles on the other, Irish women had difficulty finding space to publicly advance their interests in the 1890s. Women in the Hibernians' Ladies Auxiliary were active in the nationalist agitation, passing resolutions for Irish freedom and raising money for enemies of British imperialism like the Boers, but they played no part in American politics. Hibernian men made clear that the primary role for women, even in their own organizations, was to "assist" the men, not to operate independently or vie for leadership. Hedged in on all sides, some individual Irish women nonetheless managed to carve out public roles for themselves: Doctor Mary V. O'Callaghan became involved in school reform and even sought a nomination for the school committee in the Democratic caucuses in 1896; and Maria Dougherty continued to take the lead in community-wide causes such as the McGlynn statue. Yet no Irish organization emerged in Worcester in the 1890s to offer Irish women an important visible role in the nationalist movement, as the Ladies Land League had the decade before, or to assert women's rights to a public role in American politics.[121]

"To Show Our Strength":
The Hibernians and the Celebration of St. Patrick's Day

The aggressiveness of the Hibernians and their interest in promoting Irish culture were clearly reflected in their role in the continuing controversies surrounding the Irish celebration of St. Patrick's Day in Worcester. Irish temperance men and Hibernians fought bitterly over the observance of that holiday throughout the 1880s. The Hibernians consistently voted for a parade; the temperance men as consistently voted against it (though many marched in it, nonetheless). In the mid-1890s the AOH's rise, the decline of the temperance men, and the revival of nativism intensified the conflict between the Hibernians and the teetotallers over the parade and eventually wrecked the United Irish Societies Convention. In the wake of the convention's destruction, the Hibernians took over responsibility for the parade themselves and with the help of the Irish National Foresters and some other societies staged parades nearly every year through the first decade of the twentieth century.

The first evidence of heightening tensions between the temperance men and the Hibernians came in 1894. Delegates to the UISC were very aware of the rising tide of nativism in the city that year. At their first session in January, just a month after the APA's school committee victory, D. F. Fitzgerald, president of the convention, delivered a "scathing" attack on those "modern mongrels" or "know-nothings" called the APA. He was particularly vehement in condemning the *Telegram*'s ridicule of Irish women in the recent school elections (the *Telegram* allegedly called them "Rum Biddies").[122]

Although Fitzgerald believed that the Irish community should vigorously protest such prejudice, he did not believe that it should sponsor a parade on the upcoming St. Patrick's Day. It would be "wise and patriotic to abstain," he noted, because of the economic hard times. He and others suggested holding an evening entertainment and using the money normally spent on the parade to help the poor. T. J. McAuliffe of the St. Paul's Lyceum suggested that such a policy would be "far more creditable" than staging a parade, and delegates from the St. John's Guild agreed.[123]

The Hibernian delegates adamantly rejected such notions. They argued that despite the depression, the rising popularity of nativism in the city must be countered. John Burns of Division 2 of the AOH thundered that "this is the year we should celebrate in order to show our strength." Edward J. McMahon, representing the Washington Club in one of its infrequent appearances at the convention, retorted that the parade, a show of numbers, was not necessary to show Irish power. "Our churches tell what the Catholic Irish are doing and those good Americans [presumably Liberal Protestants] what we are." James Early concluded: "None but the Ancient Order of Hibernians seemed disposed to parade this year." The final vote confirmed his observation as the Clan na Gael and all but Division 1 of the AOH supported the parade and all the temperance societies and the Washington Club opposed it. In 1894 the numbers were still with the temperance men, and no Irishman paraded in Worcester on St. Patrick's Day that year.[124]

The following year, however, temperance forces would be considerably diminished and the shifting distribution of power within the convention proved to be severely disruptive. In 1895, only a few parish temperance societies sent representatives to the convention. Some societies like the St. John's Guild had dissolved; others like the Catholic Young Men's Lyceum may have faced more pressing problems as the depression and heightening ethnic tensions cut into their memberships. Nevertheless, delegates from the Irish Catholic Benevolent Society and the Father Mathew Society took the lead in opposing the parade. In addition to the traditional temperance arguments about the parade's extravagant waste of hard-earned resources and contribution to excessive drinking, these two societies stated that their members were simply too old to march. The Hibernians were not sympathetic. They had come to the convention determined to get their way. They heatedly denounced the opponents of the parade. John Burns again led the AOH's attack, first objecting to the convention's refusal to seat delegates from the Clan na Gael and then darkly warning the Father Mathew Society and the Irish Catholic Benevolent Society that if delegates from those societies tried to elect the marshall to a parade that they had initially opposed, the Hibernians "will pull him out of the saddle in Salem Square" in downtown Worcester. Meanwhile Thomas McGourty, a "doughty captain" of the Hibernian Guards began attacking J. Frank Quinn, an old temperance man and treasurer of the convention. Their exchange of insults grew so bitter that Quinn challenged McGourty to step into the hallway where they could settle "the matter after the fashion of Corbett and Sullivan." By then the temperance men had walked out of the convention. The Hibernians, meeting by themselves a few weeks later, concluded that they were still too weak to parade alone but raised the possibility of recruiting organizations from out of town to "make up the defection of the local societies." That option did not prove practical, and though the Hibernians controlled the convention there was no parade. The convention continued to meet, however, even after St. Patrick's Day in 1895, but the wrangles continued through "prolonged and heated discussions." As Richard O'Flynn remarked sadly, "many things were said which should have not been said."[125]

Out of habit, perhaps, but with little hope, delegates gathered once again for the annual convention in January of 1896. Immediately, James Kiely of the AOH made a motion to parade on St. Patrick's Day and launched into a pointed speech "directed towards the younger men." Kiely's challenge provoked the expected response and the debate ignited again. Yet this time it seemed clear to most of the delegates that it was "useless to continue." Kiely made a motion to abandon the convention. There was a protest that the convention's end would be "a disgrace to the Irish people of Worcester," and the delegates apparently never voted on the motion. They did not have to, for the meeting on January 14, 1896, was the convention's last.[126]

Richard O'Flynn wrote the organization's epitaph in the last pages of the convention minute books. Though a sometime critic of the American-born Irish, the immigrant O'Flynn laid the blame for the convention's demise squarely on the Hibernians and their allies. The convention's disintegration began, O'Flynn stated, with the "indiscreet language at the convention in January of 1895 at which the members of the temperance societies took offense. The delegates from the latter," O'Flynn continued, "were all young men (with few exceptions), native Americans, but were ready and willing to turn out, if the unfortunate incident had not occurred."[127]

O'Flynn clearly understood the generational division and tension that had run through the convention since at least the 1880s and had climaxed in the conflict that destroyed it in 1896, but he apparently had not detected the changing balance of power in the Irish community that was the ultimate cause of the convention's demise. The convention did not disintegrate because of the Hibernians' indiscretion but because of their power. Because of the collapse of the temperance societies and their own rapid growth, the Hibernians had less need to bargain and compromise and ultimately less need for the convention itself. They proved that by organizing and running the parade themselves in 1896 and for the next seven years, enlisting only the INF and other like-minded societies to march in the procession. In 1897, for example, the AOH marched alone, but because of the recent formation of new branches they could boast a line of march almost as long as in the parade's heyday of the 1880s. About 850 Hibernians marched that year, nearly 300 of them from new divisions, such as Divisions 34 and 35, that had been organized within the last two years. Newspapers suggested that "the revival of the parade was so successful that it is doubted if it will ever be given up again, certainly not for many years." By 1907 the parade boasted nearly 600 marchers from the Irish National Foresters as well as more than a thousand Hibernians. The triumph of the new ethnocentrism thus had a very visible sign every March 17.[128]

"Emancipation Awaits Those Who Dare to Achieve It": The Hibernians and Their Allies, Irish Nationalism, and American Foreign Policy

In the late 1890s the militance and power of the AOH and its allies became evident on issues of broader import than Worcester's St. Patrick's Day parade. In debates over questions of freeing Ireland, as might have been expected, but also, perhaps more surprisingly, in discussions of critical issues in American foreign policy as well, the strength and sharp edge of the revived ethnocentrism became clearly apparent.

After the breakup of the Parliamentary party and the failure of the Home Rule Bill in 1893, the sleepy Ireland of the late 1890s and early 1900s appeared to provide little inspiration for nationalist agitation in America. In Worcester, however, interest in nationalism, particularly physical-force militant nationalism, was still very strong during that period. The best evidence of that interest was, of course, the emergence of the Clan na Gael and its growing popularity. With the nationalist movement in Ireland stumbling through the 1890s after the defeat of Gladstone's Home Rule Bill in 1893, there were few occasions for the Worcester Clan and its allies to mobilize support for the old country's future. Nevertheless, the Clan worked hard to maintain local interest through tributes to past and present Irish revolutionaries. The O'Connell Associates, a local Clan camp or branch, for example, filled Mechanics Hall on March 4, 1899, for a celebration of the birthday of Robert Emmet, the famed nationalist revolutionary of the early nineteenth century, and Clan camps invited speakers such as Major John McBride and Maud Gonne to Worcester for fetes and speeches.[129]

Though officially neutral in the debate over nationalist tactics and goals, it appears that Worcester's AOH strongly supported revolutionary nationalism as well in the late 1890s and early 1900s. County conventions of the AOH in the early twentieth century consistently called for a free and fully independent Ireland, "not the lotus food of Home Rule concessions." Divisions of the AOH also participated in some of the Clan's symbolic activities, including the projected Gonne visit. One of the new divisions, Division 36, the *Messenger* reported with bemused pride, even passed a resolution in 1898 calling for a new invasion of Canada. Dr. Francis A. Underwood, a local physician, prominent Hibernian, and Clan leader, summed up the sentiments of the Clan, the Hibernians, and their allies on the Irish question when he spoke at the AOH-sponsored St. Patrick's Day celebration in 1904: "Nothing short of an Ireland free and independent enjoying the fullest measure of nationhood itself will satisfy the members of the Order. . . . We proclaim our faith in that deathless cause and do not subscribe to that wretched maxim that the freedom of Ireland is not worth the shedding of a drop of blood. Against that miserable maxim the noblest virtue that has served and sanctified humanity appears in judgement, and heroism has taught enslaved nations that emancipation awaits those who dare to achieve it by their intrepidity."[130]

While revolutionary nationalists grew powerful in the ethnocentric climate of the 1890s and early 1900s, moderate nationalists continued to flounder. In the spring of 1902, moderates, almost all of their leaders American-born, formed a branch of the United Irish League, a support organization run by the Irish Parliamentary party leaders to back their constitutional movement for home rule. "Local conditions," the *Messenger* explained, had caused Worcester's "delay in falling into line" with other cities, where UIL branches had been formed much earlier. Yet even after the branch's formation, "local conditions" continued to plague it. The powerful Clan and the even more powerful AOH vigorously opposed the UIL, and thus the moderate nationalism it represented found few backers in Worcester in the early 1900s.[131]

With little chance for violent revolution in the torpid Ireland of the late 1890s and early 1900s, the attentions of Worcester's restless fiery nationalists roamed around the world to find issues that would permit them to stand up for Irish principles or interests and vent their ethnic frustrations. They did so in some cases to attack Britain and thus—at least indirectly—advance Ireland's interests. The Clan, the AOH, and the *Messenger* all strongly supported the Boers in their war against the British, for example. The Hibernians passed an official resolution backing the Afrikaners in 1902 and even raised funds for them, and the *Messenger* strongly urged the application of American influence to resolve the South African conflict.[132]

The opposition of the AOH-backed *Messenger* to the proposed British-American alliance in 1898 was more important, however, for it revealed much about the ethnocentric revival and its differences from the old spirit of accommodation. This was because Joshua O'Leary in his new newspaper, the *Recorder*, had favored the alliance. O'Leary argued that the issue of the treaty "called for decision from the standpoint of American interests." Britain's cruelty to Ireland, he continued, was "somewhat beside the question of what is the proper attitude for American citizens to take regarding a matter of American policy." Thomas Kiely responded furiously to such arguments in his *Messenger*. In a rage he attacked O'Leary as the "anti-Irish Irishman . . . false to every tradition of the race from which he sprang." Kiely hardly addressed the question of the alliance's potential benefits or drawbacks for the United States; he simply found it "inconceivable" that a paper "purporting to represent Irish American sentiment and supposed to exist from the patronage given to it because of that representation editorially favors an alliance between England and the United States." Kiely almost seemed more surprised than angry that any Irish American might hesitate to attack the ancestral enemy.[133]

The same clash of perspectives seemed to separate Kiely, the Clan, and the Hibernians from old Catholic Liberals like O'Leary even on foreign policy issues that did not even remotely involve Ireland's concrete interests, such as America's own imperialist adventures. Both David Doyle and Matthew Jacobson have pointed out how America's war with Cuba and subjugation of the Philippines became critically important issues in Irish communities across America. Both have demonstrated how Irish American nationalists found the Filipino insurrection to be much like Ireland's struggle against England and thus opposed the Philippines takeover. Doyle found, however, that acculturated Irish Catholic liberals often saw imperialism solely through an American perspective and endorsed American seizure of the Philippines as a step towards America's historic destiny to became a, perhaps the, world power. This was true in Worcester too where a clash between the old Catholic Liberal Joshua O'Leary, through his *Recorder*, and the new ethnic militant, Thomas Kiely, through the *Messenger*, revealed some of the local Irish community's important fault lines.

O'Leary hailed the American takeover of the Philippines. In the *Recorder* he dismissed Philippine claims to independence and argued that the United States had as much right—indeed, moral obligation—to suppress the Philippine rebellion as the North had to preserve the Union in the Civil War. He also criticized "the absurd stories of American barbarities" in the Philippines and attacked American newspapers for stigmatizing American soldiers as "barbarians."

Kiely in the *Messenger,* and his allies in the Clan or AOH, on the other hand, consistently opposed the war in the Philippines. They had many reasons for taking this position, but they were especially moved by disheartening similarities between America's war in the Philippines and Britain's oppression of Ireland. In 1899 the *Messenger* noted that the imperialist argument that the Filipinos were "unfit for self government" was "a phrase not new but typical of the language used by British politicians about the Irish." Not long after, Kiely compared troops in the Philippines to Cromwell's troops in Ireland. The Clan na Gael perhaps best summarized the position of the militant Irish on imperialism in a 1902 resolution: "It is eminently fitting and proper that we who are banded together in the fight for Irish freedom should condemn any movement which has for its object the subjugation of a people whether in Ireland or the Philippines."[134]

Kiely, Clan, and AOH members also believed that their Irish ethnocentrism inoculated them from the dangerous fever of surging American nationalism of the late 1890s. Kiely could thus step back and dispassionately dissect the "aggressive fiery spirit" of the new patriot, "blind to the faults of his own country and refusing to see merit in other people or in other forms of government." "There is a strain of the jingo in your patriot," he concluded.[135]

All Green Institutions

The rise of the AOH and its allied ethnic militant clubs and societies was the heart of Worcester's ethnic revival, but the ethnic competition and conflict of the 1890s also moved some of the city's Irish to try to expand and strengthen their community's institutional network. Their principal achievement was to create a bank, the Bay State Bank. Founded to challenge the Yankee monopoly of financial power in Worcester and supported largely by immigrants, the new bank bore all the hallmarks of the ethnic revival. Beyond the bank, the impact of the revival on the Irish institutional framework was meager. Few new schools or charitable institutions were added to the existing range of institutions. The church, the principal source and ruler of the Irish community's institutional life, had little sympathy for the revival of Irish ethnocentrism. Though loyally Catholic, Worcester's clerics remained devoted to building an American Catholic church. Hibernians and other ethnic militants, for their part, recognized the church's hostility to their goals, and, therefore offered little help to expand it in the nineties.

The movement to establish Bay State Bank began in January of 1895. Publicly, promoters of the Bay State Bank contended that Worcester simply needed a new bank, regardless of the religion or nationality of its sponsors. James Early, Irish-born deputy sherriff of Worcester County, asserted at hearings of the state legislature's banking committee that because of the limited number of banks in Worcester, and the legal restrictions placed on the size of their individual accounts, many of his friends had been forced to deposit their savings in Boston banks.[136]

Early and other supporters of the new bank, however, also vaguely suggested at those same hearings that an unspecified elite in Worcester tightly controlled the city's banks and this oligarchy refused to grant loans to new entrepreneurs. Privately, Worcester's Irish Americans were much more explicit about the religious and ethnic character of this discrimination. Richard O'Flynn wrote in his journal in 1895 that "no young Irish American Catholic will be employed in any of the banks but Irish American Protestants find employment in them." Even more important than the question of jobs was the question of control and economic power. George McAleer, reminiscing about the formation of the Bay State Bank in 1910, recalled that Worcester's Yankee bankers in the early 1890s seemed convinced that "the strangers within the gates . . . must always remain hewers of wood and drawers of water, and be ever content to efficiently aid in the building and development of the banks, in the management of which they had no part or recognition."[137]

Bay State Bank was an immigrant Irish enterprise. Only seven of the Bank's nineteen officers in its first year who can be identified were second-generation Irishmen. The other twelve were immigrant Irishmen and most had emigrated to America as adults. In part, heavy immigrant participation in the founding of the bank simply reflected the larger trend of disproportionately strong immigrant support for all aspects of the Irish ethnocentric revival of the 1890s. It was the immigrants, not the American-born, who responded most strongly to the revival of nativism and incidents of prejudice in the 1890s. It is thus not surprising that immigrants led the efforts to found the Bay State Bank, a definably Irish bank, established as a direct and aggressive response to prejudice and discrimination by Worcester's other banks. The bank had links to the revival beyond the motives for its establishment as well. Some of the incorporators and members of the first board of trustees were also members of the Ancient Order of Hibernians, the leading organization in the renewal of Irish ethnocentrism. Moreover, the order itself officially supported the bank from its inception. Officers in the AOH waited in line the entire night before the new bank opened on July 1, 1895, to insure that the AOH would be the bank's first depositor and thus draw its first passbook. Concrete links of common leadership and symbolic identification, as well as shared motives, tied the bank to the immigrant-dominated ethnic revival.[138]

It was not only ethnic pride but the protection or advancement of their economic interests which seemed to move Bay State's immigrant founders to establish the institution. Though they were not wealthy or powerful when compared to members of the Yankee elite, the men who established the Bay State Bank were, as Richard O'Flynn noted, "the most successful Catholic businessmen in the city," the stable core of a tiny Irish business class. Fourteen of the first twenty-four officers and trustees had owned their own businesses for fifteen years or more. Almost all of them had also accumulated substantial amounts of real estate. The incorporators who can be identified averaged $10,000 a man in real estate holdings in 1895, and the original trustees and officers averaged over double that figure. In the midst of a severe depression and a rising tide of nativism, it would seem natural that these Irishmen might have grown worried about their economic interests. The vague talk before the legislature's banking committee about an elite's monopoly on banking and Richard O'Flynn's dark (and as it turned out inaccurate) predictions that the city's Yankee banks would never permit the legislature to charter an Irish bank, suggest that some Irish businessmen and property owners believed that their economic interests could be better preserved and advanced by the establishment of their own savings institution. The founding of the Bay State Bank thus revealed that many of Worcester's prominent Irish leaders understood that their economic interests differed even from those of their Yankee political allies, the bankers, real-estate developers, and others who were the core of the Yankee independents. More, it suggested that these Irish immigrants were increasingly willing to assert their own interests even at the expense of these "friends" in the Yankee elite.[139]

The ensuing history of the bank, however, also reflects the limits of this Irish challenge. Within the first six months after the Bay State Bank's "pleasant, light and airy rooms" opened in July of 1895, it drew $81,000 in deposits. By the second decade of the twentieth century, the bank had the fourth largest number of depositors of all the banks in Massachusetts. Yet though the institution became stable and prosperous, it never seriously threatened the Yankee domination of Worcester's banking industry. The Bay State Bank gained an army of depositors in the turn of the century era, but it never held over 5 percent of all the savings deposited in Worcester in that period. (By contrast, in San Francisco, where Irish upward mobility was far easier, the Hibernia Bank ranked among that city's largest and most powerful financial institutions. The difference was an instructive symbol of the very different fortunes and economic position of the Irish on the two coasts.) In the 1890s and early 1900s Irish Americans would cast off their reliance on their Yankee allies in the city's politics and mount a successful challenge to Yankee dominance of municipal government, but they would achieve no similar success in the economic realm through the turn of the century era.[140]

Beyond the bank, Irishmen built few new institutions in the late 1890s and early 1900s. St. John's parish opened a boys school in 1893 and St. Anne's built a large new elementary school for boys and girls in 1903. The effort in St. Anne's revealed some of the new Irish assertiveness. The pastor of St. Anne's, American born James Tuite (Tuite had replaced Denis Scannel as pastor in 1899 at Scannel's death) demanded that the city sell him a nearby schoolhouse. When the city refused, Tuite boasted that he would build his own school and empty all the public-school classrooms in East Worcester.[141]

This limited building effort by Irish Catholics in the late 1890s and early 1900s may seem surprising given the revival of ethnic competition and rivalry in the city, but conditions both within and without Worcester's Irish community combined to undercut any impetus for building a larger, more comprehensive, and sheltering institutional network. Albert Marble, the friend of the Irish, had been displaced as superintendent of schools, but his replacements entered office warily and sought no quick religious purge of the department. Thus though the number of Irish women appointed as teachers dipped some in the mid-1890s it never fell off precipitously. Amidst all of the charter changes, the ward-based school committee and the policy of making teaching appointments through local committeemen remained intact, ensuring some continued Irish influence in the public schools.[142]

As important, perhaps, the Hibernians and other clubs that led the ethnic revival had little reason to crusade for parochial schools or other Catholic institutions, for the church had little interest in the AOH's agenda of Irish cultural revival and preservation. Hibernians grumbled that the vast majority of local Irish American clerics paid scant attention to the teaching of Irish history and even less to the perpetuation of the Gaelic language. By 1912, after more than a decade of agitation to include Irish history in the curricula of public and parochial schools, few Catholic schools in Irish parishes devoted even minimal time to instructing their largely Celtic charges in the glories of their ancestral heritage. Without much hope for the church, Hibernian leaders tried to create their own means of preserving Irish culture among the younger generation. AOH leaders hoped their new grand hall would become a kind of Irish YMCA for Irish youngsters and founded Gaelic classes and juvenile divisions to explicitly pass on Irish culture and identity to younger generations. They did not have the same power and resources as the church, however, and without the clergy's help the Hibernians and their allies would have difficulty perpetuating the fruits of their revival in a younger generation.[143]

Americanists on the Periphery: The Beginnings of Rebirth

Indeed, there were signs, even at the revival's high point, of that younger generation's dissent from Irish ethnocentrism. Older second-generation-dominated organizations, battered or broken in the mid 1890s, revived by the end of the century and new ones emerged. The Irish temperance movement rose from the dead in the late 1890s and briefly became even more shrill and militant in its attack on the drink trade. The Washington Club, one of many local social and recreational clubs founded in the 1880s, survived and even flourished in the 1890s. More important for the future of Worcester's Irish community, a new organization, the Knights of Columbus, appeared in the city in the early 1890s and grew steadily if slowly through the decade.

Grievously wounded by the depression and the rise of the APA in the mid-1890s, Worcester's Irish temperance crusade began to slowly recover its lost strength by the end of that decade. Organizations such as the St. Stephen's Total Abstinence Society and the St. John's Temperance and Literary Guild, which had disintegrated in the turmoil of the mid-decade, revived by 1898.

Three years later those societies and ones such as the Catholic Young Men's Lyceum and the St. Paul's Lyceum that had managed to survive the troubles of the early 1890s enrolled more than 1,000 men and women in the temperance cause.[144]

In most respects the temperance societies of the late 1890s and early 1900s were similar to their predecessors in the 1880s. Clerics continued to dominate the temperance crusade. Daniel F. McGillicuddy, the new pastor of St. Stephen's, Bernard S. Conaty, who replaced his brother Thomas at Sacred Heart, and James Tuite of St. Anne's, were the local leaders of the movement. The societies of the 1890s also engaged in many of the same activities as their predecessors: participation in Catholic liturgies; debates, recitations, and concerts; night school classes; and, as before, above all else, American sports, especially baseball and track and field.[145]

The Washington Club was the only one of the many local social clubs like the Carrolltons, or Highland Associates to survive the disruptions of the mid-1890s. It did so by becoming the principal social club of Worcester's Irish elite, a kind of Celtic version of the Worcester Club or other elite men's clubs emerging in the United States in the 1880s and 1890s. Club activities, however, remained largely the same in the 1890s as they had been in the 1880s; fancy-dress balls; elaborate banquets on Washington's birthday and other occasions; and vaudeville and minstrel shows. Like the temperance men, the Washingtons showed no interest in preserving or reviving Irish culture in Worcester. Indeed, in 1894, in their only appearance at the Convention of United Irish Societies during the 1890s, delegates from the Washington Club argued vociferously against holding a St. Patrick's Day parade.[146]

More important to the future of Worcester's Irish community than either the revival of the temperance societies or the transformation of the Washington Club was the founding of a local branch of the Knights of Columbus. Founded by a second-generation Irish curate in Connecticut in 1882, the Knights spread slowly throughout New England in the next decade and a half. In 1894, a number of Worcester Irish asked for a representative from the Knights to come to the city and found a council there. The new council, Alhambra Council No. 88, grew steadily and by the first few years of the twentieth century numbered over 300 men.[147]

The Knights, like the temperance men and the Washington Club, had little sympathy for the ethnocentric revival, but they differed significantly from the older Americanist organizations as well. As with the Catholic Liberals of the 1880s, the Knights' interests centered on the United States and the Catholic church, not Ireland, but the members of the new order increasingly had little

Folding Room, Logan, Swift and Brigham Company, 1909. At the turn of the century many second-generation Irish women worked in mills and factories like the folding room at this envelope-making company.

Irish American teachers and their pupils from the sixth and seventh grades at Providence Street School c. 1905. By the second decade of the twentieth century about half of Worcester's school teachers were second-generation Irish women, while many or most of their students were the children of new immigrant Jews, Poles, Lithuanians, or Italians.

Richard O'Flynn, Irish immigrant from County Waterford, came to Worcester in the 1850s. He was Secretary of the local Conventions of United Irish Societies, leader of the Irish temperance movement in Worcester, and self-appointed chronicler of the history of the city's Irish community.

Photo: Worcester Historical Museum

Andrew Athy, Irish immigrant from County Galway, was an alderman, state legislator, chairman of the Democratic City Committee in Worcester. He was also the first Irish American nominated for mayor, prominent leader in the Ancient Order of Hibernians and Irish nationalist organizations, and the most powerful Irish politician in Worcester during the 1880s and early 1890s.

Photo: Worcester of Eighteen Hundred and Ninety Eight, ed. Franklin R. Rice.

Bishop Patrick T. O'Reilly, Irish immigrant from County Cavan, pastor of St. John's church in Worcester in the 1860s and later first bishop of the Diocese of Springfield, 1870 to 1992.

Monsignor Thomas Griffin, Irish immigrant from County Cork, pastor of St. John's church in Worcester from 1870 to 1910, Chancellor of the Springfield Diocese, built parochial schools, founded St. Vincent's Hospital, and was a powerful figure in the church in Worcester.

Photo: Worcester of Eighteen Hundred and Ninety Eight, ed. Franklin R. Rice.

Very Reverend John J. Power, second-generation Irish American, pastor of St. Anne's church, built St. Paul's church and served as its pastor from 1866 until his death in 1902. He was Vicar General of the Springfield Diocese, elected to the Worcester Public School Committee, and was a close friend of members of the Yankee elite and a consistent advocate of public schools and Americanization of immigrants.

Photo: private collection of the author

Dignitaries at St. Patrick's Day parade, c. 1890s.

Marshals gathering for the St. Patrick's Day parade, c. 1890s.

Photo: Richard O'Flynn papers, Holy Cross College.

Hibernian Guards, c. 1890, members of the Ancient Order of Hibernians.

Photo: Richard O'Flynn papers, Holy Cross College.

Irish Societies in July 4, 1892, parade. Knights of Father Mathew are dressed as Irish "gallow-glasses."

Philip O'Connell, second-generation Irish American, alderman, first Irish Catholic mayor of Worcester, elected in 1901, defeated the next year in a close race, appointed a judge in 1915.

Photo: private collection of the author

James Logan, immigrant from Scotland, self-made envelope manufacturer, mayor of Worcester, 1908 and 1911, and key figure in the creation of a powerful Republican party in Worcester municipal politics in the first two decades of the twentieth century.

Photo: Worcester of Eighteen Hundred and Ninety Eight, ed. Franklin R. Rice.

Michael J. O'Hara, Irish American Republican politician, forged a cross-ethnic coalition to reign as mayor from 1924 to 1931, but did not dampen, and may have exacerbated ethnic rivalries in the city during the tribal twenties.

Peter Sullivan, affectionately known as "Peter the Great," Irish immigrant from County Kerry, alderman, state senator, and mayor from 1920 to 1923, helped craft a new pan-ethnic Democratic party in Worcester.

sympathy for the Liberals' interest in accommodating American Protestants. Indeed by the early twentieth century, if not earlier, the Knights stood for a mixture of militant, aggressive Catholicism and almost jingoistic American patriotism.[148]

Though the Knights were hammering out a new ideology that differed from that of the temperance men and the Washington Club, the three organizations were alike in the kinds of members they attracted and, conversely, differed dramatically from the types of men who joined the Hibernians and the other ethnocentric societies. Of the Knights who joined the Alhambra Council between 1898 and 1902, for example, nearly 70 percent were white-collar workers and 65 percent were second- or third-generation Irishmen. As might be expected of a club that aspired to serve Worcester's Celtic elite, nearly all of the Worcester Club's members were white-collar workers in 1900 as well. The temperance men were not quite so prosperous. Nevertheless, most members of the St. John's Guild between 1898 and 1902, the St. Anne's Total Abstinence Association in 1902, the St. Stephen's Total Abstinence Society in 1896, and the St. Paul's Lyceum in 1899 were either white-collar workers or skilled artisans and craftsmen. The vast majority of the applicants to the St. John's Guild between 1898 and 1902 were also American-born.[149]

Though it was the Hibernians, the Clan na Gael, and their allies that dominated Worcester's Irish community in the 1890s and early 1900s, the resilience of the temperance societies and Washington Club, and the emergence of the Knights testified to the limits of Worcester's Irish ethnic revival even at its height. All three revived or survived in the midst of that revival even while articulating very different conceptions of Irish American ethnic identity and culture. All three also drew their members from the fastest-growing segments of Worcester's Irish population—the upwardly mobile, American-born. The ethnic militants flourished in the 1890s and early 1900s by mobilizing a population that was actually shrinking (proportionately in the city's Irish population before 1900; absolutely after that date): the immigrant lower class. Even as the Hibernians waxed powerful in the 1890s and early 1900s the future seemed to belong to one or the other of their Americanist rivals.

Conclusion

Irish life in Worcester entered a new phase in the 1890s. But it was not further progress down an inevitable path to assimilation. Indeed, if anything, it seemed a step back from such a fate. The Irish community lost confidence in accommodation and in cooperation across the boundaries of ethnicity and religion.

The world changed in the 1890s: Parnell fell in 1890 and died in 1891; Catholic Liberalism held on longer, but it too expired by the end of the nineties. In Parnell's place, a great cultural revival swept Ireland in the nineties, attempting to revive the Irish language and Irish customs; and after Liberalism's demise, conservatism once again reigned unchallenged in the Vatican, suspecting the adventurous and insisting on a strict orthodoxy. More important, America, Worcester, and the Irish community's position within the city changed in the 1890s. The depression of 1893 undermined optimism about easy economic advancement and ratcheted up the intensity of ethnic competition. For the Irish, that competition had already become both more complicated and more intense, as new groups, the French Canadians, the Swedes, and the British, grew in numbers, resources, political power, and anti-Irish hostility. The return of nativism during the depression undermined hopes of easy reconciliation with Yankee neighbors, just as the economic downturn dashed dreams of upward mobility or economic security. It was then, in the depression years, with nativism flourishing, that Joshua O'Leary's *Messenger* began to flounder and the temperance societies collapsed. It was then, too, that the Clan na Gael began to grow and emerged in public view for the first time, and the first new divisions of the Ancient Order of Hibernians appeared. By the end of the decade, following the bitter fight over the fountain, there would be seven new AOH divisions in the city, triple the number of six years before.

The emergence of the Irish as significant players in politics with O'Connell's election gave the second great boost to this Irish ethnic revival. Citizens' coalitions reappeared in Worcester in the mid-1890s but only briefly: the nineties were not the eighties, and both Republicans and Democrats had changed too much to sustain the old alliances. With O'Connell's dramatic victory in 1901, Irish Democrats now became open, full-fledged rivals to Yankee-Republicans in a competition for the city's biggest political prizes, not junior partners in Yankee-led coalitions, begging for political crumbs. The Irish political rising in 1901 refreshed the cultural one, which was already powerful and pervasive by that time. It convinced leaders of the Irish ethnic revival that their day had come, that a strategy of solidarity and aggressive assertion of interests was the best strategy for the community and its members to survive or even prosper. It emboldened the AOH and other men to demand more patronage, more Irish books in the library, and Irish history courses in the public schools.

Yet there were weaknesses in such a strategy and in the revival itself. O'Connell's election was not the simple result of Irish power. The Irish would still need allies to be successful in politics in Worcester. Furthermore, the revival, rooted in an immigrant base, was never able to expand beyond that base. Immigrants were the most vulnerable to the new pressures of ethnic competition and the hardships of the depression; unable to improve their economic position easily as individuals, they were the most likely to profit from the success of a strategy that improved the position of the whole community. The second-generation Irish, embittered by the revival of nativism and challenged by the new competition for power, would not return to accommodation, but they also could not go back to an Irish culture they did not know. In the twentieth century they would forge new definitions of identity and group boundaries, as well as a strategy of group relations for themselves. In 1894, the young men gathering in Red Men's hall in downtown Worcester to form the Alhambra Council of the Knights of Columbus were forging those definitions and that strategy for the twentieth century, even as the ethnic revival began its ascent to dominance in Worcester's Celtic community.

Five

The Triumph of Militant, Pan-Ethnic, American Catholicism

The Early 1900s to the 1920s

In September of 1905, Father John J. McCoy returned to Worcester. McCoy along with Thomas J. Conaty had been a leader of the Catholic temperance movement in the city in the 1880s, and in many ways the square-jawed, ex-baseball player turned cleric had embodied the American cultural perspectives, ambitions, and hopes of the second-generation Irish—his generation. McCoy was transferred out of Worcester in 1887 despite the emotional pleas of his young temperance charges. After leaving Worcester, he had served with distinction at St. Luke's parish in nearby Westboro and at Holy Name parish in Chicopee near Springfield, building a new church and gymnasium for St. Luke's and making substantial additions to the huge educational complex at Holy Name. In his spare moments he wrote a history of the Springfield diocese. Now he was returning to Worcester to become pastor of the venerable St. Anne's parish.[1]

McCoy and his generation had been hopeful when he had last lived in the city in the 1880s. They were young then, the vast majority in their teens and twenties, and they could dream of a rosy future as natives of the most powerful and progressive nation on earth. Such optimism may have been common to American-born children of immigrants of many ethnic backgrounds in their youth. Historian Sucheng Chan has suggested that even many second-generation Chinese Americans entered adult life hopeful about earning acceptance as Americans despite abundant evidence of the American racism that excluded them. The second-generation Irish of Worcester had far better reasons to be hopeful in their youth. Beyond the obvious and general advantage of their white skin, European ancestry, or Christian religion, there were the specific conditions of the Worcester environment in the 1880s. The Citizens' party alliances, the fraternal amity of Catholics and Protestants echoing from the Civil War, the rise of Liberalism in their own church, and the universal respect accorded Charles Stewart Parnell and his Home Rule party made their youthful dreams of accommodation credible.

As McCoy and other members of his generation grew older they became less confident of their acceptance, but it was not just a transformation from youthful naiveté to middle-aged realism, not just movement through the phases of the life cycle that caused them to lose hope. The whole climate of relations between religious groups changed in Worcester as they were maturing. They had lived through the APA's crusade and the emergence of Irish Yankee rivalry in the 1890s, and the chasm that had opened up again then between themselves and their Protestant neighbors would not close in the twentieth century. The city's Protestant business elite became more, not less, self-consciously exclusive, as well as more cohesive and active, tightening its hold on the local economy even as Worcester's industry became more integrated into national and international markets. Workers, as before, offered little resistance to the elite's aggressiveness and their chronic failure to build class solidarity across ethnic and religious lines continued to close down a possible alternative to the persistence, indeed escalation, of ethnic and religious tension in the city. Yet it was political rivalry not economic developments that seemed most responsible for feeding the fires of ethnic and religious antagonism in Worcester. Irish Catholic mayoral candidates led the Democratic party against Protestant Yankee or Swedish Republican nominees in every year of the twentieth century's first two decades. In the 1920s, the Yankee political elite, trying to head off the inevitable Irish capture of the city, helped create a unique political phenomenon, an exceptionally successful Irish Catholic Republican, Michael J. O'Hara. O'Hara's coalition of elite Yankees and working-class ethnic immigrants seemed much like the old Citizens' alliance that had inspired a spirit of accommodation in the Irish community in the 1880s, but O'Hara did not bridge or soften the divisions; indeed, he sharpened them and rubbed the wounds of the city raw. His rise to power frustrated and provoked thousands on both sides of the religious boundary and helped feed the fires of sectarian hatred already heated by other trends and events in the "tribal twenties."

Indeed the twenties were not merely "tribal" in Worcester, they were violently tribal, as thousands of Catholics and Protestants battled each other in the city's streets, not once but twice: in 1924 over a revived Ku Klux Klan and in 1928 over the candidacy of Alfred E. Smith.

McCoy and members of his generation, then, were older certainly, and perhaps only naturally less starry-eyed, but their world was clearly different too. Catholics had learned since those hopeful days, McCoy believed; they were wary now, suspicious of even those who talked of friendship. In 1911 he stated: "Many things of a character looking for a general uplift, at least in their modern dress, originate outside the circle of our church . . . and we mistrust them naturally. We have so often been cajoled into permitting the breach in the walls, when made in seeming kindness and we have paid for our trust . . . the world is unfair when it blames us for still 'fearing the Greeks' even though they bring us gifts." McCoy understood, as most members of his generation did, that hopes for accommodation had flickered out, that Worcester was divided by religion finally, and for as long as he or anyone could foresee, into two hostile, suspicious Catholic and Protestant camps.[2]

Yet he knew, as well, that as much as he and some members of his American-born generation might love their parents' homeland, Ireland, that faraway island was not their own country, not their native land or culture. McCoy took pride in the revival of Gaelic culture and language at the turn of the century. Like most Irish American clerics, however, he appreciated the Gaelic revival for producing evidence of the ancient glories of Ireland, not for providing a cultural blueprint for the American future of his own people. If his generation was fiercely Catholic, it was also fervently American.

Moreover, he could see no hope for continued Irish isolation in a city filling up with immigrants, the vast bulk of them from Catholic countries. He had but to look out his rectory window, down the slopes of St. Anne's hill to Shrewsbury Street and the Meadow Flats (the site of the camp that the Irish canal workers had built in 1826) to see a growing settlement of the new Italian immigrants. Only two years after he became pastor of St. Anne's these newcomers built their own Catholic church at the foot of his hill, and not long after that their *festa* processions, growing ever longer every year, snaked through the streets of his St. Anne's parish. McCoy understood, like many of his Irish contemporaries, that those people at the bottom of the hill and the Poles and Lithuanians further south in the Island were an opportunity and a threat to the Irish. The Irish might bring the newcomers into the Democratic party and Catholic community that they led and thus make both powerful enough to dominate the city politically and socially for decades to come. Yet the new immigrants might also simply overrun Irish neighborhoods, threaten Celtic jobs, and ultimately reject Irish leadership of such a new Catholic community; they might remain aloof or, worse, seek help from the Yankees, and leave the Irish a permanent, powerless minority. By the end of the 1920s, the former seemed a more likely possibility than the latter. Though the new Catholic ethnics as well as longtime Catholic settlers in the city like the French Canadians still struggled stubbornly to maintain their independence, they found themselves increasingly drawn into the orbits of both an Irish-dominated Democratic party and a Celtic-dominated American Catholic community.[3]

When McCoy returned in 1905, the ethnocentric revival that had begun in the 1890s was still in the ascendant in Worcester's Irish community. There were signs even then, however, that it would not last. Just that March, the Ancient Order of Hibernians had decided not to sponsor a parade on St. Patrick's Day. Their reason, ironically, was the same one that their temperance opponents had argued in the 1880s: the parade was too expensive and the monies squandered on it could be used for better purposes. The Hibernians would march the next year, in 1906, but the decision not to parade in 1905 was an ominous portent of Hibernian weakness.[4]

The decline hinted in that portent came rapidly. The contraction of the leading ethnocentric societies was the clearest marker of the revival's end. The county societies, the Sligo and Thomas F. Meagher (Waterford) clubs both disappeared by 1920, and the AOH suffered severe losses. Hibernian membership declined from an approximate high of 2,500 in 1901 to 2,000 in 1910 to only 900 in 1917. The strength of the Clan na Gael is harder to chart because of its secrecy. Nevertheless, though it enjoyed a brief interlude of influence during the nationalist outburst of the late 1910s, it manifested little of its previous influence through the rest of the period.[5]

As the ethnocentric societies weakened or disappeared so did their efforts to sustain or revive interest in Irish culture. The AOH continued its campaign to win acceptance for Irish history in local school curriculums and even won a small victory by convincing the new pastor of St. John's parish to add Irish history to his school's course of studies. The effort to place Irish history in the public schools, however, petered out and achieved nothing in the 1910s and 1920s. The local branch of the Gaelic League also survived, but barely. A newspaper report in 1911 suggested that it had suffered for several years and new leaders were hoping to restore its former glory. Many of the city's Gaelic football clubs had disappeared by the second decade of the twentieth century.[6]

With McCoy as one of their leaders, then, the Worcester Irish, the vast majority of them American-born, would move into a new phase in their history

in the early twentieth century and begin to define themselves and their relationship to their neighbors in a new way. John J. McCoy, their most articulate,
or perhaps simply their most indefatigable, spokesman identified the key elements of this new identity and the principal objectives of their new strategy
for relating to their neighbors. Irish Americans in Worcester in the twentieth
century would identify passionately with the United States and American culture but they would also be fiercely, belligerently—or to use their favorite
phrase—militantly Catholic. McCoy suggested, however, that they would not
be insular. They would reverse their retreat into the narrow boundaries of
their own ethnic people and define a notion of being militant American
Catholics that could conceivably include members of all other Catholic ethnic
groups. McCoy made the link between these elements very often in articles,
speeches, and sermons, never more emphatically than in 1900 when he merged
the three: "In a short time we will have ceased to hear the word Irish parish or
French parish or Polish or Italian parish. All will be one tongue. All will be
Catholic and American, and most American when most Catholic."[7]

Yet even as the second- or even third-generation Irish talked of an inclusive
Catholic identity and boundaries, they had not lost consciousness of their separate ethnic background. Thus even as the new conceptions of identity began
to dominate Worcester's Irish community, Ireland's best chance for freedom
in four centuries would set off a stunning nationalist frenzy in Worcester in the
few years after World War I. This nationalist agitation was in some sense no
more than an eddy in a strong tide flowing to redefine Irish men and women
as American Catholics, for it would disappear almost as quickly as it came. Yet
it was a powerful reminder of the situational nature of Irish ethnic identity in
Worcester.

"The Time Has Passed When We Can Go It Alone": Owners and Workers in Worcester in the Twentieth Century

The effects of Worcester's integration into a national or even international
economy had begun to appear in the 1890s but only became fully evident in the
twentieth century. The trend was to larger and larger companies with sufficient resources and scale efficiencies to compete more effectively in the new
broader markets. In some cities this meant big national companies gobbling
up local firms, but in Worcester the local Protestant elite managed to hold on
and tighten its control over local business even as the trend to consolidation
gathered momentum not only in manufacturing but in banking as well.
Worcester's factory owners and other businessmen also began to cooperate

in employers' associations and business federations on a far grander scale and with a greater effectiveness than they ever had before, as they struggled for every advantage in the new national or international economy.

Though few of Worcester's manufacturing firms were taken over by the mega corporations that emerged from the great merger movement in the late nineteenth and early twentieth centuries (the Washburn Moen Wire Company's merger into American Steel and Wire and U.S. Steel in the late 1890s was a notable exception), there was, nonetheless, a significant trend to consolidation among firms in the city at the turn of the century. Several local machinery or machine-tool manufacturers combined during this era: Whitcomb and Blaisdell; Reed and Prince; and Crompton and Knowles. The merger of the latter two forged one of the largest loom manufacturers in the nation and an employer of over 2,500 workers. Other companies simply managed to exploit the opportunities of the new economy and transform themselves from small regional firms into large manufacturers serving a national market. Wyman Gordon Company and Norton Company, both founded in the 1880s, enjoyed enormous growth in the early twentieth century. In a classic small-scale example of a national pattern of vertical integration, Norton Company, manufacturers of abrasives, expanded and systematized its plants and production, gained control of its own raw materials, developed a modern sales force, and built up or acquired complementary sideline manufacturers in other parts of the nation over the first two decades of the twentieth century. As a result its workforce increased from a few hundred to over three thousand.[8]

Integration into the national or international economy and the new conditions of business that followed, inspired many of the growing metal and machinery manufacturing companies at the heart of Worcester's economy to band together to pursue mutual interests. In 1901 several local manufacturers helped create the National Metal Trades Association and in 1902 they formed a local branch of the federation. The local NMTA performed several services for its members, such as agitating for better railroad rates and lobbying for industrial training in local schools. By the middle of the twentieth century's second decade the NMTA and a similar allied association, the National Machine Tool Builders Association, had emerged as powerful forces that exerted significant influence locally and even across the nation. In 1914, the national leaders of the NMTA and the NMTBA both recognized the prominence of Worcester's local branches by holding their national conventions in the city.[9]

The emergence of a few large firms from a field of many small ones was most evident in Worcester's manufacturing companies, but the same process occurred in other parts of the local economy in the early twentieth century

as well. In 1903, the Worcester Safe Deposit and Trust Company began gobbling up its neighbors, absorbing five other local banks in less than three
years. The new "mega bank," appropriately named the Worcester Trust, provoked the rise of a rival institution, the Merchants National. Founded in 1905,
the Merchants National Bank became the largest bank in New England outside of Boston by 1921. The Trust was originally financed by "outside" money
and, many grumbled, answered to outside control, but the Merchants National
claimed from its inception that it was "a distinctly Worcester institution. . . .
Management is entirely in the hands of Worcester directors." In banking as
in manufacturing, Worcester businessmen stubbornly retained control of the
local economy even as the city's businesses became more and more integrated
into the national economy and responded to the pressures for larger-scale
organizations.[10]

These pressures also forced Worcester businessmen from different industries to work more closely together to maintain control of the local economy.
In the 1880s the city's business community was a large and motley mix of numerous small-factory owners, a few large manufacturers, some wealthy capitalists with extensive investments in real estate and banking, and many small
and medium sized retailers. Interests diverged and even conflicted among this
diverse group of businessmen, and members of the business community
rarely spoke with one voice. By the second decade of the twentieth century,
however, manufacturing, banking, and even real estate or commercial interests had begun to blend together. The directors of the Merchants National
Bank reflected the business elite's increasing integration: nine of them were
manufacturers; two led major insurance companies; two were lawyers; one a
real estate dealer; and one a contractor. Individuals reflected this integration
as well. Lucius J. Knowles, treasurer and then president of Crompton and
Knowles, for example, also served as a director of Merchants National Bank
as well as director of the Bancroft Realty Company "and other large real estate
corporations." C. Henry Hutchins, Knowles' predecessor as president of
Crompton and Knowles, had similar diversified local interests: president of
the United States Envelope Company, director of Central National Bank, the
Worcester Trust Company, and vice president of the People's Savings Bank.[11]

The local Board of Trade reflected well the growing cohesiveness and
power of the local economic elite. Revitalized in 1891 after ten years of dor-
mancy, the Board had played an important but uneven role in the complicated politics of the 1890s. In the twentieth century, however, the Board, reorganized and renamed the Chamber of Commerce in 1913, emerged as a
sophisticated and powerful voice for Worcester business. By the beginning of

World War I it had over 1,000 members and by 1927 over 2,500 and a full-time staff of fourteen people. The Chamber advertised Worcester's products all over the world by sponsoring trade expositions, mailing lists of Worcester exports to businesses and governments overseas, and inviting foreign businessmen to visit Worcester.[12]

The rhetoric of the newly powerful Chamber of Commerce underlined the solidarity of Worcester's business class, a solidarity made increasingly necessary by the economic competition posed by other cities. The 1910 trade exposition, for example, the then Board claimed, marked "an awakening of the overstrong conservatism of the manufacturers to a desire to work together for their own and Worcester's welfare." Upon transformation of the Board into the Chamber of Commerce a few years later, the leaders of the newly reconstituted organization proclaimed: "The old Board of Trade was organized in a day of intense individualism; the new Chamber of Commerce is organized at a time when the benefits of cooperation have become clearly apparent, demonstrable and almost universally accepted."

Such brave rhetoric, however, masked persistent worries. The immediate cause for the reorganization of the Board of Trade into a new, more powerful Chamber of Commerce in 1913 was the formation of a new Western New England Chamber centered in Springfield, Massachusetts, and the "prospective creation" of a new chamber in Providence, Rhode Island. Yet the real enemies, many Worcester men had come to believe by the 1910s, were not nearby but far away in the once backward and dependent regions of the south and west. As Mayor George M. Wright suggested ominously to Chamber members: "The South and West as well as Canada are exerting their strength towards bringing our New England born and bred industries to their communities. They are holding forth every temptation." Some companies from Worcester had purchased or established factories in those cities and knew firsthand the tempting advantages they offered. Moreover, though Worcester's economy was not dependent on textile or shoe manufacturing—industries that had already begun to drift south and west—industrial machinery manufacture, its staple, would soon be outstripped in the national economy by the production of consumer durables such as cars and appliances. By the twentieth century Worcester's share of the nation's manufacturing output had already peaked and begun to decline. The Chamber understood Worcester's "struggle" as fierce and unrelenting; "We must fight for Worcester all the time," the *Worcester Magazine* stated grimly.[13]

There were other threats and challenges to meet, ones that were closer to home. Company owners realized that the growth of the early twentieth century could disrupt once intimate relations with workers and make their factories vulnerable to union organizers. Many companies thus instituted careful hiring procedures to screen out "undesirables." Several local companies also developed a broad range of welfare services for their employees to encourage company loyalty. Norton Company made the most ambitious effort: organizing festivals and picnics; sponsoring sports teams (including an eight-oared crew); and even building neat, pleasant, single-family homes for favored workers to purchase at reasonable terms.[14]

The NMTA and NMTBA also helped provide Worcester's machinery-making companies with a steady flow of skilled and docile workers as well as support in fending off unionization efforts. The NMTA set up an employment bureau in 1905, and by 1914 the local NMTA employment agency was receiving over 14,600 applications for work, the largest number from all of the NMTA employment agencies in the nation. State labor investigators determined by 1914 that the agency found work only for safe men, "blacklisting" union men and potential "troublemakers." In 1914, the local NMTA began pursuing its antiunion policies openly through an employer's association dedicated to "foster the principles of the 'open shop'" through concerted propaganda campaigns.[15]

Worcester's labor movement was also changing in response to national economic trends in the twentieth century. Trends begun in the nineties towards the development of permanent business-union locals continued and by the second decade of the twentieth century Worcester's labor movement seemed to have achieved a certain stability. Worcester's labor movement enjoyed gradual growth through the early twentieth century. In 1910 there were over 7,000 union members in Worcester and that number grew modestly over the next decade. In 1913 there were 67 union locals and that figure rose slightly over the next seven years to 74. Perhaps as important, over the same seven years only 7 of the original 67 unions had disappeared from the city. The rapid rise and fall of the Crispins and Knights of Labor in the 1860s, 1870s, and 1880s had given way to a cadre of more or less permanent trade locals by the early twentieth century.[16]

Yet if established and stable, Worcester's unions represented only a small minority of the city's workers and posed little threat to the city's business establishment. The 7,000 members that Worcester's unions boasted in 1910 were but one-tenth of the city's labor force. Though that proportion was about the average for the nation, it was also, as Roy Rosenzweig has pointed out, a far smaller percentage than in most other industrial cities in Massachusetts. In Lynn more than one-quarter of the workers were union members in 1910 and in Boston the proportion was over one in five the same year. Moreover, virtually none of the workers in Worcester's principal industries were organized. There were no organizations for the city's wireworkers and the feeble Worcester machinists local counted less than a few dozen of the city's thousands of machinists. Lacking much strength, it is not surprising that Worcester's unions were timid and ineffective through much of the first three decades of the twentieth century. Between 1906 and 1910, for example, Worcester's workers lost only 11,592 working days to strikes, one-third as many days as Holyoke, one-quarter as many days as New Bedford, one-fifth as many as Fall River or Lowell, and one-fortieth as many as the contentious union men and women of Lynn.[17]

In the 1910s the Central Labor Union, searching for other means to advance labor's cause, sought to rouse public sentiment against contractors who used nonunion labor through the publication of an "unfair list," but an ill fated attempt to use the "unfair list" against the building of a local Catholic church dramatically revealed the feebleness of the labor movement and one of the essential causes of its weakness. In 1911 the pastor of the newly created Ascension parish, James J. Farrell, chose McDermott Brothers contractors to build the new parish's first church. The second-generation Irishman McDermott had long been hostile to unions and added eight nonunion men to his team, building the church over the heated protests of the building unions. The Carpenters' District Council appointed a committee to ask Farrell to cancel the contract, but Farrell referred the committee to Bishop Beaven. On September 14 the committee wrote to Beaven complaining about the "unfair work" carried on by McDermott Brothers at both Ascension church and St. Paul's school. In his reply Beaven spoke at length about the sympathies of priests for workers, "their antecedents have brought them in touch with the life and living conditions of the laborer," but he refused to interfere with the Ascension church's construction plans—"the work in this case is too far along." On December 20, 1911, the Carpenters' District Council passed a resolution demanding that members living in Ascension parish refuse to contribute to the parish's building. Yet the council's Catholic members objected so vociferously that the council made the requirement optional and it lost all force. Nonunion firms would build five more Catholic churches in Worcester in the next decade.[18]

Given labor's weakness and management's strength, it is surprising that in the fall of 1915 Worcester's workers engaged in the largest and perhaps most bitter labor conflict in the history of the city. In June of that year, Worcester's machinists, sensing that the city's machinery manufacturers would fear a work stoppage in the midst of the rush of orders generated by World War I, and chafing under the piece-rate payment system and long hours their bosses imposed upon them, asked the International Association of Machinists to

send an organizer to Worcester. In late September, machinists in three machinery companies went out on strike, and by early November their ranks had
grown to the largest number of workers engaged in a single strike in the history of the city.[19]

These numbers masked some real weaknesses of the strikers. As Bruce
Cohen notes, they possessed very few resources to carry on a long strike. The
machinists' local had been revived only a few months before and had hastily
accumulated a small strike fund. Suffering from decades of failures and limited
growth, the Central Labor Union could offer the machinists little assistance.
More important, the machinists, so recently organized, were divided by differences among plants where they worked, skill levels, and ethnic backgrounds.
Ethnic and skill differences probably caused this fragmentation, at least in
part. A larger proportion of the machinists at Reed and Prentice, Whitcomb
Blaisdell, and Leland Gifford were American-born and more highly skilled
than those at Crompton Knowles, for example. There were also mutually reinforcing ethnic and skill differences within each of the plants that further
undermined worker solidarity. Immigrants from southern and eastern Europe
worked at lower-skill jobs in all of the shops and thus earned less pay. Organizers of the strike seemed to exacerbate these differences rather than heal
them. A Clark University graduate student studying the strike as it unfolded
reported that "all during the strike not one address or speech of any kind was
made to the Finns, French Canadians, Swedes, Armenians and so on in their
native tongue by any union organizer."[20]

It was not simply the weaknesses of the machinists, however, but the
strength of their employers that caused the strike to fail. After the strike
began, the local NMTA helped coordinate the companies' resistance and—
aside from a brief flirtation with compromise by the owners of Whitcomb
Blaisdell—maintained a solid front. A few years after the strike, John Spence,
superintendent at the Norton Grinding Machine Company, recalled in a letter
to a manager in a nearby company: "We feel that the dumping out of the
cause of most factory troubles was a great thing for us. We also feel that we
could not have done this if it had not been for a strong and just National
Metal Trades Association. Most of the members of the Metal Trades stuck to
the principle that they would not hire men who were out on strike."[21]

As early as the beginning of December the strike was in trouble. The local
Labor News estimated that as many as half to two-thirds of the strikers had
left Worcester for the plethora of jobs available in booming plants elsewhere.
By early January of 1916, the state Board of Arbitration ruled the strike dead
in most Worcester plants.[22]

Ironically, though the machinists lost their strike in 1915, their economic prospects and the prospects of most Worcester workers grew considerably brighter over the next three years. The wartime boom that had emboldened the machinists accelerated almost exponentially as America moved toward and then entered the war. In November of 1917, the *Post* estimated that the value of the city's manufacturing output had grown by an incredible 80 percent in just two years, from 100 million in 1915 to 180 million in 1917. Since the country went to war, the *Post* boasted in 1917, "Worcester is among the first dozen cities in the country in the increased value of its output and its consequent prosperity." Some observers suggested that the war created 15,000 new jobs in Worcester.[23]

The resulting tight labor market proved a boon for workers. By 1920, union membership had peaked at over 10,000 working men and women, yet workers did not need unions to enjoy the benefits of the boom. Strapped for healthy bodies, American Steel and Wire managers granted unorganized employees the eight-hour day in 1918. Even crusty George Jeppson of the Norton Company, who had taken great pleasure in breaking the machinists' strike in 1915, granted workers higher wages and better terms during the war lest labor troubles disrupt the company's rapid growth. In all, as early as 1917, the *Post* estimated that wages in Worcester had increased faster in the previous three years than at any other time in the city's history.[24]

The good times ended abruptly at the close of the war. The postwar crash was general, afflicting nearly every city and region in the United States, but in Worcester it seemed exceptionally severe. The Massachusetts Bureau of Labor Statistics reported unemployment rates among Worcester's union members that were as high as 28 percent by March of 1919. The situation continued to worsen in 1920 and 1921. By November of 1921, managers of the Golden Rule Fund estimated unemployment at 18,000 in the city and spoke fearfully of the "danger of [the depression] breaking the morale of the city." Individual firms also reflected the loss. The Norton Company, one of the largest employers in Worcester by the end of the war, reduced its work force from 4,000 to only a little over 800; managers of the company would later recall 1921, not 1929, as the real depression. Compounding the problems of workers all over the city was a severe shortage of housing that forced up rents and squeezed out prospective homeowners.[25]

Some Worcester labor leaders thought the time was ripe for another attempt at organizing the city's factories. In January of 1919, the *Labor News* hinted darkly at potential radicalism among city workers unless employers "keep as many people at work as possible." Six months later the Central Labor Union made a formal request to the AFL to send "a large corps of organizers" into Worcester "to completely organize the city." William Guilfoyle and other labor leaders believed that local discontent over the depression made the present a "most opportune time" for organizing the city.[26]

Local manufacturers responded to these developments with alarm. Though the machinists' strike had failed a few years before, local industrialists remained wary of labor's potential power, and demands for wage and hour concessions during the wartime manpower shortage had only intensified the owners' concern. The Employers Association of the NMTA, led by the militantly antiunion Jerome George, had, therefore, continued its campaign for the open shop through the war years. Several local companies themselves had also continued to fight labor inroads by hiring spies and detectives. More important, in the fall of 1918, some of Worcester's largest employers began meeting over lunch every Thursday to plot a concerted antiunion strategy. The group, Jerome George explained to Aldus Higgins of Norton Company, hoped to do something to offset the propaganda work done by the AFL.[27]

By December of 1918, the manufacturers' club had a name, the "Thursday Noon Club," and George Jeppson, Jerome George, and others began to flesh out its purview and suggest courses of action. The club hired a secret investigator to sniff out labor organizing in local mills; planted news items praising management and castigating unions in local papers; cooperated with the Chamber of Commerce in placing advertisements celebrating Worcester as an open-shop city ("Can the labor-union cities and towns of the country equal it?"); and tried to organize a boycott of the local labor newspaper, the *Labor News*.[28]

It is hard to gauge the effects of all this activity. Nevertheless, the fact that the club existed at all reflected how committed Worcester's business elite had become to concerted action. George Jeppson acknowledged that the employers had often been "individualists" in the past but that the club had to be formed because "some of us are beginning to think that the time has passed when we can go it alone on our own ideas." Such sentiments seemed particularly appropriate in the postwar years. The club members appear to have exaggerated the threat from Worcester's unions, but they were appropriately concerned about the state of Worcester business. The postwar depression seriously imperiled almost all of their companies. Many of the owners no doubt felt they were fighting for their lives, and would brook no troubles from their workers in doing it.[29]

Nevertheless, the club presented a formidable array to the feeble legions of the city's labor movement. The club's roster read like a Who's Who of Worcester business: James Logan and Louis Buckley of United States Envelope; H. G. Stoddard of Wyman Gordon; Lucius Knowles of Crompton Knowles; P. B. Morgan of Morgan Construction Company; Aldus Higgins and George Jeppson of Norton Company; J. E. White of Worcester County Bank and Trust; and F. A. Drury of Merchants National Bank.[30]

Worcester's unions wilted in the face of this opposition. The molders, long the city's best-organized industrial workers, struck firms in 1919, but months later despite sporadic violence they had accomplished little. Meanwhile union membership in the city plummeted. By 1924 it was down to 7,149, less than the number of union members in Worcester nearly fifteen years earlier. On the eve of the Great Depression, labor in Worcester was as weak and passive as it had ever been.[31]

Like the persistent weakness of the city's unions, the failure of worker or radical politics in Worcester testified to the softness of working-class sentiment in the city. The socialists never again matched the small successes of their brief surge in the late 1890s and early 1900s and their votes in city elections continued to dwindle through the first few decades of the twentieth century. Even Eugene Debs gained little support in Worcester in 1912: only 225 votes out of 21,000 cast. The city's unions attempted to found a political arm, a wage-earners club, on two occasions. The first such club appeared in 1906 but died of apathy within a few years. A second effort in 1910 suffered from similar indifference as well as rumors that some of its members accepted bribes from local politicians seeking the club's endorsement.[32]

Not surprisingly perhaps, the most significant labor success in Worcester politics in the early twentieth century came in the year of the machinists' strike, 1915. In that year John F. Reardon, a second-generation Irishman and former head of the street railway union, won the Democratic nomination for mayor. Buoyed by labor's outrage over the strike, Reardon made Mayor Wright's handling of the work stoppage his chief campaign issue. Reardon lost the election but ran a stronger race than either of the two Democratic nominees who had preceded him. He won 43 percent of the vote in the city, compared to 35 percent for Dr. Thomas Barrett, the Democratic candidate in 1913 and 33 percent for James F. Carberry, the candidate in 1914, and ran far ahead of Barrett and Carberry in virtually every ward in the city. He made particularly substantial gains in neighborhoods where many machinists lived, even ones dominated by Swedes, who had long been firmly rooted in the Republican party.[33]

Reardon's "success," however, should not be overstated. Though he fared better than either of the Democratic mayoral candidates preceding him, they had polled the lowest votes for mayor of any Democratic nominees since Philip O'Connell in 1900. Even improving on their vote total then, Reardon still lost by the near landslide margin of fourteen percentage points in both 1915 and 1916. Furthermore, when Reardon ran in 1916 he polled a much smaller vote in the Swedish precincts of Wards Two and Six than he had in 1915. In 1916, the strike was a distant memory and Swedish machinists could vote for one of their own, Pehr Holmes, a Swedish immigrant nominated for mayor by the Republicans.[34]

The decline of Reardon's Swedish vote pointed up one of the fundamental causes of organized labor's weaknesses in Worcester. Worcester's workers continued to be profoundly divided by ethnicity and religion. The refusal of the Catholic carpenters to boycott the Ascension Church fund, the ethnic fragmentation among machinists, and the slippage in Reardon's vote in Swedish neighborhoods were only the most visible signs of how those basic divisions continued to undermine mobilization of the city's workers on class lines. Ethnic divisions, of course, troubled labor movements in other cities besides Worcester, but the presence of so many Protestant workers, most notably the Swedes, seemed to split Worcester's workers more evenly and fundamentally than elsewhere in Massachusetts.

Such divisions alone were a serious obstacle to the mobilization of workers in Worcester, but they were not the only difficulties the city's union leaders or labor politicians confronted. Perhaps as important as the divisions and weaknesses of Worcester's workers were the solidarity and energy of the owners and managers who confronted them. Mostly local men, those owners employed measures like blacklists, lockouts, labor spies, and antiunion propaganda to good effect. What was perhaps most impressive is that they used such tactics in concert, not individually, through the local branch of the NMTA in 1915 and the Thursday Noon Club of the postwar era. Yet they were also very successful in winning the loyalty of their workers through corporate welfare and recreational programs for workers. Such programs at Norton Company, for example, had an even more powerful effect when they were applied selectively to reward specific groups of workers, such as skilled men and Swedes, over others such as the unskilled, Catholics, and eastern Europeans. Finally, Worcester's manufacturers and owners continued to profit from a very friendly city government throughout much of the early twentieth century. Indeed, as we shall see, long after businessmen and manufacturers had left politics in many other cities, Worcester's factory owners continued to play a prominent role in the city government and therefore insured municipal indifference or even hostility to labor's interests.[35]

Religious and Ethnic Groups: Twentieth-Century Worcester

While relations among classes changed little in Worcester in the twentieth century, relations among ethnic groups in Worcester changed significantly. The religious boundary between Catholics and Protestants remained critical, indeed became more charged over time, but it was not the city's only social or cultural boundary. Ethnic allegiances continued to distinguish and often divide groups on either side of the boundary: Yankees and Swedes on the Protestant side; Irish and French Canadians on the Catholic side. The influx of new groups into Worcester, many of them Catholic, such as Lithuanians, Italians, and Poles, increased the complexity of Worcester's ethnic relations.

The "Yankees," native-stock Americans, remained the most important of the Protestant groups in Worcester. They continued to dominate Worcester's economy, cultural life, and society, but they were not important just because of their elite control. Unlike in other New England cities like Lowell or Lawrence where their numbers had always been few, or Boston where they had been streaming out to the suburbs for several decades, Yankees were still a large group in Worcester in the early twentieth century. It is harder to measure Yankee numbers then because of the increasing number of third-generation Irish or other ethnics in the city, but the number of people in Worcester whose grandfathers had been born in America was 32,784 in 1905, or about one-fourth of the city's 128,133 people. This was a far larger proportion than in most other Massachusetts cities: in Lowell, Yankees so-defined were less than one sixth of the population, or 15,667 of 94,889; in Lawrence, they were a little more than a tenth or 7,282 of 70,050. The Yankees thus persisted as a large ethnic group, and the most powerful one, in Worcester.[36]

These Yankees, however, were less and less a rural migrant people adrift in the city, and more and more an urban or suburban middle class or elite acculturated to the city and its way of life. Migration from rural New England fell off and began to dwindle to a trickle by the early twentieth century. The farm villages and towns of northern New England had been bled dry by the constant flow of migrants through the nineteenth century. Between 1870 and 1900, the number of Worcester residents born in Maine, New Hampshire, or Vermont increased by over 135 percent or by 4,000 people; from 1900 to 1930 the number increased by only 14 percent. Yankees now more than ever were also white-collar workers, and with the advent of electrification and the rapid extension of street railways all over the city and into neighboring towns, these upwardly mobile Yankees settled in suburban-like developments on the west side and other parts of the city's periphery.[37]

As the Yankee population became more settled in Worcester it also became more acculturated to urban leisure customs and values. The cultural liberalism of the Yankee elite had become more broadly pervasive in the Yankee community by the 1910s and 1920s and evangelical fervor began to flag among the Yankee middle classes. After some initial suspicions about movies, Yankee middle classes flocked to the new movie palaces appearing downtown in the late 1910s and early 1920s. In 1915 Mayor Wright, a Yankee manufacturer, even enthusiastically agreed to take a bit part in the production of a cinema romance shot in Worcester. Dancing also won the approbation of the Congregational Ministers Association of Worcester in 1924: "Dancing," they argued, "is a proper amusement for young people" (at the same time they reported that "prayer meetings of the old fashioned variety were a thing of the past"). It was in attitudes towards drinking, however, that changes in Yankee cultural attitudes seemed most dramatic. After 1910 the no-license issue lost its edge in Worcester, as the no-license vote plummetted from an annual average of 49 percent for the first decade of the twentieth century, to 40 percent in the second. This decline in the prohibiton vote was general, but most noticeable in Ward Ten, the ward with the highest proportion of Yankee voters (native-born of native parents) in the city. Indeed, between 1910 and 1919, when prohibition became the law of the land, Ward Ten gave only a bare majority to no-license in most years, and in two years the ward actually voted against no-license. More and more native-stock Americans thus came to tolerate or even enjoy what their forbears a generation earlier had considered poison.[38]

The patterns of development of churches, social clubs, and other organizations also reflected the new rootedness of the Yankee population. Protestantism extended to the beginning of the city's history, of course, but the great Yankee migration from the countryside and the opening up of new city neighborhoods had touched off a wave of church building in the late nineteenth century. Twelve of the city's Congregational churches were organized after 1869 as well as nine of its Baptist congregations and four of its five Episcopal parishes. Most of the building had been completed by the early 1900s. In 1919 only one of the Congregationalist churches was less than ten years old and none of the Baptist churches in the city was less than fifteen years old. Fraternal societies, social clubs, sports organizations, and alumni groups had also multiplied rapidly in the late nineteenth and early twentieth centuries and were becoming established by the new century's second decade.[39]

It was among the elite, however, that the thickening of the Yankee social and institutional network was most obvious in the late nineteenth and early twentieth century. A bevy of exclusive clubs and cultural organizations helped create a distinct and entrenched elite social network that reinforced the economic trends encouraging cohesiveness among Worcester's business leaders. The Worcester Club, for example, had been virulently attacked by Protestant middle-class spokesman at its founding in 1888, but by the early twentieth century it had become well established as the principal meeting place of an exclusively Protestant business elite. It was no accident that the Thursday Noon Club held its meetings there. The Worcester Women's Club, dating from 1880, and the Tatnuck Country Club, from 1896, and the Art Museum, also from 1896 were critical elements of an elite network of exclusive clubs and institutions that had grown to maturity by the second and third decades of the twentieth century.[40]

The other Protestant groups in Worcester were changing too. Of these other groups the largest was the Swedes. Swedish migration began to die out by 1910, but the Swedes, if anything, grew more powerful and prominent in the early twentieth century as an American-born generation began to mature. In 1920, there were over 15,000 first- and second-generation Swedes in Worcester. A number of these younger Swedes and Swedish Americans enjoyed substantial success moving up the occupational ladder. Some had even penetrated into the upper reaches of the city's social and economic elite, territory that was still off-limits to almost all Irishmen. George Jeppson, the first child born in Worcester of Swedish parents, followed upon his father's success in the Norton Company and moved up to be a full partner in that rapidly growing firm. By the 1930s Swedish names sprinkled the membership lists of the elite Worcester Club as well as other high-society organizations.[41]

Some Swedes worried that such success meant the dissolution of their group and the decline of their culture, but the Swedes remained a very distinct people through the early twentieth century. Swedish neighborhoods in Quinsigamond Village, Belmont Hill, and Greendale remained vibrant centers of ethnic socializing and culture through the first two decades of the twentieth century. In 1920 over 12,000 people still called Swedish their native tongue and made the Swedes the largest foreign-language group in the city. The Swedish subsociety, a network of clubs, societies, and institutions, actually grew in the early twentieth century: in 1900 there were twenty Swedish organizations in Worcester; by 1908, there were thirty-eight and they had banded together in a Swedish federation "to keep alive Swedish culture and tradition as well as to promote the interests of the Swedish people in all activities of the community." In addition to their numerous clubs, the Swedes counted eleven churches, two old-age homes, a bank, their own hospital, and a weekly newspaper that boasted over 19,000 subscribers. Swedes, like the Irish, were eager to demonstrate their growing power in public parades and demonstrations. The visit of Prince Wilhelm of Sweden to Worcester inspired an enormous and elaborate celebration by Worcester's Swedes in 1907. Swedish Midsummer Festivals, like St. Patrick's Day for the Irish, also became annual rites. In 1912 over 4,000 Swedes, several bands, and floats depicting a Viking ship and Swedish inventor John Ericsson's Monitor, made their way down Worcester's Main Street and drew applause from tens of thousands of spectators. Finally, Swedes were slower than Yankee Protestants to abandon the evangelical cause. Quinsigamond Village, for example, earned a reputation as one of the most straitlaced neighborhoods in the city, with little or no tolerance for either drinking or dancing, and Swedish ministers and laymen continued to fight for no-license or prohibition long after many of their Yankee coreligionists had given up the battle.[42]

Until 1890, Worcester's Catholics included only the French Canadians, the Irish, and a tiny assortment of Yankee converts, wandering Germans, or emigré Frenchmen. Beginning in that decade, however, members of new Catholic ethnic groups began to trickle into the city. By the early twentieth century that trickle became a flood. All three groups of the new Catholic immigrants arrived in Worcester at roughly the same time. In 1900 the groups were large enough to attract attention but none of them yet counted more than a few hundred members in Worcester. Ten years later, however, there were at least 3,500 immigrants from each of the three nationalities in Worcester. By 1920 the number of first- and second-generation Poles and Italians had each jumped to over 8,000 and Lithuanians only slightly less, to over 7,000. This meant that by that time there were more new immigrant ethnics in Worcester than French Canadians and nearly as many as first- and second-generation Irish.[43]

Members of the three nationalities also shared roughly the same experiences in adjusting to urban and industrial life. Most of them were unskilled peasants and thus could find jobs only at the bottom of Worcester's economic hierarchy. Through the first two decades of the twentieth century nearly half of Worcester's Italian workers were simple laborers, largely in street, rail, or building construction. Poles and Lithuanians gravitated to positions in heavy industry, the foundries, wire mills, and other metalworking shops, where the vast majority of them also began in the lowest-paid unskilled jobs.[44]

Unlike the French Canadians or the Swedes who had settled on the fringes of Irish neighborhoods or in the interstices between such districts, the new Catholic immigrants invaded and overwhelmed the very core of the old Irish east side. Italian immigrants, for example, settled largely in the East Worcester and Shrewsbury Street areas in Ward Three on almost the exact spot in the Meadows where the first Irish canal-workers' camp had been located nearly ninety years before. As early as 1912 more than sixty Italian American businesses had sprung up along Shrewsbury Street there. Four years later, in 1916, Italians headed 75 of 79 households on Plum Street, 14 of the 18 families on nearby Henry Street, and 31 of the 35 on Larkin Street in East Worcester. By the 1910s and 1920s only the names of the streets, Larkin or Lyons, recalled the solidly Irish presence of the 1880s and 1890s in much of East Worcester. By that time the Italians had even begun to push up the slopes of St. Anne's Hill, an "Irish stronghold" then, an Italian American remembered years later. In 1916, seventeen Italian families already lived on Gage Street next to St. Anne's church.[45]

Poles and Lithuanians meanwhile had invaded the other historic center of Irish life in Worcester, the Island. Between 1890 and 1910 the Polish and Lithuanian proportion of the Island's families jumped from 1.2 percent to 31.8 percent. The Irish in the Island also declined as the newcomers moved in, falling from 46 percent of the neighborhood in 1890 to 26 percent by 1910. In 1920 over half the city's Lithuanian immigrants and more than two-thirds of its Polish newcomers resided in the Island neighborhood or near it in Ward Five. By 1930, a young Polish American novelist from Worcester described the Island as a "Polish village." He exaggerated somewhat, for Irish families would hang on in the Island for many decades, but the area was clearly no longer Irish-dominated.[46]

Though new immigrants were increasingly transforming Worcester life in the early twentieth century, French Canadians remained the most important non-Irish Catholic group in the city. This was true principally simply because they remained the largest single non-Irish Catholic group. In 1910, there were 14,259 foreign-stock French Canadians in Worcester, about the same number as first- and second-generation Swedes. Most of the French by that time were American-born. Immigration from French Canada slowed after 1900 though *Canadiens* continued to dribble into Worcester throughout the twentieth century. There was, however, still plentiful evidence of the persistence of French Canadian solidarity in the city. French Canadian neighborhoods on Oak Hill and around Canterbury Street in South Worcester remained vital ethnic districts. French Canadian spokesmen also continued to sound the longtime clarion call of French Canadian nationalism: *survivance.* As a curate from the French Canadian parish at St. Joseph's stated in 1907: "Let us remain French if we are to remain Catholic."[47]

Though there was broad evidence of the persistence of French Canadian ethnic identification in Worcester, there was also evidence of change in the French Canadian community. *L'Opinion Publique,* for example, frequently complained that despite all efforts many members of the new generation were losing or abandoning their language. Members of the new generation had also begun to move out along streetcar lines to new ethnically mixed residential areas in southwestern Worcester or north along Lincoln or Burncoat streets where they attended English-language churches. Meanwhile new immigrants were moving into some of the older French neighborhoods. Greeks were pouring into the earliest French district in the center of Worcester on Salem and Orange Streets, and Syrians and Italians crowded in among the *Canadiens* on Oak Hill.[48]

Irish Catholics thus confronted an increasingly complicated ethnic landscape in twentieth-century Worcester. Yankees and Swedes were ranged against them as Protestants on one side; French Canadians and the new immigrant Italians, Poles, and Lithuanians, potentially with them as Catholics, on the other. Religious divisions were critical in Worcester, as we shall see, but the dynamic of ethnic cooperation and competition that shaped Worcester's political environment over the first thirty years of the twentieth century was far too complex to characterize only in religious terms. Diverging opinions and rivalries over culture or political interest between ethnic groups on either side of the religious boundary, and even between classes within ethnic groups would, paradoxically, create that complexity, even as the religious divisions between Catholics and Protestants in Worcester grew more profound and bitter.

Protestant Republicans and Irish Democrats: The Rivalry in the Twentieth Century

When Philip O'Connell won the first mayoral election of the twentieth century, it must have seemed like a new era of triumph for Worcester's Irish Democrats. Subsequent close campaigns and John Duggan's smashing wins for mayor in 1905 and 1906 appeared to confirm those expectations. Yet the twentieth century's first two decades would belong to the Republicans, who rebuilt their party on the old Citizens' Party commitment to internal improvements and stymied Irish Democratic attempts to find allies. If Irish Democrats were unsuccessful, almost hapless at times in the twentieth century, they would never cede control of their party or consider a return to the old Citizens' alliances again. The ethnic competition for power that underlay the twentieth century's first two decades of politics was rarely publicly bruited about, but it was always present, as Irish-Catholic-led Democrats battled Protestant Yankee, Swedish, or British-led Republicans for control of Worcester at every election until the 1920s.

Factional squabbles and disputes racked the GOP through the first six years of the new century. The party remained sufficiently strong to defeat the Democrats, Philip and David O'Connell, from 1901 through 1904, but in 1905 the simmering tension between middle-class and elite Republicans exploded. In that year Melvin Overlock managed to eke out a victory over Burton W. Potter, a Harvard-trained lawyer, in a hotly contested Republican primary. Overlock gloried in his humble beginnings as a barber and his "east side cottage." In 1910 he would write *The Working People: Their Health and How to Protect It*, a book, he said, "written in a plain way by a plain man for plain people." Vaguely standing for economy in government, Overlock assailed Potter as the candidate of the wealthy. Potter ran strongest in the elite wards in the northern and western parts of the city, Wards Ten and One; Overlock won virtually everywhere else. Overlock, however, ran badly in the general election of 1905 and again in 1906, as his Democratic opponent, second-generation Irish doctor John T. Duggan, managed to peel off enough votes in the Republican elite districts to coast to two smashing victories.[49]

Overlock's defeats, however, appeared to pave the way for members of the Republican elite to seize full control of their party once and for all. Beginning in 1907 and for the next fifteen years or more a coterie of men, sometimes called the "North End Ring," led by James Logan, an envelope manufacturer, ruled the local GOP. Logan was not physically prepossessing: medium height, thinning hair, small eyes, carefully measured moustache. In pictures he looks more fastidious than charismatic. Yet he was a canny businessman and powerful politician. In 1898 he engineered the creation of the "envelope trust," a merger of ten envelope companies in Worcester and Springfield into the United States Envelope Company. By 1907, the Republicans hailed him as the "master organizer" who had rescued them from several years of "cat fighting." In addition to Logan, the ring was rumored to include at various times Louis Buckley of American Envelope Company; Chandler Bullock of State Mutual Insurance Company; George Jeppson of Norton Company; and Pehr Holmes, a metal manufacturer. Though Buckley and Bullock were Yankees, the inclusion of Holmes and Jeppson, both Swedes, and Logan, a British immigrant, though all Protestants, suggested some broadening of the ethnic definition of the Republican political elite in Worcester. More important, however, all these men were successful businessmen sitting at the very heart of economic power in the city, and ring members' occupations suggested the new unity of the local business community: James Logan, Louis Buckley, George Jeppson, and Pehr Holmes were manufacturers and Bullock was the most important leader of the city's financial interests.[50]

This new unity of Worcester's business community was an important key to the Republican party's revived success. Through the 1880s, as noted, Worcester's businessmen often split over local politics. Now commercial businessmen, bankers, insurance company owners, real estate developers and owners, and managers of the emerging large manufacturing companies, such as the machinery manufacturers, all understood the advantages of mutual association and realized that they needed to develop Worcester's infrastructure and reputation to compete in a national market. The commitment of the factory owners to a program of municipal improvements thus marked the merger of Worcester's manufacturing and commercial interests into a single, powerful business interest in Worcester's politics. Supporting the "ring" was, thus, the organized business power of Worcester's business community. It included formal organizations like the Chamber of Commerce, NMTA and the NMTBA, and informal ones like the Thursday Noon Club. After 1919 it could also boast the power of Worcester's most powerful and popular newspaper, the *Worcester Telegram,* for in November of that year the paper founded and led by the irascible Austin Christy, a Republican but always a maverick, had been sold to a group much more beholden to the local business community. Among its major new stockholders were Lucius Knowles, president of Crompton and Knowles, Paul Morgan of Morgan Construction, and other important manufacturers.

Taking up the charge to make Worcester competitive in a broad national and international market, Logan and his allies embarked on a program of heavy expenditures for municipal improvements and set about making it the keystone of the Republican party's policy in municipal politics. They were well aware that this had also been the tradition of earlier elites, even Citizens' party leaders, and they self-consciously identified with that tradition. In his very first campaign, in 1907, Logan proclaimed his philosophy crisply: "This city is to grow and we should avail ourselves of every opportunity for future growth." Republican mayoral candidates after Logan seconded his commitment to heavy expenditures and added to his agenda. George Brooks, for example, announced haughtily in 1911 that "I do not propose an administration parsimonious and mean," and George Wright, a wire manufacturer, who served as mayor from 1913 through 1916, almost cavalierly defended heavy spending on streets, sewer, and water improvements: "if such expenditure is extravagance, I am glad to be an extravagant mayor."[51]

Such statements might easily have provoked revolts among middle-class loyalists within the Republican party in years past, but under Logan and his successors these positions became the rallying cry for a united party. Overlock's defeats had done much to discredit the middle-class loyalist faction. More important, the issues that had once divided Republican independents and loyalists no longer seemed so significant. Prohibition was fading as an important issue as drinking and saloons appeared increasingly less dangerous. Divisions still existed between evangelical and liberal Protestants over drinking, but the issue was simply not important enough to trouble the Republican party much anymore. Just as important, middle-class loyalists appreciated the campaign for improvements in city services as they followed the rapidly expanding electric streetcars to all points of the city. Just as Logan and the North End Ring were taking over control of the Republican party, housing construction began to boom in Worcester, rising steadily until the First World War. Housing developments and real estate parks began to appear along trolley lines all over the west and north sides and even into the far southeast near the bordering towns of Millbury and Shrewsbury. Whether the GOP administrations stoked city growth or merely responded to it, it seems clear that their policy of improvements met a growing need or demand among the middle-class Yankees who made up much of the exodus to Lenox, Tatnuck, Franconia, and the other new peripheral neighborhoods or housing parks in Worcester. As George Wright stated in 1915: "It requires an unusually large expenditure to get the main arteries of improvements to the outskirts where these new developments are." Middle-class and elite Republicans thus both shared in the GOP's commitment to municipal improvements in the early twentieth century.[52]

Irish Democrats, of course, could hardly be happy with the changes in GOP fortunes, but there was no hint they would compromise their newly won control of the Democratic party to return to the coalitions of the 1880s. The Irish had now invested their interests totally in the Democratic party in municipal as well as state and national politics. It was their party: their political fortunes rose and fell on its success. All of the Democratic candidates for mayor between 1900 and 1919 were Irish Catholics. Yet it went deeper than that. In 1910 eight of the eleven Democratic candidates for alderman and fifteen of the twenty possible nominees for the Common Council were Irish; in 1913 eight of the party's eleven aldermanic candidates and thirteen of the twenty for the Common Council were Irish; and in 1916 eight of eleven and seventeen of twenty. Similarly, 50 of 53 in 1907, 48 of 53 in 1908, and 45 of 53 members in 1910 of the party's ward committees were first- or second-generation Irish.

Finally, every indicator suggests that Irish voters gave the Democrats lopsided majorities even as the party's vote declined among most other groups.[53]

Yet Irish Democrats could not win a citywide election on their own votes alone and thus could not pursue a strategy of ethnocentric appeals aimed at only their own voters. The situations and strategies of Worcester's Irish Democratic leaders thus differed sharply from those of fellow Celtic Democrats in Boston like James Michael Curley, who made assaults on Yankees the staple of his political campaigns. In Boston, Irish votes alone could rule in any city election. For an Irish Democrat running for citywide office in Boston, as Paul Kleppner suggests, the chief worry was factionalism and defections in the Irish vote. Ethnocentric appeals like Curley's seemed at least in part a response to that factionalism because they made voting for Yankee opponents or even compromising Irishmen tantamount to ethnic treason. In Boston it was important to "out-Irish" your opponent just as southern white politicians "out-segged" (called for segregation) their competitors. In Worcester, where the Irish population was smaller and there were so many other important groups, overt ethnocentric campaigning on the Curley model would have led a Celtic candidate to almost inevitable defeat in citywide elections.[54]

Irish Democratic candidates in early twentieth-century Worcester were thus very different men than Curley or his Boston imitators. The most successful Irish Democrat in the early twentieth century was John T. Duggan. Duggan, with his flowing white hair and luxuriant mustache, epitomized respectability. The son of an Irish immigrant policeman, Duggan attended Holy Cross and medical school in New York before opening his medical practice in Worcester. By the time he ran for mayor in 1905, he had already served on the school board for more than a decade, winning compliments from both parties for fairness and integrity. One Republican opponent acknowledged in the middle of the 1905 campaign that Duggan was a "good man and an honest man" even if from the wrong party. Duggan's speech accepting the Democratic nomination for mayor reflected his character well: "in the event of my election, I promise to the citizens a safe, a conservative and businesslike administration."[55]

Duggan's integrity and caution worked well for the Democrats when the Republicans nominated the mercurial populist Overlock, but after Logan and his allies took over the GOP, the Democrats had more difficulty finding the formula for a successful mayoral candidate. Duggan had run well on the Yankee Republican west side in his victories over Overlock in 1905 and 1906, but in 1907 Logan crushed him in the west side, in Wards One, Nine, and Ten. In 1908 the Democrats nominated Dr. Thomas Barrett, a handsome second-generation Irish dentist who appeared to have all of Duggan's virtues and then some: a Holy Cross graduate, son of an established Irish immigrant contractor, a fashionable wife from New York known for her operatic talents, and his own solid experience on the Board of Aldermen which won him bi-partisan acclaim. Barrett polled the largest Democratic vote in Worcester's history in 1908 and Logan still beat him handily; five years later George Wright routed Barrett again. After Logan's rise, Irish Democrats could no longer count on picking up enough votes from disgruntled Republican Yankees to be competitive in citywide elections.[56]

Catholic ethnics appeared to be a more promising source of allies for Irish Democrats. All the non-Irish Catholic groups seemed to vote Democratic more often than not throughout the first three decades of the twentieth century. As the French Canadian newspaper *L'Opinion Publique* and Yankee and Swedish Republican strategists all confessed, common religion was a potentially powerful bond holding the Catholic ethnics together. Moreover, as far as can be determined, all the other Catholic ethnic groups agreed with the Irish on all the issues of public morality in the period. Precinct voting data for all of the Catholic ethnics suggest consistent and strong opposition to prohibition, for example.[57]

Nevertheless, a common loyalty, shared perspectives on issues of public morality, and even similar economic circumstances did not insure the non-Irish ethnics' loyalty to an Irish-led party. Only the Poles and Lithuanians demonstrated the same kind of steady allegiance to the Democrats that the Protestant Swedes showed for the Republicans. The French continued to play a self-conscious pragmatic strategy of playing the two parties against each other, and leaders of other groups pursued the practical interests of their groups and/or themselves as well. In 1916, for example, the *Labor News* commented wryly on the tactics of Italian leader Joe De Marco, "da boss of the Meadows," who ran for councilman as a Democrat but had his son nominated for alderman as a Republican. One French Canadian leader aptly summed up the expectations and strategies of most of the city's ethnic groups: "Our city is composed of different elements or nationalities, resulting into groups, and each party is entitled to political rights. Each element should have some representation in the city government."[58]

In the twentieth century, as Republicans under Logan made significant efforts to bring French Canadians into their party, Irish Democrats did not, or perhaps could not, match the GOP's offers. In 1909 about 13 percent of the GOP city committee members were French Canadians. By contrast, there were no French Canadians on the Democratic city committee. Michael Bachand speaking at a Republican rally in 1908 suggested that these efforts proved that "the Republican party has always honored the French speaking people as much as it could." A dustup between French Canadian leaders and the GOP in 1910 and 1911 and the cagey Democratic nomination of a French Canadian for alderman at large in those years brought French Canadians back into the Democratic party briefly, but the Irish made little effort to follow up that opportunity and cement the *Canadiens* to the party. Between 1912 and 1918, the Democrats nominated only six French Canadians for city or state office; by contrast the Republicans nominated thirty-one. The Irish performed poorly in this competition, not because of a lack of interest but from a lack of resources. Yankee Republicans gave up little in nominating French Canadian or other ethnics in east side wards. Politics was a less important means of upward mobility for Yankees than for their Irish counterparts, and they had little chance of winning council, aldermanic, or state legislative seats in east side wards anyway. For Irishmen, so dependent on politics, however, those seats in heavily Democratic neighborhoods were precious and they were reluctant to yield them to the French or anyone else.[59]

Neither the Democrats nor the Republicans were very solicitous of the new Catholic ethnics in the 1900s and 1910s, perhaps because they thought these groups still too weak to matter much in municipal politics. The Republicans did stage rallies for Italian voters as early as 1909 and placed new immigrants on the city committee in 1906. Nevertheless, neither the GOP nor the Democrats were quick to slate Italians or Poles for state or city offices. Before the First World War, Republicans and Democrats each nominated two Italians for local offices, and none put up Poles or Lithuanians for municipal or state legislative posts.[60]

Irish Democratic troubles may have lain less in their willingness or capacity to recognize non-Irish Catholics than in their inability to find issues that would tie these groups to the Democratic party. In the 1910s the Irish had difficulty mobilizing Catholic ethnics around issues of common religious concern such as religious discrimination or public morality. Though there was evidence of persistent anti-Catholic discrimination in Worcester in that decade, there was no organized nativist movement substantial enough to rouse the city's non-Irish Catholics. In 1915 Irish Democrats launched an attack on Mayor Wright's appointment of a city physician who had allegedly been affiliated with anti-Catholic organizations. French Canadians and other Catholic ethnics showed no interest in the issue, however, and the *Catholic Messenger* bitterly reproached non-Irish Catholics for their indifference: "the appointment," the paper said, "has served notice on all Catholics, Irish, French, Polish, Italians . . . that their representation in our council halls are not worthy of consideration when the word is passed to snap the party whip. . . . it is hard to understand why it is that when the faith of all these nationalities is attacked publicly or otherwise the burden of defense is pushed over to the Irish Catholic and he is left alone to fight the enemy single handed and the deduction is that no one can tell who the heroes are and who the cowards until some crisis comes to put us to the test." Irish Democrats had no more success in rallying fellow Catholics against prohibition. In 1905 the state Democratic party broke open over the temperance issue as John B. Moran, an avowed enemy of the liquor interests, won the state's nomination for governor. These faction fights plagued both the state and local party through 1909 and hindered the Democrats' ability to run as a pro-license party. After 1910, of course, the liquor issue had little impact on local politics until the war.[61]

Perhaps the biggest hindrance to the Irish Democrat's appeal to other working-class ethnics, however, was their seemingly puzzling zeal for cutting costs and taxes. As the Republican party moved, first unsteadily, then with greater assurance to embrace the position of the old Citizens' party, advocating heavy expenditures for municipal improvements, the Democrats had even more quickly taken up the old Republican loyalist cry for economy in government and lower taxes. Duggan boasted freely of lowering the tax rate as the most important accomplishment of his two terms. Criticized by Logan for neglecting public improvements, Mayor Duggan replied that he did "what any sane man would do in conducting his private business, viz. guard the taxpayer's money most zealously and keep down the expenses." Even after Duggan's loss, the Democrats continued to hammer away at the GOP's spendthrift policies. David O'Connell also decried Logan's "policy of extravagance" in his 1910 campaign and assailed the Republicans in 1911 for their "fads, fancies and expensive reckless experiments."[62]

Most city Democrats had participated avidly in the Citizens' coalitions, and their sudden enthusiasm for cutting costs was, as Republicans slyly pointed out, a dramatic reversal of position. In 1911, William Lyttle, former Republican candidate for mayor, twitted David O'Connell for his opposition to increased city expenditures, noting that as an alderman in the 1890s O'Connell had regularly voted for larger sums for the same purposes. In the early 1900s, however, cutting taxes must have seemed a sound political strategy for the Democrats. Philip O'Connell and John Duggan seemed to use that issue to take advantage of internal Republican conflicts and run well in normally Republican districts. In addition to the direct appeal of low taxes, Democratic commitments to sound, conservative fiscal policies may have been reassuring to voters fearful of the potential excesses of Irish Democrats. Later Democrats, particularly

David F. O'Connell, gave the economy in government issue a populist edge by railing against bureaucratic experts in city hall and their expensive schemes.[63]

Nevertheless, in the long run the Democrats' emphasis on fiscal austerity and cutting taxes hurt them. By 1907 James Logan and his allies had reunified the GOP on a platform of public improvements and reduced the prospects of defection in Yankee Republican districts; and surely the Democrats' potential alternative working-class and lower-class constituency would be less concerned about the taxes that few of them paid directly and more interested in the jobs that new construction and an expanded city government would produce. The city employees' union, for example, openly repudiated Duggan in 1907 for cutting the city's payroll. It was the Republicans, not the Democrats, who were willing to spend money on school construction, road building, and expansion of the sewer system that not only helped city neighborhoods but provided work opportunities for unskilled laborers. James Logan's defense of his commitment to public expenditures in the depression year of 1908 appears to be a classic articulation of the philosophy of Democratic bosses, not the political principles of a Republican manufacturer turned patrician mayor. Logan said: "You have not been in the mayor's chair this year. You have not had strong, manly men come to you and plead for an appointment to work . . . they wanted to sell to this city the only thing they had to sell, the labor of their hands." In Worcester it was the Republicans who created jobs for the poorest in good times and bad.[64]

Irish Democrats were thus simply overwhelmed in municipal politics by the Logan machine and its successors through World War I, but the troubles Irish Democrats in Worcester experienced putting together a coalition of new ethnics, their difficulties with French Canadian and Italians in particular, were not uncommon among Irish Democrats in early twentieth-century urban America. In other cities with competitive Republican parties in the 1910s, like Chicago, Irish-led Democratic parties also struggled to secure the votes of the new ethnics.[65]

Moreover, at the height of Republican power, there were some signs in Worcester that the local Democrats might be able to create a broad pan-ethnic Catholic coalition in the future. Democratic candidates for president, governor, and other state offices often ran far ahead of their municipal counterparts in the 1910s. Woodrow Wilson ran very strong in the city in 1916, stronger than any Democratic presidential candidate since the Civil War, and did particularly well in the new immigrant precincts. David I. Walsh did even better in Worcester, actually carrying the city in his race for governor in 1913. The success of state and national Democrats among the new immigrants stemmed in large part from the appeal of their progressive, new urban liberal, programs to Polish, Italian, and Lithuanian workers.[66]

Even in municipal politics there was evidence of the possibility of a new Democratic pan-ethnic coalition. In 1910 David O'Connell, the free-swinging, ethnically militant, old Democratic war horse teamed with a respected French Canadian, N. B. Soulliere, on a citywide ticket for mayor and alderman at large, respectively, and ran a very close race against James Logan, himself. The next year O'Connell and Soulliere stole a victory from the Republicans. In both elections, the Democrats rolled up a particularly strong vote in east side ethnic precincts. The *Catholic Messenger* hailed this Catholic ticket's success as proof of Catholic talent and power. In truth, O'Connell's and Soulliere's victories owed as much to Republican bungling of relations with French Canadians and inept management of a municipal water crisis. Nevertheless, O'Connell and Soulliere's success revealed that groups like the French or the Italians were not at all permanently tied to the Republicans but were very much in play. Indeed, almost all of the Catholic ethnics, including the French Canadians and the Italians, voted Democrat at least as often as Republican—albeit by small margins sometimes—in the early twentieth century. As important, O'Connell's vote suggested a subtle but potentially crucial shift in the strategy of the local Democratic party: a change from Philip O'Connell's and John Duggan's older efforts to play upon GOP factionalism and lure disaffected west side Republicans to the Democratic ticket, to a possible future of establishing a Democratic majority and simply overpowering the GOP by mobilizing east side ethnics. That prospect was still well hidden in the 1910s, but it was closer to realization than anyone might have thought then.[67]

"On Account of the Catholic Vote": The Rise of Peter "the Great" Sullivan and the Prospect of a Democratic Majority

Given the state of the city and city politics in 1917 and 1918, it would have been very hard to predict either the approaching Irish political triumph in 1919 or the impending rebirth of nativism in Worcester in the early 1920s. During World War I, Worcester was caught up in the hysterical patriotism of the nation's mobilization for war, and the city's Irish Americans backed the war with no less vigor than their neighbors. Irishmen in other cities throughout the United States expressed strong support for the Central Powers before the United States entered the war in 1917, but the Worcester Irish manifested no such pro-German sentiment. Once war was declared, Worcester's Irishmen enthusiastically proclaimed their support for the American cause. Since Irish

Americans were backing the war so unstintingly and Worcester had no large population of Germans or Austrians, there was no ethnic base in the city for dissent or even reservations about the war and its relentless prosecution. (There were rumors that the Swedes were mildly pro-German but those sentiments, if they were true, never prompted local Scandinavians to protest the war.) Moreover, Worcester's factories were booming, unemployment was virtually nonexistent, and wages rose rapidly. Such prosperity encouraged unanimity. A united, prosperous city also saw no need for a change in leadership. Pehr Holmes, the Republican mayor, claimed that he had no time for politics because of the war emergency and did not even bother to campaign in the elections of 1917 and 1918. He rolled up lopsided wins over Hughie O'Rourke, his Democratic opponent, nonetheless.[68]

Though the Irish and other groups participated sincerely in the local war effort, Yankee Protestants thoroughly dominated it. Even before the war the *Labor News,* Worcester's labor weekly, had suggested that many members of the west side elite were slavish anglophiles and eager to put the country into the line on Britain's behalf. Once the war started, the same elite, men like Harry Worcester Smith, George S. Barton, and Paul Morgan and women such as Mrs. Homer Gage and Mrs. Donald Tulloch, virtually monopolized every local war committee. Of the men directing the city's last great Liberty Loan drive in September of 1918, seventeen were Yankees and only four were Protestant or Catholic ethnics.[69]

In Worcester as throughout much of America such ethnic hegemony was temporarily overlooked in a war crusade that went beyond mere patriotism and frequently degenerated into hysteria. Public rituals of conformity were frequent throughout the war period. Liberty Loan rallies, parades, and picnics occurred almost weekly, and heated rhetoric backed such rituals suggesting any but the most fervid war supporters were disloyal or treasonous. The *Post* argued, for example, that "slackers and cheapskates" in the Liberty Loan drives did not measure up to the "full standard of true Americans." Such sentiments led in Worcester as elsewhere to an attack on every vestige of German culture. Worcester's newspapers demanded that the city's schools remove the German language from their curriculum, and in 1918 the schools discharged a Commerce High School teacher and accused him of spreading war propaganda after he refused induction into the armed forces.[70]

Such crushing of dissent left little room for questioning during the war, but as shortages in virtually every commodity persisted after the Armistice, the local economy collapsed, and an influenza epidemic struck, Worcester's citizens began to stir. The new immigrants were hard hit by the postwar depression and epidemic. The *Labor News* reported that more than one thousand of Worcester's Italian immigrants returned to Italy to search for work in 1919. New immigrant resentment of the Americanization efforts and blatant nativism of the antired campaigns launched by George Jeppson at Norton Company and his allies in the Thursday Noon Club compounded the immigrants' frustrations over the hard times of the depression. Advertisements sponsored by the club repeatedly vilified aliens, and companies like Norton's were quick to dismiss new immigrants in favor of Swedish or native-stock Americans. Prohibition, another legacy of the war, also alienated the new immigrants. Through the 1910s conflicts over liquor had slipped into irrelevance, but the war made prohibition an issue once again.[71]

On the national level the Democrats bore the blame for this postwar travail, but locally the Republicans had been in power and voters held them responsible for the city's new ills. Democratic politicians and newspapers like the *Post* scalded Pehr Holmes for his failure to anticipate Worcester's need for coal during the "coal famine" in the winter of 1918–19 or for giving in to distributors on the price of milk. Italian immigrant leaders also criticized the municipal administration for not explaining its coal-rationing policy to the new immigrants, leaving many of them confused, cold, and vulnerable to the ravages of the flu epidemic. Perhaps as important, the Republicans continued to seek heavy expenditures for municipal improvements despite the shortages, the economic plunge, and the shrinking tax base. In 1919 the Holmes administration commenced a massive new sewer construction project and revived Mayor Wright's call for a grand new civic auditorium. Continuing improvements during hard times roused the Democrats and seemed to provoke grumbling within the GOP itself.[72]

Sensing Republican weakness, the Democrats put up their strongest candidate for mayor since John Duggan, perhaps their strongest candidate ever: Peter Francis Sullivan, affectionately known then and since as "Peter the Great." Born in Killarney, County Kerry, in Ireland in 1870, Sullivan emigrated to America at the age of thirteen. In the 1880s he opened a newsstand and later a steamship ticket agency that specialized in sending tickets and remittances back to Ireland (many of his customers were servant girls), but Peter the Great's real occupation was politics. Between 1901 and 1903 he represented Ward Four in the General Court in Boston and from 1907 to 1910 he served the same ward on the city's board of aldermen. When he ran for mayor in 1919 he had just won his second term in the state senate, representing the southern half of the city.[73]

Sullivan brought more to his mayoral campaign than long experience. His high forehead, strong face, and "big boned" physique could give him a severe look that belied his genial nature. He was one of the best-liked men in Worcester. Even the rabidly Republican *Telegram* acknowledged on several occasions that Peter Sullivan was "affable . . . sunny, even engaging." He loved sports, delighted in swapping stories and composing poems. His unpresumptuous easiness was a tonic to Worcester voters tired of wartime sacrifices and bitter over the decline of the economy.[74]

Sullivan brought a winning program as well as a winning personality to the election. A veteran of the Spanish American War, he had led the fight in the state senate for a veterans' "homesteading" housing bill and for veteran preference in civil service after World War I. The centerpiece of his municipal campaign was the same call for cutting costs and taxes that had been the hallmark of all previous Democratic campaigns in the twentieth century. Yet Sullivan gave his tax-cutting calls a populist dimension. His backers chided the "millionaire" leaders of the Republican ring, "men who made their pile out of the labor of children," and their wives, "ladies of leisure," who insisted on a long list of civic improvements but shunted the costs off to the small homeowner. This time the city's shrinking tax base and rampant inflation made the attack on government extravagance seem sensible to a broad segment of the public.[75]

Moreover, unlike many of his Democratic predecessors, Sullivan could credibly balance this policy with appeals to groups which might suffer under a cost-cutting administration: city workers; organized labor; and homeowners in new residential areas. Sullivan won the votes of the city's firefighters, for example, by backing their efforts to move to a two-platoon work rotation. His longtime support for organized labor underscored his criticisms of Holmes's failure to intercede in a strike by the city's molders and in other postwar labor troubles. Similarly, while on the board of aldermen, "Peter the Great" had been the city's leading advocate of public ownership of the streetcars. In the campaign for mayor he did not persist in that progressive position, but he did fight hard to hold the line on fare hikes; that, and his reputation, helped him exploit anger in the newer residential areas over high fares, poor service, and the perceived privileged treatment of the city's transit companies by the municipal government. As a friend of labor and an opponent of blue laws and prohibition, Sullivan was also an especially attractive choice for the new immigrants as well as many other Catholic workers in the city. Holmes's attempts to tie Sullivan to the Boston police strike (some said that George Jeppson of Norton Company and a mover in the Thursday Noon Club urged this strategy on Holmes) and to other postwar forces that the Republican mayor charged were "openly and firmly arrayed against the principles of law and order" probably only reinforced the resentments of new immigrants and their appreciation of the Irish Democrat.

On election day, Sullivan beat Holmes soundly, piling up the highest Democratic vote in the city's history to that time and nearly doubling the slight vote that Hugh O'Rourke, the Democratic candidate for mayor, had garnered against Holmes the year before. Sullivan ran well all over the city, making substantial gains even in normally Republican districts, but his strength lay in mobilizing the latently powerful vote in ethnic Democratic districts. Sullivan ran 27 percentage points ahead of O'Rourke in Ward Four, for example. The vast increase in Democratic voters on the east side, however, was as striking as the percentage increases. The day before the election, the *Worcester Telegram* reported that registration for the city election had risen a full 15 percent over the previous year. Much of that growth occurred in Wards Three, Four, and Five, where the Democratic vote in 1919 was 60 percent larger than an average of the three previous municipal campaigns (1,054 votes larger in Ward Four, for example; 818 in Ward Three).[76]

Sullivan's appeal in normally Republican districts was vital to his victory, but his romp to victory was really a triumph of an emerging Catholic coalition with help from some other new immigrants, such as the Jews. That was the opinion of George Jeppson, North End Ring insider, who wrote Congressman Samuel Winslow: "In going over this situation with some of those who think they know, and over the figures, I believe Sullivan won on account of the Catholic vote: the French, Irish and Italians standing behind him practically to a man." Louis Buckley, another member of the Ring, agreed, attributing Holmes's loss to the defection of the "Republican Catholic vote, the Poles, Lithuanians etc." Though Sullivan ran very well among new immigrant Catholics his most significant gains were made in French Canadian precincts. In Ward Four, precinct three, and Ward Five, precinct two, his vote jumped more than twenty percentage points over O'Rourke's proportion just a year before.[77]

Sullivan moved to bolster his newly forged Catholic coalition over the next two years by adept—if minimal—ticket balancing. His most important move was to engineer the nomination of the French Canadian Camille Trahan for alderman at large in 1920. The Republicans put up a *Canadien* for the office too, but only after a heated primary battle further alienated French Canadians from the GOP. The following year Sullivan skillfully avoided a similar conflict in his own party by persuading a popular Irishman not to challenge Trahan in the primary. Sullivan and Democratic leaders were less successful in trying to reward new Catholic immigrants with nominations. In 1921, they backed Anthony Malozzi for Common Council in Ward Three, but he was beaten by an Irishman in the Democratic primary. Still Sullivan won over 90 percent of the vote in Worcester's Little Italy in 1921, and an Italian band led the mayor's victory parade from the Knights of Columbus hall downtown to Sullivan's home on the east side's Grafton Hill.[78]

The election results suggested that Peter the Great had built a solid electoral base and would be far more difficult to defeat than any of his Democratic predecessors. In 1920, the Republicans pulled the popular ex-mayor George Wright out of retirement to face the new mayor in his reelection bid, but Sullivan clobbered him. In the next two elections Sullivan easily dispatched seasoned Republican politician Frederick Minor and narrowly defeated a successful Yankee businessman, Harry Goddard.[79]

Sullivan's success during his four-year reign marked a milestone in Irish politics in Worcester. Sullivan's east side electoral coalition differed from that of his successful Irish Democratic predecessors, Philip O'Connell and, more clearly, John Duggan. These men had run well on the east side but won only because they ran better in the normally Republican areas of the city than most state or national Democrats did. David O'Connell's victory in 1911 had hinted at a new Democratic party built on mobilization of east side voters. O'Connell's success was, however, but a hint, and after his single victory the Democratic party succumbed again to a revived Republican machine. Sullivan emerged as the city economy plunged into depression and ethnic rivalry reignited into open conflict. It was a traumatic moment in Worcester's history and it helped Sullivan construct a far more powerful and durable east side coalition than any Irish Democrat had done before him.[80]

The Crisis of the Elite and the Rise of Michael J. O'Hara

Sullivan's successes came at a difficult time for Republican business leaders. The postwar depression was the most severe blow to the local economy in decades. The city's major corporations, the Norton Company, Osgood Bradley, and many of the big foundries and machinery manufacturers, were decimated by the economic downturn and struggled merely to survive. Worcester's prominence as a manufacturing center was also beginning to recede as cities making consumer durables like cars and appliances moved to the forefront of the nation's economy ahead of machinery-manufacturing cities like Worcester. The organizational arm of Worcester business, the Chamber of Commerce, reflected the troubles of its members and the city's economy. Membership in the Chamber dropped back to a thousand in early 1922, or back to where it had been nearly a decade earlier before the war boom. An editorial in the Chamber's newsletter, *Review and Bulletin,* complained that such a small number of members was "manifestly absurd" for an industrial community of Worcester's size and stature. Sensitive to their own weakness and acutely aware of the labor revolt spreading around the country as well as Marxist revolution overseas, Worcester's business leaders braced themselves, as we have seen, for an onslaught from their own workers. That threat never materialized, but in Peter Sullivan a political threat did. Sullivan appeared to have finally achieved the long-dreaded, but long-delayed, Irish Democratic conquest of the city's politics. The problem Sullivan posed was not simply that he was Irish, Catholic, and a Democrat, however, but that he was a friend of labor (albeit a cautious one) and, perhaps most important, a populist cost- and tax-cutter, steadfastly opposed to expenditures on civic improvements.[81]

Confronting a host of problems, Worcester's business elite began to seek a means of countering or coopting emerging Irish political power in Worcester. That effort began in the business community and, more specifically, in the Chamber of Commerce itself, with the elevation of an Irish Catholic, John F. Tinsley, to a position of critical responsibility. Tinsley had taken the only apparent route available to an Irishman for corporate success in Worcester: he came from outside the city, and was appointed head of an important plant by a national firm (in this case U.S. Steel) that thus validated his ability and reliability. Having gained entry into Worcester's upper economic circles, Tinsley stayed on in Worcester after leaving his job at the wire mill and became vice president and general manager of Crompton and Knowles Company. In 1919 he was an active member in the Thursday Noon Club and in 1923 he was elected president of the Chamber of Commerce. Moreover, as Tinsley rose in the Chamber, other Irishmen—Maurice Reidy, James F. Healey, Mark Cosgrove, Thomas E. O'Connell, and Mark Carroll—rose with him, or perhaps he helped lift them up. Chamber officials, alarmed at their declining numbers and changing political circumstances in the early twenties, had stressed their organization's need to "reflect" the diversity of the community, and once in power Tinsley moved to ensure that the effort to broaden the Chamber's membership would continue. He placed Healey in charge of the membership committee and Healey in turn picked a number of Irishmen, French Canadians, and Italians to serve with him. The Chamber also made some symbolic acknowledgments of Irish power, from welcoming Senator Walsh and Mayor Sullivan in 1923 to arranging for Miss Margaret McDonnell and Miss Mae Brennan to sing at the organization's annual banquet in the same year.[82]

The selection of Tinsley and new attention to other Irish Catholics by the Chamber was not an attempt to recognize increasing Irish prominence in business, simply because such Irish prominence was not increasing. Beyond Tinsley there were scarcely any other Irishmen in the foremost ranks of Worcester industry in the early 1920s, and there were no signs that the number of Irish manufacturers would grow much in the future. In 1919, there were 8 Irish owners or managers of manufacturing companies from the 104 Irishmen listed in the biographical section of Nutt's *History of Worcester*; in 1934 there were 3 from the 63 listed in Nelson's *History of Worcester County*. The Irishmen moving up in the Chamber with Tinsley, such as Cosgrove, Coughlin, and Reidy, were successful businessmen but only medium-sized retailers, wholesalers, or real estate developers, hardly captains of industry. If Irish business power had grown little, however, Irish political power had grown enormously, and it appears that the Chamber's Irishmen were chosen to accommodate the new Celtic political potency. Maurice Reidy, second-generation Irish real estate developer and once rumored as a Democratic nominee for mayor, headed up the civic affairs committee in the early 1920s. James F. Healey, who had worked for city government as a sealer of weights and measures since 1915 joined him there. And, of course, John F. Tinsley could negotiate directly with his fellow Celt, Peter Sullivan, as the new president of the Chamber in 1923.[83]

Yet sharing power in the Chamber would not be the Yankee business elite's principal means of accommodating Irish political power, and John F. Tinsley would not be its principal vehicle. Irish power was not economic but political and it would be in the political arena that that accommodation would be struck. And the vehicle would be Michael J. O'Hara.

Portly, sporting a pencil-thin moustache, O'Hara looked like a slightly comic character actor in the movies, and, in appearance at least, was thus an unlikely candidate for his important role in Worcester politics. Born in Worcester in 1867 to Michael and Ellen (Mulvaney) O'Hara, he entered the ice business after leaving school and did not gain his first public office until after he turned forty-seven in 1914, when he was elected to the Common Council. He served there for four years, then as alderman from Ward Two for two years before winning a tight race for alderman at large in 1922. O'Hara demonstrated an impressive ability to attract votes on the east side in that election while still holding the GOP's base in the west side Yankee wards. Observers suggested that many east side Irish Democrats had ditched their own party's French Canadian candidate to vote for O'Hara. When Sullivan beat the head of the GOP's ticket, Harry Goddard, in 1922, in Sullivan's fourth consecutive victory, O'Hara emerged as the principal Republican challenger to Peter Sullivan.[84]

There is no evidence that members of the business elite had singled out O'Hara for advancement earlier in his career or had prompted his race for mayor in 1923, but comparing his vote in the Republican primary that year with his previous year's primary performance in the race for alderman at large clearly suggests that they found him an exciting, potential solution to their problem of growing Irish power. In the Republican primary for alderman at large in 1922, O'Hara had rolled up an enormous majority in his own ward, Ward Two, and hung close enough in the other wards to eke out a victory over a veteran Republican politician. In the 1923 Republican mayoral primary by contrast, O'Hara lost his home ward as Swedish voters, who had hitherto backed him, flocked to one of their own, Christian Nelson. O'Hara won the primary by winning the west side; he carried Ward Nine and, most tellingly, polled nearly four times as many votes as his nearest competitor in Ward Ten, the wealthiest and most Yankee ward in the city. Indeed, nearly one-quarter of O'Hara's vote came from Worcester's elite Ward Ten.[85]

As O'Hara rose to power, Sullivan had finally begun to appear vulnerable. French Canadians, it appears, were especially angry with Sullivan, but his biggest problem was that the parsimonious policies of his administration no longer seemed to fit the city's needs or its expectations. War and memory of its bitter sacrifices were fading. More important, the city's economy had begun to recover. A new building boom commenced in the city's peripheral neighborhoods, but Sullivan hesitated to increase city expenditures to meet the demands of the new areas for improvements.[86]

Sullivan's coalition did not crumble in 1923, but it cracked just enough to cost him a razor-thin loss. O'Hara and other Republicans were more successful than their predecessors in flogging Sullivan for his reluctance to spend more money on city streets or new schools, and yet the Catholic, culturally liberal "wet" opponent, O'Hara, also neutralized prohibition and other potentially divisive moral issues. The Republican ticket was also craftily chosen. Robert Z. Whipple, a Yankee engineer, prominent member of the Chamber of Commerce (later its president), decorated veteran of the battles at St. Mihiel and the Meuse-Argonne in World War I, won the Republican nomination for alderman at large and was O'Hara's running mate in the citywide election. Though Sullivan still rolled up majorities on the east side, O'Hara cut into Sullivan's margins there and, buoyed by Whipple, piled up exceptionally strong support on the west side to gain his victory.[87]

"A Protestant to Stand and Say He Is a Protestant": The Emergence of the Ku Klux Klan in Worcester

Though Sullivan lost, O'Hara's election meant that an Irish Catholic was still mayor of Worcester, and whether Republican or Democrat, an Irish Catholic mayor was still a symbol of dangerously growing papist power to increasing numbers of disgruntled Protestants. In Worcester as in many cities across the nation this simmering resentment inspired a new nativist crusade, the Ku Klux Klan. Like previous nativist movements in Worcester, the KKK drew its strength from middling and working-class elements of the city's Protestant population. And again like previous nativist efforts in the city, these Protestants seemed moved by economic and political grievances, more specifically by the severe economic depression of 1919–20, and the growing Irish Catholic political power in both parties. Though the KKK was very similar to prior nativist movements in many respects, there were some important differences between it and those earlier crusades. The hysterical nationalism of World War I was clearly evident in the Klansmen's xenophobic rhetoric. More important, it appears that much of the Klan's support came not just from Protestant Yankees but from Protestant Swedes and Ulster Irishmen. Indeed, the Swedish drive for political power and recognition was as important a motive cause of the new nativism as any other.

Worcester residents were aware of the Klan as early as 1921, but the first evidence that the Klan had a local following came in 1922. Most of these early members of the order were Protestant Irishmen from Ulster who resented growing Irish political power in the city. Perhaps more important to them, however, was Ireland's renewed effort to win its freedom from Britain which won enormous support from Worcester's Irish Catholics. The Klan remained insignificant until Eugene Farnsworth, King Kleagle of the KKK in Maine, appeared in Mechanics Hall in Worcester on September 20, 1923. The hall was packed that night and Farnsworth did not disappoint the thousands who came to see him. Alternating venomous diatribes against Catholics, Jews, and "Chinks" with reverent, patriotic odes backed by a quartet humming the national anthem, Farnsworth put on a show. Though members of the K. of C. had infiltrated the crowd just to heckle him, most in the hall that night were enthralled. After the Farnsworth rally, "an avalanche of members" entered Worcester's Klan Klaverns. An estimated 1,500 to 2,000 joined within the following few months.[88]

Most of these new Klansmen were middle- or working-class Protestants. Analyses of over 3,000 members of Worcester's Klaverns by Kevin Hickey have revealed that close to 60 percent were low white-collar or skilled blue-collar workers. The local Klan, therefore, drew its support from the same classes as Worcester's earlier nativist movements, the APA and the Know-Nothings. Like those earlier movements and like the Klan in other parts of the United States, the local Klaverns built on the resentments of these average Americans, not only against foreigners and Catholics but against elites of their own religion who had allegedly betrayed them.[89]

Signs of a rupture between the Protestant elite and the middle class appeared as early as 1918 in a bitter little controversy over a seemingly insignificant appointment to the city's industrial school board. When middle-class Republicans from southwestern Worcester carried the vote in the party caucus to appoint their candidate, Arthur Squires, over George Jeppson, major manufacturer and leader in the North End Ring, observers of city hall politics took notice. The Democratic *Post* sniffed a battle reminiscent of the old conflicts between the loyalist and independent, or Citizens', wings of the GOP, and Jeppson himself sensed an ominous revival of factionalism in the Republican party. After the war the Republican rupture widened. In 1920, for example, some southern districts, Ward Six and parts of Ward Seven broke against the Ring's candidate, ex-Mayor George Wright, in the Republican mayoral primary. When Farnsworth came to town, then, his antielitist rhetoric was well received: "Why they wouldn't know us . . . today America is not the land of the free. It is the land of the privileged. It is not the land where the mass rule." Disenchanted with their own elite, buffeted by the postwar depression and the housing crunch, scared by rising Irish power and inspired by prohibition's reintroduction of temperance into politics, working- and middle-class Protestants broke loose from the Logan coalition and were aflame with nativist suspicion.[90]

It is important not to overstate the antielitist dimension of the Klan's Protestant supporters. It is not clear, for example, that the new nativists objected to any economic policy of the elite. Earlier GOP loyalists had often fought over substantive economic issues, attacking the elite's heavy expenditures and urging tax cuts. Yet there is no evidence that the KKK nativists or their political spokesmen took such a position, perhaps because it had already been taken by Irish Democrats like Peter Sullivan. The elite's cultural liberalism, particularly its indifference to prohibition, must have been a more important source of resentment for the Klansmen and their sympathizers. Yet, perhaps, nothing seemed to gall them more than the elite's backing of Michael O'Hara.

Not resentment of elites or even worries over cultural change, but fears of Catholic or immigrant power were the emotional core of Klan sentiment in Worcester. The climax of Farnsworth's rally at Mechanics Hall was a call to mobilize Protestant power: "The Chinks, Jews, Italians, and Catholics all practice clannishness and help boost each other. We native born Protestant race of men who have lived honestly and paid our bills haven't a friend in the world. There isn't a member of our church that will speak to us if we get into trouble. Sixty-two per cent of all of our elected or appointed offices are occupied by

Roman Catholics. This country has got into a position where a Protestant is ashamed to stand and say he is a Protestant. . . . We want to worship in our own way without anyone insulting us."[91]

Though the religious and class backgrounds of Worcester's new nativists were much the same as the old ones, a far larger proportion of the new nativists were immigrants or the children of immigrants than in any previous nativist crusade. There were of course the Ulster Irish, but far more important were the Swedes. Klan Klaverns flourished in the Swedish neighborhoods of Greendale, Quinsigamond Village, and Bell Hill and some estimates suggest that as many as 49 percent of Worcester's Klansmen had Swedish surnames. There were several reasons for the Klan's appeal to the Swedes. Amid the general decline in evangelical fervor in Worcester, many of the city's Swedes had remained firmly committed to the old faith and its strict moralism. Indeed, when many Protestants abandoned the prohibitionist cause in the 1910s and 1920s, the Swedes emerged as the leaders and most zealous supporters of no-license. A number of Swedes were also suspicious of the new emerging forms of commercial leisure such as the movies or dance halls. In 1917, the *Telegram* reported that young people in the Swedish neighborhood of Quinsigamond Village had grown so tired of being without amusement that they had started an "agitation," but "to think that the young people in that section would want to conduct dances was too much for some of the residents."[92]

It was not just the cultural transformation of Worcester, however, but changing economic and political circumstances that made the Klan attractive to the city's Swedes. Swedes suffered heavily from the postwar depression. Many of them were machinists employed in the booming war industries that fell with a resounding crash when the war ended. The Norton Company, the largest employer of Swedes in twentieth-century Worcester, laid off 75 percent of its work force from 1918 to 1922. Many of these men flocked to the Klan. Of the members of the Klan who could be identified, no less than 62 percent worked, or had worked, for the Norton Company.[93]

This economic hardship only aggravated Swedish frustrations over their changing political fortunes. Though the Swedes seemed classic Republican partisans they were well aware of their own interests and pursued them doggedly in twentieth-century Worcester politics. As far back as Philip O'Connell's time, Swedes had periodically threatened to bolt the Republicans if they did not receive sufficient political recognition. In 1911 the Democrats successfully lured some Swedes in Quinsigamond Village out of Republican ranks when they nominated their own Swedish candidate, Charles Orstrom, for state representative. In 1912, hundreds of Swedish workers in Bell Hill and Quinsigamond

Village bolted the Republican party to vote for Teddy Roosevelt and his Progressives, and in 1915 Swedish defections rose again in Reardon's election during the machinists' strike. Republican leaders, sensing Swedish impatience and perhaps scared by the defections to Reardon in 1915 countered by nominating Pehr Holmes, the Swedish immigrant, for mayor in 1916 and by electing Axel Magnuson chairman of the party's city committee. The party reaped the benefits of that recognition when the Swedish precincts once again became Republican strongholds in local elections.[94]

Even after Holmes's election and Magnuson's appointment, Swedes still felt alienated, and relations between Swedes and Yankees remained strained. In 1917, the *Labor News* reported Swedish complaints that when "a Swede wants anything [from the Republican party] he is quickly reminded that he is a Swede and it is up to him to keep out of the glare of bright lights." As the Republican party broke open in 1920, Swedish districts voted by more than two to one against George Wright and the remnants of the North End Ring in the Republican primary. Their appetite for power and recognition had been whetted and they remained eager for greater gains.[95]

Yet they were forced to make way for their old antagonists, the Irish. Mutual hatred between Swedes and Irish remained virulent in the early twentieth century. Peter Sullivan's victory in 1919 was a bitter blow to the Swedes, both because Sullivan was an Irish Catholic, one of their old enemies, and because he had abruptly checked rising Swedish power by vanquishing Pehr Holmes. As George Jeppson and his friends suggested, Holmes's Swedish support stood firm in that election even as other parts of the Republican coalition disintegrated. Michael O'Hara's election was, perhaps, even more galling, however, for O'Hara and his Yankee allies had taken over the Swedes' own Republican party. In 1923, O'Hara faced off with Christian Nelson in the Republican mayoral primary and beat him with a combination of west side Yankee and east side Irish and French votes. O'Hara would face Swedish or Yankee evangelical rivals at every succeeding primary election until 1931, and would defeat them in every one of those contests with the backing of the same coalition allying the Yankee elite and east-side Catholics. The Swedes, frustrated and furious, looked to the Klan in 1924 as an outlet for their cultural fears, economic insecurities, and political frustrations.[96]

Drawing from Swedes and middle-class Yankees, the Klan grew stronger and bolder in Worcester through 1924. Some estimates suggest that there were as many as 5,000 Klansmen in Worcester by the end of 1924. Intrepid KKK sympathizers even dared to burn crosses on Bell Hill, which overlooked the long-entrenched Irish settlement of East Worcester, or in front of the

Convent of the Sisters of Notre Dame de Namur near Lake Quinsigamond. In October of 1924, cocky Klan leaders organized a mass "Klonvocation" at the fairgrounds in the Swedish neighborhood of Greendale in north Worcester. An enormous crowd of more than 15,000 people, at least 1,000 of them in full Klan regalia, flocked to the Klonvocation (one Klansman arrived by horse with his robes packed in his saddle bag). There they listened to speeches attacking Catholic candidates in the upcoming state elections, and when night fell they cheered a giant burning cross made up of flares and stretching 200 by 350 feet over the fairgrounds turf.[97]

If the Klan had grown stronger and bolder, however, so had its opponents. The wave of cross burnings prompted retaliatory attacks on Klan members or suspected Klan members throughout Worcester County. Small riots, fistfights, and rock-throwing battles became commonplace. Meanwhile Catholics and Jews organized a boycott of suspected Klan sympathizers. This effort was so successful it nearly drove one of the city's leading bakeries out of business.[98]

When the KKK called for its Klonvocation at the city fairgrounds in October of 1924, then, its opponents were ready. Little trouble occurred during the day of the Klan rally, but as the sun went down and Klan sympathizers began to leave the meeting and head home, they were attacked with rocks and other "missiles." The violence was not confined to the fairgrounds or even to the Greendale neighborhood. As Klan sympathizers rode through the city, men and boys pelted them with rocks or even jumped on the running boards of their cars and dragged them into the streets and beat them mercilessly. (In the midst of the chaotic melee, a biplane with KKK emblazoned on its fuselage made a forced landing near the fairgrounds. Rumors raced through the Klonvocation that it had been shot down by Klan opponents; the pilot revealed later that he had merely run out of gas.)[99]

Michael O'Hara and the Politics of Ethnic Frustration

The ethnic tensions reflected in pitched battles between the Klan and its opponents were played out in city politics as well as on the streets. Initially, the Klan riot and its portent of a city descending into a maelstrom of ethnic violence appeared to inspire support for tolerance on both sides of the partisan and religious divide. As an Irish Catholic Republican, Michael J. O'Hara seemed aptly suited to bridge differences in the city and bring its factions together. O'Hara would prove very resilient in Worcester politics—his reign as mayor would last until 1931—but it would not be because he unified the city or bridged its ethnic chasms. By building an independent power base through popular policy positions and old-fashioned machine tactics, O'Hara was able to skillfully negotiate between Worcester's antagonistic ethnic forces but his administration did little to dampen their antipathy. Indeed, by frustrating both Swedish Republicans and Irish Catholic Democrats, O'Hara seemed to further inflame the mutual hatreds, not resolve them. By 1928 the city would be primed once again for an explosion of ethnic and religious rancor.

Soon after the fairgrounds riot, Klan members began to rally around Arthur Squires as candidate for mayor in the Republican primary. A former alderman from Ward Seven in the southwest part of the city, Squires never claimed to be a member of the Klan or to hold to its principles, but when rumors tagged him as the Klan candidate he did not deny it. "If the organization saw fit to support him the members would be exercising their right to vote for any candidate whose name is on the ballot" he told the *Telegram*. By the day of the primary election, Squires and the evangelical Protestant ministers supporting him had grown less coy, openly appealing to Protestants to vote for the Protestant Squires over the Catholic O'Hara.[100]

The Republican elite, however, quickly moved to bolster O'Hara. The *Telegram*, which was owned by the city's largest industrialists and was the city's most popular paper, battered Squires, attacking him directly on the issue of prejudice. On the day of the election the *Telegram* assailed Squires for the "low business" of his religious appeals, particularly his assertion of the "sanction of a peculiarly Protestant God." Meanwhile, business leaders like Chandler Bullock and Zelotes W. Combes organized the campaign for O'Hara. They signed up a number of prominent Swedes, including former mayor Pehr Holmes, George Jeppson, and even O'Hara's antagonist from the previous year, Christian Nelson, to back the Irish mayor. With virtually the entire Republican party hierarchy behind him, O'Hara rolled to an easy victory in the primary election; indeed, he won every ward. Squires ran well in the Swedish Quinsigamond Village, and in his own Ward Seven where working and middle-class Yankees dominated. Yet if O'Hara ran strongly everywhere, his vote was particularly impressive in the wealthy Yankee west and north side wards, Ten and One, and in the Catholic east side districts. A number of Irish and other Catholic Democrats re-registered as Republicans to vote for O'Hara in the primary. Thus his vote in Wards Three, Four, and Five almost doubled his totals in the previous year's primary election. Even this increase did not reflect the number of Irish and other Democrats who wanted to vote for O'Hara against Squires in the GOP primary. The *Telegram* reported the next day that "many ordinarily Democratic voters desired to cast ballots for Mayor O'Hara only to find it impossible" because election rules permitted only voters registered as Republicans or independents to vote in the GOP primary.[101]

The outpouring of Democratic support for O'Hara in the primary did not bode well for the chances of the Democratic challenger, Francis P. McKeon, in the general election. McKeon, a past Grand Knight of the local Knights of Columbus, had seized on the issue of the Klan immediately after the riot. He attacked the Klan as the "most anti American thing in America." He complained that "it should never have been allowed to meet in Worcester" and that it was "absolutely unfair" of O'Hara to ask the largely Catholic police to defend men who hated their "race" and religion. It became increasingly difficult for McKeon to depict O'Hara as a defender of the KKK while the mayor was under attack from the Klan's own candidate, Arthur Squires. The day after O'Hara's victory in the Republican primary, the *Telegram* smugly announced: "It has been made obvious that if the government of Worcester is ever to be determined by racial and religious affiliations that lamentable condition will be accomplished by some organization other than the Republican party." McKeon desperately began to seek out other issues to fire his campaign, such as condemning O'Hara as a front man for the NMTA, before returning to the Democratic staples: cutting expenditures and lowering taxes. O'Hara beat him in a landslide, running well in almost all parts of the city, particularly on the east side, where he even captured Ward Four, an Irish Democratic stronghold and Peter Sullivan's home district.[102]

The next year O'Hara smashed the Democrat John J. Walsh in the mayoral election of 1925. It was the biggest Republican landslide in a quarter-century and one of the largest margins in the city's history, for the mayor carried all but two of the city's ten wards. He appeared to have become the indispensable man in Worcester politics, the man at the center, who had isolated the ethnic extremists in both parties.[103]

O'Hara would remain in power for the next six years, but it would never again be as easy for him as it was in 1924 and 1925 because he would never again be a unifying force in Worcester politics. He faced increasing dissension in his own party as the Swedes and middle- and working-class Yankees became more and more frustrated and more and more hostile. Christian Nelson ran against him in the 1925 primary and polled enough votes, particularly in Swedish districts, to achieve a respectable loss. By 1927, however, the Swedes had rallied around another one of their own, Roland Frodigh, president of the Common Council, who lived in a three-decker in the Swedish neighborhood, Quinsigamond Village. Frodigh vaguely criticized O'Hara for reckless spending on city improvements, but he was never consistent on that issue and that was not the principal rationale for his candidacy. What really made Swedes angry was that O'Hara and his west side friends had taken over the Republican party and blocked their own path to power. As a "Swedish American" wrote to the *Post*: "We can be loyal to the Republican party but we cannot and will not be loyal to the O'Hara party or to his political machine which has excluded us during its existence." In the 1927 GOP primary, Frodigh rolled up four- or five-to-one majorities in the Swedish neighborhoods of Greendale, Bell Hill, and Quinsigamond Village against O'Hara and shaved 4,000 votes and over ten percentage points off the Irishman's margin over Nelson of two years earlier.[104]

Once past the primary, O'Hara confronted another challenge in the revitalized Democratic party. In the off-year elections of 1926, the Democratic party of Massachusetts had bounced back from demoralizing defeats in 1922 and 1924 and began the construction of a new multiethnic coalition under the leadership of David I. Walsh. In 1927 the local Democrats revived as well, and mounted a strong campaign against O'Hara behind John C. Mahoney. Mahoney's broad face, slightly turned-up nose, and thick brogue (lace-curtain Irish from the west side delighted in mimicking his speech: "Me hands are tied and me arse is against the wall") marked him as distinctly Irish, and, indeed, he came from Boherbue, County Cork, in Ireland. At the age of seventeen he emigrated to Worcester where he began life at the bottom of the city's occupational ladder as a coal shoveler and laborer. Unlike the vast majority of his immigrant contemporaries, he escaped to become a clerk, earn a law degree, and win political success as a state representative, common councillor, and alderman. In the 1927 municipal campaign, as city Democrats had since Philip O'Connell in 1900, Mahoney ran on a platform of cutting city expenditures and lowering taxes. In his first campaign speech in 1927, he promised to eliminate the "deadwood" from the city payrolls and stop construction of "gorgeous school palaces." This position did not play well in a city where business boomed and new residential parks were popping up in vacant fields in every corner of the city. Mahoney also lacked some of the political grace and wit of his predecessor, Peter Sullivan. Nevertheless, he was a dogged campaigner and by 1927 the Democratic party had regained some of its old strength. Mahoney lost to O'Hara that year by only a little less than 1,700 votes in over 47,000 cast.[105]

If O'Hara only barely survived challenges from the Swedes and Irish Democrats, he nonetheless did survive. He still occupied the center, and the antagonism between his Swedish and Irish opponents was simply too great for them to ally against him. He suceeded, in part, because on the principal bread-and-butter issue of Worcester policy, he firmly backed municipal improvements, and neither his Swedish primary nor Irish Democratic opponents, because of long-term Republican loyalist or Democratic party tradition, did, or could. Michael O'Hara was, perhaps, the greatest builder of any mayor in the city's history. In 1929 he claimed that his administration had laid fifty-nine new miles of sewer pipe and fifty-four miles of water pipes, and in 1931 a supporter added that Mayor O'Hara's administration had spent nearly six million dollars on new schools and over one million in repairs of old ones. Worcester's housing industry skyrocketed in the 1920s. By the middle of the decade the annual number of building permits in Worcester had almost doubled the previous prewar high. The numbers (largely single-family homes) not only had never been so high, they would never be so high again. It would be the biggest construction boom in Worcester's history. O'Hara's emphasis on improvements thus pleased a whole host of players in the new boom, real estate developers, new homeowners, contractors, construction unions, and the Chamber of Commerce, which had long backed city development. In the vibrant Worcester economy of the mid-1920s, this support for city spending offered O'Hara a clear and unique advantage over both his opponents.[106]

It was not the popularity of O'Hara's positions alone that secured his rule in Worcester, however; the strength of his organization was also critical. O'Hara's biggest political problem was that as an Irish Catholic Republican he had no natural base of support. He relied on the west side elite, but unlike Logan or many of the Republican mayors before him, he was not of that elite; the GOP's other important constituencies, the Swedes and middle-class Yankees hated him, and his own people, the Irish and other Catholics, were in the other party. In 1925, therefore, he set out to re-register enough Irish and other ethnic Democrats as Republicans or independents to give him a base of support in the Republican primary. In 1925, 694 Democrats became Republicans and 300 more registered as independents; two years later the numbers were 836 and 250 respectively, and in 1929 770 Democrats re-registered to vote in the Republican primary. It might be expected that most of these crossovers were upwardly mobile Irish Democrats living on the east side periphery or on the west side who found O'Hara an easy excuse for moving into a party that seemed to better represent their economic interests. Yet the preponderance of Irish Democrats (504) re-registering in 1927 came from the heart of the east side, not the new neighborhoods of the west side or zones of emergence on the border of east and west. Moreover, the vast majority of re-registrants in Ward Four (where the number of switches was largest) were low white-collar (44 percent) or blue-collar workers (37 percent), a cut above their neighbors, perhaps, but hardly an ambitious and upwardly mobile cutting edge seeking new political, social, and cultural space. The Republican Irishman ran as strong or stronger among French Canadians and new immigrants as among his fellow Irish in the GOP primaries. Over the course of O'Hara's career, these votes from Irish and other Catholic ethnics in the east side wards became increasingly critical to him in the Republican primaries. From 1925 to 1929, O'Hara's primary vote in those three wards rose from 1,690 to 3,059. By the 1929 primary election, O'Hara's west side vote had fallen off from its 1925 totals, and the three east side wards, accounting for nearly a quarter of his total vote, had become his critical base.[107]

O'Hara built this east side base through old-fashioned political machine tactics. The mayor's city department heads were also his political lieutenants and through them he organized city employees into a personal following. At least one in seven of the Democrats in Ward Four who re-registered as Republicans or independents in 1927 worked for the city or had spouses who were city workers. In turn, the spendthrift O'Hara generously rewarded city workers: the police department had more senior officers drawing high salaries than the "Mexican army," the *Post* charged in 1927. In addition to building an organization among city workers, O'Hara did not hesitate to use patronage to forge powerful alliances or coopt opponents. In 1927, he appointed Major Thomas Foley, a popular Irish Catholic war hero and a once-rumored candidate for mayor, as deputy chief of police, bumping him up over other policemen higher on the civil service list. In the same year he found Arthur Squires—the same Arthur Squires who had run against him in 1924 as the Klan candidate—a job in the traffic department. As he rebuilt the city's roads and sewers, and constructed new schoolhouses all over the city, O'Hara also produced a bevy of contracts and private construction jobs.[108]

Throughout this effort O'Hara solidified his appeal to new Catholic ethnics through canny political recognition. In a concerted effort to cut into the Democratic party's east side stronghold in 1925 the Republicans nominated a French Canadian to run against an Irishman for alderman in Ward Four and an Italian against a Celt for alderman in Ward Three. Later, French Canadian Louis Grenier played a vital role in the mayor's impressive campaign to re-register Democrats as Republicans in 1927. He alone, the *Post* contended, was responsible for the party switches of over 200 voters. Moreover, the O'Hara administration seemed especially generous to French Canadian firms in doling out city contracts. Lezime Rochford, a second-generation *Canadien,* and his sons built the new million-dollar Providence Street Junior High School, two elementary schools, and additions on several other city buildings during the O'Hara administration.[109]

In short, Michael O'Hara came as close to creating a political machine as Worcester had ever had. His remarkable success in that regard enabled him to perform a delicate balancing act and retain his rule over a city seething with ethnic tension and hatred that his rule did little to allay and seemed actually to exacerbate. Yet as open ethnic conflict broke out again in 1928, O'Hara was pushed to the brink.

"To Defy Al Smith and the Puppets of Rome": The 1928 Election in Worcester

In 1928, the Democratic Party's national convention, meeting in Houston, nominated Alfred E. Smith, the Roman Catholic governor of New York, to oppose Herbert Hoover in the election for president of the United States. The effect on Worcester's ethnic relations of this electoral contest would be extraordinary. Feelings ran so high that the campaign precipitated one of the worst riots in Worcester's history on the day before the election. Yet the election itself was also critical, breaking records for registration and turnout, and ultimately ending in almost a dead tie. The Smith election, even more than the KKK riots or other tumultuous events of the 1920s, both reflected and reinforced the sharp divisions between Catholics and Protestants in Worcester.

The excitement rose early in the 1928 election. The *Catholic Messenger*, indifferent to presidential politics for nearly three decades, began pumping Smith's candidacy even before the nomination and sent a reporter to the Democratic convention to report on Smith's historic triumph. By October, a broad-based and passionate constituency had mobilized behind Smith's candidacy in Worcester. Nearly 40,000 people crowded into Washington Square in East Worcester, for example, to catch a glimpse of the candidate as his train stopped in Worcester for a few minutes on its way to Boston. More important, perhaps, 15,000 new voters registered for the election, over 10,000 of them women.[110]

With both Catholic Democrats and Swedish and Yankee Republicans straining for victory, the 1928 presidential campaign became increasingly fevered and tense. On Halloween the Republicans "filled every nook and corner" of Mechanics Hall's two auditoriums for their biggest rally in several years. Two nights later the Democrats filled the same building for a wildly enthusiastic rally featuring United States Senator David I. Walsh of nearby Clinton. More ominous, however, sporadic violence had begun to mar the campaign. Scuffles broke out between young Harvard men for Smith and Hoover backers on the night of the Republican rally. The right provocation threatened to spark the city's simmering ethnic and partisan tensions into an explosion.[111]

The spark came on the day before the election when the Republican party sponsored a massive parade through downtown Worcester. Political parades seem to have fallen out of favor in local politics in the early twentieth century, but, perhaps inspired by wartime demonstrations, they became a regular feature of Worcester politics in the 1920s. Peter Sullivan celebrated his victory in 1921 with a parade through his old neighborhood led by a band playing the "Wearin' of the Green" and "How Dry I Am." John C. Mahoney kicked off his campaign in 1927 with an old-fashioned torchlight procession. The Republicans also held a large victory parade led by Governor Alvin Fuller after the victories of Fuller and Coolidge in 1924. That was their first major partisan parade since a torchlight procession marking McKinley's victory in 1896. Just as in 1924, the Republicans organized their 1928 procession by manufacturing companies: workers and managers from Norton Company, Heald Machine, Whittall Carpet Mills, and other firms, all marching behind their company banners. The 1928 parade differed from its predecessor, however, in several ways. It was far larger than the 1924 march. Some observers estimated that as many as 15,000 men and women marched or rode in the 1928 parade compared to the few thousand four years earlier. The 1928 line of march also included a variety of trucks and searchlights. More important, the 1928 parade occurred *before* the most hotly contested presidential election in the city's history, not, as in 1924, after a predictable Republican landslide. Finally, and most important, in 1928 the GOP planned the parade to march into East Worcester, the very heart of the city's Catholic and Democratic east side.[112]

The parade's size and even its timing may have produced only minor trouble, but its route virtually assured a major incident. The marchers started their parade among friends when they stepped out from Lincoln Square at the north end of Main Street and proceeded south for about a quarter-mile to City Hall. Just after City Hall they wheeled left into Franklin Street and their troubles began. Crowds lining the sidewalk began to boo and jeer. Smith backers taunted some marchers: "Afraid to lose your job if you don't march?" By the time the parade reached Trumbull Square, near the AOH hall and just east of City Hall, some onlookers had already begun to throw tomatoes and rocks. The marchers pressed forward, however, through Washington Square down Shrewsbury Street. There all order collapsed and the procession and the jeering crowd of onlookers dissolved into a gigantic melee. Shrewsbury Street was "packed in all the way from Washington Square to East Park." (The *Post* estimated that at least 30,000 people were milling about on Shrewsbury Street and in the park by then.) One observer claimed it looked like a huge subway tunnel filled with people. Antagonists were hurling tomatoes and eggs at the marchers and dropping bottles on them from rooftops. George Jeppson, the grand marshall of the parade was battered by tomatoes and eggs (His friends would later jokingly note this as one of the great honors of his career, "Grand Marshall . . . Decorated by Shrewsbury St. Citizens with the Order of the Overripe Tomato"). Little boys—"Smith campaigners," the Republican *Telegram* charged—tore the sashes from the "Heald Girls for Hoover." The searchlights on the Norton Company truck were smashed. The wife of the former county chairman of the GOP was assaulted; her attacker hit her over the head with her own Hoover sign. The marchers gave as good as they got, however. A woman would later be treated for burns from a marcher's torch, and police broke up one fight where the antagonists were "jousting with long sticks." Police Chief Foley claimed the riot was "the greatest spectacle Worcester has ever witnessed and therefore the greatest the police department has ever been called upon to handle." It was like the Armistice in 1918, he stated, adding—oblivious to the irony—"except the attitude of the people was entirely different." His men struggled to bring the rival mobs under control but could not subdue the rioters until that evening. Finally, after hours of pitched battle, Shrewsbury Street began to empty and the rioters dispersed. In all at least twenty people were seriously injured and scores were arrested.[113]

A poem written by a Heald Machine Company employee underlined the riot's meaning for Protestant Hoover backers:

> Last nite in a column ten thousand strong,
> We gathered for Hoover and marched along,
> Down Salisbury Street, then to City Hall,
> We paraded and received the cheers of all.
>
> Then to the depot and on to the park,
> Most men and women there carried a mark,
> Home on their back from things there thrown,
> From rotten eggs to fish and stones.
> All because they would leave their homes
> To defy Al Smith and the puppets of Rome.
>
> A vote for Al is a vote for rum,
> A vote to empower America's scum.
> A vote for intolerance and bigotry,
> In a land of tolerance and of the free.
>
> We welcome them in these foreign gangs,
> And now we feel their poisoned fangs,
> Our symbols of liberty they cannot see,
> They are loyal to a potentate across the sea.
>
> . . . If Al was a protestant we wouldn't see,
> Last night such acts of bigotry,
> Let historians write "Smith also ran"
> Now its time to support the Ku Klux Klan.

The Irish and other Catholics for their part were just as outraged by the calcu-
lated "Protestant invasion" of their neighborhoods.[114]

After such chaos on the eve of the vote, the election itself might have
seemed an afterthought, but it and not the riot proved to be the grand climax
of an extraordinary campaign. Hoover won in Worcester, as throughout the
nation, marking but another in a long line of victories for Republican presidential candidates in the city that extended back to 1856. Yet Hoover's victory
margin was but .2 percent, or only 201 votes out of 74,156 cast. The latter figure
dwarfed the number of people who had voted in any previous Worcester
election. Half the city had already voted by eleven o'clock in the morning, the
Telegram reported, and by early evening "voters residing on whole streets and
blocks of streets voted without a single unchecked name on the checklist . . .
crippled, ill or blind, voters had walked, driven or been carried to the polls."
Turnout was especially high in the Swedish precincts of Ward One and the
Irish and Italian precincts in Ward Three. In the latter ward, all but a hundred
of the 7,930 registered voters turned out, and the ward's vote went overwhelmingly for Smith.[115]

The city's enormous turnout and the virtual tie vote suggested how much
the Smith-Hoover election had roused the people of Worcester. The Catholic
Smith's candidacy drew out not only the partisan competitiveness between
Republicans and Democrats but the ethnic and religious rivalries that underlay the partisan division. The 1928 election revealed like no other election
before it in Worcester's history the city's deep division between Catholic and
Protestant. Even before the election, observers could sense the massive swell
of interest in Smith that was building in French Canadian and new immigrant
neighborhoods. "Reliable" sources, the *Post* reported on November 3, three
days before the election, estimated "that this year from 75 to 90 percent" of
Italian and French Canadian votes would go to Smith. The final percentages
were almost exactly that, ranging from a low of 70 percent in one of the
French-dominated precincts to nearly 90 percent in Little Italy along Shrewsbury Street. As impressive was the tremendous increase in turnout on the
heavily Catholic east side. On the whole, the number of Democratic votes more
than tripled in Wards Three, Four, and Five, the city's Irish, French, Italian,
Polish, and Lithuanian bastions, from 1924.[116]

The importance of the Smith election to Worcester politics is hard to underestimate. The violence and the enormous vote suggest that the election was a
defining point in the history of the city's ethnic and religious groups. The lines
were drawn: Catholics on one side; Protestants on the other. It also suggested
the beginning of a change: the emergence of a Catholic Democratic majority

that would dominate the city. Historians have long talked about an "Al Smith revolution" in American politics, a sudden and dramatic shifting of Catholic and other immigrants and second-generation ethnics, into the Democratic party. Such a revolution seemed evident in Worcester as the city appeared to reach a turning point.

Nevertheless, if the effects of Smith on Worcester's electorate were indeed dramatic, they were perhaps the climax of a long evolution rather than a sudden revolution. Samuel Gamm, John Allswang, and others have argued persuasively that Catholic Democratic coalitions evolved slowly in the complicated electoral changes of several groups over a number of elections, not dramatically in one election. This seems to have been the case in Worcester, too. Members of some groups, like the Irish and the Poles, were Democrats almost from their arrival. Others, like the French Canadians, Italians, and Jews, moved back and forth between the parties through the 1910s and 1920s. Most groups, even the most loyal Democrats, pursued pragmatic policies of attempting to maximize returns of patronage or political recognition. In Peter Sullivan's victories in the early twenties and Smith's dramatic near-triumph in 1928 these groups had finally moved into the orbit of the Democratic party and begun to see that as the vehicle for achieving their goals. They would, however, continue to pursue their own ethnic interests, still sometimes fracturing Democratic unity and leaving openings for the Republicans.[117]

Furthermore, if the Al Smith election was a turning point, it would take time to complete the turn. Michael O'Hara and his odd political coalition was proof of that. In 1929, Roland Frodigh challenged O'Hara again in the Republican primary, reviving their rivalry that had become "a war unto the knife" as a newspaper would later characterize it. Swedes and other Republican loyalists were incensed at O'Hara for his handling of the Smith riot and, perhaps even more, for his endorsement of Smith. O'Hara survived the primary, but just barely, winning by a majority of only 752 votes in over 28,000 cast. Swedish precincts again delivered lopsided majorities for Frodigh, and Swedes remained so angry after the primary that the local Swedish newspaper, *Svea*, urged its readers to vote for the Irish-born Democrat, Mahoney, in the general election just to spite O'Hara. The continued slide of O'Hara's vote in west side Wards Nine and Ten was probably more troubling for the mayor. Though both wards still gave O'Hara majorities, his percentage of the vote fell by 12 points in Ward Nine and 14 points in Ward Ten from the 1927 primary. As Worcester chose up sides along religious lines, many, even among liberal elite Republicans who favored O'Hara's policies of municipal improvements, could no longer back him. It was the east side Republicans, the men and women of his machine, who saved him, as his totals rose in Wards Three, Four, and Five by over 700 votes from 1927 to 1929.[118]

Having barely staved off Frodigh for the second time, the wounded O'Hara nonetheless managed to again confront and edge out his Democratic opponent, John C. Mahoney, in the general election as well. Though Mahoney ran as many as 35 to nearly 40 percentage points ahead of Smith's 1928 vote in some Swedish precincts (he carried Quinsigamond Village with 51 percent of the vote; Smith had polled only 12 percent there), the Corkman fell far below Smith's vote on the east side, especially in Wards Four and Five.[119]

Smith had wounded but not killed O'Hara, but the depression and the Democratic tide that followed it, finally did the mayor in. As the city plunged into depression, Frodigh opened up a steady attack on the mayor's "extravagances." He and other opponents raised questions about corruption in O'Hara's street department, rigged assessments for the wealthy, city hall insurance frauds, and construction rakeoffs. As O'Hara reeled under these attacks, his organization caved in and some of his former lieutenants, most notably Louis Grenier, jumped to Frodigh. O'Hara finally fell to Frodigh in the Republican primary as west siders joined Swedes and middle-class Yankees in turning against him. John C. Mahoney, however, trumped Frodigh in turn. With the Catholic, "wet" O'Hara out of the race and Frodigh insisting on massive cuts in expenditures, Mahoney finally rolled up big majorities on the east side that nearly equalled Smith's of three years earlier and revitalized the Catholic Democratic coalition in local politics that Peter Sullivan had forged in the early 1920s.[120]

The O'Hara phenomenon was over. At the very least the phenomenon suggests the complexity of ethnic politics in Worcester and the continuing flexibility of the Yankee elite in pursuit of its interests. O'Hara, however, was no agent of a new reconciliation or bridge for a new rapprochement in Worcester. His appeal to Irish and elite voters may have appeared similar to the coalitions of the 1870s and 1880s, but the circumstances of the 1920s were radically different. The Irish in the mid-twenties were not a humble minority eager for the few scraps an alliance with powerful Yankees might give them. Most Irish and other Catholics had no need for such a coalition, nor any interest in it after the specter of the Klan had passed. Most voted for their own Irish-led Democratic party, a party that before O'Hara emerged seemed well on its way to becoming Worcester's majority party. Nor did O'Hara provide a viable permanent bridge for Protestants to reconcile with their Catholic neighbors. The Yankee elite supported O'Hara, but as a useful tool, not as an overture to share power with Catholics or admit them as social equals. As ethnic and religious tensions rose in the city, O'Hara's elite support declined and melted away altogether at the end of his embattled reign. (Rapprochement between

Yankee elites and Irish Catholics may have been difficult to sustain for a long time at any but the most pragmatic level anyway, as issues of public morality ultimately shifted from prohibition to birth control and abortion.) More important, O'Hara's hold on the Republican party in the 1920s frustrated Swedish and some middle- and working-class Yankee Protestants, intensified their antagonism towards Catholics, and helped push the battles between Catholics and their religious antagonists into the streets. Michael O'Hara did little to prevent the "tribal twenties" from engulfing Worcester; indeed, by frustrating Swedish and Irish Democrats' political aspirations, he may have unwittingly abetted such tribalism.

Relations between groups in early twentieth-century Worcester were complicated then, but there were some clear patterns: the endurance and intensification of hostility between Catholics and Protestants and the drifting to a rough, tenuous unity among Catholic ethnics. How would the Irish shape their conceptions of themselves, their group boundaries and identities, to these patterns? They would not persist in the Irish ethnocentrism of the 1890s, nor return to the accommodationist Catholic Americanism of the 1880s; they would craft a new definition of themselves to meet the new constraints of their times and reflect the perspectives of a rising American-born generation. This definition began with a fervent American patriotism, a celebration of American culture and identity. That first principle would now be combined with a militant separatist Catholicism. The boundaries of this new Catholicism would be broad enough to encompass Catholics of all ethnic backgrounds under Irish leadership but would be fiercely defended against Protestants and other suspected enemies.

Making George Washington a Catholic:
The Worcester Irish against Socialism

The first principle of the new militant American Catholics was loyalty to their native country, the United States. By the second decade of the twentieth century, Thomas Kiely's concerns about the excesses of American patriotism or jingoism had long been forgotten. Twentieth-century militant Irish American Catholics would be unabashedly patriotic Americans, "devoted to unadulterated Americanism." In part, this patriotism was the natural expression of the now dominant second-generation Irish. After all, they had been born in America; it was their country. Yet as the *Columbiad,* the state's Knights of Columbus newsletter, conceded in 1899: "Protestant . . . opinion induces us to protest our patriotism too much." Self-conscious that their patriotism was suspect, the new militant American Catholics went to great lengths to prove the essential harmony of their faith and patriotism, to demonstrate that in McCoy's phrase they were "most American when they were most Catholic." Some of these efforts were ludicrous, such as contrived attempts to rewrite American history. In 1912 the *Catholic Messenger* asked "Was Washington really a Catholic?" and presented a full page of evidence, which suggested an affirmative answer. A more serious effort to demonstrate the harmony of nation and faith—and one with more far-reaching consequences—was the crusade Worcester's twentieth-century Irish Catholics mounted against socialism.

Worcester's Irish did not become conservative reactionaries in the twentieth century. They would best be described as "urban liberals" very much like the Irish and other ethnic Democrats that John Buenker found emerging throughout northern industrial states in the first two decades of the twentieth century. In Worcester, as in many parts of the country in the early twentieth century, the Irish dominated the local labor movement. In 1906 12 of the 22 delegates to the Central Labor Union were Irish. In 1913, 37 percent (25 of 67) of the secretaries of the city's unions were Irish and in 1920 at least 27 of 74 or at least 36 percent. Both the *Post* and the *Messenger* (renamed the *Catholic Messenger* in 1907) consistently advocated labor's cause. During the 1915 strike the *Post* pushed hard for arbitration and sharply condemned the employers and the mayor for avoiding a peaceful and equitable resolution of the walkout. Both papers and many of Worcester's Irish Democratic state or national office backed a full range of progressive economic and political reforms, including old-age and mothers' pensions, the income tax, regulation of hours and wages for women and children, utility regulation, the referendum, the initiative, and even public housing. (James Mellen, in fact, played a critical role in pushing the first state-sponsored public housing bill in American history through the Massachusetts legislature.) In municipal politics most Democrats were more conservative, but the *Messenger* and some Democratic aldermen pushed for public ownership of utilities and the street railways and Irish Democratic candidates for mayor campaigned for a city-owned market and free medical clinics, as well as other reforms.[121]

Worcester's Irish Americans, however, were liberals, not radicals, and their antagonism towards the latter became increasingly shrill in the early twentieth century. The flirtations with socialism of the late 1890s seemed very distant by the second decade of the twentieth century. By then Irish suspicions of radicals and socialists had become articles of political and religious faith. The *Catholic Messenger* repeatedly denounced socialism in the 1910s as an enemy of Catholic Americans as sinister as the organized nativism of "APAism." The paper attacked socialism so frequently, and with such vehemence, that one reader complained in 1912 that its attacks were becoming tedious. The *Catholic*

Messenger, however, was not alone in the crusade against socialism. The Irish-owned daily, the *Post*, attacked the socialists too, if with slightly less obsessive vigor than the *Catholic Messenger*. Leaders of the city's Irish Catholic community, priests, and politicians also weighed in against radical ideologies. John J. McCoy's boasting in 1914 was typical of his clerical colleagues: "The [Catholic] schools will not breed anarchists or socialists. From the beginning and through all their days at school our children are made to look to God standing there back of the law. And in our pulpits this we teach and the Catholic church will yet be hailed as the impregnable bulwark of law and order."[122]

Irish politicians condemned radicals in much the same terms. In his campaign for reelection as mayor in 1912 David O' Connell alluded frequently to the role of the Industrial Workers of the World (the IWW) in the Lawrence strike of that year. According to the *Post*, O'Connell noted the Wobbly banners in Lawrence and thundered: "they would not be allowed to carry such banners through the streets here. He would . . . prevent with all the force in him and all the force of the police department the advance of such radicals."[123]

There had never been many Irish radicals in Worcester even in the 1880s and 1890s. Even James Mellen, who had invoked the language and principles of working-class republicanism to excoriate "mill aristocrats" in the 1880s, had condemned anarchists and socialists with equal vigor then. The anti-radical liberalism of the Irish in the early twentieth century was, therefore, not entirely new, but before the twentieth century there had been no persistent campaign against radicalism like the *Catholic Messenger's* antisocialist crusade. Without abandoning a sympathy for labor, endorsement of greater popular access to government, or a commitment to using the power of the state to control the greedy or ameliorate the conditions of the poor and workers, the Worcester Irish seemed to have become more determinedly and openly hostile to radicalism in the early twentieth century than ever before.[124]

There were several reasons for the increasing Irish antagonism to socialism. Irishmen in Worcester had made substantial economic progress even from the 1880s. The second generation now dominated, and they had achieved significantly higher status by the 1900s than their immigrant parents or cousins had enjoyed in the 1880s. Even many of the blue-collar workers among them had achieved skilled status and saw their interests better protected by their bread-and-butter craft unions and a liberal state than by the seemingly distant promises of socialism. Moreover, the Irish antagonism to socialism was strongly influenced by their rising political power. By the early twentieth century the Irish had become far more politically powerful than they had been in the 1880s. They could now compete for control of the city and reap the rich benefits of patronage such control could assure. Irish opposition to radicalism thus reflected the fears of people who saw a threat to a system that had already worked for many of them and held out the promise of future rewards.[125]

Yet it was not only the threat to their material interests that inspired this new Irish assault. Though socialism seemed a real threat to Irish political power in Worcester in the very first few years of the twentieth century, it was less so a decade later as the local socialists faded into political irrelevance. Material interests, then, were a reason for the Irish opposition to socialism in the 1910s, but they do not entirely explain the new-found fury of that opposition.

Some of that emotion came from Irish fears of socialism's effects on sexual behavior and family life. Irish attacks on socialism repeatedly condemned its alleged atheism and immorality and its threat to the traditional family. Worcester's Irish Catholics had never seemed entirely comfortable with capitalism's effect on community and family, either. Even priests seemed wary of the havoc that unlimited ambition let loose in a free market might wreak on the bonds of their community, and inveighed repeatedly against the dangers of materialism. Yet Catholics were even more fearful about socialism's links to cultural modernism and the threats it posed to traditional conceptions of women's roles and sexual morality.

The new intensity of Irish antagonism to socialism, however, seemed to also grow out of the need for American-born Irish to prove their patriotism, or more precisely out of their obsessive concern with proving the harmony, indeed, intrinsic unity of Catholicism and Americanism, as when John J. McCoy would say "most American when most Catholic." In a sense, perhaps, socialism played the role of a defining target for the Irish as they strove to hammer out their new militant American and Catholic identity. Their opposition to socialism seemed proof of their American loyalty, proof, as McCoy had hinted, that Catholics were, in fact, the best kind of Americans. David F. O'Connell echoed this point in his diatribe against the Wobblies in 1912: "No man or band of men shall ever parade on our streets bearing banners on which is inscribed the words, 'No God or Country.' If Worcester authorities allowed this it would be allowing a blow to be struck at the very foundation of our liberties. Our motto is and shall be: 'For God and Country.'"[126]

"Something Must Be Done or We Will Not Hold the Boys":
Making a Catholic Ghetto in Worcester

The Worcester Irish, however, were very clear that it was a Catholic God they worshiped, and in the twentieth century they made no secret of their unyielding antagonism to anyone who worshiped another. Their efforts to reconcile their faith and patriotism may have been attempts to prove they were as good Americans as any Yankee but they were not attempts to assimilate into a Protestant-dominated mainstream. Their American patriotism now suggested a belligerent competitiveness—we are as good as you—not humble proof of worthiness for acceptance. In the early twentieth century Worcester's Irish Catholics no longer sought an accommodation with the Protestant-dominated host society; they were at war with it. They no longer sought to be simply a Catholic alternative version of being American; they had become actively opposed to Protestant America.

In the early twentieth century, Irish Catholic attitudes in Worcester crystalized into what later became known as a "Catholic ghetto mentality." Irish Catholics in the city began to suspect every Protestant or Protestant-dominated organization. Worcester's Irish had expressed such suspicions before, but these fears had never seemed as codified or systematized as they would become in the first few decades of the twentieth century. In the 1880s and early 1890s, after all, Joshua O'Leary and Father John J. Power could praise Protestant or secular organizations and question the further development of the Irish network of institutions and organizations. The rise of the APA and the ethnic conflict of the 1890s marked a turning point, however; thereafter there would be no talk of reconciliation. Memories of the 1890s, cultural conflicts, political rivalries, the revival of nativism, and growing conservatism in the Catholic church would not permit the gap between Protestants and Catholics to close again. By the early twentieth century Worcester's Irish had clearly drawn the boundary between themselves and their enemies. Institutions and organizations beyond the boundary, even apparently innocuous ones, were suspect; those within the boundary needed to be expanded and strengthened so that the Catholic subsociety could meet all of its people's needs.

The battles of the 1890s continued to echo in Worcester long after the decade's closing. For John J. McCoy the memory of the APA remained as vivid, sharp, and painful in 1914 as it had in 1907 or even 1899. In 1914 he vividly recalled that "in our own day our ears have grown accustomed to the hissing in the night of the new reptilian brood, the treasonable order of the APA." Once Irish Americans in Worcester had labeled every new instance of anti-Catholic prejudice as "Know-Nothingism," testifying to the powerful impact of that crisis on their common memory. Now they labeled such instances "new" or "revived" "APAism." The APA had seemed particularly galling and threatening to the American-born Irish. The Know-Nothings had risen against people who were largely immigrant and alien; the APA as McCoy said, "cursed spirit that would make me, an American born and bred, and of citizen sire, make me because I was of the old faith suspected, make me, a man branded, make me a man not to be trusted where my country or my neighbor's life was concerned."[127]

New instances of anti-Catholic prejudice in the twentieth century reinforced
the image of a hostile, threatening Protestantism derived from those memories of the 1890s. Catholics were quick to take note of every evidence of Protestant prejudice in the early twentieth century. In 1905 priests at St. John's complained of a Protestant mission established in the Island to lure Catholic
children away from their faith with "free ham sandwiches." In 1910 the *Catholic
Messenger* reported that members of Worcester's First Presbyterian Church
were circulating a petition asking the United States government to prohibit
nuns from wearing clerical garb while teaching in the Indian schools. That
year, too, Protestants in the elite area of the old west side near Elm Park organized to prevent the Catholic diocese from purchasing Park Congregational
Church and transforming it into a Catholic parish. New examples of anti-
Catholic feeling cropped up throughout the 1910s as well: reports of the appearance of Tom Watson's anti-Catholic weekly, *The Menace* in Worcester, for
example; or rumors of boycotts against Catholic businesses in 1915; or efforts
by a Protestant congregation in Webster Square to prevent Catholics from
building the new Our Lady of Angels church across the street from their own
place of worship in 1917.[128]

As we have seen, these alleged instances of anti-Catholic discrimination
took place in a changing environment of ethnic and religious conflict. Public
debate of cultural issues had grown complicated in this era as the city and the
country at large were making a transition from old conflicts, over drinking or
playing sports on Sunday, to new debates about the family and sexuality, such
as birth control and abortion. The church had spoken on issues of drinking,
of course, but its support for temperance was defensive and apologetic and
came close to tacit agreement or even open alliance with Protestants and opposition to most of its faithful. The conflicts over temperance thus sometimes
put strains on clerical authority and did not help reinforce the church's distinction between Catholics and Protestants. On the new issues, particularly
birth control and abortion, however, the church claimed to speak authorita-
tively, and Catholics drew sharp distinctions between themselves and others.
In Michigan, Leslie Tentler found some evidence of cooperation between
Catholics and Protestants on these issues, but in Worcester, Irish Catholics delighted in assailing Protestants for their "race suicide" moral failures. In 1903
a *Messenger* editorial blamed the decline in the Yankee birth rate on the physical decline of Yankee Protestant women. Their excessive cultivation of "brain
power" made them so nervous and weak that they could not bear children,
the paper claimed. Ten years later the *Catholic Messenger* attacked again, suggesting that Protestant missionaries abandon their overseas efforts and "try

first to gather native congregations [in America] and teach them the law of the lord" on the reproductive responsibilities of marriage. Throughout these assaults the *Messenger* and its successor, the *Catholic Messenger,* were quick to point out that Protestants themselves had confessed their own people's moral dissolution and had made many of the same charges. As early as 1910, G. Stanley Hall of Clark University, pleading for better understanding between the city's two religions, summed up their divisions by suggesting that "we want to get away . . . from the question as to whether the Catholics have a few more crimes and the Protestants a few more abortions." These issues were just emerging as prominent cultural conflicts between religious groups in Worcester as Hall spoke; it would not be until the 1940s that birth control would emerge as a ballot issue. Nevertheless, differences over birth control, abortion, divorce, and even movie censorship and regulation of dance halls, had begun to give Catholics added reasons for limiting contacts with Protestants and other non-Catholics. Marriage to members of other religions would not only be wrong in its own right, Irish Catholic spokesmen argued, but a first step to further sins of birth control, abortion, and divorce, or other sins of immorality.[129]

Yet as the history of Worcester's economy and politics in the early twentieth century revealed, it was not culture alone, but power relations and the contest for power among groups that also heightened ethnic tension and reinforced and strengthened religious boundaries in the twentieth century. An important underlying source of tension between Protestants and Catholics was the persistent Protestant monopolization of economic power in Worcester. Worcester's Irish Catholics, led by American-born generations, were far more economically successful in the early twentieth century than they had been in the 1880s, but they were not necessarily more economically powerful. Even as late as the 1920s, they had little or no presence in the boardrooms of the city's major manufacturers or banks and there was no hint then that they would play a larger role in Worcester industry in the future. If anything, the local Protestant elite seemed even more solidly entrenched in the early twentieth century than it had ever been. Local Protestant businessmen had skillfully negotiated the integration of Worcester's economy into the national economy without losing control of the city's industry. They had also forged a new economic and social cohesiveness through their bigger companies, businessmen's associations, and networks of social clubs. Catholics had not yet begun to even challenge Protestant economic power or social dominance.

Irish Catholics were, of course, more successful in politics, but their successes here also fostered increasing religious tension. The emergence of Irish

Catholics in open competition with Yankees and other Protestants in city elections through the century's first two decades, and then the explosion of anti-Catholic feeling in the twenties, had a profound effect on Worcester's Irish Catholics. Though they were incensed by the Ku Klux Klan and other manifestations of nativism, it was Al Smith's campaign and defeat that seemed to have the most significant impact. Older Irish Catholics remember even today that just wearing a Smith button seemed an important symbolic statement, a badge of identity asserted in an environment that permitted no ambiguity or compromise. Smith's defeat, though it must have been expected, was nonetheless a bitter blow. Former mayor Philip O'Connell, a judge by 1928, wept when he heard of Smith's loss, his son recalls. Six weeks after the election, an officer of the Worcester Alhambra Council of the Knights of Columbus, read out "The Brown Derby," an article by Father Leonard Feeney published in the Jesuit magazine, *America*, to the Knights gathered for their general meeting.

> It goes without saying, Al, that we Catholics were a tremendous liability to you in your recent campaign. . . . We are sorry that you have been so humiliated on our account. We are wholly to blame and we know it. But if you remember we told you it would be that way. We told you what it would cost to be a Catholic: the insults, the ingratitude, the mudslinging. . . . Maybe you didn't hear about the man who tends our railroad crossing who was found weeping in his shack the night you went down to defeat. I could tell you also about the nuns who made a novena, not that you would be elected—but in order that you wouldn't be assassinated. . . . I might mention, too, the old lady who stayed up till three o'clock saying her rosary and begging the Blessed Mother of God, "not to let Al go broken hearted." The night of November sixth was a night of sixteen million tragedies and it may cheer you, Al, to know that when you went to bed that night, you did not lie awake alone.

The sentiments may seem maudlin now, but Worcester's Knights did not think so then; they had not only requested that the article be read out in full at their monthly meeting but then "voted unanimously" to have it reprinted in the January issue of their own magazine, the *Cable*. Three months later a *Cable* editorial charged: "We deceive ourselves if we think that the traditional bigotry [anti-Catholicism] is of the slightest extent. Recent events have shown that it is strong not only in certain but in all sections of our country."[130]

Michael O'Hara's support cut across Worcester's deep religious division, of course, but there was no reflection of O'Hara's political coalition in the social and cultural life of the Worcester Irish. O'Hara was hardly an agent of reconciliation after the mid-1920s; his hold on the mayoralty frustrated religious enemies on either side and provoked conflict rather than healed it. For his upper-class Yankee allies, his coalition appeared to be little more than political expediency; there was no evidence that they wished to open their company boardrooms and social clubs to Irish Catholics. O'Hara also did little to better relations between Catholics and middle- and working-class Protestants. Indeed, his success seemed to merely stoke their rising anti-Catholic hatred. On the Catholic side, O'Hara did not appeal to ambitious middle-class and upper-class Catholics who might have been eager for acceptance by their Yankee neighbors. His Irish support came largely from lower-middle and working-class Irish from the east side. His coalition, then, of these east side working- and middle-class Catholics and wealthy Yankees would have been hard to replicate in Worcester's social and cultural arena. Finally, when pushed by the election of 1928—as all Catholics and Protestants in Worcester were pushed—O'Hara came down on the Catholic side and backed Al Smith.

O'Hara's coalition points up, nonetheless, that local politics in Worcester was neither a perfect reflection of religious and ethnic boundaries, nor, conversely, the sole determinant of them. There were other causes of the Catholic ghetto besides local social conflicts or contests for power. In the 1880s local trends in power relations had neatly coincided with emerging factions and ideologies in the Catholic church to nurture Worcester's version of Catholic Liberalism. In the twentieth century increasing centralization of power in the church and its growing conservatism combined with the local political rivalry between Irish Catholics and Protestants and the revival of nativism to produce the Irish Catholic ghetto, or "militant" Catholicism in Worcester.

These trends to conservatism and centralization varied from diocese to diocese, but in general there was a noticeable movement towards a more conservative, ultramontane, and authoritarian Catholic church in the early twentieth century. The Vatican slowly retreated from its brief flirtation with liberalism in the 1890s, to attack it finally in Leo's encyclical *Testem Benevolentiae* at the end of the decade. Leo's successor, Pius X, followed shortly thereafter by condemning "modernism" in 1907 in his encyclical *Pascendi Dominici Gregis*.

The Vatican coupled these reassertions of doctrinal orthodoxy with efforts to control the American church. New rules introduced in the early twentieth century severely reduced the power of American priests and prelates in selecting new American bishops. Roman patronage became the critical key to securing a see for ambitious priests as never before, and a whole generation of bishops, almost entirely dependent on Rome, like William O'Connell of Boston, came to rule the American church. As Rome centralized power, so in turn did local bishops. As Edward Kantowicz and David O'Brien have pointed out, a kind of "organizational revolution" swept through many American dioceses in the early and middle years of the twentieth century. Bishops created new bureaucracies to centralize control of schools and charitable agencies. They also fought to gain greater control over their priests. New technologies of communication and transportation and new rules set by the Vatican or adopted by American bishops, including a revised code of Canon Law issued in 1918, helped the bishops in this effort. Moreover, in eastern dioceses like Boston and Springfield, bishops may also have profited from a surfeit of priests that encouraged curates to vie for diocesan favor lest they live out their lives as assistants or as exiles in rural backwaters. In 1910 Monsignor Thomas Griffin wrote Bishop Beaven about one priest's reluctance to accept a transfer: "We have hard work with Fr. Foley who is much disinclined to go to Montague [a small town in rural western Massachusetts] afraid that he will never leave it alive."[131]

Whether the church's growing conservatism made Worcester's Irish Catholics more belligerent in dealing with their Protestant neighbors and more likely to read deep-rooted and pervasive prejudice into every act of anti-Catholic aggressiveness, or whether their rivalry with Protestants and the revival of nativism gave credence to the church's suspicions and calls for obedience, is not clear. Most likely the two trends worked together to nurture the ghetto mentality which flourished among the Irish in early twentieth-century Worcester.

For it was clear that such a mentality had not only taken root but become widely pervasive among the city's Irish in the early twentieth century. The attack on Catholic Liberals in this period grew unrelenting and vicious. The *Messenger* assailed Liberal Catholics as "Nominal Catholics . . . who practice their religion after a fashion but [are] not bigoted you know," who go to mass, "but as to saying the rosary, wearing the scapular or making the way of the cross, the very suggestion provokes a smile and a shrug and the non-Catholic friend is informed that for their part they attach no importance to them." The paper charged "the Catholic who caters to Protestant prejudices—trimming his connections and opinions with a view to making himself more tolerable to them—wins . . . nothing but the contempt and distrust he deserves." Worcester's Irish Catholics in the early twentieth century were not liberal but "militant" Catholics, those who, according to the *Catholic Messenger* in 1915, "in our parish life . . . strengthen our societies . . . in our social life break down barriers of bigotry rampant around us . . . and in our public life . . . [fight] the prejudice which holds a Catholic under disability in seeking public office." Confronted by "bitter opponents" and "weighty odds," Worcester's new militant Irish Catholics were not "truculent or domineering," but "made a positive stand upon principles."[132]

Embattled and angry, Worcester's Irish Catholic spokesmen worried that virtually every organization or institution outside their own subsociety, even the apparently neutral or harmless, might endanger the faith of Catholics who joined them. Catholic priests inveighed against Protestant and secular colleges, predicting that those who attended such institutions severely endangered their faith. Concerns of clerical and lay spokesmen extended also to the Boy Scouts, boys clubs, fraternal societies like the Elks, and the YMCA. The *Catholic Messenger* stated in 1912 that "this paper is in favor of that juvenile organization [the Boy Scouts] only when companies are formed entirely or almost exclusively of Catholics and when some moderate and restraining Catholic authority has supervision over them." Father John J. McCoy revealed similar opinions about the newly opened Worcester Boys Club in a letter to Bishop Beaven in 1908: "I make bold to send you the enclosed clipping from this morning's *Telegram*. It will show you the danger for our boys who are under Protestant influence all the while even if the influence is hidden under the name and profession of resurrection work. We are doing nothing while the enemies of the faith are moving heaven and earth and are coming closer together every day. Kindly read it well. Something must be done or we will not hold the boys."[133]

Celtic fears of Protestant or secular influences and concerns about sexual immorality seemed to combine and reinforce the desire to keep Irish Catholic women segregated from Protestants and other non-Catholics. The *Catholic Messenger* frequently contended that Catholic women who married Protestants or non-Catholics usually lost their faith and easily fell into the sinful practices of birth control or abortion, or ended their marriages in divorce. This mix of fears of both apostasy and sexual immorality inspired a campaign by the *Catholic Messenger* in 1913 to warn Irish Catholic women away from non-Catholic boardinghouses or hotels. Such establishments run by Protestants or other non-Catholics did not offer the "proper life for reputable women." The paper ran a list of Catholic boardinghouse keepers, each one endorsed by a Catholic pastor, who could presumably offer Irish Catholic women safe and "proper" accommodations.[134]

It was not just women and children but men too who needed to be wary of threatening Protestant and secular environments around them. Though the *Catholic Messenger*'s campaign against boardinghouses aimed its warnings principally at women, the paper acknowledged that men too could profit from such advice. Moreover, the societies listed in the church's decrees against Catholic membership in secret organizations were all male fraternal orders. The *Catholic Messenger* frequently reprinted this mandate, but in the 1910s it also began to question Catholic membership in the Elks, a society that Irish Catholics dominated in many cities (John Patrick Sullivan, an Irish Catholic, was elected national president in 1911). The paper argued: "I have known Catholic men who are Elks to pass by unnoticed an assault upon the church but who would instantly take up the cudgels were one to say the least word against this popular organization."[135]

It was the YMCA, however, more than the boys clubs, any of the non-Catholic fraternal groups, or perhaps any other single Protestant or secular institution that most concerned Worcester's Irish Catholics in the twentieth century. Joshua O'Leary had gone out of his way to praise the YMCA in calmer days when Catholic Liberalism was still in fashion. Those days were long gone by 1909 when the AOH building committee explicitly argued for creating a gymnasium at AOH Hall to offset the enticements of the YMCA for young Catholics. O'Leary's old paper, the *Catholic Messenger*, however, voiced the new suspicions of the YMCA even more pointedly in 1915: "We regret to say that these zealous campaigners imprison in their net many Catholic men and youth who enter unaware of the real character of the YMCA organization or brazenly risk their faith and invite spiritual disaster."[136]

One result of this rising suspicion of non-Catholics and a concomitant new militancy was the stunning upswing in Catholic devotionalism. Memberships in Holy Name societies and clubs skyrocketed, novenas to St. Francis Xavier and St. Theresa Lisieux turned patrons away, and annual pilgrimages such as the trek to Nazareth in nearby Leicester doubled in size and doubled again. In Worcester, as in many other parts of the country, Catholics took to giant devotional celebrations in the 1920s and 1930s, both to rally the faithful and advertise Catholic power. In 1932, 25,000 people from all the parishes in the city packed Holy Cross College's Fitton Field to demonstrate the church's commitment to evangelization, that "the many who are in error [may] be brought back." It was, Thomas O'Leary, bishop of Springfield, claimed, "an amazing spectacle . . . the most amazing example of faith I have ever seen."[137]

Another result of the new militance among Irish Catholics was a reinvigorated commitment to building up their own societies and institutions. Like others in the late nineteenth or early twentieth century Irish Americans in Worcester felt the need for organization, yet the need for organization took on a special urgency in the competitive and hostile religious atmosphere of the early twentieth century. "It is the age of organization—everybody is a joiner," said the *Columbiad* in 1899: "The enemy is highly organized; but we are behind the age." Promoters of Worcester's council of the K. of C. argued similarly in 1916: Catholics needed to foster societies such as theirs so that "there would be no need for Catholic men and women to cast eyes longingly towards those proscribed by the church."[138]

In the twentieth century Catholics would establish many organizations clearly parallel to ones found in Protestant or mainstream society. One notable example of a parallel association was the Catholic Women's Club. The ubiquitous John J. McCoy founded the club in 1907 as an alternative to the Yankee-dominated Worcester Women's Club. The *Catholic Messenger* reported at the club's establishment in 1907 that Worcester Catholic women had attended the public lectures sponsored by the Worcester Women's Club "in large numbers" and admired some of its lectures for their "wholesome mental food." Like the Worcester Women's Club, Catholic Women's Club's members came from the upper ranks of Worcester's Irish society: 70 percent of its members in 1911 were white-collar workers or married to white-collar workers. McCoy organized the club, he said, to promote the "talents for leadership and the arts" among Worcester's Catholic women; it was—and was meant to be—the most prominent social and cultural club for Catholic women in Worcester, just as the Worcester Women's Club was the height of social and cultural prominence for the city's Yankee Protestant women.[139]

The development of parochial education in Worcester afforded, perhaps, the best example of how changing lay attitudes combined with new energy and authority in the diocesan offices worked to expand and strengthen the Irish subsociety. Both clerics and laymen alike displayed little interest in parochial education through the 1880s and 1890s. As late as 1900 only one of the city's Irish parishes, St. John's, had built a parochial school. By 1910 there were 2,200 children in parochial schools at St. John's or St. Anne's, but 2,600 first- and second-generation Irish children and countless third-generation Irish in the city's public schools. In the 1910s and 1920s, however, renewed diocesan pressure and changing lay attitudes produced a virtual explosion of Catholic schools in Worcester. Between 1912 and 1927, five of the city's Irish parishes built elementary schools, and two of them added high schools as well. By 1930 there were over 4,300 children in the schools of the Irish parishes.[140]

The diocese's new commitment and activity in advancing the cause of parochial education was one important reason for the upsurge in parochial school construction in Worcester. The bishop's establishment of a central diocesan office of education and the institution of diocesan-wide examinations in 1907 reflected the diocese's increasing effort to assert its authority in education. More important were the direct efforts of the bishops to pressure Worcester's pastors to comply with the mandate of the 1884 Baltimore Council and build schools in their parishes. Older pastors often proved resistant but new appointees were eager to please. New pastors at old parishes like St. Peter's, St. Paul's, St. Stephen's, and Sacred Heart all erected the first schools at those parishes in the 1910s and 1920s. Pastors in new parishes were also quick to respond to the bishops' new urgency. In 1912, Beaven had advised William Ryan, pastor of the new parish of Blessed Sacrament, to build a parochial school before constructing a church—and then to hold services in the school until the church could be completed. This had been a common practice in other dioceses like Chicago but it had never before been attempted in Worcester. Ryan later thanked the bishop: "because of your advice, in three years or four at most the parish will be complete in every way. It will have its church, school and parochial residence."[141]

Not just pressure for parochial schools from above, but a new receptiveness from lay Irish Catholics below, helped produce the explosion of Irish school-building in the twentieth century. In the 1880s and 1890s, the Catholic Liberal Joshua O'Leary and the *Messenger* grudgingly defended Catholic rights to build parochial schools, but the liberal editor had little use for them and frequently praised public education. Thomas Kiely, spokesman for the ethnic revival in the 1880s and 1890s, was also only slightly more sympathetic to parochial education, perhaps reflecting a sense among Irish nationalists that parochial schools did almost nothing to preserve Irish culture. Yet the succession of new editors at the *Messenger* (renamed the *Catholic Messenger*) who succeeded Kiely after he left in 1906 were all enthusiastic supporters of Catholic education. In 1911 the paper claimed that "worldliness and atheism will conquer if Catholic schools are left to deteriorate." Further editorials and articles praised Catholic education, denigrated the materialistic curriculum of public schools, and reminded Catholic parents that the Third Baltimore Council's decrees ordered them to send their children to Catholic schools. Supporters of Catholic education acknowledged in the twentieth century—as opponents had pointed out in the nineteenth—that public or private secular schools might be better equipped to train students for success than parochial schools. In the new world of the militant Church, however, discrepancies in quality no longer mattered; only loyalty to the church and its institutions did. To attend public or private schools was now "desertion" or treason. Changes in Catholicism had left little cultural space and no language for criticizing the church or debating its policies. "The Catholic parent who receives the claims of the Catholic school with a dubious shake of his head," the *Catholic Mirror* noted smugly in 1930, "has all but disappeared from our midst." The battles of the twenties between Protestants and Catholics, the KKK riots, and the Smith election reinforced that rigidity; it was more than a coincidence that five of the city's new Catholic schools opened during the turbulent "tribal twenties."[142]

The church's obsession with creating an all-encompassing world was not entirely successful. The growing ghetto did not hermetically seal off Irish Catholics from their Protestant neighbors. There were some social spaces, a handful of fraternal groups, civic clubs, or art or cultural organizations, where Irish men and women might mix with non-Catholics. The Worcester Country Club was the most notable example of an ethnically mixed social organization. The club had middle- and upper middle-class Yankees, Swedish, and Irish members from its inception in 1902. Nevertheless, the Worcester Country Club was an exception. Irish Catholics were almost unknown in most other prominent social clubs, particularly the Tatnuck Country Club and Worcester Club, the city's premier social organizations. For their part, many Yankee matrons blanched at the thought of their daughters or sons marrying an Irish Catholic. Mrs. Milton Higgins, wife of the Norton Company president, suspecting the background of her daughter's beau, Sanford Riley, had his genealogy thoroughly investigated before their marriage in 1904. Only when she found "not a drop of Irish blood in him" did she agree to the union. Even in the fraternal societies, the Irish tended to join clubs that they dominated, such as the Elks or certain circles of the Foresters. Many Irish people who grew up in Worcester in the 1910s and 1920s remembered having Protestant friends, but they also remembered hostile neighbors, separate sororities in high school, and concerns about dating non-Catholics. One man who grew up in one of the new ethnically mixed neighborhoods created by the trolley cars in the 1920s, said, "when I think it over I cannot remember ever going out with a girl that [sic] was not an Irish Catholic." After early childhood, Catholics were often self-conscious about relations with Protestants even when they were attempting to be amicable.[143]

As important, there were no organizations in Worcester's Irish community that suggested the possibility of reconciliation with Protestant neighbors. The men and women who might have been expected to seek acceptance from Protestant neighbors, the families who joined the Worcester Country Club, or perhaps a John F. Tinsley, the only Irishman to penetrate the very top rungs of the economic and social elite, could find no organization expressing their hopes for religious moderation, compromise, or accommodation. In twentieth-century Worcester, the leading Catholic organizations, the Federation of

Catholic Societies, the Knights of Columbus, and almost all others, spoke constantly of "war" and struggle against the "weighty odds" of entrenched Protestants and other enemies. The local Irish weekly, the *Messenger*, epitomized the complicated, changing spirit of the Worcester Irish, from accommodationists to ethnic chauvinists to militant Catholic Americans. In 1907, the new editors and owners abandoned the narrow Irish ethnocentrism of Thomas Kiely, sought out clerical approval, and changed the name of the paper to the *Catholic Messenger* to reflect the "broad Catholic field" of its interests. Yet the paper pledged a militant, not liberal, Catholicism. The new *Catholic Messenger* claimed in 1911 that "when the people of other denominations made attacks on the Catholic faith [the editors] would be ever ready to take up the defense of that faith they love so dearly." Through a succession of owners and editors over the next twenty-odd years, it stuck to that position and reflected well the new religious militancy of its people.[144]

"We All Worship the One God in the Same Way": Building a Pan-Ethnic Catholic World

If Irish Catholics continued to turn their backs on Protestants in the twentieth century, they did not continue to remain alone in ethnocentric isolation. As the city filled up with new Catholic immigrants, the Irish began to emphasize their broader Catholic rather than narrowly Irish loyalties; or put another way, they pushed out the defined limits of their group to its Catholic boundaries and identified themselves as militant American Catholics. They might have done this even had there been no new Catholic immigrants. American-born Irish Catholics, the dominant proportion of the Irish community's population, may have lost hope of acceptance by their Yankee neighbors—hence their militant Catholicism—but they still knew that they had no future as Irishmen: they were Americans and could not and did not wish to forsake their native United States and its—their—culture. Yet even if the American-born Irish came to this emphasis on the broader religious and national aspects of their identity on their own, the practical benefits of extending the boundaries of their identity to include new groups also became increasingly clear to many of them in the early twentieth century. Broad Catholic loyalties were, as we have seen, the foundation of the Irish Democratic ascent to power through Peter Sullivan and later Al Smith. Irish churchmen or lay leaders of Catholic clubs or institutions also profited from the manpower and money the new immigrants and an emerging French Canadian second generation offered. Through the first three decades of the twentieth century Irish institutions and organizations opened up to accommodate members of the new groups, and many Irishmen sought to foster cooperation and unity among Worcester's Catholic peoples.

The mingling of Catholic ethnics in common institutions or their cooperation in joint efforts can be traced as far back as the very first days of St. John's and St. Anne's, but the real beginnings of a modern pan-ethnic Catholicism in Worcester appear to date more accurately to the 1890s. St. Vincent's sought and received substantial support from Worcester's Yankee Protestant community, but the financial pressures caused by the building of three new hospital buildings in the hospital's first seven years prompted Monsignor Griffin and the Sisters of Providence, who ran St. Vincent's, to seek help from all available sources among non-Irish Catholics as well. Thus they added both a French Canadian cleric and a *Canadien* layman to the hospital's board of trustees by 1899. From its founding in 1895, the Bay State Bank had also solicited aid from non-Irish Catholics. Alexander Belisle, a member of Worcester's most prominent French Canadian family, served as one of the bank's first vice presidents and Joseph G. Vaudreil, a French Canadian contractor, was one of its first trustees. An Italian caterer and a Polish baker were also among the first incorporators. Struggling to establish itself against well-entrenched competitors, the Irish-dominated Bay State Bank grudgingly extended its market within the Catholic community.[145]

The most striking example of the trend to increasing cooperation among the Irish and Worcester's other Catholic nationalities in the 1890s, however, was the creation of the St. Francis Home for the Aged. In the early nineties, an order of French Canadian nuns, officially the Little Franciscans of Mary, often called simply the "Brown Nuns," had become embroiled in a wrenching controversy with Worcester's French Canadian clergy over the nuns' management of an orphanage in the city. Estranged from the French Canadian elite, they sought help from the city's Irish population in their efforts to maintain the orphanage. By 1896 the sisters resolved their conflicts with the French clergy, though only after pursuing appeals to the bishop, the papal legate in Washington, and even to the Vatican. The final decision decreed that the sisters should give up their orphanage and establish an old-age home in Worcester. The nuns won strong support from the Irish in their new effort. In 1898, the president and many of the officers of the St. Francis Home Aid Association were Irish. This support, no doubt, stemmed in part from the sisters' earlier cultivation of Irish financial resources, but it was also motivated by the real needs of the Irish community. Prominent Irish priests and laymen had bandied about proposals for an Irish old-age home since at least 1890. Thus when the

Brown Nuns opened their home, the Irish seized this solution to what the *Messenger* called in 1890 "a long felt need." By 1900, eighteen of the thirty-four aged living in the new St. Francis Home were Irish.[146]

The trend among Irish-dominated or Irish-controlled organizations to include non-Irish Catholic members gained considerable momentum in the twentieth century. Institutions founded in the 1890s such as St. Vincent's Hospital and the Bay State Bank added more French Canadians and Italians to their boards of trustees in the first two decades of the twentieth century. In 1915, the bank announced the election of a recent Italian immigrant to the board, praising him as a fine example of an American success story.[147]

As important, non-Irish Catholics began filtering into the original Irish churches, creating ethnically mixed congregations. As early as 1899 the *Messenger* had noted that numbers of non-Irish Catholics were deserting their national parishes for English-speaking churches. The archives of the diocese of Springfield and of some of the older parishes suggest that this trend increased substantially in the first three decades of the twentieth century. French Canadians or new immigrants seeking to leave their national parishes, or Irish priests concerned about the proper procedure for admitting them into their congregations often petitioned the diocese for permission to make the transfer in order to forestall objections by pastors of national churches. Most of the petitioners in these early decades of the twentieth century were French Canadians. Invariably they complained that they or their children no longer spoke French and thus worship in the national parishes made no sense. In 1905, one couple explained simply: "We are American born." Others claimed that the old language simply seemed irrelevant to them. They were committed to the faith, however, and recognized that they shared that commitment with Catholics of all nationalities. One French Canadian justified his request for a transfer from Notre Dame des Canadiens to St. Paul's by arguing "We all worship the one God in the same way." Newer ethnics were understandably slower to move into the old Irish churches, but as early as 1905 and 1906, Father John J. McCoy was asking the diocese to permit some Lithuanian couples to join his parish. McCoy explained to the diocesan chancellor that "all speak English . . . the men especially well." By the late 1920s and 1930s, French Canadian and Italian names had begun to appear on the parish rolls of St. Peter's and on the sacramental registers of St. John's. By the 1940s St. John's parish began to celebrate St. Joseph's Day for its Italian parishioners, as well as St. Patrick's Day for its Irish churchgoers. Gradually, almost invisibly then, some of the oldest institutions in the Irish community were becoming ethnically heterogeneous.[148]

Many of the new churches established in Worcester's peripheral sections outside its immigrant neighborhoods in the early twentieth century were ethnically mixed from the outset. The bishop did not plan most of these new English-language churches as mixed parishes but almost all of them attracted French Canadians and other non-Irish ethnics from the moment they opened. In 1918, the wife of one of the city's wealthiest French Canadian businessmen petitioned the diocese to permit her family to attend the six-year-old Blessed Sacrament parish near her home on the west side, rather than Notre Dame, the inner-city French national parish. The parish records of Our Lady of the Angels established on the far southwest in 1917 suggest that large numbers of French Canadians as well as Irish attended that church from its beginnings as well. St. Margaret Mary's, founded in 1922 among new housing developments on the far eastern edge of the city near Lake Quinsigamond, quickly attracted Italians and other new immigrants as well as French Canadians and Irish Catholics to its services.[149]

While most new parishes on the city's periphery became integrated naturally, the diocese self-consciously formed Holy Rosary parish to serve an ethnically diverse population. Founded in 1913, Holy Rosary was located near the Greendale section on the far north side of Worcester. Before the twentieth century the area had attracted very few Catholic residents, and when the parish began only six hundred Irish and French Catholics were living within its borders. Neither group had enough people in the area to support a church on its own, but the combined numbers of Irish and French warranted a new Catholic parish in the neighborhood.[150]

Nevertheless, the diocese approached the establishment of the new church gingerly, for no parish in the city had been explicitly created to serve a mixed ethnic congregation before, and New England's Catholic history was fraught with similar experiments gone awry. The first four pastors of the parish were French, despite an Irish majority among the parishioners, and the priests offered services in both French and English until at least the 1920s. When the bishop finally appointed an Irish pastor in 1919, he was bilingual, educated in Canada, and seasoned by extensive service in French parishes in western Massachusetts. Despite these concessions to Holy Rosary's divided population, the parish, nonetheless, reflected the gradual triumph of a broad religious identification over more narrowly defined ethnic allegiances.[151]

Irish societies and clubs also began to invite Catholics of all nationalities into their ranks in the late nineteenth and early twentieth centuries. The AOH, the Clan na Gael, and the Irish National Foresters, restricted their memberships to the Irish-born or Irish descendants, but the parish temperance societies and local clubs such as the Washington Club set no such rules or restrictions. These societies had been almost exclusively Irish in the past because of custom or their close affiliation with parishes. Nevertheless, by the 1890s,

names such as Nordi, Josti, and Beaudette began appearing on the membership rolls of groups such as the St. Stephen's Total Abstinence Association and
the Washington Club.[152]

New societies appearing in the twentieth century were usually open to non-
Irish Catholics from their founding. Women's societies such as the Catholic
Women's Club, the St. Agnes Guild, or the Ladies Catholic Benevolent Association were open to Catholic women of all backgrounds. Though dominated by
the Irish, all of these organizations attracted other Catholic ethnics such as
French Canadians, Italians, or Lithuanians. In 1917 the Ladies Catholic Benevolent Association opened branches in the Shrewsbury Street neighborhood
that mixed Irish, Italian, and French members.[153]

Perhaps as significant as the opening up of individual societies to multiethnic membership were the efforts to bring clubs and organizations of all
Catholic ethnics together to pursue common purposes. Some of these efforts
were temporary, such as the multiethnic parade and ceremonies honoring
James Cardinal Gibbons when he came to Worcester in 1907, the uniting of
church choirs from parishes across the city into a "Catholic" chorus in 1916,
and the Mission Crusade meeting at Holy Cross College's Fitton Field in 1932.
The attempt to create a local branch of the Federation of Catholic Societies
was far more ambitious, for it meant to permanently unite Catholics of every
ethnic background. The national federation had been founded in 1901 to
cement "the bonds of fraternal union among the Catholic laity and Catholic
societies of the United States," and to foster "Catholic interests" as well as to
achieve other goals. Worcester was slow to join the movement, but in 1909,
Father John J. McCoy enlisted the help of Father Bernard S. Conaty, pastor of
Sacred Heart, and Thomas McAvoy, a second-generation Irish layman, to form
a branch of the organization in Worcester. Representatives of virtually all the
Irish societies, including the Ancient Order of Hibernians, gathered for the
first meeting in early November. The project lagged through the winter until
Conaty took the lead and called for a second meeting in April of 1910. At this
second conclave Father Zwickerath, S.J., from Holy Cross College gave the
principal address. Zwickerath proclaimed that the purposes of the organization were to "knit closer together those of the same faith, but of various races
who too often fail to understand each other," providing an "external expression to the unity of faith and sentiment which binds them inwardly together."
"Such union will give the Catholics strength," he predicted, in their "war of de-
fence," "fight for rights," and moral crusades against immorality and divorce.[154]

Though slow and halting, the trend towards ethnic mixing and pan-ethnic
cooperation among Catholics in Worcester was, nonetheless, steady. There

were many reasons for this. Most of the institutions were run by the church: they were founded on a common loyalty and could invoke a common authority. That the members of these groups felt a part of this single institution and more or less bowed to its authority was a powerful force in uniting them into a single group. This sometimes, of course, exacerbated intra-Catholic friction as it had in nearby North Brookfield or elsewhere around the country when French Canadians, Germans, or Poles felt an Irish-led church ignored or dismissed their claims. On the other hand, most Catholic ethnics often thought twice before risking the church's condemnation in order to fight for ethnic interests. Clerics risked more concrete rewards like prize posts if they defied their bishops too strenuously. Moreover, American Catholics of almost all ethnic backgrounds recognized the Vatican's ultimate sovereignty. Over the course of the late nineteenth and early twentieth centuries, respect for the popes evolved into a virtual cult of the papacy, and the Vatican, in turn, exerted more and more direct influence over the American church.

Catholicism, however, meant more than a shared loyalty to a common institution or authority; it also meant shared values, ideas, and rituals. As the French Canadian man who sought to attend St. Paul's stated: "We all worship the one God in the same way." Such beliefs—from such specific tenets as the real presence of Christ in the Eucharist or papal infallibility, to the broader values of sacramentalism or communalism—not only linked them together but distinguished them from Protestants. Ethnically specific rituals, devotions, prayers, and elaborations on common liturgies like the mass, had often been a source of divisiveness among American Catholics. From the late nineteenth through the mid-twentieth centuries, however, "post-ethnic" devotions, to use Robert Orsi's phrase, devotions to St. Theresa of Lisieux, Our Lady of Lourdes, the Sacred Heart, or St. Jude became popular among Catholic ethnics of all ethnic backgrounds and provided a style of Catholic worship amenable to people of all nationalities.[155]

Catholics of many ethnic backgrounds also shared perspectives on issues of public morality, experiences of discrimination and prejudice, and some of the same material and political interests. Catholics of all ethnic backgrounds seemed to take the same positions on the fading question of drinking as well as the emerging questions of sexual morality, women's roles, birth control, and abortion. Most Catholic ethnics in Worcester also experienced or understood the Protestant prejudice against them as shown by the Klan or the nativists backing Hoover. Moreover, though there were clear class divisions not only within the Irish community but distinguishing the Irish and to a lesser extent the French from the poorer new groups, Catholics as a group were not as wealthy as Protestants, lived in the city's poorer districts, and often had less access to the offices that controlled the city's companies than even the recently arrived Protestant immigrants such as the Swedes or British. Finally, if Catholic ethnics vied with the Irish and each other for political recognition, the steady, if halting, forging of a Democratic Catholic coalition both drew on and reinforced the effort to create a unified Catholic subcommunity. Irish church and community leaders also had advantages over Celtic political leaders: the religious loyalties of the French and new immigrants were rooted in centuries of history, not just recent calculations of interest; and the Irish churchmen's competitors for those loyalties were a zealous but small and underfinanced band of Protestant missionaries, not the well-oiled Republican machine.[156]

If Catholic ethnics had much in common, Irish Catholics had good reasons for capitalizing on those shared loyalties and values to draw non-Irish ethnics into a single Celtic-led subsociety. For Irish leaders of the church and other institutions it made practical sense to seek the widest base of support. It certainly made sense for the Bay State Bank and St. Vincent's Hospital to seek non-Irish Catholics as trustees and thus as possible entrees to new customers, investors, or donors in the French Canadian, Italian, or other new immigrant communities. For the French Canadian nuns at the St. Francis Home, however, the need for Irish help was also clear and the sisters did not hesitate to seek Celtic aid. Pastors of new Irish parishes in peripheral parts of the city, struggling with the financial burdens of constructing new churches and schools, could use any new parishioners, no matter what their nationality. Also, since the populations in the new districts were so dispersed and mixed, it was impossible for the diocese to create new national parishes in these burgeoning residential districts. Necessity, as much as an ideological commitment to an American church, demanded the Holy Rosary experiment, for example.

For the Irish, however, it was not merely the calculation of current practical interest but visions of future power that moved them to integrate fellow ethnics in their organizations or try to gather them in federations. The *Catholic Messenger* was very conscious of growing Catholic strength in Worcester. In 1903 and 1904, the paper repeatedly boasted that Catholics had become a majority among Worcester's citizens. The paper then, and throughout the first three decades of the twentieth century, took great pleasure in listing the large and growing number of Catholic institutions as evidence of the might of the "one true faith." Invariably such lists began with Worcester's Irish churches and institutions, but the paper proudly detailed French Canadian, Italian, Polish, and Lithuanian churches and societies as well. In the effort to establish a branch of the Federation of Catholic Societies the Irish were perhaps most candid about the potential power they saw in their coreligionists. The *Catholic Messenger*, in promoting the branch, admitted the lack of solidarity often manifested by Catholics because churches are set apart "for people of the different races . . . who [therefore] often fail to understand each other." But "a fraternal organization . . . united on most intimate lines of charity, unity and fraternity," the paper gushed, "would exert an influence for the well being of the church and our country beyond calculation." Others suggested that the federation might serve as the precursor to a Catholic political party in America. Few Irishmen would go that far, but many were optimistic about the potential power of a growing and united church.[157]

Yet if the Irish could see advantages in expanding their subsociety it was not clear, perhaps even to them, what they wanted from these non-Irish ethnics. Their frequent praise of French Canadian, Polish, or other groups' institutions suggested some respect for the cultural and social integrity of these non-Irish ethnics. Organizers of the federation also sometimes talked in innocent terms of merely providing an opportunity for members of the "different" Catholic parishes and societies to come together "from time to time." Yet just as often Irish Catholics spoke of creating a new single group of American Catholics, melting down and remaking other Catholic ethnics in the image of the American Catholic ideal, the Irish American. Words or phrases like "melting pot," "assimilation," and "amalgamation" filled the rhetoric of Irish orators or writers when they discussed new immigrants in the second decade of the twentieth century. Such terms undoubtedly reflected the broader drive for Americanization which became increasingly rabid throughout the United States as the nation moved towards war in the second decade of the twentieth century. Yet it also reflected the powerful identification of American-born Irishmen and women with America, and their resulting disdain for the foreignness of the new immigrants. In 1919, the *Catholic Messenger* bluntly chastised new immigrants for remaining "apart" from "all American influences" and thus persisting in ignorance of "our [American] customs and institutions." Some of the new multiethnic organizations like the Catholic Federation also explicitly stated their goal of promoting the use of English among the new Catholic ethnics. Even clearer were the motives of the young Irish men and women who took over the Sunday school at the Italian parish of Mount Carmel in 1916, intent on turning the Italian children there into "fine little Catholic American citizens." Furthermore, Worcester's Irish Catholics candidly rejoiced that the roots of that Catholic American identity lay in Ireland and not elsewhere. As one Worcester priest proclaimed in 1915: "It is a special blessing of the church in this country that it has been founded along the lines of the Irish church and no matter how great the flood of immigrants may be in the years to come, the tradition and custom has been established and it will continue along the lines of the dear church of Ireland."[158]

Even as the Worcester Irish sought to forge all Catholic ethnics into a powerful new American group, they never lost a sense of their own identity as a people distinct from these other Catholic newcomers. Worcester's Irish Catholics almost always saw themselves as leaders of this new group, as arbiters and models of proper American Catholic behavior. The city's Irish understood that other Catholic ethnics served a useful purpose in bolstering their power by joining the Irish-led subsociety, but they never seemed convinced that other groups could measure up to their own standards, either in devotion to the church or loyalty to America. Contests for power within the church and outside in city politics or in the competition for jobs helped keep such a sense of distinctiveness alive. In local politics as in the church and, indeed, many institutional arenas in the early twentieth century, Irishmen always fought two battles: to unite other Catholic ethnics behind them against Protestants and to fend off the challenges of those new ethnics for supremacy in this pan-ethnic coalition. Moreover, a distinctive Irish ethnic culture did not die in the twentieth century. The efforts to revive Irish sports and language never succeeded in attracting the interest of the second generation, but a commercialized Irish American ethnic culture of Tin Pan Alley songs and urban theater plays or vaudeville skits did. This Irish ethnic culture was not a critical part of the American-born generation's everyday life. That was structured by their faith's dictums and rituals and the values and customs of American culture, but these Irish American songs and plays provided some cultural substance to help the second-generation Irish mark themselves off as different from other Catholic ethnics. Thus, though the Worcester Irish in the twentieth century thought of themselves as American Catholics, never tired of proclaiming that identity, and worked hard and sincerely to create a pan-ethnic Catholic subsociety, they still knew themselves as different from other American Catholics. Under the right circumstances even the American-born's Irish loyalties could still revive— as we shall see.[159]

An intra-Catholic ethnic dispute in nearby Rhode Island in the mid-1920s that spilled over into Worcester vividly exposed the combination of aggressive Irish Americanization and non-Irish Catholic resistance that complicated the creation of a new pan-ethnic Catholic people in Worcester. In 1926, the bishop of Providence, William Hickey, a native of Worcester, demanded that French Canadians and all other members of his diocese contribute to the establishment of English-language, "American" high schools. French Canadian laymen in Woonsocket, led by Alfred Daigneault, editor of the *Sentinelle* news-paper, objected strongly to forcing *Canadiens* to pay for schools that would ultimately destroy their culture. Many of Worcester's French Canadians and *L'Opinion Publique* backed the Sentinellists and invited their leading spokes-man, Alfred Daigneault, to the city to speak at Mechanics Hall. Local Irish Catholics were furious at this entertaining of Catholic renegades in the city. The *Catholic Messenger* objected strongly to Daigneault's presence in Worcester and traded insults with him and local French Canadians over the Sentinellist protest for over a month. The thrust of the *Messenger's* attack on Daigneault was that French Canadians and all Catholic ethnics of whatever background should be "Americanized." The paper claimed to find it "ridiculous" and "un-believable" that any Catholic would not contribute money to schools that teach in English, the nation's language; it declared solemnly, "all patriotic American Catholics will readily subscribe to this patriotic program of the American bishops." It was, nonetheless, clear that this was an ethnic dispute between the Irish and the French Canadians. Daigneault attacked the *Catholic Messenger* as an Irish paper defending the Irish stranglehold on the church, and the weekly, in turn, attacked Daigneault as "an anti Irish Catholic." Yet in a telling example of how the Irish understood their ethnicity in the creation of the new Catholic group, how they distinguished themselves against other Catholic ethnics not as Irish but as model American Catholics, the *Catholic Messenger* suggested that Daigneault's real offense was not that he was anti-Irish but "un American." Even as news from counties in Ireland ran on its back pages, the weekly denied that it was an Irish paper at all, only an "ordi-nary" American Catholic newspaper: "Let a native of the United States dis-agree with him [Daigneault] and he promptly labels him Irish. Let a Catholic newspaper which has given many examples of unadulterated Americanism endeavor to tell the facts about an intolerable situation in Woonsocket and that publication immediately becomes an Irish newspaper published by dirty Irish."[160]

As incidents like the dustup over Daigneault reveal, French Canadian, Italian, and other Catholic ethnics in Worcester remained suspicious of their Irish neighbors and the Americanizing intentions of the Irish. Thus, though more and more non-Irish ethnics joined the clubs and institutions of a new Catholic subsociety as the twentieth century wore on, many still resisted, re-luctant to abandon their own cultures and interests to Irish ambitions. Be-cause of this reluctance, the Federation of Catholic Societies folded after only a few meetings. Though the Irish organizers extended invitations to French Canadian and Lithuanian societies, it is not clear that any of them or other non-Irish associations participated in the federation. For French Canadians and the new immigrants, the intentions of McCoy and other Irish leaders to "knit closer together those of the same faith" often seemed an effort to swallow them whole in the name of Catholic unity.[161]

The best evidence of the French and new immigrant reluctance to be incorporated into a new Irish-led subsociety was their efforts to build up their own networks of institutions and clubs. By the 1920s, the Lithuanians had already built a large new church for their original parish, St. Casimir's, a parish school of the same name, and a second parish church, Our Lady of Vilna; and the city's Poles had constructed their own St. Mary's parish and a school which taught Polish and enrolled over 700 pupils. Worcester's Italians had established their own parish, Our Lady of Mount Carmel, and a number of societies by then, though they never built a parochial school.[162]

The French Canadian subsociety, meanwhile, remained large and complex through the 1910s. At the end of that decade, there were four councils of the St. Jean de Baptiste Society in Worcester, five circles of Les Artisans Canadienne as well as thirteen other private clubs, a band, a philharmonic society, ten military companies, and three naturalization clubs. As important, Worcester had become a primary center of French-language culture in New England when the Assumptionist Fathers founded Assumption College in Worcester in 1904. Though the Assumptionists were from France and not Canada, their college quickly became the intellectual center for French Canadians throughout New England.[163]

Clearly, then, neither the French nor the new immigrant ethnics were willing to abandon their ethnic loyalties for absorption into an Irish-led American Catholic subsociety. In 1911, *L'Opinion Publique,* Worcester's French Canadian daily, expressed their concerns bluntly, complaining that Irish "assimilators" seemed intent on trying "to tear from us piece by piece, the last vestiges of our national heritage." For their part, the Irish (model American Catholics in their own minds) were also reluctant to bring these other ethnics into such a community as equals. Ethnic distinctions thus would persist within Worcester's Catholic community until long after World War II.[164]

Nevertheless, it would be a mistake to underestimate the degree of merging that occurred among Catholics in the early twentieth century and what it portended for the future. The number of Irish-run institutions and associations that opened up to the French and new immigrants was impressive and grew ever larger over the first three to four decades of the new century. Moreover, resistance by the French or other groups to Irish absorption had an ambiguous effect on the Irish. Though it sometimes made them more conscious

of their own ethnic group identity, it often appeared to push them to proclaim even more energetically the broader American Catholic conception of
their loyalties in order to justify their assimilationist crusades. The *Catholic
Messenger*'s remarkable denial of its Irish roots and shrill assertion of its unqualified Catholic Americanism during the Sentinelle controversy is a good
example. Finally, though Italian, Lithuanian, and Polish ethnics would continue to expand their subsocieties through World War II, there were signs that
the growth of the French Canadian subcommunity had passed its peak much
earlier: no new French Canadian parishes were founded in Worcester after
1904, and by the 1930s *L'Opinion Publique,* Worcester's French-language paper,
long prominent throughout New England as well as in the city, had ceased
publication. The broader Irish-led Catholic subsociety would continue to evolve
in tandem with the Celtic-led Catholic political coalition in the Democratic
party, feeding it and feeding off it. Its growth, like that coalition's development, would be halting—boundaries dividing Catholic ethnics would not
disappear—but the Catholic boundaries that embraced the French, Italians,
Poles, and Lithuanians, and divided them from non-Catholics, relentlessly, if
slowly and irregularly, thickened and hardened.

"The Service of God and Country": The Knights of Columbus as Leaders of Pan-Ethnic, Militant American Catholicism

As before in the history of the Irish in turn of the century Worcester, one association emerged in the early twentieth century which seemed to best embody
the themes of changing Irish identity in the new era, became the principal pro-
ponent of them, and thus rose to dominate the community. In the 1880s, temperance societies perhaps best reflected Irish conceptions of their place in
Worcester. In the turbulent 1890s, the AOH and its allies, the Clan na Gael and
others, thrived as advocates of the new bellicose Irish ethnocentrism. By the
1910s the successor to the temperance societies and the Hibernians began to
emerge to dominate Worcester's Irish community: the Knights of Columbus.

The Knights had been founded in 1894 and enjoyed steady, if unspectacular,
growth through the early 1900s. About the middle of the twentieth century's
first decade, the K. of C.'s membership began to take off. At the turn of the
century there were only a few hundred Knights in Worcester. By 1914 there
were 1,400, or nearly five times as many. In the latter year, as a sign of their
growing strength and rising confidence in their future, the Knights purchased
the old YMCA on Elm Street for their headquarters. The building, with its numerous halls, rooms, and gymnasium, the *Catholic Messenger* suggested in 1915,

was "a splendid monument to the enterprise and ambition of the Catholic men of Worcester." It was the war, however, and the Knights role in it, that proved the greatest stimulus to the order's growth. By 1921, Worcester's Alhambra Council would boast over 5,000 members—the largest K. of C. council in the world at the time.[165]

Their rapid growth and vast numbers notwithstanding, the Knights came from a very distinct, if large and rapidly expanding, part of the Irish population in Worcester. They were, for example, almost all American-born. As noted in the last chapter 83 percent of the Knights who joined the order at the turn of the century and could be traced in the 1900 census had been born in America; 60 percent of them were second-generation Irish. The Knights' appeal was limited, even among the American-born Irish. The Knights attracted the upwardly mobile, middle-class, American-born Irish. Of the 782 applicants to the order between 1905 and 1915, 62.7 percent were white-collar workers. Moreover, 10 percent were professionals, such as doctors and lawyers, and another 16 percent were managers or supervisors.[166]

The Knights were attractive to these successful American-born Irishmen, at least in part, because they celebrated and promoted respectability and achievement. The Alhambra Council offered classes to prepare members or their relatives for the police, post office or other civil service examinations, and courses in bookkeeping or commercial law for Knights pursuing careers in business. The K. of C. promoted these classes as "an excellent opportunity for advancement" for the "young man with aspirations after the higher things in life." Verse by John Boyle O'Reilly printed on the cover of the program for the Knights' eleventh anniversary banquet in 1905 summed up the attitude they hoped to encourage among their members: "A man is not the slave of circumstances. . . . He makes his own events, not time nor fate their logic his: not creature but creator."[167]

The Knights not only encouraged achievement among their members, they also demanded a strict respectability that they believed should mark every Knight. In 1916, the Alhambra Council suggested that it sought to make "desirable actions . . . automatic and habitual" and "guard carefully against growing into ways . . . likely to be disadvantageous." The order did not pledge its members to temperance, but through the 1890s and early 1900s it did refuse to admit saloonkeepers or any liquor dealers to its ranks. Officers of the association also set strict rules about smoking, gambling, or drinking in the meeting rooms and encouraged good grooming and proper dress among members. Rules of morality and respectability extended to the Knight in his home as well. The Knights strongly endorsed Church teachings against divorce and backed proscriptions of indecent books and movies. The K. of C., the *Catholic Messenger* stated in 1916, "stamps its members in the opinion of the public as men of sobriety, progress and public spirit, living good home lives and raising their children to the service of God and country."[168]

It was not their respectability, however, so much as their definition of "service to God and country" that made the Knights the dominant organization in Worcester's Irish community in the early twentieth century. The Knights were enthusiastic American patriots, almost jingoes, but also militant, fervent Catholics. This combination as well as their openness to Catholics of all ethnic backgrounds fitted them perfectly for leadership of Irish efforts to forge a new, pan-ethnic, militant, American Catholicism in early twentieth-century Worcester.

Like the temperance men, the Knights enthusiastically embraced many aspects of American popular culture. The K. of C. sponsored activities including minstrel shows, dance parties, vaudeville reviews, and band concerts. In 1929 the K. of C.'s annual minstrel show featured "a number of modern and old time melodies . . . and some very clever dancing numbers." George (Ducky) Rogers sang "I Left My Ginger," and Ralph Berthiaume sang "Bells of the Sea." Following the show, the floor was cleared for general dancing to music played by "Eddie Murphy's Bohemian Orchestra." The Knights were also interested, as earlier Catholic teetotallers were, in American athletics. The K. of C. organized teams or leagues for members or their sons in a wide variety of sports, fielding strong basketball teams in particular.[169]

The Knights' commitment to the United States went beyond a mere embrace of its customs to a vigorous, almost fanatical, assertion of what they perceived to be American interests. In a 1929 listing of the reasons why Catholic men should join the K. of C., Worcester's Alhambra Council listed patriotism among the most important, "because it is a patriotic organization, upholding governmental institutions." Patriotic rhetoric or symbols or both marked virtually every K. of C. event. Flags and red, white, and blue bunting even draped the walls at minstrel shows and dinners. The Knights' patriotism was active and aggressive, not merely rhetorical. Like many Catholic associations in this era, they were vociferously opposed to radicalism. In the same 1929 list of reasons to join the K. of C., Worcester's Knights suggested "because of its [the K. of C.'s] battle against socialism and communism." The Knights sponsored frequent lectures condemning socialism, including speeches by the noted Catholic convert and antisocialist activist, David Goldstein.[170]

The best evidence of the depth of the K. of C.'s patriotism came during World War I. Even before the American entry into the War, the Knights in Worcester enthusiastically backed American "preparedness" efforts. Once the United States entered the war in April of 1917, the Knights threw themselves into the war effort with abandon. Over 750 Knights from the Alhambra Council joined the armed forces and at least twelve died overseas. At home the Alhambra Council raised over $25,000 to "comfort" soldiers moving through Worcester or staying at nearby military installations. The council converted two large halls in its headquarters into dormitories capable of housing seventy-five men "and as a result more than 7,500 men were furnished lodging and breakfast while en route to and from cantonments" during the war. Finally, Worcester's Knights purchased over half a million dollars worth of War Bonds and organized numerous local patriotic meetings and lectures.[171]

The Knights of Columbus were not just Americans but "Catholic" Americans, and the modifier was critical to them. Devotion to the church was written into the very rituals of the K. of C., and the entire Alhambra Council and its constituent committees frequently attended mass and received communion in a body. The council also organized an annual retreat for its members, sponsored frequent lectures on aspects of the church, and provided instruction in the faith and encouragement in its private practice through its newsletter or other literature. In 1928 the council newsletter assured members that by assisting devoutly at mass "you kneel amidst a multitude of holy angels," earn a "higher degree of glory in heaven," and, perhaps, even gain a blessing for "your temporal goods and affairs." The Knights also made their new clubhouse, a huge building with many rooms, into "the Catholic social center of the city." Because of efforts by the K. of C. in Worcester and around the nation, spokesmen for the Alhambra Council boasted in 1915 that "thousands of young men have been kept from being drawn away from Holy Mother Church."[172]

The Knights' faith was not a passive, private devotion, but a public crusade. The K. of C. took pride in calling themselves a "militantly Catholic" society ever "vigilant, watchful and awake in those matters which effect its members or their religion." Their first notable effort in that regard took place in 1907 when they organized a meeting of Worcester Catholics to protest the passage of new laws by the government of France for the Republic's Catholic institutions and clergy. Although a group of Assumptionist priests, recent refugees from France, were the featured guests of the meeting, the largely Irish Knights ran it. Over 2,000 people, including a number of prominent Irish and French Canadian politicians, turned out for the protest and "voted to pass resolutions condemning the attitude of the government of France towards the Catholic church."[173]

The Knights would also later organize local protests against revolutionaries in Mexico, but they focused most of their attention in the 1910s and 1920s on the defense of Catholic interests at home. As the Massachusetts K.

of C.'s magazine trumpeted in 1908, the K. of C. was steadfastly committed to preventing Protestants from "getting the upper hand." The Knights' motto, the magazine declared was: "We want the same rights and privileges as the Protestants." Thus the Knights led the fight locally and nationally against distribution of the *Menace,* an anti-Catholic newspaper in the 1910s. In 1915, Worcester's Knights hinted broadly that they had also fought against efforts by local nativists to boycott or isolate Catholic businessmen: "No business-man can be boycotted successfully today on the grounds of his faith and the businessman and the professional man owe a debt of gratitude to the Knights of Columbus for this one activity alone." We have been, the Knights claimed, "the bulwark against the hostile attacks of bigots."[174]

The Knights would truly become the bulwark of the Irish and Catholic community in Worcester as ethnic and religious tensions flared in the 1920s. The Knights repeatedly denied any involvement in politics, but their opponents were not convinced. The Knights were closely identified with Peter Sullivan's triumphs in the early 1920s. After Sullivan's victory in 1919, Lewis Buckley, Protestant manufacturer and member of the Republican North End Ring, wrote bitterly to Republican Congressman Samuel Winslow about the "de-fection of the Republican Catholic vote among the Poles, Lithuanians etc. due to the K. of C. activities among those classes." The *Catholic Messenger* noted that the K. of C. was also the first organization to congratulate Peter Sullivan on his victory in 1919, and a delegation of Knights escorted Sullivan to the K. of C. hall where more than a thousand people stood in line to shake his hand and honor him in a way "that will never be forgotten by those on hand." Sullivan celebrated subsequent victories at the K. of C. hall as well, starting his victory parade from there in 1922, for example. Francis P. McKeon, Democratic may-oral candidate in 1924, was, if anything, even more closely identified with the K. of C., having been a prominent member for years and even serving as the state Grand Knight.[175]

The Knights were also in the forefront of the campaign against the Klan and other nativists in the 1920s. K. of C. members monitored KKK rallies, identi-fied Klan members from the license plates on cars parked at Klan meetings, and later organized boycotts against businessmen they had identified as Klansman. Knights of Columbus were also rumored to have spread fraudulent tickets for Eugene Farnsworth's first big Klan meeting at Mechanics Hall in 1923. The Knights played no official role in the Smith campaign four years later, but the religious prejudice unleashed against the New York governor deeply disturbed them. After the presidential campaign of 1928, Frank Cham-pagne, Grand Knight of the Alhambra Council, argued that "when our church is vilified, we are vilified" and announced an effort by all the K. of C. councils in Massachusetts to counteract this prejudice through a series of radio broadcasts that would give a "systematic, intelligent and clear exposition" of Catholicism. "The public utilities should not be used to vilify and calumniate us," Champagne argued, and Catholics should respond aggressively to anyone who attempts to use them for that purpose.[176]

The Knights drew a sharp boundary between themselves and non-Catholics, but they welcomed Catholics of every nationality into their ranks. Some of the earliest Knights in the 1890s and early 1900s had been French Canadian. Though the organization remained overwhelmingly Irish throughout the next three decades, the K. of C. continued to attract Catholics of diverse ethnic backgrounds. From January of 1912 to December of 1914, sixty French Canadians, Italians, Poles, and Lithuanians applied for admission to the Alhambra Council. This was a small minority of the men applying to the K. of C. in that period, but it suggested both the Knights' commitment to the principle of ethnic inclusiveness and the willingness of some non-Irish Catholics—many of them upwardly mobile French Canadians—to take advantage of it. John J. McCoy expressed that principle in grand terms in an address to Worcester's Knights: "You are like the mother church in that you do not limit your membership to men of any one nationality or color or like condition but have room for all who have grace hot from the heart of God, [and] make one heart in the service of God."[177]

In 1915, the Knights, no longer content to merely accept non-Irish Catholics who applied to the organization, began an active search for members among the new Catholic immigrants. In September of that year, Knights officials instructed the council's membership committee to "see to it that all desirable citizens of this locality, no matter what nationality, are Knights and there are many desirable men who would make fit Knightly timber among the peoples who have come to this country." The next month the council set up a committee, including three Italian Americans and eight French Canadians, to seek new members.[178]

At the same time the Knights launched a much more ambitious "Americanization" program for all adults in these new immigrant Catholic communities. Proclaiming that the "Alhambra Council does not wish to fall within the class which has not done anything toward the assimilation of the newcomer to this country," the Knights organized naturalization classes and courses in English and the "fundamentals of religion" for new immigrant adults. Later, the council formed a committee of laymen to work with pastors of the national parishes to make sure that the new immigrants did not emerge from the "melting pot . . . polluted with false ideas about religion and pernicious notions of citizenship" and would remain true to their faith as they were "transformed into American metal." It is clear, then, that the Knights, like other Irish-dominated associations in this era, were committed, even actively committed, to the creation of an American Catholic people, a new, broad group, from people of diverse backgrounds, sharply defined by its religious, not ethnic, boundaries.[179]

"Columbus Day Belongs to Our Catholic People . . . an Imposing Demonstration of Catholic Power": Columbus Day Parades in Worcester

Perhaps the principal effort mounted by the Knights to forge this ethnically diverse but religiously united American Catholic community in Worcester was their promotion of a parade on Columbus Day. Columbus, the Knights and other Catholics in Worcester believed, was a critically important figure for American Catholics. He was not only the first American (America's native people were irrelevant to them); he was the first American Catholic. He thus stood as a kind of symbolic ancestor for all American Catholics.[180]

Despite Columbus's significance, few Catholics in Worcester, Irish or otherwise, made much of the anniversary of his "discovery" until the early twentieth century, but in 1910 Worcester's K. of C. organized a mammoth parade, made up largely of Knights but with a scattering of Irish and non-Irish ethnic societies, to celebrate Columbus as an American Catholic hero. Observers took special note of the "picturesque" uniforms of two of the Polish organizations. The following year the parade had grown far larger to include thousands of marchers in six divisions—French and Italian divisions among them—tramping from City Hall down Main Street to Lincoln Square. By 1912 and 1913 more than 10,000 men and women participated in the parade, including virtually all of the parish Holy Name Societies in Worcester and branches of the Ladies Catholic Benevolent Association. Some of Worcester's non-Irish Catholic ethnics marched again as they had in earlier parades. The Polish division even featured a float with young Polish men and women dressed in traditional peasant costumes.[181]

The size and broad ethnic diversity of the parades should not suggest that they were welcomed by all in Worcester. The parade almost immediately became the focus of intergroup controversy and conflict. The first battle was between Catholics and non-Catholics. Organizers of the first four parades clearly saw them as Catholic processions honoring a Catholic hero. The *Catholic*

Messenger argued in 1910 that "Columbus Day is essentially a Catholic holiday" and the parade "a golden opportunity to let the people of Worcester witness an imposing demonstration of Catholic sentiment" in the city. In 1911, however, the K. of C. sought not merely to display Catholic power but to exert it as well and sent a committee around to local merchants to ask them to close down on Columbus Day. Most merchants refused and the Merchants Association became the spokesman for their resistance. John J. McCoy made light of the controversy. Noting that the city's Swedes had been particularly opposed to the Catholic commemoration of Columbus, he taunted: "Let us have a Leif Ericson Day as well as a Columbus Day and we will join our Swedish friends in honoring his memory because Ericson was just as good a Catholic and as honorable a man as Columbus." With tongue in cheek, he added: "And certainly we can have St. Brendan who was not only an Irishman and a Catholic but a Kerryman as well." Many other Catholics, however, were not amused by the Merchant Association's objections. The *Catholic Messenger* and others read the merchants' refusal as "an anti Catholic action" and "an insult for the Catholic organizations." "It is time now," the paper warned vaguely, "that the Catholics of Worcester demand every consideration to which they are entitled." The Knights themselves were more specific and straightforward; they appealed to "all Catholics to refrain from business dealings with the merchants during the day."[182]

The conflict between Catholics and non-Catholics sparked by the parade may not have troubled the Knights so much as the controversy the procession provoked within the Catholic community. On September 5, 1912, spokesmen for Worcester's Italian societies announced that they had declined the K. of C.'s invitation to march in the parade. The Italians decried the Knights' attempt to make Columbus Day a "denominational and not a general" holiday, claimed that some members of their own Italian societies were not Catholic, and objected to taking part in what had been called a Catholic demonstration. They also asked why the K. of C. had never joined them in honor of Columbus when they had been celebrating his day for years, and they bitterly resented that no one seemed to pay much attention to their own parades, the first public commemorations of the great discoverer and his achievements in Worcester. (A Knights of Columbus spokesman hinted untactfully that those processions must have been so small no one *could* notice.) About the same time leaders of the city's French societies also expressed displeasure over the Knights' handling of arrangements for the procession. Rumors flew that the French Canadians felt slighted by the Knights' organizers. Some sources also suggested that the French were eager to "throw down" the K. of C.'s invitation because

Irishmen in Canada had objected to the appointment of a French Canadian as bishop of Halifax. The Knights were largely successful in overcoming these controversies in 1912. The *Worcester Telegram* reported on September 9, 1912, that "if the French society delegates thought they had any grievances or were being made too little of in the preliminary meetings they spoke their minds and what differences of opinion there might have been were adjusted satisfactorily to all." Many non-Irish Catholic societies marched in the Knights' parades in 1912 and 1913 and the intrareligious conflicts seemed resolved.[183]

Perhaps because of these controversies or because the Knights were on the verge of purchasing a new headquarters and worried about the parade's costs, or because the war drained off resources and energy, the Knights gave up the parade for several years, but in 1920 the Knights of Columbus once again took responsibility for the processions. The parade that year took on a special aura in the midst of the "Red Scare" as the K. of C. dedicated the parade to the campaign against Bolshevism; but, as before, it was, and was meant to be, a demonstration of pan-ethnic Catholic power and unity. The parade's 5,000 participants and eight divisions that year included 2,800 Knights and marchers from the Union of St. Jean Baptiste, the Sons of Italy, and the Lithuanian and Polish Holy Name Societies, as well as members of the AOH, the Irish National Foresters, and the Catholic Women's Club. In the mid-1920s the city's Italian societies began playing a more prominent role in organizing the parade. In 1923 and 1924, they "cooperated" with the Knights in making the preparations and then led the procession, followed by "a long column of Knights." In 1927, the Italian organizations took over the celebration, staging fireworks at East Park and a parade of their own associations down Main Street. By 1929, however, the Knights had returned to the streets to honor their patron's day. Six thousand people, most of them Knights but some of them members of the Italian societies, marched on October 12 that year. The Poles joined them again this time, and organizers bowed to growing Polish importance in Worcester by claiming that the procession was a "joint celebration" honoring both Columbus and Casimir Pulaski.[184]

Even by the end of the 1920s, then, and through a number of controversies the Knights had not given up their effort to make Columbus Day a Catholic holiday and the parade in his honor a demonstration of Catholic unity and power. That they were not wholly successful reflected some of the enduring tensions and suspicions that continued to divide Catholic ethnics of diverse backgrounds. Yet the persistence of the K. of C.'s effort was equally significant, for it reflected well the earnest desire of Worcester's Irish Catholics not only to strengthen the bonds of Catholic unity but to shape a new identity or conception of themselves. It was no coincidence that the last St. Patrick's Day parade took place in 1911, the year after the Knights launched the first Columbus Day procession. St. Patrick's Day spoke to an ethnic exclusiveness of the past; Columbus Day to a militantly Catholic but pan-ethnic American future led by the models of militant American Catholicism—Irish Americans.[185]

A Principle "Which is Our Very Own . . . People Have a Right to Rule Themselves": The Revival of Irish American Nationalism in Worcester

If Worcester's Irish Americans seemed ready to abandon a narrow Irish ethnic identity for a broader American Catholic one, that trend was still in process, not yet accomplished by the second decade of the twentieth century, and Ireland, the ancestral homeland, still lingered in their memory. At the close of World War I, it would once again become their passion, not just for Irish immigrants in Worcester but all generations of Irish Americans. In 1918, Worcester's Irish community erupted in a frenzy of Irish nationalist activity that lasted nearly three full years and surpassed every previous nationalist movement in Worcester—even the Land League agitation. Events in Ireland, the rebellion in 1916 that gave birth to the revolution of 1918, clearly encouraged this nationalist revival. The city's Irish gradually grasped that this new uprising gave their ancestral homeland its best chance for a measure of real independence since the Elizabethan wars in the sixteenth century. Events in Ireland not only seemed to inspire the movement but, as in the 1880s, set the pace for its development and, ultimately dictated its demise. As before, however, American conditions also had a critical impact on the nationalist movement in Worcester. American war aims, articulated in terms of self-determination for all nations, provided the American-born Irish with a crucial means of harmonizing Ireland's quest for independence with their American patriotism. Patriotic appeals to American ideals thus echoed and re-echoed through the rhetoric of Worcester's new postwar Irish nationalists just as they had in the speeches of local home-rulers forty years before. The new, nearly unanimous and vocal support of the Catholic hierarchy for Irish nationalism—from old liberals like James Cardinal Gibbons to new militant conservatives like William Cardinal O'Connell—also helped convince the American-born Irish to commit themselves to the movement. In the new nationalist crusade as in the 1880s the clergy would play a prominent role. Ethnic tensions and conflict building up through the war and exploding after it also helped provoke Irishmen to take a new interest in their ancestral home as well. Those tensions, however, also discouraged them from seeking help from Yankee and other Protestant neighbors. In the postwar movement, then, unlike the Home Rule crusade of the 1880s, the Worcester Irish would seek and receive support only from their co-religionists, fellow Catholics.

In the 1910s, the Worcester Irish displayed little interest in the cause of their homeland. Groups like the AOH passed annual resolutions endorsing independence for Ireland but the Hibernians and their allies were in decline, and clubs and associations on the ascendant, like the K. of C., paid little attention to Ireland's cause. Even the Easter rebellion in Dublin in April of 1916, or, more accurately, the executions that followed it, roused Worcester's Irish only briefly. The city's Irish scarcely noticed the rebellion itself but like much of the rest of the country began to react after the British government executed some of the rebel leaders a few months later. As the sentences came down, individual AOH divisions in Worcester passed resolutions condemning Britain, and the branch of a new nationalist organization formed before the rebellion, the Friends of Irish Freedom, organized a mass meeting on June 15, 1916. The meeting condemned England for her brutal suppression of the rebellion and demanded "imperatively . . . that England restore to Ireland her absolute freedom and independence not fifty years hence, not twenty-five years hence, not ten years hence but now." Though the protest meeting was well attended, participation in the agitation seemed limited to the AOH and its allies. The *Catholic Messenger*, while sympathetic to the protest, was wary of Irish American attempts to encourage continued armed rebellion in Ireland. In July of 1916, the paper condemned "zealots . . . on this side of the Atlantic" who sought to rouse the Irish in Ireland to "foolish deeds." In the midst of the protest agitation, the *Catholic Messenger* had reaffirmed the local Irish community's commitment to an American Catholic identity. Acknowledging that it had been attacked in the past "because of its not taking up discussions of racial issues," the *Catholic Messenger*, "desired to bring attention to the fact that the *Messenger* is a Catholic paper and its policy is to confine itself to questions on the theological and social sides of Catholic life."[186]

American entry into the war seemed only to further bury Ireland's problems for the Worcester Irish. In some cities like Butte, Montana, Irishmen protested openly against American participation in the war, but in Worcester and in most cities across the country, Thomas Rowland suggests, Ireland's future seemed irrelevant to the vast majority of Irish Catholics who threw themselves enthusiastically into the American war effort. The Irish-owned *Worcester Post* demanded of its east side readers: "Be a full wool yard American. Be a true blue Worcesterite." A few articles criticizing British rule in Ireland appeared in the *Catholic Messenger* in the first few months after the United States entered the war in 1917, but by the fall of 1917, and through all of 1918, the weekly paid no attention to Ireland. Irish organizations sympathetic to Irish nationalism either maintained a careful silence or dutifully gave their full backing to the Allied cause. The Friends of Irish Freedom, if it still existed, had no public presence during the war. The AOH passed resolutions endorsing the president and the war effort and enlisted in fundraising campaigns to provide comforts to the soldiers at the front. On March 17, 1918, J. P. Dalton, a curate at St. Peter's parish, reminded the Hibernians gathered for their annual St. Patrick's Day celebration that "Catholic Faith warmed by Celtic blood begets a true American patriotism." Dalton scarcely mentioned Ireland or its future; the United States and its struggle was the center of concern.[187]

American participation in the war may have temporarily closed debate on Ireland in Worcester, but, ironically, the war effort also helped pave the way for the postwar outburst of Irish nationalism. The nation's war aims, for example, would provide Worcester's Irish Americans with the ideological justification for the backing of Ireland's nationalist aspirations. In July of 1917, John J. McCoy told some Irish American soldiers that they were embarking on a crusade to "free small nations" oppressed by a ruthless "imperialism . . . heedless of centuries of differences in blood, in native tongue and in sacred memories of past racial glories." Presumably McCoy was speaking of Belgium and the peoples of the Austro-Hungarian empire, but the old Irish nationalist might well have intended a parallel to Ireland's own situation; more important, whether he intended it or not, many of his listeners could no doubt draw the parallel. In his famous peace proposal, Woodrow Wilson transformed that parallel into a broad and patently American ideal of self-determination for all nations. To Irish Americans, if not to the president himself, it appeared self-evident that this new American ideal applied to Ireland.[188]

While conditions favorable to a rebirth of Irish nationalism ripened in Worcester during the war, the cause of national independence was steadily gaining ground in Ireland. After the executions of the Easter Week rebel leaders, the Irish Parliamentary party, heir to Parnell's party and long invincible in southern Ireland, imploded, as its goal of home rule increasingly appeared to be but a weak accommodation to the British oppressor. Through the latter half of 1916 and 1917, Sinn Fein, a nationalist movement committed to an independent Irish Republic, became more and more powerful. British efforts to impose conscription on Ireland in April of 1918 provoked massive and nearly unanimous resistance and assured Sinn Fein's triumph. By the end of the War in November 1918, Sinn Fein was the power in Ireland in fact; it awaited only a parliamentary election to be the power in name as well.[189]

The effect of these events on the Irish in America was electric. By the end of November of 1918, Irish American politicians, associations, and individuals—

finally free from the war's rigid strictures on political debate—were flooding the White House and Congress with appeals and memorials pleading Ireland's cause. In the second week of December, hearings on Irish independence opened in Congress and elections took place in Ireland. Mass meetings were thus organized throughout the United States to lobby Congress and show support for the nationalists in Ireland. On December 10 in New York, over 25,000 people jammed Madison Square Garden to hear James Cardinal Gibbons, William Cardinal O'Connell, and others demand freedom for Ireland. The participation of Gibbons and O'Connell was critical. Gibbons, the old liberal, had long been suspicious of Irish and other nationalist movements and had played little or no public role in the Home Rule cause in the 1880s and early 1890s. O'Connell was the leader of the new, conservative, militant American Catholicism. Their enlistment in the nationalist crusade both testified to the broad popularity of the cause and gave it added legitimacy for thousands of American Irish. The congressional hearings resulted in a careful resolution of sympathy for the Irish cause that later passed the House overwhelmingly. More important, Sinn Fein won a smashing triumph over the old Irish Parliamentary party and all other opponents in December of 1918. The new Sinn Fein members of Parliament refused to take their seats in the House of Commons in Westminster and instead convened as the parliament of a new Irish Republican government, assuming the ancient Irish name the Dail. Within little over a month after the end of the war, then, Ireland was in revolt and much of Irish America was mobilizing to support her.[190]

Worcester's Irish community, indifferent to Ireland's cause throughout most of the twentieth century, now plunged into the nationalist crusade with a furious energy. The *Catholic Messenger* reflected well the community's sudden turnabout as it quickly became a passionate advocate of Irish nationalism. From the very beginning of the nationalist revival in November of 1918, the paper set the principal theme for the movement in Worcester: the link between the American war aim of self-determination for all nations and Ireland's fate. In a front-page article on November 29, 1918, the paper stated simply: "Through our President we have asked again and again for the self determination of foreign ruled nationalities. Ireland has never willingly submitted to English rule." The paper went on to argue: "The President's championship of oppressed people was all inclusive. There was no exception." The Irish thus had as much right as the Poles, Czechs, or southern Slavs or any other people in Europe to win their freedom, the *Catholic Messenger* claimed. Indeed, the sacrifices of Irish Americans in the armed forces of the United States (they made up one-third of the American army, the *Catholic Messenger* asserted), should have earned Ireland special consideration. Indifference to Ireland's claims, the weekly contended, would undermine "the whole moral structure of the Allied cause."[191]

The easy integration of American ideals and patriotism into nationalist rhetoric would be an important key to nationalism's success in Worcester; the Catholic clergy's strong support would be another. On December 13, 1918, the *Catholic Messenger* reported that the Catholic hierarchy of the Springfield diocese and all the priests of Worcester were "unanimous" in support of Ireland's independence. Whether following the lead of Cardinal O'Connell of Boston, the head of their province, or pursuing their own passions or interests free from fear of hierarchical scrutiny, Bishop Beaven and his priests made the new Irish nationalism a Catholic as well as an American crusade.[192]

On December 22, 1918, the Worcester Irish staged their first rally in the new nationalist campaign. A large crowd filled Mechanics Hall to cheer speakers, vote resolutions of protest, and demonstrate commitment to the "great work of Irish freedom." Yet it was not just the size of the crowd but its composition that suggested the broad appeal of the nationalist revival. The chairman of the meeting was John F. McGrath, an American-born Irish lawyer and Democratic politician. John T. Duggan, the second-generation ex-mayor, was the principal speaker and John F. O'Connor, second-generation Irish school principal and longtime prominent figure in various Irish organizations, chaired the committee of resolutions (O'Connor had written poetry for Father Conaty's *School and Home Magazine* and participated in temperance and moderate nationalist organizations since the late 1880s). Every member of O'Connor's committee was American-born, and it included such notables as John J. McCoy; Philip O'Connell, now a judge; two school principals; a doctor who had been a war hero; and a Yale-educated lawyer. Finding inspiration—or at least legitimization—in the new nationalism's link to American ideals and its backing by the Catholic hierarchy, the American-born Irish, so long indifferent to Ireland's fate, now made the homeland the focus of their energy and passion.[193]

The enthusiastic participation of the Knights of Columbus in the new nationalism was, perhaps, the best evidence of its broad support in the Irish community. American-born and upwardly mobile, the Knights had studiously avoided ethnic issues for the quarter century of their history in Worcester. As Irish nationalist fervor swept Worcester following the war, however, the Knights abandoned their strict commitment to ethnic neutrality and took up the Irish cause. The K. of C.'s recently purchased clubhouse quickly became the headquarters for the movement. The Grand Knight of Worcester's Alhambra branch, James A. Crotty, spoke frequently on behalf of the nationalist effort and served on the committee to raise money for the FOIF's Victory Fund. The K. of C. even published announcements urging all members to attend the protest meeting at Poli's in April of 1919, and some Knights suggested that the order divert funds left over from their war work to buy the bonds of the newly proclaimed Irish Republic. There is no evidence that the Knights did that, but the arguments made for such a policy were telling. Nationalist Knights claimed that the K. of C. had been founded by men of Irish ancestry and that "the order is 80 percent Irish from a racial point of view . . . so the order owes something to Ireland."[194]

The Catholic clergy's strong support and, indeed, prominent leadership of the nationalist movement was, no doubt, one reason why devout and militant Catholics like the Knights so quickly embraced the nationalist cause. Throughout 1919 the clergy's role in the movement expanded substantially. In March, during the Victory Fund drive, pastors Thomas Donohue of St. John's and James J. Farrell of the new Ascension parish, a few blocks away up Vernon Hill, devoted their Sunday sermons to Irish independence. Those parishes were in or near old Irish neighborhoods on the east side and an endorsement of Irish nationalism might have been expected there, but William Ryan, pastor of Blessed Sacrament, the new parish on the city's middle-class west side, also preached the Irish cause from his Sunday pulpit that month. Ryan later organized protest meetings in his parish hall. The pastors of the north side parishes, George Flynn of the newly created St. Bernard's and Michael J. Coyne of the old Immaculate Conception, also publicly backed the independence effort in the newspapers. Flynn spoke of his Irish-born parents and proclaimed that he was "heart and soul in favor of the independence of Ireland." Coyne announced: "We who have found happiness and success in America exclaim in fervent patriotism: 'America First.' We who have within our veins the royal blood of the Gael prayerfully add to this sentiment 'then Ireland.'" Donohue, Farrell and some of their clerical colleagues also gave generously to the Victory Fund and later fundraising efforts. Most impressive, Father Dalton, curate at St. Peter's parish, headed one of the largest affiliates of the FOIF in the city, the Padraic Pearse branch, and thus emerged as one of the principal leaders of the nationalist movement in Worcester.[195]

As the nationalist movement expanded in Worcester, the city's Irish Americans grew ever more insistent that American ideals demanded Ireland's independence. Some, like Philip O'Connell, invoked the Declaration of Independence just as Thomas Conaty and the home-rulers had done four decades earlier. Most new nationalists, however, found Woodrow Wilson's war aim of self-determination for small nations a more relevant and powerful justification for Irish independence and their own backing of it. Indeed, virtually every Irish American who spoke on the Irish question in Worcester cited self-determination in making their case for Irish freedom. "Self determination for every people and every country meant just that," Thomas Barrett, the stuffy and conservative ex-alderman and mayoral candidate, argued: "if the millions of American men who fought . . . find now that it meant self determination for every country save Ireland, they will be justified in feeling that they had been deceived." Worcester's Irish Americans thus almost without exception made Irish independence an American cause, a goal of America's war effort, and the only just recompense for Irish American participation in it. In a speech to the FOIF state convention, Father Dalton argued that Ireland was fighting for a principle "which is our very own—namely that people have a right to rule themselves," a principle so American "that we fought a war for it."[196]

Such statements suggest how easily Worcester's Irish harmonized their nationalist efforts with their American patriotism, but they do not fully explain why they embraced Ireland's cause with such enthusiasm after ignoring it for decades. It was the rebirth of the heated rivalry with their Protestant rivals that seemed to give the nationalist movement in Worcester its special intensity, its emotional edge. In the 1880s nationalists in Worcester had drawn heavily on Yankee support. The nationalist movement, at least the conservative home-rule version that came to dominate the local Irish community, reflected well the broad cooperation between Yankee and Celt that characterized that age. The political alliance between Yankee and Irish had long since died; at the end of World War I Protestants and Irish Catholics were about to enter a decade of bitter conflict. There were, moreover, few Yankees in Worcester in the 1910s who were still suspicious of the United Kingdom or her imperial ambitions. In the 1880s the United States and Britain still eyed each other warily, and it was possible, even likely in provincial cities like Worcester, that native-stock Americans looked upon England's monarchy, aristocracy, and colonialism as the antithesis of American republicanism. Soon, however, Britain and America became closely tied and Anglo-Saxon ethnocentrism developed into a powerful ideological bond nourishing Yankee esteem for their English cousins. When war broke out in Europe in 1914, Worcester's Yankees knew whose side they were on. As the *Labor News* reported in 1916, "the most enthusiastic among those who were active in shouting for the success of the allies were those who represent the wealthy section of the city and who claim connection in some way or other with the Pilgrims who landed on Plymouth Rock." Shortly thereafter, wealthy west siders sponsored a series of balls in Worcester to raise money for England.[197]

Even after the war many Yankees remained devoted to America's ally, England, and they suspected Irish nationalists of treacherously endangering her in her time of peril. As the Irish nationalist movement began to pick up momentum in early 1919, for example, Jerome George, the hatchetman of the Worcester industrialists' antilabor circle, the Thursday Noon Club, pointedly called the attention of his fellow businessmen to a wartime *Labor News* editorial that had mildly endorsed Irish national aspirations and branded the editorial a vicious attack on a faithful ally, Britain. About the same time eight Yankee and Swedish common councilors voted against a city government resolution endorsing freedom for Ireland.[198]

It was not until late 1919, however, that the Irish nationalist movement became an open point of contention between the Worcester Irish and their Protestant neighbors. In the fall of 1919, a British-American Association stepped forward as the city's leading opponent of Irish nationalism and began to grow by leaps and bounds. One hundred fifty-two men and women joined the association in November alone, raising its membership to over 800. The visit of Eamon de Valera, leader of the Sinn Fein revolutionaries, to Worcester in 1920 galvanized Protestant opposition. The Common Council had invited de Valera the previous year with no opposition and the Republican mayor, Swedish American Pehr Holmes, had endorsed the invitation enthusiastically. But early in 1920, Republican members of the council voted against sending the Irish leader a formal invitation to visit the city. Newspaper reports suggested that the Republican councilmen considered de Valera an outlaw, a revolutionary, and the instigator of needless violence. A few days after the council vote, three Worcester ministers, Charles Fisher of First Presbyterian, Benjamin Wyland of Union Church (Congregational), and William McNutt of First Baptist publicly proclaimed their opposition to both de Valera and Irish independence. McNutt wrote to the newspapers that "no good can come from this [de Valera's] visit" and argued that if de Valera came to Worcester, someone should invite an Irish unionist as well, to counter his lies.[199]

This Yankee hostility to de Valera seemed rooted in the general circumstances feeding postwar ethnic hostility and rivalry: wartime patriotic hysteria, fears of radicalism, resentment of ethnic groups clamoring for local and international recognition, and the hardships of the depression. De Valera was but another episode in the ethnic war of attack and counterattack that spiralled ultimately into the clashes over the KKK and the tumult of the Hoover-Smith campaign. The Irish, of course, gave as good as they got in this ethnic war and it would be a mistake to see the intensity of the nationalist movement simply as a defensive reaction to nativist prejudice. It seems likely, for example, that the nationalist movement fed, and fed off, the Irish rise to political power under Peter Sullivan. There was no formal connection between the two, but Sullivan, an immigrant whose ticket agency served immigrants, was closely identified with Ireland and played a prominent part in the nationalist crusade. Most important, the nationalist movement exploded in the same year as Sullivan rose to power. For many, perhaps most, local Irish, there must have been an emotional, if not publicly proclaimed, relation between Ireland's struggle for independence and their imminent successful takeover of Worcester's politics.[200]

Worcester's postwar nationalist movement, then, differed radically from the city's last great nationalist crusade, the Land League and Home Rule agitations of the 1880s, when local Irish nationalists sought Yankee cooperation and that help was readily given. The Irish were a poor, largely foreign people then, grateful for the recognition and patronage bestowed on them by their Yankee allies. They were now modestly prosperous, far more numerous and politically powerful; indeed, they were reaching the height of their political power in 1919 and 1920. Ireland's cause now was not another opportunity for reconciliation in an age of accommodation, but a new field of battle in an era of rivalry.

There was another important difference between the nationalist movement of the eighties and the postwar crusade for Ireland. Nearly four decades before, a large faction of Irish nationalists in Worcester had sought the economic transformation of Ireland as well as its freedom. Yet no one in the city spoke of such changes in 1919 or 1920. The landlords, it is true, had almost been eliminated in the old country, but a labor movement had emerged in Ireland during the last years of World War I and had forced Sinn Fein's leaders to promise a thorough restructuring of the economy in a future Irish Republic. There was, then, a root in Ireland for economically radical nationalism. Moreover, nationalist radicalism did reemerge—at least briefly—in Irish American communities as diverse as Butte, Montana, and New York City. Given the severity of the postwar depression in Worcester why was there no similar revival of radical nationalism there?[201]

One important reason, perhaps, was the changing nature of radicalism itself. By the twentieth century the homegrown working-class republicanism of the 1870s and 1880s had all but disappeared from Worcester. Radicalism in the city and throughout much of the United States had come to be defined as ideological socialism. Butte and New York City both had strong socialist traditions in the twentieth century even though Irish Americans may have had only tangential connections to them. There was no such socialist movement in Worcester to inspire or sustain radical nationalists. In Worcester, socialism was hapless, organized labor timid and weak, and the assault on radicalism during and after the war efficiently organized, well financed, and virtually unopposed.

Radical ideologies had changed, then, but so had the Worcester Irish themselves. The city's labor movement had been weak and timid in the early 1880s, too, but radical nationalism became popular then in spite of, or almost because of, labor's weakness. Yet at that time the vast bulk of Irish Americans in Worcester were immigrants fresh from an impoverished rural Ireland and lodged at the bottom of Worcester's economic hierarchy. The Worcester Irish of the 1920s were largely American-born, scarcely rich, but often comfortably situated in skilled blue-collar or modest white-collar jobs. Socialism seemed a threat not only to their modest economic prosperity but their growing political power. Organizations such as the K. of C., which represented the new Irish-American middle class and the Irish-led Catholic church, had thus spent much of the 1910s articulating a new definition of Irish identity focused on American patriotism and militant Catholicism that categorically and vociferously excluded sympathy for socialism. Flirtations with radical solutions for Ireland, however, not only meant a rejection of their own definitions of themselves but in the Red Scare climate of 1919 and the 1920s might have made them exceedingly vulnerable to attacks on their patriotism from outsiders. That the Irish were clearly sensitive to such charges seems evident in their obsessive efforts to justify their commitment to Ireland on the basis of loyalty to American ideals. Support for the aspirations of a foreign country was already difficult for men and women whose devotion to the United States bordered on jingoism; support for radicalism would have been far too risky.

Despite his allegedly radical tinge and Yankee opposition, Eamon de Valera came to Worcester anyway in February 1920. Mayor Sullivan pointedly ignored the Common Council's resolution rejecting the Irish hero and warmly greeted him. Major Thomas Foley, war hero and later police chief, led a parade in his honor and thousands lined the streets to cheer him despite a howling blizzard. About the same time the Friends of Irish Freedom launched a drive to sell bonds for the new Irish Republic. Within two weeks the branch had sold $6,000 in bonds. By April it claimed to have sold over $130,000. Over the next year public activity in behalf of the nationalist cause flagged somewhat, but on November 1, 1920, 10,000 nationalist sympathizers marched from City Hall in the center of Worcester to Fitton Field, the Holy Cross football stadium, to honor Terence MacSwiney, the mayor of Cork, who had died in a hunger strike against the British government. Twenty thousand other mourners met the marchers at the stadium, where Father Farrell of Ascension parish officiated at a funeral mass for the dead Irish hero.[202]

By the time of MacSwiney's funeral, the Irish nationalist movement in Worcester and throughout the United States faced a major crisis. A simmering feud between de Valera and Judge Daniel Cohalan of New York, national leader of the FOIF, had broken into open conflict and de Valera had abandoned the Friends of Irish Freedom and created his own American nationalist organization, the American Association for the Recognition of the Irish Republic (AARIR). Worcester's movement split too, with most of the city's nationalist supporters backing de Valera's AARIR. This internal bickering and confusion took some of the momentum out of the nationalist movement in Worcester. The new AARIR engaged in little public agitation over the next year though it claimed branches in all of Worcester's ten wards. The movement seemed to lose some of its luster as well; the prominent community leaders who rushed to the standard in the frantic days of 1919 and in early 1920 were less visible and presumably less active by 1921.[203]

On December 6, 1921, representatives of Sinn Fein and the British government signed a treaty ending the Irish revolution. The treaty was controversial: it created the Irish Free State, a dominion within the British Empire, politically autonomous but still loyal to the British crown, and retained six counties in Ulster as part of the United Kingdom while suggesting that a future boundary commission would make further adjustments in the northern border.[204]

De Valera and many other Sinn Fein leaders opposed the treaty provisions that acknowledged loyalty to the British king and cut Ulster out of the new Free State. Though the parliament of the new Free State, the Dail, accepted the treaty on January 14, 1922, de Valera and his supporters refused to acknowledge the legitimacy of that vote. By the early summer of 1922, civil war had broken out in Ireland, pitting men and women who had recently fought the British against each other. Some backed the treaty and the new Free State; others sought to overthrow both.

In Worcester and in most of the United States, the signing of the treaty marked the end of the nationalist movement. Initially many Irish men and women in Worcester opposed compromises on the questions of Ireland's full independence and territorial integrity. On the day the treaty was signed 1,200 Irish nationalists gathered in Worcester to hear speakers hail the resolve of the revolutionaries to see their fight through to the end. "Cheer after cheer," the *Telegram* reported, went up after every declaration against compromise. Even the day after the signing, Father Thomas McLaughlin, pastor of St. Stephen's, and Father Stephen O'Donoghue, pastor of St. John's, expressed their skepticism about the treaty. McLaughlin stated that it is "by no means certain that the question has been settled." Yet within a few weeks most of Worcester's Irish seemed eager to accept the treaty as the final chapter in the long saga of Ireland's struggle for independence. On December 15, 1921, the *Catholic Messenger* glossed over the issues of fealty to the king and Ulster as unimportant or remediable and claimed an "old wrong has been swept away . . . the centuries-old struggle between England and Ireland has at last been happily terminated." The next week the paper simply sighed: "The Irish Question has been settled. We thank God for it."[205]

Some in Worcester, like de Valera in Ireland, refused to accept the treaty but most viewed the ensuing civil war in the old country as an embarrassment or tragedy and turned their backs for good on Ireland's politics. When Philip O'Connell, the former mayor, heard that Michael Collins, the great Sinn Fein and Free State leader, had been killed by fellow Irishmen in the civil war, one of O'Connell's sons recalled, he was so disgusted that he disavowed any further interest in Ireland's political fate. The close of the civil war in 1923 did not revive the interest of the Worcester Irish in their ancestral home. When de Valera visited the city in 1927, the embers of nationalist fervor had grown so cold that the great Irish leader, Ireland's revolutionary hero and its future president, passed through Worcester with scarcely any notice.[206]

Conclusion

Nationalism's sudden explosion in Worcester and just as sudden evaporation was as good an example as any of how the intensity and definitions of Irish identities could change in Worcester. The right circumstances, a successful revolution in Ireland, the congruence of Ireland's goals and American war aims, a revival of ethnic tension in Worcester, and clerical backing of the Irish cause made support for Irish nationalism nearly unanimous and extraordinarily emotional among the city's Irish population. The end of the Irish revolution and the fragmentation of Ireland's nationalist movement into literally warring factions just as quickly burst the nationalist bubble in Worcester.

Yet if the rise and fall of nationalism was a good example of fluidity of identities, ultimately it offered few clues about where Irish conceptions of identity and group boundaries were going and why. The postwar frenzy of activity in behalf of Ireland was nationalism's last gasp in the city. Never again would it provide an important focus for community activity and self-definition. The vast majority of Worcester Irish in the future would define themselves through their church and their native America. They would call themselves militant American Catholics. Nationalism's demise helped clear space for the new definition; nationalist movements no longer competed with the church for the attention of most Irish Americans after the early 1920s. Yet this change would have happened anyway, indeed, was happening until the eruption of nationalist feeling briefly interrupted. It happened because American-born generations now dominated Worcester's Irish community. They were certainly sympathetic to Ireland—hardly the forgetting "rebels" against their past that Marcus Lee Hansen described—but they were born in America, bred in its culture and proud to call themselves American. They were also bred into an institutionally devotional Catholicism that met their needs to create respectable American lives still true to their traditions far better than Irish nationalism did.

It was, however, the circumstances the new generation found themselves in that also shaped their definitions of themselves. In the 1880s, Irish men, especially American-born Irish men, seemed tentatively willing to accommodate their Catholic Americanism to their neighbors and win some acceptance for an alternative Catholic version of being American. In the twentieth century that no longer seemed possible; by the 1920s it must have seemed more remote than ever. Prejudice and political rivalry outside (Michael O'Hara notwithstanding), and increasing church conservatism inside the Irish community, doomed such dreams. Worcester's Irish men would not accommodate and seek some reconciliation in the twentieth century; they would fight and remain defiantly separate. In the 1910s, they would vastly expand the "Catholic ghetto," making a real commitment for the first time to parochial schools.

They would remain separate, but not alone. An influx of newer Catholic ethnics into Worcester changed the population composition of the city and transformed its ethnic balance of power. If the Irish could weld these many ethnics together they could build a vast self-contained Catholic world and forge a Catholic majority in Worcester. Protestants would be irrelevant, or, better, useful bogeymen to encourage Catholic solidarity in response. As time passed, the political bonds tying Catholic ethnics together grew stronger as they all moved to a political home in the Democratic party, emerging first in Peter Sullivan's reign, confirmed in Al Smith's near miss, and made permanent when Franklin Roosevelt swept the city by increasing majorities in his four elections. The trend towards such Catholic mingling also gained increasing momentum over the course of the first three decades of the twentieth century in institutions and organizations as various as the Bay State Bank; the new peripheral parishes of Holy Rosary, Our Lady of the Angels, and Saint Margaret Mary's; and the Ladies Catholic Benevolent Association. If the Irish wished to forge a new group out of a diverse array of ethnics and defend their leadership of it, they would have to emphasize what they had in common with their Catholic neighbors and not what distinguished them as Irishmen. The Knights of Columbus sought to do exactly that through their pan-ethnic, militant Catholic Americanism. The advent of new Catholic ethnics thus made the new self-conception of militant American Catholic practically sensible, just as the cultural change among the American-born made it culturally satisfying.[207]

In forging this new people the Worcester Irish were working to raise the importance of Catholic boundaries and play down the significance of ethnic borders among all American Catholics. These internal boundaries did not disappear, however. Members of other groups often resisted Irish assimilation. French Canadians, Italians, Poles, and Lithuanians were committed to the preservation of their own ethnic groups, the maintenance of their cultures and social autonomy. Like the French, the new groups wanted their own churches and schools and often stubbornly opposed the efforts of Irish churchmen to interfere in their affairs. Politics both fed and fed off this desire for autonomy as groups mobilized in search of political recognition and often came up against their co-religionists, the Irish, in the rough and tumble political arenas of the east side.

The Irish themselves were also ambivalent. They were never quite sure whether they simply wanted to lead a coalition of Catholic ethnics or forge an entirely new people. Furthermore, even as they struggled to create a new American Catholic people, they themselves retained a sense of ethnic distinctiveness. While they worked to make a pan-ethnic Catholic group, they insisted on their own privileged place in it.

Nevertheless, the influx of new immigrants and persistence of Protestant-Catholic rivalry and tension structured a new world for the Worcester Irish and thus inspired and shaped their efforts to create a new sense of group identity, of boundaries and strategy for making their way in this new environment. In the twentieth century, they would neither try to accommodate their Protestant neighbors as they had in the 1880s, nor retreat into ethnocentric isolation as they had in the 1890s and early 1900s. They would instead try to draw Catholics of all nationalities into a new group, a group militantly, oppositionally, Catholic and patriotically American. For all their own ambivalence about their purposes, the Irish would persist in trying to forge this new group and thus this new definition of their own identity and group boundaries into the middle of the twentieth century. Despite the continuing wariness and suspicion of other Catholic ethnics about Irish intentions, Worcester's Irish would be remarkably successful in this effort and the new identity would prove impressively durable.

Conclusion

Archbishop, soon to be Cardinal, Richard Cushing of Boston intoned the text in his own distinctive nasal drone and it rang out through St. Paul's Church in Worcester: "Behold I make all things new." It was March 7, 1950, and Cushing was there to install a new bishop in a new diocese in an old church that had finally become a cathedral. The new bishop was John J. Wright, Auxiliary Bishop of Boston. Stocky, even fleshy at only forty years, but strikingly dark-haired and dark-eyed, the smoothly mannered and elegant Wright was a rising star in a church triumphant. The new diocese was the diocese of Worcester, made up entirely of Worcester County sliced out of the old Springfield diocese. Wright had chosen St. Paul's for his cathedral, and its huge white marbeled interior, grandly Gothic granite towers, and location on the slope of a western hill just above Main Steet, made it an apt choice. Reverend John J. Power, the first pastor of St. Paul's parish, had dreamed of all this over eighty years before: dreamed himself a bishop, mitered and sceptered, marching up the aisle of the church he had built so vastly beyond the needs of its congregation to be the cathedral of a new diocese. Power had been disappointed, for another man had been chosen bishop, another church in another city chosen to be his cathedral. In 1950 Power was long gone, dead nearly half a century. But a new era in the history of Worcester Catholicism had begun, so at least Cushing promised.[1]

John Wright certainly seemed eager to make it a new era. Secretary to Cushing and to Cushing's predecessor, William Cardinal O'Connell, Wright had learned all the tricks of exercising power. Intent on proving himself in this his first independent command, he would not hesitate to practice what he had learned. The nine years of Wright's reign in Worcester stretching over the decade of the fifties were thus a whirlwind of activity. He established thirty new parishes in the diocese; seven in Worcester alone, a city that already seemed filled with more than a score of Catholic churches when he arrived. As early as the mid-1950s, his new white, wood-frame, or red or yellow brick parish churches, scattered throughout central Massachusetts, had made a visible and powerful impression of the diocese's dynamism. "A stranger travelling around the Diocese today," *Jubilee* magazine declared in 1956, sees them [churches] "everywhere, springing up even in the smallest hamlets." The centerpiece of Wright's building program, however, was a new St. Vincent's Hospital. Rising up on the crest of Vernon Hill and overlooking the city's east side, the new white brick structure housed over 400 beds and cost over nine million dollars to build.[2]

Mindful of the lessons of his mentors, Wright reorganized the new diocese and tightened his control of it even as he vastly expanded its size. Since the early twentieth century, the trend throughout American Catholic dioceses had been to the rationalization of administration and increasing concentration of power in the hands of local bishops. Wright quickly brought his new little diocese into line with that trend: gathering a motley mix of day-care centers, clinics, orphanages, and old-age homes into a single new diocesan agency, an office of Catholic Charities; making a number of parish high schools over into centrally controlled, diocesan high schools; founding a new diocesan newspaper, the *Catholic Free Press* (and burying forever the heretofore amazingly resilient *Catholic Messenger*); and forging diocesan-wide councils of lay Catholic women, men, and adolescents.[3]

Wright seemed to bring not only a new energy and efficiency to Catholicism in Worcester, but a new image of success and confidence. Though a hard-nosed administrator and ambitious builder, he was no simple reincarnation of an old Irish brick-and-mortar priest; he had the energy and craftiness, perhaps, of Worcester's own Monsignor Thomas Griffin of St. John's, but his world and vision were larger. Born the son of a second-generation Irish factory clerk amid the tenements and three-deckers of Dorchester, Massachusetts, Wright had sedulously set about to make himself something far grander. Brilliant success in school at Boston Latin, Boston College, and St. John's seminary in Brighton, Massachusetts, earned him the opportunity to study overseas at the North American College and Gregorian University in Rome. He earned a doctorate at the latter and became well known as a Catholic intellectual, writing with facility on a wide range of Catholic issues, including why there were not more Catholic intellectuals like himself—a burning issue in the American church of the 1950s. He spent time in France, developed a love of

French high culture, and a devotion to Joan of Arc. He became worldly, genteel, and urbane. He spoke, for example, in a deep voice accented by Boston Brahmin and "Romanita" inflections, exuding confidence and charm. He brought an apparent gentility to Catholicism in Worcester that it had never seen before. The scale and pace of new church construction, the sure-handed efforts at diocesan reorganization, the charming, refined bishop, suggested a new standard of power, efficiency, and grace for a people who could still remember the bewilderment, insecurity, and poverty of immigrant pasts. Wright pointed up this progress when he told—as he often did—humorous stories about the "provincialism" of the Dorchester Irish of his youth. Recounted in his cultivated diction and genteel accents, such anecdotes were more than nostalgic reminiscences or disarming self-deprecations; they were subtle but powerful reminders of how far both he and his people had come.[4]

In the 1950s, Worcester's Catholics entered an era of growth and rising power unparalleled in their history. Led by their new young bishop, it was an era of triumph and glory. This was true not just in Worcester, however, but across the country: churches and schools sprouted in cities and suburbs; seminaries and novitiates filled to overflowing with future priests and nuns; mammoth new hospitals and charitable instititions multiplied. America was awash in Catholic yellow brick, nuns' habits, and school uniforms.

But it was not the beginning of a new era in Worcester, or anywhere else for that matter; it was an old Catholicism at high tide, a ghetto church triumphant. It was the height of the old order, not the beginning of a new one.

For the Irish Catholics who dominated this church in Worcester, the 1950s were the full flowering of the militant Catholic American identity that they had defined for themselves a half century earlier. After stumbling through the tumult of the turn of the century era, shifting rockily from one conception of themselves and their place in Worcester society to another, they had finally settled on that identity in the 1910s and 1920s, and through the upsets of depression and world war it remained serviceable and appropriate. By the 1950s they were still fervent, even militant, Catholics, since the old reasons for their passionate Catholicism—a hunger for respectability and suspicion of Protestant enemies—remained. Yet that identity continued to permit them to embrace most aspects of American culture and to proclaim the American loyalties that had become almost second nature to them. It also permitted, indeed encouraged, the Worcester Irish to include non-Irish Catholic ethnics in their world and that effort gained considerable momentum as new American-born generations of Italians, Poles, and Lithuanians emerged, moved up the occupational ladder and out of old neighborhoods to multiethnic areas on the west side or other parts of Worcester and thus became more receptive themselves to an American Catholic identity.

Wright's people, particularly the Irish members of his flock, were intensely Catholic. The churches sprouting up all over Worcester and its suburbs, the new hospital, the flourishing organizations all testified to that. There was more direct evidence as well. As late as 1969, a survey revealed, an astounding 78 percent of the Worcester diocese's Catholics attended mass every week.[5]

The church's pomp and pageantry, evidence of its broad power and ancient roots, continued to appeal to a people still mindful of their past poverty and powerlessness, a people still new and uncertain members of the postwar middle class. Wright, of course, with his elegant bearing and fondness for ritual was particularly adept at satisfying that hunger for the regal and the splendid.

The reverse side of the church's appeal—its rigorous morality and discipline—also fed a continuing need. Monitoring movies and other forms of popular culture in its newspaper, laying down rules of behavior from church pulpits, inculcating discipline in parochial classrooms, the church remained the premier moral guide and enforcer of the moral norms of respectability for its people. Sociologist Ellen Horgan Biddle, who grew up in an Irish parish in Worcester in the 1930s and 1940s, remembers that the American-born Irish still delayed marriages "as long as possible" to ensure they made a "good match." Such delays continued to require the discipline the church could best provide.[6]

Yet it was probably the persistence of interreligious tension more than anything else that gave the intense Catholicism of Worcester's Irish and other Catholics its edge. Biddle recalls that almost all the Irish in her parish were convinced that Yankee Protestants hated them and took every opportunity to discriminate against them. She also remembers that her fellow parishioners returned that hatred with equal fervor. Protestants were aware of Worcester's persistent religious tensions too. Wallace Robbins, a Unitarian minister, was appalled at the interreligious conflicts he met when he came to Worcester in 1956: "Protestants feared the Catholics and Catholics feared the Protestants." Both religious groups were conscious of the boundaries between them and eager to maintain those borders. Much of Wright's expansion testified to the desire of his church and people to maintain a parallel, separate Catholic society. He established, for example, a whole series of Catholic societies for different occupational groups, St. Appollonia for dentists, St. Thomas More for lawyers, even Our Lady of the Bell for telephone workers, paralleling existing professional or occupational associations. *Jubilee* cited St. Vincent's Hospital as evidence of a budding new ecumenism in Worcester. Yet the hospital had been supported and staffed by non-Catholics since its inception. Rather than a sign of some new trend, the hospital remained an old, isolated example of interreligious cooperation from a distant past, an anachronism that actually better reflected how little, not how much, progress had been made since it had been founded by Protestants and Catholics over sixty years earlier.[7]

As in the early twentieth century, Worcester's Irish and many other Catholics mixed this fervent Catholicism with an equally passionate American patriotism. By the 1950s, most of Worcester's Irish ethnics were third- or fourth-generation, and American popular culture and an American loyalty had become second nature to them. The temperance society sports teams might have long since disappeared, but Worcester's Catholic high schools had moved to the forefront of local athletic competition. By the mid-twentieth century, St. John's High School, part of St. John's parish on Temple Street, had emerged as a local athletic powerhouse in almost all sports, and its competition with St. Peter's High School of St. Peter's parish in Main South, was the city's most storied high school athletic rivalry. American patriotism came naturally to local Irish Catholics too, but during the Cold War it ran at an especially high pitch. As before, Worcester's Catholics continued to proclaim the essential identity of Catholic and American goals and values. The *Official Reference and Information Guide* of the new Catholic diocese of Worcester proclaimed in 1951 that the Declaration of Independence was a "Catholic document" and listed with pride the Catholic heroes who had fought in the Revolution, the Civil War, and World Wars I and II. The *Guide* also suggested that socialism was "a very real and very present danger" to the church and the nation and that "there could be no good socialism any more than there can be a good counterfeit dollar." Worcester's Irish and other Catholics thus continued to insist on Catholicism's harmony with Americanism and to fuse their American and Catholic loyalties through opposition to Marxist radicalism.[8]

An American Catholic identity could be stretched to include more than just Irish Americans. Indeed, the breadth of its boundaries had been critical to American-born Irish men and women in the early twentieth century who sought to gather Catholic ethnics of all backgounds into a grand Catholic American group. Many among the other Catholic ethnic groups such as the French Canadians, the Italians, Poles, and Lithuanians remained skeptical of their Irish co-religionists, and ethnic rivalries within the Catholic fold persisted into the 1950s. Cognizant that he and over half his clergy were Irish, Bishop Wright stepped gingerly amidst these ethnic hostilities. Showing "his genuine regard for the various nationality groups in his diocese and his reluctance to force their assimilation," *Jubilee* magazine claimed in 1956, Wright took pains to recognize all of the city's major and minor ethnic groups through appearances at their events and support for parish undertakings. The diocesan paper, the *Catholic Free Press,* also published columns in four languages, French, Italian, Polish, and Lithuanian. Still, Wright thought assimilation and the merger of Catholics of various nationalities into a single Catholic group "inevitable." There was plentiful evidence in Worcester to support such a conclusion. Catholic parishes on the city's periphery, new parishes like St. Charles Borromeo or St. Andrew as well as old ones like Blessed Sacrament or Holy Rosary, were increasingly multiethnic. Yet the trend was noticeable even in older downtown parishes like St. John's. In that church, the oldest Irish church in the city, more than two-thirds of all marriages in 1947 included non-Irish partners. When Wright departed from Worcester in 1959 to become bishop of Pittsburgh, he pointedly noted that Pittsburgh was like Worcester: "a place of diverse and strong peoples united under one Lord, by one faith, and one baptism."[9]

If the Worcester Irish still defined themselves as militant American Catholics, it was because key elements in their environment that had produced that definition remained more or less unchanged and continued to hold it in place. Irish nationalism had faded away after the post–World War I outburst and efforts to bring Ulster into the new Irish Republic roused none but the most diehard Celts of Worcester or elsewhere through the 1960s. The Vatican's persistent conservatism and commitment to Catholic separatism would have a more profound effect on the city's Irish. Wright mingled amiably with Protestant or other non-Catholics, but Rome insisted that laymen, priests, or even bishops continue to recognize and respect the boundaries that set Catholics apart. Intermarriage was discouraged and official ecumenical efforts frowned upon. Worcester's new diocese disappointed many of the city's Protestant ministers by publicly refusing to join the local council of churches. Nevertheless, it was not Vatican policy as much as the imbalance of power in Worcester's local economy and competition in the city's local politics that continued to stoke the long-burning fires of mutual suspicion between Catholics and Protestants and, therefore, to keep alive the old identity of militant American Catholicism. Even the Great Depression of 1929 and the subsequent New Deal, or the introduction in the late 1940s of city-manager, nonpartisan government—an entirely new set of rules in local politics—would not change that fundamental religious divide. A Protestant elite would continue to rule the city's economy, unions would remain feeble, and religion and ethnicity would still figure prominently in local elections.[10]

Through the depths of the Depression, the heights of World War II prosperity, and subsequent economic ups and downs, essential features of Worcester's economy remained remarkably the same. Machinery manufacturing and metalworking remained its heart: in 1950 nearly half the city's industrial workers labored in those branches of manufacture. To a remarkable degree, Worcester's biggest manufacturing companies also remained in the hands of the local Yankee families that had started them. Norton Company had expanded both abroad and in Worcester over the course of the twentieth century, opening operations in several countries overseas and enlarging its Worcester plant to employ over 5,000 workers. Wyman and Gordon, and Morgan Construction, both machinery manufacturers, were other examples of such locally owned firms that remained powerful players in the city's economy. Yankees also retained ownership and the top positions in Worcester's most important banks and insurance companies. A distinct Yankee business elite thus continued to dominate Worcester's economy. Exclusive clubs like the Tatnuck Country Club or the Worcester Club, and cultural institutions like the Art Museum also flourished through the 1950s, reinforcing the boundaries of this elite and helping it maintain its social and cultural cohesiveness.[11]

The Yankee business elite continued to fend off challenges not only from socially mobile Irish or other ethnics seeking to join their ranks, but from Worcester's ethnically diverse working class that sought to curb the elite's economic power. During the Depression, union organizers scored few successes in Worcester. The CIO through vigorous grassroots efforts and the help of nationwide agreements managed to organize the work force at U.S. Steel's American Steel and Wire plant (the former Washburn and Moen Wire Company). But unions had difficulty penetrating the locally owned companies that were the city's economic backbone. At the Norton Company ownership's adept manipulation of paternalist rewards, company spies, and Swedish ethnic loyalties kept the company free of unions through the late twentieth century. Sources suggest that Norton's workers were more restive in the 1920s than in the 1930s. Wyman Gordon's owners also staved off unionization attempts through the 1930s, and Alden Reed of Reed and Prince closed down his plant in 1937 for over a year rather than accept a union. Organizing efforts among shoeworkers were also largely unsuccessful in that decade. By the end of the 1950s, labor remained weak in Worcester, boasting no more than 2,500 workers pledged to the unions of the local labor council, and having little representation in the core industries of the local economy. Class solidarities and identities, never a viable option for most of Worcester's Irish and other workers in the turn of the century era, did not became any more viable in subsequent decades.[12]

Political competition, like persisting trends of Protestant dominance, tended to reinforce Worcester's religious and ethnic divisions. Franklin Roosevelt rolled to victory in Worcester in the 1930s and 1940s, following up and securing the gains among Massachusetts ethnics made by United States Senator David I. Walsh and presidential candidate Al Smith in the 1920s. By the 1950s, Democrats usually delivered big majorities in most statewide and national elections (Dwight Eisenhower was a lone but notable exception in his two campaigns for president), majorities made up largely of Worcester's 100,000 Catholics. It took longer for the Democratic party to turn the tide in local elections for Congress or the state legislature, but by 1946 the Democrats had elected a congressman from Worcester, Harold D. Donohue, and by the 1950s they dominated the local legislative delegations. The Democratic party in Worcester, or throughout Massachusetts, was by no means an efficient or even unified force. The party committees had little authority and the party leadership and rank and file were riven by personality and ethnic conflicts. Still, party lines tended to follow confessional divisions and thus reinforced the Catholic-Protestant boundary that ran through Worcester's society.[13]

As before, Worcester's municipal politics played out very differently than state and national contests. Throughout the 1930s and 1940s Democrats and Republicans competed on nearly even terms for control of City Hall. John C. Mahoney was ousted from the mayoralty in 1935, and thereafter Democrats and Republicans fought a number of close, bitter battles. After the war, however, the tide seemed to turn in the Democrats' favor. They not only elected a mayor, Charles F. "Jeff" Sullivan, but finally wrested control of both branches of the city's legislature, the Board of Aldermen, and the Common Council. At the same time, however, a municipal reform movement began picking up strong support among Worcester's Yankee and Swedish middle classes. With some help from young lace-curtain Irish Catholics, this reform movement completely restructured Worcester's politics by pushing through "Plan E" government, a city-manager system with a nine-person city council elected in nonpartisan, at large, proportional representation elections.[14]

The Yankee business elite had not been the moving force in the Plan E reform movement. It was not that they were not interested in such reforms, but they had tried on their own to push through a reform charter in the 1930s only to be thoroughly repudiated. They had thus been reluctant to try again. But once Worcester's voters ratified the Plan E charter, the local Yankee elite became strong backers of it. Relying less on their old political vehicle, the Chamber of Commerce, members of the business elite and their allies among the Yankee, Swedish, and Jewish middle classes worked through the new Citizens for Plan E Association (CEA) to shape local municipal politics. Worcester's local daily newspapers, the *Worcester Telegram* and *Worcester Evening Gazette* (the Democratic *Evening Post* had gone out of business), also became strong advocates of Plan E. Owned by the conservative Republican owner of the Wyman

Gordon Company, the *Telegram* and the *Gazette*'s editorials "harmonized so well with [the CEA's] philosophy that they could be CEA leaflets."[15]

Plan E was a dramatic recasting of the rules of Worcester's politics, and its effect on the roles of the city's ethnic and other social groups in local politics was complicated. Labor unions remained a negligible force in municipal politics, but ethnic allegiances in the new nonpartisan, proportional representation elections seemed—if anything—to become even more important. Throughout the 1950s Worcester's nine-person city council had clearly designated Yankee, Swedish, and Italian seats. The new charter thus helped to reinforce ethnic rivalries. The charter itself was perhaps the biggest source of ethnic division. Robert Binstock, in a report on the city's politics in 1959 for the Harvard-MIT Joint Urban Studies Project, suggested that "preventing Irish Catholic rule" was at least one of the important reasons why many Yankees, Swedes, and even middle-class Jews backed the Plan E charter, and bitter exchanges over the charter's disadvantages for Irish Catholics often disrupted local council meetings.[16]

Irish Catholics, however, were hardly shut out of power under the new charter. Through the 1950s, they still held more seats than any other group on the City Council. In 1951, the council also appointed Francis J. McGrath, an Irish Catholic and local school official, as city manager. Even more than Michael O'Hara, or even Andrew Athy many years before, McGrath would eventually become the key figure in local politics, mediating craftily between the city's ethnic politicians and bureaucrats and its Yankee elite. Moreover, many west side, middle-class Irish had helped bring Plan E to Worcester and they and others continued to play important roles in the CEA thereafter.[17]

Just as before the Plan E charter, Worcester's municipal politics in the 1950s thus still exacerbated ethnic and religious divisions, but they also continued to afford the city's Yankee elite and its allies opportunities to forge partnerships and alliances across ethnic or religious lines and shape the nature of politics in a largely Catholic and ethnic city.

On January 28, 1959, the new pope, John XXIII, appointed John J. Wright as bishop of the diocese of Pittsburgh. It was another step forward for the rising star of American Catholicism and was to be expected, but many people in Worcester, Protestant and Catholic alike, understood it as an epochal event. Wright had presided over a church triumphant in Worcester during the 1950s, and now at the end of the decade he would be leaving it at new heights of power and prestige.[18]

If Worcester's residents, particularly Catholic residents, understood that their lives would change in the next decade, they could hardly have expected how much. Yet it was hardly Wright's passing on to Pittsburgh that made the difference. His successor, Bernard J. Flanagan, was less aggressive and ambitious, though some would say more pastoral, sincere, and earnest. But no amount of ambition and energy would have changed the outcome for Worcester's Irish and other Catholics in the 1960s and 1970s. The definition of themselves that they had hammered out in the early twentieth century and that had proved so durable through the 1950s—militant Catholic Americanism—became useless for all but a few diehards by the 1960s and 1970s. The ghetto church, the institutional embodiment of that definition, cracked and crumbled. The Protestant-Catholic boundary that had been so critical in Worcester became less and less distinct or charged. Religious or even ethnic differences among Worcester's white people would not disappear, but contests over those differences would occur infrequently, and the borders that divided different white groups would be easily and often crossed.[19]

In the 1960s, several international or national events and movements hammered at the walls separating white ethnics from one another and cracked and broke open old group identities. Even as Wright was leaving Worcester in January of 1959, the movements and events that would transform the lives of the Worcester Irish were already evident. That month, the new pope, John XXIII, announced he would convene a great council of Catholic bishops that would self-consciously seek a rapprochement with Protestants and other non-Catholics and undermine at a stroke the rationale for the ghetto church and the militance of American Catholics. John F. Kennedy was also well on his way to securing the Democratic nomination for the presidency; his election as president and then his assassination helped to break down barriers of anti-Catholic hostility and suspicion. Finally, the civil rights movement, building momentum from the early fifties, flourished in the 1960s and won several notable victories in its war on Jim Crow in that decade. Civil rights may have seemed irrelevant to how Irish Catholics might define themselves, but it actually had powerful effects on them and other white ethnics. By introducing and promoting new standards of tolerance it delegitimized old hatreds: if prejudice against African Americans had been discredited, then, Catholic-Protestant enmity seemed archaic, perhaps even silly. More troubling, perhaps, African, Asian, and Latino American efforts to achieve equality made white ethnics more conscious of the boundary between whites and these minorities and, in turn, less concerned about the differences that may have distinguished them from other whites.[20]

These events and movements had such a shattering effect on differences among white ethnics because they built upon several longterm economic and social trends in Worcester. Some were trends occurring around the country as well as in Worcester. Catholic ethnics, for example, continued to move up the economic ladder and into the middle class, moving out of old neighborhoods into suburban areas, as they moved up. In Worcester, the relocation of St. John's High School in 1962 from its original site next to the old church on Temple Street to a new, leafy campus in suburban Shrewsbury, seemed to symbolize well this new Catholic prosperity and the final demise of the old Irish neighborhoods.[21]

The economy in Worcester as well as in the rest of the nation was also transformed. Machinery manufacturing continued to dominate the local economy into the 1960s, but the city's machinery-making companies were already suffering from competition in other parts of the nation and the world. Through the next two decades, many of the machinery manufacture companies closed down, relocated, or were bought out by outsiders. By the 1980s machinery and metalworking no longer dominated the city's economy. The number of manufacturing workers in the city shrunk from 33,000 (42 percent of Worcester's total workforce) in 1950 to 23,000 (30 percent of the workforce) in 1982. This trend had many ramifications, but one of the more important was that it undermined the old Yankee elite's economic domination of the city just as the revolutions of the sixties were discrediting its ethnic exclusiveness.[22]

Finally new groups, African Americans, Latinos from Puerto Rico, Mexico, and Central America, and Asians from Indochina, Korea, and Taiwan began moving to the city in increasing numbers. In Worcester, this migration was small compared to that in other cities. Even today, Worcester is over 90 percent white. Nevertheless, there was a noticeable immigration of Latinos, largely from Puerto Rico, in the late 1960s and 1970s. Those immigrants began to build up communities in the old Main South area and other parts of the east side. By the 1990s, St. Peter's church would officially be called San Pedro as well as St. Peter's, and St. Paul's and a number of other parishes offered masses in Spanish. Yet there were also tensions between white Catholic ethnics and these Latino newcomers. Old enmities between whites softened as they encountered new enemies—or at least new "others"—the Latinos among them.[23]

It was the first St. Patrick's Day parade in Worcester in more than seventy years. On a cold March 13, 1983—the last Sunday before the seventeenth— the parade lined out for miles along Main Street from its starting point in the south near St. Peter's church to its end in the north at Lincoln Square. No established organization, no convention claiming to speak for the Irish people of Worcester sponsored this march. An ad hoc committee, not elected, appointed, or delegated—there were, in fact, few organizations left to elect, appoint, or delegate—put on this parade. As late as the September before the parade, the "committee" could boast but three members, and even as its numbers grew, most acknowledged that they were "literally 'green' when it came to organizing a parade." Many of the members of the new parade committee were women—a sharp departure from earlier years at the turn of the century. Indeed, the key figure was a woman, Elizabeth Mullaney, descendant of a longtime Worcester Irish family, daughter of a Worcester mayor, and herself an important person in local Democratic party reform politics (she was a Michael Dukakis Democrat). She "conceived" of the parade, organized the committee, and directed its efforts.[24]

There was no single compelling vision of Irish identity in that committee, or even clear factions with competing, compelling visions. Nor was there a single definition or even a few such clear definitions out in the Irish community. For the Irish immigrants on the committee, an Irish identity was assumed, but its meanings varied somewhat according to their ages, when they left Ireland, or the experiences they had had in America. Immigrants played an important role on the parade committee, but they did not dominate it and they were now only a tiny part of Worcester's Irish population. The Worcester Irish were now an overwhelmingly American-born people and the committee was largely American-born. For these American-born Celts of many generations, meanings of Irishness were now much more wildly various than for the Irish-born and much more numerous than they had ever been. For some older people, perhaps, or Irish Catholics feeling themselves threatened by neighborhood encroachment, or by the emergence of new groups or rapidly changing values, the old identity of militant American Catholicism, flecked with some Irish green, remained a rallying cry to mobilize against suspected enemies. Yet for many of Elizabeth Mullaney's contemporaries, third-, fourth-, or fifth-generation, being Irish might mean no more than a day's celebration, a few jokes, an occasional movie, snatches of remembered conversations with grandparents. If it meant more to them than that, it was because they had decided that it should mean more, and they fashioned such meanings to meet their individual needs. They might thus find in their ancestry a cultural anchor in a rootless society, or a touch of premodern innocence in a society commercialized and cynical, but whatever their reasons, they were not compelled to think of themselves as Irish. There were few enemies now who would bar them from employment or fight with them for political spoils. The boundaries of their ethnicity and even their faith were easy to cross (many of them or their parents had already crossed them to marry non-Irish or even non-Catholic spouses) and had none of the charge and meaning they once had. Indeed, the parade committee that first year was deeply moved by non-Irish neighbors who not only gave "encouragement" but stepped into roles of "active participation." The committee itself included a Baltas, a Perrone, and a Cote scattered among the McGinns, O'Sullivans, Madigans, and O'Malleys.[25]

Nor would the parade itself resemble those ranks of marching men, the "gallowglasses" and Hibernian rifles, and row after row of members of the Ancient Order of Hibernians stepping out in martial grandeur. Not everyone now would even be Irish. The Sunday school from the Armenian church would march; so would the Knights Templars and Temple Emmanuel Boy Scouts. The Greek church, St. Spyridon's, would sponsor a float. The parade would include everyone from the Redheads of Worcester to the La Femmina Modeling Agency to McDonald's Restaurants of Greater Worcester. There would be Bubbles the Clown, Shriners in go-carts, riding clubs, marching bands, Marine details, and a seemingly endless number of firetrucks. The firetrucks (eighteen of them), in fact, outnumbered the AOH divisions (four) in the line of march.[26]

The parade, once revived, has become a tradition in Worcester. Succeeding parades have included as many as 8,000 participants and 100,000 onlookers. The parade's goal, as its organizers suggested, was to be a "family event" to help bring the entire city of Worcester together, and it remained a sometimes chaotic mix of groups of every background. In 1996, a *Telegram* reporter suggested that the assembly area before the parade "resembled an outdoor movie studio." "People dressed as bears mingled with pipers wearing kilts," he noted, "clowns stood next to children dressed as dalmatians (and Cruella De Vil), people from Oz boarded the O'Rourke's Welding Co. float, and Shriners brandished swords next to muskets of the Federal Blues of Rhode Island Pipe and Drum."[27]

And yet for all its changes, and for all the changes in the Irish community it was supposed to represent, the parade is still a focus of controversy today. The controversy is not the same as in Boston or New York where gay Irishmen and lesbian Irishwomen are struggling with older Celtic traditionalists about the nature of Irish identity. In Worcester, the controversy centers on the parade's very effort to avoid controversy: specifically, after the parade in 1996, the parade committee banned any signs from the parade that might be considered "a social or political protest." Signs borne by members of Worcester's St. Francis-St. Therese Catholic Workers organization calling for peace in Northern Ireland were the provocation for this rule. Those signs condemned the violence by both sides in Ulster and urged an immediate end to the bloodshed: "Killing," one sign said, "cannot be with Christ." The Catholic Workers were banned from the parade in 1997 but still lined the route of march bearing their signs.[28]

By the end of this century, the Worcester Irish had changed radically since the end of the last one. They had changed because older generations had grown up, grown old, and passed away, and new generations emerged with new understandings of themselves as Irish and American and Catholic. They had also changed because Worcester had changed; its economy, its alignment of different racial and ethnic groups, its distribution of political and economic power, all were transformed and transformed again, and the nation and the world had also changed in important ways too numerous to count. And yet as the Catholic Workers' protest suggests, definitions of Irishness, even debates over Ireland's fate, still meant something in Worcester in 1997, and even then the parade was still the site for contesting those definitions, for engaging in those debates. It had been over a century since the men of the St. Paul's Total Abstinence Society debated so "hotly" whether to join the St. Patrick's Day parade or not; but whether to march on St. Patrick's Day— or on the Sunday before it—was still an important question in Worcester.

Notes

Introduction

1. Richard O'Flynn MSS, "Records of the Convention of United Irish Societies," vol. 2, p. 205, clipping, no citation, March 17, 1890, Holy Cross College Archives (HCC). On the importance of cultural festivals and parades to group consciousness, see Mary Ryan, "The American Parade: Representations of the Nineteenth Century Social Order," in Lynn Hunt, ed., *The New Cultural History* (Berkeley: University of California Press, 1989); Susan Davis, *Parades and Power: Street Theater in Nineteenth Century Philadelphia* (Philadelphia: Temple University Press, 1986); Kathleen Neils Conzen, "Ethnicity as Festive Culture: Nineteenth Century German America on Parade," in Werner Sollors, ed., *The Invention of Ethnicity* (New York: Oxford University Press, 1989), pp. 44–76; Eric Hobsbawm and Terence Ranger, eds., *The Invention of Tradition* (Cambridge: Cambridge University Press, 1985). For St. Patrick's Day parades, see John Bodnar, *Remaking America: Public Memory, Commemoration and Patriotism in the Twentieth Century* (Princeton: Princeton University Press, 1992), pp. 65–70; Sallie Marston, "Public Rituals and Community Power: St. Patrick's Day Parades in Lowell, Massachusetts, 1848–1874," *Political Geography Quarterly* 8, no. 3 (July 1989), pp. 255–69; and Kenneth Moss, "St. Patrick's Day Celebrations and the Formation of Irish American Identity, 1845–1875," *Journal of Social History* 29, no. 1 (Fall 1995), pp. 125–48.

2. "Souvenir of the United Catholic Total Abstinence Societies Coffee Party, January 15, 1896," Worcester organizations file, American Antiquarian Society (AAS).

3. O'Flynn MSS, "Records of the Convention," vol. 2, p. 205, clipping, March 17, 1890, HCC Archives.

4. O'Flynn MSS, "Records of the Convention," vol. 2, p. 83, January 5, 1890, p. 195, February 16, 1890. See Timothy J. Meagher, "'What Should We Care for a Walk in the Mud?': St. Patrick's and Columbus Day Parades in Worcester, Massachusetts,

1845–1915," *New England Quarterly* 58, no. 1 (March 1985), pp. 5–26, and Chapter 3 this book.

5. William Shannon, *The American Irish: A Political and Social Portrait* (New York: Macmillan, 1963), pp. vii–xii.

6. Ibid., p. 145.

7. Ibid., pp. 132, 145.

8. Nathan Glazer and Daniel Patrick Moynihan, *Beyond the Melting Pot* (Cambridge: MIT Press, 1963), p. 217. For overviews of this period, see Kerby Miller, "Class, Culture and Immigrant Group Identity in the United States: The Case of Irish American Ethnicity," in Virginia Yans-McLaughlin, ed., *Immigration Reconsidered* (New York: Oxford University Press, 1990), pp. 96–129. The best survey of the turn of the century period in Irish American history is Kerby A. Miller, *Emigrants and Exiles* (New York: Oxford University Press, 1985), pp. 492–555. Miller is the only author to examine the broad range of Irish life in that era, including religion, politics, nationalism, and labor. David Doyle has provided a useful examination of Irish American occupational status at the turn of the century as well as insight into the ideas of the Irish about American imperialism in *Irish Americans: Native Rights and National Empires, 1890–1901* (New York: Arno Press, 1976). Important local studies of the Irish in this era include Victor Walsh, "Across the Big Wather" (Ph.D. diss.: University of Pittsburgh, 1983); Emmons, *The Butte Irish* (Urbana: University of Illinois Press, 1989); David Brundage, "The Making of Working Class Radicalism in the Mountain West: Denver, Colorado, 1880–1903" (Ph.D. diss.: UCLA, 1983); Dale Light, "Class, Ethnicity and the Urban Ecology in a Nineteenth Century City: Philadelphia's Irish, 1840–1890" (Ph.D. diss.: University of Pennsylvania, 1979); Margaret Connors Harrigan, "Their Own Kind: Family and Community Life in Albany, New York, 1850–1915" (Ph.D. diss.: Harvard University, 1975). Walsh and Light end their studies before the 1890s and thus before the Gaelic Revival and the hardening of the Catholic ghetto.

The literature that touches on various dimensions of Irish American life at the turn of the century is vast. The following is a sampling of some of the best works that appeared in the late 1980s and the 1990s. Many more works from this and earlier eras appear in later notes. On nationalism, see Matthew Jacobson, *Special Sorrows: The Diasporic Imagination of Irish, Polish, and Jewish Immigrants in the United States* (Cambridge: Harvard University Press, 1995). On religion, see Jay P. Dolan, "The Search for an American Catholicism," *Catholic Historical Review* 82, no. 2 (April 1996), pp. 169–86; James M. O'Toole, *Militant and Triumphant: William Henry O'Connell and Catholicism in Boston, 1859–1944* (Notre Dame: University of Notre Dame Press, 1992); Brian Clarke, *Piety and Nationalism: Lay Voluntary Associations and the Creation of an Irish Catholic Community in Toronto, 1850–1895* (Toronto: McGill-Queen's University Press, 1993); Leslie Woodcock Tentler, *Seasons of Grace: A History of the Catholic Archdiocese of Detroit* (Detroit: Wayne State University Press, 1990); Paula Kane, *Separatism and Subculture: Boston Catholicism, 1900 to 1920* (Chapel Hill: University of North Carolina Press, 1994); and Hugh McLeod, *Piety and Poverty: Working Class Religion in Berlin,*

London and New York, 1870–1914 (New York: Holmes and Meier, 1996). On Irish American women, see Janet Nolan, *Ourselves Alone: Women's Emigration from Ireland, 1885–1920*
(Lexington: University Press of Kentucky, 1989). On mobility, see Joel Perlmann,
*Ethnic Differences: Schooling and Social Structure among the Irish, Italians, Jews and
Blacks in an American City, 1880–1935* (New York: Cambridge University Press, 1988),
and Suzanne Model, "The Ethnic Niche and the Structure of Opportunity: Immi-
grants and Minorities in New York City," in Michael Katz, ed., *The Underclass Debate:
Views from History* (Princeton: Princeton University Press, 1992).

Studies of turn of the century workers where the Irish figure prominently include
James Barrett, *Work and Community in the Jungle: Chicago's Packinghouse Workers,
1894–1922* (Urbana: University of Illinois Press, 1990); William Hartford, *Working
People of Holyoke: Class and Ethnicity in a Massachusetts Mill Town, 1850–1960* (New
Brunswick: Rutgers University Press, 1990); and David Brundage, *The Making of
Western Labor Radicalism: Denver's Organized Workers* (Urbana: University of Illinois
Press, 1994).

On politics, see Thomas O'Connor, *The Boston Irish: A Political History* (Boston:
Northeastern University Press, 1995); Christopher McNickle, *To Be Mayor of New
York: Ethnic Politics in the City* (New York: Columbia University Press, 1993); Daniel
Czitrom, "Underworlds and Underdogs: Big Tim Sullivan and Metropolitan Politics
in New York, 1889–1913," *Journal of American History* 78, no. 1 (September 1991),
pp. 536–48; Steven Erie, *Rainbow's End: America and the Dilemmas of Urban Machine
Politics, 1840–1985* (Berkeley: University of California Press, 1988).

Deborah Dash Moore is one of the few historians to address the experience of
second-generation white ethnics in *At Home in America: Second Generation New York
Jews* (New York: Columbia University Press, 1981). Her conclusions are similar to the
results of this study, although her approach is very different. For recent works on
the second generation of minorities like Japanese and Mexican Americans, see Valerie
Matsumoto, *Farming the Home Place: A Japanese American Community in California,
1919–1982* (Ithaca: Cornell University Press, 1993), and George J. Sanchez, *Becoming
Mexican Americans: Ethnicity, Culture and Identity in Chicano Los Angeles, 1900–1945*
(New York: Oxford University Press, 1993). Oscar Handlin edited a collection of readings on the first American-born generation, *The Children of the Uprooted* (New York:
G. Braziller, 1966). I edited a book on six Irish American communities at the turn of
the century: Lowell and Worcester in Massachusetts; Philadelphia; Chicago; St. Louis;
and San Francisco; see Timothy J. Meagher, *Irish American Communities at the Turn of
the Century, 1880 to 1920* (Westport, Conn.: Greenwood Press, 1986). There is an older
and richer sociological tradition focusing on second-generation ethnics and generational transitions. It includes marginal-man literature such as Everett E. Stonequist,
The Marginal Man: A Study in Personality and Culture Conflict (New York: Scribners,
1937). Other sociological studies on generations include Irwin L. Child, *Italian
or American? The Second Generation in Conflict* (New Haven: Yale University Press,
1943); Vladimir Nahirny and Joshua Fishman, "American Immigrant Groups, Ethnic

Identification and the Problem of Generations," *Sociological Review* 13, no. 3 (December 1965), pp. 311–26; Sidney Goldstein and Calvin Goldscheider, *Jewish Americans: Three Generations in a Jewish Community* (Englewood Cliffs: Prentice-Hall, 1968).

9. Marcus Lee Hansen, "The Problem of the Third Generation Immigrant," in Peter Kivisto and Dag Blanck, eds., *American Immigrants and Their Generations: Studies and Commentaries on the Hansen Thesis After Fifty Years* (Urbana: University of Illinois Press, 1990), p. 195. See also Peter Kivisto, "Ethnicity and the Problem of Generations in American History," pp. 1–10; Philip Gleason, "Hansen, Herberg and American Religion," pp. 85–103 also in Kivisto and Blanck, *American Immigrants*. Will Herberg, *Protestant, Catholic, Jew: An Essay in American Religious Sociology* (Garden City: Doubleday, 1955), pp. 6–71; Hansen argued in his famous Rock Island speech that the second-generation son "wanted to forget everything: the foreign language that left an unmistakable trace in his speech, the religion that continually recalled childhood struggles, the family customs that should have been the happiest of memories": Hansen, "The Problem," in Kivisto and Blanck, *American Immigrants*, p. 193. Herberg spent little time on the second generation except to echo Hansen in his overall explanation of the generational dynamic. He is more equivocal about the second-generation Irish experience, suggesting that American-born Irish men and women may have developed an American Catholic identity by World War I: Herberg, *Protestant, Catholic, Jew*, pp. 28, 148. Milton Gordon, *Assimilation in American Life: The Role of Race, Religion and National Origins* (New York: Oxford University Press, 1964); Kazal, "Revisiting Assimilation," pp. 450–51; John Higham, "Ethnic Pluralism in Modern American Thought," in Higham, *Send These to Me: Immigrants in Urban America* (New York: Atheneum, 1975), pp. 196–230; Milton Gordon, "Toward a General Thesis of Racial and Ethnic Group Politics," in Daniel P. Moynihan and Nathan Glazer, eds., *Ethnicity: Theory and Experience* (Cambridge, Mass.: Harvard University Press, 1975), pp. 84–110. Milton Gordon also suggested a model for explaining how ethnicity could persist even as ethnic group members changed. He made a distinction between behavioral, structural or social, and identificational assimilation, suggesting that a group's assimilation through these dimensions occurred in roughly that order of sequence. I am not aware of any full-scale historical study of a white American ethnic group or community that has used Gordon as its conceptual framework. Ewa Morawska has pointed to its potential usefulness in "In Defense of the Assimilation Model," *Journal of American Ethnic History* 13 (Winter 1994), pp. 76–87. Yet Gordon assumed that acculturation was "overwhelming," and his notions of the assimilation process suggested that groups might move through various steps of the process he had identified, or not move through them, but he allowed no room for a group to move back after moving forward or for the creation of an entirely new group, as happened in Worcester. I originally attempted to analyze the Worcester Irish using Gordon's framework but abandoned that conceptualization because of its shortcomings. See Gordon, *Assimilation in American Life*, pp. 60–83.

10. Rosenzweig, *Eight Hours for What We Will*, pp. 171–227; Gerstle, *Working Class Americanism*, pp. 1–8, 41–60, 153–94; Barrett, "Americanization from the Bottom Up,"

pp. 997–1020; Cohen *Making a New Deal*, pp. 4–7, 100–158, 334–49; See, for example, Rosenzweig, *Eight Hours for What We Will*, pp. 2–3, 227–28; Cohen, *Making a New Deal*, pp. 3–6, 362–68, 324–59; Gerstle, *Working Class Americanism*, pp. 1–12, 230–36; Barrett, "Americanization from the Bottom Up," pp. 998, 1007–1120. None of these works focus narrowly on moments of class solidarity. Indeed, it is the richness and breadth of their analyses that makes them useful here. Gerstle's book actually spends much more time on the conditions leading up to working-class Americanism and its later unraveling than to the decade of the 1930s itself and discusses in detail the unfolding of understandings of ethnic and American identities among Woonsocket's French Canadians throughout the twentieth century. My point is that the questions they are seeking to answer concern the conditions that encourage workers' solidarity and the creation of cultures and languages of resistance among workers. Gerstle describes the purpose of his book: "this study has tried to demonstrate the centrality of the language of Americanism to the political consciousness of American workers in the post World War I period" (*Working Class Americanism*, p. 331). Cohen describes the purpose of hers: "This book is devoted to explaining how it was possible and what it meant for industrial workers to become effective as national political participants in the 1930s" (*Making a New Deal*, p. 5). For discussions of new approaches to problems of class analysis in labor history, see Kazin, "Struggling with Class Analysis," pp. 497–514, and for French labor history, Lenard Berlanstein, *Rethinking Labor History: Essays on Discourse and Class Analysis* (Urbana: University of Illinois, 1993), especially the essays by Berlanstein (Introduction, pp. 1–15) and by Ronald Aminzade ("Class Analysis, Politics and French Labor History," pp. 90–113). Kazal notes the similarities of the labor historians' Americanization to the religious Americanization of Herberg and others: "One could argue that they [labor historians like Gerstle and Cohen] revived the postwar conviction that ethnic groups were assimilating along certain lines, but they made those lines ones of class rather than confession" ("Revisiting Assimilation," p. 468). See him also on racial Americanism, pp. 468–471, and Gerstle, "The Working Class Goes to War," *Mid America* 75, no. 3 (October 1993), pp. 315–16. Moore found a religious Americanism among New York's second-generation Jews not unlike the Catholic Americanism of the second-generation Irish in Worcester, in *At Home in America*, pp. 11–17.

11. I have drawn on the following books and articles from this literature: Frederick Barth, *Ethnic Groups and Boundaries: The Social Organization of Cultural Difference* (Boston: Little, Brown, 1969); Donald L. Horowitz, *Ethnic Groups in Conflict* (Berkeley: University of California Press, 1985); Abner Cohen, ed., *Urban Ethnicity* (London: Tavistock, 1974); idem, *Two-Dimensional Man: An Essay on the Anthropology of Symbolism and Power in Complex Society* (Berkeley: University of California Press, 1974); idem, "Variables in Ethnicity," and Richard Trottier, "Charters of Pan Ethnic Identity: Indigenous American Indians and Immigrant Asian Americans," in Charles Keyes, ed., *Ethnic Change* (Seattle: University of Washington Press, 1986), pp. 272–331; Michael Banton, *Racial and Ethnic Competition* (New York: Cambridge University Press, 1983); Michael Hechter, "Towards a Theory of Ethnic Change," *Politics and*

Society (Fall 1971), pp. 21–31; Lurie Kay Sommers, "Inventing Latinismo: The Creation of Hispanic Pan-ethnicity in the United States," *Journal of American Folklore* 104 (Winter 1991), pp. 32–53; William Yancey, Eugene Erickson, and Richard Juliani, "Emergent Ethnicity," *American Sociological Review* 41, no. 3 (June 1976), pp. 391–403; Anya Patterson Royce, *Ethnic Identity: Strategies and Diversity* (Bloomington: Indiana University Press, 1982); Ulf Hannerz, *Exploring the City: Inquiries Toward an Urban Anthropology* (New York: Columbia University Press, 1980); Donald G. Baker, *Race, Ethnicity, and Power: A Comparative Study* (London: Routledge and Keegan Paul, 1983); Michael E. Meeker discusses segmented opposition in his *Literature and Violence in North Arabia* (Cambridge University Press, 1979); Werner Sollors, *Beyond Ethnicity: Consent and Descent in American Culture* (New York: Oxford University Press, 1986); Yen Le Espiritu, *Asian American Panethnicity: Bridging Institutions and Identities* (Philadelphia: Temple University Press, 1992); Milton J. Esman, *Ethnic Politics* (Ithaca: Cornell University Press, 1994); Susan Olzak and Joane Nagel, eds., *Competitive Ethnic Relations* (Orlando, Fla.: Academic Press, 1986).

12. Conzen et al., "Invention of Ethnicity," pp. 5, 13, 5. See also Vecoli, "An Interethnic Perspective," pp. 226–27.

13. Conzen et al., "Invention of Ethnicity," p. 5, p. 31.

14. Ibid., p. 31. Such emphases harmonize well with calls over the last two decades to restore narrative to history, particularly social history, and also to connect social history and political history. See William Cronon, "A Place for Stories: Nature and Narrative" *Journal of American History* 78, no. 4 (March 1992), pp. 1347–76.

15. Kazal, "Assimilation, Rise, Fall, and Reappraisal," p. 471. David Gerber, *The Making of an American Pluralism: Buffalo, 1825–1860* (Urban: University of Illinois Press, 1989). There have been others employing this framework. Stanley Nadel has applied this literature in his recent book on German Americans, *Little Germany: Ethnicity, Religion and Class in New York City, 1845–1880* (Urbana: University of Illinois Press, 1990), but he has focused on the immigrant generation of Germans, not the later ones. April Schultz uses it to study an ethnic revival among Norwegian Americans, but she never identifies the generation: Schultz, "The Pride of Race Had Been Touched: The 1925 Norse American Immigration Centennial and Ethnic Identity," *Journal of American History* 77, no. 2 (March 1991), pp. 1265–95. Ethnic history, instead of moving forward to study American ethnic generations, has tended to move back into the European background of the migrants. Good examples of this work that have painstakingly traced immigrants back into Europe and assessed the effects of their homelands' culture on their American adjustment include: Jon Gjerde, *From Peasants to Farmers: The Migration from Balestrand, Norway, to the Upper Middle West* (New York: Cambridge University Press, 1985); Donna Gabaccia, *Militants and Migrants: Rural Sicilians Become American Workers* (New Brunswick: Rutgers University Press, 1988); Kerby Miller's magisterial *Emigrants and Exiles*; Victor Walsh, "Across the Big Wather," and Walsh, "A Fanatic Heart: The Cause of Irish American Nationalism in Pittsburgh during the Gilded Age," *Journal of Social History* 15, no. 2 (Winter 1981), pp. 187–204.

16. Ethnocultural analyses generally see culture affecting politics and influencing voting behavior, but not politics shaping identity. See Kleppner, *Cross of Culture*, or McSeveney, *Politics of Depression*, for example. For the best recent overview of the ethnocultural school and its critics, see Ronald Formisano, "The Invention of the Ethnocultural Interpretation," *American Historical Review* 99, no. 2 (April 1994), pp. 453–77.

17. Students of ethnicity have defined ethnic groups or communities in various ways. Many have pointed, in particular, to group members' shared understandings of boundaries and common cultural traits, interests, and sense of destiny or peoplehood as essential elements of any ethnic group or community. These elements help define the notion of ethnic community or group informing this study of the Worcester Irish at the turn of the century.

18. For discussions of regional distinctions in Irish American and other ethnics' experiences, see Timothy J. Meagher, Introduction, in Meagher, ed., *From Paddy to Studs*; John Higham, "Another Look at Nativism," *Catholic Historical Review* 44, no. 2, (1958), pp. 155–58; Dennis Clark, *Hibernia America: The Irish and Regional Cultures* (Westport: Greenwood Press, 1986).

For distinctions between Irish environments in the West and the East, see Lawrence McCaffrey, *The Irish Diaspora in America* (Bloomington: Indiana University Press, 1976), pp. 77–79; David N. Doyle, "The Regional Bibliography of Irish America, 1880 to 1930: An Addendum," *Irish Historical Studies* 13, no. 1 (May 1983), pp. 254–55; James Walsh, "The Irish in the New America: Way Out West," in David N. Doyle and Owen Dudley Edwards eds., *The American Identity and the Irish Connection* (Westport: Greenwood Press, 1976); and Shannon, *The American Irish*, pp. 182–200.

Other works suggest a reading of Irish environments in New England and elsewhere that attributes less to an East-West continuum and more to a complex of environmental variables: Meagher, Introduction, *From Paddy to Studs*, pp. 5–7, 9, 181–83; Martin Towey, "Kerry Patch Revisited: Irish Americans in St. Louis in the Turn of the Century Era," in Meagher, ed., *From Paddy to Studs*, pp. 139–57; Brian C. Mitchell, *The Paddy Camps: The Irish of Lowell* (Urbana: University of Illinois Press, 1988); Geoffrey Blodgett, "Yankee Leadership in a Divided City: Boston, 1860–1910," and Paul Kleppner, "From Party to Factions: The Dissolution of Boston's Majority Party, 1876–1908," in Ronald Formisano and Constance Burns, eds., *Boston 1700–1980: The Evolution of Urban Politics* (Westport: Greenwood Press, 1984), pp. 87–110; Peter K. Eisinger, "Ethnic Political Transition in Boston, 1884–1933: Some Lessons for Contemporary Cities," *Political Science Quarterly* 93 (Summer 1978), pp. 217–39; Donna Merwick, *Boston Priests, 1848–1910* (Cambridge: Harvard University Press, 1973), pp. 69–110.

19. David R. Roediger, *The Wages of Whiteness: Race and the Making of the American Working Class* (New York: Verso, 1991), on the Irish specifically, pp. 133–63; Noel Ignatiev, *How the Irish Became White* (New York: Routledge, 1995); Moses Rischin, "Immigration, Migration and Minorities in California: A Reassessment," *Pacific Historical Review* 41, no. 1 (1973); Kazin, *Barons of Labor*, pp. 146–48; Alexander Saxton, *The Indispensable Enemy: Labor and the Anti-Chinese Movement in California* (Berkeley: University of California Press, 1971); John Kuo Wei Tchen, "Quimbo Appo's Fear of

Fenians: Chinese-Irish-Anglo Relations in New York City," in Ronald Bayor and Timothy J. Meagher, eds., *The New York Irish* (Baltimore: Johns Hopkins University Press, 1996), pp. 125–52. On African Americans in Worcester, see Nick Salvatore, *We All Got History: The Memory Books of Amos Webber* (New York: Random House, 1996). As late as the 1990s, Worcester's population was over 93 percent white: Kenneth Moynihan, "Worcester: Point of No Return," *Worcester Magazine* (June 5, 1996), p. 10.

20. Emmons, *Butte Irish*. Irishmen in many other cities helped forge stronger labor movements in the 1880s and early 1900s, and though too little is known to be sure there is evidence that the Irish ethnic revival flourished in some but not all parts of the nation as much as it did in Worcester in the 1890s. For Irish participation in successful labor movements, see Kazin, *Barons of Labor*; Fink, *Workingmen's Democracy*; On ethnic revivals, see Miller, *Emigrants and Exiles*, pp. 533–37. AOH membership rose from 89,901 in 1895 to 185,715 in 1906: John O'Dea, *History of the Ancient Order of Hibernians and Ladies Auxiliary* (New York: National Board of the AOH, 1923) vol. 3, pp. 1129, 1358.

One. The Immigrant Irish

1. John R. Stillgoe, *Common Landscape in America: 1580 to 1845* (New Haven: Yale University Press, 1982), pp. 43–58, 135–208; J. B. Jackson, *American Space: The Centennial Years, 1865–1876* (New York: Norton, 1972), pp. 87–138 (on the return of the forest see p. 89); "The Great Blizzard of 1888," *Worcester Magazine* 16, no. 3 (March 1913), p. 87.

2. Eugene Moriarty, biographical clipping file, WHM; Henry McDermott, biographical narrative written by James A. McDermott (1905?) in the possession of Andrew and Katherine McDermott, Worcester, Massachusetts.

3. Roy Foster, *Modern Ireland: 1600–1972* (New York: Penguin, 1989), pp. 195–225, 318–44; Cormac O'Grada, *Ireland: A New Economic History, 1780–1939* (New York: Oxford University Press, 1994), pp. 3–272; Kevin O'Neill, *Family and Farm in Pre-Famine Ireland: The Parish of Killishandra* (Madison: University of Wisconsin Press, 1984), pp. 3–31, 60–186; Miller, *Emigrants and Exiles*, pp. 26–101.

4. Miller, *Emigrants and Exiles*, pp. 26–101, 353–426; on manufacturing workers, pp. 364, 363.

5. Jonathan Prude, *The Coming of the Industrial Order: Town and Factory Life in Rural Massachusetts, 1810 to 1860* (Cambridge: Cambridge University Press, 1983), pp. 3–132; pp. 183–216; Christopher Clark, *The Roots of Rural Capitalism: Western Massachusetts, 1780–1860* (Ithaca: Cornell University Press, 1990); John Brooke, *The Heart of the Commonwealth: Society and Political Cultures in Worcester County, Massachusetts, 1713–1861* (Cambridge: Cambridge University Press, 1989), pp. 269–309; Charles G. Washburn, *Industrial Worcester* (Worcester: Davis Press, 1917); David Jaffee, "Peddlers of Progress and the Transformation of the Rural North," *Journal of American History* 78, no. 2 (September 1991), pp. 511–35, 555.

6. William Lincoln, *History of Worcester, Massachusetts From Its Earliest Founding to September 1836* (Worcester: Hersey, 1862); Brooke, *The Heart of the Commonwealth*, pp. 17–130; Robert A. Roberge, "The Three Decker: Structural Correlate of Worcester's Industrial Revolution" (M.A. thesis: Clark University, 1965), p. 22; "old graves" in "Charles Dickens in Worcester," *Worcester Magazine* (April 1908), p. 74; *Worcester City Directory* (Worcester: Drew Allis, 1882), p. 24; Weiss, "Patterns and Processes," pp. 79–80; Stephen Salisbury, *The State, the Investor and the Railroad: The Boston and Albany Railroad, 1825–1867* (Cambridge, Mass.: Harvard University Press, 1967), pp. 9–15; Washburn, *Industrial Worcester*, pp. 205–300, p. 49.

7. Grady Oscar Tucker, "Development of the Central Business Area: Worcester, Massachusetts, with special reference to the retail Sales Function" (Ph.D. diss.: Clark University, 1957), pp. 84–90; "Worcester's Greatest Needs," *Worcester Magazine* (January 1901), p. 26; Roberge, "Structural Correlate," pp. 22, 71–72.

8. Elbridge Kingsley, *Picturesque Worcester* (Springfield: W. F. Adams, 1895); In 1875, Worcester boasted 108 steam engines generating 8,000 horsepower for manufacturing, compared to 721 horsepower produced by the city's 27 waterwheels: *Census of Massachusetts: 1875*, vol. 2, "Manufactures and Occupations" (Boston: Wright and Potter, 1877), p. 351. On three-deckers, see Roberge, "Structural Correlate," pp. 18–22, and Marilyn Spear, *Worcester's Three Deckers* (Worcester: Bicentennial Commission, 1977), p. 7; Tucker, "Development of the Central Business Area," pp. 1–90.

9. David Fitzpatrick and W. P. Vaughn, *Irish Historical Statistics: Population, 1821–1971* (Dublin: Irish Academy, 1978), pp. 260–64, 282–336. See Miller, *Emigrants and Exiles*, and David Fitzpatrick, *Irish Emigration: 1801–1921* (Dublin: Economic and Social History Society of Ireland, 1984).

10. Miller, *Emigrants and Exiles*, pp. 137–279; Lawrence McCaffrey, *The Irish Diaspora* (Bloomington: Indiana University Press, 1976), pp. 59–69.

11. Vincent Powers, "Invisible Immigrants: The Pioneer Irish of Worcester, Massachusetts, 1826 to 1860" (Ph.D. diss.: Clark University, 1976), pp. 94–124, 150–205, 240–97; numbers from different counties, p. 332.

12. McCaffrey, *The Irish Diaspora*, pp. 59–69; S. H. Cousens, "Regional Patterns of Emigration during the Great Irish Famine: 1846–1851," *Transactions and Papers of the Institute of British Geographers* no. 28 (1960), pp. 119–30; idem, "Demographic Change in Ireland, 1851–1861," *Economic History Review* 14 (Spring 1961), pp. 275–88; Miller, *Emigrants and Exiles*, pp. 280–344, 284–88. There are serious disagreements about the importance of the Famine to the Irish economy. Foster emphasizes transportation change and suggests that changing markets beginning in 1815 had the most critical effect on the spread of Irish pasturage. Whelan and O'Grada suggest that the Famine's devastation was essential in permitting the spread of the Irish new agriculture: Whelan, "Born Astride a Grave"; Foster, *Modern Ireland*, pp. 318–44; Cormac O'Grada, *Ireland: A New Economic History*, pp. 3–272.

13. Powers, "Invisible Immigrants," app. 2, chap. 1, pp. 186, 150–205, 332, 240–382; Miller, *Emigrants and Exiles*, p. 299, and tables, pp. 574, 576, 579. According to

Powers's figures, Worcester seemed to have received a higher proportion of immigrants from Mayo and other western counties than would be expected from those areas.

14. Powers, "Invisible Immigrants," pp. 290–341.

15. Ibid., pp. 286–332; *Ninth Census of the United States*, vol. 1, *The Statistics of the Population of the United States* (Washington: G.P. O., 1872), p. 389; *Abstract of the Census of the Commonwealth of Massachusetts, 1865*, pp. 80–81.

16. Charles Chauncey Buel, "The Workers of Worcester: Social Mobility and Ethnicity in a New England City, 1850–1870" (Ph.D. diss.: New York University, 1974), pp. 157–58. Samples taken from the census manuscript schedules of the 1880 and 1900 censuses: one of every nine Irish immigrants over age eighteen listed in the schedules for 1880, 966 men and women, and one of every twelve Irish immigrants over age eighteen listed in 1900, 1,218 men and women.

17. Immigrant Sample: 1900 U.S. Census Manuscript Schedules; Miller, *Emigrants and Exiles*, pp. 345–492; Fitzpatrick, *Irish Emigration*, pp. 3–30; McCaffrey, *The Irish Diaspora*, p. 70; Robert Kennedy, *The Irish* (Berkeley: University of California Press, 1973), p. 75; Donald Jordan, "Land and Politics in the West of Ireland: County Mayo, 1846–1882" (Ph.D. diss.: University of California at Davis, 1982).

18. Kennedy, *The Irish*, pp. 8–10, 52–54, 150–62, 55–61; Hasia Diner, *Erin's Daughters in America: Irish Immigrant Women in the Nineteenth Century* (Baltimore: Johns Hopkins University Press, 1983), 1–42; Gearoid O'Tuathiagh, "The Role of Irish Women under the English Order," Joseph Lee, "Women and the Church Since the Famine," and Mary T. W. Robinson, "Women in the New Irish State," in Margaret MacCurtain and Doncha O'Corrain, eds., *Women in Irish Society: The Historical Dimension* (Westport: Greenwood Press, 1979), pp. 26–36, 37–45, 58–70, 75–84, 168–70.

19. Miller, *Emigrants and Exiles*, pp. 380–413; Fitzpatrick, *Irish Emigration*, pp. 9–10.

20. Immigrant Sample: 1900 U.S. Census Manuscript Schedules. Over 60 percent of Irish immigrants in Worcester in 1900 came to the United States after the age of eighteen. Only about a fifth of married Irish immigrants in Worcester in 1900 had married in Ireland. Less than 30 percent of Irish immigrant families in 1880 or 1900 had children born abroad or in foreign countries. Evidence of county origins: Monsignor Kavanagh to Bishop John J. Wright, 1950, St. Paul's parish archives; Herbert Sawyer, *History of the Department of Police*, pp. 194–206; and O'Flynn, MSS, notebooks, HCC Archives. Clubs formed in the late nineteenth century for Waterford men and women, Sligo men and women, and Kerry men and women: *Messenger*, November 11, 1899, *Evening Post*, November 26, 1898.

21. Rev. Eldridge Mix, "Cosmopolitan Worcester," *Worcester Magazine*, (February 1901), p. 99, pp. 99–101.

22. Miller, *Emigrants and Exiles*, pp. 350–51, 580. In 1900 even in the most heavily Irish districts of the city, no Irish immigrants told census-takers that they could not speak English.

23. Quotation from Miller, *Emigrants and Exiles*, pp. 72, 414–24, quotation from Plunkett, in Miller, *Emigrants and Exiles*, p. 416; Louis Cullen, *Six Generations of Life*

and Work in Ireland from 1790 (Cork: Mercier Press, 1970); T. Crofton Croker, *Researches in the South of Ireland* (New York: Barnes and Noble, 1969; first published in 1824), pp. 228–31; Samuel Clark and James Donnelly, eds., *Irish Peasants: Violence and Political Unrest, 1780–1914* (Madison: University of Wisconsin Press, 1983); Charles Townshend, *Political Violence in Ireland: Government and Resistance Since 1848* (Oxford: Clarendon Press, 1983); McCaffrey, *The Irish Diaspora*, pp. 71–76.

24. Gaelic Sports Day in O'Flynn MSS, folio 2, July 5, 1880, pp. 608–12, HCC Archives. Moriarty quotations in *Boston Globe* July 11, 1880, and Michael Horan in *Worcester Daily Times,* July 12, 1880.

25. Donald Akenson, *The Irish Education Experiment: The National System of Education in Ireland in the Nineteenth Century* (Toronto: University of Toronto Press, 1970); P. J. Dowling, *The Hedge Schools* (Cork: Mercier Press, 1968); O'Flynn MSS, Richard O'Flynn notes written in 1900, vol. 3, HCC Archives.

26. O'Flynn MSS, O'Flynn notes written in 1900, vol. 3, HCC Archives; Akenson, *The Irish Education Experiment*, pp. 49–51, 136–40; Dowling, *The Hedge Schools.*

27. Akenson, *The Irish Education Experiment*, pp. 49–51, 136–40, 120–80; McCaffrey, *The Irish Diaspora*, p. 76; Immigrant Samples: 1880 and 1900 U.S. Census Manuscript Schedules.

28. David Miller, "Irish Catholicism and the Great Famine," *Journal of Social History* 9 (1975), pp. 81–98; S. J. Connolly, *Priests and People in Pre-Famine Ireland, 1780–1845* (Dublin: Gill and Macmillan, 1982), pp. 264–78; Emmet Larkin, "The Devotional Revolution in Ireland," *American Historical Review* 78, no. 3 (June 1972), pp. 625–52; "Notes from Folklore Commission," *County Louth Archeological Journal* 14, no. 1, pp. 111–20.

29. Larkin, "The Devotional Revolution in Ireland," pp. 626–27. See also James Donnelly, "The Marian Shrine at Knock: The First Decade," *Eire-Ireland* 28 (Summer 1993), pp. 54–97; Hugh McLeod, *Religion and the People of Western Europe* (Oxford: Oxford University Press, 1981), pp. 205–6.

30. Powers, "Invisible Immigrants," pp. 247–52, 302–22, 331–32, 314, 341–49, 360–63.

31. Timothy J. Meagher, *To Preserve the Flame: Saint John's Parish and 150 Years of Catholicism in Worcester* (Worcester: St. Johns, 1984), pp. 28–30; Peter Joyce, "The History of Saint John's Church, Worcester, Massachusetts: 1826–1861" (M.A. thesis: Catholic University, 1982), pp. 74–92; O'Flynn MSS, folio 2, *Telegram*, July 17, 1889; O'Flynn MSS, folio 2, notes August 16, 1883; folio 12, *Telegram* February 18, 1890, HCC Archives.

32. O'Flynn MSS, Sacred Heart folio, 1879, HCC Archives; McCoy MSS, "Christmas Sermon," n.d., HCC Archives.

33. *Messenger*, March 18, 1904; O'Flynn MSS, Convention Records, vol. 2, following the meeting of February 16, 1890, HCC Archives.

34. On Tom Moore Club, see O'Flynn MSS, Societies Folio, HCC Archives; St. John's Announcement Books, May 25, 1879, St John's parish archives; O'Flynn MSS, Concert of Irish Songs, June 2, 1888, program, folio 18, HCC Archives; *Spy*, November 26, 1890;

O'Flynn MSS, Convention Records, vol. 3, clipping, March 18, 1895. John F. Mc Grath, third-generation Irish man from Worcester, said of Moore: "Moore, if Ireland had no other, is lyricist enough for her." McGrath also praised Samuel Lover and claimed his mother used to sing "Cruiskeen Lawn" to him: John F. McGrath "Ireland's Contribution to English Literature," in Thomas McAvoy, ed., *A Course of Lectures on Irish History* (Worcester: Messenger Publishing Company, 1914), p. 315; Thomas Flanagan, "Nationalism: The Literary Tradition," and Mary Helen Thuente, "The Folklore of Irish Nationalism," in Thomas E. Hachey and Lawrence McCaffrey, eds., *Perspectives on Irish Nationalism*, pp. 66–72 and 42–60; William H. A. Williams, *'Twas Only an Irishman's Dream: The Image of Ireland and the Irish in American Popular Song Lyrics, 1800–1920* (Urbana: University of Illinois Press, 1996). On connections to Ireland, see *Messenger*, January 15, 1890, February 6, 1891, April 21, 1890; *Catholic Messenger*, February 5, 1910. People went back to Ireland to visit, *Worcester Daily Times*, August 23, 1880, or sent money back to care for graves in Ireland, *Spy*, November 28, 1890. On Irish plays, see *Messenger*, December 7, 1900; Broadside, "St. Stephen's Dramatic Club," March 16, 1893, St. Stephen's parish archives; *Messenger*, March 11, 1893, March 30, 1900; *Worcester Sunday Telegram*, March 18, 1896; O'Flynn MSS, folio 1, p. 467, folio 3, St. Anne's, March 17, 1887, HCC Archives; Littleton Diaries, vol. 4, February 6, 1891, AAS; Saint John's parish announcements, July 22, 1877, October 13, 1878, Saint John's parish archives.

35. *Messenger*, March 18, 1904; *Worcester Daily Times*, March 17, 1882; O'Flynn MSS, Convention Records, vol. 2, clipping, March 1, 1898, HCC Archives.

36. O'Flynn MSS, Convention Records, vol. 2, p. 206, HCC Archives.

37. Michael Hechter, *Internal Colonialism: The Celtic Fringe in British National Development* (London: 1975), pp. 265–93; Samuel Clark, *Social Origins of the Land War* (Princeton: Princeton University Press, 1979); Tom Garvin, *The Evolution of Irish Nationalist Politics* (New York: Holmes and Meier, 1981); John Hutchinson, "Irish Nationalism," in D. George Boyce and Alan O'Day, eds., *The Making of Modern Irish History: Revisionism and the Revisionist Controversy* (London: Routledge, 1996), pp. 100–19. See chapter 3 for a full discussion of the Land League and Worcester's reaction to it.

38. R. V. Comerford, *The Fenians in Context: Irish Politics and Society, 1848–1882* (Dublin: Wolfhound Press, 1985); Roy Foster, *Modern Ireland: 1600–1972* (New York: Penguin, 1989), pp. 392–95; T. W. Moody, *The Fenian Movement* (Cork: Mercier Press, 1968).

39. *Worcester Daily Times*, November 26, 1881, March 17, 1882; *Messenger*, March 18, 1904; John J. Duggan, "The Irish Contribution to America," in McAvoy, ed., *A Course of Lectures on Irish History*, pp. 255–57. On Athy, see Rice, ed., *Worcester of 1898*, pp. 548–51.

40. Miller, *Emigrants and Exiles*, pp. 474, 35–351, 427–35; O'Flynn MSS, January 3, 1886, folio 2, Gaelic folio, HCC Archives; *Messenger*, April 18, 1899, February 17, 1900, February 10, 1905, May 19, 1905; *Catholic Messenger*, June 28, 1907, December 11, 1907, January 1, 1915, January 22, 1915; Stephen Littleton Diaries, vol. 1, November 7, 1889, AAS; Dance program, Company B, Hibernian Rifles, September 4, 1905, Worcester organization file, AAS.

41. Elizabeth Malcolm, *Ireland Sober, Ireland Free: Drink and Temperance in Nineteenth Century Ireland* (Syracuse: Syracuse University Press, 1986), pp. 321–34, quotation by priest, pp. 300, 299–303.

42. *Thirteenth Census of the United States Taken in the Year 1910*, vol. 1, "Population," p. 865; *Reports of the Immigration Commission* vol. 18, "Immigrants and Crime," pp. 159–78; O'Flynn MSS, "Humorous Sketches," folio 21, HCC Archives; *Worcester Globe*, February 12, 1888.

43. *Worcester Daily Times*, April 20, 1885; *Messenger*, April 15, 1910; O'Flynn MSS, vol. 1, "Rumsellers," HCC Archives; Roy Rosenzweig, *Eight Hours for What We Will: Workers and Leisure in an Industrial City, 1870–1920* (Cambridge: Cambridge University Press, 1983) pp. 40–46.

44. O'Flynn MSS, vol. 1, "Rumsellers," William Foley, HCC Archives; Dennis Moore in *Daily Times*, August 26, 1880, April 2, 1885; *Catholic Messenger*, May 17, 1907, April 15, 1910; O'Flynn MSS, Sacred Heart parish folio, notes, October 9, 1882, St. Anne's parish folio, October 25, 1886, HCC Archives; Rosenzweig, *Eight Hours*, pp. 40–64.

45. O'Flynn MSS, vol. 1, "Rumsellers," HCC Archives; *Daily Times*, April 21, 1885; *Messenger*, April 6, 1901. See, for example, M. J. Finnegan listed in Dun and Bradstreet Reports, vol. 105, p. 1277, Baker Library, Harvard University Business School; Rosenzweig, *Eight Hours*, pp. 40–64, see especially pp. 57–64.

46. M. E. Francis, "Dinny and St. Anthony," *Annals of St. Anthony's Shrine* (June 1900), pp. 20–25; *Annals of St. Anthony's Shrine* (June 1899), p. 3. See also O'Flynn MSS, Sacred Heart folio, 1879, HCC Archives; McCoy MSS, "Christmas Sermon," n.d., HCC Archives; Robert Orsi, *The Madonna of 115th Street: Faith and Community in Italian Harlem, 1880–1950* (New Haven: Yale University Press, 1985); idem, *Thank You St. Jude: Women's Devotion to the Patron Saint of Hopeless Causes* (New Haven: Yale University Press, 1996); Joseph Chinnici, *Living Stones: The History and Structure of Catholic Spiritual Life in the United States* (New York: Macmillan, 1989), pp. 35–85; Leslie Tentler, *Seasons of Grace: History of the Catholic Archdiocese of Detroit* (Detroit: Wayne State University Press, 1990); Anne Taves, *The Household of Faith: Roman Catholic Devotions in Mid-Nineteenth Century America* (Notre Dame: University of Notre Dame Press, 1986); Thomas Wangler, "Catholic Religious Life in Boston in the Era of Cardinal O'Connell," in James M. O'Toole and Robert E. Sullivan, eds., *Catholic Boston: Studies in Religion and Community, 1870 to 1970* (Boston: Archdiocese of Boston), pp. 239–78; Timothy Meagher, ed., *Urban American Catholicism: Culture and Identity of the American Catholic People* (New York: Garland Press, 1988).

47. Quotation, "a father," in *Annals of St. Anthony's Shrine* (June 1899), pp. 45 and 44–45; *Annals of St. Anthony's Shrine* (June 1901), pp. 47–48; *Annals of St. Anthony's Shrine* (June 1902), pp. 41–42. Conlin sermon in *Annals of St. Anthony's Shrine* (June 1901), p. 11.

48. *Annals of St. Anthony's Shrine* (June 1900), p. 23; *Annals of St. Anthony's Shrine* (June 1902), p. 18; See McDannell, *Material Christianity*, pp. 132–63, and Orsi, *Madonna of 115th Street*.

49. Quotation from Miller, *Emigrants and Exiles*, p. 428; See also Donnelly, *Land and People of Cork*, pp. 219–86; Clark, *Social Origins of the Land War*, pp. 193–255; Bew, *Land and the National Question*, pp. 34–73. Communal values were, of course, common among most peasant immigrants and were reinforced here in the United States for most of those groups. See, for example, John Bodnar, *The Transplanted: A History of Immigrants in Urban America* (Bloomington: Indiana University Press, 1985), pp. xv–xxi, 91, 57–116; John Bukowcyk, *"And My Children Did Not Know Me:" A History of Polish Americans* (Bloomington: Indiana University Press, 1987), pp. 22–57; Herbert Gans, *The Urban Villagers: Group and Class in the Life of Italian Americans* (New York: The Free Press, 1962), pp. 229–81.

50. Miller, *Emigrants and Exiles*, p. 357; O'Flynn MSS, folio 18, pp. 38, 204, 210–11, HCC Archives.

51. Immigrant Samples: 1880 and 1900 U.S. Census Manuscript Schedules.

52. Of the Irish-born women in industrial work in 1900 65 percent lived with their parents, siblings, or both: Immigrant Sample, U.S. Census Manuscript Schedules. "Trained and Supplemental Employees for Domestic Service," *Thirty Seventh Annual Report of the Bureau of Statistics of Labor* (Boston: 1907), pt. 2, pp. 89–123; David Katzman, *Seven Days a Week: Women and Domestic Service in Industrializing America* (New York: Oxford University Press, 1978), pp. 3–4; Theresa McBride, "Social Mobility for the Lower Classes: Domestic Servants in France," *Journal of Social History* 4, no. 4 (Fall 1974), pp. 70–71; Laurence Glasco, "The Life Cycles and Household Structures of American Ethnic Groups: Irish, Germans, and Native Born Whites in Buffalo, New York," in Tamara Hareven, ed., *Family and Kin in Urban Communities: 1790–1930* (New York: New Viewpoints, 1977), pp. 135–36.

53. *Evening Spy,* August 21, September 12, 1884; *Worcester Daily Times,* October 16, 1881; Katzman, *Seven Days a Week,* pp. 98–99; The House of Mercy, according to the Sisters of Mercy, provided classes in cooking, cleaning, and sewing, "preparing the young girls for domestic employment": Annals of the Sisters of Mercy, p. 141, Sisters of Mercy Archives, Worcester, Massachusetts. In 1904, the home admitted 120 women: U.S. Bureau of the Census, *Census of Benevolent Institutions* (Washington, D.C.: G.P. O., 1904).

54. From December 12 to December 15, 1880, eight of fifteen people purchasing tickets from O'Flynn were women: O'Flynn MSS, folio 18, pp. 38, 164, 204, 210–11. "Father Walsh paid a special compliment to the living out girls of those days and of today. He expresses his deep gratitude for the assistance received from them in building up the parish and says that the history of the Immaculate Conception in this respect is the history of New England. The Irish immigrant girl has been a tower of strength to the church.": *Messenger,* October 28, 1899. See also *Catholic Messenger,* March 13, 1908. Immigrant girls were also praised at the laying of the cornerstone of St. Anne's for their generosity, "it was indeed characteristic of the pure and religious daughters of Erin.": O'Flynn MSS, St Anne's parish folio, 1884, HCC Archives. O'Flynn MSS, Convention Records, HCC Archives.

55. *Messenger,* June 2, 30, 1900, October 11, 1902, February 12, 1905, August 25, 1905; *Catholic Messenger,* November 11, 1915; Ladies Auxiliary County Convention, September 18, 1906, pamphlet file, AAS; Bylaws Ladies Auxiliary, Ancient Order of Hibernians, Division 11, 1900, Worcester organizations file, AAS; Bylaws of the Ladies Auxiliary, Division 17, Ancient Order of Hibernians, Worcester, Mass., 1907, Worcester organizations file, AAS; Irish National Foresters Benefit Subsidary Council general rules, April 1, 1902, Worcester organizations file, AAS. Bylaws of Branch Charles Stewart Parnell, no. 453, Irish National Foresters, Worcester, Massachusetts, 1905, pamphlet file, Worcester Historical Museum, (WHM). The Irish National Foresters enrolled women in separate courts. They became very popular in Worcester around 1900. They sponsored many Irish jig and reel dances, as well as concerts of Irish music for their members (see chapter 5).

56. *Fourth Annual Report of the Associated Charities of Worcester, October 15, 1894* (Worcester: Charles Hamilton Press, 1894), p. 6.

57. Several historians, most notably John Bodnar and Tamara Hareven, have pointed to the vital role family networks played in helping Polish, Italian, or French Canadian immigrants secure work. David Emmons has also recently pointed to the ethnic associational and friendship networks that helped Irish miners in Butte claim and defend a virtual monopoly over work in the copper mines of Butte. Recently Walter Licht has called into question the importance of friendship networks in finding work, noting that large proportions of workers—even Italian and Irish workers—in New Deal Philadelphia secured jobs on their own initiative without the help of friends or family. Licht concedes, however, that family and friendship networks probably played a more critical role in the late nineteenth century than they did in the 1920s and 1930s: Walter Licht, *Getting Work: Philadelphia, 1840–1950* (Cambridge: Harvard University Press, 1992). John Bodnar, Roger Simon, and Michael Weber, *Lives of Their Own: Blacks, Italians and Poles in Pittsburgh, 1900–1960* (Urbana: University of Illinois Press, 1982), pp. 55–87; David Emmons, *The Butte Irish: Class and Ethnicity in an American Mining Town, 1875–1925* (Urbana: University of Illinois Press, 1989), pp. 61–254; Tamara Hareven, *Family Time and Industrial Time: The Relationship Between Family and Work in a New England Industrial Community* (New York: Cambridge University Press, 1982), pp. 126–29; 154–217. For wire and brewery workers, see vol. 64, time books, February, March, May, 1882, April 1887, American Steel and Wire Collection, Baker Library; and dues book, AOH Division 36, AOH Archives, Worcester, Mass., traced into 1900 U.S. Census Manuscript Schedules.

58. Thomas N. Brown, "Nationalism and the Irish Peasant," *Review of Politics* 15, no. 4 (October 1953), pp. 403–45; O'Tuathaigh, *Ireland Before the Famine,* pp. 42–74; Lee, *The Modernization of Irish Society,* pp. 82–86; Samuel Clark, *Social Origins of the Irish Land War* (Princeton: Princeton University Press, 1979), pp. 246–326.

59. *City Document no. 35,* p. 455; Sawyer, *History of the Department of Police,* pp. 194–206; U.S. Bureau of the Census, *Census Bulletin no. 20* (Washington, D.C.: G.P.O., 1905), pp. 68–69, 166; "Annual Report of the Fire Department," *City Document no. 61,*

p. 1161; *City Document no. 77*, p. 553; Fire Service of Worcester Souvenir Program, Fireman's Ball, December 9, 1887, Boston Public Library; Rice, ed., *Worcester of 1898*, p. 249; *A Tribute to the Columbian Year*, pp. 32–34; "Inaugural Address of Mayor James Logan," *City Document no. 64*, p. 21.

60. Rice, ed., *Worcester of 1898*, pp. 549–51, 650–51; Nutt, *History of Worcester* vol. 3, p. 103; Nelson, *History of Worcester County*, vol. 3, p. 293; *Evening Post*, September 29, 1918, October 25, 1919.

61. *Messenger*, June 2, 1905; Immigrant Samples: 1880 and 1900 Census Manuscript Schedules; Sawyer, *History of the Department of Police*, pp. 194–200.

62. O'Flynn MSS, vol. 1, p. 233, HCC Archives; *Worcester Daily Times*, December 5, 1883, December 22, 1882, November 20, 1882. Murphy in *Worcester Telegram*, December 25, 1887, June 24, 1888.

63. Sawyer, *History of the Department of Police*, pp. 194–206; *Post*, November 26, 1898; *Constitution and Bylaws of the Thomas Francis Meagher Club, Organized February 26, 1899*, pamphlet file, AAS; *Messenger*, November 11, 1899; *Nineteenth Annual Report of Massachusetts Bureau of Labor Statistics* (1888), p. 187.

64. R. A Burchell, *The San Francisco Irish: 1848–1880* (Berkeley: University of California Press, 1980); David Doyle, *Irish Americans: Native Rights and National Empires* (New York: Arno Press, 1976), 86–95, 182–200; David N. Doyle, "The Regional Bibliography of Irish America, 1800–1930: A Review and Addendum," *Irish Historical Studies* 23, no. 90 (November 1982), pp. 254–83.

65. Washburn, *Industrial Worcester*, pp. 299–310, 231–46; U.S. Census Office, *Report on the Manufactures of the United States, 1880* (Washington, D.C.: G.P.O., 1883), pp. 404–7; *Twelfth Census of the United States, 1900: Manufactures*, part 2, vol. 7 (Washington, D.C.: G.P.O., 1902), pp. 662–65.

66. *Report on Manufactures, 1880*, pp. 404–5; *Twelfth Census, Manufactures*, pp. 662–65.

67. Immigrant samples: 1880 and 1900 U.S. Census Manuscript Schedules.

68. In 1900, the proportions of female manufacturing workers in Lowell, Lawrence, and Fall River, Massachusetts, were 71 percent, 76 percent and 82 percent respectively: *Twelfth Census of the United States, 1900*, part 2, vol. 2, "Population," pp. 563, 571, 574, 599–601; *Tenth Census of the United States*, vol. 1, "Population," p. 909. Worcester was not unique in the high proportion of Irish-born women in service. In 1900, nationwide, 54 percent of Irish immigrant women in the workforce were servants: *Reports of the Immigration Commission, Senate Documents, 61st Congress, 2d Session, Document no. 282, Volume 28*, "Occupations of the First and Second Generation Immigrants in the United States," p. 83; Rice, ed., *Worcester of 1898*, pp. 449–54.

69. Buel, "Workers of Worcester," p. 87; Immigrant Sample: 1880 U.S. Census Manuscript Schedules; *Eighteenth Annual Report of the Bureau of Statistics of Labor* (December 1887), p. 215; *Report on the Population of the United States at the Eleventh Census, 1890*, part 2 (Washington, D.C.: G.P.O., 1897), p. 743; U.S. Bureau of the Census, *Spe-*

cial Report: Occupations, 1900, pp. 760–63; Nutt, *History of Worcester*, vol. 3, p. 214, vol. 4, p. 539.

70. Washburn, *Industrial Worcester*, p. 313.

71. Ibid.; L. P. Richard, Castle Garden, New York, to Messrs. Washburn and Moen, March 28, 1882, American Steel and Wire, Industrial Museum Collection, Baker Library; Wahlstrom, "A History of the Swedish People," p. vii; *Times*, April 29, 1886, June 25, 1886; Charles W. Estus and John F. McClymer, *"ga till Amerika": The Swedish Creation of an Ethnic Identity for Worcester, Massachusetts* (Worcester Historical Museum, 1994), pp. 11–99.

72. *Evening Spy*, November 19, 24, December 6, 19, 1894; August 20, 21, September 12, 22, 1881.

73. O'Tuathaigh, *Ireland Before the Famine*, pp. 117–26; Miller, *Emigrants and Exiles*, p. 367, table 14, p. 582; Donald Jordan, "Land and Politics in the County of Mayo, 1846–1882" (Ph.D. diss.: University of California at Davis, 1982), pp. 9–11; Carol Groneman, "Working Class Immigrant Women in Mid-Nineteenth Century New York: The Irish Women's Experience," *Journal of Urban History* 4, no. 3 (May 1978), p. 259; *Reports of the Immigration Commission*, vol. 1, "Statistical Review of Immigration to the United States, 1820 to 1910," p. 98; Hasia Diner, *Erin's Daughters in America*, pp. 1–42, 80–97; Kennedy, *The Irish*, pp. 8–10, 52–54, 159–62, 55–61; MacCurtain and O'Corrain, eds., *Women in Irish Society*, pp. 26–45, 58–70, 168–70, 75–84.

74. Immigrant Samples: 1880 and 1900 U.S. Census Manuscript Schedules; Rice, ed., *Worcester of 1898*, pp. 650–51; Dun and Bradstreet reports, vol. 105, p. 1050, Baker Library; O'Flynn MSS, "Biographical Sketches," vol. 1, HCC Archives.

75. *Messenger*, September 20, 1902, October 27, 1905; *Catholic Messenger*, May 20, June 18, 1915; *Dedication Souvenir of A.O.H. Hall*, p. 69; Stephen Littleton Diaries, vol. 4, entry February 17, 1891, AAS; Cousin Ruth, "Gleanings for Children," *Catholic School and Home Magazine* (February 1896), p. 311.

76. Immigrant Samples: 1880 and 1900 U.S. Census Manuscript Schedules.

77. Buel, "Workers of Worcester," pp. 106–7; Immigrant Sample: 1900 U.S. Census Manuscript Schedules.

78. Moriarty, clipping, biographical clipping file, WHM; Rice, ed., *Worcester of 1898*, pp. 650–51.

79. Thirty-six and three-tenths percent of those still paying their mortgages and 42.9 percent of the families who owned their own homes free had at least two working children: Immigrant Samples: 1900 U.S. Census Manuscript Schedules.

80. *Sixth Annual Report of the Massachusetts Bureau of Labor: Public Document no. 13* (Boston: Wright and Potter, 1875), pp. 438–55; *Thirty-Second Annual Report of the Massachusetts Bureau of Labor: Public Document no. 15*, "Price and Cost of Living," pt. 3 (March 1902), pp. 151, 215; In 1911, Mrs. Ethel Shepherd of Central Congregational Church found that many Worcester families ate meat but once a week, used lard instead of butter, and could not afford blankets: *Worcester Telegram*, November 16, 1911; *Times*, March 3, 1882.

81. "American Steel and Wire" *Worcester Magazine* (May 1902), pp. 173–74; *Worcester Daily Times*, June 28, 1882, January 1, April 23, 1885.

82. *Eighteenth Annual Report of the Massachusetts Bureau of Labor Statistics: Publication no.15* (Boston: Wright and Potter, 1887) pp. 215, 151; *Daily Times*, June 28, 1882, April 10, 1885; *Twenty-Fourth Annual Report of the Massachusetts Bureau of Labor Statistics* (Boston: Wright and Potter, 1897) pp. 121, 131; Immigrant Samples: 1880 and 1900 U.S. Census Manuscript Schedules; vol. 64, time books, February, March, May, 1882, April 1887, Baker Library.

83. "Report of the Overseers of the Poor," *City Document no. 54*, p. 13; *City Document no. 55*, pp. 5, 56, 6; *Worcester Daily Times*, January 19, 1885; George W. Haynes, "A Businessman's Proposition," reprint of *Worcester Magazine* article, November 1909, p. 5, pamphlet file, WHM; *Eleventh, Twelfth, Thirteenth, Fourteenth, Fifteenth, Sixteenth, and Seventeenth Annual Reports of the Associated Charities of Worcester, 1901, 1902, 1903, 1904, 1905, 1906, 1907* (Worcester: Lewis Goddard); *Worcester Evening Post*, February 19, 1898.

84. K. H. Connell, *Irish Peasant Society: Four Historical Essays* (Oxford: Clarendon Press, 1961), pp. 114–47; Kennedy, *The Irish*, pp. 142–56; Timothy Guinnane, *The Vanishing Irish: Households, Migration and the Rural Economy in Ireland* (Princeton: Princeton University Press, 1997), pp. 34–58, 193–286; K. H. Connell, *The Population of Ireland*, pp. 47–85; Albert Gibbs Mitchell Jr., "Irish Family Patterns in the Nineteenth Century: Ireland and Lowell, Massachusetts," Ph.D. diss.: Boston University, 1976); Michael Katz, *The People of Hamilton, Canada West: Family and Class in a Mid-Nineteenth-Century City* (Cambridge: Harvard University Press, 1975), pp. 279–90; Timothy Guinnane, "Rethinking the Western European Marriage Pattern: The Decision to Marry in Ireland at the Turn of the Century," *Journal of Family History* 16, no. 1 (1991), pp. 48–64; O'Neill, *Family and Farm*, pp. 125–92. Figures are from Miller, *Emigrants and Exiles*, p. 403.

85. Connolly, *Priests and People in Pre-Famine Ireland*, pp. 175–218; Kennedy, *The Irish*, pp. 151–52, 146; Connell, *The Population of Ireland*, pp. 47–83. Quote from Patrick K. Egan, *The Parish of Ballinasloe* (Dublin: 1960), p. 28; Connell, *Irish Peasant Society*, p. 121. For German parallels, see Jonathan Sperber, *Popular Catholicism in Nineteenth-Century Germany* (Princeton: Princeton University Press, 1984), pp. 10–89, 91–93.

86. Immigrant Samples: Census Manuscript Schedules, 1900; Sample from U.S. Census Manuscript Schedules, 1900, of a one in twenty sample of all persons over age eighteen native-born of native parents.

87. Kennedy, *The Irish*, pp. 143–44; Samples from the 1900 U.S. Census Manuscript Schedules; *Twelfth Census of the United States, 1900* vol. 2, "Population," p. 348. In 1900, 15.8 percent of native-stock men aged 35 to 44 and 10.3 percent aged 45 to 54 remained unmarried compared to 15.1 percent and 9.9 percent of Irish immigrant men respectively; for women, the native-stock figures were 18 percent aged 35 to 44 and 14.4 percent aged 45 to 54 and 12.9 percent aged 35 to 44 and 9 percent aged 45 to 54 for Irish immigrants.

88. Mitchell, "Irish Family Patterns," p. 293; Katz, *People of Hamilton, Canada West*, pp. 279–80; Miller, *Emigrants and Exiles*, pp. 403–8; Coakley and wife in *Messenger*, January 6, 1900.

89. In 1880, 50 percent of immigrant men aged 20 to 24 were boarders; in 1900 39.1 percent. In 1880 38.4 percent lived with parents; in 1900, only 10.8 percent. In 1900, 47 percent of immigrants aged 30 or more lived with four or more boarders compared to 33 percent of those aged 20 to 24: Immigrant Samples: 1880 and 1900 U.S. Census Manuscript Schedules.

90. "Trained and Supplemental Employees," *Thirty-Seventh Annual Report*, pp. 84–123, quotes, p. 122; "Hours of Labor in Domestic Service and Their Objections to Domestic Service," *Labor Bulletin of the Commonwealth of Massachusetts*, no. 8 (October 1898), pp. 1–24, quote, p. 29. Servant unions in *Recorder*, July 1, 1898; *Evening Post*, January 13, 23, 1904; *Labor News*, October 30, 1909; Immigrant Sample: 1880 and 1900 U.S. Census Manuscript Schedules.

91. *Reports of the Immigration Commission, Document no. 665* (Washington, D.C.: G.P.O., 1911), vol. 35, "Immigrants as Charity Seekers," p. 1136; Rev. Thomas J. Conaty, "Temperance Idea in Public Instruction," *Catholic School and Home Magazine* (March 1895), p. 8; "Silver Jubilee of the CTA Union of America," *Catholic School and Home Magazine* (September 1895), p. 171; *Catholic Messenger*, October 28, 1910; Sullivan fight, *Worcester Telegram*, December 2, 1897; O'Flynn MSS, folio 1, "Rumsellers," HCC Archives; Sawyer, *History of the Department of Police*, p. 134.

92. In 1900, three-quarters of immigrants with all children over age seven had one working child at home, one-half had two or more working children: Immigrant Samples: 1880 and 1900 U.S. Census Manuscript Schedules; O'Flynn MSS, folio 1, clipping, November 7, 1890, HCC Archives; Byrne quote, *Messenger*, February 2, 1901; debate on marriage, *Messenger*, April 14, 1900.

93. Immigrant Samples: 1880 and 1900 U.S. Census Manuscript Schedules.

94. Ibid.

95. O'Flynn MSS, folio 1, clipping, November 7, 1890, HCC Archives; *City Document no. 46*, pp. 466–70; Immigrant Samples: U.S. Census Manuscript Schedules, 1880 and 1900.

96. Immigrant Samples: U.S. Census Manuscript Schedules, 1880 and 1900.

97. Powers, "Invisible Immigrants," p. 144.

98. Ibid., pp. 235–37; 242–53.

99. Kingsley, *Picturesque Worcester: Illustrated Business Guide, 1880* (Boston: Inwood, Man and Co., 1880); Witherspoon, "Housing Conditions," p. 81; Matt Babinski, *By Raz 1937* (Worcester, n.p., 1937), pp. 18–19; "Cosmopolitan Worcester," *Worcester Magazine* 18, no. 8 (August 1915), p. 80; Immigrant Samples: U.S. Census Manuscript Schedules, 1880 and 1900.

100. Weiss, "Patterns and Processes," pp. 154, 159; Roberge, "Structural Correlate," pp. 27, 80; Washburn, *Industrial Worcester*, pp. 143–48; Olive Higgins Prouty, *Pencil Shavings* (Boston: Riverside Press, 1961), p. 43.

101. Segregation indices for Irish immigrants measuring their segregation from all other residents in Worcester were 46 in 1880 and 41 in 1900: Immigarnt Samples from U.S. Census Manuscript Schedules, 1880 and 1900; *Worcester Telegram*, December 6, 1893.

102. Weiss, "Patterns and Processes," pp. 140–54; Roberge, "The Three Decker," pp. 29–30.

103. *Census of the Commonwealth of Massachusetts, 1895* vol. 1, "Population and Social Statistics" (Boston: Wright and Potter, 1896), p. 779; *Fifteenth Census of the United States, 1930* (Washington, D.C.: G.P.O., 1931), vol. 6, "Families," p. 632; Witherspoon, "Housing Conditions," pp. 80–81; Spear, *Worcester's Three Deckers*, pp. 7, 23, 29, 15–24, 27; City Planning Board of Worcester, *Building Zone Ordinance for the City of Worcester* (Worcester: Harrigan Press, 1923), pp. 13–19, and attached map. In the 1920s and 1930s the construction of three-deckers in the city declined as more of Worcester's residents found single-family homes affordable. Yet even as late as 1945, a study of Worcester's housing found that half of the city's rental units were in three-deckers, a proportion far larger than that of other cities such as Providence, Rhode Island, or Hartford, Connecticut, where three-deckers were also common.

104. Harrison Eddy, "Sewerage and Sewer Disposal," *Worcester Magazine* (January 1901), pp. 51, 111–12; "Sewers of Worcester," *Worcester Magazine* (February 1901), p. 31; City of Worcester, *Worcester Sewerage and Blackstone River Hearings* (Worcester: Band Aberry and Co., 1872), p. 6; O'Flynn MSS, vol. 1, "Rumsellers," HCC Archives; Babinski, *By Raz*, p. 19; Rosenzweig, *Eight Hours for What We Will*, p. 137.

105. See "Reports of the Board of Health," *City Document no. 34*, pp. 332–37, *City Document no. 54* p. 31, *City Document no. 74*, pp. 957–61; *Catholic Messenger*, January 11, 1907; Edward D. King to M. Dunn, April 24, 1884, St. Vincent de Paul Society, St. John's Parish Conference Records, St. John's parish archives.

106. *Times*, August 22, 1885; *Telegram*, November 6, 1893; "Invisible Immigrants," pp. 43–55. On January 13, 1900, the *Messenger* reported that the Kerry-born Daniel Sullivan had died. "During the troublesome times of the moonlighting escapade," Sullivan "got into trouble" and had fled to Canada. O'Flynn MSS, folio 1, "Rumsellers," folio 21, "Humorous Sketches," HCC Archives; *Telegram*, May 19, 1890, May 26, 1890. Sawyer, *History of the Police Department*, pp. 186–87; *Worcester Telegram*, January 24, 25, 27, 1910, February 1, 5, 7, 1910; "Cosmopolitan Worcester," *Worcester Magazine* (August 1916), p. 180; "Report of the City Marshal," *City Document no. 44*, p. 134; "Report of the Chief of Police," *City Document no. 76*, p. 349; *Catholic Messenger*, December 17, 1909, March 22, 1907.

107. List of Achonry natives from *Irish World*, March 18, 1882, traced into *Worcester City Directory* (Worcester: Drew Allis Co., 1882); St. Vincent de Paul, St. John's Conference, August 15, 1882, St. John's parish archives; Kerryville in *Worcester Telegram*, December 12, 1893.

108. *Worcester City Directory of 1899* (Worcester: Drew Allis Co., 1899), pp. 533–35; Alexander Keysar, *Out of Work: The First Century of Unemployment in Massachusetts*

(New York: Cambridge University Press, 1986), pp. 163, 163–65; Littleton diaries, vol. 4, January 16, 17, 18, 1891, AAS; Interview with Peter Sullivan, August 24, 1989.

109. McCoy, *History of the Diocese of Springfield*, pp. 240–71; O'Flynn MSS, Sacred Heart folio, June 26, 1881, September 21, 1884, February 4, 1889, HCC Archives; Nutt, *History of Worcester*, vol. 2, p. 871.

110. O'Flynn MSS, vol. 1, "Rumsellers," HCC Archives.

111. St. John's parish announcement books, February 13, 1881, quote, April 20, 1879, St. John's parish archives; *Spy*, October 7, 1890.

112. *Recorder*, April 8, 1898; St. Vincent de Paul, St. John's Conference, 1879–87, report copy, July 5, 11, 1882, Year-end reports, December 31, 1882, and 1883, Griffin diary, March 7, 1880, St. John's parish archives.

113. O'Flynn MSS, folio 1, August 16, 1883, Sacred Heart folio, July 20, 1880, April 22, 1887, August 31, 1885, February 23, March 16, 1886; St. Anne's folio, August 15, 1886, November 10, 1890, HCC Archives; *Worcester Telegram*, April 16, 1887; *Messenger*, October 14, 1893.

Two. The Second-Generation Irish

1. *Catholic Messenger*, March 25, 1926.

2. *Worcester Daily Times*, November 26, 1881; Rev. Thomas J. Conaty, "The Ideal American," *Catholic School and Home Magazine*, (April 1895), p. 56; idem, "Address Delivered at Taunton, Massachusetts, May 30, 1890" (Worcester: Charles Hamilton Press, 1890); Major John Byrne, "Talks to Catholic Young Men," *Catholic School and Home Magazine* (1892), p. 190; Lawler in *Worcester Evening Spy*, February 12, 1895; John J. Riordan to George F. Hoar, October 17, 1884, Hoar papers, Massachusetts Historical Society.

3. *Worcester Daily Times*, November 26, 1881; January 14, 1882.

4. Quotation in O'Flynn MSS, "Sacred Heart," folio 3, HCC Archives; "Dedication Souvenir of AOH Hall by the United Divisions of the Ancient Order of Hibernians of Worcester, April 8, 1901," p. 69; *Catholic Messenger*, February 13, 1914; *Messenger*, March 2, 1906.

5. Immigrant and Second-Generation Samples: 1900 U.S. Census Manuscript Schedules. Second-generation samples, one in every eight, supplemented by one in twenty of American-born men and women of an Irish-born father age eighteen and over in 1880, 671 men and women; and one in every twelve American-born men and women of an Irish-born father over age eighteen in 1900, 797 men and women.

6. "Dedication Souvenir," p. 69; *Catholic Messenger*, February 13, 1914.

7. Howard in *Worcester Telegram*, March 17, 1901; McCoy in O'Flynn MSS, "Convention Records," vol. 3, March 18, 1897, clipping, HCC archives; Donnelly in *Worcester Evening Spy*, March 19, 1900. McCoy, O'Flynn MSS, clipping, March 18, 1897, HCC Archives; Thomas McAvoy, ed., *A Course of Lectures on Irish History* (Worcester: Messenger Printing Co., 1915).

8. *Worcester Daily Times*, November 26, 1881; Corcoran in clipping, March 17, 1892, O'Flynn MSS, "Records of the Convention," vol. 2; Dowd *Worcester Evening Post*, March 11, 1909; *Worcester Telegram*, March 18, 1901.

9. *Worcester Telegram*, March 17, 1891, March 19, 1895, March 18, 1901; *Worcester Evening Spy*, March 19, 1901; *Worcester Evening Post*, March 18, 1915; Vladimir Nahirny and Joshua Fishman, "American Immigrant Groups, Ethnic Identification and the Problem of Generations," *Sociological Review* 13, no. 3 (December 1965), pp. 311–26. John Duggan, "Ireland's Contribution to American Progress," in McAvoy, ed., *A Course of Lectures*, p. 257; *Worcester Telegram* March, 18, 1890.

10. Reverend Woodley, Baptismal Register, October 11, 12, 1828, Archives of the Archdiocese of Boston.

11. Second-generation samples: 1880 and 1900 U.S. Census Manuscript Schedules.

12. Robert D. Cross, *The Emergence of Liberal Catholicism in America* (Cambridge: Harvard University Press, 1958), pp. 28–36; Joseph P. O'Grady, *How the Irish Became Americans* (New York: Twayne, 1973).

13. Nutt, *History of Worcester*, vol. 2, pp. 665–70, 1119–25; *Messenger*, October 28, 1899; F. Bradley Nutting, "Worcester Learns to Play: The Development of Public Entertainment, 1820–1860," Unpublished paper, pamphlet file, WHM, p. 11; *Worcester Daily Times*, September 1, 1879, January 9, 1880; vaudeville more legitimate, *Messenger*, October 28, 1899. See chapter 3.

14. Albert Southwick claims that Thayer wrote the poem to celebrate the pitching exploits of the indisputably Yankee and later Worcester congressman, Samuel Winslow Jr. Yet, of course, it is not the pitcher but the batter Casey who is remembered. Thayer could have called him anything, even Winslow, but did not. Albert Southwick, *Once Told Tales of Worcester County* (Worcester: Worcester Telegram and Gazette, 1985), pp. 74–76.

15. Souvenir of United Catholic Total Abstinence Societies of Worcester Coffee Party, January 15, 1896, Mechanics Hall, AAS; St. John's Temperance and Literary Guild records, vol. 2, August 31, 1885, February 8, 21, March 21, April 28, June 6, 1886, St. John's parish archives; McCoy, "Morals of Athletics," address at Worcester English High School, March 4, 1910, McCoy MSS, HCC Archives; Diocesan field day, *Worcester Evening Spy*, September 3, 1895; *Worcester Telegram*, December 6, 1897; *Recorder*, April 8, 1898.

16. *Messenger*, May 5, 1894; *Worcester Telegram*, December 2, 1893, November 2, 1929, April 23, 1961; "Rosy Ryan of Worcester wins first game in the World Series for the Giants," *Worcester Evening Gazette*, October 11, 1923; *Worcester Evening Spy*, August 29, 1895; *Worcester Evening Post*, July 31, 1926; Nutt, *History of Worcester*, vol. 2, pp. 1118–29.

17. *Messenger*, August 4, 11, 1888, August 17, 31, 1895, August 6, 30, 1898, August 28, 1899, July 21, 1900, August 1, 15, 22, 1903; *Catholic Messenger*, August 15, 22, 1913; quotation, "everybody," *Alumna*, August 1886, p. 4; *Messenger*, September 9, 1899.

18. *Messenger*, July 27, 1886, August 13, 20, 26, 1898; *Catholic Messenger*, August 15, 22, 1913, traced into the *Worcester City Directories* of 1898 and 1913. Father Mathew

Total Abstinence Cabaret, "I'm Makin for Macon, Georgia," "Crossin the Mason Dixon Line": *Catholic Messenger,* February 12, 1915; "Piano Forte Recital by Pupils of Gertrude Maude Wilson, June 15, 1903 at Saulsbury Hall," program file, WHM.

19. *Messenger,* February 24, 1900; Program, Worcester Theater, June 6, 1905, program file, Worcester Historical Museum; *Worcester Evening Spy,* November 26, 1890; *Catholic Messenger,* June 3, 1915; St. John's Temperance and Literary Guild, February 24, 1884, November 10, December 29, 1901; St. Stephen's parish minstrel show program, October 24, 25, 1907, program file, WHM; *Recorder,* May 13, 1898; *Labor News,* January 18, 1914; John J. Riordan, "A Prosperous Catholic Club in Central Massachusetts," *Donahoe's Magazine* (December 1897), pp. 139–42.

20. *Worcester Sunday Telegram,* January 3, 1886, May 2, 1886; *Worcester Evening Spy,* December 22, 1885, March 15, 1886; *Worcester Daily Times,* January 1, 14, 1886, January 20, 1887; *Catholic Messenger,* February 12, 1915; *Worcester Sunday Telegram* January 3, 1886; O'Flynn MSS, folio 1, clipping, October 26, 1892, HCC Archives; O'Flynn MSS, societies folio, clipping, March 5, 1887, HCC Archives; *Worcester Telegram,* April 23, 1961; Riordan, "A Prosperous Club," pp. 140–42; *Messenger,* February 23, 1895; *Worcester Daily Times,* March 31, 1882, January 20, 1887, November 27, 1884.

21. *Messenger,* May 5, 1888; Sacred Heart parish announcements, handbill, "Our Boys: An Original Comedy in Three Acts," n.d., parish announcements, Archives of the Archdiocese of Los Angeles; Sacred Heart parish announcements, March 18, 1885, Archives of the Archdiocese of Los Angeles; Souvenir of the United Catholic Total Abstinence Society, 1896, Worcester organization file, AAS; Program, "St. John's Lyceum Presents the College Freshmen," May 29, 1912, pamphlet file, AAS; *Catholic Messenger,* May 18, 1916.

22. *Catholic Messenger,* September 13, 1909, February 18, 25, March 25, July 1, September 2, 16, November 18, 1910, April 15, 1912, June 3, 1915; *Messenger,* March 3, 1901, May 25, 1901, April 7, September 22, 1905.

23. Sperber, *Popular Catholicism,* pp. 92–98; Brian Clarke, *Piety and Nationalism: Lay Voluntary Associations and the Creation of an Irish Catholic Community in Toronto, 1850–1895* (Toronto: McGill-Queen's University Press, 1993); Taves, *The Household of Faith;* Dolan, *The American Catholic Experience,* pp. 221–40; Jay P. Dolan, *The Immigrant Church: New York's Irish and German Catholics, 1815–1865* (Baltimore: Johns Hopkins University Press, 1975), idem, *Catholic Revivalism: The American Experience, 1830–1900* (Notre Dame: University of Notre Dame Press, 1978); Joseph Chinnici, *Living Stones: The History and Structure of Catholic Spiritual Life in the United States* (New York: Macmillan, 1989) pp. 35–147; Joseph Chinnici, ed., *Devotion to the Holy Spirit in American Catholicism* (New York: Paulist Press, 1985), pp. 3–90; Ralph Gibson, *A Social History of French Catholicism, 1789–1914* (New York: Routledge, 1989); Leslie Woodcock Tentler, *Seasons of Grace: A History of the Catholic Archdiocese of Detroit* (Detroit: Wayne State University Press, 1990), pp. 59–71, 166–218; Robert A. Orsi, *Thank You, St. Jude: Women's Devotion to the Patron Saint of Hopeless Causes* (New Haven, Connecticut: Yale University Press, 1996), and idem, *The Madonna of 115th Street: Faith and Community in Italian Harlem, 1880–1950* (New

Haven: Yale University Press, 1985), pp. xiii–xxiii, 50–74, 163–233; Hugh McLeod, *Religion and the People of Western Europe, 1789–1970* (New York: Oxford University Press, 1981), pp. 47–53.

24. *Annals of St. Anthony's Shrine* (June 1899), p. 4; quotation, "praying," in Chinnici, *Living Stones,* p. 65; Clarke, *The Irish in Toronto;* Taves, *The Household of Faith,* pp. vii–x, 102–20; Dolan, *American Catholic Experience,* pp. 319–20; 247–48, 259–60; Sperber, *Popular Catholicism,* pp. 92–98; David Miller, "Irish Catholicism and the Great Famine," *Journal of Social History* 9 (1975), pp. 81–98; S. J. Connolly, *Priests and People in Pre-Famine Ireland, 1780–1845* (Dublin: Gill and Macmillan, 1982), pp. 264–78; Emmet Larkin, "The Devotional Revolution in Ireland," *American Historical Review* 78, no. 3 (June 1972), pp. 625–52.

25. Dolan, *American Catholic Experience,* pp. 101–270; Thomas W. Spalding, *The Premier See: A History of the Archdiocese of Baltimore, 1789–1994* (Baltimore: Johns Hopkins University Press, 1989), pp. 62–63, 145–46; Donna Merwick, *Boston Priests, 1848–1910: A Study of Social and Intellectual Change* (Cambridge: Harvard University Press, 1973), pp. 1–59, 78–99.

26. McCoy, *History of the Springfield Diocese,* pp. 8–9, 246, 250; Peter Joyce, "The History of St. John's Church, Worcester, Massachusetts, 1826–1862," (M.A. thesis, Catholic University, 1982), pp. 19–24. On Irish Catholic ritual, see Dolan, *Immigrant Church,* pp. 59, 80.

27. *St. Peter's Jubilee: Seventy-Fifth Anniversary History,* St. Stephen's parish; "The Correct in Church" 1904, St. Stephen's parish archives; *Worcester Daily Times,* January 2, 1882; O'Flynn MSS, St. Anne's parish folio, October 18, 1884, HCC Archives; St John's parish announcements, July 3, 1892, St. John's parish archives.

28. Conaty in Sacred Heart parish announcements, May 24, 1885, Archives of the Archdiocese of Los Angeles; O'Flynn MSS, St. Anne's folio, October 18, 1887; Corpus Christi described in *Alumna,* 1, no. 3, July 1886, and *Worcester Telegram,* June 9, 1890; St. John's parish announcements, June 16, 1878, April 3, 1881, June 19, 1881; *Worcester Evening Spy,* July 4, 1889.

29. Vespers in *Alumna,* October 1886, p. 3; *Alumna,* March 1887, p. 4; Novenas in *Annals of St. Anthony's Shrine* (June 1899), pp. 6–11; Sacred Heart parish announcements, novenas, May 24, 1880, letter from Bishop Patrick O'Reilly to Pastors, January 25, 1886, September 11, 1887, feasts of great devotion, June 28, 1885, September 13, 1885, Archives of the Archdiocese of Los Angeles; Forty Hours devotion in *Sacred Heart Calendar,* October 1891; St. John's parish announcements, November 13, 1910, St. John's parish archives.

30. Sacred Heart parish announcements, Memorial of the Mission given by Frs. Smith, O'Kane, and Campbell of the Society of Jesus at Sacred Heart, December 1894, pamphlet attached to announcements book, Archives of the Archdiocese of Los Angeles; "Mission Chronicles," vol. 4, April 5–19, 1891, vol. 5, April 28–May 12, 1895, Paulist Archives, Washington, D.C.; *Sacred Heart Parish: Work of Decade* (Worcester: February 1890), pp. 14–15, Worcester Room, Worcester Public Library; quotation, "a mission," in *Messenger,* April 20, 1895; Dolan, *Catholic Revivalism,* pp. 1–112.

31. Quotation, "packed," in Griffin diary, March 21, 1886, St. John's parish archives; "Mission Chronicles," vol. 4, April 5–19, 1891; "enthusiasm never flagged," in "Mission Chronicles," vol. 4, March, 1892; "Mission Chronicles," vol. 3, January 6–13, 1884; "Mission Chronicles" vol. 5, April 28–May 12, 1895; "Mission Chronicles," vol. 3, May 19–June 2, 1899.

32. Parish annual reports, St. Anne's, 1860, Archives of Archdiocese of Boston. "Mission Chronicles," vol. 3, February 19–March 4, 1888; *Catholic Messenger,* September 19, 1924; St. John's parish announcement book, November 3, 1910, St. John's parish archives. Quotation, "large and flourishing," in "Mission Chronicles," vol. 3, May 19–June 2 1889; *Sacred Heart Calendar,* April 1891; "Mission Chronicles," vol. 3, February 19–March 4, 1888; *Sacred Heart: Work of a Decade,* pp. 14–15; St. John's parish announcements, April 28, 1875, St. John's parish archives.

33. Quotation, "novena is ended," in St. John's parish announcements, November 3, 1910, St. John's parish archives; Sacred Heart parish announcements, May 24, 1885, Archives of the Archdiocese of Los Angeles; Sacred Heart parish announcements, *Men's League of Sacred Heart,* March 1891, pamphlet attached to book, Archives of the Archdiocese of Los Angeles.

34. *Catholic Messenger,* July 8, 1920; Quotation, "The crucifix is," *Annals of St. Anthony's Shrine* (July 1900), p. 11. See Colleen McDannell, *Material Christianity* (New Haven: Yale University Press, 1995), pp. 18–57. Pictures, statues, and other artifacts were not ends in themselves, Catholic leaders believed, but rather means to create the proper environment for prayer and sacrifice. The purpose of having a crucifix in the home, the *Annals* pointed out, was to prompt family members to spend a "little time" every day in prayer before it.

35. *Catholic Messenger,* May 1, 1919, October 2, 1919, October 14, 1920; Griffin diary, February 18, 1877, St. John's parish archives; *Catholic School and Home Magazine,* October 1896, pp. 170–71. In 1885 Conaty urged his parishioners: "parents should recite it [the rosary] in the family every evening if possible after supper," Sacred Heart parish announcements, October 4, 1885, Archives of the Archdiocese of Los Angeles.

36. Quotation, "all our young people," in *Monthly Calendar of the Church of Sacred Heart,* vol. 1, no. 3, May 1891, p. 5; "Mission Chronicles," vol. 3, January 6–13, 1884; vol. 4, March 1892.

37. "Mission Chronicles," vol. 5, April 29–May 12, 1895, vol. 6, May 24–June 7, 1908; Quotation, "gleaming candles," in *Annals of St. Anthony's Shrine* (July 1940), pp. 17–20; *Annals of St. Anthony's Shrine* (June 1910), pp. 18–19 ; St. John's parish announcements, clippings, October 11, 1927, and October 3, 1929, February 12, 25, October 25, 1934, St. John's parish archives; *Catholic Messenger,* April 30, 1915; July 20, 29, August 12, 19, 1920, November 17, 1921, September 19, 1924; *Worcester Telegram,* November 1, 1920.

38. Canonical Visitation of Blessed Sacrament, c. 1913, Blessed Sacrament file, parish files, Springfield Diocesan Archives; *Messenger,* September 16, 1899, May 5, 1900; *Catholic Messenger,* October 25, 1912, February 19, 1920, September 19, 1924.

39. St. John's parish announcements, November 13, 1881, St. John's parish archives; St. John's Temperance and Literary Guild, vol. 2, December 17, 1896, St. John's parish archives; *Catholic Messenger,* September 19, 1924.

40. *Cable,* December 1929, March 1929; historian's report, July 1943, Alhambra Council, no. 88, Knights of Columbus Archives.

41. *Sacred Heart: Work of a Decade,* p. 11; McCoy MSS, Sermon, Notre Dame Convent Dedication, November 12, 1899, HCC Archives; Bishop O'Connor, Newark-South Orange Diocese, to Bishop Thomas Beaven, August 22, 1907, Beaven correspondence, Springfield Diocesan Archives; *Messenger,* February 3, May 19, 1900; *Catholic Messenger,* July 8, September 30, 1920; *Sacred Heart Review,* November 14, 1896. In the 1895–96 school year 49 of 252 students attending Holy Cross were from Worcester: *Catalogue of the College of Holy Cross, 1895–1896* (Worcester: Hamilton Press, 1896); in the 1915–16 school year 110 of 597 students were from Worcester: *College of the Holy Cross, 1915–1916* (Worcester: 1916). Of 998 Irish Americans who attended Holy Cross between 1870 and 1917 who reported their occupation in the *Alumni Directory* in 1917, 354 (35.5 percent) had become priests and 12 of them bishops: Holy Cross Alumni Association, *Holy Cross Alumni Directory, 1917,* pp. 21–64, Holy Cross College Archives; "List of Holy Cross Alumni Elevated to the Episcopate," pp. 1–2, manuscript, Holy Cross College Archives; Robert E. Sullivan, "Beneficial Relations: Toward a Social History of the Diocesan Priests of Boston, 1875 to 1944," in Robert E. Sullivan and James M. O'Toole, eds., *Catholic Boston: Studies in Religion and Community, 1870 to 1970* (Boston: Archdiocese of Boston, 1985), pp. 204–5. In 1900 over half of the Sisters of Notre Dame in Worcester, two-thirds of the Xaverian Brothers and two-thirds of the Sisters of Providence were American-born Irish: 1900 U.S. Census Manuscript Schedules. Mary Oates, "Organized Voluntarism: The Catholic Sisters in Massachusetts, 1870–1940," Paper delivered at the New England Historical Association Meeting, April 30, 1977.

42. *Sacred Heart Monthly Calendar,* June 1891; O'Connor, in *Catholic School and Home Magazine* (January 1895), p. 263, and *Catholic School and Home Magazine* (April 1896), p. 25; McKeon in *Catholic School and Home Magazine* (December 1895), p. 237. See McKeon in *Catholic School and Home Magazine* (May 1895), p. 55.

43. Stephen Littleton diaries, vol. 1, "My Life to January 1, 1890," AAS; *Labor News,* September 13, 1918.

44. Ibid., vol. 2, December 8, 1889; vol. 3, March 4, 7, 9, 10, 12, 1890; vol. 4, December 25, 28, 1890, AAS.

45. Ibid., vol. 4, December 31, 1890; vol. 3, April 6, 1890; vol. 4, April 12, 1891, AAS.

46. Ibid., vol. 4, January 4, 1891, AAS.

47. Ibid., vol. 3, February 2, 11, March 7, April 3, 1890; vol. 4, December 25, 1890, January 4, 1891, AAS.

48. Dolan, *American Catholicism,* pp. 232–33.

49. Quotation, "good boys," in McCoy MSS, "Temperance," n.d., Holy Cross College Archives; Rosenzweig, *Eight Hours for What We Will,* p. 188; *Worcester Evening Post,*

April 1, 1913. The Moonlight Gang, led by Jack Ryan, roamed the Temple Street area in the same period. See Herbert Sawyer, *History of the Department of Police Service* (Worcester: Worcester Police Relief Service, 1900), p. 186. Second-generation Irish men constituted 9.3 percent of Massachusetts' population in 1910 but over 29 percent of the men arrested for drunkenness in the state in 1908: *Reports of the Immigration Commission*, vol. 18, "Immigrants and Crime," pp. 159–78 and *Thirteenth Census of the United States Taken in the Year 1910*, vol. 1, "Population," p. 865.

50. *Worcester Telegram*, November 4, 1920; "Mission Chronicles," vol. 3, Mission on February 19–March 4, 1888, vol. 4 Mission on April 5–19, 1891, Mission on March 6–20, 1892; St. John's parish, announcement book, November 13, 1881, St. John's parish archives; men led in Forty Hour devotion, in *Sacred Heart Calendar* October 1891, p. 7. There were over a thousand members of parish temperance societies in 1888 and 200 men in the Confraternity of the Blessed Sacrament at St. John's the same year: *Messenger*, July 7, August 25, September 8, 1888. Hugh McLeod has found "quite a strong tradition of male piety among Irish New Yorkers" at the turn of the century: Hugh McLeod, *Piety and Poverty: Working Class Religion in Berlin, London and New York, 1870–1914* (New York: Holmes and Meier, 1996) p. 172.

51. Leslie Tentler "Present at the Creation: Working-Class Catholics in the United States," in Rick Halperin and Jonathan Morris, eds., *American Exceptionalism? U.S. Working-Class Formation in an International Context* (New York: St. Martin's, 1997), p. 136; Christopher Kauffman, *Faith and Fraternalism: The History of the Knights of Columbus, 1882–1892* (New York: Harper and Row, 1982), pp. 176, 227; Dolan, *American Catholicism*, p. 233; Clarke, *Piety and Nationalism* (Montreal: McGill-Queen's University Press, 1993), pp. 12, 224–53.

52. *Messenger*, October 28, 1893; quotation, "despite many changes and upsets," in *Catholic Messenger*, February 16, 1906; *Sacred Heart Calendar*, March 1891; O'Flynn MSS, St. John's folio, September 28, 1886, HCC Archives; "Mission Chronicles," vol. 3, January 6–13, 1884. See also "Mission Chronicles," vol. 3, May 19–June 2, 1889. On women as fundraisers see Colleen McDannell, "Going to the Ladies' Fair: Irish Catholics in New York City, 1870–1900," in Ronald H. Bayor and Timothy J. Meagher, *The New York Irish* (Baltimore: Johns Hopkins University Press, 1996), pp. 234–51.

53. Quotation, "aimed to prevent," in *Our Church and Country: The Catholic Pages of American History* (New Haven: Catholic Historical League, 1905), p. 703, see also pp. 704–5. *Messenger*, February 16, 1906; *Catholic Messenger*, February 8, 15, 1907, January 27, 1911, January 17, 1913, March 7, 1913, February 26, March 31, April 16, June 18, August 5, October 21, 28, November 4, 1915, April 5, 1918. *Worcester Evening Post*, November 3, 1906; Leslie Woodcock Tentler, *Seasons of Grace: A History of the Archdiocese of Detroit* (Detroit: Wayne State University Press, 1990), pp. 213–14.

54. Clarke, *Piety and Nationalism*, pp. 11–12, 72–96, 224–53, 259; Both St. Anne's and St. John's boasted rosary and scapular societies for women by the middle of the nineteenth century: Parish annual reports, St. Anne's parish 1860, 1865, St. John's parish, 1865, Archives of the Archdiocese of Boston; Joyce, "St. John's Parish," pp. 70–92.

55. Paula Kane, *Separatism and Subculture: Boston Catholicism, 1900–1920* (Chapel Hill: University of North Carolina Press, 1994), pp. 7–8, 324; Taves, *The Household of Faith*, pp. vi–viii; Dolan, *The American Catholic Experience*, pp. 236–40; Josef Barton, "Religion and Cultural Change in Czech Immigrant Communities: 1850–1920," in Randall Miller and Thomas D. Marzik, eds., *Immigrants and Religion in Urban America* (Philadelphia: Temple University Press, 1977), pp. 3–24.

56. See appeal of saints in *Annals of St. Anthony's Shrine*, July 1900, p. 11; "Anna," *Catholic School and Home Magazine* (June 1896), pp. 80–81. See below, this chapter, for second-generation economic status.

57. See, for example, the development of the elaborate White City amusement park along Lake Quinsigamond in Shrewsbury: Rosenzweig, *Eight Hours for What We Will*, pp. 180–83. Thomas Buckley, second-generation Irishman and inventor of the lunch cart, created the White House Café, the "most elaborate restaurant in the city, plate mirrors, polished brass and when bathed at night it looked like a fairy grotto," *Worcester Telegram*, December 1, 1903.

58. Quote, "He who does not feel," in *Catholic School and Home Magazine* (December 1896), p. 219; quote, "Take the saints," in *Annals of St. Anthony's Shrine* (June 1902) p. 1; McCoy, "Sermon: Notre Dame Convent," November 12, 1899, McCoy MSS, Holy Cross College Archives; *Messenger*, December 24, 1898; quote, "Now New England knows," in McCoy, *History of the Springfield Diocese*, p. 31.

59. James M. O'Toole, *Militant and Triumphant: William Henry Cardinal O'Connell and the Catholic Church in Boston, 1859–1944* (Notre Dame: University of Notre Dame Press, 1992), pp. 228, 227–50; quotation, "so deeply woven," in Doris Kearns Goodwin, *The Fitzgeralds and the Kennedys* (New York: Simon and Schuster, 1987) p. 27; see also pp. 25–27.

60. David Gerber, "Ambivalent Anti-Catholicism: Buffalo's American Protestant Elite Faces the Challenge of the Catholic Church, 1850–1860," *Civil War History* (1984), pp. 120–43; Gerber, *The Making of an American Pluralism*, p. 284. Stephen Earle specialized in building stone Gothic or Romanesque churches for Protestant denominations in Worcester. Over his career he designed new churches for three Episcopal congregations and three of the city's biggest Congregational churches. *Stephen C. Earle: Architect Shaping Worcester's Image* (Worcester: Worcester Historical Museum and Worcester Heritage Preservation Society, 1887).

61. McKeon quotation in *Catholic School and Home Magazine* (May 1895), p. 55; McCoy, *History of the Springfield Diocese*, pp. 1, 262, 272. When the new St. Bernard's church was dedicated in 1921, five years after the parish was founded, a ten-piece orchestra and 600 children, each carrying an American flag, lined the streets and greeted the guest speaker, Bishop Louis Walsh of Maine: *Worcester Telegram*, November 5, 1921. In 1887, second-generation Irish R. H. Mooney "called attention to the growth of his people in this respect to property and emphatically denied that they were improvident and reckless. Such buildings could not have been built by them if this were true": O'Flynn MSS, Sacred Heart folio, February 2, 1887, HCC Archives. See also O'Flynn MSS, Sacred Heart folio, September 21, 1884, HCC Archives.

62. "Mission Chronicles," vol. 3, May 19–June 2, 1889, vol. 4, April 5–19, 1891; Griffin, diary, March 1, 1876, St. John's parish archives; *Sacred Heart Monthly Calendar,* vol. 1, no. 3, May 1891.

63. *Annals of St. Anthony's Shrine,* June 1900, p. 9.

64. Quotation in Hugh McLeod, "Catholicism and the New York Irish, 1880 to 1910," in Jim Obelkevich et al., eds., *Disciplines of Faith: Studies in Religion, Politics, and Patriarchy* (New York: Routledge, 1987) p. 350; See also McLeod, *Piety and Poverty.*

65. *Catholic Messenger,* November 1, 1928.

66. Kerby Miller, "Class, Culture, and Immigrant Identity in the United States: The Case of Irish American Ethnicity," in Virginia Yans McLaughlin, ed., *Immigration Reconsidered* (New York: Oxford University Press, 1990), pp. 96–130; Kane, *Separatism and Subculture,* pp. 89–95, 104–7.

67. *Messenger,* October 28, 1893, February 16, 1906; quotation, "to the letter," in *Catholic Messenger,* February 8, 1907, January 27, 1911, December 19, 1913.

68. Quotation in O'Flynn MSS, John F. O'Connor, "Address to the St. John's Temperance Society," clipping, March 18, 1899, Convention Records, vol. 3, HCC Archives. Professionals and high managers were 14.3 percent of native-stock Yankees and 6.4 percent of second-generation Irish: U.S. Bureau of the Census, *Special Report: Occupations, 1900,* pp. 760–63, and second-generation samples: 1900 U.S. Census Manuscript Schedules.

69. O'Connor quote in O'Flynn MSS, "Address to the St. John's Temperance Society"; quote, "If we are not careful," in *Catholic Messenger,* July 25, 1913. Thomas Fitzpatrick in the *Messenger* of 1905 also felt that more recent immigrants were threatening to surpass the Irish: *Messenger,* May 3, 1905.

70. Immigrant and second-generation samples: 1880 and 1900 U.S. Census Manuscript Schedules.

71. The table below includes data from the Community Studies Program at Assumption College drawn from a Swedish and a French Canadian neighborhood in Worcester in 1902:

Occupational Status, 1902	Swedes	French Canadians
Professional	.9%	1.0%
High managerial	.9%	.9%
Small proprietor	3.0%	8.5%
Clerical	8.5%	8.5%
Skilled blue-collar	29.4%	37.0%
Semi-skilled and operatives	29.7%	18.2%
Unskilled	24.2%	18.4%
Other	3.0%	6.5%

See also Reports of the Immigration Commission, vol. 28, "The Occupations of the First and Second Generation Immigrants in the United States," pp. 352–61. In 1919, over 77.1 percent (30 of the 36) Swedes listed in the biographical section of Nutt's *History of Worcester* owned their own businesses or factories: Nutt, *History of Worcester,* vols. 2, 3.

72. Quote, Major John Byrne, "Talks to Catholic Young Men," *Catholic School and Home Magazine* (July 1892), p. 190; quote, "nothing to stop our young people," in *Catholic Messenger*, July 25, 1913. See also *Worcester Evening Spy*, February 12, 1885; Rev. John J. McCoy speech, clipping, March 18, 1897, Convention Records, vol. 3, Holy Cross College Archives; *Worcester Evening Post*, March 18, 1909; *Worcester Evening Spy*, March 18, 1892; Rev. John J. McCoy, "Volunteers of 82" speech, McCoy MSS, Holy Cross College Archives; Dr. John T. Duggan, "Ireland's Contribution to American Progress," *Lectures in Irish History*, p. 189, p. 286.

73. St. John's Literary and Temperance Guild Records, vol. 1, February 28, 1884, St. John's parish archives: *Catholic Messenger*, April 15, 1910; Walsh, "The Irish in the New America: 'Way Out West,'" in Doyle and Edwards, eds., *America and Ireland, 1776–1996*; Dennis Clark, *Hibernia America: The Irish and Regional Cultures* (New York: Greenwood Press, 1986); Burchell, *The San Francisco Irish*; Vinyard, *The Irish on the Urban Frontier;* Patrick Blessing, "West Among Strangers: Irish Migration to California, 1850 to 1880" (Ph.D. diss.: University of California at Los Angeles, 1977); Martin Towey, "Kerry Patch Revisited: Irish Americans in St. Louis in the Turn of the Century Era," and Timothy Sarbaugh, "Exiles of Confidence: The Irish American Community of San Francisco, 1880 to 1920," in Meagher, ed., *From Paddy to Studs*, pp. 139–60, 161–80. In 1880 13 percent of all second-generation Irishmen in Worcester worked in boots and shoes compared to 11 percent of the Irish-born. By 1900, only 2.5 percent of the second-generation worked in boots and shoes. The proportion of the second-generation Irish in iron and steel fell from 16 percent in 1880 to 11.4 percent in 1900. Statistics from second-generation samples: 1880 and 1900 U.S. Census Schedules.

74. Quotation, "the banks," in O'Flynn MSS, March 18, 1899; R. M. Washburn, *Smith's Barn: A Child's History of the West Side*, p. 42; O'Flynn's notes in O'Flynn MSS, folio 1, January 28, 1895, Holy Cross College Archives; *Catholic Messenger*, January 3, 1916.

75. *Boston Post*, February 21, 1895; *Catholic Messenger*, December 2, 1915; list of buildings constructed by McDermott Brothers Contractors, 1884–1925, in possession of James A. McDermott Jr., Worcester; Tinsley biography in Nutt, *History of Worcester*, vol. 4, p. 511.

76. Quotation, "Where if I," in O'Flynn MSS, March 18, 1899. See also complaints of discrimination against Worcester doctors, in Sisters of Providence, Annals of the Mission, 1942, Sisters of Providence Archives, Holyoke, Massachusetts; *Catholic Messenger*, December 22, 1911, July 25, 1913; *Alumna*, June 1886.

77. Griffin diary, March 28, 1877.

78. Stephan Thernstrom, *Poverty and Progress: Social Mobility in a Nineteenth Century City* (Boston: Atheneum, 1972), pp. 156–57; Stephan Thernstrom, *The Other Bostonians: Poverty and Progress in the American Metropolis, 1880–1970* (Cambridge: Harvard University Press, 1973), pp. 168–75; Joel Perlman, *Ethnic Differences: Schooling and Social Structure among the Irish, Italians, Jews, and Blacks in an American City, 1880 to 1935* (New York: Cambridge University Press, 1988), pp. 56–59. See also Andrew

Greeley, "The Success and Assimilation of Irish Protestants and Catholics in the United States," *Social Science Research* 72, no. 4 (1988), pp. 229–35.

79. *Catholic Messenger,* July 1, 1899; second-generation samples: 1880 and 1900 Census Manuscript Schedules. In 1871 there were 425 American-born children of Irish parents in elementary schools, but only 3 in secondary schools. By contrast, there were 2,862 native-born children of native-born parents in elementary schools and 233 in secondary schools. Thirty years later, in 1901, there were 3,419 second-generation Irish in elementary schools and 314 in secondary schools, and 8,903 native-born children of native-born parents in elementary school and 1,157 in secondary schools. Sources: *City Document no. 26,* p. 98; *City Document no. 46,* p. 410; *City Document no. 56,* p. 145.

80. Walter Meagher and William J. Gratton, *The Spires of Fenwick: A History of the College of the Holy Cross, 1843–1963* (New York: Vantage Press, 1966), pp. 208, 285; Quotation, "send your," in *Alumna,* September 1886, p. 2; *Catholic Messenger,* July 25, 1913; *City Document no. 24, 1870,* "Superintendent's Report," pp. 65–66. In 1914 the *Catholic Messenger* urged parents to send their children to college "if you don't need their support": *Catholic Messenger,* November 6, 1914. Between 1880 and 1900 the number of Irish immigrant multiple-income families rose by 70 percent: Immigrant Samples: 1880 and 1900 U.S. Census Manuscript Schedules.

81. Robert Kolesar, *Urban Politics and Social Conflict* (New York: Praeger, forthcoming), pp. 198–200; *City Document no. 22,* pp. 68–70; Nutt, *History of Worcester* vol. 2, pp. 725–29, 721; Quotation, "Are we to," in *City Document no. 21,* "Report of the Superintendent of Schools of Worcester," p. 50; *City Document no. 23,* "Superintendent's Report"; quotation, "cultivate," *City Document no. 26,* "School Committee Report," p. 109.

82. Quotation, "Boys the future," in Littleton diary, vol. 3, February 22, 1891; *Catholic Messenger,* October 27, 1911; quotation, "industry and a good life," in *Sacred Heart Monthly Calendar,* vol. 1, no. 3 (May 1891).

83. Rev. John J. McCoy, "Christmas Sermon," McCoy MSS, HCC Archives; quotation, "only to be," in *Sacred Heart Monthly Calendar,* vol. 1, no. 3 (May 1891). For other examples see Griffin diary, January 2, 1876, June 9, 1885, February 9, 1886, March 2, 1887, March 9, 1887, St. John's parish archives; McCoy MSS, "Synopsis," Holy Cross College Archives; *Catholic Messenger,* August 26, 1915; *Alumna,* July 1886.

84. McCoy, *History of the Springfield Diocese,* p. 32; *Messenger,* September 20, 1902; quotation, "traitors," in John H. Meagher scrapbook, clipping (1900?), in author's possession. See also *Dedication Souvenir of A.O.H. Hall,* p. 69.

85. Second-generation samples: 1900 U.S. Census Manuscript Schedules; Nutt, *History of Worcester,* vols. 3, 4.

86. Quotation, "lack of Catholic men," in *Catholic Messenger,* December 22, 1911; quotation, "so few of them," in *Catholic Messenger,* July 25, 1913; *Catholic Messenger,* July 23, 1912.

87. John Brooke, *The Heart of the Commonwealth: Society and Political Cultures in Worcester County, Massachusetts, 1713–1861* (Cambridge: Cambridge University Press,

1989), pp. 269–309; Charles G. Washburn, *Industrial Worcester* (Worcester: Davis Press, 1917); Kenneth Solokoff, "Inventive Activity in Early Industrial America: Evidence from Patent Records, 1790–1846," *Journal of Economic History* 48, no. 4, pp. 824, 829, 832; David Jaffee, "Peddlers of Progress and the Transformation of the Rural North," *Journal of American History* 78, no. 2 (September 1991), pp. 511–35; Washburn, *Industrial Worcester*, pp. 28, 70–71, 85–93, 118, 144–62, 292–99; Washburn, *Industrial Worcester*, pp. 301–10; Mildred Tymeson, *Two Towers: The Story of Worcester Tech, 1865–1965* (Worcester: Worcester Polytechnic Institute, 1965); Joshua Chasan, "Civilizing Worcester: The Creation of Institutional and Cultural Order in Worcester, Massachusetts, 1848–1876" (Ph.D. diss.: University of Pittsburgh, 1974).

88. Classical High School, *Classic Myths: Class of 1925* (Worcester: Classical High School, 1925), Worcester Room, Worcester Public Library; *The Academe*, June 15, 1886, January 19, 1886. It was 110 of 597, or 18.4 percent in 1916 and 49 of 252 or 19.4 percent in 1896: *College of the Holy Cross Catalogue: 1915–1916* (Worcester: Harrigan Press, 1916); *Catalogue of the College of Holy Cross, 1895–1896* (Worcester: Hamilton Press, 1896).

89. Edward Quinn, non-graduate, 1887, and Robert Gallagher of 1885 worked for Morgan Construction Company but not in executive positions: *Journal of the Worcester Polytechnic Institute* 25, no. 1 (October 1931); Tymeson, *Two Towers*, p. 43; Herbert Foster Taylor, *Seventy Years of the Worcester Polytechnic Institute* (Worcester: published privately, 1937), p. 106.

90. Timothy J. Meagher, "The Irish Americans at Georgetown and Holy Cross" (Undergraduate senior thesis, Georgetown University, 1971); *A Catalogue of the Graduates of the College of Holy Cross* (Worcester: Harrigan Press, 1916).

91. *Alumna*, September 1886, p. 2; *Messenger*, December 2, 1893; *Catholic Messenger*, December 22, 1911, July 25, 1913, November 6, 1914, June 3, 1915, August 26, 1915; Littleton diary, vol. 3, February 22, 1891; *Catholic Messenger*, January 8, June 17, June 24, 1915, August 26, 1915, July 19, 1918; *Golden Conquest*, p. 158; Kolesar, *Urban Politics* p. 200.

92. *Messenger*, November 3, 1905; *Catholic Messenger*, December 22, 1911; Nutt, *History of Worcester*, vols. 3, 4; Lee, *Modernization of Ireland*, pp. 16–17. *Alumna*, September 1886.

93. Tymeson, *Two Towers*, pp. 46–50, 90; Washburn, *Industrial Worcester* pp. 301–10, 177, 270–72; Nutt, *History of Worcester*, vol. 4, pp. 776–77, vol. 2, pp. 38, 361.

94. *Journal of the Worcester Polytechnic Institute* 25, no. 1 (October 1931). See also Mildred Tymeson, *The Wyman Gordon Way, 1883–1958* (Worcester: n.p. 1959); Harry Gilpin Stoddard, *The Seventy Year Saga of a New England Enterprise at Industrial Worcester* (New York: Newcomen Society of North America, 1952).

95. Nutt, *History of Worcester*, vol. 4, p. 511. Worcester does not conform to patterns laid out by Oliver Zunz, *Making America Corporate, 1870 to 1920* (Chicago: University of Chicago Press, 1990). Zunz argues (p. 9) that corporate middle-level managers "devised ways of working and adopted new living patterns that weakened the

significance of geographical boundaries within regions and reduced the de facto cultural autonomy that had characterized many communities." See also Burton W. Folsom, *Urban Capitalists: Entrepreneurs and City Growth in Pennsylvania's Lackawanna and LeHigh Regions, 1880 to 1920* (Baltimore: Johns Hopkins University Press, 1981).

96. *Messenger,* June 2, 1905; quotation, "naturally cut out," in *Catholic Messenger,* January 21, 1910, and "higher salary," *Catholic Messenger,* September 23, 1915; collective biography from Nutt, *History of Worcester,* vols. 2, 4—for examples, see vol. 2, pp. 381, 403, vol. 4, pp. 528, 554; Rice, ed., *Worcester of Eighteen Ninety Eight,* p. 151; second-generation sample: 1900 U.S. Census Manuscript Schedules; Lyceum nine in *Worcester Evening Post,* July 31, 1926.

97. *Catholic Messenger,* January 21, 1910.

98. Second-generation sample: 1880 and 1900 U.S. Census Manuscript Schedules.

99. Immigrant samples: 1880 and 1900 U.S. Census Manuscript schedules; second-generation samples: 1880 and 1900 U.S. Census Manuscript Schedules; *Reports of the Immigration Commission, 61st Congress, 3d Session, Document no. 247,* "Abstracts of the Reports of the Commission," vol. 2, pp. 58–59; Nutt, *History of Worcester,* vol. 3, p. 300, vol. 4, p. 485.

100. Nutt, *History of Worcester* vol. 3, pp. 300, 185.

101. "Mission Chronicles," vol. 3, January 6–13, 1884.

102. Second-generation sample: 1900 U.S. Census Manuscript Schedules; U.S. Bureau of the Census, *Special Report on Occupations,* pp. 760–63.

103. *Worcester Evening Gazette,* January 21, 1891; *American,* January 2, October 10, 24, 1893; *Messenger,* May 23, 1903; quotation, "I believe," in *Worcester Telegram,* November 16, 1905.

104. Quotation, "a grand avenue," in *Messenger,* June 18, 1898; *Messenger,* June 23, 1901; McCoy, *History of the Springfield Diocese,* p. 257 ; Rev. Thomas J. Conaty, "Educator's View on the Education of Women," *Donahoe's Magazine,* February 1901, p. 178. In 1900, 11 percent of the Irish women aged 18 to 21 were in school compared to 8 percent of the second-generation Irish men of the same age.

105. Anna, "Nobility of the Working Girl," *Catholic School and Home Magazine* (March: 1896), p. 13; *Catholic Messenger,* July 4, 1913.

106. *Messenger,* October 28, 1899; *Catholic Messenger,* July 1, 1815, July 4, 1913; second-generation-sample: 1900 U.S. Census Manuscript Schedules.

107. *Messenger,* February 11, 1888; *Catholic Messenger,* July 1, 1915; quotation, "who dares to be," in Anna, "Nobility of the Working Girl," p. 13; J. Michael Moore, "Irish American School Teachers and Cultural Change: Worcester, Massachusetts, 1875–1915," unpublished paper, October 22, 1994, WHM.

108. Quotation, "her . . . the light," in *Alumna,* July 1886; *Catholic Messenger,* July 25, 1913; *Catholic Messenger,* July 1, 1915; second-generation sample: 1900 U.S. Census Manuscript Schedules. The *Sacred Heart Calendar,* for example, reminded girls in 1891 that "your mission in life is a beautiful one: that of angels of the home": *Sacred Heart Calendar,* April 1891. See also Anna, "Home Corner," *Catholic School and Home*

Magazine, March 1894, pp. 43–44; Anna, "Home Corner," *Catholic School and Home Magazine,* November 1893, pp. 251–52; Anna, "Home Corner," *Catholic School and Home Magazine,* June 1895, pp. 95–96; Anna, "Home Corner," *Catholic School and Home Magazine,* December 1896, pp. 210–12. See Paula Kane, *Separatism and Subculture.*

109. Abigail L. O'Hara, "Women in the Twentieth Century," *Catholic School and Home Magazine* (June 1894), p. 92; Moore, "Irish American School Teachers," pp. 10–17.

110. *Worcester Magazine* (June 1901), p. 335.

111. Second-generation and immigrant samples: 1900 U.S. Census Manuscript Schedules.

112. Second-generation sample: 1900 U.S. Census Manuscript Schedule; Irish figures from Robert E. Kennedy, *The Irish,* pp. 143–44; Sources: *Twelfth Census of the United States Taken in the Year 1900,* vol. 2, "Population," pt. 2, p. 348; Immigrant and second-generation samples: 1900 U.S. Census Manuscript Schedules.

113. Quotation, "get rich," in *Catholic Messenger,* April 16, 1915; *Messenger,* February 2, 1901; immigrant and second-generation samples: U.S. Census Manuscript Schedules 1880 and 1900.

114. Nutt, *History of Worcester,* vol. 4, pp. 798–99, 522–23, 763–64, 528–29; vol. 3, pp. 184–85.

115. In 1900, for example, 53.8 percent of the second-generation white-collar men, 52.2 percent of the skilled blue-collar workers and 55.6 percent of the semi- and un-skilled workers aged 30 to 34 were single: second-generation sample: 1900 U.S. Census Manuscript Schedules.

116. In 1900, for example, 60.9 percent of second-generation Irish men aged 25 to 29 were living at home with their parents, compared to 7.6 percent of the immigrant men in that age category. Similarly 51.8 percent of the second-generation Irish women were living at home with their parents compared to 9.5 percent of immigrant daughters: immigrant and second-generation samples: 1880 and 1900 U.S. Census Samples.

117. Quotation, "young people," in *Catholic Messenger,* February 2, 1913; examples from 1880 and 1900 U.S. Census Manuscript Schedules.

118. Second-generation samples: 1900 U.S. Census Manuscript Schedules.

119. Quotation, "young people," in *Catholic Messenger,* February 2, 1913; *Messenger,* September 12, 1896; *Catholic Messenger,* May 1, 1908, January 24, 1913.

120. Quotation, "it is the foolish," in *Catholic Messenger,* February 2, 1913; *Catholic Messenger,* June 20, 1913.

121. Immigrant samples: 1900 U.S. Census Manuscript Schedules; 80 percent of widows over age 70 lived with married children in 1900: immigrant sample: 1900 U.S. Census Manuscript Schedules. Second-generation samples: 1900 U.S. Census Manuscript Schedules. On children's obligations to parents, see O'Flynn MSS, folio 1, clipping, November 7, 1890, Holy Cross College Archives.

122. *Catholic Messenger,* June 20, 1913; *Catholic Messenger,* July 5, 1918; *Donahoe's Magazine* vol. 12, no. 1 (July 1884), p. 64.

123. Number of children of women over age forty-five and married ten to twenty years

No. of children	Native stock in Rhode Island	Worcester Irish immigrants	Worcester second- generation
None	20.0%	8.3%	7.0%
2 or fewer	58.4%	16.6%	19.3%
Over 5	9.2%	44.8%	35.1%
(n)		(96)	(57)

Note: In 1900, 83.5 percent of all married immigrant Irish women, 80 percent of the second-generation women, and 34 percent of Yankee, native-stock women from Worcester, had two or more children.

Sources: Reports of the Immigration Commission, 61st Congress, Second Session, no. 282, volume 28, "Fecundity of Immigrant Women," pt. 1, Rhode Island, pp. 741–57; immigrant and second-generation samples: 1900 U.S. Census Manuscript Schedules.

Regression statistics reveal that there was little difference in the fertility rates between first- and second-generation Irish in Worcester in 1900 when the number of years married was held constant.

By generation	Beta	F
Age	.28	11.16
Number of years married	.78	85.79
Generation	.03	.69

Generation measures the deviation from an immigrant norm.

By occupation of the head of household	Beta	F
Age	-.27	10.7
Number of years married	.78	89.4
White collar	-.01	.07
Unskilled and semiskilled	-.05	1.68

White-collar and unskilled-semiskilled measure the deviation from a skilled norm.

Sources: Immigrant and second-generation samples: 1900 U.S. Census Manuscript Schedules.

124. Of the second-generation Irish men 25 percent remained unmarried after age 45, compared to 11 percent of second-generation women, 10.3 percent of native-stock men, 9.9 percent of Irish immigrant men, 9.0 percent of Irish immigrant women, and 14.4 percent of native-stock women: *Twelfth Census of the United States,* vol. 2,

"Population," pt. 2, p. 348; immigrant and second-generation samples: 1900 U.S. Census Manuscript Schedules.

125. St. John's Temperance and Literary Guild, vol. 1, St. John's parish archives.

126. O'Hara, "Women in the Twentieth Century," p. 91; second-generation samples: 1900 U.S. Census Manuscript Schedules.

127. Littleton diary, vol. 3, entry for February 5, 1890; *Messenger,* June 29, 1903; *Catholic Messenger,* May 14, 1913. See also *Catholic Messenger,* May 1, 1908, October 2, 1913, May 14, 1915; *Messenger,* February 2, 1901.

128. *Worcester Daily Times,* January 3, 1881; McCoy, *History of the Springfield Diocese,* p. 259; Littleton diary, vol. 3, entry for April 19, 1890.

129. K. H. Connell, *Irish Peasant Society: Four Historical Essays* (Oxford: Clarendon Press, 1961), p. 121; Nancy S. Landale and Stewart E. Tolnay, "Generation, Ethnicity and Marriage: Historical Patterns in the Northern United States," *Demography* 30, no. 1 (February 1993), pp. 112–15. Tolnay and Landale found that second-generation Irish women and especially Irish men were more likely to delay marriage than almost any other ethnic group. Scandinavian women and Austro-Hungarian men were the closest.

130. *Messenger,* July 27, 1898; "Mission Chronicles," vol. 3, January 6–13, 1884, Paulist Archives; 79.7 percent of second-generation Irish men married first- or second-generation Irish women and 76.3 percent of second-generation Irish women married first- or second-generation Irish men in 1900. In 1880 the figures were 91.7 percent and 81.2 percent respectively. In 1900, 80 percent of second-generation women marrying white-collar workers married first- or second-generation Irish (n=31). Of the 17 second-generation Irish women who married Yankees in the sample in 1900, four married white-collar workers, two married skilled workers, and ten married semi- or unskilled blue-collar men. In 1900, of second-generation women marrying white-collar workers, 16.1 percent married Irish immigrants, 64.5 percent married fellow second-generation Irish, 12.8 percent married Yankees, and 6.5 percent married other ethnics. By comparison, of those marrying semi- or unskilled workers, 35.8 percent married Irish immigrants, 37.7 percent married fellow second-generation Irish, 18.9 percent married Yankees, and 5.7 percent other ethnics. For white-collar men the proportions were 14.3 percent married Irish immigrants, 64.3 percent married second-generation Irish, and 7.1 percent married Yankees; by contrast, 25.7 percent semi- or unskilled second-generation Irishmen married Irish immigrants, 51.4 percent married fellow second-generation Irish, and 11.4 percent married Yankees: second-Generation samples: 1880 and 1900 U.S. Census Manuscript Schedules.

131. Immigrant and second-generation samples: 1880 and 1900 U.S. Census Manuscript Schedules.

132. Proportion of the second-generation Irish in each of the Irish Worcester neighborhoods in 1900: North End, 4.3 percent; Washington Square, 13.9 percent; Island, 23.1 percent; South Worcester, 8.2 percent. In 1900, 64.4 percent of the immigrant Irish household heads but 49.2 percent of the second-generation Irish

household heads and 53 percent of the immigrant boarders, but 33 percent of the second generation boarders lived in Irish Worcester. Sources: immigrant and second-generation Irish samples: 1880 and 1900 U.S. Census manuscript Schedules.

133. Of all second-generation Irish 60 percent continued to live somewhere on the east side: immigrant and second-generation samples: 1900 U.S. Census Manuscript Schedules.

134. *Atlas of Worcester, 1896,* plates 13, 14, and 15. See also the Fitch, Stark, and Girest homes. According to Weiss, "Patterns and Processes," p. 150, 32 percent of the elite homes were located in Main South or Chandler-May in 1870. In plate 3, 10 of the 17 house lots on La Grange were over 9,000 square feet. See also statistics for Ward Six, *Census of the Commonwealth of Massachusetts, 1895,* vol. 1, "Population and Social Statistics," pp. 778–79. Ward Six homes had fewer persons per room, more rooms, and more single-family homes than the city as a whole. On all these counts it approximated the West Side Wards Seven and Eight. See also Roberge, "Three Decker," pp. 16, 25, 54; Weiss, "Patterns and Processes," p. 154; Rice, ed., *Worcester of Eighteen Ninety Eight,* p. 467.

135. The Irish immigrant families that moved into Main South were also more prosperous than most of their fellows remaining back in the old districts: a disproportionate number of them were headed by skilled blue-collar workers; and more than 40 percent had three or more working members: immigrant and second-generation samples: 1900 U.S. Census Manuscript Schedules.

136. *Worcester City Directory* (Worcester: Drew Allis Co., 1882); "Mission Chronicles," vol. 5, April 28–May 12, 1895, Paulist Archives; *Messenger,* September 1887; Bishop P. T. O'Reilly to Rev. John Power, April 26, 1886, St. Paul's parish archives, Worcester; McCoy, *History of the Springfield Diocese,* pp. 274–76; *Centennial Echoes: The First 100 years of St. Peter's Parish in Worcester, Massachusetts.*

137. Weiss, "Patterns and Processes," pp. 114, 250; *Le Worcester Canadien* (Worcester: Roy, 1902), p. 208; Second-generation sample: 1900 U.S. Census Manuscript Schedules.

138. *Atlas of Worcester, 1896,* plates 17 and 22. Plate 22, for example, contained no industries at all and many farms; plate 17 was more developed but also contained no factories. On plate 17, almost all of the lots on Mendon Street were over 9,000 square feet; lower on Jefferson Street and Ingalls Street were 5,000 square feet or more. See plate 22 for the Crompton, Ballard and Heywood estates. See also *Messenger,* August 28, 1902.

139. Immigrant and second-generation samples: 1900 U.S. Census Manuscript Schedules.

140. Ibid.; *Worcester House Directory* (Worcester: Drew Allis Co., 1904), pp. 405, 313, 403, 348.

141. *Catholic Messenger,* July 14, 1911, November 17, 1916; McCoy, *History of the Springfield Diocese,* pp. 276–77; *Messenger,* May 5, 1900; O'Flynn MSS, "St. Stephen's," June 30, 1887, Holy Cross College Archives.

142. O'Flynn MSS, folio 2, p. 269, Holy Cross College Archives; McCoy, *History of the Springfield Diocese,* pp. 264–67.

143. Balk, "The Expansion of Worcester," pp. 93–94; Roberge, "The Three Decker," pp. 22–24; *The Worcester Index: A Bureau of Information Showing in Detail Official Plans of Real Estate and Maps from Latest Surveys* (Worcester: Index Publishing Co., 1901), pp. 101–21. "Montvale" on the West Side, for example, had sold only 18 of 65 lots by 1901 and Mountain View, Ingleside, and Ashmont had sold none: *The Worcester Index 1901,* pp. 101, 105, 106, 108; 1900 U.S. Census Manuscript Schedules.

144. Quotation, "eyesores," in *Worcester Sunday Telegram,* July 7, 1889; Weiss, "Patterns and Processes," p. 125; *Worcester Telegram,* December 13, 1893; *Catholic Messenger,* December 6, 1893; Powers, "Invisible Immigrants," p. 433; *Worcester Telegram,* September 27, 1923; *Catholic Messenger,* February 22, 1907, December 8, 1911, February 19, 1915, March 26, 1915, July 8, 22, 1921. In the southwest, Ward Seven, precinct two, voted 492 to 328 for school committee candidates backed by the APA and Ward Seven, precinct three, voted 661 to 245 for candidates backed by the APA. Leaders of the nativists, David O. Mears, pastor of Piedmont Congregational Church, and George Hatch, head of the Order of United American Mechanics, lived in the southwest: Nutt, *History of Worcester,* vol. 2, p. 815; *American,* April 17, 1894. In 1901, residents of South Worcester tried to block appointment of principals in the area: *Messenger,* June 8, 1901. See chapter 4 for fuller discussion.

145. Second-generation samples: 1880 and 1900 U.S. Census Manuscript Schedules; *Worcester City Directory* (Worcester: Drew Allis Co., 1900), pp. 236, 242.

146. Thompson, "Cultural Ties as Determinants of Immigrant Settlement," pp. 111, 145; "The Growth of a Worcester Neighborhood," Worcester Polytechnic Institute, Interactive Qualifying Project, 1980, p. 20, pamphlet file, Worcester Historical Museum; *Public Document no. 14: Thirty-Second Annual Report of the Railroad Commissioners* (Boston: Wright and Potter, 1901), p. 816; *Public Document no. 14: Forty-Fourth Annual Report of the Railroad Commissioners* (Boston: Wright and Potter, January 1915), p. 473; *Richard's Standard Atlas of the City of Worcester, Massachusetts* (Springfield: Richards Map Co., 1911). Plate 10 shows twenty-seven new homes in Montvale and plate 27 shows thirteen new homes in Franconia; "New Homes for Worcester," *Worcester Magazine* (May 1916), p. 105; *Fourteenth Census of the United States,* 1920, vol. 3, "Population: Composition and Characteristics of the Population by States," p. 479.

147. Quotation, "surprisingly large," in *Catholic Messenger,* August 11, 1911. *Worcester City Directory* (Worcester: Drew Allis Co., 1907), p. 472; Oral history interview with Louise McDermott Salisbury, January 1982; interview with Eleanor O'Donnell, August 24, 1989; collective biographical file of 104 first-, second- and third-generation Irishmen attending Catholic parishes from Nutt, *History of Worcester* vols. 3, 4. For Blessed Sacrament, *Richard's Atlas of Worcester,* plate 25, traced into *Worcester House Directory* (Worcester: Drew Allis Co., 1912); for Our Lady of the Angels, plate 11 traced into the *House Directory*; quotation "as fortune favors" in *Catholic Messenger,* August 11, 1911.

148. *Catholic Messenger,* August 12, 1910; Rev. William Goggin to Bishop Beaven, June 3, 1912, Blessed Sacrament file, parish files, Springfield Diocesan Archives; Powers, "Invisible Immigrants," p. 433; *Worcester Telegram,* September 27, 1923; Eleanor O'Donnell interview, August 24, 1989; Lawrence O'Connell interview, August 29, 1989; Louise Salisbury interview, January 1982.

149. *Catholic Messenger,* August 11, 1911, June 24, 1915, November 17, 1916, February 19, 1920, June 10, 17, 1926; *Worcester Telegram,* June 24, 1912, June 7, 1926; *Alumna,* December 1886, Creveling, "Cultural Geography in Worcester," p. 39; Ellen Skerret "The Catholic Dimension," in McCaffrey, ed., *The Irish in Chicago,* pp. 36–55. The church was estimated to cost $300,000 according to John F. X. Gleason, *Blessed Sacrament Church, 1912–1987,* pp. 1–7; pamphlet file, Blessed Sacrament scrapbook, Worcester Historical Museum. In 1936, the *Catholic Messenger* reported that "It is only 24 years since Father Ryan established Blessed Sacrament. There are five [Sunday] masses at Blessed Sacrament and they are usually overcrowded. Worshippers may be found kneeling behind the back pews and the choir gallery is crowded with others": *Catholic Messenger,* August 22, 1936.

150. *Catholic Messenger,* May 15, 1913. See also *Catholic Messenger,* March 22, 1907, April 15, 1910; *Messenger,* April 13, 1901; *Worcester Daily Times,* January 12, 1885.

Three. The Search for Accommodation: The 1880s and Early 1890s

1. *Messenger,* January 28, 1893.

2. Immigrant sample: 1880s U.S. Census Manuscript Schedules.

3. Nutt, *History of Worcester,* vol. 1, pp. 27–29; Thomas J. MacDonagh, "The Origins of the Parochial Schools of This City," *The Catholic Directory and History of Worcester and Suburbs* (Worcester: n.p., 1887), p. 30; Powers, "Invisible Immigrants," pp. 188–209, 273, 259–62, 274–75; O'Flynn MSS, HCC Archives, vol. 1, p. 258.

4. Powers, "Invisible Immigrants," pp. 210, 218–21, 248–50, 257–60, 275–78. An example of these good relations: Pat Doyle, reputed to be heavyweight champion boxer and Canal Company employee, lived in William Lincoln's mansion (Powers, "Invisible Immigrants," p. 231). For similar close Irish-Yankee relations in the antebellum era, see Brian Mitchell, *The Paddy Camps: The Irish of Lowell, 1821–1861* (Urbana: University of Illinois Press, 1988), pp. 34–77.

5. George Haynes, "A Chapter from the Local History of Know-Nothingism," *New England Magazine* 13, no. 1 (September 1896), p. 83; *Worcester Daily Evening Journal,* November 14, 1854; *Worcester Evening Spy,* March 2, 8, 1896. See Tyler Gregory Anbinder, *Nativism and Slavery: The Northern Know Nothings and the Politics of the 1850s* (New York: Oxford University Press, 1992).

6. The Free Soil party collapsed between 1853 and 1854 in Worcester. Though all parties lost voters to the new party, the Free Soilers seemed to lose the most. The Free Soil vote for governor, for example, fell from 1,296 votes to 234. See *Worcester Daily*

Evening Journal, November 14, 1854; *Worcester Transcript,* November 19, 1853. *Worcester Daily Evening Journal,* January 3, 1855, March 26, 1855. On occupational analysis of the Know-Nothing lodge, see Haynes, "A Chapter," p. 87, table 5 on p. 96. Quotations in *Worcester Daily Evening Journal,* February 7, 1855, April 13, 16, 1855.

7. For Plunkett and O'Neil's story and quote, see A. P. Marvin, *History of Worcester in the War of the Rebellion* (Worcester: privately published, 1870), pp. 160, 234, 506–9; for enlistments and casualties, see Powers "Invisible Immigrants," pp. 442–44, and on the home front see Buel, "Workers of Worcester," pp. 77–78.

8. Robert H. Lord, John E. Sexton, and Edward T. Harrington, *A History of the Archdiocese of Boston* (New York: Sheed and Ward, 1944), vol. 2, pp. 602–7.

9. *Celebration of the 200th anniversary of the Naming of Worcester, October 14 and 15, 1884* (Worcester, 1885), pp. 68–75; *Dedication of the Soldiers Monument at Worcester, July 15, 1874* (Worcester, 1875), pp. 16–17; Nutt, *History of Worcester* vol. 2, pp. 645, 674. Richard O'Flynn to George Frisbie Hoar, October 16, 1884, and John J. Riordan to George Frisbie Hoar, October 17, 1884, Hoar Papers, Massachusetts Historical Society. See Gerald F. Linderman, *Embattled Courage: The Experience of Combat in the American Civil War* (New York: The Free Press, 1987), pp. 266–97 for discussion of memories of the war.

10. Rev. A. Z. Conrad, "Protestant Churches," and Nathaniel Paine, "Literary, Scientific and Historical Societies," in Rice, ed., *The Worcester of Eighteen Hundred and Ninety Eight,* pp. 289–91 and 221–35; U.S. Census Office, *Report on Statistics of Churches in the United States at the Eleventh Census: 1890s* (Washington, D.C.: G.P.O., 1894), p. 112; Nutt, *History of Worcester,* vol. 2, pp. 782–96; R. M Washburn, *Smith's Barn: A Child's History of the West Side of Worcester* (Worcester: Commonwealth Press, 1923), pp. 13–14; Stephen Salisbury, box 67, volume 8, February 20, 21, 22, 24, March 8, 14, 1886, Salisbury Papers, American Antiquarian Society; Arthur Prentice Rugg Papers, box 63, diary, "Through England and Ireland," Massachusetts Historical Society; William A. Koelsch, *Clark University, 1887–1987: A Narrative History* (Worcester: Clark University Press, 1987), pp. 1–42. For changes in native-stock Protestant society in another city, see Frank Couvares, *The Remaking of Pittsburgh: Class and Culture in an Industrializing City, 1877–1919* (Albany: The State University of New York Press, 1984), pp. 31–50, 96–126. For a general discussion of changing culture of Protestant society, see T. Jackson Lears, *No Place of Grace: Antimodernism and the Transformation of American Culture, 1880s to 1920* (Pantheon: New York, 1981).

11. Nutt, *History of Worcester,* vol. 2, pp. 793–95, 1119–23; Nutting, "Worcester Learns to Play," p. 12; *Light,* May 10, August 2, 30, September 6, 1890; *At the End of Fifty Years: The Worcester Club* (Worcester: privately published, 1938); Salisbury Family Papers, box 67, volume 8, diary, March 8, 14, 1886; Worcester Club clippings, club file, Worcester Historical Museum; Washburn, *Smith's Barn,* p. 109.

12. Worcester Club clippings, club file, Worcester Historical Museum; Washburn, *Smith's Barn,* p. 109; William Koelsch, *Clark University, 1887–1987* (Worcester: Clark University Press, 1987), pp. 32–34; *Worcester Methodist* 1, no. 1 (April 1888), p. 4. Higgins in Charles Cheape, *Family Firm to Modern Multinational: Norton Company, A New England Enterprise* (Cambridge, Mass.: Harvard University Press, 1985), pp. 6–8, and

Olive Higgins Prouty, *Pencil Shavings*, pp. 19–20; *Worcester Methodist* 1, no. 1 (April 1888), p. 4, vol. 1, no. 8 (November 1888), p. 5. See Robert Snyder, *Voice of the City* (New York: Oxford University Press, 1990), pp. 129–54.

13. Conrad on churches in Rice, ed., *Worcester of Eighteen Ninety Eight*, pp. 289–91, 652; U.S. Census Office, *Report on Churches*, p. 112; William Woodward, *Historical Sketch of Piedmont Congregational Church* (Worcester: Piedmont Church, 1922); Dr. David Otis Mears, *An Autobiography* (Boston: Pilgrim Press, 1920), pp. 106–12.

14. As many members of the elite were Unitarians or Episcopalians as Congregationalists in 1905, based on biographical information on 82 of 172 members of the Worcester Club traced into Nutt's *History of Worcester*, vols. 3 and 4. *Manual of the Piedmont Congregational Church of Worcester, Massachusetts, 1883* (Massachusetts State Library), traced into *Worcester City Directories*.

15. *Census of the Commonwealth of Massachusetts, 1875*, vol. 3, "Population and Social Statistics" (Boston: Wright and Potter, 1879), pp. 144, 283. Native stock sample: 1900 U.S. Census Schedules. Statistics based on 432 heads of households drawn from census samples, one in every twenty native-born of native parents over age eighteen, 1900 United States Census. *Census of the Commonwealth of Massachusetts, 1885*, vol. 1, "Population and Social Statistics" (Boston: Wright and Potter, 1889), p. 445. On rural migration and rural society in New England, see Hal S. Barron *Those Who Stayed Behind: Rural Society in Nineteenth Century New England* (New York: Cambridge University Press, 1984).

16. Clippings, June 19, 1881, January 17, 1884, clipping file, Worcester Historical Museum; *Worcester Daily Spy*, February 19, 1876; *Worcester Evening Gazette*, February 19, 1876; *Worcester Daily Times*, January 27, 1882; Poem, no date, Sons and Daughters of Vermont, Third Annual Reunion of the Sons and Daughters of Vermont, February 18, 1876, Seventh Annual Reunion of Sons and Daughters of Vermont, January 20, 1880, Nineteenth Annual Reunion of the Sons and Daughters of Vermont, January 15, 1889, pamphlet file, WHM.

17. *Worcester Daily Spy*, February 19, 1876; Poem, no date, Sons and Daughters of Vermont; *Light*, September 6, 1890, November 8, 1890.

18. *Annual Report of the Banking Commissioners, 1890s: Public Document no. 5* (Boston: Wright and Potter, 1891), pp. 442, 632–41; *Annual Report of the Commissioner of Savings Banks, 1873: Public Document no. 5* (Boston: Wright and Potter, 1874), pp. 138–39; for discussions of elites in politics and definitions of class interest, see Michael H. Frisch *Town into City: Springfield, Massachusetts and the Meaning of Community, 1840–1880s* (Cambridge: Harvard University Press, 1972), pp. 117–250; David C. Hammack, *Power and Society: Greater New York at the Turn of the Century* (New York: Columbia University Press, 1987), pp. 130–91; Steven P. Erie, *Rainbow's End: Irish Americans and the Dilemmas of Urban Machine Politics, 1840–1985* (Berkeley: University of California Press, 1988), pp. 45–66; Terrence J. McDonald, *The Parameters of Urban Fiscal Policy: Socioeconomic Change and Political Culture in San Francisco, 1860–1906* (Berkeley: University of California Press, 1986).

19. Rice, ed., *Worcester of 1898*, pp. 406–10.

20. The Bureau reported a strike of 1,875 workers in Lowell in 1885, in New Bedford of 800 workers in 1881 and 812 in 1884, and a citywide Lawrence strike in 1882 when 5,255 men and women quit 150 factories for five months: Commissioner of Labor, *Third Annual Report, 1887* (Washington, D.C.: GPO, 1888), pp. 228–54; *Tenth Annual Report, 1906* (Washington, D.C.: GPO, 1907), pp. 364–414; *Worcester Daily Times*, April 3, 1882, April 10, 1882, October 7, 1882; *Eighteenth Annual Report of the Massachusetts Bureau of Labor Statistics: Public Document no. 15* (Boston: Wright and Potter, December 1887), pp. 151, 215; Jonathan Garlock, *Guide to the Local Assemblies of the Knights of Labor* (Westport: Greenwood Press, 1982), pp. 184–85; 189–91; 206–7.

21. New Bedford, another city much smaller than Worcester, had over 360 Knights that same year, and Lynn had twenty-six councils with hundreds of members: Garlock, *Guide to the Local Assemblies*, pp. 184–85, 189–91, 206–7. *Worcester Daily Times*, June 30, 1885, quoted in Rosenzweig, *Eight Hours for What We Will*, p. 21; *Worcester Telegram*, January 11, 25, 27, 28, 29, 31, February 4, 5, 7, 9, 10, 16, 18, 19, 1887. Maguire quoted in Rosenzweig, *Eight Hours for What We Will*, p. 20.

22. Rosenzweig, *Eight Hours for What We Will*, pp. 86–87; *Manual of the Piedmont Congregational Church, 1883*, Massachusetts State Library; Petition for Samuel Hildreth, Republican candidate for mayor: *Worcester Daily Spy*, December 3, 1882. Of a sample of one in six names from the petition, 16 percent were machinists and 35.4 percent were blue-collar workers.

23. One in six of signers of the petition for Hildreth listed in the *Worcester Daily Spy*, December 3, 1883. Ward Seven had the highest average vote for the Republicans in city campaigns of all the wards in the city: 67 percent of the two-party vote in 1883–84. The strongest precincts for the Republicans in 1883–84 were clustered in the southwest, Chandler May, and Main South districts: 69 percent in Ward Eight, precinct two; 65 percent in Ward Seven, precinct two; 66 percent in Ward Six, precinct one. Moreover, over one-third of the signers of the Hildreth petition in 1883 lived in the Main South or Chandler May neighborhoods and a little less than one-third worked there. Manufacturers signing the petition included Philip L. Moen, Philip W. Moen, C. H. Hutchins, George F. Hutchins, L. J. Knowles, F. B. Knowles, Calvin Colvin, Loring Coes, C. C. Houghton, V. F. and A. F. Prentice, George S. Barton, David Manning, E. P. Curtis, Samuel Winslow, and H. C. Graton: Hildreth petition, *Worcester Daily Spy*, December 3, 1883. Robert Kolesar in his dissertation, "Politics and Policy," has examined this era in Worcester city politics in great detail and was the first to point out the conflict between Yankee factions over city improvements. He suggests a more straightforward conflict between middle-class Yankee loyalists and Yankee elite independents, but I believe the elite itself was divided, manufacturers wavering between the two factions as I have noted here. Roy Rosenzweig has found strong support among manufacturers for temperance in this era: *Eight Hours For What We Will*, pp. 93–126. For a broad discussion of successful cross-party alliances and third parties in the "Party Period" of the late nineteenth century, see Ronald P. Formisano, "The 'Party Period' Revisited," and Mark Voss-Hubbard, "The 'Third

Party Tradition' Reconsidered: Third Parties and American Public Life, 1830–1900," in "Round Table: Alternatives to the Party System in the 'Party Period, 1830–1890,'" *Journal of American History* 86, no. 1 (June 1999), pp. 93–150. I first wrote about such alliances in Worcester in 1985: Meagher, "Irish All the Time," and "What Care We for a Walk in the Mud."

24. Petition for Stoddard in *Worcester Daily Spy,* December 7, 1883. In 1883–84, Citizens' candidates for mayor ran 119 votes ahead of the Democratic-Peoples party turnout in Ward One, precinct one, on the northwest side; 120 votes ahead in Ward Two, precinct two, in the small elite district just north of Belmont Street (Senator Hoar's home district), and 145 votes ahead in Ward Eight, precinct one, the heart of the elite district on the west side. Conversely they ran less than 40 votes ahead in Ward Six and Seven precincts in the southern part of the city.

25. *Worcester Daily Times,* November 24, 1879, November 30, 1881, September 2, 1882, November 2, 1883; The state census revealed that 2,800 Irish immigrants had become naturalized and registered by 1885: *Massachusetts Bureau of Labor Statistics,* vol. 19, p. 187. There were 14,843 legal voters in the city that year. Given the youth of the second-generation Irish in the 1880s, they probably added no more than a few thousand to those immigrant numbers, second-generation samples, 1880s, U.S. Census. On French Canadians see *Worcester Daily Times,* November 9, 1882, October 25, 1883. The state census found only 284 French Canadians naturalized in Worcester in 1885: *Massachusetts Bureau of Labor Statistics,* vol. 19, p. 187. On French Canadian voting loyalties, see Ronald A. Petrin, *French Canadians in Massachusetts Politics, 1885–1915: Ethnicity and Political Pragmatism* (Philadelphia: Balch Institute Press, 1990), pp. 36, 73, 92–93.

26. Kolesar, "Politics and Policy," pp. 58–69; *Worcester Evening Gazette,* November 29, 1876, November 30, 1877, December 3, 7, 1877; *Worcester Daily Spy,* December 12, 1876; *Worcester Daily Times,* October 17, 1883, November 14, 1883; Nutt, *History of Worcester,* vol. 1, pp. 396–98.

27. The Irish vote became more important in 1883 and 1884 than it had been earlier, as the Yankee Citizens' vote declined in the Republican southern wards and precincts from 50 percent between 1878 and 1882 to 36 percent in 1883 and 1884. In 1883 and 1884 the vote in the three Democratic wards averaged 74.6 percent.

28. Kolesar, *Urban Politics,* pp. 128–46. See also Robert Kolesar, "The Politics of Development: Worcester Massachusetts in the Late Nineteenth Century," *Journal of Urban History* 16, no. 1 (November 1989), pp. 4–12.

29. Richard O'Flynn papers, vol. 1, p. 171; *Worcester Daily Spy,* November 26, 1884. Kolesar, *Urban Politics,* pp. 118–46.

30. O'Flynn MSS, vol. 1, p. 233, HCC Archives; *Worcester Daily Times,* December 5, 1883, December 22, 1882, November 20, 1882; *Worcester Telegram,* December 25, 1887, June 24, 1888; Kolesar, *Urban Politics,* pp. 118–46.

31. Paul Kleppner, *The Third Electoral System, 1853 to 1892* (Chapel Hill: University of North Carolina Press, 1979), pp. 348–52; 198–297; Samuel McSeveney, *The Politics*

of Depression in the Northeast, 1893–1896 (New York: Oxford University Press, 1972), pp. 10–26; Kolesar, "Politics and Policy," pp. 69–70; Geoffrey Blodgett, "Yankee Leadership in a Divided City," in Ronald Formisano and Constance Burns, eds., *Boston, 1700–1980: The Evolution of Urban Politics* (Westport: Greenwood Press, 1984), 87–110.

32. Kolesar, *Urban Politics*, pp. 155–82; Rosenzweig, *Eight Hours for What We Will*, pp. 40–43, 93–103; *Worcester Daily Times*, September 15, 1882; *Worcester Daily Spy*, December 6, 8, 9, 1882, December 4, 1884, November 26, 1885.

33. *Worcester Daily Times*, November 24, 1879, October 19, 1883, November 21, 30, 1881, December 5, 1881, November 21, 1883, December 8, 1882, December 11, 1882; *Worcester Evening Spy*, November 3, 1882; *Worcester Evening Gazette*, October 13, 1876, September 17, 1878, November 5, 1879; *Worcester Daily Times*, January 18, November 27, 1883, July 22, September 12, 25, 30, 1884.

34. Restlessness about control by the liquor interests among Democrats extended back to the early 1880s: *Worcester Daily Times*, December 11, 1882, May 22, 1882, December 22, 1882, January 9, 1883; *Worcester Daily Spy*, December 9, 11, 14, 1885. The vote for license fell by 125 votes in Ward Three, 108 votes in Ward Four, and 221 in Ward Five, while no-license votes rose by 139, 89, and 176 votes, respectively, in the three wards: *Worcester Daily Spy*, December 14, 1885.

35. Kolesar, *Urban Politics*, pp. 157–92. The Republicans had a severe caucus fight that may have scared Winslow into being more amenable. Winslow in his inaugural address in 1888 claimed, "Fortunately the welfare of our school system is not entrusted to any party, creed or set of men. In our schools supported by all, irrespective of nationality or faith, our future citizens are being trained in sentiments of mutual forbearance and respect. During my two years of service I have been pleased to note the singular absence of friction, both in the meetings of the committee and the schools themselves." *City Document no. 42*, p. 312. In 1890 a special committee of the school board reported that 40 of 157 teachers appointed in the previous five years were Irish Catholics. In the late 1880s and 1890s the Citizens' tickets were revived but unsuccessful. In the most hotly contested of those elections in 1889, it is important to note, the Republicans made strong and somewhat successful appeals to Irish Democrats.

36. *Messenger*, January 11, 1890, February 1, 1890, November 7, 1891, November 21, 1891, March 29, 1892, July 25, 1891, March 11, 1893. Quotations from October 8, 1892, and November 26, 1892.

37. The length of tenure for Worcester's pastors were as follows: John J. Power, 1866–1902; John J. Griffin, 1870–1910; D. H. O'Neill, 1885–1916; R. S. J. Burke 1887–1896; Thomas J. Conaty, 1878–1896; Robert Walsh, 1872–1908; Dennis Scannell, 1870–1899. For discussions of priests' power in the hierarchy, see Robert E. Sullivan, "Beneficial Relations: Towards A Social History of the Diocesan Priests of Boston, 1875–1944," in Robert E. Sullivan and James M. O'Toole, eds., *Catholic Boston: Studies in Religion and Community* (Boston: Archdiocese of Boston, 1985), pp. 201–38; and for general discussions of the priesthood in the United States, John Tracy Ellis, *The Catholic Priest in the United States: Historical Investigations* (Collegeville: St. John's University Press,

1971), and Leslie Woodcock Tentler, *Seasons of Grace: A History of the Catholic Arch-diocese of Detroit* (Detroit: Wayne State University Press, 1990), pp. 34–55, 137–65.

38. Donna Merwick, *Boston Priests 1848–1910: A Study of Social and Intellectual Change* (Cambridge: Harvard University Press, 1973); Sullivan, "Beneficial Relations," Sullivan and O'Toole, eds., *Catholic Boston*, pp. 201–38; Thomas H. O'Connor, *Fitzpatrick's Boston, 1846–1866: John Bernard Fitzpatrick, Third Bishop of Boston* (Boston: Northeastern University Press, 1984); 1880 U.S. Census Manuscript Schedules; *Sacred Heart Review*, November 14, 1896; curriculum vitae of pastors in the Springfield Diocesan Archives prepared by Monsignor Roger Vian and sent to the author, October 12, 1976.

39. O'Flynn MSS, Records of the United Irish Societies, vol. 3, November 24, 1867, March 10, 1871, HCC Archives; McCoy, *History of the Springfield Diocese*, pp. 261–62; *Messenger*, November 7, 1891, March 19, 1892, April 20, 1895; *Worcester Telegram*, February 22, 25, 1891; Parish announcement book, January 19, 1890, St. John's parish archives; "Mission Chronicles" vol. 3, January 6–13, 1884, February 19, 1888, May 19–June 2, 1989; vol. 4, April 5–19, Paulist Archives, Washington D.C. On Liberalism there is a voluminous literature. For recent discussions, see Jay P. Dolan, "The Search for an American Catholicism," *Catholic Historical Review* 82, no. 2 (April 1996), pp. 169–86; and an entire issue of the *U.S. Catholic Historian*, "The Americanist Controversy: Recent Historical and Theological Perspectives," *U.S. Catholic Historical Society* 11, no. 3 (Summer 1993). In the latter, see especially Philip Gleason, "The New Americanism in Catholic Historiography," pp. 1–18.

40. McCoy, *History of the Springfield Diocese*, pp. 263, 271, 275–77; *Messenger*, August 15, 1903; *St. Peter's Parish, Seventy-Fifth Anniversary Jubilee Memorial*, St. Peter's parish archives; O'Flynn MSS, folio 14, clipping, February 21, 1891, HCC Archives; *Catholic Messenger*, December 16, 1910. The *Boston Herald*, quoted in the *Messenger*, June 30, 1905; McCoy, *History of the Springfield Diocese*, p. 258; Diocesan Reports, 1905–10, St. John's parish archives.

41. McCoy, *History of the Springfield Diocese*, p. 261; McGratty, *The Life of the Very Rev. John J. Power D.D.*, pp. 10, 21–27, 69, 52–53, 264.

42. McGratty, *The Life of Power*, pp. 10, 11, 17, 21–26, 72, 141; Merwick, *Boston Priests*; O'Connor, *Fitzpatrick's Boston*.

43. Nutt, *History of Worcester*, vol. 2, pp. 869–71; McCoy MSS, sermon, August 15, 1880, Holy Cross College Archives. On schools, see *Messenger*, July 14, 29, 1888, McCoy MSS, sermon, Notre Dame, November 12, 1899, Holy Cross College Archives, and McCoy, *History of the Springfield Diocese*, pp. 27, 272–73. Conaty led the counterattack on schools against Rev. David O. Mears: *Messenger*, February 11, July 28, August 11, 25, 1888. On McCoy's ambition, see Monsignor John F. Reilly, "Memories of Beloved Worcester Priests," typewritten MSS of speech delivered at the Catholic Women's Club, March 6, 1955, Worcester Public Library; O'Flynn MSS, Sacred Heart folio, September 21, 1884, Holy Cross College Archives; Robert Cross, *The Emergence of Liberal Catholicism in America* (Cambridge: Harvard University Press, 1967) p. 126.

44. The number of families with three or more working members rose by 80 percent between the 1880s and 1900: Immigrant and second-generation samples; 1880 and 1900 U.S. Census Manuscript Schedules; Larkin, "The Devotional Revolution," pp. 626–27.

45. McGratty, *Life of Power,* p. 13; *The Second Annual Report of St. Vincent's Hospital,* AAS.

46. *Catholic Free Press,* September 24, 1959; O'Flynn MSS, folio 1, clippings, November 7, 10, 17, 1890, Holy Cross College Archives; *City Document no. 46,* pp. 466–70; Rice, ed., *Worcester of 1898,* p. 241; O'Flynn MSS, "St. Stephen's" folio, January 30, 1887, Holy Cross College Archives; Mother Mary of Providence, "History of the Community," typewritten MSS, vol. 1, pp. 158, 160–69; Mission Annals of the Sisters of Providence, Worcester, "An Account of the Founding of St. Vincent's Hospital," Sisters of Providence Archives, Holyoke, Massachusetts; Mother Mary of Providence, "History of the Community," typewritten MSS, vol. 1, pp. 160–61. White-collar Irish donors gave $1,335 and priests $1,200 to the project in 1894: *First Annual Report of the Sisters of Providence Hospital for the Year Ending December 31, 1894* traced into the *Worcester City Directory* (Worcester: Drew-Allis, 1895); *Sixth Annual Report of St. Vincent's Hospital for the Year Ending, December 31, 1899.* Trustees traced into the clipping files of the American Antiquarian Society and Worcester Historical Museum and biographical sections of Nutt, *History of Worcester* vols. 3, 4; Rice, ed., *Worcester of 1898;* Nelson, *History of Worcester County,* vol. 3, and 1900 U.S. Census Manuscript Schedules.

47. *Messenger,* September 23, 1893, June 9, 1894; *Worcester Evening Spy,* September 10, 1895; *Catholic Messenger,* April 12, 1904; "Appeal for Funds" clippings, November 1919, Sisters of Providence Archives; *First Annual Report of the Sisters of Providence Hospital; Fifth Annual Report of St. Vincent's Hospital for the Year Ending December 31, 1898.* Mother Mary, "History of the Community," pp. 169–78; On the need for a new hospital, see "Report to Mayor Rufus Dodge by the Trustees of City Hospital, November 30, 1900," T. Hovey Gage Papers, AAS; *City Document no. 74,* p. 505; *City Document no. 44,* pp. 275–76.

48. *Messenger,* June 9, 1894; *Worcester Evening Spy,* September 10, 1895.

49. Thomas McAvoy, *A History of the Catholic Church in the United States* (Notre Dame: University of Notre Dame Press, 1969), p. 260; For the building of schools in other dioceses, see Dennis Clark, *The Irish in Philadelphia: Ten Generations of Urban Experience* (Temple University Press, 1974), pp. 94–95; James W. Sanders, *The Education of an Urban Minority, 1933–1965* (New York: Oxford University Press, 1977), p. 4; Robert E. Curran, S.J., *Michael Augustine Corrigan and the Shaping of Conservative Catholicism in America, 1878–1902* (New York: Arno Press, 1978), pp. 507–8. In the 1890s only four of the largest twenty dioceses had built fewer schools than the Boston archdiocese, and only one—the diocese of Santa Fe—had constructed fewer schools than Worcester's diocese, the diocese of Springfield. By 1905 the two dioceses still lagged far behind: Boston, 13th, and Springfield, 17th of 19. See the *Messenger,* January 11, 1890; *Official Catholic Directory, Almanac and Clergy List* 19 (1905), p. 965, and

James W. Sanders, "Catholics and the School Question: The Cardinal O'Connell Years," in James M. O'Toole and Robert Sullivan, eds., *Catholic Boston*, pp. 121–69. There were 1,100 children in St. John's school in 1884 and 3,700 first- and second-generation Irish in public schools that year: *City Documents no. 59*, p. 98.

50. Mary J. Oates, "The Professional Preparation of Parochial School Teachers, 1870s-1940," *Historical Journal of Massachusetts* 12, no. 1 (January 1984), pp. 60–61; McCoy, *History of the Springfield Diocese*, pp. 13–18; Annals of the Sisters of Mercy, p. 31, Sisters of Mercy Archives, Worcester, Mass.; Sister Miriam of the Infant Jesus, *The Finger of God: History of the Massachusetts Province of Notre Dame de Namur, 1849–1963* (Boston: Mission Church Press, n.d.), p. 32; Brother Julian, CFX, *Deeds of the Xaverian Brothers in America* (New York: Macmillan), pp. 1–15; 1900 U.S. Census Manuscript Schedules.

51. McGratty, *Life of Power*, pp. 82, 104, 34–36, 72–82; *Messenger*, May, 1887, February 11, July 28, August 25, 1888; O'Flynn MSS, Sacred Heart folio, February 4, 1889, September 12, 1887, HCC Archives: *Sacred Heart Monthly Calendar*, May 1891.

52. *Alumna* (January 1987), p. 3; *Alumna* (May 1886), p. 2; *Alumna* (June 1886), p. 3; *Alumna* (September 1886), p. 2; *Messenger*, November 21, 1891, August 3, 1894; O'Flynn MSS, vol. 1, p. 467, HCC Archives.

53. *Messenger*, March 22, 1890, November 21, 1891, May 13, June 16, 1892; *Alumna* (May 1886), p. 2; O'Flynn MSS, convention records, vol. 2, HCC Archives.

54. Kolesar, *Urban Politics*, pp. 192–219. Marble's policies included disciplining principals or teachers who appeared to favor Protestant students, sensitivity to Bible reading in the public schools, and hiring Catholic teachers. Littleton diaries, March 15, 1890, AAS; *Alumna* (May 1886), p. 4; See also *City Document no. 41*, pp. 342–43; *City Document no. 23*, p. 73.

55. *Messenger*, March 19, 1892, November 7, 1891, April 20, 1895, January 13, 1900, April 21, 1900; announcement book, 1889–95, January 19, 1890, St. John's parish archives. On McGlynn's speech, see *Worcester Telegram*, February 22, 25, 1891.

56. *Messenger*, August 3, 1895, March 22, 1890: October 8, 1892, March 11, 1893, November 26, 1892.

57. L. M. Cullen, *Six Generations of Life in Ireland*, p. 22; Carleton, *Tales and Stories of the Irish Peasantry*, p. 449; T. Crofton Croker, *Researches in the South of Ireland* (New York: Barnes and Noble, 1969; first published in 1924), p. 228; H. R. Augustine, *In the Footprints of Father Mathew* (Dublin: Gill and Son, 1947), p. 567; Connell, *Irish Peasant Society*, p. 47; Egan, *Parish of Ballinasloe*, pp. 274–75; Elizabeth Malcolm, *"Ireland Sober, Ireland Free": Drink and Temperance in Nineteenth-Century Ireland* (Syracuse: Syracuse University Press, 1986); Richard Stivers, *A Hair of the Dog: Irish Drinking and American Stereotype* (University Park: Pennsylvania State University Press, 1976).

58. *Messenger*, June 17, 1904; O'Flynn MSS, societies, HCC Archives; "Fiftieth Anniversary of Rev. Theobald Mathew Total Abstinence Society, Father Mathew Hall, November 15, 1899" (Worcester, Mass.: Harrigan Brothers, 1899); St. John's parish announcements, March 9, 1879, St. John's parish archives.

59. St. John's parish announcement books, April 28, 1878, St. John's parish archives; Richard O'Flynn MSS, folio 2, p. 286, St. John's parish archives. The Father Mathew Society, as we shall see, played a critical role in the organization of the St. Patrick's Day parades: O'Flynn MSS, folio 1, p. 534, HCC Archives; *Messenger*, June 24, 1904.

60. *Messenger*, May 12, July 7, 1888; *Catholic Messenger*, April 20, 1916.

61. "Harvest Festival Souvenir, St. Stephen's Parish, May 1900," St. Stephen's parish archives; O'Flynn MSS, folio 1, Program, Coffee Party, St. Anne's T. A. Society and St. Anne's Guards, HCC Archives; St. Paul's Temperance and Literary Lyceum, Tenth Anniversary Harvest Festival Program, November 22, 1899; Littleton diaries, vol. 1, December 11, 1889, AAS; O'Flynn MSS, St. John's Cadets, folio 6, HCC archives; *Worcester Telegram*, April 19, 1887; Records of St. John's Temperance and Literary Guild, vol. 1, December 2, 1883, March 6, 1887, February 6, 1887, March 4, 1888, January 22, 1888, May 6, 1888, vol. 2, October 18, 1896.

62. For other priests, see George McAleer, "Very Reverend John J. Power, D.D. V.G.," *Worcester Magazine* (April 1902), p. 2; diary, Monsignor Griffin, March 1, 1876, September 29, 1878; *Worcester Daily Times*, April 20, 1888; *Catholic Messenger*, April 3, 1908, October 22, 1909. Rev. Daniel F. McGillicuddy served as president of the national Catholic Total Abstinence Union. On Conaty and McCoy, see *Catholic Messenger*, October 28, 1910; McCoy MSS, "Temperance," sermon file, no date, HCC Archives; *Worcester Daily Times*, April 20, 1885; *Sacred Heart Monthly Calendar*, March 1891.

63. St. John's parish announcements, March 9, 1879, St. John's parish Archives; St. John's Temperance and Literary Guild, records, vol. 1, January 11, 1885; T. J. Conaty, "Temperance Idea in Public Instruction," *Catholic School and Home Magazine* (March 1895), p. 8; Rev. James Cleary, "Silver Jubilee of the CTAU of America," *Catholic School and Home Magazine* (September 1895), p. 170.

64. *Worcester Evening Journal*, November 11, 1854, October 28, 1854; *Worcester Telegram*, March 2, 1888, May 19, 1890, November 14, 1893; *American*, August 8, 1893; *Worcester Daily Spy*, December 15, 1884, November 24, 1882, November 27, 1882, November 28, 1882, December 5, 1882; O'Flynn MSS, folio 21, May 1896, HCC Archives.

65. Littleton diaries, vol. 2, December 11, 1889, American Antiquarian Society; T. J. Conaty, "Father Mathew," *Catholic School and Home Magazine*, October 1896, p. 164; O'Flynn MSS, convention records, vol. 2, clipping, March 17, 1887, HCC Archives; *Worcester Daily Times*, April 20, 1885; Cleary, "Silver Jubilee of the CTAU of America," p. 170.

66. T. J. Conaty, "Temperance Idea in Public Instruction," *Catholic School and Home Magazine* (March 1895), p. 8; Cleary, "Silver Jubilee of the CTAU of America," p. 170.

67. *Messenger*, February 3, 1900; O'Flynn MSS, folio 1, St. Anne's T.A. Society, HCC Archives; St. John's Temperance and Literary Guild Records, volume 1, January 3, 1887, March 6, 1887, March 28, 1887, October 18, 1887, St. John's parish archives; *St. Aloysius Echo*, March 17, 1887.

68. O'Flynn MSS, folio 1, St. Anne's T.A. Society, HCC Archives; *St. Aloysius Echo*, vol. 1. no. 1, March 17, 1888; St. John's Temperance and Literary Guild, records, vol. 1,

March 2, 1884, July 4, 1886, December 13, 1888, March 16, 1887, May 8, 1887, vol. 2, June 27, 1897, St. John's parish archives; *Messenger,* October 28, 1893, February 16, 1906.

69. St. John's Temperance and Literary Guild, records, vol. 1, April 4, 1886; *Messenger,* July 29, 1893; *Worcester Daily Times,* February 26, 1886; *Worcester Daily Spy,* April 4, 1887, August 29, 1895, September 3, 1895; *Worcester Telegram,* August 15, 1887, December 2, 1893; *Worcester Post,* July 31, 1926; *Alumna* (May 1886), p. 2; The St. John's Temperance and Literary Guild, records, vol. 1, September 5, 24, 1886; February 6, 1887, February 8, 1885; "Souvenir of the United Catholic Total Abstinence Societies Coffee Party, January 15, 1896," AAS. In 1898, the *Messenger* reported that local Protestant churches had banned bowling and billiards at Worcester's YMCA: *Messenger,* June 18, 1898; Rosenzweig, *Eight Hours for What We Will,* pp. 106–7. For Catholic embrace of sports, see Tentler, *Seasons of Grace,* p. 150.

70. O'Flynn MSS, convention records, vol. 2, clipping, March 18, 1886, HCC Archives.

71. Of the 33 temperance delegates to the United Irish Societies Conventions between 1884 and 1895, 26, or 79 percent, were American-born of Irish parents: O'Flynn MSS, records of the convention, vols. 2, 3, HCC Archives. Roy Rosenzweig found that two-thirds of the members of the St. John's Temperance and Literary Guild whom he traced into the 1880s census manuscript schedules were American-born: Rosenzweig, *Eight Hours for What We Will,* p. 259. Of 44 members of the St. John's Temperance and Literary Guild from 1897 to 1898 traced into the 1900 census, 39 (88 percent) were second-generation Irish. For characterizations of the temperance men as American-born, see O'Flynn MSS, records of the convention, vol. 2, pp. 78, 133, 148, 103, 169; vol. 3, pp. 201–4, HCC Archives. For the Father Mathew members, see Rosenzweig, *Eight Hours for What We Will,* p. 108. Of the 13 Father Mathew delegates who could be traced into the census manuscript schedules, 10, or 77 percent, had been born in Ireland: O'Flynn MSS, convention records, vols. 2, 3, HCC Archives. In 1906, of 19 women in the CYWL listed in the *Messenger,* 8, or 42.0 percent, were teachers and 3 more, 15.7 percent, were bookkeepers or clerks: *Messenger,* February 16, 1906.

72. *Constitution and By-laws of the St. Peter's Mutual Advancement Society* (Messenger, 1893), AAS; *Messenger,* May 25, November 2, 16, 1895, April 11, 1896, May 23, 1896. For the women's Lady Fullerton Society, see *Messenger,* May 30, 1896.

73. *Worcester Daily Times,* January 1, 14, 1886; *Worcester Daily Spy,* March 15, 1886, December 22, 1885, April 17, 1887; *Worcester Sunday Telegram,* May 2, 1886; O'Flynn MSS, "Societies" folio, clipping, March 5, 1887, HCC Archives; *Worcester Telegram,* April 23, 1961; *Worcester Sunday Telegram,* January 3, 1886; O'Flynn MSS, folio 1, clipping, October 26, 1892, HCC Archives; *Worcester Telegram,* April 23, 1961; John J. Riordan, "A Prosperous Club," *Donahoe's Magazine* (December 1897), pp. 140–42; *Messenger,* February 23, 1895; *Worcester Daily Times,* March 31, 1882, January 20, 1887, November 27, 1884; *Worcester Evening Spy,* April 12, 1887.

74. *Worcester Daily Spy,* January 6, 1886, July 15, 1886; *Messenger,* February 27, 1892, October 12, 1895.

75. Carrolltons listed in the *Worcester Daily Spy,* May 2, 1886, and Washingtons in the *Worcester Sunday Telegram,* January 3, 1886. See also *Messenger,* February 23, 1895.

76. *Worcester Telegram,* November 2, 1895.

77. Of the 216 AOH delegates in that period, 59 or 27.1 percent were white-collar workers, 49 or 22.1 percent were semiskilled or unskilled: O'Flynn MSS, convention records, vols. 2, 3, traced into *Worcester City Directories.* On the AOH's commitment to ethnocentrism, see the next chapter.

78. On the history of the AOH see *Dedication Souvenir of AOH Hall, 1901,* pp. 30–33, Worcester Historical Museum. The AOH mustered out 290 men for the St. Patrick's Day parade in 1884, 234 men for the parade in 1889, 253 men in 1890 and 235 men in 1891: *Worcester Daily Spy,* March 18, 1884, March 18, 1890, March 18, 1891; O'Flynn MSS, records of the convention, vol. 2, clipping, March 18, 1889, HCC Archives.

79. John O'Dea, *History of the AOH and Its Ladies Auxiliary* (New York: National Board of the A.O.H., 1923) pp. 1062–1100; Rev. John J. Power to Father Cuddihy, July 2, 1878, St. Paul parish archives; McGratty, *Life of Power,* pp. 90–92.

80. O'Flynn MSS, folio 1, Rumsellers, HCC Archives. *Messenger,* August 23, 1902; Rosenzweig, *Eight Hours for What We Will,* pp. 74–81.

81. Powers, "Invisible Immigrants," pp. 247–52, 301–14, 331–32, 341–49, 360–63; *Messenger,* June 24, 1904; O'Flynn MSS, folio 1, p. 534, HCC Archives.

82. O'Flynn MSS, records of the convention, vol. 2, p. 3, HCC Archives; *Worcester Evening Gazette,* March 17, 1873. For the effect of the Fenians and the depression on the parade, see *Worcester Evening Gazette,* March 13, 1867 and March 17, 1873.

83. Drawn from O'Flynn MSS, convention records, vol. 2, HCC Archives. See also *Worcester Daily Spy,* March 18, 1884, March 18, 1890; *Worcester Telegram,* March 18, 1891.

84. O'Flynn MSS, convention records, vol. 2, pp. 44, 74, and vol. 3, p. 150; *Irish World,* February 12, 1881, and *Worcester Daily Times,* March 1, 1881.

85. O'Flynn MSS, convention records, vols. 2, 3, HCC Archives. This includes the following parish temperance societies: St. Anne's Guards; St. Anne's Cadets; St. Anne's Total Abstinence Society; St. John's Cadets; Catholic Young Men's Lyceum; St. John's Temperance and Literary Guild; St. Aloysius Temperance Society, Sacred Heart Benevolent Society; St. Paul's Temperance Lyceum.

86. O'Flynn MSS, convention records, vol. 2, pp. 20–22, quote from O'Flynn on p. 205. For priests "reaction," see *Worcester Daily Times,* April 20, 1885, March 13, 1882; *Worcester Telegram,* March 16, 1903; Littleton diaries, vol. 2, December 11, 1889, AAS.

87. O'Flynn MSS, records of the convention, vol. 2, frontispiece, pp. 123, 205, and vol. 3, p. 180; Rosenzweig, *Eight Hours for What We Will,* pp. 103–11.

88. O'Flynn MSS, records of the convention, vol. 2, p. 21; *Messenger,* August 23, 1902; Rosenzweig, *Eight Hours for What We Will,* pp. 74–81.

89. O'Flynn MSS, convention records, vol. 2, p. 102, 220, and vol. 3, p. 144.

90. Ibid.

91. Ibid., vol. 1, pp. 20, 39, 78, 105, 133, 169.

92. O'Flynn MSS, convention records, vol. 2, p. 97. For temperance men marching, see descriptions of parades: *Worcester Daily Spy*, March 18, 1884, March 18, 1890, March 18, 1891, and O'Flynn MSS, convention records, vols. 2, 3, HCC Archives.

93. For discussions of St. Patrick's Day celebrations in Ireland, see Robert Jerome Smith, "Festivals and Calendar Customs," in Harold Orel, ed., *Irish History and Culture* (Lawrence: University of Kansas, 1976), pp. 129–37; Gary Owens, "'A Moral Insurrection': Faction Fighters, Public Demonstrations, and the O'Connellite Campaign, 1828," *Irish Historical Studies* 30, no. 120 (1997) pp. 513–41; For discussions of American parades and ethnic parades, see Ryan, "The American Parade," in Hunt, ed., *The New Cultural History*, pp. 131–53; Conzen, "Ethnicity as Festive Culture: Nineteenth Century German America on Parade," in Werner Sollors, ed., *The Invention of Ethnicity* (New York: Oxford University Press, 1989), pp. 44–76; Eric Hobsbawm and Terence Ranger, eds., *The Invention of Tradition* (Cambridge: Cambridge University Press, 1985). For St. Patrick's Day parades, see Dennis Clark, *Irish Relations: Trails of an Immigrant Tradition* (East Brunswick: Associated University Presses, 1982), pp. 193–98; John Bodnar, *Remaking America: Public Memory, Commemoration, and Patriotism in the Twentieth Century* (Princeton: Princeton University Press, 1992), pp. 65–70; Sallie Marston, "Public Rituals and Community Power: St. Patrick's Day Parades in Lowell, Massachusetts, 1848–1874," *Political Geography Quarterly* 8, no. 3 (July 1989), pp. 255–69; and Kenneth Moss, "St. Patrick's Day Celebrations and the Formation of Irish American Identity, 1845–1875," *Journal of Social History* 29, no. 1 (Fall 1995), pp. 125–48.

94. Conzen suggests that German parades were performed less as the invented traditions of an ethnic interest group than the invocation of an old country custom to create a fraternal, solidary community: Conzen, "Ethnicity as Festive Culture," pp. 44–77.

95. Marvin, *Worcester in the War of the Rebellion*, pp. 350–51; O'Flynn MSS, "Societies," June 17, 1859, HCC Archives; Powers, "Invisible Immigrants," p. 440; R. V. Comerford, *The Fenians in Context: Irish Politics and Society, 1848–1882* (Wolfhound Press: Dublin, 1985), pp. 11–66; Tom Garvin, *The Evolution of Irish Nationalist Politics* (New York: Holmes and Meier, 1981) pp. 54–57, 59–64. Thomas N. Brown, *Irish American Nationalism: 1870–1890* (New York: Lippincott, 1966), pp. 21–39; O'Flynn MSS, folio 2, "Societies," HCC Archives; William D'Arcy, *The Fenian Movement in the United States, 1858–1886* (Washington, D.C.: Catholic University of America Press, 1947), pp. 1–98.

96. Comerford, *Fenians in Context*, pp. 101–60; Garvin, *The Evolution*, pp. 59–64; T. Desmond Williams, "John Devoy and Jeremiah O'Donovan Rossa," in T. W. Moody, ed., *The Fenian Movement* (Dublin: Mercier, 1969), pp. 89–98; D'Arcy, *The Fenian Movement*, pp. 98–369; Brown, *Irish American Nationalism*, pp. 15, 38–41, 65–74; Comerford, *The Fenians in Context*, pp. 161–220; Garvin, *The Evolution*, 59–64; O'Flynn MSS, folio 2, "Societies," HCC Archives; Powers, "Invisible Immigrants," pp. 37–55, 435–45; *Worcester Evening Gazette*, March 18, 1867.

97. T. W. Moody, *Michael Davitt and Irish Revolution, 1846–1882* (New York: Oxford University Press, 1981), pp. 222–70, in Worcester, p. 260; Brown, *Irish American Nationalism*, pp. 84–85; O'Flynn MSS, folio 2, "Societies," HCC Archives.

98. Moody, *Michael Davitt*, pp. 271–327; Brown, *Irish American Nationalism*, pp. 95–105; Samuel Clark, *Social Origins of the Irish Land War* (Princeton: Princeton University Press, 1979), pp. 225–44; Paul Bew, *Land and the National Question in Ireland* (Dublin: 1978), pp. 1–119; idem, "The National Question, Land and Revisionism: Some Reflections," in D. George Boyce and Alan O'Day, eds., *The Making of Modern Irish History: Revisionism and the Revisionist Controversy* (London: Routledge, 1996), pp. 90–99; Donald Jordan, "Land and Politics in the West of Ireland: County Mayo, 1846–1882" (Ph.D. diss.: University of California at Davis, 1982).

99. Brown, *Irish American Nationalism*, pp. 95–105; Brundage, *Making of Western Labor Radicalism*, pp. 40–52.

100. Brown, *Irish American Nationalism*, pp. 85–108; Eric Foner, "Class, Ethnicity and Radicalism in the Gilded Age: The Land League and Irish America," *Marxist Perspectives* 1, no. 2 (Summer 1978), pp. 9–24; Moody, *Michael Davitt*, pp. 383–84, 382–416. As we shall see, there was significant variation across the country and even within cities in support for these factions, just as there was within Worcester's Irish community. Victor Walsh found that factions in the nationalist movement in Pittsburgh correlated roughly by neighborhood and ultimately by region of origin in Ireland, eastern Irish immigrants backing the conservative nationalists and southwestern Munster immigrants backing the Ford radicals: Victor Walsh, "'A Fanatic Heart': The Cause of Irish American Nationalism in Pittsburgh during the Gilded Age," *Journal of Social History* 15, no. 2 (Winter 1981), pp. 191–92. The western Rocky Mountain states were a stronghold of radicalism (Leadville, Virginia City, Butte), but in Denver nationalism was "dominated by city's Irish American middle class." The Ladies Land League was strong in Denver, however: David Brundage, *The Making of Western Labor Radicalism: Denver's Organized Workers, 1878–1908* (Urbana: University of Illinois Press, 1994), pp. 40–52. In Chicago, the Clan na Gael faction was most powerful: Michael Funchion, *Chicago's Irish Nationalists* (New York: Arno Press, 1976).

101. *Worcester Daily Times*, December 5, 1879; O'Flynn MSS, folio 1, p. 624, HCC Archives; O'Flynn MSS, folio 1, pp. 624–25, HCC Archives; *Pilot*, March 13, 1880.

102. O'Flynn MSS, folio 1, pp. 624–27; *Boston Pilot*, March 6, 13, August 14, 1880. Worcester County's AOH divisions contributed $2,081 and the Father Mathew Society gave $200: *Boston Pilot*, May 15, 29, 1880.

103. Brown, *Irish American Nationalism*, pp. 83–111; O'Flynn MSS, folio 1, p. 620, HCC Archives; *Worcester Evening Gazette*, April 24, 1880; Matthew McCafferty chaired the committee to form the Land League branch.

104. On the Clan na Gael, see *Irish World*, July 2, October 1, 1881; O'Flynn MSS, folio 2, November 17, 1880, February 6, 1881, pp. 618, 620, HCC Archives; *Irish World*, January 22, March 12, 1881; *Worcester Daily Times*, February 21, 1881; Margaret Ward, *Unmanageable Revolutionaries*, pp. 5–21.

105. O'Flynn MSS, folio 2, p. 620, HCC Archives; Brown, *Irish American Nationalism*, pp. 109, 156.

106. *Worcester Daily Times*, January 7, February 4, 11, 1881; *Boston Pilot*, January 1, 1881, February 5, 1881, March 12, 1881, January 13, 1882, February 25, 1882.

107. *Worcester Daily Times,* January 7, 1881; Patrick Collins papers, Thomas J. Conaty to Patrick Collins, February 26, 1881, Irish Collection, Burns Library, Boston College, Boston, Massachusetts; *Worcester Evening Post,* January 5, 1909; *Worcester City Directory* (Worcester: Drew-Allis, 1881); *Worcester Daily Times,* January 5, 12, 15, 1881; *Irish World,* January 22, 1881.

108. *Worcester Daily Times,* January 22, February 2, 22, 1881; *Irish World,* January 5, 22, March 12, 1881.

109. *Worcester Evening Post,* January 5, 1909; O'Flynn MSS, folio 2, *Land League Advertiser,* HCC Archives.

110. *Worcester Evening Post,* May 31, 1906.

111. *Worcester Evening Post,* May 31, 1906; Hasia Diner, *Erin's Daughters in America: Irish Immigrant Women in the Nineteenth Century* (Baltimore: Johns Hopkins University Press, 1983) pp. 128, 150.

112. Brown, *Irish American Nationalism,* pp. 115–22; Moody, *Michael Davitt,* pp. 437–85, pp. 304–49; Bew, *Land and the National Question,* pp. 166–216; Charles Townshend, *Political Violence in Ireland: Government and Resistance Since 1848* (Oxford: Clarendon Press, 1983), pp. 148–49; Ward, *Unmanageable Revolutionaries,* pp. 21–23.

113. *Worcester Daily Times,* October 14, 15, 17, 18, 1881.

114. O'Flynn MSS, folio 2, p. 621, HCC Archives; *Worcester Daily Spy,* October 24, 1881; *Irish World,* November 5, 19, 1881.

115. *Irish World,* December 10, 31, 1881, January 7, 1882.

116. See also *Irish World,* March 18, 1882.

117. *Donahoe's Magazine* 7, no. 1 (January 1882), pp. 97–101; *Worcester Daily Times,* January 13, 1882. On the central branch, see *Worcester Daily Times,* January 20, February 3, 1882; *Worcester Daily Times,* January 13, 1882.

118. *Worcester Daily Times,* January 4, February 13, 14, 15, 16, 17, 1882; O'Flynn MSS, folio 2, p. 621, HCC Archives; *Irish World,* March 25, 1882.

119. *Worcester Daily Spy,* February 18, 1882; *Worcester Daily Times,* February 18, 1882; *Irish World,* March 25, 1882.

120. *Worcester Daily Spy,* February 18, 1882; *Worcester Daily Times,* February 18, 1882.

121. O'Flynn MSS, folio 2, p. 621, HCC Archives; *Worcester Daily Times,* February 22, 1882.

122. *Worcester Daily Times,* February 22, March 18, 20, 21, 1882.

123. *Irish World,* May 13, 1882; *Worcester Daily Times,* April 26, May 1, 5, 1882.

124. Brown, *Irish American Nationalism,* pp. 122–29; F. S. L. Lyons, *Charles Stewart Parnell* (New York: Oxford University Press, 1977), 177–237; Moody, *Michael Davitt,* pp. 520–45; Ward, *Unmanageable Revolutionaries,* pp. 31–39; Bew, *Land and the National Question,* pp. 304–49.

125. Moody, *Michael Davitt,* pp. 522–40.

126. *Worcester Daily Times,* May 6, 23, 26, 27, 29, June 2, 1882. Almost simultaneously with Parnell's release, members of an Irish revolutionary band fell upon Frederick Cavendish, the chief secretary for Ireland, and Thomas Burke, the under secretary, in Phoenix Park in Dublin with knives and killed them both. Moderate nationalists in

America and Ireland were quick to denounce the act. Worcester was no exception. Monsignor Griffin condemned the Invincibles as "snakes and vipers," the *Times* condemned them as "reckless, cowardly enemies of Ireland," and even Eugene Moriarty of the Clan na Gael denounced "the foul deed." See *Worcester Daily Times,* May 8, 10, 12, 1882.

127. *Irish World,* June 3, 1882; *Worcester Daily Times,* May 9, 10, 14, 28, 1882; *Worcester Evening Post,* May 31, 1906, January 5, 1909.

128. *Worcester Daily Times,* June 10, 14, 17, 28, 30, July 3, 18, 1882, July 28, 31, August 17, September 7, October 9, 1882.

129. *Worcester Daily Times,* November 26, 1881, January 14, 1882; Brown, *Irish American Nationalism,* pp. 23–25.

130. *Irish World,* March 18, June 3, 1882.

131. *Irish World,* April 23, 1881, January 7, March 18, June 3, 1882.

132. Foner, "Class, Ethnicity and Radicalism," pp. 24–47; Paul Buhle, "The Knights of Labor in Rhode Island," *Radical History Review* 17 (1978), pp. 39–73; time books, North Works, 1882, 1887, American Steel and Wire Collection, Baker Library, Harvard Business School; *Worcester Evening Post,* May 31, 1906, January 5, 1909; *Worcester Telegram,* July 3, 1926; Nutt, *History of Worcester* vol. 3, p. 300. O'Callaghan also seemed to inspire her niece to become a doctor: Nutt, *History of Worcester,* vol. 4, p. 85.

133. *Worcester Daily Times,* January 4, June 11, June 28, July 7, 13, 1883; O'Flynn MSS, folio 2, "Call for a State Convention of the National Hibernian Benevolent Organizations of Massachusetts," June 7, 1883, HCC Archives; O' Donovan Rossa Papers, Box 3, Ledger of Subscribers to the *United Irishmen,* pp. 390–92, Catholic University of America Archives; *Worcester Daily Times,* November 26, 1880, July 6, 1883, July 28, September 16, 18, 1884; O'Flynn MSS, convention records, vol. 2, HCC Archives. For opposition to the Clan, see the *Messenger,* February 2, June 15, June 22, 1889.

134. O'Flynn MSS, records of the convention, vol. 2, February 14, 1886, HCC Archives; O'Flynn MSS, folio 2, November 23, December 5, 1885, HCC Archives; *Worcester Daily Spy,* March 1, 1886.

135. O'Flynn MSS, folio 1, p. 173, HCC Archives.

136. Ibid.; *Worcester Daily Spy,* March 1, 9, 1886; November 30, 1887.

137. *Alumna,* May 1887, p. 3; *Worcester Daily Spy,* November 30, 1887.

138. *Worcester Daily Telegram,* November 14, 1890.

Four. Ethnic Revival: The 1890s and Early 1900s

1. *Worcester Telegram,* February 20, 1901.

2. F. S. L. Lyons, *Charles Stewart Parnell* (London: Collins, 1977), pp. 452–567; Foster, *Modern Ireland,* pp. 423–25; Paul Bew, *Land and the National Question in Ireland* (Atlantic Highlands: Humanities Press, 1979); T. W. Moody, *Michael Davitt and the*

Irish Revolution, 1846–1882 (Oxford: Clarendon Press, 1982), p. 546; Conor Cruise O'Brien, *Parnell and His Party: 1880–1890* (Oxford: Oxford University Press, 1964), pp. 277–346; Emmet Larkin, *The Roman Catholic Church in Ireland and the Fall of Parnell: 1888–1891* (Chapel Hill: University of North Carolina Press, 1979), pp. 191–288.

3. Clipping, "Anniversary of the Death of Parnell," *Evening Post*, n.d., scrapbook, Meagher MSS; *Evening Spy* quote condemns Parnell in November 26, 1890, November 28, 1890, December 1, 6, 1890; *Messenger*, February 28, March 21, April 4, November 7, December 5, 1891.

4. Lyons, *Ireland Since the Famine*, pp. 196–98; Bew, *Land and the National Question*; Foster, *Modern Ireland*, pp. 423–26; Miller, *Emigrants and Exiles*, p. 540; Hachey, *Britain and Irish Separatism*, pp. 31–36; Alan O'Day, "Home Rule and the Historians," in Boyce and O'Day, eds., *Making of Modern Irish History*, pp. 141–62.

5. *Evening Spy*, March 7, quotations in April 4, April 6, 1893; *Messenger*, March 4, April 1, 1893.

6. *Messenger*, July 7, 1894; St. Stephen's Total Abstinence and Benevolent Society, pamphlet, n.d., St. Stephen's archives; "Catholic Total Abstinence Union of Springfield, Thirtieth Annual Field Day and Games at Holy Cross College, Worcester, Massachusetts" (Boston: 1907), pp. 12–20, Worcester organizations file, AAS.

7. The new *Messenger* bought out O'Leary's *Recorder* in September of 1899, about one year after the *Recorder* appeared: *Recorder* quotes in March 25, September 17, 1898; *Messenger*, September 19, 1899.

8. Thomas T. McAvoy, *The Great Crisis in American Catholic History, 1895–1900* (Chicago: Henry Regnery, 1957), pp. 261–343; Cross, *Liberal Catholicism*, pp. 182–224; Curran, *Michael Augustine Corrigan*, pp. 395–515; John Tracy Ellis, *The Life of James Cardinal Gibbons: Archbishop of Baltimore, 1834–1921* (Milwaukee: Bruce, 1952), vol. 2, pp. 1–80.

9. *Messenger* quotation, "nominal Catholic," in July 28, 1900, February 9, 1901, February 10, 1905, quote, "avowed enemy," in March 18, 1905; *Recorder* quotation backing Liberalism in July 15, 1898.

10. Powers, "Invisible Immigrants," pp. 454–55; *Worcester Evening Gazette*, July 16, 1941; Nutt, *History of Worcester*, vol. 1, pp. 869, 871, vol. 3, p. 100, vol. 4, p. 562; Rice, ed., *Worcester of 1898*, p. 549; McCoy, *History of the Springfield Diocese*, pp. 236–37; Cross, *Catholic Liberalism*, p. 126; Peter Hogan, *The Catholic University of America: The Rectorship of Thomas J. Conaty* (Washington, D.C.: Catholic University of America Press, 1949), pp. 1–27.

11. *Worcester Telegram*, August 5, 21, October 29, 1893; *Thirty-Fifth Annual Report of the Massachusetts Bureau of Labor Statistics: Public Document no. 15* (Boston: Wright and Potter, 1896), p. 315; *Report on the Population of the U.S. at the Eleventh Census*, pt. 2 (Washington, D.C.: G.P.O., 1897), p. 743; U.S. Bureau of the Census, *Special Report: Occupations, 1900*, pp. 760–63.

12. *Worcester Telegram*, August 5, October 29, 1893; *Fourth Annual Report of the Associated Charities* (Worcester: Charles Hamilton Press, 1894), p. 21.

13. Washburn, *Industrial Worcester*, pp. 70–71, 90–93, 102–6, 148, 176–83, 208–10, 218–19, 250–51; Roberge, "Three Decker," pp. 16–18.

14. Washburn, *Industrial Worcester*, quotation, "a large foreign business," pp. 126, 176–83, 218–19, 246–47; Cheape, *From Family Firm*, pp. 13–36. See Anthony Patrick O'Brien, "Factory Size, Economies of Scale, and the Great Merger Wave of 1898–1902," *Journal of Economic History* 48, no. 3 (December 1988), pp. 639–49.

15. *A Tribute to Worcester in the Columbian Year*, p. 68; Rice, ed., *Worcester of 1898*, pp. 409–10.

16. *Worcester of 1898*, pp. 409–10; *Annual Report of the Worcester Board of Trade* (Worcester: Felt Press, 1898), pp. 31, 15–18; *Annual Report of the Worcester Board of Trade* (Worcester: Felt Press, 1897), pp. 13–17, 34–37; *Annual Report of the Worcester Board of Trade, 1901* (Worcester: Felt Print, 1901), pp. 14–15; *Annual Report of the Worcester Board of Trade* (Worcester: Gilbert Davis Printer, 1896), pp. 8–9, 17–21. In 1893, of the 21 officers and directors, 11 were manufacturers, 1 was in insurance, 1 in real estate, 2 ran lumber yards, 1 was a contractor, 2 were lawyers: *A Tribute to Worcester in the Columbian Year*, p. 68, traced in the *Worcester City Directory* (Worcester: Drew-Allis, 1893).

17. *Annual Report of the Worcester Board of Trade, 1898*, p. 31; *Annual Report of the Worcester Board of Trade, 1897*, quotation on p. 14, pp. 13–22; *Annual Report of the Worcester Board of Trade, 1896*, pp. 14–21; Tucker,"Development of the Central Business Area," pp. 83–89; Washburn, *Industrial Worcester*, p. 263; Nutt, *History of Worcester*, vol. 2, p. 1003; "Worcester's Greatest Needs," *Worcester Magazine*, January 1901, p. 26.

18. "NMTA: Tenth Annual Reunion and Banquet, Wednesday, March 6, 1912 Program," Worcester Room, Worcester Public Library; Donald Tulloch, "Worcester: City of Prosperity," *Worcester Magazine* (May 1914), p. 122; *Annual Report of the Worcester Board of Trade, 1896*, pp. 7–8.

19. *Illustrated History of the Central Labor Union and Building Trades Council of Worcester and Vicinity* (Worcester: 1899), pp. 126, 130–31, 135; C. F. Johnson, "History of the Central Labor Union" (M.A. thesis, Clark University, 1913), pp. 1–18.

20. *Worcester Telegram*, June 21, 25, 28, 1890.

21. Mark Ehrlich, *With Our Hands* (Philadelphia: Temple University Press, 1986), pp. 46–47; *Worcester Telegram*, June 27, 28, 1890, July 1, 3, 8, 11, 1890.

22. Ehrlich, *With Our Hands*, pp. 46–47, McDermott quote on p. 46; *Worcester Telegram*, June 24, 28, quotation, Prince Edward Island men, July 3, 8, 1890.

23. *Labor World*, March 1, 8, 1890; *Worcester Globe*, January 30, 1890; Amos Webber diaries, March 4, 1892, American Steel and Wire Collection, Baker Library, Harvard School of Business.

24. *Worcester Labor* (self-described "Associated Worker party paper"), February 5, 26, 1895; *Worcester Telegram*, November 23, 1895; *Worcester Telegram*, November 30, 1897; *Evening Spy*, October 12, 19, 1899, November 3, 1903.

25. *Worcester Telegram*, November 30, December 3, 1897; *Evening Post* quotation about former populists in December 11, 1900. See numerous Swedes and Yankees on

nomination papers for Socialist candidates, and Swedish and Yankee nominees for office. For example: *Worcester Telegram,* December 3, 1898, and *Evening Post,* November 28, 1900. Socialist votes tended to be strongest in Ward Five, particularly in precincts two and three (the highest Socialist vote in the city in 1897 and the highest Socialist Labor vote in 1898 was Ward Five, precinct three) in or near Quinsigamond Village, and some other votes in Ward Two, near Bell Hill. These votes were, nonetheless, still slight: *Evening Post,* December 14, 1898; *Worcester Telegram,* December 15, 1897. As late as 1907 a Socialist candidate, Addison W. Barr, garnered over 3,000 votes in the citywide elections for aldermen, more than some of the weaker Democratic candidates: *Worcester Telegram,* December 15, 1907.

26. Nutt, *History of Worcester,* vol. 1, p. 398. In 1907, Socialist candidate for alderman, Addison W. Barr, received 3,779 votes: *Worcester Telegram,* December 15, 1907; For Socialist party city committee, see *Worcester City Directory* (Worcester: Drew-Allis, 1907), p. 861; Henry Bedford, *Socialism and the Workers in Massachusetts, 1886–1912* (Amherst: University of Massachusetts Press, 1966), pp. 137–60; James Weinstein, *The Decline of Socialism in America, 1912–1925* (New York: Vintage, 1969), pp. 16–26; Nicholas Salvatore, *Eugene V. Debs: Citizen and Socialist* (Champaign-Urbana: University of Illinois Press, 1984), pp. 283–85. *Worcester Telegram,* November 22, 1897, December 12, 1899; *Evening Gazette,* December 15, 1897, December 14, 1898; Bedford, *Socialism and the Workers,* pp. 83–97, 137–41; *Illustrated History of the C.L.U.,* quote in pp. 247–49; *Evening Spy,* October 21, 1899, November 3, 1903; *Messenger,* December 19, 1903.

27. Immigrant and second-generation samples: 1880 and 1900 U.S. Census Manuscripts Schedules.

28. McCoy, *History of the Diocese of Springfield,* pp. 4–7; Nutt, *History of Worcester* vol. 1, pp. 311–13; Alexandre Belisle, *Histoire De La Presse Franco Americaine* (Worcester: L'Opinion Publique Publishers, 1911), p. 424; Report of the Immigration Commission, Senate Document no. 756, 61st Congress, "Distribution of Immigrants" (Washington, D.C.: GPO, 1911), p. 530; L'Abbé Chandonett, *Notre Dame Des Canadiens et Les Canadiens aux Etats Unis* (Montreal: George E. Des Barres, 1872); *Thirteenth Census of the United States Taken in the Year 1910,* vol. 3, "Population: Reports by States," p. 896; *Le Worcester Canadien* (Worcester: Roy, 1906), p. 7; Alexandre Belisle, *Livre D'Or Des Franco Americaines de Worcester, Massachusetts* (Worcester: Le Compagnie de Publication de Belisle, 1920), pp. 19–60; Mason Wade *The French Canadians: 1760–1967* (Toronto: Macmillan, 1968), vol. 1, pp. 276–392; Gerard J. Brault *The French Canadian Heritage in New England* (Hanover: University Press of New England, 1986), pp. 51–64; Richard Sorrelle, "The Sentinelle Affair and Militant Survivance: The Franco American Experience in Woonsocket, Rhode Island," (Ph.D. diss.: University of Buffalo, 1975), pp. 52–83.

29. "Special Report: Occupations, 1900," pp. 760–63; Power, "Invisible Immigrants," pp. 299–312. Data gathered by the Community Studies Program at Assumption College also reveals a high proportion of skilled workers among the

French: 37 percent of the French foreign stock in the Oak Hill area were skilled workers in 1902, for example.

30. *The Growth of a Worcester County Neighborhood*, WPI Interactive Qualifying Project, p. 20, pamphlet file, WHM; Chandonnet, *Notre Dame Des Canadiens*, p. 120; *Thirteenth Census of the United States: 1910*, "Population," p. 896; *Le Worcester Canadien*. p. 7.

31. *Le Worcester Canadien*, pp. 4–12; *Worcester House Directory* (Worcester: Drew-Allis, 1890), pp. 361–63; *Worcester House Directory* (Worcester: Drew-Allis, 1904), p. 411; immigrant and second-generation samples: U.S. Census Manuscript Schedules 1880 and 1900.

32. Belisle, *Livre D'Or*, pp. 71, 119–20, 130, 167–79.

33. *L'Opinion Publique* quotation from August 16, 1907, June 4, 1907; Belisle, *Histoire De La Presse Franco Americaine*, pp. 93–107; Wade, *French Canadians*, vol. 1, pp. 220–393; Brault, *French Canadian Heritage*, pp. 7–8, 65–66; Rumilly, *Histoire Des Franco Americaines* (Montreal: Union De St. Jean de Baptiste D'Amerique, 1958), pp. 84, 148, 185; Sorrelle, "The Sentinelle Affair," pp. 1–84.

34. Quotation from Emile Tardivel in 1892 cited in *L'Opinion Publique*, August 7, 1907; on O'Leary, see *Messenger*, May 30, 1896; Rumilly, *Histoire Des Franco Americaines*, pp. 108, 121–23, 184–85, 209, 203, 257.

35. Rumilly, *Histoire Des Franco Americaines*, pp. 106–8, 177–78; *L'Opinion Publique*, October 22, 1900; Berger in *L'Opinion Publique*, October 22, and Perrault in October 29, 1900; Ronald Petrin, "Ethnicity and Political Pragmatism: The French Canadians in Massachusetts, 1885–1915" (Ph.D. diss.: Clark University), pp. 284–85.

36. Petrin, "Ethnicity and Political Pragmatism," pp. 180–86.

37. Esther Wahlstrom, "A History of the Swedish People of Worcester" (M.A. thesis, Clark University, 1947) pp. 19–20, figures on p. 240.

38. Washburn, *Industrial Worcester*, pp. 150–60; L. P. Richard, Castle Garden, New York to Mr. Moen of Washburn and Moen Co., March 28, 1882, American Steel and Wire Industrial Museum Collection, Baker Library, Harvard University; Wahlstrom, "A History," p. vii; Charles Esthus and John McClymer, *ga Till Amerika*, pp. 11–99, quotation on p. 22.

39. Esthus and McClymer, *ga till Amerika*, pp. 11–99.

40. *Tenth Census of the United States 1880*, "Population" p. 908; Washburn, *Industrial Worcester*, pp. 30–31, 156; Census of Norton Company, Emery Wheel Co. employees, November 1, 1899, Norton Company papers, Worcester Historical Museum; volume 64, time books, February, March, May 1882, April 1887, American Steel and Wire Collection, Baker Library, Harvard University Business School.

41. *Worcester Daily Times*, April 29, June 25, 1886.

42. Wahlstrom, "A History," pp. v–vii, 241; *Thirteenth Census of the United States, 1910*, vol. 2, "Population: Report By States," p. 896. Esthus and McClymer, *ga Till Amerika*, pp. 11–99.

43. *Worcester House Directory* (Worcester: Drew-Allis, 1888), Thenius Street, pp. 316, 328; immigrant and second-generation samples: Census Manuscript Schedules, 1880 and 1900; Rosenzweig, *Eight Hours for What We Will*, pp. 88–89; Esthus and McClymer, *ga till Amerika*, p. 38.

44. *Worcester Telegram*, December 11, 1907; Wahlstrom, "A History," pp. 63–79, 21, 121; *Worcester Daily Times*, April 29, July 30, 1886; Rosenzweig, *Eight Hours for What We Will*, pp. 88–90; Esthus and McClymer, *ga till Amerika*, pp. 101–21.

45. Wahlstrom, "A History," pp. 121–29; Esthus and McClymer, *ga till Amerika*, pp. 101–21.

46. *Census of Massachusetts: 1885*, vol. 1, "Population and Social Statistics" (Boston: Wright and Potter, 1887), pp. 562–63; *Census of Massachusetts, 1895*, vol. 2, "Population and Social Statistics" (Boston: Wright and Potter, 1897), p. 691; U.S. Census Office, "Report on the Population of the United States at the Eleventh Census: 1890," pt. 1 (Washington, D.C.: GPO, 1895), pp. 672–73; *Census of the Commonwealth of Massachusetts, 1905* vol. 1, "Population and Social Statistics" (Boston: Wright and Potter, 1909), p. 495; *Special Report on Occupations, 1900*, pp. 760–63; Washburn, *Industrial Worcester*, p. 101; Nutt, *History of Worcester*, vol. 2, pp. 327, 347; *American*, March 7, 1893. There were 792 in Ward Five and 766 in Ward Six of 3,113 English in the city in 1910: *Thirteenth Census of the United States, 1910*, vol. 2, "Population: Report By States," p. 896.

47. *Messenger*, January 28, 1888; Nutt, *History of Worcester*, vol. 1, pp. 327–29, 855–56.

48. Meagher MSS, clipping, November 8, 1898; *Recorder*, September 17, October 1, 22, 1898; *Messenger*, October 29, November 19, 1898, October 22, November 1906; *Recorder*, September 17, 1898, October 1, 22, 1898; *Worcester Evening Post*, October 17, 22, 24, 1898.

49. *Worcester Evening Post*, October 22, 24, November 9, 1898; *Worcester Telegram*, November 9, 21, 1898; *Messenger*, November 1906.

50. *Worcester Evening Post*, October 22, 24, November 9, 1898; *Worcester Telegram*, November 9, 21, 1898; *Messenger*, November 1906.

51. Robert H. Lord, John E. Sexton, and Edward F. Harrington, *A History of the Archdiocese of Boston* (New York: Sheed and Ward, 1949), vol. 3, pp. 107–16; Lawrence Kennedy, "Power and Prejudice: Boston Political Conflict, 1885–1895" (Ph.D. diss.: Boston College, 1989), pp. 191–224; *Worcester Evening Spy*, December 1, 1890; *City Document no. 42* (Worcester: 1888), p. 312; John T. Galvin, "The Dark Ages of Boston Politics," *Proceedings of the Massachusetts Historical Society* 89 (1979), pp. 88–111; *Boston Globe*, October 6, 1887.

52. Kolesar, *Urban Politics and Social Conflict*, p. 198.

53. Ibid., pp. 14–16; Between 1881 and 1888, 151 boys who had graduated from the Worcester High School went to college; 33 went to Holy Cross, 44 to Worcester Polytechnic Institute, 19 to Amherst, and 16 to Harvard: *City Document no. 43*, pp. 331, 387.

54. Kolesar, *Urban Politics*, pp. 13–16.

55. *Worcester Evening Spy*, December 13, 20, 31, 1888, January 14, 1889; O'Flynn MSS, folio 17, HCC Archives; *Worcester Telegram*, July 7, 1890; quotation, "names not American," *Worcester Evening Spy*, December 3, 1890; O'Flynn MSS., folio 12, *Worcester Evening Spy*, n.d., and O'Flynn MSS folio 17, *Worcester Evening Spy*, December (n.d.) 1890, HCC Archives.

56. *Worcester Telegram,* December 3, 1890; *City Document no. 45,* pp. 460–62; *Worcester Evening Gazette,* January 2, 7, 1891.

57. *Worcester Telegram,* November 17, 19, 25, 1890; *American,* November 1, 1892; Kolesar, *Urban Politics,* pp. 13–16, 192–201.

58. *American,* October 24, November 14, December 5, 1893.

59. Kolesar, *Urban Politics,* pp. 201–19.

60. Kolesar, *Urban Politics,* pp. 201–19; *Worcester Evening Spy,* November 14, 21, December 14, 1893, October 29, 31, November 1, 2, 3, 1894; *Messenger,* November 9, 1893; *American,* December 12, 1893; *Worcester Telegram,* December 9, 1893.

61. Kolesar, *Urban Politics,* pp. 201–13; Kinzer, *An Episode in Anti-Catholicism,* p. 148; *Worcester Evening Spy,* October 17, November 6, December 3, 11, 1895; *Worcester Telegram,* December 4, 1895; Minutes of the Massachusetts Women Suffrage Association, vol. 98, folder 1069, May 1894, October 1895, Women's Rights Collection, Schlesinger Library, Harvard University; Lois Bannister Merk, "Massachusetts and the Woman Suffrage Movement," (Ph.D. diss.: Radcliffe College, 1956), p. 260; Nutt, *History of Worcester,* vol. 1, p. 502; suffrage won only in the two strongest anti-Marble precincts: Ward Seven, precinct three, and Ward Eight, precinct two, *Worcester Evening Spy,* November 6, 1895 (see note 71 below). For antiethnic sentiments among suffragettes, see *Worcester Evening Gazette,* November 12, 1896. James Kenneally, "Catholicism and Woman's Suffrage in Massachusetts," *Catholic Historical Review* 3, no. 1 (April 1967), pp. 46–51.

62. *American,* October 3, 1893, April 25, 1893, December 19, 1893, January 23, 1894.

63. Of OUAM members, 267 were identified and traced into the city directory: 3 percent (8) were professionals; 8 percent (22) were managers; 11 percent (31) were small proprietors; 21 percent (55) were clerical workers; 44 percent (117) were skilled workers; 8 percent (22) were semiskilled workers; 4 percent (12) were unskilled: Souvenir of the Fifty-first Annual Convention of the OUAM, Worcester, Mass., September 8 to 14, 1896, pamphlet file, Worcester Public Library, traced into *Worcester City Directory* (Worcester: Drew-Allis, 1897); *American,* December 5, 1893, June 19, July 17, 1894.

64. *American,* November 1, 1892, March 22, April 11, 1893; quotation, "foreign labor," in *American,* August 14, 1894.

65. See chapter 2 for Irish movement into Main South. *American,* April 17, 1894. Mears, Conrad, and Atkinson, all ministers from South Worcester, were listed on the masthead of the *American*—see February 28, 1893, and Nutt, *History of Worcester,* vol. 2, pp. 815, 832, 840, 848. Ward Seven, precinct three, went 73 percent to 27 percent for Marble, the strongest anti-Marble vote in the city. Ward Eight, precincts two and three, also voted almost two to one against Marble. Together these were the three strongest anti-Marble precincts in the city: Kolesar, *Urban Politics,* p. 205.

66. Quotation, "Why is it," in *American,* April 4, 1893.

67. Quotation, "why should," in *American,* April 10, 1894; *American,* April 3, 17, 1893.

68. *American,* October 3, 1893; *Messenger,* August 10, November 16, 1895. On the British, see *American,* March 7, 1893, and on the Armenians, see *American,* January 9, 1894. On the Swedes, the *American* said on November 7, 1893, that the celebration of the Swedish Tercentenary has "brought these worthy people with the interesting and instructive history of their national country before the Worcester public. They are staunch Protestants and in their uncompromising opposition to Catholic aggression might be bracketed with Scotch Irish Orangemen. They are very industrious, law-abiding people and make first class American citizens. They can give an intelligent reason for the faith they hold and good ground for their attitude towards all forms of ecclesiastical tyranny": *American,* November 7, 1894.

69. Quotation, "suck their thumbs," in *American,* October 3, 1893; quotation, "foreign episcopate," in *American,* November 28, 1893; *American,* August 8, November 14, 1893; the list of associate editors included Rev. Thomas Atkinson (First Presbyterian); Rev. A. Z. Conrad (Old South Congregational); Rev. Dr. David O. Mears (Piedmont Congregational); Rev. C. H. Pendleton (no information); Rev. J. D. Pickles (Methodist). List drawn from *American,* February 28, 1893, and traced into Nutt, *History of Worcester,* vol. 2, pp. 815, 832, 840, 848; Rice, ed., *Worcester of 1898,* p. 284.

70. Geoffrey Blodgett, *The Gentle Reformers: Massachusetts Democrats in the Cleveland Era* (Cambridge: Harvard University Press, 1966); Paul Kleppner, *The Third Electoral System, 1853–1892: Parties, Voters, and Political Cultures* (Chapel Hill: University of North Carolina Press, 1979); idem, "From Party to Factions: The Dissolution of Boston's Mayoralty Party, 1876–1908," in Ronald Formisano and Constance Burns, eds., *The Evolution of Urban Politics: Boston 1700–1980* (Westport: Greenwood Press, 1984); Samuel McSeveney, *The Politics of Depression: Political Behavior in the Northeast, 1893 to 1896* (New York: Oxford University Press, 1972).

71. *Worcester Evening Spy,* November 25, December 8, 10, 11, 1893. The *Messenger* always saw the school battles as the results of nativist concerns about the appointment of Catholic school teachers: *Messenger,* October 7, November 25, 1893.

72. *Worcester Evening Spy,* November 25, 1899, December 1, 1899, November 22, 1901, November 13, 19, 1903.

73. Quotation in *Addison Archer's Interviews Regarding the Character, Circulation and Advertising of the Leading Publications in Worcester and Fitchburg, Massachusetts* (Boston: n.p., 1898), p. 5, pamphlet file, American Antiquarian Society.

74. Ibid., pp. 2–6; Nelson, *History of Worcester County,* vol. 2, p. 598. The *Post's* predecessor, the *Times,* collapsed in the late 1880s and had always existed on a shoe-string: *Worcester Evening Post,* August 26, 1930; N. W. Ayer and Sons, *American Newspaper Annual and Directory* (Philadelphia: N. W. Ayer and Sons, 1889), p. 1323.

75. Quotations, George F. Hoar to Rockwood Hoar, December 6, 1903, and Rockwood Hoar to George F. Hoar, December 10, 1903, folder, December 1–10, 1903, Box 15, George Frisbie Hoar Papers, Massachusetts Historical Society; *Worcester Evening Gazette,* records, vol. 1, p. 9, Salisbury family papers, American Antiquarian Society; *Worcester Evening Spy,* November 16, 1901; *Worcester Telegram,* November 17,

1898; *Addison Archer Interviews,* pp. 2–5; Nutt, *History of Worcester,* vol. 2, pp. 1107–10. On changes in the political role of the press, see Michael E. McGerr, *The Decline of Popular Politics* (New York: Oxford University Press, 1986), pp. 107–38.

76. Nutt, *History of Worcester* vol. 1, p. 398, average of total votes for mayor, 1896 election to 1899, was 13,258. The total registered vote was much higher, of course, 21, 128 in 1895, 21,201 in 1900, and 23,786 in 1904: *Manual of the General Court, 1896,* p. 344; *Manual of the General Court, 1901,* p. 225; *Manual of the General Court, 1905,* p. 244; estimate of votes by group, *Worcester Evening Post,* December 9, 1899. For disputes, see *Worcester Telegram,* November 25, 1895, November 30, 1897, December 1, 1897, November 8, 1899; *Worcester Evening Spy,* December 11, 1895, November 14, 27, 1896, November 27, 1902; *Worcester Evening Gazette,* November 17, 1896, October 18, 1899, December 1, 1899; *Worcester Evening Post,* November 27, 1899.

77. *Worcester Telegram,* November 29, 1895. See also *Worcester Telegram,* November 18, 1895, December 16, 1896; Nutt, *History of Worcester* vol. 1, p. 397; *Worcester Telegram,* November 19, 1895; quotation, "the city," *Worcester Telegram,* November 19, 1895. See also *Worcester Telegram,* November 18, 27, 28, 29, 30, 1895, and *Worcester Evening Spy,* November 19, 20, 28, December 11, 1895; *Worcester Evening Post,* November 8, 1897. A canvas of 25 Republican leaders in Ward Six found only 10 for Dodge. Most wanted a businessman, other than Dodge or Pinkerton: *Worcester Telegram,* November 18, 19, 1895. Quotation, "Several thousand," in *Worcester Evening Gazette,* November 20, 1896. Businessmen in the Sprague movement included A. W. Parmlee and Caleb Colvin, manufacturers and important figures in the Board of Trade, and F. E. Reed, Enoch Earle, P. W. Moen and W. B. McIver, also prominent manufacturers: *Worcester Evening Gazette,* November 23, 1896. See *Worcester Evening Spy,* November 16, 18, 27, 1896; *Worcester Evening Gazette,* November 11, 1896. *Worcester Telegram,* November 30, December 3, 4, 1895, November 27, 1897; *Worcester Evening Spy,* November 24, December 4, 1895, November 16, 27, December 3, 1896; *Worcester Evening Gazette,* November 16, 17, 20, 1896; *Annual Report of the Board of Trade, 1897,* pp. 14–16, 34–38. Committee listed in *Worcester Evening Spy,* November 23, 1896, and traced into Rice, ed., *Worcester of Eighteen Hundred and Ninety Eight,* pp. 735, 644, 725, 579, 386, 497, 554, 765. *Worcester Evening Spy* described Sprague backers as the "best elements" in the city: November 22, 1896. *Worcester Evening Spy,* December 8, 1895, November 18, 1896; *Worcester Telegram,* December 2, 1897.

1896 Elections: A Comparison of the City and Presidential Votes in Republican Wards

	Sprague	Bryan	Winslow	McKinley
Ward 1	523	384	732	1472
Ward 2	469	334	656	1710
Ward 7	560	256	732	1719
Ward 8	692	116	816	1772

Source: Worcester Evening Spy, November 4, 1896, December 9, 1896.

78. In 1895 the three Democratic wards, Wards Three, Four, and Five accounted for 46 percent of the Citizens' vote for mayor. The Democratic presidential vote in Wards Three, Four, and Five fell from Cleveland's 3,512 in 1892 to Bryan's 2,816 in 1896, and from 367 in Ward Eight to 116. The Democratic presidential vote did recover from a citywide total of 4,232 in 1896 to 6,194 in 1900. See also Petrin, "Ethnicity and Political Pragamatism," pp. 290–301. Quotation, "how many Democrats," in *Worcester Evening Gazette,* November 11, 1896. Quotation, "sound money men," in *Worcester Evening Gazette,* November 13, 1896. See also *Worcester Evening Spy,* November 11, 1896.

79. *Worcester Evening Gazette,* December 15, 1897; *Worcester Telegram,* December 13, 1897. See also *Worcester Telegram,* November 1, 10, 1897, December 4, 7, 8, 1897; *Worcester Evening Post,* November 22, 1897, December 1, 1897; *Worcester Evening Spy,* December 9, 1896. Sprague lost 245 votes in Ward Four and 397 votes in Ward Five from his 1896 totals.

In 1895 Dodge defeated Sprague:

462 to 240 in Ward Seven, precinct two;
611 to 265 in Ward Seven, precinct three;
317 to 155 in Ward Eight, precinct two;
419 to 191 in Ward Eight, precinct three.

All of these precincts were located in the fast-growing areas of the southwestern part of the city and most of them on the city's periphery.

In 1896 those same precincts voted for Winslow but the votes were far closer:

325 to 267 in Ward Seven, precinct two;
334 to 230 in Ward Seven, precinct three;
347 to 260 in Ward Eight, precinct two;
324 to 244 in Ward Eight, precinct three.

Sprague thus won in 1896 by picking up votes in Dodge's old bastion in the southwestern part of the city but lost ground to Winslow in Wards Three, Four, and Five on the east side. Sources: *Worcester Evening Spy,* December 11, 1895, December 9, 1896.

80. Quotation, "apathy," in *Worcester Evening Gazette,* December 15, 1897; *Worcester Telegram,* November 8, 1897. The city's debt rose by almost 40 percent under Sprague: from $2,530,368.44 in 1895 to $3,498,803.02 in 1897: *City Document no. 52,* p. 1. See also *Worcester Telegram,* November 1, 16, 24, 29, December 10, 11, 13, 14, 1897; *Worcester Evening Post,* November 4, 29, 1897. *Report of the Special Committee on Street Railways,* p. 13. Sprague's vote fell 44 percent in Ward Eight, 33 percent in Ward Seven, and 30 percent in Ward Six, all strong Republican districts, Wards Seven and Eight on the west side and Six on the southeast. His biggest dropoff was in the southwestern peripheral areas: 52 percent decline in Ward Seven, precinct two; 43 percent in Ward Seven, precinct three; 40 percent in Ward Eight, precinct two and 49 percent in Ward Eight, precinct three. Dodge's vote actually declined from Winslow's in six of the city's

eight wards. He fell off heavily in Wards Three, Four, and Five: down 24 percent in Ward Three; 15 percent in Ward Four; and 13 percent in Ward Five. The only wards where he ran ahead of Winslow were Ward Six by 1 percent and Ward Seven by 2 percent. Sprague lost the election: Dodge did not win it.

81. *City Document no. 54, 1900*, p. 54; *City Document no. 52, 1898*, pp. 8–9, 11, 18; Report of the Special Committee on Street Railways of the City of Worcester, 1897, pamphlet file, Worcester Room, Worcester Public Library; *Worcester Evening Post*, November 15, 1897, November 21, December 5, 8, 11, 12, 1899; *Worcester Telegram*, December 15, 1897, November 14, 22, 1898, November 17, 22, 23, 1899; *Worcester Evening Spy*, November 30, 1899; *Worcester Evening Gazette*, November 20, 1899.

82. On November 16, 1899, the *Gazette* claimed that it is "doubtful if in the history of the Democratic party in Worcester so much trouble has been experienced in finding a candidate for mayor." That same day the paper reported that Albert Roe said "he wouldn't want to injure his standing in the Republican party by becoming a Citizens' candidate and running against the regularly nominated Republican candidate": *Worcester Evening Gazette*, November 16, 1899. For Sprague's decline of a rumored nomination, see *Worcester Evening Post*, November 22, 1899. See also *Worcester Evening Gazette*, November 13, 17, 20, 1899; *Worcester Evening Spy*, October 6, 8, 18, November 30, 1899; *Worcester Telegram*, November 11, 15, 22, 1898, November 23, 1899; *Worcester Evening Post*, November 17, 23, 1898, November 21, 1901.

83. *Worcester Telegram*, November 19, 30, 1897, November 6, 1898, November 17, 1899; *Worcester Evening Gazette*, November 25, 1899; *Worcester Evening Spy*, October 8, 15, 1899; *Worcester Evening Post*, November 19, 1897. Nutt, *History of Worcester*, vol. 4, p. 580; Sullivan in *Worcester Evening Post*, December 9, 1899; *Worcester Evening Gazette*, December 11, 1899. See also *Worcester Telegram*, November 17, 1898; *Worcester Evening Post*, November 30, 1897, December 9, 1899; *Worcester Telegram*, November 27, 1899, December 4, 1899; *Worcester Evening Spy*, November 20, 1895; *Worcester Evening Spy*, November 23, 1901. *Worcester City Directory* (Worcester: Drew-Allis Co., 1909). Aldermen elected included Daniel Fitzgerald, Philip J. O'Connell, David F. O'Connell, James H. Mellen, Thomas Barrett, and James F. Carberry; Quotation, "squeezed out," in *Worcester Evening Post*, December 9, 1899; *Worcester Evening Gazette*, October 3, 1898, December 11, 1899; *Worcester Telegram*, November 17, 1899, October 28, 1899.

84. Quotation, "annihilation," in *Worcester Evening Post*, December 10, 1898; *Messenger* attacks provincial "foolishness" even American-born, November 11, 1899. See also *Worcester Evening Spy*, November 30, December 5, 8, 1899. Steven Erie, *Rainbow's End: Irish Americans and the Dilemmas of Urban Machine Politics, 1840–1985* (Berkeley: University of California Press, 1988), pp. 67–106.

85. Projected on the basis of samples from the census manuscript schedules of 1880: 671 second-generation Irish in 1880 (one of every five supplemented by one of every twenty); and 797 in 1900 (one of every 12 over age eighteen): second-generation samples: 1880 and 1900 United States Census Manuscript Schedules. Immigrants in 1900 based on 1,218 immigrant Irish (one in every nine). Immigrant sample, 1900 U.S. Census Manuscript Schedules.

86. Nutt, *History of Worcester,* vol. 3, Meagher, p. 306, Carberry, p. 389, vol. 4, O'Connell, p. 798, Ratigan, p. 554; Rice, *History of Worcester of Eighteen and Ninety Eight,* Barrett, p. 142; Thomas McAvoy, ed., *A Course of Lectures on Irish History* (Worcester: Messenger Printing, 1915), McMahon, p. 186, Duggan, p. 252. *Worcester Telegram,* November 10, 1897.

87. Quotations, "time for the party" and "party suicide," *Worcester Evening Post,* November 27, 1900. See also *Worcester Evening Post,* November 21, 24, quotation by O'Connell in November 26, 1900.

88. Ward Three, precinct one, had a majority of Irish-stock households, 60 percent, and Ward Four, precinct two, 51 percent. O'Connell picked up an additional 109 votes in Ward Three, precinct one, between the December and February elections (the highest number of additional votes in the city) and 83 votes in Ward Four, precinct two (the fifth highest for any precinct). O' Connell ran ahead of Thayer: 309 to 247 in Ward Three, precinct one; 454 to 310 in Ward Four, precinct two. In general, O' Connell ran a whopping 550 votes ahead of Thayer, 1,330 to 880 in Ward Three; 644 votes, 1,770 to 1,126, in Ward Four; and 375 votes, 1,206 to 831, in Ward Five.

89. On November 24, 1901, the *Worcester Evening Spy* claimed O'Connell had won because of Republican factionalism. In 1899, for example, the *Gazette* claimed that the Swedes wanted an alderman but the French did too: "Many Republicans think that the party cannot turn down French voters this year in view of the large draft of French Americans from the Democratic to the Republican fold": *Worcester Evening Gazette,* November 4, 1899. See also fights over Swedish claims for aldermen: *Worcester Evening Gazette,* October 18, November 3, 4, 1899; Swedish dissatisfaction, *Worcester Telegram,* December 9, 1903. Lyttle as possible Citizens' in *Worcester Evening Spy,* November 27, 1896. Other fights over aldermen nominations: *Worcester Evening Gazette,* December 1, 1899; *Worcester Evening Post,* November 27, 1899. Later conflicts split Republicans: *Worcester Evening Spy,* November 19, 1902; *Worcester Telegram,* November 23, 1901, December 1, 5, 1903. In 1903 the Republicans had a tough fight in their caucuses for mayor between Blodgett and Dean: *Worcester Evening Spy,* November 18, 1903. See also unrest among independents, Swedes, and French: *Worcester Evening Spy,* November 24, 1901; *Worcester Telegram,* December 5, 9, 1903.

90. Quotation, "Were he without," in *Worcester Evening Spy,* November 23, 1901. See also *Worcester Evening Spy,* November 23, 24, 26, 1901, November 26, 1902. *Worcester Telegram,* November 15, 1901. The *Spy* estimated the citywide normal Republican vote was 11,000 and the normal Democratic vote 7,500: *Worcester Evening Spy,* December 10, 1901. See also *Boston Herald,* October 6, 1898. The average Democratic vote for mayor, 1900 to 1904, exceeded the average Democratic vote in the two presidential elections, 1900 and 1904, by at least 5 percent in every precinct in the city and over 15 percent in 22 of the city's 42 precincts: *Evening Spy,* November 5, 1902, December 10, 1902, November 9, 1904; *Worcester Telegram,* December 14, 1904.

91. *Worcester Telegram,* March 18, 1901; *Messenger* on February 23, 1901, delighted in O'Connell, "Catholic not of the milk and water type," and scoffed at broadminded Protestants: "Why shouldn't he vote for a Catholic as well as the Catholic votes for a

Protestant? Hasn't the Catholic an equal right to the suffrages of his fellow citizens as anyone else? To come to the point isn't half the population of this city Catholic and what is there to wonder at in choosing a Catholic mayor": *Messenger,* February 23, 1901. See also *Messenger,* October 24, 31, November 7, 21, 28, 1903, January 6, 29, 1904.

92. *Worcester Evening Spy,* November 28, 1901, December 31, 1901, December 6, 1902; The *Spy* claimed in 1901 that O'Connell "has not been partisan . . . he has been modest and conservative": *Worcester Evening Spy,* November 12, 1901. See also *Worcester Evening Spy,* November 23, 28, December 31, 1901; *Worcester Telegram,* November 28, 1901. Efforts by Board of Trade and businessmen led by James Logan: *Worcester Telegram,* November 15, 1901; *Worcester Evening Spy,* November 15, 1901; factionalism in the Democratic party undermines Philip O'Connell: *Worcester Evening Spy,* November 14, 16, 1901, December 10, 12, 1901; quotation, "treachery," in December 10, 1902.

93. Between December 31, 1895, and October 10, 1897, the membership of the Worcester County divisions of the AOH rose from 2,345 to 3,123, and over 1,300 new members were initiated from 1896 to 1898: *Messenger,* March 18, 1899, August 23, 1902; *Worcester Evening Spy,* March 16, 1903; *Dedication Souvenir of the Ancient Order of Hibernians Hall by the United Divisions of Worcester Hibernians, April 8, 1901.*

94. *Messenger,* March 26, 1898, July 15, 1899, May 16, 1903. On Kiely, see the *Worcester Evening Gazette,* December 1, 1924.

95. *Dedication Souvenir of AOH Hall*; *Messenger,* August 4, 25, 1900; Records of the AOH Building Association, Act of Incorporation, March 9, 1898, Division 36 records, Worcester.

96. *Messenger,* June 22, August 12, 1893, June 23, 1894, June 8, 1895, January 13, 1905, February 17, 1907; Program for Emmet Festival, Worcester, July 1, 2, 3, 1905, Program File, WHM.

97. Irish National Foresters Benefit Society, Subsidiary Council, General Rules, April 1, 1902, Worcester organization file, AAS; *Messenger,* October 11, 1902, August 26, 1904, August 25, 1905; *Catholic Messenger,* January 1, 22, April 23, 1915; Bylaws of Branch Charles Stewart Parnell, no. 453, Irish National Foresters, Worcester, 1905, pamphlet file, WHM; *Worcester Telegram,* February 27, 1907; *Worcester Evening Spy,* November 10, 1902.

98. *Messenger,* April 9, 1898, April 8, 1899, November 11, 1899, December 7, 1901, July 5, 1902, March 17, 24, May 26, July 30, November 17, 1905; Records of the Biennial County Convention, AOH Divisions of Worcester County, September 16, 1902, pamphlet file, WHM; Constitution and Bylaws of the Star, G.A.A. Football Club, organized April 1905, pamphlet file, WHM.

99. "Gratifying" quotation in *Messenger,* May 12, 1900; see also *Messenger,* June 8, 1895. In 1899, three of five second-generation Irish running for alderman were members of the AOH or the Clan na Gael or both. In 1899 all five of the second-generation Irishmen slated for state or county offices were members of the AOH or the Clan na Gael, and Philip O'Connell was a member of the AOH. In 1900 the *Telegram* accused

the AOH and the Clan of being a secret political machine working for O'Connell: *Worcester Sunday Telegram,* October 26, 1901; *Worcester Telegram,* November 26, 1899, November 27, 1900, December 1, 1900.

100. Sources: O'Flynn MSS, Convention records, vols. 2, 3, HCC Archives; *Messenger* March 18, 1899, August 23, 1902; Official Convention Souvenir, AOH of Worcester, Massachusetts: August 25 to 28, 1902; dues book of Division 35 AOH, Division 36 Archives; attendance book, Division 36 Archives.

101. *Messenger,* March 18, 1899, September 6, 1902, April 9, 1908; *Illustrated History of the Central Labor Union, 1899,* pp. 172–242; *Labor News,* March 17, June 9, 1906. The Central Labor Union was founded in the old AOH meeting rooms: O'Flynn MSS, "History of the Central Labor Union," HCC Archives. And five unions met in the new rooms in 1916: *Forty Seventh Annual Report on the Statistics of Labor for the Year 1916: Public Document no. 15,* pt. 1, "Thirteenth Annual Directory of Labor Organizations in Massachusetts: 1916," pp. 57–59; *Messenger,* January 14, 1898, September 24, 1898, May 28, 1898, January 3, 1899, April 9, 1899, May 27, 1899, September 23, 30, 1899; *Messenger,* January 28, 1898; laborers quotation, *Messenger,* July 22, 1904; city laborers quotation, *Messenger,* July 23, 1899.

102. *Messenger,* April 9, 1898, May 14, 1898, June 11, 1898, November 26, 1898; *Worcester City Directory* (Worcester: Drew-Allis, 1898); Doyle running for office: *Worcester Evening Spy,* October 21, 23, 1899; *Worcester Telegram,* October 28, 1899.

103. On continued commitment to labor causes, see: *Messenger,* July 7, 21, 1900, May 11, 1901, August 30, 1902, March 25, July 22, 29, 1904, April 24, 1905. For anti-socialism see *Messenger,* November 7, 1903; *Messenger,* October 24, November 7, December 19, 1903, January 1, 15, 29, April 22, 1904. See Henry Bedford, *Socialism and the Workers in Massachusetts, 1886–1912* (Amherst: University of Massachusetts Press, 1966), pp. 184–91.

104. Burke in *Messenger,* January 21, February 4, August 24, 1899; Erie, *Rainbow's End,* pp. 45–106; Mark Karson, *American Labor Unions and Politics: 1900–1918* (Carbondale: Southern Illinois University Press, 1958), pp. 212–44; David Montgomery, *Fall of the House of Labor,* pp. 302–10; Charles Lienenweber, "Class and Ethnic Bases of New York City Socialism: 1904–1915," *Labor History* 22, no. 1 (Winter 1981), p. 47. Irish nationalism also provided little support for radicalism after the 1880s. Patrick Ford, for example, became increasingly conservative: James Rodechko, *Patrick Ford and His Search for America: A Case Study of Irish American Journalism, 1870–1913* (New York: Arno Press, 1976).

105. *Messenger,* March 26, 1898; AOH Building Association, records, 1898, AOH Division 36 Archives.

106. *Messenger,* January 1, 1904.

107. *Recorder,* September 17, 1898, October 1, 22, 1898; quotation, "outrage" and "desecration," in *Messenger,* October 22, 1898. See also *Messenger,* October 29, 1898, November 19, 1898; *Worcester Evening Post,* October 22, 1898; Meagher MSS, clipping, November 8, 1898, in possession of the author.

108. *Messenger,* November 3, 1900, February 16, 1901, October 26, 1901; quotation on O'Connell in October 23, 1901; December 12, 19, 1903, January 29, 1904, November 24, 1905.

109. *Messenger,* December 12, 19, 1903; quotation, "unparalleled," in January 16, 1904; "if [they] do not unite" in January 29, 1904.

110. *Messenger,* September 6, 1902, March 26, May 26, 1905, March 21, 1906; *Catholic Messenger,* February 1, 8, March 1, 8, 15, 1907, February 12, 1915; quotation on demand for Irish history, March 1, 1907. *Worcester Telegram,* February 25, 1907, September 7, 1912; *Worcester Evening Post,* February 25, 1907; O'Dea, *History of the A.O.H.,* pp. 1171, 1196, 1274, 1434–37.

111. *Worcester Evening Post,* March 11, 1904.

112. Records of the Biennial County Convention of the AOH Divisions of Worcester County, Massachusetts, September 16, 1902, Worcester organizations file, AAS; Records of the Biennial County Convention of the AOH Divisions of Worcester County, Massachusetts, September 18, 1906, Worcester organizations file, AAS; John O'Dea, *History of the Ancient Order of Hibernians,* vol. 3, p. 1296; *Messenger,* March 11, 1893, March 30, 1900; *Catholic Messenger,* March 29, 1907; St. Stephen's Dramatic Club, March 16, 1893, St. Stephen's parish archives; *Worcester Sunday Telegram,* June 24, 1888, March 18, 1896; O'Flynn MSS, folio 3, St. Anne's, March 17, 1887, HCC Archives.

113. Lyons, *Ireland Since the Famine,* pp. 219–92; F. S. L. Lyons, *Culture and Anarchy in Ireland, 1890 to 1939* (Oxford: Clarendon Press, 1979), pp. 27–83; Oliver MacDonagh, *States of Mind: A Study of Anglo-Irish Conflict, 1780–1980* (London: George Allen Press, 1983), pp. 104–25; W. F. Mandle, *The Gaelic Athletic Association and Irish Nationalist Politics, 1884–1924* (Dublin: Gill, 1987); Janet Dunleavy, *Douglas Hyde: A Maker of Modern Ireland* (Berkeley: University of California Press, 1991).

114. O'Flynn MSS, folio 2, pp. 608–11, HCC Archives; *Worcester Evening Spy,* July 5, 6, 1880; *Boston Sunday Herald,* July 11, 1880; *Messenger,* January 5, March 30, May 25, September 14, November 30, 1895; quotation, American football "brutish," in January 2, 1895; quotation concern about competition in April 9, 1898; quotation, "immigrants lately arrived," in August 4, 1900; quotation, "prettiest exhibition," in June 7, 1902; July 27, 1901, August 23, 1902; *Catholic Messenger,* June 28, 1907; bylaws of the Star G.A.A. Club, Worcester organizations file, AAS.

115. *Records of the Convention of the AOH Divisions 1908; Records of the Biennial County Convention of the AOH Divisions of Worcester County, September 16, 1902; Records of the Biennial County Convention of AOH Divisions of Worcester County May 28, 1900; Messenger,* April 6, 27, May 28, 1899. O'Dea, *History of the A.O.H.,* pp. 1131, 1269–74; Quotation in *Messenger,* February 17, 1900; See also *Messenger,* April 8, 1899, September 14, 1901, March 17, November 17, 24, 1905; *Messenger,* February 17, June 16, December 29, 1900; Star-Spangled Banner in Gaelic in January 20, 1900; Minnie McCarthy in *Messenger,* February 24, 1900, December 7, 1901.

116. Company B Hibernian Rifles, Order of Dances, September 4, 1905, Worcester organizations file, AAS; *Messenger,* February 17, 1900; June 28, 1907; *Messenger,* De-

cember 20, July 26, August 23, September 27, 1902, August 29, 1903; advertisements in December 4, 1906; support for drinking in *Messenger,* December 1, 1900, January 5, 1901, December 5, April 28, 1903; *Worcester City Directory* (Worcester: Drew-Allis, 1902), pp. 230, 304, 700.

117. *Messenger,* November 5, 16, 1895; *Messenger,* May 14, 1898; On Dolan incident, see *Worcester Evening Spy,* November 13, 1895; Rosenzweig, *Eight Hours for What We Will,* pp. 74–80.

118. See Richard Stott, *Workers in the Metropolis: Class, Ethnicity and Youth in Antebellum New York City* (Ithaca: Cornell University Press, 1990); Michael T. Isenberg, *John L. Sullivan and His America* (Urbana: University of Illinois Press, 1988), pp. 39–59; Rosenzweig, *Eight Hours for What We Will,* pp. 49–81.

119. Quotation about women's suffrage in *Messenger,* April 30, 1898. Division 17, Ladies Auxiliary AOH, for example, was formed by the male Division 35; Dr. Joseph A. Smith was reported to be "the prime mover," *Messenger,* May 25, 1901. Quotation, "what was expected of them," *Messenger,* March 31, 1894. See also *Messenger,* April 21, 1904.

120. *Messenger,* June 18, 1898, October 28, 1899, June 6, 23, 1900, June 22, 1901; Cliona Murphy, *The Women's Suffrage Movement and Irish Society in the Early Twentieth Century* (Philadelphia: Temple University Press, 1989), pp. 14–89. See also Joanna Bourke, *Husbandry to Housewifery: Women, Economic Change and Homework in Ireland, 1890–1914* (New York: Clarendon Press, 1993), and chapter 1 of this book; Kennedy, *The Irish,* pp. 8–10, 52–54, 150–62, 55–61; Hasia Diner, *Erin's Daughters in America: Irish Immigrant Women in the Nineteenth Century* (Baltimore: Johns Hopkins University Press, 1983), pp. 1–42; Gearoid O'Tuathiagh, "The Role of Irish Women under the English Order," Joseph Lee, "Women and the Church Since the Famine," and Mary T. W. Robinson, "Women in the New Irish State," in Margaret MacCurtain and Donncha O'Corrain, eds., *Women in Irish Society: The Historical Dimension* (Westport: Greenwood Press, 1979), pp. 26–36, 37–45, 58–70, 75–84, 168–70.

121. Maria Dougherty, in *Messenger,* March 10, 1900; Nutt, *History of Worcester* vol. 3, p. 300; *Worcester Evening Gazette,* November 14, 1896.

122. O'Flynn MSS, convention records, vol. 2, January 10, 1894, HCC Archives.

123. Ibid.

124. Ibid.

125. O'Flynn MSS, convention records, vol. 2, January 5, May 1, 1895.

126. Ibid., January 14, 1896, pp. 200–201.

127. Ibid.

128. Ibid., March 18, 1896, quotation, "so successful," clipping, March 18, 1897, March 13, 17, 1898, March 17, 1898, March 17, 1901, March 18, 1904, HCC Archives; *Messenger,* March 14, 1903, January 20, 1905, March 2, 1906; *Catholic Messenger,* March 15, 22, 1912, March 16, 1916; *Worcester Evening Gazette,* March 16, 1901; *Worcester Evening Post,* March 14, 1903, March 17, 1905, March 9, 1907. *Worcester Telegram,* March 18, 1899, March 18, 1903, February 27, 1907.

129. *Messenger,* March 4, 1899, December 30, 1899, March 2, 9, April 6, 13, November 16, 1901, February 15, March 8, 1907. The AOH and the Clan na Gael also organized to raise money for a monument to the 1798 rebellion: *Worcester Telegram,* November 7, 1897.

130. Quotation, "lotus food," in AOH County Convention Records, 1906, Worcester organizations file, AAS; quotation, "Nothing short," *Messenger,* March 18, 1904. *Messenger,* October 29, 1898, February 3, 1900, September 30, 1904, October 5, 1906; *Worcester Evening Post,* October 31, 1906.

131. *Messenger,* May 10, August 30, October 11, 18, 25, 1902, October 26, November 2, 1906.

132. *Messenger,* December 30, 1899, January 20, February 3, 10, March 10, June 23, 30, September 29, 1900, April 12, June 14, August 30, 1902.

133. Quotation, "American interests," in *Recorder,* July 8, 1898; quotation, "beside the question" in July 1, 1898; quotation, "purporting," in *Messenger,* July 8, 1899.

134. Quotation, "phrase not new," *Messenger,* February 4, 1899; quotation, "eminently fitting," in *Messenger,* March 8, 1902, *Messenger,* February 18, 1899, September 1, 1901. The *Messenger* also compared American troops in the Philippines to Cromwell's troops in Ireland: *Messenger,* August 5, 1894; Quotation, "absurd stories," in *Recorder* June 10, 1899.

135. *Recorder,* May 20, 27; *Messenger,* September 3, December 10, 1898, March 4, July 8, 1899, September 1, June 21, October 27, November 3, 1900, February 1, March 12, November 2, 1901, February 1, March 22, 1902; quotation, "jingo," in *Messenger,* November 17, 1900. See David Doyle, *Irish Americans: Native Rights and National Empires* (New York: Arno Press, 1976), pp. 227–34; Matthew Jacobson, *Special Sorrows: The Diasporic Imagination of Irish, Polish, and Jewish Immigrants in the United States* (Cambridge: Harvard University, 1995), pp. 177–216.

136. O'Flynn MSS, folio 6, January 28, 1895, HCC Archives; *Boston Post,* February 21, 1895.

137. Quotation, "no young Irish American Catholic," in O'Flynn MSS, folio 6, January 29, 1895, HCC Archives; quotation, "hewers of wood," in *Worcester Sunday Telegram,* March 9, 1910; *Bay State Bank Celebrates Its Seventieth Anniversary* (Worcester: n.p., 1965); *Boston Post,* February 21, 1895.

138. Original officers and trustees listed in *Bay State Bank Celebrates Its Seventieth Anniversary* traced into Nutt, *History of Worcester* vols. 2, 4; Nelson, *History of Worcester County* vol. 3; Rice, ed., *Worcester of 1898*; clipping files, AAS and WHM biographical files; O'Flynn MSS, folio 6, clipping, July 2, 1895, HCC Archives.

139. List from *Bay State Bank Celebrates Its Seventieth Anniversary* traced into *Worcester City Directory* (Worcester: Drew-Allis, 1895), and *Worcester House Directory* (Worcester: Drew-Allis, 1896); Fourteen of twenty-four officers and trustees traced from *Bay State Bank Celebrates Its Seventieth Anniversary* into Nutt, *History of Worcester,* vols. 2, 4, and Nelson, *History of Worcester County,* vol. 2; Rice, ed., *Worcester of 1898*; and clipping files of AAS and WHM; *Worcester City Directory* and *Worcester House Directory* had

been in business for at least fifteen years and had accumulated an average of $20,430 in real property. For second-generation demographics see chapter 2.

140. O'Flynn MSS, folio 6, *Worcester Telegram*, July 1, 1895, Holy Cross College Archives; *Bay State Bank Celebrates Its Seventieth Anniversary*; *Public Document no. 7: Twenty-first Annual Report of the Banking Commissioners of Massachusetts* (Boston: Wright and Potter, 1896), pp. 30–31; *Catholic Messenger*, June 8, 1915.

141. *Messenger*, July 28, 1900, July 12, December 6, 13, 1902; *Worcester Telegram*, June 7, 8, 1903; St. Anne's 1899, pamphlet file, American Antiquarian Society.

142. Of the 55 teachers appointed between September 1, 1894, and April 1, 1895, 8 had Irish names; of 27 teachers appointed between September 1, 1896 and April 1, 1897, 6 had Irish names: *City Document no. 49*, p. 347; *City Document no. 51*, p. 368.

143. *Messenger*, February 12, 1895, February 17, 1900, September 1, 1902, March 17, 1905; *Catholic Messenger*, March 1, 1907; *Worcester Evening Post*, February 21, March 16, 1907; *Records of the A.O.H. Building Association*, October 15, 1907; *Worcester Telegram*, September 7, 1912.

144. *Catholic Messenger*, March 20, 1908; St. John's Temperance and Literary Guild, records of meetings, vol. 2, October 4, 1896; St. Stephen's Festival Program, May 1900, St. Stephen's parish archives; *Worcester Telegram*, November 25, 1907; *Thirtieth Annual Field Day and Games, 1907*, Worcester organizations file, AAS, pp. 12–20.

145. *Messenger*, May 7, 1898, June 9, October 13, 1900, September 8, 1905; *Worcester Evening Post*, November 28, December 4, 7, 8, 1900, August 31, 1907; St. Stephen's Harvest Festival, May 1900, St. Stephen's parish archives; St. John's Temperance and Literary Guild, records, March 13, 1898, April 3, 1898, St. John's parish archives.

146. *Recorder*, May 13, 1898; John J. Riordan, "A Prosperous Club," *Donahoe's Magazine* (December 1897), pp. 140–42; *Catholic Messenger*, August 19, 1915; *Worcester Telegram*, April 23, 1961; O'Flynn MSS, folio 6, "History of the Grattan Literary Association," by James Early, clipping, Holy Cross College Archives; O'Flynn MSS, Convention Records, vol. 2, January 10, 1894, HCC Archives. By 1900 virtually all Washington Club members were white-collar workers and nearly a quarter of them were professionals or prominent businessmen. List drawn from *Worcester House Directory* (Worcester: Drew-Allis, 1900), p. 517, and traced into the *Worcester City Directory* (Worcester: Drew-Allis, 1901).

147. Christopher Kauffman, *Faith and Fraternalism: The History of the Knights of Columbus, 1882–1982* (New York: Harper and Row, 1982), pp. 1–72; Knights of Columbus Massachusetts State Council, "Report of the Annual Convention in Boston, May 5, 1903"; *Messenger*, February 17, 1894, October 19, 1901, September 29, 1905; *Historian's Report Ending July 1, 1943*, Alhambra Council archives, Worcester Massachusetts; *Cable*, May 1929.

148. Kauffman, *Faith and Fraternalism*, pp. 73–94.

149. For the Knights, list drawn from *Cable* (September, October, November 1929), traced into *Worcester City Directories* (Worcester: Drew-Allis) for 1899, 1900, 1901, and 1902 and the 1900 U.S. Census Manuscript Schedules. Of St. John's Temperance and

Literary Guild applicants, 1894–98, traced into Worcester City Directories 22 percent were white-collar workers, and 41 percent were skilled blue-collar workers; 75 percent of St. Stephen's Total Abstinence men were white-collar or skilled blue-collar workers; 88 percent of St. John's Temperance and Literary Guild applicants traced into Census Manuscript Schedules were second-generation; 41 percent of St. Paul's members (18 of 44) traced were low white-collar workers and 35 percent (16 of 44) skilled blue-collar workers; 38 percent of St. Anne's Total Abstinence members were low white-collar workers (22 of 58), and 25 percent were skilled blue-collar workers (15 of 58). Lists drawn from records of St. John's Temperance and Literary Guild, 1897–1898, vol. 2, traced into *Worcester City Directories* and United States Census Manuscript Schedules. St. Paul's Temperance and Literary Lyceum: Eleventh Anniversary Souvenir, Harvest Festival, November 20, 1900, St. Stephen's Temperance Festival, 1896; St. Anne's Total Abstinence Society Souvenir, 1902, all from Worcester organizations file, AAS, traced into *Worcester City Directories*.

Five. The Triumph of Militant, Pan-Ethnic, American Catholicism: The Early 1900s to the 1920s

1. McCoy, *History of the Diocese of Springfield*; *Messenger*, September 29, 1905; McCoy MSS, on Gaelic Revival, n.d., Holy Cross College Archives.

2. Rev. John J. McCoy, "Catholic Viewpoint of the Present French Crisis: Address Before the Congregational Club" (Worcester: 1907), pp. 1–2; McCoy MSS, "The Playground Movement," 1911, Holy Cross College Archives.

3. *Berkshire County Eagle*, February 18, 1914; *Messenger*, September 1, 1902; *Evening Post*, February 21, 1907; *Worcester Telegram*, September 7, 1912.

4. *Messenger*, January 16, 1905. In 1917 when the AOH was running concerts to celebrate St. Patrick's Day, the reporter from the *Catholic Messenger* took pains to preface his enthusiasm by stating: "It was my fortune to be born in this great land of room enough": *Catholic Messenger*, March 23, 1917.

5. *Catholic Messenger*, January 13, 1916, March 30, 1916.

6. *Catholic Messenger*, December 22, 1911; *Worcester Telegram*, March 8, 1907, March 8, September 7, 1912, March 13, 1913.

7. McCoy, *History of the Diocese of Springfield*, p. 33; Quotation in *Columbiad*, vol. 6, no. 11 (November 1899), p. 4.

8. *Report of the Manufactures of the United States 1880*, p. 445; Washburn, *Industrial Worcester*, pp. 93, 201; Industrial Museum Committee, American Steel and Wire Company, "Genesis of American Steel and Wire Company of New Jersey, 1897–1899" (Industrial Museum Committee: Worcester, 1929), p. 18; Cheape, *From Family Firm*, p. 25. Norton Company sales expanded from $412,000 to $16,643,000 in 1918, p. 91. By 1920, Worcester manufacturing companies averaged 72 workers and $298,000 in capital apiece: *Fourteenth Census of the United States*, vol. 9, "Manufactures," pp. 662–63.

9. Donald Tulloch, *Worcester City of Prosperity*, pp. 10–21; Donald Tulloch, "Worcester: City of Prosperity," *Worcester Magazine* (May 1914), p. 122; "Synopsis of the Proceedings of the Sixteenth Annual Convention," *National Metal Trades Association Convention: Worcester, Massachusetts, April 21 and 22, 1914*, pp. 47–48; Cohen, "Machinists' Strike," pp. 163–64. By 1946, nine of the top ten manufacturing firms in Worcester were companies formed in the late nineteenth century like Norton Company, Morgan Construction, and Wyman and Gordon, or were started earlier but emerged out of the pack in the early 1900s through merger and/or expansion, like Graton and Knight, Reed and Prince, Reed and Prentice, Crompton and Knowles, or Rice Barton: David Eisenthal, "The Origins of Charter Reform in Worcester with Particular Attention to Plan E" (Honors thesis, Clark University, 1983), Appendix 2.

10. Mildred McClary Tymeson, *Worcester Bankbook: From County Barter to County Bank, 1804 to 1966* (Worcester: Worcester County National Bank, 1966), quotation, "a distinctly," on p. 77, pp. 54–92; see Naomi Lamoreaux, "Bank Mergers in Late Nineteenth Century New England: The Contingent Nature of Structural Change," *Journal of Economic History* 51, no. 3 (September 1991), pp. 537–57.

11. Nutt, *History of Worcester*, vol. 2, p. 1012, vol. 4, pp. 43–44, 52; Tymeson, *Worcester Bankbook*, p. 77. For a discussion of changes in banking in New England, see Naomi Lamoreaux, *Banks, Personal Connections and Economic Development in Industrial New England* (New York: Cambridge University Press, 1994).

12. *Review and Bulletin* (February 1923; April 1926); *Worcester Magazine* (January 1910), p. 9; *Synopsis of the National Metal Trades Association Convention, 1914*, pp. 90–92; Nutt, *History of Worcester*, vol. 2, pp. 1029, 1031. Anne Keating, *Building Chicago: Suburban Developers and the Creation of a Divided Metropolis* (Columbus: Ohio State University Press, 1988), pp. 36–37; Jon Teaford, *The Unheralded Triumph: City Government in America* (Baltimore: Johns Hopkins University Press, 1984), pp. 174–209, and Teaford, *The Twentieth Century American City* (Baltimore: Johns Hopkins University Press, 1986); Burton Folsom, *Urban Capitalists: Entrepreneurs and City Growth in Pennsylvania: Lackawanna and Lehigh Regions, 1800–1920* (Baltimore: Johns Hopkins University Press, 1981); Carl V. Harris, *Political Power in Birmingham, 1871–1921* (Nashville: University of Tennessee Press, 1977) pp. 39–56, 96–145; David Hammack, *Power and Society: Greater New York at the Turn of the Century* (New York: Columbia University Press, 1987), pp. 31–58, 130–57, 230–58; Harold L. Platt, *The City Building in the New South: The Growth of Public Services in Houston, Texas, 1830–1910* (Philadelphia: Temple University Press, 1983); John Mollenkopf, *Dual City: Restructuring New York* (New York: Russell Sage, 1991), and idem, *The Contested City* (Princeton: Princeton University Press, 1983); William Issell, "Citizens Outside the Government: Business and Urban Policy in San Francisco and Los Angeles, 1890–1932," *Pacific Historical Review* 57, no. 2 (Spring 1988), pp. 117–42.

13. Quotation, "individualism," in "Editorial Reflections," *Worcester Magazine* (March 1913), p. 90; Henry Knapp, "I Believe in Worcester," *Worcester Magazine* (May 1913), pp. 150–53. See also Tulloch, *City of Prosperity*, pp. 23–42; Wright in *Worcester*

Magazine (April 1913), p. 111; "Editorial Reflections," *Worcester Magazine* (March 1913), pp. 89–90. In "To Have and To Hold," *Worcester Magazine* (April 1913), pp. 109–10, the Chamber of Commerce suggested that New England's sons and daughters were being awakened "to a fuller realization of the dangers that threaten their traditional industrial eminency on every side," "Editorial," *Worcester Magazine* (January 1910), pp. 13–14.

14. Cohen, "Worcester Machinists," pp. 154–58; Cheape, *From Family Firm*, pp. 131–39; Stephen W. Tener, "How a Great Corporation Is Solving the Safety and Welfare Problems of Its Employees," *Worcester Magazine* (April 1913), pp. 110–11.

15. "Synopsis of the Proceedings of the Sixteenth Annual Convention," *National Metal Trades Association Convention: Worcester, Massachusetts, April 21 and 22, 1914*, pp. 47–48; Cohen, "Machinists' Strike," pp. 163–64; quotation, "foster," in Tulloch, *Worcester: A City of Prosperity*, p. 218.

16. *Annual Report of the Massachusetts Bureau of Labor Statistics, 1913*, pp. 55–57; *Annual Report of the Massachusetts Bureau of Labor Statistics, 1920*, pp. 66–68.

117. Rosenzweig, *Eight Hours for What We Will*, p. 23; Cohen, "Worcester's Machinists," pp. 154–57; C. F. Johnson, "History of the Central Labor Union, Worcester, Massachusetts" (M.A. thesis, Clark University, 1935), pp. 15–35; Rosenzweig, *Eight Hours for What We Will*, p. 22; *Annual Report, 1913*, pp. 55–57. Forty of the city's sixty-seven unions were building-trades, transportation, service-industry, or textile locals. Bruce Cohen, "The Worcester Machinists' Strike of 1915," *Historical Journal of Massachusetts* (Summer 1988), pp. 155–56.

18. C. F. Johnson, "History of the Central Labor Union," pp. 39–43; John Harrigan, P. B. Keefe, and James Flavin to Bishop Beaven, September 14, 1911; Bishop Beaven to John Harrigan, September 15, 1911, St. Paul's parish file, Parish Files, Springfield Diocesan Archives.

19. Cohen, "Worcester Machinists' Strike," pp. 157–59; William Edward Zeuch, "An Investigation of the Metal Trades Strikes of Worcester, 1915," (M.A. thesis, Clark University, June 1916).

20. Cohen, "Worcester Machinists' Strike," pp. 165–66; Zeuch, "An Investigation," pp. 6–22, 32–33, 35–37, on "not one address," p. 35.

21. Cohen, "Worcester Machinists' Strike," pp. 160–65, quote on p. 164; Zeuch, "An Investigation," p. 36; Charles W. Cheape, *From Family Firm to Modern Multinational: Norton Company, A New England Enterprise* (Cambridge: Harvard University Press, 1985), pp. 125–28.

22. Cohen, "Worcester Machinists' Strike," pp. 165–70.

23. *Evening Post*, November 24, 1917; Cheape, *From Family Firm*, pp. 125–29.

24. Bruce Cohen, "Worcester, Open Shop City: The National Metal Trades Association and the Molders Strike of 1919," in Kenneth Fones-Wolf and Martin Kauffman, eds., *Labor in Massachusetts: Selected Essays* (Westfield, Mass.: Institute for Massachusetts Studies, 1990), pp. 169–73; *Labor News*, October 25, 1918; *Annual Report of the Bureau of Labor Statistics, 1920*, pt. 3, "Labor Organizations," p. 19. Worcester's union population rose to 9,423 by the end of 1917: *Annual Report of the Bureau of Labor Sta-*

tistics, 1917, pt. 4, "Labor Organizations," p. 47. See also Cheape, *From Family Firm*, pp. 128–30; *Labor News*, May 24, 1918; *Evening Post*, September 24, 1918.

25. Sales at Norton plunged from $18.8 million in 1920 to $4.3 million in 1921: Cheape, *From Family Firm*, pp. 120–21; *Fifty-first Annual Report of the Massachusetts Bureau of Labor Statistics, 1921* (Boston: Wright and Potter, 1921), pt. 2, p. 44; *Evening Post*, September 4, 1918, December 2, 1920; *Review and Bulletin* (January 1920), "Annual Report"; "Annual Report" (January 1921); "Annual Report" (February 1920); (September 1921); (October 1921); *Labor News*, November 21, 1919; on 18,000 unemployed, see *Worcester Telegram*, November 12, 1921.

26. *Labor News*, January 10, June 6, 1919.

27. Cheape, *Norton Company*, p. 128; *Labor News*, September 20, 1918. Memorandum, George N. Jeppson, "Thursday Noon Club," October 15, 1918; Frederick Babcock, Worcester Chamber of Commerce, to all members, August 11, 1919, Norton Company papers, WHM.

28. Memorandum for Thursday Noon Club, George Jeppson, December 26, 1918, Norton Company papers; F. D. Babcock to all members of Chamber of Commerce, August 11, 1919, Norton Company papers; Frank Dresser to George Jeppson, August 1, 1919, Norton Company papers; Jerome George to George Jeppson, October 18, 1919, Norton Company papers; Aldus Higgins to Jerome George, October 19, 1918, Norton Company papers. Jerome George to Samuel Woodward, December 17, 1919, Woodward papers, box 6; Cohen, "Open Shop City," pp. 179–83.

29. Jeppson to Dresser, August 4, 1919; F. D. Babcock to all members, August 11, 1919; Babcock to Jeppson, July 25, 1919; quotation, "some of us," in George Jeppson to Chester E. Reed, November 8, 1919, Norton Company papers.

30. Memorandum, George Jeppson, "Thursday Noon Meeting, Worcester Club, 12:30," May 8, 1919, Norton Company papers. This memorandum listed names, telephone numbers and agreement to attend.

31. *Evening Post*, September 23, 24, 28, 1920; *Labor News*, September 26, 1919; *Worcester Telegram*, November 1, 3, 4, 1921, December 7, 1922; *Annual Report of the Statistics of Labor for the Year Ending November 30, 1925*, pt. 3, "Statistics of Labor Organizations in Massachusetts, 1923 and 1924," p. 9; Strikes around the country: *Worcester Telegram*, November 11, 1921; *Evening Post*, October 9, 1921, November 9, 1919; Cohen, "Worcester Open Shop City," pp. 176–93.

32. In 1897 Socialist Rostow Wood had polled 1,139 votes in the local election for mayor. After 1910 no Socialist candidate for mayor received more than 379 votes; see Nutt, *History of Worcester*, vol. 1, p. 398; Johnson, "History of the Central Labor Union," pp. 25–26; *Labor News*, April 26, 1917; *Evening Post*, December 10, 1917; Democrat O'Rourke backs raises for teachers, *Worcester Telegram*, November 27, 1917; Republican Holmes favors eight hours for city workers, *Labor News*, November 16, 1916, *Worcester Telegram*, December 4, 1916. In 1918 the *Labor News* claimed "Fortunately in Worcester men selected by the Democrats have always proved loyal to the cause of labor and this may have been responsible *in a large measure* for the lack of interest in

making any real move toward the formation of a local labor party": *Labor News*, November 15, 1918. *Evening Post* November 8, 1919.

33. Cohen, "Worcester Machinists' Strike," pp. 160–66; *Worcester Telegram*, December 11, 14, 1915, October 30, 1916; *Evening Post*, December 9, 10, 11, 13, 1915, December 5, 1916; *Labor News*, December 4, 18, 1915; Barrett had won Ward Three, 1,071 to 856; won Ward Five, 1,033 to 635 in 1913; lost Ward Six, 1,519 to 800. Carberry had lost Ward Three, 937 to 965, won Ward Five, 992 to 627, and lost Ward Six, 1,639 to 744 in 1914. Reardon won Ward Three, 1,294 to 814 (223 votes more than Barrett and 357 more than Carberry), won Ward Five, 1,217 to 445 (184 more than Barrett and 225 more than Carberry), and lost Ward Six, 1,066 to 1,397 (266 more than Barrett and 322 more than Carberry). *Worcester Telegram*, December 4, 13, 1916; *Labor News*, November 9, 16, 23, 30, December 7, 14, 21, 1915. On Machinists' homes, see Roberge, "Structural Correlate," pp. 80, 25–27, 54, 16; Weiss, "Patterns and Processes," p. 154.

34. The Democratic percentage for the Swedish neighborhood on Bell Hill, Ward Two, precinct four, rose from 14 percent to 24 percent from 1914 to 1915, and fell back to 17 percent the next year. The Democratic percentage rose from 7 percent to 16 percent from 1914 to 1915 in Quinsigamond Village, Ward Six, precinct three, and fell back to 9 percent the following year. *Worcester Telegram*, December 13, 1916; *Labor News*, November 9, 16, December 7, 1916.

35. Cheape, *From Family Firm*, pp. 130–41. On elite and businessmen in politics, see later in this chapter.

36. *Census of the Commonwealth of Massachusetts, 1905*, "Population and Social Statistics," (Boston: Wright and Potter, 1909) pp. 252, 445; Washburn, *Industrial Worcester* pp. 24, 180, 253, 301–10.

37. *Thirteenth Census of the United States Taken in the Year 1910*, vol. 2, "Population: Reports by States with Statistics for Counties, Cities, and Other Civil Divisions: Alabama to Montana," (Washington, D.C.: GPO, 1913), p. 896; Rose Zeller, "Changes in the Ethnic Composition and Character of Worcester's Population" (Ph.D. diss.: Clark University, 1940), p. 67. In 1910, five wards exceeded the Yankee proportion of the city population and all five were on the west side. See also Weiss, "Patterns and Processes," pp. 74, 107–12, *Richard's Standard Atlas of the City of Worcester, Massachusetts* (Springfield, Mass.: Richard's Map Co., 1911), plate 10 and plate 27; "New Homes for Worcester," *Worcester Magazine* (May 1916), p. 105.

38. Rosenzweig, *Eight Hours for What We Will*, pp. 187, 206–15; *Labor News*, November 16, 1916, December 6, 1916; *Worcester Telegram*, March 26, December 11, 1918, June 12, December 12, 1910; *Worcester Telegram*, December 1, 1917, October 15, 1924, November 8, 1922, December 8, 1924; quotation in *Evening Gazette*, November 7, 1924; *Evening Post*, November 20, 1923.

39. Nutt, *History of Worcester*, vol. 2, pp. 797–850; 757–78; 895–976.

40. Ibid., vol. 3, pp. 17, 61–64, 67–69, 241; vol. 2, p. 947, 953, 963, 783–84; *At the End of Fifty Years* (Worcester: privately published, 1938). A study of the Worcester Club membership of 1905 reveals an overlapping of membership among the elite institu-

tions and clubs. Of the Worcester's Club members, for example, 52.4 percent were also members of the Tatnuck Country Club, and 14.6 percent were linked to the Worcester Art Museum: study of members of Worcester Club in 1905 based on biographical information on 82 of 172 members located in Nutt's *History of Worcester*, vols. 3, 4. See also P. P. Swan, "Personal Histories of Worcester's Social and Industrial Leaders with Certain Sociological Interpretations" (M.A. thesis, Clark University, 1929), p. 76; Stanley Hull, "Social Selection in Worcester, Massachusetts" (M.A. thesis, Clark University, 1947), pp. 62–67.

41. *Thirteenth Census of the United States, 1910*, "Population by States," p. 868; Wahlstrom, "A History of the Swedish People of Worcester," pp. 19–20, 240–41; Karl J. Karlson, "The Swedish Population of Worcester: A Study in Social Survey" (M.A. thesis, Clark University, 1910); *Fourteenth Census of the United States, 1920*, vol. 2, "Population: Report by States," p. 896. Collective biographical file: Nutt, *History of Worcester*, vols. 3, 4; Nutt, *History of Worcester*, vol. 1, p. 353. Four Swedes were members of the Worcester Club, for example, in 1932: *The Blue Book for Worcester and Nearby Cities* (Springfield Gardens, N.Y.: Blue Book Co., 1932), pp. 105–6.

42. Wards One, Two, and Six contained over 79 percent of the Swedish foreign-born population in 1920: *Fourteenth Census of the United States Taken in the Year, 1920*, vol. 3, "Population: Composition and Characteristics of the Population by States" (Washington, D.C.: GPO, 1922), p. 896. Wahlstrom, "History of Swedish People," pp. 19–20, 32, 240, 63–79, 114, 93–94, 50–121; *Evening Gazette*, August 26, 1907; *Worcester Telegram*, December 13, 1916. On language, *Fourteenth Census, 1920*, "Population," pp. 1010–11; *Labor News*, November 16, 1916, December 6, 1913; *Worcester Telegram*, March 26, December 11, 1918, June 12, December 12, 1910.

43. B. W. Lamphear, "The Italian Population of Worcester" (M.A. thesis, Clark University, 1909), p. 8; Zeller, "Changes in the Ethnic Composition," pp. 81–83, 138; Bryan Thompson, "Cultural Ties Determinants of Immigrant Settlement in Urban Areas" (Ph.D. diss.: Clark University, 1971), pp. 94–95; *Thirteenth Census, 1910*, vol. 1, "Population," pp. 1010–14.

44. *Fourteenth Census, 1920*, vol. 2, "Population by States," p. 470.

45. Thompson, "Cultural Ties," pp. 94–95; *Fourteenth Census, 1920*, "Population," p. 896; *Worcester House Directory* (Worcester: Drew-Allis, 1916), pp. 426, 240, 288–90. "Cosmopolitan Worcester," *Worcester Magazine* (August 1916), p. 181; Thompson, "Cultural Ties," p. 145. By 1916, 17 Italian households had moved in among the 41 families who lived on Gage Street on St. Anne's Hill: *Worcester House Directory, 1916*, p. 195.

46. "The Growth of a Worcester Neighborhood," Worcester Polytechnic Institute, Interactive Qualifying Project, 1980, p. 20, pamphlet file, WHM; "Cosmopolitan Worcester," *Worcester Magazine* (August 1916), p. 181; Babinski, *By Raz*, p. 23; *Fourteenth Census, 1920*, "Population," p. 896; "Cosmopolitan Worcester," *Worcester Magazine* (August 1916), p. 181; "The Growth of a Worcester Neighborhood," p. 20.

47. Of these, 9,249 were second-generation: 5,010 were immigrants: *Thirteenth Census, 1910*, "Population by States," p. 868. *Fourteenth Census, 1920*, "Population,"

p. 896. In 1903, more than a quarter of all French voters in Worcester lived in two precincts, Oak Hill, Ward Three, precinct four, and South Worcester, Ward Five, precinct one: *Le Worcester Canadien, 1903.* Quotation "let us remain," in *L'Opinion Publique,* August 16, 1907.

48. "Cosmopolitan Worcester," *Worcester Magazine* (August 1916), pp. 180–82; Holy Rosary in *Messenger,* June 27, 1906; *Catholic Free Press,* November 20, 1961; St. Margaret Mary in *Catholic Messenger,* June 24, 1921; *L'Opinion Publique,* August 7, 1907, September 4, 1907, February 16, 1908; Marriage Records, 1917 to 1921, Our Lady of the Angels parish archives, Worcester, Massachusetts.

49. *Worcester Telegram,* November 15, 16, 18, 20, 22, 1905; Rice, ed., *Worcester of 1898,* pp. 141–42; Melvin Overlock, *The Working People: Their Health and How to Protect It* (Worcester: Blanchard Press, 1910), p. 9; *Worcester Telegram,* November 25, 28, December 7, 11, 12, 13, 1905, December 5, 6, 7, 12, 1906.

50. *Evening Post,* October 28, 1920; *Worcester Telegram,* November 27, 1907; Nutt, *History of Worcester,* vol. 3, p. 361; Mildred Tymeson, *The Story of Worcester Tech, 1865–1965* (Worcester: W.P. I., 1965), pp. 90–91.

51. *Worcester Telegram,* November 22, 23, first quotation from Logan on 26, second quotation on 27, December 5, 7, 1907, December 7, 8, 1908, December 4, quotation by Brooks on 6, 1911; *Evening Post,* December 7, 1908, December 3, 5, 9, 1910, December 4, 1913, quotation by Wright on December 9, 1915; *City Document no. 66* (Worcester: Belisle Printing, 1911), pp. 31–32.

52. *City Document no. 66,* pp. 31–32. The number of building permits rose from less than 700 in 1907 to over 1,800 in 1912: Roberge, "Structural Correlate," pp. 95, 173. The Republicans claimed that the city was fifth in building growth of all cities in the nation during this time and that it was prompted by improvements: *Worcester Telegram,* December 11, 1911, *Worcester Evening Post,* December 5, 1913, Wright quotation on December 9, December 10, 1915. Between 1900 and 1912 the miles of track for Worcester's street railways rose from 46 to 251 miles and passengers from 14 million to 59 million: *Annual Report of Railroad Commissioners,* pp. 473, 385.

53. Lists of nominees from election day covered: *Worcester Telegram,* December 11, 1912, December 10, 1913, December 9, 1914, December 8, 1915, December 13, 1916, December 11, 1918; lists of party committee members in *Worcester City Directory* (Worcester: Drew-Allis, 1910), p. 829; *Worcester City Directory* (Worcester: Drew-Allis, 1908), p. 882; *Worcester City Directory* (Worcester: Drew-Allis, 1907), p. 861.

54. Geoffrey Blodgett, "Yankee Leadership in a Divided City, 1860–1910," Paul Kleppner, "From Party to Factions: The Dissolution of Boston's Majority Party, 1876–1908," and Charles H. Trout, "Curley of Boston: The Search for Irish Legitimacy," all in Ronald Formisano and Constance Burns, ed., *Boston 1700–1980: The Evolution of Urban Politics* (Westport: Greenwood Press, 1984); Jack Beatty, *The Rascal King: The Life and Times of James Michael Curley, 1874–1958* (Reading, Mass.: Addison-Wesley, 1992); Joseph Dineen, *The Purple Shamrock: The Honorable James Michael Curley of Boston* (New York: 1949); Alec Barbrook, *God Save the Commonwealth: An*

Electoral History of Massachusetts (Amherst: University of Massachusetts Press, 1973), pp. 15–58. James J. Connolly in his recent book, *The Triumph of Ethnic Progressivism: Urban Political Culture in Boston, 1900–1925* (Cambridge: Harvard University Press, 1998), suggests that the Boston Irish took up the language of the Progressive assault on vested interests and employed it for ethnic purposes, but the Irish in Worcester seemed too confused by their need to endorse fiscal caution to embrace Progressive rhetoric with any enthusiasm. Only Peter Sullivan, as we shall see, and David O'Connell, as we have seen, appeared to marry a biting Progressive rhetoric with ethnic solidarity, and they were far more cautious than their Boston counterparts.

55. *Worcester Telegram,* November 25, 1905, December 4, 11, 1905; *Labor News,* October 20, 1906, November 27, 28, 1907; Duggan's parents were born in Dublin, Ireland: Thomas A. McAvoy, *Course of Lectures on Irish History* (Worcester: Messenger Printing, 1915), p. 252.

56. *Evening Post,* November 19, 28, December 7, 1907, December 3, 4, 1913; *Worcester Telegram* September 8, 1908. Duggan polled 2,206 votes, or 42 percent of the total, in Wards One, Nine, and Ten in 1906. He polled 1,707 votes, or 28 percent, in 1907. Barrett also polled 28 percent in 1908.

57. *L'Opinion Publique,* June 28, 1907, October 22, 1924; *Le Worcester Canadien* (Worcester: J. Arthur Roy, 1891), p. 175: George Jeppson to Samuel Winslow, December 11, 1919, Norton Company papers.

Votes on license among Catholic ethnics:

French Canadians	Ward 3, precinct 4:	476 yes, 196 no in 1911
		360 yes, 107 no in 1914
	Ward 4 precinct 3:	308 yes, 104 no in 1918
		444 yes, 132 no in 1919
Italians	Ward 3 precinct 3:	272 yes, 34 no in 1918
		455 yes, 83 no in 1919
Poles	Ward 5 Precinct 3:	309 yes, 87 no in 1918
		437 yes, 93 no in 1919

In 1942 Catholic ethnic districts voted strongly against the dissemination of birth control information: Italian Ward Three, precinct three and precinct eight, against 251 to 80 and 329 to 94 respectively; Polish and Irish Ward Six, precinct three, against 439 to 138; and French and Irish Ward Four, precinct 4, against 448 to 132. Votes in *Worcester Telegram,* November 4, 1942. In 1891, *Le Worcester Canadien* claimed: "In the years just past, a grave association was publicly made against our emigrated compatriots. Certain journals have claimed the French Canadian families who live in the American union are not as prolific as those in the home country, and that, little by little, they are imitating their Yankee fellow citizens by limiting the number of children in the family. Nothing could be more false. Our compatriots have not degenerated in this respect, and they scrupulously preserve the traditions of their ancestors. It is not rare to find in Worcester families with 8 to 12 children. Is that the way it is in the large Canadian cities with populations the size of Worcester's? . . . If we are to believe the reports published in the press, the population of our old parishes of the Province of Quebec is decreasing at an alarming rate, while that of our Canadian parishes in the U.S. is growing rapidly . . .": *Le Worcester Canadien* (Worcester: J. Arthur Roy, 1891), p. 175. Few aspects of Irish American history have received more attention than Irish efforts to gather other ethnics into the Democratic party. See Erie, *Rainbow's End*; Thomas McLean Henderson, *Tammany Hall and the New Immigrants: The Progressive Years* (New York: Arno Press, 1976); Edgar Litt, *Beyond Pluralism: Ethnic Politics in America* (Glencoe: Scott Foresman, 1970), pp. 26–28; J. Joseph Huthemacher, *Massachusetts People and Politics, 1919–1933* (Cambridge: Belknap Press, 1959). In a broader sense the forging of a multiethnic Democratic party coalition has also been a critical issue in American political history. See Paul Kleppner, *Continuity and Change in Electoral Politics, 1893–1928* (Westport: Greenwood Press, 1987); Gerald H. Gamm, *The Making of New Deal Democrats: Voting Behavior and Realignment in Boston, 1920–1940* (Chicago: University of Chicago Press, 1990); Alan Lichtman, *Prejudice and the Old Politics: The Presidential Election of 1928* (Chapel Hill: University of North Carolina Press, 1979); John Allswang, *A House For All Peoples* (Lexington: University of Kentucky Press, 1971).

58. In the Polish-dominated Ward Five, precinct three, the Democratic municipal vote fluctuated between 66 percent and 86 percent from 1911 to 1924. Italian Ward Three, precinct three, and French Canadian precincts, Ward Three, precinct four (which later became Ward Four, precinct three), fluctuated much more wildly, from 33 percent to 90 percent and 37 percent to 80 percent, respectively. *Labor News*, November 30, 1916, quote from Trahan in Petrin, "Ethnicity and Political Pragmatism," p. 293.

59. *Messenger* August 6, 1898, April 1, 1899, October 17, December 2, 16, 1899; Petrin, "Ethnicity and Political Pragmatism," pp. 283–90; *Worcester Evening Post*, December 9, 1899; *Worcester Evening Gazette*, December 11, 1899. *Worcester Telegram*, November 17, 1898. Lists of nominees from election day covered: *Worcester Telegram* December 11, 1912, December 10, 1913, December 9, 1914, December 8, 1915, December 13, 1916, December 11, 1918; Petrin, "Ethnicity and Political Pragmatism," pp. 291–94; quotation from Bachand in *Worcester Telegram*, December 8, 1908; *Evening Post*, November 29, 30, December 1, 1910; *Catholic Messenger*, December 15, 1911; *Worcester Telegram*, December 12, 1911.

60. *Worcester Telegram*, December 11, 1909. The Republicans had two Jews and an Armenian on their city committee in 1908: *Worcester City Directory* (Worcester: Drew-Allis, 1908), p. 881. Democrats nominated William Nardi in 1916 and Anthony Lepore for Common Council in 1913, and Republicans nominated Joseph Cussone and Luciano Manzi for the same offices in 1916. Nardi and Lepore won, illustrating the Irish dilemma: Republicans could nominate Italians on the east side without taking seats

from their strong supporters; Irishmen had to be sacrificed for Italians in sure seats: *Worcester Telegram*, December 10, 1913, December 13, 1916.

61. *Catholic Messenger*, February 19, 1915, quotation, "served notice," from March 5, 1915; *Evening Post*, November 24, 27, December 1, 3, 5, 6, 8, 10, 1906.

62. *Worcester Telegram*, December 14, 1910, December 4, 1911, December 5, 1916; *Evening Post* December 3, 1913, December 10, 1915; *Worcester Telegram*, quotation from Duggan, November 26, November 27, 28, 1907, December 4, 5, 6, 1911. *Evening Post*, November 19, 28, December 4, quotation from Barrett, December 7, 8, 10, 1908, December 2, quotation from O'Connell, December 5, 1910, December 6, 1912.

63. As noted earlier, Duggan's votes in Wards One, Nine, and Ten dropped from 42 percent to 28 percent from 1906 to 1907. See below, note 97; *Worcester Telegram*, December 6, 1911.

64. Logan also noted in his speech the "constant stream of mothers" who came to him in hard times: *Worcester Telegram*, quotation from Logan, December 8, 1908; *Worcester Telegram*, November 27, 1907. David O'Connell talked of building waiting stations for trolley riders, a high school on the east side, medical clinics, and a city market: *Worcester Telegram*, December 4, 5, 6, 9, 1911.

65. Allswang, *A House for All Peoples*; Chris McNickle, *To Be Mayor of New York: Ethnic Politics in the City* (New York: Columbia University Press, 1994); Steven Erie, *Rainbow's End: Irish Americans and the Dilemmas of Urban Machine Politics, 1840–1985* (Berkeley: University of California Press, 1988).

66. Erie, *Rainbow's End*, pp. 79–91; Allswang, *A House for All Peoples*, pp. 21–35; Kleppner, *Change and Continuity*, pp. 125–31. In 1910, Eugene Foss, Democratic candidate for governor, carried Worcester by 1,603 votes, the first Democrat to carry the city since Butler. John A. Thayer also carried the city in his successful race for Congress, and liberal Cornelius Carmody barely lost his race for state senate: *Worcester Telegram*, November 9, 1910. David Walsh carried the city by even more, 2,464 votes, over Charles Sumner, the Progressive candidate, in 1913. Walsh ran as much as five or six to one over Sumner in Wards Three, Four, and Five. Hugh O'Rourke won for the state senate in the same election, carrying Ward Four by 753 votes: *Worcester Telegram*, November 5, 1913. Wilson ran better than any Democratic candidate since at least the 1870s, losing the city by only 1,166 votes, 11,764 to 10,598. Frederick Mansfield, the Democratic candidate for governor, lost by only 1,900 votes and John F. Fitzgerald, candidate for the Senate, by only 1,406, 11,477 to 10,051: *Worcester Telegram*, November 1, 1916.

67. *Catholic Messenger*, December 15, 1911, January 19, 1912, December 15, 1921. In the Italian district, Ward Three, precinct three, for example, the Democratic vote rose 7 points from 1908–9 to O'Connnell's elections, 1910–12, and declined 19 points from the 1910–12 average to the 1913–18 average. On the whole, O'Connell ran better in the east side ethnic wards, Three, Four, and Five, in his victory in 1911 than Duggan did, on average, in his two wins in 1905–6: 78 percent to 72 percent, 86 percent to 80 percent and 85 percent to 78 percent respectively. He ran worse in the northwest Yankee wards, One and Ten: 31 percent to 49 percent and 32 percent to 41 percent respectively.

68. Francis M. Carroll, *American Opinion and the Irish Question, 1910–1923: A Study in Opinion and Policy* (New York: Gill and Macmillan), pp. 26–36; 46–54; 89–99; Emmons, *The Butte Irish,* pp. 349–86; Dennis Clark, *The Irish in Philadelphia: Ten Generations of Urban Experience* (Philadelphia: Temple University Press, 1973), pp. 148–52. An Irish company, the Emmet Guards, "the first to go when the stars and stripes were imperilled and the last to leave the border" during Pershing's Mexican incursion, were greeted by 75,000 people when they returned: *Worcester Telegram,* November 7, 1916. George Jeppson said "All Swedish people were considered more or less pro German at the beginning of the war four years ago, but that is changed now": *Worcester Telegram,* November 5, 1918. *Evening Post,* October 29, November 19, December 1, 7, 10, 11, 1917, September 9, 15, 28, 1918, November 29, 1918. *Catholic Messenger,* AOH pledge for support of the war April 13, 1917, January 11, 18, 25, February 8, 22, 1918.

69. *Labor News,* November 23, 1916, October 2, 6, 1918; *Evening Post,* September 11, 14, 16, 18, 20, 24, 1918.

70. *Evening Post,* October 23, November 1, 1917, September 2, 15 quotation, "slackers," September 18, 1918, October 12, 1918; *Labor News,* August 30, 1918; *Evening Post* October 25, 29, November 1, 5, 1917, September 2, 12, 16, 28, October 2, 6, 1918.

71. *Worcester Telegram,* December 2, 3, 1917; *Labor News,* September 13, 1918, October 4, 1918; *Evening Post,* December 4, 1917, October 30, 1917; *Labor News,* September 13, October 25, November 15, 1918, February 7, March 21, April 25, October 10, December 26, 1919; *Worcester Telegram,* November 22, 1919, December 6, 1919; *Evening Post,* September 4, 7, 14, 1918, September 2, 1920.

72. *Labor News,* October 4, 1918, September 26, November 28, December 5, 1919; *Worcester Telegram,* December 6, 1919; *Evening Post,* October 11, November 8, 22, December 6, 8, 10, 1919. For the weakness of the Democrats on the national and state levels: Kleppner, *Change and Continuity,* pp. 45–48; Huthemacher, *Massachusetts: People and Politics,* pp. 19–76.

73. *Evening Post,* September 29, 1918, October 25, 1919.

74. Interview with Peter Sullivan Jr., August 24, 1989; "Mayor Sullivan's Inaugural Address," *City Document no. 74,* p. 17; *Evening Post,* November 1, 1920, December 1, 3, 1920; *Worcester Telegram,* December 1, 2, 3, 4, 15, 1920.

75. *Worcester Telegram,* September 13, December 2, 4, 6, 10, 15, 1920; *Evening Post,* quotation, "ladies of leisure," December 13, 1920, November 26, 1918, October 25, November 1, 1920; *Evening Post,* October 28, November 3, 4, 6, 8, 1920. Housing construction would not reach prewar highs again until 1924: Roberge, "Structural Correlate," p. 95a. *Worcester Telegram,* November 4, 21, 1921, December 3, 9, 12, 1921, November 9, December 5, 6, 1922.

76. *Evening Post,* October 9, 1919, November 8, 22, December 6, 1919; *Labor News,* December 5, 1919; *Worcester Telegram,* December 6, 10, 1919; George Jeppson to Samuel Winslow Jr., December 11, 1919, Norton Company papers; *Evening Gazette,* November 1, 4, December 14, 1910; *Labor News,* September 26, October 10, November 28, December 5, 1919; *Evening Post,* October 9, 11, November 8, 22, December 6, 1919; *Worcester*

Telegram citing Holmes on law and order, December 5, 8, 1919. The number of registered voters rose from 26,890 to 30,050: *Worcester Telegram* December, 9, 10, 1919.

77. Lewis Buckley to Samuel Winslow Jr., December 11, 1919; quote from George Jeppson to Samuel Winslow Jr., December 15, 1919, Norton Company papers. O'Rourke had lost the French precinct, Ward Four, precinct three, 248 to 163; Sullivan carried it, 402 to 186. O'Rourke won the Italian precinct, Ward Three, precinct three, 220 to 85; Sullivan won it, 391 to 103.

78. The Sullivan vote in the Italian Ward Three, precinct three, rose from 79 percent in 1919 to 89 percent in 1920 and 91 percent in 1921. Sullivan's vote in the French Canadian Ward Four, precinct three, increased from 68 percent in 1919 to 84 percent in 1920 and 1921. *Evening Post,* November 4, 1920; *Worcester Telegram,* December 13, 15, 1920, November 11, 24, December 4, 1921.

79. Lewis Buckley to Samuel Winslow Jr., December 11, 1919, George Jeppson to Samuel Winslow Jr., December 15, 1919; *Catholic Messenger,* November 11, December 9, 1920, December 15, 1921; *Worcester Telegram,* December 14, 1921, December 4, 1922.

80. Duggan, for example, won an average of 49 percent of the vote in Ward One and 41 percent in Ward Ten in his two victories in 1905 and 1906, and rolled up majorities of 72 percent, 80 percent and 78 percent, respectively, in Wards Three, Four, and Five. David O'Connell won 31 percent in Ward One and 32 percent in Ward Ten, and 78 percent, 86 percent, and 85 percent, respectively, in Wards Three, Four, and Five. During his years of triumph, 1920, 1921, and 1922, Sullivan's percentages averaged 39 percent in Ward One, 36 percent in Ward Ten, and 88 percent, 85 percent and 91 percent in Wards Three, Four, and Five.

81. *Review and Bulletin* (January 1920, February 1920, September 1921, October 1921), quotation "manifestly absurd" in January 1922, April 1922; George Jeppson to Calvin Coolidge, January 9, 1919, Norton papers. Jeppson said that Osgood Bradley had laid off 1,100 of 2,200 workers, Norton 700 of 3,500, Graton and Knight 750 of 3,100, American Steel and Wire 800 of 5,500 by that date and the city's foundries were working at 25 percent capacity.

82. Nutt, *History of Worcester,* vol. 4, pp. 511–12; Memorandum for G. N. Jeppson, May 8, 1919, Thursday Noon Club Meeting, Norton Company papers; *Review and Bulletin* (January 1920, January 1922, December 1922), invite Sullivan and singers (June 1923), invite Walsh (September 1923), appoints Healey (April 1924, May 1924, January 1925, February 1926, November 1927); Clippings: John F. Tinsley, October 24, 1926, January 16, 1927, November 16, 1931; Biographical file, WHM; *Worcester Telegram,* November 21, 1952; John F. Tinsley, "Looms for the World: Crompton Knowles in Textile Machinery Manufacture since 1837," pamphlet, 1949, pamphlet file, WHM.

83. Collective biographical file, Nutt, *History of Worcester,* vols. 3, 4; collective biographical file, Nelson, *History of Worcester County,* vol. 3; Nutt, *History of Worcester,* vol. 3, pp. 324, 97, vol. 4, p. 674; *Review and Bulletin* (April 1924, January 1920); *Evening Post,* November 1, 1918.

84. Nelson, *History of Worcester County*, vol. 3, p. 353; *Worcester Telegram*, November 22, December 4, 5, 6, 1922, December 8, 12, 1923; *Evening Post*, December 7, 1923; *Evening Gazette*, October 25, 1923. O'Hara ran 145 votes ahead of Harry Goddard, the Republican mayoral candidate, in Ward Three, 296 votes ahead of him in Ward Four, and 136 votes ahead of him in Ward Five.

85. *Worcester Telegram*, November 22, 1922. In the 1922 primary, O'Hara racked up 1,143 votes in his own Ward Two, to 295 for his opponent Corliss. He ran much closer in the other wards: losing Wards Three, Five, Seven, Eight, and Nine, and winning Ward One, 267 to 232, Ward Four, 51 to 34, Ward Six, 403 to 359, Ward Ten, 546 to 494. *Evening Gazette*, November 19, 1923; endorsed by prominent Republican women, *Worcester Telegram*, November 20, 1923. The *Telegram* said in 1923 that it is "evident that many of the voters anxious for a return of a Republican administration had taken into consideration the vote getting ability of Mr. O'Hara": *Worcester Telegram*, November 21, 1923. Nelson, *History of Worcester County* vol. 3, p. 99.

86. *Worcester Telegram*, September 29, October 9, 16, 17, 25, 27, 29, November 17, 19, 23, 24, December 1, 6, 8, 12, 1923; *Evening Post*, December 7, 1923; *Evening Gazette*, September 29, October 9, November 17, 19, 1923. *Labor News*, November 30, 1923. Building permits and construction rose rapidly in the mid-1920s. By 1924 they had risen far above prewar levels: Roberge, "Structural Correlate," p. 95a; Weiss, "Patterns and Processes," p. 173. The *Review and Bulletin* of the Chamber Of Commerce noted in 1922 that "not for several years has there been so much building in Worcester . . . new residences are springing up in every part of the city" (May 1922).

87. *Worcester Telegram*, October 9, 1923, November 17, 21, December 8, 12, 1923. O'Hara ran as well in Wards Nine (60 percent), Ten (71 percent), and One (67 percent), as Goddard had in 1922, but finished 6 percentage points ahead of Goddard in Ward Four, 3 points ahead in Ward Three, and 2 points ahead in Ward Four, to win the election. The *Telegram* noted: "the vote for mayor in the Democratic precincts was particularly significant and gave an indication of the dissatisfaction of the mayor's supporters." They pointed out that Sullivan won Ward Four by 3,064 votes in 1922, but only by 2,347 in 1923: *Telegram*, December 12, 1923.

88. *Worcester Sunday Telegram*, November 12, 1978; *Catholic Messenger*, September 29, October 21, 28, November 17, 1921. *Worcester Telegram*, December 4, 1922. Charged with KKK sympathies, Goddard claimed on December 9, 1922, "I am sick of denying this": *Worcester Telegram*, December 9, 1922; *Gazette*, October 8, 1923. Southwick, *Twice Told Tales*, p. 139; *Worcester Sunday Telegram*, September 12, 1978; *Evening Post*, September 26, 27, 28, 1923; *Worcester Telegram*, September 27, 28, 1923.

89. Kevin Hickey, "The Immigrant Klan: A Socio-Economic Profile of the KKK Membership in Worcester, Massachusetts," Appendix E, unpublished paper, American Association for Geographers Meeting, April 20, 1981. From the larger of two lists of members identified by Klan opponents and provided by Vincent Powers, Hickey found that 30.0 percent were low white-collar workers, 27.9 percent were skilled blue-collar, 28 percent were semiskilled blue-collar and 8 percent were unskilled blue-collar workers. For interpretations of the Klan as a populist movement, a good overview is

Stanley Coben, *Rebellion Against Victorianism: The Impetus for Cultural Change in 1920s America* (New York: Oxford University Press, 1991), pp. 136–58.

90. *Evening Post,* December 17, 1918; George Jeppson to F. W. Stearns, January 6, 1919, Norton Company papers; *Worcester Telegram,* September 28, 1923.

91. *Worcester Telegram,* September 28, 29, 1923; *Evening Post,* quotation in September 28, 1923.

92. Hickey, "The Immigrant Klan," summary tables and p. 8; *Worcester Telegram,* December 4, 11, 1916, quotation in December 1, 1917, November 3, 1921, November 6, 1924; *Evening Post,* October 17, 1925.

93. Hickey, "The Immigrant Klan," summary table; Cheape, *From Family Firm to Multinational,* pp. 120–31.

94. *Worcester Telegram,* November 9, 1910. Roosevelt polled well in Swedish Greendale, Ward One, precinct four, 226 to Taft's 253, and on Swedish Bell Hill, Ward Two, precinct four, 278 to 306. He carried Quinsigamond Village, Ward Six, precinct three, 326 to 165. See above, note 34, on votes for Reardon.

95. *Labor News,* November 9, 16, 23, December 7, 1916, January 11, 1917; *Evening Post,* November 8, 1920; *Worcester Telegram* November 5, 1918. Minor won Ward Six 1,060 votes to 570 over Wright. He rolled up one-quarter of his total vote in the primary in Ward Six, 1,060 of 4,656 votes: *Worcester Evening Post,* November 24, 1920.

96. *Worcester Telegram,* November 21, 1923.

97. Estimate of 5,000 in *Worcester Sunday Telegram,* November 12, 1978; Hickey, "Immigrant Klan," Appendix E, identified 2,897 members in the city between 1922 and 1925. *Worcester Telegram,* October 22, 29, November 13, 1924; *Worcester Telegram,* October 18, 19, 20, 21, 1924; *Catholic Messenger,* October 24, 1924; *Evening Post,* October 17, 18, 1924.

98. *Worcester Telegram,* October 22, 29, 1924; *Catholic Messenger,* November 14, 1924: "The KKK and the Catholic Church" delivered in Union Church, Worcester Massachusetts, November 9, 1924, pamphlet file, WHM; Huthemacher, *Massachusetts People and Politics,* pp. 76–115.

99. *Worcester Telegram,* October 18, 19, 20, 21, 1924; *Evening Post,* October 17, 18, 1924; *Catholic Messenger,* October 24, 1924.

100. *Worcester Telegram,* October 24, 25, 28, November 10, 12, 13, 15, 18, 19, 20, quote in 21, 1924. Squires carried Ward Six, precinct two, with 53 percent of the vote and Ward Seven, precinct four, with 57 percent of the vote (both in Main South, Southwestern Worcester area), and won 48 percent of the vote in Ward Six, precinct four (Quinsigamond Village).

101. *Worcester Telegram,* November 10, quotation, "low business," in November 12, November 13, 15, 18, quotation on "Irish who went to vote" in November 19, 20, 1924. O'Hara won 866 votes on the east side in the 1924 primary compared to 463 in the 1923 primary, an increase of 187 percent.

102. *Worcester Telegram,* October 21, 1924; quotation in *Catholic Messenger,* October 24, 1924; *Worcester Telegram,* quotation in November 19, 1924, December 6, 8, 10. McKeon complained that the Chamber of Commerce and the NMTA controlled

O'Hara and backed his campaign with their economic might: *Worcester Telegram*, December 8, 10, 1924.

103. O'Hara beat Walsh 26,492 to 11,616: *Worcester Telegram*, December 9, 10, 1925.

104. *Evening Gazette*, October 17, 28, November 9, 1927; *Evening Post*, November 18, 1925, October 1, 10, 13, 15, 1927, October 9, 16 1929, November 2, 4, 5, 6, 1929. Nelson lost by 15,714 to 8,444 and carried Ward Six which included the Swedish neighborhood, Quinsigamond Village: *Evening Post*, November 19, 1925. George Nelson, a Frodigh supporter, told a Frodigh rally in 1927: "affairs have come to a sad pass when a Republican mayor surrounded himself with a herd of left-handed Republicans and then expects the regular Republicans to go out and elect the nominee. The time has come when the West Side resents this high handed procedure": *Evening Post*, October 1, 1927. In the 1925 primary O'Hara polled 7,253 votes in Wards Nine, Ten, and One; in the 1927 primary he polled 5,763 votes there; in the 1929 primary he polled 5,182.

105. *Worcester Telegram*, October 28, 1927; Nelson, *History of Worcester County*, vol. 3, p. 293; On Mahoney's speech, Honorable John H. Meagher to the author; J. Joseph Huthemacher, *Massachusetts: People and Politics, 1919–1933* (Boston: Belknap Press, 1959); Allswang, *A House for All Peoples* pp. 123–49.

106. *Worcester Telegram*, October 28, 1931; *Worcester Evening Post*, October 9, 1929; October 13, 1927, October 10, 12, 1929; *Worcester Telegram*, November 9, 1927; *Bulletin of Worcester's Taxpayers Association*, vol. 1, no. 2 (February 1932); Roberge, "Structural Correlate," p. 95a; Weiss, "Patterns and Processes," p. 173. The *Boston News Bureau*, a financial newspaper, declared Worcester's industries in "fine condition," fully recovered from the postwar depression by 1927: *Evening Post*, October 17, 1927.

107. *Evening Post*, October 19, 1925, October 8, 11, 12, 13, 14, 15, 16, 17, 1927, October 16, 1929. Of 1,086 changes in 1927, 564 came from Wards Three, Four, and Five. Of the re-registrants that year, the following numbers by wards had Irish names: 50 in Ward One; 68 in Ward Two, 70 in Ward Three, 73 in Ward Four, and 41 in Ward Five. A one in three sample of the re-registrants in Ward Four produced 56 names: 6 small proprietors; 25 low white-collar; 11 skilled blue-collar; 6 semiskilled; 7 unskilled. A small sampling of 1 in 15 of the re-registrants in Ward Nine produced the following result: 1 small proprietor; 4 clerks; 1 semiskilled worker. *Evening Gazette*, October 25, 1923; *Worcester Telegram*, November 17, December 8, 10, 12, 1923, December 7, 9, 1925. *L'Opinion Publique*, October 25, 1924; *Evening Post*, October 13, 14, 15, 1927, November 3, 1927. The Democratic vote in Ward Five, precinct three, fell off from 82 percent in 1923 to 75 percent in 1924 to 62 percent in 1925. In the Italian Ward Three, precinct three, it fell off from 82 percent in 1923 to 69 percent in 1924 to 58 percent in 1925; *Evening Gazette*, October 17, November 9, 1927; *Evening Post*, November 18, 1925, October 1, 10, 13, 15, 1927, October 9, 16, 1929, November 2, 4, 5, 6, 1929.

108. *Evening Post*, November 18, 1925, October 8, 11, 12, quotation on "Mexican army" in October 13; see also October 14, 15, 16, 17, 1927, October 10, 12, 14, November 1, 1929, October 9, 1931.

109. *City Document no. 82* (1928) pp. 110–11; *City Document no. 81* (1927) pp. 104–9; *Worcester Telegram,* November 17, 1924, December 7, 9, 1925; *Evening Post,* October 11, 1927. In 1927, Republicans put up French Canadians for alderman, council, and school committee in Ward Four, but no new immigrants: *Evening Post,* November 9, 1927, and no French Canadians or new immigrants for state representative or state senator in 1928: *Worcester Telegram,* November 7, 1928.

110. *Catholic Messenger,* July 5, 1928, September 6, 1928, October 25, 1928. Between March 9, 1928, and October 17, 1928, 10,442 women registered to vote: *Women's Voter List,* Board of Registrars, City Hall, Worcester Massachusetts. On October 17, the *Evening Gazette* reported that 62,439 people in the city were registered to vote; on November 8, 1928, the paper reported that there were 77,543 registered voters in Worcester.

111. Leland Maynard to A. P. Rugg, October 23, 1928, Box 28, Rugg papers, Massachusetts Historical Society; A. P. Rugg diary, November 2, 1928, Massachusetts Historical Society. *Worcester Telegram,* October 31, November 2, 1928. Author's interview with Eleanor O'Donnell, August 24, 1989; author's interview with Lawrence O'Connell, August 29, 1989.

112. *Worcester Telegram,* December 4, 1921, November 7, 1924, October 28, 1927, November 6, 7, 8, 1928; *Evening Post,* November 6, 7, 1928; *L'Opinion Publique,* October 30, 31, November 1, 5, 6, 1928.

113. *Worcester Telegram,* November 6, 7, 8, 1928; *Evening Post* November 6, 7, 1928; Esthus and McClymer, *ga till Amerika,* p. 123.

114. *Evening Post,* November 6, 1928; *Catholic Messenger,* November 22, 1928; Esthus and McClymer, *ga till Amerika,* p. 137.

115. *Worcester Telegram,* November 7, 1928; *Evening Post,* November 8, 1928.

116. In the heavily Italian precinct, Ward Three, precinct three, the proportion of the Democratic vote rose from 45 percent to 87 percent, 1924 to 1928. In the heavily French Canadian precincts, Ward Four, precinct three, and Ward Five, precinct four, the increases were 29 percent to 70 percent and 44 percent to 82 percent. The vote in the east side wards rose 15,710 over 1924. *Evening Post,* November 3, 6, 8, 1928; *Worcester Telegram,* November 7, 1928.

117. Alan Lichtman, *Prejudice and the Old Politics: The Presidential Election of 1928* (Chapel Hill: University of North Carolina Press, 1979); Gerald H. Gamm, *The Making of New Deal Democrats: Voting Behavior and Realignment in Boston* (Chicago: University of Chicago Press, 1989); Samuel Lubell, *The Future of American Politics* (New York: Harper, 1952); Allswang, *A House for All Peoples*; Paul Kleppner, *Continuity and Change in Electoral Politics, 1893–1928* (New York: Greenwood Press, 1987); Huthemacher, *Massachusetts People and Politics*; McNickle, *To Be Mayor of New York,* pp. 1–52; Steven Erie, *Rainbow's End: Irish Americans and the Dilemma of Urban Machine Politics, 1840–1985* (Berkeley: University of California Press, 1988), pp. 91–106; Peter Tuckel and Richard Maisel, "Voter Turnout Among European Immigrants to the United States, " *Journal of Interdisciplinary History* 24, no. 4 (Winter 1994), pp. 410–11.

118. Frodigh won in Ward One by 3,038 to 1,208; in Ward Two, 2,712 to 1,581; and in Ward Six, 2,264 to 985: *Evening Gazette*, October 19, 1927, *Evening Post*, October 16, 1929. *Evening Post*, November 2, 5, 6, 1929. The *Post* claimed "voters of Swedish extraction in 1927 did not like the political methods of Mayor O'Hara . . . the reaction against O'Hara even more pronounced this year and is so strong that the leading Swedish paper has advised its readers to vote outright and en masse for Mahoney": *Evening Post*, November 2, 1929.

119. Mahoney polled 651 votes to O'Hara's 636 in Quinsigamond Village, Ward Six, precinct four, but carried Ward Four by only 62 percent polling 3,235 votes and Ward Five by only 58 percent polling 2,530, compared to Smith's 77 percent and 5,861 and 78 percent and 4,885, respectively: *Evening Post*, November 6, 1929; *Worcester Telegram*, November 7, 1928; *Evening Post*, November 8, 1928.

120. The number of building permits issued plunged from over 2,000 in 1930 to less than 1,000 in 1931: Weiss, "Patterns and Processes," p. 173. *Worcester Telegram*, October 9, 10, 13, 14, 28, 31, November 2, 3, 4, 1931. In 1927, against O'Hara, Mahoney had carried Ward Four by only 62 percent with 3,235 votes and Ward Five by 58 percent with 2,530 votes. In 1931 against Frodigh, Mahoney carried Ward Four by 85 percent with 5,827 votes, Ward Five by 82 percent with 4,664 votes; Smith had carried Ward Four by 77 percent with 5,861 votes and Ward Five by 78 percent with 4,885 votes: *Evening Post*, November 6, 1929; *Worcester Telegram*, November 7, 1928; *Evening Post*, November 8, 1928; *Worcester Telegram*, October 9, 10, 13, 14, 28, 31, November 2, 3, 4, 1931.

121. *Labor News*, August 18, 1906; "Directory of Labor Organizations," *Massachusetts Bureau of Labor Statistics*, pp. 55–57; "Directory of Labor Organizations," pt. 1, *Annual Report of the Massachusetts Bureau of Labor Statistics, 1920*. Swedes headed five unions, Italians two, French four, and Jews three in 1920. Other union leaders bore either Yankee or English names or names that could not be identified; *Evening Post*, August 9, 1897, October 25, 1898, January 2, February 23, 1904, February 6, 1907. *Catholic Messenger*, September 2, 1909, March 26, May 14, 1915, July 19, 1918. For the support for municipal ownership, see *Messenger*, January 12, 1906, and *Evening Post*, October 22, 1906. The *Post*'s support for strikers, September 22, 1915. Mellen introduced housing legislation in 1907 and got the urban homestead commission established. For Mellen's role in public housing, see *Labor News*, November 22, 1917, and Roy Lubove, *Community Planning in the 1920s* (Pittsburgh: University of Pittsburgh Press, 1965), pp. 5–12. The *Post* also supported the income tax, initiative and referendum, and nationalization of railroads, November 1, 1909, November 25, 1912, October 23, 1918. In 1906, James F. McGovern backed limited working hours for women and children, prolabor antistrike legislation, and regulation of railroads in his campaign for Congress: *Evening Post*, November 2, 3, 1906. John F. McGrath, candidate for Congress, backed the eight-hour day: *Evening Post*, October 31, 1918. Cornelius Carmody, candidate for the state senate supported limited hours for women, direct election of senators, and the income tax: *Worcester Telegram*, November 1, 1910. Peter Sul-

livan, who was an alderman, state senator, and later became mayor, was an advocate of municipal ownership of street railways while on the board of aldermen and of public housing in the legislature: *Evening Post,* November 26, 1918. Florence Donohue, Democratic candidate for the Constitutional Convention, supported the initiative, referendum, municipal ownership of utilities, urban home rule "and all other progressive measures": *Labor News,* April 26, 1917.

122. The *Post* decried socialism, for example, as too "narrow and cramped" for Americans, September 14, 1918. *Catholic Messenger,* November 10, 1911, March 29, 1918, April 19, 1918, May 22, 1919, July 17, 24, 31, 1919, October 16, 23, 30, 1919, November 6, 27, 1919, January 8, 15, 1920, June 13, 1924, March 15, 1912, September 30, 1915, December 16, 1915, October 7, 1910, December 22, 1917, April 18, 1913, March 30, 1916, January 20, 1916, July 10, 1914, August 5, 1915, April 26, 1918, March 7, 1915, January 19, 1912, December 7, 1913, for the complaint of a reader about too much antisocialism, see May 15, 1912. McCoy quotation in *Berkshire County Eagle,* February 18, 1914. For other examples of Catholic antisocialism, see *Labor News,* November 30, 1916; *Worcester Telegram,* November 29, 1923.

123. *Evening Post,* November 30, 1912. See also December 6, 1912.

124. See chapter 3.

125. Donald Cole, *Immigrant City: Lawrence, Massachusetts, 1845–1921* (Chapel Hill: University of North Carolina Press, 1963), pp. 184–85; Henry F. Bedford, *Socialism and the Workers in Massachusetts, 1886–1912* (Amherst: University of Massachusetts Press, 1966), pp. 185–93; Mark Karson, *American Labor Unrest and Politics* (Carbondale: University of Southern Illinois Press, 1958), pp. 212–84; David Emmons, *The Butte Irish: Class and Ethnicity in an American Mining Town* (Urbana: University of Illinois Press, 1989), pp. 180–291; David Montgomery, *The Fall of the House of Labor* (Cambridge: Cambridge University Press, 1989), pp. 306–10; Charles Leinenweber, "The Class and Ethnic Bases of New York City Socialism, 1904–1915," *Labor History,* vol. 22 (1981), p. 47; John McKivigan and Thomas Robertson, "The Irish American Worker in Transition, 1877–1914: New York City as a Test Case," in Timothy Meagher and Ronald Bayor, eds., *The New York Irish* (Baltimore: Johns Hopkins University Press, 1996), pp. 301–21.

126. *Catholic Messenger,* January 19, 1912, March 15, 1912, December 7, 1913, April 8, 1913, April 8, 1913, March 30, 1916, May 22, 1919, July 17, 24, 31, 1919, January 18, 1920, January 15, 1920, April 26, 1928, May 3, 1928; *Columbiad,* May 1899. On Washington as a Catholic, see *Catholic Messenger,* May 17, 1912. McCoy quotation in McCoy, *History of the Springfield Diocese* p. 33; McCoy quotation in *Berkshire County Eagle,* February 18, 1914. O'Connell quote in *Evening Post,* December 6, 1912.

127. *Messenger,* June 8, 1901; *Catholic Messenger,* April 30, May 7, 1915, June 10, 1920, November 25, 1921; McCoy, "Catholic Viewpoint on the Present French Crisis," p. 3; *Berkshire County Eagle,* February 18, 1914.

128. *Catholic Messenger,* February 22, 1907, December 8, 1911, February 19, 1915, March 26, 1915, July 8, 22, 1921; *Messenger,* June 8, 1901; St. John's parish announcement book, May 28, 1905, St. John's parish archives; *Labor News,* March 29, 1917.

129. *Messenger,* April 4, 1903, July 27, 1903, November 18, 1903, July 27, 1905; *Catholic Messenger,* June 20, 1913, quotation, "try first," in May 16, 1913; *Catholic Messenger,* G. Stanley Hall quotation in July 1, 1910.

130. Interview with Lawrence O'Connell, August 29, 1989; *Cable* (January 1929), p. 10, (March 1929), p. 1.

131. R. Scott Appleby, *Church and Age Unite: The Modernist Impulse in American Catholicism* (Notre Dame: University of Notre Dame Press, 1992); Jay P. Dolan, *The American Catholic Experience: A History From Colonial Times to the Present* (Garden City: Doubleday, 1985), pp. 308–20; William Halsey, *The Survival of American Innocence: Catholicism in an Era of Disillusionment, 1920–1940* (Notre Dame: University of Notre Dame Press, 1980); Robert E. Sullivan and James M. O'Toole, *Catholic Boston: Studies in Religion and Community, 1870–1970* (Boston: Archdiocese of Boston, 1985); James M. O'Toole, *Militant and Triumphant: William Henry O'Connell and the Catholic Church in Boston* (Notre Dame: University of Notre Dame Press, 1992), pp. 9–120; Tentler, *Seasons of Grace,* pp. 297–300, 408–14, 426–66; Robert Trisco, "Bishops and Priests in the United States," pp. 109–292, and Michael Gannon, "Before and After Modernism: The Intellectual Isolation of the American Priest," pp. 292–376, in Ellis, ed., *The Catholic Priest in the United States*; James Hennessy, *American Catholics: A History of the Roman Catholic Community in the United States* (New York: Oxford University Press, 1981), pp. 204–53; Edward Kantowicz, *Corporation Sole: Cardinal Mundelein and Chicago Catholicism* (Notre Dame: University of Notre Dame Press, 1983), pp. 10–98, 237–41; Gerald Fogarty, *The Vatican and the American Hierarchy from 1870 to 1965* (Stuttgart: Anton Hiersemann, 1982), pp. 177–277; Monsignor Thomas Griffin to Bishop Beaven, May 27, 1910, St. John's parish file, Springfield Diocesan Archives.

132. *Messenger,* July 28, 1900, September 20, 1902; *Catholic Messenger,* February 10, 1907, April 9, 1915, September 23, 1915; *Columbiad,* vol. 7, no. 1 (January 1900), p. 3.

133. Clipping, Alumni Reception, Holy Cross, book of clippings 1896 to 1903, John H. Meagher scrapbooks in author's possesion; *Catholic Messenger,* March 10, 1908, March 24, 1911, May 17, June 21, 1912, September 20, 1912, October 25, 1912; Quote in Rev. John J. McCoy to Bishop Beaven, March 10, 1908, St. Anne's file, parish files, Springfield Diocesan Archives.

134. *Catholic Messenger,* October 3, 1913, March 20, 1914.

135. *Catholic Messenger,* quotation about Catholic Elks, August 11, 1911, October 3, 1913, March 20, 1914, November 22, 1918; Bishop Beaven to Mgr. Thomas Griffin, January 10, 1895, St. John's parish archives; *Messenger,* July 5, 1902, October 19, 1906.

136. Ancient Order of Hibernians Building Association Minutes, October 15, 1909, AOH Division 36, archives, Worcester Massachusetts; quotation on YMCA in *Catholic Messenger,* October 7, 1915.

137. *Worcester Evening Gazette,* October 10, 1932.

138. *Columbiad* quotation in vol. 6, no. 11 (November 1899), p. 6; see also vol. 6, no. 10 (October 1899), p. 10; *Catholic Messenger* May 24, 1912, May 4, 1916, June 21, 1918.

139. *Catholic Messenger,* quotation, "mental food," February 8, 1907, February 15, 1907, January 27, 1911, December 19, 1913, August 15, 1915, March 9, 1917; Catholic

Women's Club, pamphlet, pamphlet file, WHM; *Catholic Free Press,* September 10, 1954, January 6, 1956; John F. Coughlin to Pastors, May 10, 1907, St. John's parish file, parish files, Springfield Diocesan Archives. One of five Catholic Women's Club members drawn from list in *Catholic Messenger,* January 27, 1911.

140. St. Anne's pamphlet, 1899, pamphlet file, AAS; *Worcester Telegram,* June 7, 8, 1903; *Messenger,* July 12, 1902, June 6, 13, 1903; *Catholic Messenger,* September 2, 1921, *Catholic Free Press,* April 16, 1957, April 17, 1970; *City Document no. 65,* p. 1042; "Annals of the Sisters of Mercy, Worcester," p. 121, Sisters of Mercy Archives, Worcester, Massachusetts; McCoy MSS, "Examination Records of Parochial Schools in the Springfield Diocese," Holy Cross College Archives. The new schools, St. Stephen's, St. Peter's, Blessed Sacrament, St. Paul's, and Sacred Heart, enrolled 2,596 students in 1930: *Records of the School Committee of the City of Worcester, 1931,* June 5, 1931, p. 259.

141. *Centennial Echoes: The First One Hundred Years of St. Peter's Parish in Worcester, Massachusetts, 1884–1954;* "Annals of the Sisters of Mercy," p. 121; McCoy, "Examination Records"; Rev. John F. Conlon to pastors, St. John's parish file, parish files, Springfield Diocesan Archives; Rev. William Ryan to Bishop Beaven, August 28, 1912, Blessed Sacrament parish file, parish files, Springfield Diocesan Archives; *Records of the School Committee of Worcester of 1919,* December 5, 1919, p. 384; *Records of the School Committee of Worcester, 1931,* June 5, 1931, p. 259; *Catholic Mirror: A Century of Catholicism in Western Massachusetts* (Springfield: Mirror Press, 1930), pp. 21–22.

142. *Catholic Messenger,* quotation, "atheism," in November 10, 1911; see also July 29, 1915; February 12, 1915, June 24, 1915, September 2, 1915, October 28, 1910, July 1, 1910, May 13, 1910, March 24, 1911, June 21, 1918; *Messenger,* December 25, 1903, January 8, 1904; Meagher MSS, clipping, Holy Cross Alumni Banquet; *Golden Conquest,* p. 231; *Catholic Mirror: A Century of Catholicism in Western Massachusetts* (Springfield: Mirror Press, 1930), p. 22.

143. *Catholic Messenger,* November 25, 1910, August 11, 1911, March 5, 1915, October 7, 1915; quotation, "dating," William Kelleher to author, July 6, 1993; Mary O'Reilly to author, June 30, 1993; F. A. Jaques to author, June 12, 1993; Rev. Thomas McDermott to the author, June 20, 1993; Arthur Sheedy to the author, June 15, 1993. Among the Foresters of America Courts in Worcester, the Irish dominated the Cunningham, Heart of the Commonwealth, and Quinsigamond courts, but there were separate French, Swedish, and Italian courts and Yankee-dominated Court Damascus: lists of dead in "Associated Courts, F. of A. of Worcester, Memorial Services, AOH Hall, June 11, 1905," Worcester organizations file, AAS; *Blue Book,* 1932. Olive Higgins Prouty, *Pencil Shavings,* p. 13.

144. *Catholic Messenger,* March 29, 1907, February 22, 1907, April 22, 1910, November 10, 1911.

145. *Sixth Annual Report of St. Vincent's Hospital, 1899; Evening Spy,* May 17, 1895; *Bay State Bank Celebrates Its Seventieth Anniversary;* Polachi and Rebboli traced into *Worcester City Directory* (Worcester: Drew-Allis, 1898) pp. 395, 402.

146. Sister Marie Michael Archangel, *"By This Sign You Will Live": History of the Congregation of the Little Franciscans of Mary, 1889–1955* (Worcester: 1964), pp. 243–316;

Recorder, October 29, 1898; *Messenger,* October 28, 1898; Mother Mary of Providence, "History of the Community," vol. 1, p. 158; O'Flynn MSS, clipping, November 7, 10, 17, 1890, folio 1, Holy Cross College Archives; Census Manuscript Schedules: 1900 Census.

147. *Seventeenth Annual Report of St. Vincent's Hospital Conducted by the Sisters of Providence, Year Ending December 31, 1911*; *Catholic Messenger,* June 8, 1915; clipping file, August 27, 1925, WHM.

148. *Messenger,* February 18, 1899; Rev. Robert Ahearn to Rev. William Goggin, November 12, 1909; Rev. William Ryan to Bishop Beaven, October 27, 1913; Angelina Yando to Rev. Robert Ahearn, May 26, 1925; Bishop Beaven to Rev. William Goggin, November 22, 1916; Rev. L. Grenier to Rev. William Goggin, February 6, 1919, and November 20, 1916; George H. Miller to Bishop O'Leary, April 9, 1922; Mrs. Prosper Handfield to Rev. James F. Ahéarn, November 11, 1909, St. Paul's parish archives; Mrs. J. G. Vaudreil to Bishop Beaven, April 3, 1910, Blessed Sacrament parish files; Mr. Fred Bove to Bishop Beaven, September 20, 1908; Mr. Fred Rondeau to Bishop Beaven, September 28, 1909; Mr. George Shapp to Bishop Beaven, September 27, 1909, St. Paul's parish file, Springfield Diocesan Archives. There were at least eleven such names on the list for St. Peter's: St. Peter's parish monthly collection, November 1929 to October 1930, Worcester organizations file, AAS; Rev. John J. McCoy to Rev. Ahearn, March 24, 1906, January 1, 1907, March 30, 1908, St. Anne's file, Springfield Diocesan Archives; St. John's announcement books, 1941–45, 1946–50, St. John's parish archives.

149. Mrs. J. G. Vaudreil to Bishop Beaven, April 3, 1910, Blessed Sacrament files; *Catholic Mirror,* p. 72; *Catholic Messenger,* June 24, 1926; Marriage records, Our Lady of the Angels parish, 1917–21, Our Lady of the Angels parish archives, Worcester; *Worcester Telegram,* November 27, 1922.

150. *Catholic Messenger,* June 27, 1926; Belisle, *Livre D'Or,* pp. 153–55; *Catholic Free Press,* November 20, 1961.

151. *Catholic Messenger,* September 21, 1922, June 27, 1926.

152. St. Stephen's Total Abstinence Society, Festival Souvenir, May 1900, St. Stephen's parish archives, Worcester.

153. *Catholic Messenger,* June 27, 1915; *Worcester Telegram,* November 3, 1917.

154. *Catholic Messenger,* June 21, 1907, March 9, 1916; *Catholic Messenger,* November 5, 1909, February 11, 1910, quotations in April 22, 1910, August 22, 1913, February 6, 1914, April 24, 1914; *Evening Post,* April 18, 1910; *Messenger,* April 20, December 21, 1901; quotation about Catholic Federation goals in Dolan, *Catholic Experience,* p. 341.

155. Orsi, *Thank You St. Jude,* pp. 7–22.

156. Kantowicz, *Corporation Sole,* pp. 65–83; O'Toole, *Militant and Triumphant,* pp. 143–72; Hennessy, *American Catholics,* pp. 195–96; Colman Barry, *The Catholic Church and German Americans* (Milwaukee: Bruce, 1953), pp. 131–277; Charles Shanabruch, *Chicago's Catholics: The Evolution of an American Identity* (Notre Dame: University of Notre Dame Press, 1981), pp. 1–30; 104–232.

157. *Catholic Messenger,* November 5, 1909, quotation, "beyond calculation," April 22, 1910, July 8, 1926; *Messenger,* October 10, 1903.

158. *Catholic Messenger,* quotation, "along the lines of church in Ireland," May 14, 1915, quotation on Italian Sunday school, March 2, 1916, quotation, "apart," May 8, 1919, April 29, 1910, November 5, 1909, April 22, 1910, September 30, 1915, December 16, 1915, March 31, 1915, December 2, 1915.

159. "Irish Night" at the Knights of Columbus in 1917 revealed the popularity of the new Irish American culture. Five hundred members and friends attended to listen to a mix of Tom Moore tunes and Tin Pan alley Irish American music: *Messenger,* March 16, 1917.

160. *Catholic Messenger,* February 4, February 25, quotation on March 24, 1926.

161. *Catholic Messenger,* November 5, 1909, April 22, 1910, April 22, 1913; *Evening Post,* April 18, 1910.

162. *Evening Post,* November 2, 1906; Nutt, *History of Worcester,* vol. 1, pp. 309, 344–46; "Diamond Jubilee of St. Casimir's Parish," pp. 54–56; John F. Quigley to Rev. Thomas H. McLaughlin, 1910, St. Stephen's parish archives; Thompson, "Cultural Ties as Determinants," pp. 136–49; *Worcester Sunday Telegram,* November 15, 1981.

163. Alexandre Belisle, *Livre D'Or Des Franco Americaines de Worcester, Massachusetts* (Worcester: Le Compagnie de Publication de Belisle, 1920), pp. 19–60, 71, 119–20, 130–32, 147–48, 171–74, 175–77, 167–79, 225–26, 225–65.

164. *L'Opinion Publique* quotation on "vestiges," August 24, 1911, October 29, 1900, June 5, 1911, August 22, 1911; Rumilly, *Histoire Des Franco Americaines,* pp. 176, 189, 204, 222; *Catholic Messenger,* March 15, 1907.

165. *Messenger,* February 23, 1901; *Catholic Messenger,* May 1, 1914, April 31, May 4, 1915, August 5, 1921; "The New Home of the K. of C.," *Worcester Magazine* (December 1914), pp. 337–41; *Cable* (March 1921).

166. Members drawn from *Cable,* September, October, and November issues in 1929 and traced into the 1900 Census Manuscript Schedules. See also *Cable* (March 1921); "Recorder: Minutes of Meetings and Lists of proposed Members, 1905–1915," Alhambra Council, K. of C. Archives, Worcester, Massachusetts. Ellen Skerrett, "The Religious Dimension," in McCaffrey, ed., *The Irish in Chicago,* pp. 47–49.

167. *Catholic Messenger,* May 24, 1912, December 11, 1914, June 24, quotation, young man's aspiration," September 23, 1915; "Eleventh Anniversary Banquet, Alhambra Council, no. 88, K. of C. February 14, 1905," in private possession of Eleanor O'Donnell, Worcester, Massachusetts; "Recorder," January 26, 1909, K. of C. Chaplain's report, 1909, Alhambra Archives, Worcester, Massachusetts; *Evening Gazette,* February 9, 1910.

168. *Catholic Messenger,* quotations, "desirable actions" and "stamps its members," March 30, 1916, June 24, 1912; "Recorder," September 24, 1912, March 11, 1912, January 28, 1913, K. of C. Chaplain's Report, 1909, Alhambra Council Archives; *Cable* (September 1928).

169. *Catholic Messenger* July 22, 1915, November 25, 1915, November 30, 1917, August 5, 1921; *Cable* (April 1928, October 1928, November 1928, December 1929, September 1930).

170. *Cable* (March 1929, December 1929); "Recorder," May 20, 1929, Alhambra Council Archives; *Catholic Messenger,* May 21, 1915; *Messenger* February 6, 1895, February 23, 1901. At a banquet in 1916 all the members of the order wore American flags in their lapels and were regaled by a program of "patriotic and popular music": *Worcester Telegram,* November 4, 1916; *Cable* quotation in (March 1929); *Catholic Messenger,* January 20, 1916; *Messenger,* February 16, 1895.

171. *Catholic Messenger,* December 22, 1915; *Worcester Telegram,* November 4, 1916; *Evening Post,* November 7, 12, 1917; *Catholic Messenger,* December 22, 1915, April 6, 1917, June 1, 1917, January 25, February 22, April 19, 1918; Historian's Report, July 1943, Knights of Columbus, Alhambra Council Archives, Worcester, Massachusetts. See also description of Irish activities in World War I earlier in this chapter.

172. *Cable* (April 1928, June 1928), quotation about mass (August 1928, March 1929, December 1932); *Catholic Messenger,* March 28, 1914, December 9, 30, 1915, March 30, 1916, quotation, "social center," March 16, 1916; Bishop Beaven to Rev. John J. McCoy, December 12, 1913, Alhambra Council Archives; "Recorder," March 26, 1911, April 9, 1912, January 28, 1913, Alhambra Council Archives; K. of C. Chaplain's Report, 1909, Alhambra Council Archives; *Evening Gazette* February 9, 1910.

173. *Cable* (May 1928, August 1928); *Catholic Messenger,* May 14, 1915, February 17, 22, 1907, January 8, December 2, 1915; *Evening Gazette,* February 18, 1907; *Cable* (March 1929), quotation, "vigilant," August 1929. See also *Columbiad,* vol. 7, no. 1 (January 1900), p. 3.

174. *Columbiad,* vol. 16, no. 4 (March 1908), p. 3; *Catholic Messenger* quote on boycotts December 2, 1915, January 8, 1915.

175. *Cable* (April 1928, May 1928, June 1928, August 1928); "Recorder," February 16, 1895, October 8, 1912, April 31, 1915; Lewis Buckley to Samuel Winslow, December 11, 1919, Norton Company papers, WHM; *Catholic Messenger,* December 11, 1919; *Evening Post,* October 21, 1919; *Worcester Telegram,* December 14, 1921, December 3, 1922.

176. Hickey, "Immigrant Klan," pp. 1–4, *Cable* (January 1929), quotation from Champagne in March 1929; *Catholic Messenger,* October 24, November 17, 24, 1924; *Worcester Telegram,* September 28, 1923; *Evening Post,* September 27, 28, 1923.

177. Ten non-Irish in 1912, 23 in 1913, 27 in 1914: "Recorder," 1912 to 1914, Alhambra Archives. Quote from McCoy in McCoy MSS, K. of C., address, Holy Cross College Archives.

178. *Catholic Messenger,* September 30, April 30, November 11, 1915, March 16, 1916.

179. *Catholic Messenger,* December 16, September 30, 1915.

180. Kauffman, *Faith and Fraternalism,* pp. 16, 28, 79–81; Thomas Schlereth, "Columbia, Columbus, and Columbianism," *Journal of American History* 79, no. 3 (December 1992), pp. 957–59.

181. *Messenger,* October 19, 1901; *Worcester Telegram,* September 5, October 12, 1912; *Catholic Messenger,* September 16, 1910, October 14, 1910, October 13, 14, Polish pic-

turesque uniforms in 20, 27, October 10, 11, November 2, 1912, September 19, October 17, 1913; "Recorder," August 22, 1911, Alhambra Archives.

182. *Catholic Messenger*, October 14, 1910, McCoy quotations in October 20 and 27, 1911, quotation, "anti-Catholic Catholics," in October 20, 1911; "Recorder," October 10, 1911, Alhambra Archives.

183. *Worcester Telegram*, quotation, "golden opportunity," September 9, 1912; *Worcester Telegram*, on Italians, September 6, 1912, on French Canadians September 9, 1912; *Worcester Telegram*, September 5, 1912; *Catholic Messenger*, October 11, 1912, November 2, 1912, September 19, 1913, October 17, 1913.

184. *Catholic Messenger*, May 22, September 11, October 9, 16, 1914, October 7, October 14, 1915; *Catholic Messenger*, October 9, 1919, October 14, 1920, October 9, 17, 1924; *Worcester Telegram*, October 13, 1924; *Evening Post*, October 12, 1923, October 12, 1927, October 13, 1929; *Evening Gazette*, October 11, 1923, October 12, 1924, October 12, 1927; *Cable* (November 1929).

185. The last St. Patrick's Day parade before recent times was in 1911. *Catholic Messenger*, February 3, 1911; *Worcester Telegram*, March 18, 1912, March 17, 1913, March 21, 1914.

186. *Catholic Messenger*, April 3, 1908, December 22, 1911, February 27, March 27, May 29, June 5, 12, July 3, 24, September 18, 25, October 2, 1914, June 8, 1916; quotation, "racial issues," in June 15, 1916, quotation, "zealots," in July 21, 1916, February 10, March 16, June 15, July 7, 21, August 11, 1916; *Labor News*, November 23, 1916; *Evening Post*, September 10, October 27, November 24, 1906, March 8, 1907; *Worcester Telegram*, September 7, October 4, 1912.

187. *Catholic Messenger*, April 13, May 11, May 25, July 20, 1917, Dalton quotation in March 22, April 12, 1918. There was no mention in the *Catholic Messenger* of the conscription crisis in Ireland: *Catholic Messenger*, April to May 1918; *Evening Post*, September 27, 1918.

188. McCoy MSS, "Prayer to Soldiers," July 29, 1917, Holy Cross College Archives; Carroll, *American Opinion*, pp. 121–30; Arthur Link, *Wilson the Diplomatist* (Chicago: Quadrangle Books, 1957), pp. 91–125.

189. F. S. L. Lyons, *Ireland Since the Famine* (London: Weidenfeld and Nicolson, 1971), pp. 358–436; Joseph J. Lee, *Ireland, 1912–1985: Politics and Society* (Cambridge: Cambridge University Press, 1989), pp. 1–55; Foster, *Modern Ireland*, pp. 461–93; D. George Boyce, "Interpreting the Rising," in Boyce and O'Day, *The Making of Modern Irish History*, pp. 163–87; George Dangerfield, *The Damnable Question: A Study in Anglo-Irish Relations* (Boston: Little, Brown, 1976), pp. 264–304; David Fitzpatrick, *Politics and Irish Life 1913–1921: A Provincial Experience of War and Revolution* (Dublin: Gill and Macmillan, 1977), pp. 107–59; Francis Carroll, *American Opinion and the Irish Question, 1910–1923: A Study in Opinion and Policy* (Dublin: Gill and Macmillan, 1978), pp 112–30.

190. Carroll, *American Opinion* pp. 121–48; Thomas Hachey, *Britain and Irish Separatism: From the Fenians to the Free State, 1867–1922* (Chicago: Rand McNally, 1977), pp. 143–290; Charles Callan Tansill, *America and the Fight for Irish Freedom* (New York: Devon-Adair, 1957), pp. 215–83.

191. *Catholic Messenger,* November 29, 1918.

192. Ibid., December 13, 1918, March 28, September 19, 1919.

193. Ibid., December 27, 1918.

194. Ibid., April 4, 1919, quotation about Knights in February 19, 1920, August 5, 1920.

195. Ibid., March 21, 28, July 17, December 11, 1919; *Worcester Telegram,* December 6, 1921.

196. *Catholic Messenger,* November 29, December 13, 1918, March 7, 21, quotation from Barrett in 28, July 17, 1919, quotation from Dalton in September 25, 1919.

197. *Labor News,* quote in December 7, 1916. Bradford Perkins, *The Great Rapprochement: England and the United States, 1895–1914* (New York: Atheneum, 1968); Barbara Miller Solomon, *Ancestors and Immigrants: A Changing New England Tradition* (Cambridge: Harvard University Press, 1956).

198. Jerome George to Samuel Woodward, December 17, 1919, and December 30, 1919, box 6, Woodward papers, WHM; *Catholic Messenger,* March 21, 1919; Edward Cuddy, "The Irish Question and the Revival of Anti-Catholicism in the 1920s," *Catholic Historical Review* 67, no. 2 (April 1981), pp. 236–55.

199. *Worcester Telegram,* November 29, 1919; *Catholic Messenger,* January 22, 1920; *Evening Post,* January 20, 22, 23, 1920. See Cuddy, "The Irish Question and the Revival of Anti-Catholicism," pp. 236–55, and Cuddy, "'Are the Bolsheviks Any Worse Than the Irish': Ethno-Religious Conflict in America During the 1920s," *Eire* 11, no. 3 (Autumn 1976), pp. 13–32.

200. *Catholic Messenger,* January 22, 1920.

201. *Hibernian,* March 2, 1915. Emmons, *Butte Irish,* pp. 340–97; Joe Doyle, "Striking for Ireland on the New York Docks," in Bayor and Meagher, eds., *New York Irish,* pp. 357–73; Michael Laffan, "Labor Must Wait: Ireland's Conservative Revolution," in Patrick Corish, ed., *Radicals, Rebels and Establishments* (Belfast: Appletree Press, 1983), pp. 203–22; Fitzpatrick, *Politics and Irish Life,* pp. 254–73. Patrick Ford, as noted earlier, had become much more conservative over time: Rodechko, *Patrick Ford and His Search for America,* pp. 91–182.

202. *Catholic Messenger,* January 22, February 5, 19, March 4, 11, April 15, September 23, 30, October 28, November 4, 1920; *Worcester Telegram,* November 1, 1920; *Evening Post,* September 1, 2, 4, 5, 6, 9, 27, 28, October 5, 8, 19, 20, 25, 28, 1920.

203. *Catholic Messenger,* November 25, 1920; *Evening Post,* November 20, 22, December 6, 7, 9, 10, 1920; *Worcester Telegram,* November 26, 1921.

204. Lyons, *Ireland Since the Famine* pp. 436–62; Carroll, *American Opinion,* pp. 177–93; Hachey, *Britain and Separatism,* pp. 282–310; Lee, *Ireland, 1912–1985,* pp. 56–69; Tansill, *American and the Fight,* pp. 340–95, 426–42.

205. *Worcester Telegram,* December 5, 6, quotations describing meeting in December 7, 1921; *Catholic Messenger* quote in December 15 and 22, 1921; Carroll, *American Opinion and the Irish Question,* pp. 177–88.

206. Interview, Lawrence O'Connell, August 29, 1989; *Worcester Telegram,* November 24, 1922, November 8, 1928; *Evening Post,* November 8, 1928; Clipping, de Valera, April 30, 1927, clipping file, WHM.

207. Smith actually remained more popular than Roosevelt in Worcester in 1932, but FDR carried the city after he was nominated. Curley's pro-Roosevelt slate polled between 876 and 1,086 votes in each ward in the presidential primary in Worcester; David I. Walsh's pro-Smith slate polled between 4,702 and 4,999 in each ward in the presidential primary in Worcester: *Election Statistics, 1932–1934, Public Document no. 43*, pp. 52, 58; registration rose to 79,125 by the time of the presidential election in 1932: *Evening Post* November 7, 1932. *Evening Post*, November 4, 5, 7, 8, 1932; *Evening Gazette*, November 7, 8, 1932.

Conclusion

1. Robert Reynolds, "Worcester: A New Diocese in the New England Scene," *Jubilee* 3, no. 10 (February 1956), p. 11; O'Flynn MSS, folio 2, p. 269, Holy Cross College Archives; McCoy, *History of the Springfield Diocese*, pp. 264–67; *Worcester Evening Gazette*, March 7, 1950, April 19, 1975; McGratty, *The Life of Power*, pp. 9–11, 99–104.

2. Quotation, "a stranger," in Reynolds, "Worcester: A New Diocese," p. 9; *Worcester Telegram*, January 29, 1959.

3. Reynolds, "Worcester: A New Diocese," p. 11; *Worcester Telegram*, January 29, 1959.

4. Reynolds, "Worcester: A New Diocese," p. 9.

5. Ellen Horgan Biddle, "The American Irish Catholic Family," in Charles Mindel and Robert W. Habenstein, eds., *Ethnic Families in America* (New York: Elsevier Press, 1976), pp. 103–5; *The Impact of Vatican II: A Survey of the Laity of the Diocese of Worcester* (Boston: Becker Research Corporation, 1969), p. 134; *Catholic Free Press*, June 28, 1956; *Worcester Telegram*, January 29, 1959; Reynolds, "Worcester: A New Diocese," pp. 10–14.

6. Ellen Horgan Biddle, "The American Irish Catholic Family," p. 107; For Catholic concerns about sexual morality in the movies, see *Catholic Free Press*, January 28, June 10, June 17, and June 24, 1955. For Legion of Decency ratings in the same paper, see *Catholic Free Press*, July 11, 18, 1952, and January 21, 28, 1955. See Andrew Greeley, *The Irish Americans: The Rise to Money and Power* (New York: Harper and Row, 1981), p. 124.

7. Biddle, "The American Irish Catholic Family," p. 114; quotation, "Protestants feared," in *Worcester Sunday Telegram*, November 29, 1981; Reynolds, "Worcester: A New Diocese," p. 11. Catholics also continued to decry "liberals" among them who compromised too much to please non-Catholics; see *Catholic Free Press*, January 28, 1966.

8. *Catholic Free Press*, March 4, 1955, March 9, 1962; *Worcester Telegram*, January 18, 21, 1959; quotation, "Catholic document," in *Official Reference and Information Guide: Diocese of Worcester, 1951*, vol. 1, p. 247; quotation, "no good socialism," in *Reference Guide*, p. 333. See also *Reference Guide*, pp. 189, 191, 193, 195, 291. The *Catholic Free Press* printed a weekly column called "The Reds—What Now?" *Catholic Free Press* January 21, 28, 1955. The paper also attacked communist aggression persistently, in

Vietnam, for example: *Catholic Free Press*, March 11, 18, 1955. Timothy J. Meagher, *To Preserve the Flame: St. John's Parish and 150 Years of Catholicism in Worcester* (Worcester: St. John's Parish, 1984), pp. 47–49.

9. Quotation, "shown genuine regard," in Reynolds, "Worcester: A New Diocese," p. 15, and see also pp. 6, 13; quotation, "a place of diverse," in *Worcester Telegram*, January 29, 1915; Biddle, "The American Irish Catholic Family," p. 114. On the mixed congregations in the new peripheral parishes, see the French, Irish, Polish, and Italian names of members of the women's clubs and guilds in St. Charles Borromeo parish, St. Joan of Arc parish and Our Lady of the Angels parish: *Catholic Free Press*, June 10, April 1, 8, 1955. On St. John's, see Meagher, *To Preserve the Flame*, p. 46.

10. *Worcester Sunday Telegram*, November 29, 1981; Roger Finke and Rodney Starke, *The Churching of America, 1776–1990: Winners and Losers in Our Religious Economy* (New Brunswick: Rutgers University Press, 1992), pp. 255–58; Steven Avella, *The Confident Church: Catholic Leadership and Life in Chicago, 1940–1965* (Notre Dame: University of Notre Dame Press), pp. 71–109; Eileen McMahon, *What Parish Are You From? A Chicago Irish Community and Race Relations* (Lexington: University Press of Kentucky, 1995), pp. 75–96.

11. Robert N. Binstock, *A Report on Politics in Worcester, Massachusetts* (Cambridge: Harvard and MIT Joint Center for Urban Studies, 1960), pp. V-5–V-9, V-12.

12. Alice V. Emerson, "The Failure of Organized Labor in Worcester, 1930–1940" (M.A. thesis, Clark University, 1963), pp. 9–11, 46–47 ; James P. Hanlan, "Grinding Out Dissension: The Evolution of Labor Relations at Norton Company, 1914–1944," pp. 3–6, 16–18; Binstock "A Report on Politics," pp. V-15, V-16.

13. Binstock, "A Report on Politics," pp. V-13–V-16. Alec Barbrook, *God Save the Commonwealth: An Electoral History of Massachusetts* (Amherst: University of Massachusetts Press, 1973), pp. 79–106; Murray B. Levin, *The Compleat Politician: Political Strategy in Massachusetts* (Indianapolis: Bobbs-Merrill), pp. 15–54.

14. Binstock, "A Report on Politics," pp. I-80, III-14. In 1959, 44 percent of Worcester's voters were registered Democrats, 29 percent were Republicans; and 27 percent were Independents: Binstock, pp. III-7, I-21 to p. I-25. David Eisenthal, "The Origins of Charter Reform in Worcester with Particular Attention to Plan E" (Honors thesis, Clark University, 1983), pp. 30–36, 38–49, 52.

15. Eisenthal, "The Origins," pp. 41, 48–49, 52; Binstock, *A Report on Politics*, pp. V-1 to V-2, V-7 to V-9, II-44 to II-50; quotation "editorials harmonize" in p. II-48. Barbrook, *God Save the Commonwealth*, pp. 79–106.

16. Binstock, *A Report on Politics*, pp. V-14 to V-16, II-50, III-1 to III-6, VI-14 to VI-16; quotation, "preventing," p. II-50.

17. Eisenthal, "The Origins," pp. 51–52; Binstock, *A Report on Politics*, pp. V-13 to V-14, II-46, I-17, III-9, III-2 to III-5. On McGrath, see *Worcester Telegram*, November 15, 19, 1993.

18. *Worcester Telegram*, January 29, 1959.

19. *Worcester Sunday Telegram*, November 29, 1981; *The Impact of Vatican II*, pp. 90–107. For Flanagan, see Joy Anderson, ed., *The American Catholic Who's Who, 1978–1979* vol. 22 (Washington, D.C.: National Catholic News Service, 1978), p. 194.

20. Dolan, *The American Catholic Experience*, pp. 420–54; David J. O'Brien, *The Renewal of American Catholicism* (New York: Oxford University Press, 1972); Jay P. Dolan, R. Scott Appleby, Patricia Byrne, and Debra Campbell, *Transforming Parish Ministry: The Changing Roles of Catholic Clergy, Laity and Women Religious* (New York: Crossroads, 1990), pp. 79–108, 154–99, 253–80; Leslie Woodcock Tentler, *Seasons of Grace: A History of the Archdiocese of Detroit* (Detroit: Wayne State, 1990), pp. 519–27; Steven Avella, *The Confident Church: Catholic Leadership and Life in Chicago, 1940–1965* (Notre Dame: University of Notre Dame Press) Eileen McMahon, *What Parish Are You From? A Chicago Irish Community and Race Relations* (Lexington: University Press of Kentucky, 1995), pp. 116–89; Barry A. Kasmin and Seymour P. Lachma, *One Nation Under God: Religion in Contemporary American Society* (New York: Harmony Books, 1993), pp. 255–56; Lawrence H. Fuchs, *John F. Kennedy and American Catholicism* (New York: Meredith Press, 1967); John T. McGreevy, *Parish Boundaries: The Catholic Encounter with Race in the Twentieth-Century Urban North* (Chicago: University of Chicago Press, 1996); Andrew Greeley, William McCready, and Kathleen McCourt, *Catholic Schools in A Declining Church* (Kansas City: Sheed and Ward, 1976), pp. 103–54. Greeley claims the biggest impact on changing church attendance came from the encyclical *Humanae Vitae*, not the Council. Robert Wuthnow, *The Restructuring of American Religion: Society and Faith Since World War II* (Princeton: Princeton University Press, 1988), pp. 132–214. For political changes in Massachusetts, see Edgar Litt, *The Political Cultures of Massachusetts* (Cambridge: MIT Press, 1965), pp. 47–55, 152–74, 201–11, and Barbrook, *God Save the Commonwealth*, pp. 159–65. For ethnic changes and the emergence of whiteness, see Mary C. Waters, *Ethnic Options: Choosing Identities in America* (Berkeley: University of California Press, 1990), and Richard Alba, *Ethnic Identity: The Transformation of White America* (New Haven: Yale University Press, 1990); Thomas Byrne Edsall, *Chain Reaction: The Impact of Race, Rights, and Taxes on American Politics* (New York: Norton, 1991). See also Arnold R. Hirsch, "Massive Resistance in the Urban North: Trumbull Park, Chicago, 1953–1966," pp. 522–50; Thomas J. Sugrue, "Crabgrass-Roots Politics: Race, Rights, and the Reaction against Liberalism in the Urban North, 1940–1964," pp. 551–78, and Gary Gerstle, "Race and the Myth of the Liberal Consensus," pp. 579–86 all in *Journal of American History*, 82, no. 2 (September 1995). For the Irish specifically, see McCaffrey, "The Irish Dimension," pp. 17–18 and Skerrett, "The Catholic Dimension," pp. 51–55 in Lawrence McCaffrey, Ellen Skerret, Michael F. Funchion, and Charles Fanning, *The Irish in Chicago* (Urbana: University of Illinois Press, 1987); Meagher and Bayor, Introduction, pp. 2–8, and David M. Reimers, "Overview: An End and a Beginning," pp. 419–38, in Ronald Bayor and Timothy Meagher, eds., *The New York Irish* (Baltimore: Johns Hopkins University Press, 1996); *The Impact of Vatican II*, pp. 91, 107; *Catholic Free Press* April 17, 1970, May 29, 1970.

21. *Catholic Free Press*, March 4, 1955, March 9, 1962; Harold Creveling, "The Cultural Geography of Worcester," p. 26. By 1980 nearly 30 percent of the heads of Massachusetts families claiming only Irish ancestry held professional or managerial occupations: *Census of Population, 1980*, pt. 15, pp. 145, 148. By 1989, one source

claimed that Tatnuck Country Club had more Irish than Yankees: Amy Zuckerman and Andy Baron, "Prejudice Finds Its Targets in Worcester," *Worcester Magazine,* March 1, 1989, p. 12.

22. "Worcester's Future," *Holy Cross Quarterly,* vol. 5, nos. 3–4, pp. 155–56. See also Margaret Erskine, *Heart of the Commonwealth: Worcester* (Woodland Hills, Calif.: Windsor Publications, 1981), p. 129; U.S. Bureau of the Census, *County and City Data Book, 1952* (Washington, D.C.: GPO, 1953), p. 468; Bureau of the Census, *County and City Data Book, 1988* (Washington, D.C.: GPO, 1988), pp. 660–61.

23. Kenneth Moynihan, "Worcester: Point of No Return," *Worcester Magazine,* June 5, 1996, p. 10. Moynihan reported a Latino population of 4 percent in 1990 and a black population of 2 percent. In 1980, Worcester had 5,433 Puerto Rican residents, 4,625 African Americans, and 311 Vietnamese. Latino leaders complained of anti-Latino sentiment and stereotypes leading to job, housing, and educational discrimination: Zuckerman and Baron, "Prejudice Finds Its Targets," p. 11. See also Erskine, *Heart of the Commonwealth: Worcester,* p. 132, and Morris Cohen, "Worcester's Ethnics," *Holy Cross Quarterly,* vol. 5, nos. 3–4 (1973), p. 47.

24. *Worcester County St. Patrick's Day Parade, Sunday, March 13, 1983,* Program, pamphlet file, WHM.

25. Ibid. For discussions of white ethnic identity today, see Richard Alba, *Ethnic Identity: The Transformation of White America* (New Haven: Yale University Press, 1990), and Mary C. Waters, *Ethnic Options: Choosing Identities in America* (Berkeley: University of California Press, 1990).

26. *Worcester County St. Patrick's Day Parade, March 13, 1983,* Program.

27. *Worcester Sunday Telegram,* March 16, 1997; *Worcester Telegram,* March 17, 1997.

28. *Worcester Sunday Telegram,* March 16, 1997; *Worcester Telegram,* March 17, 1997.

Bibliography

Primary Sources

Manuscript Collections

American Antiquarian Society
    Pamphlet File
    Stephen Littleton Diaries
    Stephen Salisbury Papers
    Worcester Organizations File

Archives of the Archdiocese of Boston
    Parish Reports

Catholic University of America Archives
    Fenian Papers (Jeremiah O'Donovan Rossa) Papers

College of the Holy Cross Treasure Room
    Richard O'Flynn Papers

Harvard University Business School Baker Library
    American Steel and Wire Collection
    Dun and Bradstreet Collection

Massachusetts Historical Society
    George Frisbie Hoar Papers

Worcester Historical Museum
   Biographical File
   Norton Company Papers
   Pamphlet File

Newspapers and Periodicals

   Alumna
   American
   Annals of St. Anthony's Shrine
   Boston Pilot
   Cable
   Catholic School and Home Magazine
   Irish World
   Labor News
   Light
   Messenger (after 1906, *Catholic Messenger*)
   Review and Bulletin
   Worcester Daily Spy
   Worcester Daily Times
   Worcester Evening Journal
   Worcester Evening Gazette
   Worcester Magazine
   Worcester Post
   Worcester Sunday Telegram
   Worcester Telegram

Government Documents

Reports of the Immigration Commission (Washington: GPO, 1911)
   Volume 1, *Statistical Review of Immigration to the United States, 1820–1910.*
   Volume 18, *Immigrants and Crime.*
   Volume 28, *Fecundity of Immigrant Women.*
   Volume 35, *Immigrants as Charity Seekers.*

Census of the Commonwealth of Massachusetts, 1875 (Boston: Wright and Potter, 1879).
   Volume 3, *Population and Social Statistics.*

Census of the Commonwealth of Massachusetts, 1885 (Boston: Wright and Potter, 1887).
   Volume 1, *Population and Social Statistics.*

Census of the Commonwealth of Massachusetts, 1895 (Boston: Wright and Potter, 1897).
   Volume 2, *Population and Social Statistics.*

Ninth Census of the United States, 1870. (Washington: GPO, 1872).
The Statistics of the Population of the United States.

Tenth Census of the United States, 1880.
Volume I, *Population.*

Twelfth Census of the United States, 1900. (Washington: GPO, 1902).
Part 2, Volume 7, *Manufactures.*
Part 2, Volume 2, *Population.*

Thirteenth Census of the United States Taken in the Year 1910 (Washington: GPO, 1913).
Volume 3, *Population: Report by States.*

Fifteenth Census of the United States, 1930 (Washington: GPO, 1931).
Volume 6, *Families.*

Secondary Sources

Akenson, Donald. *The Irish Education Experiment: The National System of Education in Ireland in the Nineteenth Century.* Toronto: University of Toronto Press, 1970.

Allswang, John. *A House for all Peoples.* Lexington, Kentucky: University of Kentucky Press, 1971.

Anbinder, Tyler Gregory. *Nativism and Slavery: The Northern Know Nothings and the Politics of the 1850s.* New York: Oxford University Press, 1992.

Appleby, R. Scott. *Church and Age Unite: The Modernist Impulse in American Catholicism.* Notre Dame, Indiana: University of Notre Dame Press, 1992.

Archangel, Sister Marie Michael. *"By This Sign You Will Live": History of the Congregation of the Little Franciscans of Mary, 1889–1955.* Worcester: privately published, 1964.

Augustine, H. R. *In the Footprints of Father Mathew.* Dublin: Gill and Son, 1947.

Baker, Donald G. *Race, Ethnicity and Power: A Comparative Study.* Boston: Routledge and Kegan Paul, 1983.

Banton, Michael. *Racial and Ethnic Competition.* Cambridge: Cambridge University Press, 1983.

Barbrook, Alec. *God Save the Commonwealth: An Electoral History of Massachusetts.* Amherst: University of Massachusetts Press, 1973.

Barron, Hal S. *Those Who Stayed Behind: Rural Society in Nineteenth-Century New England.* New York: Cambridge University Press, 1984.

Barry, Colman. *The Catholic Church and German Americans.* Milwaukee: Bruce, 1953.

Barth, Frederick. *Ethnic Groups and Boundaries: The Social Organization of Cultural Difference.* Boston: Little, Brown, 1969.

Bayor, Ronald, and Timothy J. Meagher, eds. *New York Irish.* Baltimore: Johns Hopkins University Press, 1996.

Beatty, Jack. *The Rascal King: The Life and Times of James Michael Curley, 1874–1958.* Reading: Addison-Wesley, 1992.

Bedford, Henry. *Socialism and the Workers in Massachusetts, 1886–1912.* Amherst: University of Massachusetts Press, 1966.

Belisle, Alexandre. *Histoire De La Presse Franco-Americain.* Worcester: L'Opinion Publique Publishers, 1911.

———. *Livre D'Or Des Franco-Americaines de Worcester, Massachusetts.* Worcester: Le Compagnie de Publication de Belisle, 1920.

Berlanstein, Lenard, ed. *Rethinking Labor History: Essays on Discourse and Class Analysis.* Urbana: University of Illinois Press, 1993.

Bew, Paul. *Land and the National Question in Ireland.* Atlantic Highlands: Humanities Press, 1979.

Binstock, Robert N. *A Report on Politics in Worcester, Massachusetts.* Cambridge: Harvard and MIT Joint Center of Urban Studies, 1960.

Blessing, Patrick. "'West Among Strangers': Irish Migration to California, 1850 to 1880." Ph.D. diss.: University of California at Los Angeles, 1981.

Blodgett, Geoffrey. *The Gentle Reformers: Massachusetts Democrats in the Cleveland Era.* Cambridge: Harvard University Press, 1966.

Bodnar, John, Roger Simon, and Michael Weber. *Lives of Their Own: Blacks, Italians and Poles in Pittsburgh, 1900–1960.* Urbana: University of Illinois Press, 1982.

———. *Remaking America: Public Memory, Commemoration and Patriotism in the Twentieth Century.* Princeton: Princeton University Press, 1966.

———. *The Transplanted: A History of Immigrants in Urban America.* Bloomington: Indiana University Press, 1985.

Bourke, Joanna. *Husbandry to Housewifery: Women, Economic Change, and Homework in Ireland, 1890–1914.* New York: Clarendon Press, 1993.

Boyce, D. George, and Alan O'Day, eds., *The Making of Modern Irish History: Revisionism and Recent Controversy.* London: Routledge, 1996.

Brault, Gerard. *The French-Canadian Heritage in New England.* Hanover: University Press of New England, 1986.

Brooke, John. *The Heart of the Commonwealth: Social and Political Cultures in Worcester County, Massachusetts, 1713–1861.* Cambridge: Cambridge University Press, 1989.

Brown, Thomas N. *Irish-American Nationalism, 1870–1890.* New York: Lippincott, 1966.

Brundage, David. *The Making of Western Labor Radicalism: Denver's Organized Workers, 1878–1908.* Urbana: University of Illinois Press, 1994.

Buel, Charles Chauncey. "The Workers of Worcester: Social Mobility and Ethnicity in a New England City, 1850–1870." Ph.D. diss.: New York University, 1974.

Buhle, Paul. "The Knights of Labor in Rhode Island," *Radical History Review* 17 (1978), pp. 39–73.

Bukowcyk, John. *"And My Children Did Not Know Me": A History of Polish Americans.* Bloomington: Indiana University Press, 1987.

Burchell, R. A. *The San Francisco Irish, 1848–1880.* Berkeley: University of California Press, 1980.

Carroll, Francis. *American Opinion and the Irish Question, 1910–1923: A Study in Opinion and Policy.* New York: St. Martin's Press, 1978.

Catholic Mirror: A Century of Catholicism in Western Massachusetts. Springfield: Mirror Press, 1930.

Chandonett, L'Abee. *Notre Dame Des Canadiens et les Canadiens Aux Etats Unis.* Montreal: George E. Des Barres, 1872.

Chasan, Joshua. "Civilizing Worcester: The Creation of Institutional and Cultural Order in Worcester, Massachusetts, 1848–1876." Ph.D. diss.: University of Pittsburgh, 1974.

Cheape, Charles. *Family Firm to Modern Multinational: Norton Company, A New England Enterprise.* Cambridge: Harvard University Press, 1985.

Child, Irwin. *Italian or American? The Second Generation in Conflict.* New Haven: Yale University Press, 1943.

Chinnici, Joseph. *Devotion to the Holy Spirit in American Catholicism.* New York: Paulist Press, 1985.

———. *Living Stones: The History and Structure of Catholic Spiritual Life in the United States.* New York: Macmillan, 1989.

Clark, Christopher. *The Roots of Rural Capitalism: Western Massachusetts, 1780–1860.* Ithaca: Cornell University Press, 1990.

Clark, Dennis. *Hibernia America: The Irish and Regional Cultures.* Westport: Greenwood Press, 1976.

———. *The Irish in Philadelphia: Ten Generations of Urban Experience.* Philadelphia: Temple University Press, 1974.

———. *Irish Relations: Trials of an Immigrant Tradition.* East Brunswick: Associated University Presses, 1982.

Clark, Samuel. *Social Origins of the Irish Land War.* Princeton: Princeton University Press, 1979.

Clarke, Brian. *Piety and Nationalism: Lay Voluntary Associations and the Creation of an Irish Catholic Community in Toronto, 1850–1895.* Toronto: McGill Queen's University Press, 1993.

Coben, Stanley. *Rebellion Against Victorianism: The Impetus for Cultural Change in 1920s America.* New York: Oxford University Press, 1991.

Cohen, Abner. *Two-Dimensional Man: An Essay on the Anthropology of Symbolism and Power in a Complex Society.* Berkeley: University of California Press, 1974.

Cohen, Bruce. "The Worcester Machinist Strike of 1915." *Historical Journal of Massachusetts* 16, no. 2 (Summer 1988), pp. 154–71.

Cole, Donald. *Immigrant City: Lawrence, Massachusetts, 1845–1921.* Chapel Hill: University of North Carolina Press, 1963.

Comerford, R. Vincent. *The Fenians in Context: Irish Politics and Society, 1848–1882.* Dublin: Wolfhound Press, 1985.

Connell, K. H. *Irish Peasant: Four Historical Essays.* Oxford: Clarendon Press, 1961.

Connolly, S. J. *Priests and People in Pre-famine Ireland, 1780–1845.* Dublin: Gill and Macmillan, 1982.

Conzen, Kathleen Neils. "Ethnicity as Festive Culture: Nineteenth Century German America on Parade," in Werner Sollors, ed. *The Invention of Ethnicity*. New York: Oxford University Press, 1989.

Corish, Patrick, ed. *Radicals, Rebels, and Establishments*. Belfast: Appletree Press, 1983.

Cousens, S. H. "Demographic Change in Ireland, 1851–1861," *Economic History Review* 14 (Spring 1961), pp. 275–88.

Couvares, Frank M. *The Remaking of Pittsburgh: Class and Culture in an Industrializing City, 1877–1919*. Albany: State University of New York Press, 1984.

Croker, T. Crofton. *Researches in the South of Ireland*. New York: Barnes and Noble, 1969.

Cronon, William T. "A Place for Stories: Nature and Narrative." *Journal of American History* 78. no. 4 (March 1992), pp. 1347–76.

Cross, Robert. *The Emergence of Liberal Catholicism in America*. Cambridge: Harvard University Press, 1967.

Cullen, Louis. *Six Generations of Life and Work in Ireland from 1790*. Cork: Mercier Press, 1970.

Curran, Robert Emmett. *Michael Augustine Corrigan and the Shaping of Conservative Catholicism in America, 1878–1902*. New York: Arno Press, 1978.

D'Arcy, William. *The Fenian Movement in the United States, 1858–1886*. Washington: Catholic University of America Press, 1947.

Davis, Susan. *Parades and Power: Street Theater in Nineteenth Century Philadelphia*. Philadelphia: Temple University Press, 1986.

Diner, Hasia. *Erin's Daughters in America: Irish Immigrant Women in the Nineteenth Century*. Baltimore: Johns Hopkins University Press, 1983.

Dinneen, Joseph. *The Purple Shamrock: The Honorable James Michael Curley of Boston*. New York, 1949.

Dolan, Jay. *The American Catholic Experience: A History from Colonial Times to the Present*. Garden City: Doubleday, 1983.

———. *Catholic Revivalism: The American Experience, 1830–1900*. Notre Dame: University of Notre Dame Press, 1978.

———. *The Immigrant Church: New York's Irish and German Catholics, 1815–1865*. Baltimore: Johns Hopkins University Press, 1975.

———. "The Search for an American Catholicism." *Catholic Historical Review* 82, no. 2 (April 1996), pp. 169–86.

Dolan, Jay, R. Scott Appleby, Patricia Byrne, and Debra Campbell. *Transforming Parish Ministry: The Changing Roles of Catholic Clergy, Laity, and Women Religious*. New York: Crossroads, 1990.

Donnelly, James, and Samuel Clark, eds. *Irish Peasants: Violence and Political Unrest, 1780–1914*. Madison: University of Wisconsin Press, 1983.

Dowling, P. J. *The Hedge Schools*. Cork: Mercier Press, 1968. •

Doyle, David N. *Irish America: Native Rights and National Empires, 1890–1901*. New York: Arno Press, 1976.

———. "The Regional Bibliography of Irish America, 1880 to 1930: An Addendum." *Irish Historical Studies* 13, no. 1 (May 1983), pp. 254–83.

Doyle, David, and Owen Dudley Edwards, eds. *America and Ireland, 1776–1976: The American Identity and the Irish Connection*. Westport: Greenwood Press, 1976.

Dunleavy, Janet. *Douglas Hyde: A Maker of Modern Ireland*. Berkeley, California: University of California Press, 1991.

Edsall, Thomas Byrne. *Chain Reaction: The Impact of Race, Rights, and Taxes on American Politics*. New York: Norton, 1991.

Ehrlich, Mark. *With Our Hands*. Philadelphia: Temple University Press, 1986.

Ellis, John Tracy. *The Life of James Cardinal Gibbons: Archbishop of Baltimore, 1834–1921*. Volumes 1 and 2. Milwaukee: Bruce, 1952.

Ellis, John Tracy, ed. *The Catholic Priest in the United States: Historical Investigations*. Collegeville: St. John's University Press, 1971.

Emmons, David M., *The Butte Irish: Class and Ethnicity in an American Mining Town, 1875–1925*. Urbana: University of Illinois Press, 1989.

Erie, Steven P. *Rainbow's End: Irish-Americans and the Dilemmas of Urban Machine Politics, 1840–1985*. Berkeley, California: University of California Press, 1988.

Esman, Milton J. *Ethnic Politics*. Ithaca: Cornell University Press, 1994.

Estus, Charles W., and John W. McClymer. *"ga till amerika": The Swedish Creation of an Ethnic Identity in Worcester, Massachusetts*. Worcester: Worcester Historical Museum, 1994.

Finke, Roger, and Rodney Starke. *The Churching of America, 1776–1990: Winners and Losers in Our Religious Economy*. New Brunswick: Rutgers University Press, 1992.

Fitzpatrick, David. *Irish Emigration, 1801–1921*. Dublin: The Economic and Social History Society of Ireland, 1984.

Fitzpatrick, David, and W. P. Vaughn. *Irish Historical Statistics: Population, 1821–1971*. Dublin: Irish Academy, 1978.

Fogarty, Gerald. *The Vatican and the American Hierarchy from 1870 to 1965*. Stuttgart: Anton Heiresman, 1982.

Folsom, Burton W. *Urban Capitalists, Entrepeneurs, and City Growth in Pennsylvania's Lackawanna and Lehigh Regions, 1880 to 1970*. Baltimore: Johns Hopkins University Press, 1981.

Foner, Eric. "Class, Ethnicity and Radicalism in the Gilded Age: The Land League and Irish America." *Marxist Perspectives* 1, no. 2 (Summer 1978), pp. 6–55.

Fones-Wolf, Kenneth, and Martin Kauffman, eds. *Labor in Massachusetts: Selected Essays*. Westfield: Institute for Massachusetts Studies, 1990.

Formisano, Ronald P. "The Invention of the Ethnocultural Interpretation." *American Historical Review* 99, no. 2 (April 1994), pp. 453–77.

Formisano, Ronald P., and Constance M. Burns, eds. *Boston, 1700–1980: The Evolution of Urban Politics*. Westport: Greenwood Press, 1984.

Foster, Roy. *Modern Ireland, 1600–1972*. New York: Penguin, 1989.

Frisch, Michael H. *Town into City: Springfield, Massachusetts and the Meaning of Community, 1840–1880s*. Cambridge: Harvard University Press, 1972.

Fuchs, Lawrence. *John F. Kennedy and American Catholicism*. New York: Meredith Press, 1967.

Funchion, Michael. *Chicago's Irish Nationalists*. New York: Arno Press, 1976.

Gabaccia, Donna. *Militants and Migrants: Rural Sicilians Become American Workers*. New Brunswick: Rutgers University Press, 1988.

Gamm, Gerald H. *The Making of New Deal Democrats: Voting Behavior and Realignment in Boston, 1920–1940*. Chicago: University of Chicago Press, 1990.

Gans, Herbert. *The Urban Villagers: Group and Class in the Life of Italian-Americans*. New York: Orbis Press, 1962.

Garlock, Jonathan. *Guide to the Local Assemblies of the Knights of Labor*. Westport: Greenwood Press, 1982.

Garvin, Tom. *The Evolution of Irish Nationalist Politics*. New York: Holmes and Meier, 1981.

Gerber, David. *The Making of an American Pluralism: Buffalo, 1825–1860*. Urbana: University of Illinois Press, 1989.

———. "Ambivalent Anti-Catholicism: Buffalo's American Protestant Elite Faces the Challenge of the Catholic Church, 1850–1860." *Civil War History* 30, no. 2 (1984), pp. 120–43.

Gerstle, Gary. "Race and the Myth of the Liberal Consensus." *Journal of American History* 82, no. 2 (September 1995), pp. 579–86.

———. "The Working Class Goes to War," *Mid-America* 75, no. 3 (October 1993), pp. 303–22.

———. *Working Class Americanism: The Politics of Labor in a Textile City, 1914–1960*. New York: Cambridge University Press, 1989.

Gibson, Ralph. *A Social History of French Catholicism, 1789–1914*. New York: Routledge, 1989.

Gjerde, Jon. *From Peasants to Farmers: The Migration from Balestrand, Norway to the Upper Middle West*. New York: Cambridge University Press, 1985.

Gleason, Philip. "The New Americanism in Catholic Historiography." *US Catholic Historian* 11, no. 3 (Summer 1993), pp. 1–18.

Goldscheider, Calvin, and Sidney Goldstein. *Jewish Americans: Three Generations in a Jewish Community*. Englewood Cliffs: Prentice-Hall, 1968.

Goodwin, Doris Kearns. *The Fitzgeralds and the Kennedys*. New York: Simon and Schuster, 1987.

Gordon, Milton. *Assimilation in American Life: The Role of Religion and National Origins*. New York: Oxford University Press, 1964.

Grattan, William J. *The Spires of Fenwick: A History of the College of the Holy Cross, 1843–1963*. New York: Vantage Press, 1966.

Greeley, Andrew. "The Success and Assimilation of Irish Protestants and Catholics in the United States." *Social Science Research* 72, no. 4 (1985), pp. 229–35.

Greeley, Andrew, William McCready, and Kathleen McCourt. *Catholic Schools in a Declining Church*. Kansas City: Sheed and Ward, 1976.

Groneman, Carol. "Working Class Immigrant Women in Mid Nineteenth Century New York: The Irish Woman's Experience." *Journal of Urban History* 4, no. 3 (May 1978), pp. 255–74.

Guinnane, Timothy. "Rethinking the Western European Marriage Pattern: The Decision to Marry in Ireland at the Turn of the Century." *Journal of Family History* 16, no. 1 (1991), pp. 47–64.

———. *The Vanishing Irish: Households, Migration, and the Rural Economy in Ireland.* Princeton: Princeton University Press, 1997.

Hachey, Thomas. *Britain and Irish Separatism: From the Fenians to the Free State, 1867–1922.* Washington, D.C.: Catholic University of America Press, 1984.

Hachey, Thomas, and Lawrence McCaffrey. *Perspectives on Irish Nationalism.* Lexington: University Press of Kentucky, 1989.

Hammack, David C. *Power and Society: Greater New York at the Turn of the Century.* New York: Columbia University Press, 1987.

Handlin, Oscar, ed. *The Children of the Uprooted.* New York: G. Braziler, 1966.

Hannerz, Ulf. *Exploring the City: Inquiries Toward an Urban Anthropology.* New York: Columbia University Press, 1980.

Hareven, Tamara. *Family Time and Industrial Time: The Relationship Between Family and Work in a New England Industrial Community.* New York: Cambridge University Press, 1982.

Hareven, Tamara, ed. *Family and Kin in Urban Communities: 1790–1930.* New York: Viewpoints, 1977.

Harrigan, Margaret Connors. "'Their Own Kind: Family and Community Life in Albany, New York, 1856–1915." Ph.D. diss.: Harvard University, 1975.

Harris, Carl V. *Political Power in Birmingham, 1871–1921.* Nashville: University of Tennessee Press, 1977.

Haynes, George. "A Chapter from the Local History of Know-Nothingism." *New England Magazine* 13, no. 1 (September 1896).

Hechter, Michael. *Internal Colonialism: The Celtic Fringe in British National Development, 1536–1966.* Berkeley: University of California Press, 1975.

———. "Towards a Theory of Ethnic Change." *Politics and Society* (Fall: 1971), pp. 21–31.

Henderson, Thomas McLean. *Tammany Hall and the New Immigrants, 1910–1921.* Charlottesville: University of Virginia Press, 1973.

Herberg, Will. *Protestant, Catholic, and Jew: An Essay in American Religious Sociology.* Garden City: Doubleday, 1955.

Higham, John. "Another Look at Nativism." *Catholic Historical Review* 44, no. 2 (1958), pp. 147–158.

Hobsbawm, Eric, and Terence Ranger. *The Invention of Tradition.* Cambridge: Cambridge University Press, 1985.

Hogan, Peter. *The Catholic University of America: The Rectorship of Thomas J. Conaty.* Washington, D.C.: Catholic University of America Press, 1949.

Illustrated History of the Central Labor Union and Building Trades Council of Worcester and Vicinity. Worcester: Private Publisher, 1899.

Isenberg, Michael T. *John L. Sullivan and His America.* Urbana: University of Illinois Press, 1988.

Issell, William. "Citizens Outside the Government: Business and Urban Policy in San Francisco and Los Angeles, 1890–1932," *Pacific Historical Review* 57, no. 2 (Spring 1988), pp. 117–42.

Jackson, J. B. *American Space: The Centennial Years, 1965–1876*. New York: Norton Press, 1972.

Jacobson, Mathew. *Special Sorrows: The Diasporic Imagination of Irish, Polish, and Jewish Immigrants in the United States*. Cambridge: Harvard University Press, 1995.

Jaffee, David. "Peddlers of Progress and the Transformation of the Rural North." *Journal of American History* 78, no. 2 (September 1991), pp. 511–35.

Jordan, Donald. "Land and Politics in the West of Ireland: County Mayo, 1846–1882." Ph.D. diss.: University of California at Davis, 1982.

Joyce, Peter. "The History of St. John's Church, Worcester, Massachusetts: 1828–1862." M.A. thesis: Catholic University of America, 1982.

Julian, Brother, C.F.X. *Deeds of the Xaverian Brothers in America*. New York: Macmillan, 1930.

Kane, Paula. *Separatism and Subculture: Boston Catholicism, 1900–1920*. Chapel Hill: University of North Carolina Press, 1994.

Kantowicz, Edward. *Corporation Sole: Cardinal Mundelein and Chicago Catholicism*. Notre Dame: University of Notre Dame Press, 1983.

Karlson, Karl. "The Swedish Population of Worcester: A Study in Social Survey." M.A. thesis: Clark University, 1910.

Karson, Marc. *American Labor Unrest and Politics*. Carbondale: University of Southern Illinois Press, 1958.

Katz, Michael. *The People of Hamilton, Canada West: Family and Class in a Mid-Nineteenth-Century City*. Cambridge: Harvard University Press, 1975.

Kauffman, Christopher J. *Faith and Fraternalism: The History of the Knights of Columbus, 1882–1982*. New York: Harper and Row, 1982.

Keating, Anne. *Building Chicago: Suburban Developers and the Creation of a Divided Metropolis*. Columbus: Ohio State University Press, 1988.

Kennedy, Lawrence. "Power and Prejudice: Boston Political Conflict, 1885–1895." Ph.D. diss.: Boston College Press, 1989.

Keysar, Alexander. *Out of Work: The First Century of Unemployment in Massachusetts*. New York: Cambridge University Press, 1986.

Keyes, Charles, ed. *Ethnic Change*. Seattle: University of Washington Press, 1986.

Kingsley, Elbridge. *Picturesque Worcester*. Springfield: W. F. Adams, 1895.

Kivisto, Peter, and Dag Blanck, eds. *American Immigrants and Their Generations: Studies and Commentaries on the Hansen Thesis after Fifty Years*. Urbana: University of Illinois Press, 1990.

Kleppner, Paul. *Continuity and Change in Electoral Politics, 1893–1928*. Westport: Greenwood Press, 1987.

———. *The Third Electoral System, 1853 to 1982*. Chapel Hill: University of North Carolina Press, 1979.

Koelsch, William A. *Clark University, 1887–1997: A Narrative History*. Worcester: Clark University Press, 1987.

Kolesar, Robert, "The Politics of Development: Worcester, Massachusetts in the Late Nineteenth Century." *Journal of Urban History* 16, no. 1 (November 1989), pp. 3–28.

Kosmin, Barry A., and Seymour Lachma. *One Nation Under God: Religion in Contemporary American Society*. New York: Harmony Books, 1993.

Lamoreaux, Naomi. "Bank Mergers in Late Nineteenth Century New England: The Contigent Nature of Structural Change." *Journal of Economic History* 53, no. 1 (September 1991), pp. 537–57.

———. *Banks, Personal Connections, and Economic Development in Industrial New England*. New York: Cambridge University Press, 1994.

Lamphear, B. W. "The Italian Population of Worcester." M.A. thesis: Clark University, 1909.

Landale, Nancy S., and Stewart Tolnay. "Generation, Ethnicity, and Marriage: Historical Patterns in the Northern United States." *Demography* 30, no. 1 (February 1993), pp. 103–27.

Larkin, Emmett. "The Devotional Revolution in Ireland." *American Historical Review* 77, no. 3 (June 1972), pp. 625–52.

———. *The Roman Catholic Church in Ireland and the Fall of Parnell, 1888–1891*. Chapel Hill: University of North Carolina Press, 1979.

Lears, T. Jackson. *No Place of Grace: Antimodernism and the Transformation of American Culture, 1880s to 1920*. New York: Pantheon, 1981.

Leinenweber, Charles. "The Class and Ethnic Bases of New York City Socialism, 1904–1915." *Labor History* 22, no. 1 (1981), pp. 31–56.

Levin, Murray B. *The Compleat Politician: Political Strategy in Massachusetts*. Indianapolis: Bobbs-Merrill, 1962.

Le Worcester Canadien. Worcester: Roy Press, 1900.

Licht, Walter. *Getting Work: Philadelphia, 1840–1950*. Cambridge: Harvard University Press, 1992.

Light, Dale. "Class, Ethnicity, and the Urban Ecology in a Nineteenth Century City: Philadelphia's Irish, 1840–1910," Ph.D. diss.: University of Pennsylvania, 1979.

Lincoln, William. *History of Worcester, Massachusetts from Its Earliest Founding to September 1836*. Worcester: Hersey, 1862.

Linderman, Gerald F. *Embattled Courage: The Experiences of Combat in the American Civil War*. New York: The Free Press, 1987.

Litt, Edgar. *Ethnic Politics in America: Beyond Pluralism*. Glencoe: Scott, Foresman, 1970.

Lord, Robert H., John E. Sexton, and Edward T. Harrington. *A History of the Archdiocese of Boston*. Volumes 1 and 3. New York: Sheed and Ward, 1944.

Lubell, Samuel. *The Future of American Politics*. New York: Harper, 1952.

Lubove, Roy. *Community Planning in the 1920s*. Pittsburgh: University of Pittsburgh Press, 1963.

Lyons, F. S. L. *Charles Stewart Parnell*. New York: Oxford University Press, 1977.

———. *Culture and Anarchy in Ireland, 1890 to 1939.* Oxford: Clarendon Press, 1979.

MacCurtain, Maragaret, and Doncha O'Currain. *Women in Irish Society: The Historical Dimension.* Westport: Greenwood Press, 1979.

MacDonagh, Oliver. *States of Mind: A Study of Anglo-Irish Conflict, 1800–1980.* London: George Allen Press, 1983.

MacDonagh, Thomas J. "The Origins of the Parochial Schools of This City," *The Catholic Directory and History of Worcester and Suburbs.* Worcester: n.p., 1887.

Malcolm, Elizabeth. *"Ireland Sober, Ireland Free": Drink and Temperance in Nineteenth-Century Ireland.* Syracuse: Syracuse University Press, 1986.

Mandle, W. F. *The Gaelic Athletic Association and Irish Nationalist Politics, 1884–1924.* Dublin: Gill, 1987.

Marvin, A. P. *History of Worcester in the War of the Rebellion.* Worcester: privately published, 1870.

Matsumoto, Valerie. *Farming the Home Place: A Japanese American Community in California.* Ithaca: Cornell University Press, 1993.

McAvoy, Thomas. *A History of the Catholic Church in the United States.* Notre Dame: University of Notre Dame Press, 1969.

McBride, Theresa. "Social Mobility for the Lower Classes: Domestic Servants in France." *Journal of Social History* 4, no. 4 (Fall 1974), pp. 63–78.

McCaffrey, Lawrence, ed. *The Irish in Chicago.* Urbana: University of Illinois Press, 1987.

———. *Irish Diaspora in America.* Bloomington: Indiana University Press, 1976.

McDannell, Colleen. *Material Christianity.* New Haven: Yale University Press, 1995.

McDonald, Terrence J. *The Parameters of Urban Fiscal Policy: SocioEconomic Change and Political Culture in San Francisco, 1860–1906.* Berkeley: University of California Press, 1986.

McGreevy, John T. *Parish Boundaries: The Catholic Encounter with Race in the Twentieth-Century Urban North.* Chicago: University of Chicago Press, 1996.

McLaughlin, Virginia Yans, ed. *Immigration Reconsidered.* New York: Oxford University Press, 1990.

McLeod, Hugh. "Catholicism and the New York Irish: 1880 to 1910," in Jim Obelkevich et al., eds. *Disciplines of Faith: Studies in Religion, Politics, and Patriarchy.* New York: Routledge and Kegan Paul, 1987.

———. *Piety and Poverty: Working Class Religion in Berlin, London, and New York, 1870–1914.* New York: Holmes and Meier, 1996.

———. *Religion and the People of Western Europe.* Oxford: Oxford University Press, 1981.

McMahon, Eileen. *What Parish Are You From? A Chicago Irish Community and Race Relations.* Lexington: University Press of Kentucky, 1995.

McNickle, Chris. *To Be Mayor of New York: Ethnic Politics in the City.* New York: Columbia University Press, 1994.

McSeveney, Samuel. *The Politics of Depression in the Northeast, 1893–1896.* New York: Oxford University Press, 1972.

Meagher, Timothy, ed. *From Paddy to Studs: Irish-American Communities at the Turn of the Century, 1880 to 1920.* Westport: Greenwood Press, 1986.

———. *Urban American Catholicism: Culture and Identity of the American Catholic People.* New York: Garland Press, 1988.

Mears, David Otis. *An Autobiography.* Boston: Pilgrim Press, 1920.

Meeker, Michael. *Literature and Violence in North Arabia.* Cambridge: Cambridge University Press, 1979.

Merk, Lois Bannister. "Massachusetts and the Women's Suffrage Movement," Ph.D. diss.: Radcliffe College, 1956.

Merwick, Donna. *Boston Priests, 1848–1910: A Study of Social and Intellectual Change.* Cambridge: Harvard University Press, 1973.

Miller, David W. "Irish Catholicism and the Great Famine." *Journal of Social History* 9, no. 1 (1975), pp. 81–98.

Miller, Randall, and Thomas D. Marzik, eds. *Immigrants and Religion in Urban America.* Philadelphia: Temple University Press, 1977.

Mitchell, Albert Gibbs. "Irish Family Patterns in Nineteenth Century Ireland and Lowell, Massachusetts." Ph.D. diss.: Boston University, 1976.

Mitchell, Brian C. *The Paddy Camps: The Irish of Lowell, 1821–1861.* Urbana: University of Illinois Press, 1988.

Mollenkopf, John. *The Contested City.* Princeton: Princeton University Press, 1983.

———. *Dual City: Restructuring New York.* New York: Russell Sage, 1991.

Montgomery, David. *The Fall of the House of Labor.* Cambridge: Cambridge University Press, 1989.

Moody, T.W. *The Fenian Movement.* Cork: Mercier Press, 1968.

———. *Michael Davitt and Irish Revolution, 1846–1882.* New York: Oxford University Press, 1981.

Moore, Deborah Dash. *At Home in America: Second Generation New York Jews.* New York: Columbia University Press, 1981.

Moss, Kenneth. "St. Patrick's Day Celebrations and the Formation of Irish American Identity, 1845–1875." *Journal of Social History* 29, no. 9 (Fall 1995), pp. 125–48.

Nahirny, Vladimir, and Joshua Fishman. "American Immigrant Groups, Ethnic Identification, and the Problem of Generations." *Sociological Review* 13, no. 3 (December 1965), pp. 311–26.

Oates, Mary J. "The Professional Preparation of Parochial School Teachers, 1870s to 1940s." *Historical Journal of Massachusetts* 12, no. 1 (January 1984), pp. 60–72.

O'Brien, Anthony Patrick. "Factory Size and Economies of Scale and the Great Merger Wave of 1898–1902." *Journal of Economic History* 48, no. 3 (December 1988), pp. 639–49.

O'Brien, Conor Cruise. *Parnell and His Party, 1880–1890.* Oxford: Oxford University Press, 1964.

O'Brien, David. *The Renewal of American Catholicism.* New York: Oxford University Press, 1972.

O'Connor, Thomas H. *Fitzpatrick's Boston, 1846–1866: John Bernard Fitzpatrick, Third Bishop of Boston.* Boston: Northeastern University Press, 1984.

O'Dea, John. *History of the Ancient Order of Hibernians and Its Auxiliary.* New York: National Board of the A.O.H., 1923.

O'Grada, Cormac. *Ireland: A New Economic History, 1780–1939.* New York: Oxford University Press, 1994.

O'Grady, John. *How the Irish Became Americans.* New York: Twayne, 1973.

Olzak, Susan, and Joanne Nagel, eds. *Comparative Ethnic Relations.* Orlando: Florida Academic Press, 1986.

O' Neill, Kevin. *Family and Farm in Pre-famine Ireland: The Parish of Killashandra.* Madison: University of Wisconsin Press, 1984.

Orel, Harold, ed. *Irish History and Culture.* Lawrence: University of Kansas, 1976.

Orsi, Robert. *The Madonna of 115th Street: Faith and Community in Italian Harlem, 1880–1950.* New Haven: Yale University Press, 1985.

———. *Thank You St. Jude: Women's Devotion to the Patron of Hopeless Causes.* New Haven: Yale University Press, 1996.

O'Toole, James M. *Militant and Triumphant: William Henry O'Connell and Catholicism in Boston, 1859–1944.* Notre Dame: University of Notre Dame Press, 1992.

Petrin, Ronald A. *French Canadians in Massachusetts Politics, 1885–1915: Ethnicity and Political Pragmatism.* Philadelphia: Balch Institute Press, 1990.

Powers, Vincent. "Invisible Immigrants: The Pioneer Irish of Worcester, Massachusetts, 1826–1860." Ph.D. diss: Clark University, 1976.

Platt, Harold L. *City Building in the New South: The Growth of Public Services in Houston, Texas, 1830–1910.* Philadelphia: Temple University Press, 1983.

Prude, Jonathan. *The Coming of the Industrial Order: Town and Factory Life in Rural Massachusetts, 1810–1860.* Cambridge: Cambridge University Press, 1983.

Rischin, Moses. "Immigration, Migration and Minorities in California: A Reassessment." *Pacific Historical Review* 41, no. 1 (1972), pp. 71–90.

Roberge, Robert A. "The Three-Decker: Structural Correlate of Worcester's Industrial Revolution." M.A. thesis: Clark University, 1965.

Rodechko, James. *Patrick Ford and His Search for America: A Case Study of Irish-American Journalism, 1870–1913.* New York: Arno Press, 1976.

Roediger, David. *The Wages of Whiteness: Race and the Making of the American Working Class.* New York: Routledge, 1995.

Rosenzweig, Roy. *Eight Hours for What We Will: Workers and Leisure in an Industrial City, 1870–1920.* Cambridge: Cambridge University Press, 1983.

Royce, Anya Patterson. *Ethnic Identity: Strategies and Diversity.* Bloomington: Indiana University Press, 1982.

Salvatore, Nicholas. *Eugene V. Debs: Citizen and Socialist.* Urbana: University of Illinois Press, 1984.

———. *We All Got History: The Memory Books of Amos Webber.* New York: Random House, 1996.

Sanchez, George. *Becoming Mexican American: Ethnicity, Culture and Identity in Chicano Los Angeles, 1900–1945.* New York: Oxford University Press, 1993.

Sanders, James W. *The Education of An Urban Minority: Catholics in Chicago, 1833–1965.* Chicago: University of Chicago Press, 1977.

Saxton, Alexander. *The Indispensable Enemy: Labor and the Anti-Chinese Movement in California.* Berkeley: University of California Press, 1971.

Schlereth, Thomas. "Columbia, Columbus, and Columbianism," *Journal of American History* 79, no. 3 (December 1992).

Shannabruch, Charles. *Chicago's Catholics: The Evolution of an American Identity.* Notre Dame: University of Notre Dame Press, 1981.

Snyder, Robert, *The Voice of the City.* New York: Oxford University Press, 1990.

Sollors, Werner. *The Invention of Ethnicity.* New York: Oxford University Press, 1989.

Sorrelle, Richard. "The Sentinelle Affair and Militant Survivance: The Franco-American Experience in Woonsocket, Rhode Island." Ph.D. diss.: University of Buffalo, 1975.

Southwick, Albert. *Once Told Tales of Worcester County.* Worcester: Worcester Telegram and Gazette, 1985.

Spear, Marilyn. *Worcester's Three Deckers.* Worcester: Bicentennial Commission, 1977.

Stilgoe, John R. *Common Landscape of America, 1580 to 1845.* New Haven: Yale University Press, 1982.

Stivers, Richard. *A Hair of the Dog: Irish Drinking and American Stereotype.* University Park: Pennsylvania State University Press, 1971.

Stoddard, Harry Gilpin. *The Seventy-Year Saga of a New England Enterprise in Industrial Worcester.* New York: Newcomen Society of North America. 1952.

Stonequist, Everett. *The Marginal Man: A Study in Personality and Culture Conflict.* New York: Scribner's, 1937.

Stott, Richard. *Workers in the Metropolis: Class, Ethnicity, and Youth in Antebellum New York City.* Ithaca: Cornell University Press, 1990.

Sugrue, Thomas J. "Crabgrass Politics: Race, Rights, and the Myth of the Liberal Consensus." *Journal of American History* 82, no. 2 (September 1995), pp. 551–78.

Sullivan, Robert E., and James W. O'Toole, eds. *Catholic Boston: Studies in Religion and Community.* Boston: Archdiocese of Boston, 1985.

Taves, Anne. *The Household of Faith: Roman Catholic Devotions in Mid-Nineteenth-Century America.* Notre Dame: University of Notre Dame Press, 1986.

Taylor, Herbert Foster. *Seventy Years of the Worcester Polytechnic Institute.* Worcester: Published privately, 1937.

Teaford, Jon. *The Unheralded Triumph: City Government in America.* Baltimore: Johns Hopkins University Press, 1986.

Tentler, Leslie. "Present at the Creation: Working Class Catholics in the United States," in Rick Halperin and Jonathan Morris, eds., *American Exceptionalism: U.S. Working Class Formation in an International Context.* New York: St. Martin's Press, 1997.

Tentler, Leslie Woodcock. *Seasons of Grace: A History of the Catholic Archdiocese of Detroit.* Detroit: Wayne State University Press, 1990.

Thompson, Bryan. "Cultural Ties as Determinants of Immigrant Settlement in Urban Areas." Ph.D. diss.: Clark University, 1971.

Townshend., Charles. *Political Violence in Ireland: Government and Resistance Since 1848.* Oxford: Clarendon Press, 1983.

Tuckel, Peter, and Richard Maisel. "Voter Turnout Among European Immigrants to the United States. " *Journal of Interdisciplinary History* 24, no. 3 (Winter 1994), pp. 407–30.

Tucker, Grady Oscar. "Development of the Central Business Area: Worcester, Massachusetts, with Special Reference to the Retail Sales Function." Ph.D. diss.: Clark University, 1957.

Tymeson, Mildred M. *Men of Metal.* Worcester: Worcester Stamped Metal Co., 1954.

———. *Two Towers: The Story of Worcester Tech, 1865–1965.* Worcester: Worcester Polytechnic Institute, 1965.

———. *The Wyman-Gordon Way, 1883–1958.* Worcester: Privately published, 1959.

———. *Worcester Bankbook: From County Barter to County Bank, 1804 to 1966.* Worcester: Worcester County National Bank, 1966.

Wade, Mason. *The French Canadians: 1760–1917.* Toronto: Macmillan, 1968.

Walsh, Victor. "'Across the Big Wather': Irish Community Life in Pittsburgh and Allegheny City, 1850–1885." Ph.D. Thesis. University of Pittsburgh, 1983.

———. "A Fanatic Heart: The Cause of Irish American Nationalism in Pittsburgh During the Gilded Age." *Journal of Social History* 15, no. 2 (Winter 1981), pp. 187–204.

Washburn, Charles G. *Industrial Worcester.* Worcester: Davis Press, 1917.

Waters, Mary C. *Ethnic Options: Choosing Identities in America.* Berkeley: University of California Press, 1990.

Weinstein, James. *The Decline of Socialism in America, 1912–1925.* New York: Vintage, 1969.

Williams, William H. A. *'Twas Only an Irishman's Dream: The Image of Ireland and the Irish in American Popular Song Lyrics, 1800–1920.* Urbana: University of Illinois Press, 1996.

Woodward, William. *Historical Sketch of Piedmont Congregational Church.* Worcester: Piedmont Church, 1922.

Wuthnow, Robert. *The Restructuring of American Religion: Society and Faith Since World War II.* Princeton: Princeton University Press, 1988.

Yancey, William, Eugene Erickson, and Richard Juliani. "Emergent Ethnicity." *American Sociological Review* 4, no. 3 (June 1976), pp. 391–403.

Zunz, Oliver. *Making America Corporate, 1870 to 1920.* Chicago: University of Chicago, 1990.

Index

abortion, 323, 328–29, 333, 343

accommodation, 4, 11, 323; and Catholic Church, 152–62, 204–5; deviations from, 134; end of, 13, 202–7, 265, 271; and institutional networks, 3–4, 156–72, 337–38; trends toward, 133–36, 199–200. *See also* assimilation; Citizens' Alliance

African Americans, 15, 383

Alden, George, 109

Allswang, John, 321

American, 224–25, 229

American Association for the Recognition of the Irish Republic (AARIR), 368

American Federation of Labor (AFL), 281

Americanism, 133, 363; of American-born Irish, 68–71; and Knights of Columbus, 351–52, 354–55, 367; Leo XIII's condemnation of, 205; and pan-ethnic Catholic cooperation, 4, 338–39, 345–49; in social clubs, 169–70; in temperance movement, 167–68. *See also* patriotism

American Land League, 180–81, 184. *See also* Land League

American Protective Association (APA), 206, 227; and Ancient Order of Hibernians, 247; and high school controversy, 254; impact of, 244, 327; Ku Klux Klan compared to, 307; leadership of, 128

American Steel and Wire Company, 274, 280, 379, 469n81

Ancient Order of Hibernians (AOH), 170–72, 240–44; and American Protective Association, 247; and Bay State Bank, 261; and Catholic Church, 171, 260, 263; communalism of, 36, 48–49; decline of, 162, 172, 272; on denial of heritage, 68–69; and Federation of Catholic Societies, 342; and fountain controversy, 247–48; fundraising for Ireland by, 438n102; Gaelic cultural revival and, 4, 34, 202, 250–51, 263; gender role attitudes of, 252–53; and Irish nationalism, 256–58, 359–60; Irish stereotyping fought by, 249–50; labor movements and, 245–46; membership of, 2, 10, 42, 170–71, 241–43, 272, 341; political participation of, 247–49; and St. Patrick's Day celebrations, 2–3, 134, 172–78, 253–56, 272, 385; teaching of Irish history proposed by, 249, 263, 272; and temperance movement, 171–72, 251–52, 253–56; on U.S. foreign policy, 258–59; women's auxiliaries of, 41, 241, 245, 252–53

Anthony of Padua, Saint, 29, 37–38, 80, 86

anti-Catholicism: of British immigrants, 221; in high school controversy, 224–25; and

anti-Catholicism *(continued)*
  Knights of Columbus, 102, 353–54;
  of native-stock Yankees, 136–37, 229,
  327–28, 376; and pan-ethnic cooperation,
  295–96; and presidential campaigns, 271,
  330–31, 382. *See also* discrimination;
  nativism
anti-German sentiments, 299
antimaterialism, 105, 108, 326
apostasy, 105, 333
Armenian immigrants, 229
Les Artisans Canadienne, 348
Art Museum, Worcester, 139, 286, 379
Art Society, 139
Ascension parish, 86, 127, 278, 363
Asians, 15, 269–70, 383
assimilation, 6, 11, 130, 134, 216, 378. *See also*
  accommodation
Associated Charities, 51–52, 60
Assumption College, 348
Athy, Andrew: accommodationist leadership of, 206; as Ancient Order of Hibernians member, 172; fund-raising of, 182,
  197–98; home and exile for, 33; and Irish
  nationalism, 183, 203; mayoral election
  of, 152; political activities of, 43, 151–52
Athy, Annie, 185
Atkinson, Thomas, 228

Bachand, Michael, 294–95
Baltimore Council, 158, 161, 205, 336
banks, 102, 260–62, 275, 339–40, 344
Baptist Church, 141, 220, 285
Barnard, Lewis, 144
Barrett, James, 6–7
Barrett, Thomas J., 237, 282, 293–94, 364,
  450n83
Barry, John, 70
Barton, George S., 299
baseball, 74–75, 111, 140, 167, 264
basketball, 75, 351
Bay State Bank, 260–62, 339–40, 344
Beaven, Thomas, 88; and Irish nationalism,

362; on labor problems, 278; and North
  Brookfield controversy, 216; on parochial
  school construction, 336; on veneration
  of saints, 37
Belisle, Alexander, 339
Bell Hill neighborhood, 219, 309–10
Belmont Hill neighborhood, 286
Berger, L'Abbé, 217
bicycling, 140
Biddle, Helen Horgan, 376
Binstock, Robert, 381
birth control, 323, 328–29, 333, 343, 465n57
Blackstone Canal, 22–23, 58–59, 136
Blessed Sacrament parish, 129–30, 336, 341,
  363, 378
blue-collar workers: in Ancient Order of
  Hibernians, 243; in Blessed Sacrament
  parish, 129; Irish as, 45–46, 106, 118, 159;
  and Irish nationalism, 188–89; as KKK
  members, 307; nativism of, 227–28;
  political participation of, 147; in social
  clubs, 169; in temperance movement, 168
boarding houses. *See* housing
Board of Trade, 144, 209–10, 225–26,
  275–76. *See also* Chamber of Commerce
Boaz, Franz, 140
Bodnar, John, 401n57
Boer War, 258
Bohemian Club, 139
Boland, Tobias, 59
boot- and shoe-making industry, 46, 101–2,
  112, 145–46, 276, 379
Boston Pilot, 181, 183–85
Bowler Brothers (brewery), 42, 211
Boyle, Daniel, 2, 176
Boyle, Katie, 93
Boy Scouts, 333
Briden, Dennis, 119
Bridget, Saint, 29, 68–69, 72
British-American Association, 221, 365
British immigrants, 12, 206, 212, 214, 220–22
Brooks, George, 291
Brown, Push, 201, 248

Brown, Thomas, 183, 193
Brown Nuns, 339–40, 344
Bryan, William Jennings, 233, 238
Bryne, John, 101
Buckley, Louis, 282, 290–91, 302, 353
Buckley, Thomas, 414n57
Buenker, John, 324
Buffington, Mr. and Mrs. E. D., 140
Bullock, Augustus G., 197, 233
Bullock, Chandler, 290–91, 312
Burke, Richard, S.J., 57, 246, 430n37
Burke, Thomas, 439n126
Burns, John, 196, 254–55
business elites: in banking, 102, 260; class
    solidarity of, 275–76; dominated by
    Yankee Protestants, 15, 45, 143–44, 273,
    329, 379–80, 383; Irish as, 106, 110, 305,
    329; and market integration, 275; politi-
    cal activities of, 303–6, 380; and Worces-
    ter Polytechnic Institute, 107–10
Butler, Benjamin, 150–51
Butler, James, 188
Butte, Montana, 16, 44–45, 359, 366–67,
    401n57

Callahan, Charles, 89
Canada, Fenian invasions of, 179
Carberry, James F., 237, 239, 282, 450n83
Carmody, Annie, 88
Carmody, Cornelius, 467n66, 474n121
Carpenters' District Council, 278
carpenters' strike (1890), 211–14
Carroll, Charles, 77, 169
Carroll, Mark, 304
Carrolltons, 168–69, 264
Cassidy, Mary, 36
Catholic Church: and accommodation,
    152–62, 204–5; administration in, 331–32,
    374; and Ancient Order of Hibernians,
    171, 260, 263; antimaterialism of, 105,
    108, 326; conservatism of, 331–33, 378;
    devotional revolution in, 11, 28–29,
    36–37, 79–81, 85–86, 93; and French

Canadians, 216–17, 288; and Irish iden-
    tity, 93–94; liturgical rituals in, 81–83,
    95–96, 343, 376; and pan-ethnic parishes,
    340–41, 344, 378; parish missions in,
    83–84, 86; self-discipline in, 97–98,
    122–23, 376; and temperance movement,
    156, 163–64, 328; and women's roles,
    98–99. See also anti-Catholicism; priests;
    saints, veneration of
Catholic Liberalism movement, 154–55; and
    parochial schools, 161, 204; reining in of,
    204–5, 266, 331–32, 483n7; temperance
    attitudes of, 162, 164, 170
Catholic Messenger: boosterism of, 344, 349;
    editorial policy of, 338; end of, 374; and
    Irish nationalism, 359, 361; labor cover-
    age in, 324; and presidential politics, 317.
    See also Messenger
Catholic School and Home Magazine, 164
Catholic Women's Club, 86–87, 92–93, 99,
    335, 342
Catholic Young Men's Lyceum, 75, 91, 163–64,
    166, 255, 264
Catholic Young Women's Lyceum, 74, 86, 92,
    99, 166, 195
Cavendish, Frederick (chief secretary for Ire-
    land), 196, 439n126
Central Labor Union (CLU), 210–11, 278–79,
    280–81, 324
Chamber of Commerce, 275–76, 291, 303–5,
    315, 471n102. See also Board of Trade
Champagne, Frank, 353–54
Chan, Sucheng, 269–70
Chandler May neighborhood, 141, 228–29
charities, 51–52, 64, 181–83, 207–8
charter reforms, city, 225–26, 236–38,
    380–81
Chase, Charles, 157–58, 197
Chatham Club, 168
Chenoweth, B. P. (superintendent of
    schools), 104
childbearing, 53, 120, 328, 465n57
child labor, 50, 56–58, 104, 119–20

Chinese Americans, 15, 269–70

Chinnici, Joseph, 80

Christy, Austin, 291

Churchill, James K., 235, 239

Citizens' Alliance, 135, 146–52, 161, 178, 206, 230–35, 296

Citizens for Plan E Association (CEA), 380–81

city charter reforms, 225–26, 236–38, 380–81

civil rights movement, 382

Civil War, U.S., 70, 135, 137–38, 173, 182

Clan na Gael: decline of, 272; emergence of, 241–42; Gaelic cultural revival and, 4, 202, 240–41; as Gaelic League supporter, 251; and Irish nationalism, 180–81, 257–58; labor movements and, 245; membership of, 242–43, 272, 341; and St. Patrick's Day celebrations, 254–55; on U.S. foreign policy, 259

Clarke, Bryan, 93

Clark University, 140

Classical High School, 107

class solidarity, 135, 143–46, 213–14, 244–47, 270, 275–76, 379, 391n10

Cleary, James, 165

clerical occupations, 45–46, 113

Cleveland, Grover, 150–51

Coakley, John F., 42, 54

Coakley, Michael, 42

coal famine (1918–19), 300

Cody, Michael, 188

Coes, Loring, 146

Coffey, James C., 197

Cohalan, Daniel, 368

Cohen, Abner, 7

Cohen, Bruce, 279

Cohen, Liz, 6

Cold War, 377

College of the Holy Cross. See Holy Cross College

Collins, Michael, 369

Collins, Nellie, 77

Collins, Patrick, 181, 184

Columba, Saint, 29

Columbus Day celebrations, 3, 355–58

Colvin, Caleb, 448n77

Combes, Zelotes W., 312

comedians, Irish, 249–50

Conaty, Bernard S., 37, 264, 342

Conaty, Thomas J., 156, 430n37; accommodationist leadership of, 156, 206; Americanism of, 68, 363; and Catholic Young Women's Lyceum, 99; on devotional rituals, 82; fund-raising of, 196–98, 203, 208; on industriousness, 105; and Irish nationalism, 183–84, 187, 189–91, 196–98; Littleton on, 90; and parish missions, 84, 86; on parochial schools, 156, 159; and St. Vincent's Hospital, 158; temperance leadership of, 156, 164–66, 269

confraternities, 28, 84–85

Congregational Church, 138–39, 141, 220, 285

Congregational Ministers Association, 285

Congress of Industrial Organizations (CIO), 379

Conlin, John, 38

Conlin, Peter, 231

Connell, K. H., 122

Connolly, James J., 465n54

Conrad, A. Z., 228–29

conscription crisis, 360, 481n187

construction employment, 22–23, 43–44, 278

Conzen, Kathleen, 7–9

Coolidge, Calvin, 318

Corcoran, Edward, 70

Corpus Christi, 81–82, 94

Cosgrove, Mark, 304

Courtney, D. J., 176

Courtney, Daniel, 44

Coyne, Michael J., 363

Crescents, 168

crew racing, 74–75

crime, 24, 62, 91, 219

Crispins, 277

Crompton, George, 126

Crompton and Knowles Loom Works, 124, 274, 279

cross burnings, 310–11

Crotty, James A., 363

Cuba, 259

Cuddihy, Patrick Huntington, 171

Cullen, Paul (Archbishop of Dublin), 28

cultural persistence, studies of, 6

Curley, James Michael, 293, 483n207

Curran, Patrick, 35

Curtis, Edwin, 209

Curtis Machine Shop, 207

Cushing, Richard, 373

Cussone, Joseph, 466n60

Daigneault, Alfred, 347

Dalton, J. P., 360, 363–64

Daly, Jim, 35

dancing, 26, 77, 285

Davitt, Michael, 134, 179–80, 185, 191–93

death rates, 61

Debs, Eugene V., 282

De Marco, Joe, 294

Democratic Party, 44, 292–98; as Catholic party, 320–21; and Citizens' Alliance, 146–52, 233–35, 296; and city charter reforms, 225–26, 236–37; dominance of, in 1950s, 380; and economy in government/ tax cut policies, 296–97, 301, 313–14; and French Canadians, 217; Irish membership in, 136, 235–40, 322; labor movement impact on, 212; and nativism, 226; and pan-ethnic Catholic cooperation, 320–21, 344; and postwar ills, 300; and re-registration as Republicans, 315; revitalization of, 314; and Socialists, 246

department stores, 210

depressions, economic: 1870s, 173; 1880s, 144–45; 1890s, 206–14; post–WWI, 280, 299–300, 303–4, 472n106; Great, 322, 378–79

de Valera, Eamon, 68, 365, 367–69

devotional revolution, 11, 79–81, 85–86, 93; in Ireland, 28–29, 36–37

Devoy, John, 179, 181

Dickens, Charles, 20

Diner, Hasia, 120, 186

Diocesan Temperance Union, 156

discrimination: and changes in neighborhood patterns, 128–30; in economic opportunity, 47–48, 101–2, 113–14, 260–61; in patronage appointments, 248–49; shared understanding of, 295, 343. See also anti-Catholicism; nativism

diseases, 61–62, 95

Dodge, Rufus, 233–35, 238

Dolan, Harry, 252

Dolan, Jay, 80, 83–84, 91, 94

domestic servants, 40–41, 46–47, 54–55, 111–12, 218–19

domestic violence, 55

Donohue, Florence, 475n121

Donohue, Harold D., 380

Donohue, Thomas, 127, 363

Dougherty, Maria, 184–86, 188, 190, 192, 245, 253

Dowd, Martin, 40

Dowd, Mary, 40

Dowd, Thomas, 70

Doyle, David, 245–46, 259

Doyle, James, 153

Doyle, Pat, 425n4

drama societies, 77–78

Drennan, John, 183–84

drinking: as communal activity, 34–36; as cultural characteristic, 26, 162, 251; as domestic problem, 55; as public problem, 91, 343; Yankees' view of, 140, 165, 172, 285. See also liquor license referenda; prohibition; temperance movement

Drury, F. A., 282

Duggan, John T.: Americanism of, 70–71; economy in government/tax cut policies of, 296–97; and Irish nationalism, 362; mayoral elections of, 289–90, 293; on neighborhood patterns, 60; political activities of, 237, 240, 303

Dungarvan Hill. See Oak Hill neighborhood

Dunleavy, Honora, 67

Eagan, Mary, 185
Earle, Enoch, 448n77
Earle, Stephen, 414n60
Early, James, 176, 254, 260
Early, Michael, 40
Easter rebellion (1916), 359
East Worcester neighborhood, 59, 124; churches in, 63; hospitals in, 157; non-Irish in, 215, 219, 288; parades in, 63, 318–19; settlement patterns in, 62; street gangs in, 91
economic conditions: of American-born Irish, 95, 99–116, 156–57, 325; of immigrant Irish, 41–52, 119–20, 149; in Ireland, 19, 32; in Worcester, 19–20, 143–46, 208–10, 273–76, 280, 378–79, 383
economy in government/tax cut policies, 296–97, 301, 313–14
education: and Bible reading in public schools, 138; and high school controversy, 223–26; impact of Irish on public, 262–63; Irish children enrolled in public, 103–4, 335; and Irish history curricula, 249, 263, 272; of women, 114. See also parochial schools
Eisenhower, Dwight D., 380
Elks (fraternal order), 333–34
Elliott, Walter, 155
Elm Park neighborhood, 128, 328
Emerald Bazaar, 189–90
Emmet, Robert, 257
Emmet Guards, 75, 82, 468n68
Emmons, David, 16, 401n57
England. See Great Britain
envelope industry, 112, 290
Episcopal Church, 138–39, 141–42, 285
Esthus, Charles, 218
ethnic competition. See specific ethnic groups
ethnicity and ethnic change, studies of, 6–9
ethnocentrism, 4, 12–13, 323; and Catholic networks, 338–49, 376–77; and Irish networks, 260–63, 327, 334–37; labor movements and, 244–46; opposition to ac-

commodation, 134–35; social organizations and, 170–78, 240–44, 272
evangelism, 133, 141–42, 285, 287, 334, 342
Evening Gazette, 148, 231, 380–81

F. E. Reed (machinery manufacturer), 209, 218
Fairmount Hill neighborhood, 59
fairs, 26, 42, 64–65
family size, 53, 120, 328, 465n57
Fanning, David Hale, 226
Farnsworth, Eugene, 307–8, 353
Farrell, James J., 278, 363, 367
Father Mathew Cadets, 163–64, 167
Father Mathew Total Abstinence Association, 163, 167–68, 173, 255, 438n102
Federation of Catholic Societies, 337–38, 342, 344–45, 347
Fenians, 33, 173, 179–80
fertility rates. See childbearing
Finnish immigrants, 212
Fisher, Charles, 365
Fishman, Joshua, 70
Fitton, James, 162
Fitzgerald, Clara, 113, 118
Fitzgerald, D. F., 254
Fitzgerald, Daniel, 450n83
Fitzgerald, Edward, 173
Fitzgerald, John F., 96, 467n66
Fitzpatrick, John, 171
Fitzpatrick, Thomas, 415n69
Flaherty, Martin, 75
Flanagan, Bernard J., 382
Flynn, George, 363
Flynn, Hugh, 251
Foley, Frank H., 332
Foley, Jeremiah, 36
Foley, John, 57
Foley, Thomas, 316, 319, 367
folk culture, 26–27, 33–34, 142–43, 228–29
football: American, 75, 140, 167; Gaelic, 167, 250, 272
Foran, William, 111

Ford, Ellen, 183, 185

Ford, Patrick: attacks on position of, 189, 192; Ladies Land League and, 185–86, 188; as radical nationalist, 134, 181, 194, 453n104

Foss, Eugene, 467n66

Foster, Roy, 33

fountain controversy, 221, 247–48

Fourth of July celebrations, 172, 175, 179

fox hunting, 140

Francis Xavier, Saint, 29, 334

fraternal societies, 205, 333–34, 337. *See also specific societies*

Free Soil Party, 137, 425n6

French Canadians, 214–17, 287–89; anti-Irish antagonism of, 62, 216–17, 346–47; and carpenters' strike, 211–12; Catholic Church and, 216–17, 288; and Columbus Day celebrations, 3, 356–57; as competitors, 12, 15, 100, 111, 206, 215; immigration patterns of, 214; naturalization rate of, 44, 429n25; neighborhood patterns of, 62, 126, 214–15, 288–89; occupations of, 113; and pan-ethnic Catholic cooperation, 4, 339–49, 354, 377–78; political participation of, 148, 214, 217, 232, 233–34, 238, 294–95, 298, 302, 320–21; as potential marriage partners, 58

friends and kinship networks, 401n57; of American-born Irish, 95, 109; centers of, 36, 62; of immigrant Irish, 39–42, 401n57

Friends of Irish Freedom, 359–60, 363, 367–68

Frodigh, Roland, 313–14, 321–22

Fuller, Alvin, 318

Gaelic Athletic Association, 250

Gaelic language, 4, 26, 33–34, 251, 263

Gaelic League, 33–34, 240, 242, 250–51, 272

Gaelic Sports Day (1880), 26–27

Gage, Homer, 158

Gage, Mrs. Homer, 299

Gallagher, Francis, 211

Galvin, C. O'Connell, 203

gambling, 35

Gamm, Samuel, 321

gangs, street, 24, 62, 91, 219

Gannon, John, 111

Geary, Margaret, 185–86

generational studies, 6, 9

George, Henry, 192

George, Jerome, 281, 365

Gerber, David, 7, 9

Germans, 299, 468n68

Gerstle, Gary, 6–7, 391n10

ghetto mentality, Catholic, 326–38

Gibbons, James, 135, 342, 358, 361

Gibson, Matthew, 29, 81

Gladstone, William, 197–98, 202

Gleason, Maurice, 39

Gleason, Sara, 39

Goddard, Harry, 303, 305, 470n88

Goggin, William, 87

Goldstein, David, 351

Gonne, Maud, 257

Goodwin, Doris Kearns, 96

Gordon, Lymna, 109

Goulding, Frank, 197

government employment, 42–43, 110–11, 149. *See also* patronage, political

Grafton Country Club, 140

Graton and Knight (belt manufacturers), 208, 469n81

Great Britain, 19, 32, 258–59, 364–65. *See also* nationalism, Irish

Greek immigrants, 289

Green, John, 155

Green, Samuel Swett, 159

Greendale neighborhood, 286, 309, 311

Grenier, Louis, 316, 322

Griffin, John J., 430n37

Griffin, Thomas: accommodationist leadership of, 155; and Church administration, 332; construction projects of, 127; on devotional rituals, 82; fund-raising of, 183; and Irish nationalism, 439n126; and

Griffin, Thomas (continued)
parish missions, 83; and St. Vincent's
Hospital, 127, 339; temperance leadership of, 165
grocery stores, 63
Guilfoyle, William, 281
gymnastics, 74

Hagberg, John G., 220
Hall, G. Stanley, 155, 329
Halloran, Michael, 118
Hanrahan, Thomas, 164
Hansen, Marcus Lee, 6, 8, 370
Hareven, Tamara, 401n57
Harrington, Francis, 222
Harrington and Richardson (firearms manu-
facturer), 207
Hatch, George, 424n144
Healey, James F., 304–5
Healy, Jim, 89
Healy, Richard, 49–50
Hechter, Michael, 32
Hecker, Issac, 155
hedge schools, 27
Henry, James, 194
Henry, Paul, 194
heroes, Irish American, 70, 198
Heywood, Charles, 233
Hibernians. See Ancient Order of Hibernians
Hickey, Kevin, 307
Hickey, William, 76, 346
Higgins, Aldus, 282
Higgins, Milton, 109, 141–42
Highland Associates, 168, 264
high school controversy, 223–26, 254
Hildreth, Charles, 224, 226
Hildreth, Samuel, 142, 146–47
Hoar, George F.: on demise of Spy, 231–32;
and Irish nationalism, 198; and praise for
the Irish, 138, 167; as St. Wulstan's
member, 155; on J. A. Thayer, 151; and
women's suffrage, 226
Hoar, Rockwood, 139, 231–32

Holmes, Pehr: and coal famine, 300; and
de Valera visit, 365; mayoral elections of,
283, 299, 310; municipal improvement
policies of, 300; North End Ring mem-
bership of, 290–91; political activities of,
299–302, 312
Holy Cross College, 75, 107–9, 334, 342,
445n53
Holy Name of Jesus Church, 126, 215
Holy Name societies, 87, 92, 334, 355
Holy Rosary parish, 130, 341, 344, 378
home rule. See nationalism, Irish
Home Rule bill, 197, 203–4, 257
Home Rule party, 180, 196–97, 202–3
Hoover, Herbert, 317–20, 343
Horan, Jerry, 27
Horan, Michael, 251
Hormly, Margaret, 119
Horowitz, Donald, 7
horse racing, 140
hospitals: Protestant/Catholic cooperation
on, 133, 339–40, 376–77; St. Elizabeth's,
63, 157; St. Vincent's, 127, 157–58, 339,
344, 374, 376–77
House of Mercy, 41
housing, 60–61, 128; boarding, 39–40, 54,
333; construction booms, 292, 315; living
at home, 118–19, 124; taking in boarders,
56
Huntington, Rev., 182
Hurley, Michael, 42
hurling (game), 26–27, 167, 250
Hutchins, C. Henry, 209, 275

Immaculate Conception parish, 41, 63, 86,
159, 184, 363
immigration patterns: British, 220; French
Canadian, 214; Irish, 22–25, 39, 41; non-
white groups, 383; Swedish, 217–18
industrial school board controversy, 308
Industrial Workers of the World (IWW),
325–26
institutional networks: and accommodation,

3–4, 156–72, 337–38; Irish, 260–63, 327, 334–37; pan-ethnic Catholic, 338–49, 376–77; Swedish, 286–87; Yankee/Protestant, 285–86, 327, 333–34. *See also specific societies and organizations*

Ireland: Catholic Church in, 28–29, 36–37; conscription crisis in, 360, 481n187; Easter rebellion in, 359; economic change in, 19, 32; education in, 27–28; fundraising for, 181–83, 188–90, 196–98, 203, 438n102; Gaelic culture in, 33–34; labor movements in, 366; nationalism movement in, 32–33, 134, 178–98, 202–4, 256–58, 358, 360, 368; Potato Famine in, 23, 93; St. Patrick's Day in, 177; temperance movement in, 162

Ireland, John, 135, 161–62, 164

Irish Americans, American-born, 10–11; Catholicism of, 78–99, 122–23; communalism of, 93–95; demographics of, 73, 134, 421nn123–24, 422n130; dual loyalties of, 5, 67–71, 176–77, 271, 345–46, 362, 384; economic conditions of, 95, 99–116, 156–57, 325; education of, 103–4, 114; friends and kinship networks of, 95, 109; and Irish nationalism, 134; leisure activities of, 73–78, 168–70; neighborhood patterns of, 123–31; occupations of, 101–2, 106, 108–9, 111–13, 116, 118; political participation of, 44, 110–11, 186, 237, 325–26; predominance of, 73; and temperance movement, 134, 167–68

Irish Americans, immigrant: and Bay State Bank, 261–62; Catholicism of, 29, 37, 63–65; communalism of, 22, 34–39, 41, 48–49, 57–58, 62–65, 177–78; conflicts among, 24, 29; demographics of, 134, 421nn123–24, 422n130; economic conditions of, 41–52, 119–20, 149; and ethnic militancy, 244, 261; ethnocentric clubs, membership in, 243–44; friends and kinship networks of, 36, 39–42, 62, 401n57; home and exile for, 10, 17–18, 21, 30–33,

67–68, 244, 345–46, 384; immigration patterns of, 22–25, 39, 41; and Irish nationalism, 134, 188–89, 193–95; naturalization rate of, 44, 429n25; neighborhood patterns of, 58–65; occupations of, 22–23, 40–46, 50, 149; political participation of, 44; skills, lack of, 21–22, 47–48, 103, 113; and temperance movement, 134, 168

Irish Catholic Benevolent Society, 255

Irish Free State, 368–69

Irish National Federation, 203

Irish National Foresters, 41, 240, 242, 251, 254, 341

Irish Parliamentary Party, 33, 203, 257–58, 360–61

Irish Republican Brotherhood, 180

Irish World, 181, 186, 188

Island neighborhood, 59, 124; churches in, 63; gangs in, 62, 91; non-Irish in, 215, 271, 288; Protestant mission in, 328; sewage disposal in, 61, 150; temperance societies in, 163

Italians: and coal famine, 300; and Columbus Day celebrations, 3, 356–57; as competitors, 12, 100, 271–72; neighborhood patterns of, 128, 271, 287–89; and pan-ethnic Catholic cooperation, 4, 340–49, 354, 377–78; political participation of, 295, 298, 302–3, 320–21; unemployment of, 300

Jacobson, Matthew, 259

Jandron, John, 217

Jeppson, George: and anti-red campaigns, 300; and 1928 election parade, 318; elite status of, 286; and industrial school board controversy, 308; and labor movements, 280; North End Ring membership of, 290–91; political activities of, 301–2, 310, 312; on Swedes' pro-German attitudes, 468n68; Thursday Noon Club membership of, 281–82

Jews, 100, 302, 311, 321, 380–81

Jillson, Clark, 142
John the Baptist, Saint, 94
John XXIII, 381–82
Joyce, Josie, 76
Jude, Saint, 343

Kane, Paula, 93–94
Kantowicz, Edward, 332
Kazal, Russell, 9
Keane, John, 155
Kearny, Philip, 70
Kelley, William R. (mayor), 182, 187
Kellor, Frances, 40
Kennedy, J. Joseph, 75
Kennedy, John F., 382
Kent, George W., 221
Keysar, Alexander, 63
Kiely, James, 255
Kiely, Thomas: home and exile for, 30–31, 33,
    67; and labor movements, 245–46; and
    Messenger, 241; and parochial schools,
    336; political activities of, 248–49; on
    rowdy masculinity, 252; on U.S. foreign
    policy, 258–59, 323
Kilmainham Treaty, 191–92, 195
Kleppner, Paul, 293
Knights of Columbus, 263–65, 338, 349–55;
    Americanism of, 351–52, 354–55, 367;
    and anti-Catholicism, 102, 353–54; and
    Columbus Day celebrations, 3, 355–58;
    and Irish nationalism, 359, 362–63; and
    Ku Klux Klan, 307, 353–54; leisure activi-
    ties and, 75, 77, 351; membership of, 10,
    86–87, 350, 354–55; political participa-
    tion of, 353; religious devotion of, 92,
    352–53; and self-improvement, 350; and
    socialism, 351; and temperance move-
    ment, 350; and World War I, 351–52
Knights of Father Mathew, 163, 174
Knights of Labor, 145, 194, 208, 210, 277
Knights of Pythias, 205
Knights of Robert Emmet, 242
Knights of St. Patrick, 173

Knights Templars, 170
Knowles, Lucius J., 144, 275, 282, 291
Know-Nothings, 135–37, 173, 307, 327
Kolesar, Robert, 149, 161, 428n23
Ku Klux Klan, 271, 306–13, 330, 343, 353–54

labor movements, 208, 276–83, 304; and
    Ancient Order of Hibernians, 245–46;
    bootworkers' strike, 145–46; carpenters'
    strike, 211–14; and Clan na Gael, 245; and
    Democratic Party, 212; and domestic ser-
    vants, 55; and ethnocentrism, 244–46; in
    Ireland, 366; Irish domination of, 324;
    and Land League, 194–95; machinists'
    strike, 278–79, 324; political participa-
    tion of, 212–14; and radical nationalism,
    367; union organizing in, 144–45, 210–12,
    277–78, 280–82, 379
Ladies Catholic Benevolent Association, 93,
    342, 355
Ladies Land League, 183–86, 188, 190–91,
    195, 438n100; in Ireland, 185, 187–88, 192
Lady Fullerton Circle, 168
Landale, Nancy, 122
Land League, 33, 134, 180–81, 183–84, 187–92,
    194–95, 366
Larkin, Emmet, 28
Larkin, William, 67
Larkin, William J., 67–68
Latinos, 383
Lawler, Thomas Bonaventure, 68
Lee, Joseph, 105, 108
leisure activities, 73–78, 139–41, 309; dancing,
    26, 77, 285; fairs, 26, 42, 64–65; Knights
    of Columbus support of, 75, 77, 351;
    minstrel shows, 77, 169, 351; movies,
    285; music and songs, 26, 31, 76–77, 81,
    139–40; sports, 26–27, 74–76, 140–41,
    166–67, 250, 264, 377; theater, 31, 74,
    77–78, 122, 139, 249–50; vacationing, 74,
    76, 140; vaudeville, 74, 122, 139. *See also*
    social clubs and societies
Leland Gifford (manufacturing firm), 279

Leonard, Dennis, 36

Leo XIII, 205, 331

Lepore, Anthony, 466n60

Licht, Walter, 401n57

Lincoln, Edward, 58

Lincoln, William, 136

liquor license referenda: and Ancient Order of Hibernians, 251; origin of, 150–51; Swedish support for, 220, 287, 309; and temperance movement, 164–65, 170; Yankee support for, 222–23, 285. *See also* drinking; prohibition; temperance movement

literacy, 28

Lithuanians, 287; as competitors, 12, 15, 271–72; neighborhood patterns of, 128, 288; and pan-ethnic Catholic cooperation, 342, 347–49, 354, 377–78; political participation of, 294

Little Franciscans of Mary, 339–40, 344

Littleton, Stephen, 62–63, 88–90, 95–96, 121, 161, 165

Logan, James: business career of, 109, 209; mayoral elections of, 293–94; municipal improvement policies of, 296–97; North End Ring membership of, 290–91; Thursday Noon Club membership of, 282

Lonergan, Danny, 89

Long, Margaret, 36

Lyttle, William, 296

machinists' strike (1915), 278–79, 324

MacSwiney, Terence, 367

Magnuson, Axel, 310

Maguire, P. J., 145

Mahoney, John C., 380; economy in government/tax cut policies of, 314; mayoral elections of, 43, 314, 317–18, 321–22

Main South neighborhood, 124–26, 141, 215, 228–29, 383

Malcolm, Elizabeth, 34

Malozzi, Anthony, 302–3

Mansfield, Frederick, 467n66

manufacturing industries, 45–47, 378–79; decline of, 276, 303, 383; labor movements in, 143–45; and market integration, 208–9, 274; and 1890s depression, 207–9

Manzi, Luciano, 466n60

Marble, Albert, 104, 161, 223–26, 228, 262

Marble, J. O., 197

marriage patterns: of American-born Irish, 98, 116–23, 376; of immigrant Irish, 53–58, 116–17; in Ireland, 34, 52–53, 117; mixed, 329, 333, 337, 378, 385; of native stock Yankees, 53, 116

Marsh, Henry, 183, 197, 225–26

Marxism, 245, 377

masculinity, attitudes about, 166–67, 252

Mathew, Theobald, 162–63

mayoral elections. *See individual candidates*

McAleer, George, 260

McAuliffe, T. J., 254

McAvoy, Thomas, 342

McBride, John, 257

McCafferty, Matthew, 43; accommodationist leadership of, 152, 206; as Ancient Order of Hibernians member, 172; fund-raising of, 182; and Irish nationalism, 187; and Land League, 438n103

McCaffrey, Lawrence, 26, 33

McCarthy, Katie, 185

McCarty, Bridget, 36

McCaughan, W. C., 49

McClymer, John, 218

McCoy, John J.: accommodationist leadership of, 156, 206, 269–71; Americanism of, 69, 272–73, 324, 326; on American Protection Association, 327; and Catholic Women's Club, 99, 335; on Columbus Day celebrations, 356; on dangers of street gangs, 91; on devotional rituals, 95–96; on ethnic inclusiveness, 340, 354; and Federation of Catholic Societies, 342; and Irish nationalism, 187, 191, 360, 362;

McCoy, John J. (*continued*)
and Ladies Land League, 183; on leisure activities, 122; on neighborliness, 48; on Protestantism's lure, 105, 271, 333; on socialism, 325; temperance leadership of, 156, 164, 167, 269
McDannell, Colleen, 85
McDermott, Henry, 18
McDermott, James A., 118, 129, 211
McDermott, James T., 77
McDermott Brothers Contractors, 102, 211, 246, 278
McDowell, Hannah, 76
McDowell, Julia, 76
McGillicuddy, Daniel F., 87, 264, 434n62
McGillicuddy, Ellen T., 118
McGillicuddy, Mary Agnes, 112–13, 118
McGlynn, Edward, 155, 161, 192, 245
McGourty, Thomas, 175–76, 255
McGovern, James F., 474n121
McGrath, Francis J., 381
McGrath, John F., 362, 474n121
McGrath, Mary, 56
McHugh, Francis, 40
McIver, W. B., 448n77
McKeon, Francis, 88, 96, 313, 353
McKinley, William, 233, 318
McLaughlin, Delia, 88
McLaughlin, Thomas, 368
McLeod, Hugh, 97
McMahon, Edward J., 221, 254
McNally, Ann B., 40
McNally, William, 40
McNamara, Andrew, 39
McNamara, Bridget, 39
McNutt, William, 365
Meadows neighborhood, 59, 271
Meagher, John H., 237
Meagher, Mrs. Dennis, 76
Mears, David O., 141, 424n144; educational opinions of, 159, 224; as nativist leader, 228; and women's suffrage, 226
Mehan, John, 36
Melican, Dennis, 42

Mellen, James: as alderman, 236, 450n83; Citizens' Alliance opposition of, 234; fund-raising of, 182; on Irish loyalties, 31, 33, 68, 70; and Irish nationalism, 69, 184; and labor movements, 145, 325; public housing supported by, 324; on Swedes as Irish competitors, 219
men: Catholicism of, 90–92; and drinking, 34, 91; economic conditions of, 45–46, 99–111, 113; housing arrangements for, 39–40, 54, 118–19, 333; immigration patterns of, 24–25; and masculinity, attitudes about, 166–67, 252; political participation of, 44, 110–11; Protestant influences on, 333–34; as widowers, 55
Men's League of the Sacred Heart, 91
Merchants Association, 356
Merchants National Bank, 275
Merriman, Daniel, 139, 141
Merwick, Donna, 154
Messenger: and accommodation, 133, 153; cessation of, 201, 204; coverage of Ireland, 30–31; editors of, 30, 133, 336; revival of, 241, 248; socialism opposed by, 245–46; and women's suffrage, 252. *See also Catholic Messenger*
Messenger Hill neighborhood, 59
Methodist Church, 220
Mill, John Stuart, 191
Miller, F. H., 102
Miller, Kerby, 26, 31, 33, 38, 388n8
Minor, Frederick, 303
minstrel shows, 77, 169, 351
Mission Crusade (1932), 334, 342
M.J. Finnegan Company (brewery), 42
Moen, Philip L., 142, 144, 218
Moen, Philip W., 128, 147, 209, 218, 233, 448n77
Molloy, William, 36
Mooney, John F. H., 197
Mooney, Richard H., 167–68, 176–77, 414n61
Moore, Deborah Dash, 9, 389
Moore, Thomas, 31
Moran, John B., 296

Morgan, P. B., 282, 291, 299

Morgan Construction (machinery manufacturer), 379

Moriarty, Eugene: and high school controversy, 224; home and exile for, 18; on hurling game at Gaelic Sports Day, 26–27; and Irish nationalism, 439n126; political activities of, 49, 183; *Worcester Post* purchased by, 231

Mostgeen, John, 40

Mostgeen, Michael, 40

Mount Carmel parish, 345

movies, 285

Moynihan, Daniel Patrick, 5

Mullaney, Elizabeth, 384

municipal improvements: business backers of, 210; and Citizens' Alliance, 150; Republican Party and, 289, 291–92, 296–97, 300, 314–15

Murphy, Anna, 116, 118

Murphy, Connie, 75

Murphy, Jeremiah, 43, 149–50, 182–83, 197

Murphy, John L., 149

Murren, John, 194

music and songs, 26, 31, 76–77, 81, 139–40

Mutual Benefit Society, 91

Nahirny, Vladimir, 70

names: in high school controversy, 224; as symbol of Irishness, 68–69, 72

Nardi, William, 466n60

National Catholic Total Abstinence Union, 156, 162

nationalism, Irish, 4, 32–33, 134, 178–98, 385–86, 453n104; and Ancient Order of Hibernians, 256–58, 359–60; blue-collar workers' support of, 188–89; and Clan na Gael, 180–81, 257–58; collapse of moderate, 202–4; fund-raising to support, 181–83, 188–90, 196–98, 203, 438n102; and Irish Free State treaty, 368–69; and Kilmainham Treaty, 191–92, 195; and Knights of Columbus, 359, 362–63; and Ku Klux Klan, 307; priests and, 183–84,

190, 358, 362–63; revival of, 13, 273, 358–69; Yankees' support of, 4, 187–88, 197, 364–66. *See also* Ladies Land League; Land League

National Machine Tool Builders Association (NMTBA), 274, 277, 291

National Metal Trades Association (NMTA), 274, 277, 279, 281, 283, 291, 313

nativism, 12–13; of American Protective Association, 206, 227; Hibernians' efforts to counteract, 253–54; of high school controversy, 223–26; of Know-Nothings, 135–37; of Ku Klux Klan, 306–11; of native-stock Yankees, 206, 222–30, 364; overcome by Citizens' Alliance, 135. *See also* anti-Catholicism; discrimination

neighborhood patterns: American-born Irish, 123–31; British, 220; discrimination in, 128–30; French Canadian, 62, 126, 214–15, 288–89; immigrant Irish, 58–65; movement out of strictly Irish, 123–31, 382–83; native stock Yankees, 128, 228; non-white immigrant groups, 383; other Catholic immigrant groups, 128, 271, 287–89; Swedish, 214, 219, 286

neighbors. *See* friends and kinship networks

Nelson, Christian, 306, 310, 312–13

Nelson, George, 472n104

newspapers, 231–32. *See also specific papers*

"no-license" issue. *See* liquor license referenda

No Rent Manifesto, 187–90, 192

North Brookfield controversy, 216–17, 343

North End neighborhood, 59, 63, 124, 219

North End Ring (informal political group), 290–91, 302, 308, 310

Norton Company, 109; employees as KKK members, 309; expansion of, 274, 379; and postwar depression, 303; Swedish employees of, 47, 218, 379; and union organizing, 277, 283, 379; workforce reductions of, 280, 309, 469n81

Notre Dame des Canadiens Church, 215, 340–41

Oak Hill neighborhood, 62, 124, 215, 288

O'Brien, David, 332

O'Brien, Richard, 176

O'Brien, William, 198, 202

O'Callaghan, Mary V., 113, 116, 118, 185–86, 253

O'Connell, Daniel, 177–78

O'Connell, David F.: economy in government/tax cut policies of, 296–97; mayoral elections of, 239, 248, 290, 298, 303; political activities of, 43, 237, 450n83; and Progressivism, 465n54; on the Wobblies, 325–26

O'Connell, Philip J.: AOH, Clan na Gael membership of, 243; delayed marriage of, 116, 118; economy in government/tax cut policies of, 296; and Hoover/Smith election, 330; and Irish nationalism, 362–63, 369; mayoral elections of, 116, 237–39, 248, 303; political activities of, 118, 201–2, 237–40, 289–90, 450n83

O'Connell, Thomas E., 304

O'Connell, William, 96, 358, 361, 373

O'Connell Associates, 242, 257

O'Connor, Jeremiah, 39

O'Connor, John, 39

O'Connor, John F., 88, 99–100, 102, 114, 160, 362

O'Connor, Thomas Power, 198, 202

Odd Fellows, 205

O'Donoghue, Stephen, 368

O'Flynn, Richard: on Ancient Order of Hibernians, 171; on Bay State Bank, 261; on church construction, 29; on discrimination against the Irish, 102, 260; on drinking, 35–36, 55; education of, 26–27; on fund-raising to support Irish nationalism, 182; home and exile for, 30, 67–68; on St. Patrick's Day parades, 174–75, 176; as steamship agent, 39; on United Irish Societies Convention, 255–56

O'Gorman, John, 182

O'Hara, Abigail L., 116, 121

O'Hara, Michael, 188

O'Hara, Michael J.: and Catholic/Protestant relations, 270, 330–31; corruption charges against, 322; and Ku Klux Klan, 308; mayoral elections of, 305–6, 310–16, 321–23; municipal improvement policies of, 313–15

old age homes, 57, 339–40, 344

O'Leary, Joshua: accommodationist leadership of, 153, 199, 204–6, 248, 327; on parochial schools, 160–62, 336; on rowdy masculinity, 252; on U.S. foreign policy, 258–59; on YMCA, 334

O'Leary, Thomas, 334

O'Malley, Elizabeth, 114

O'Neill, D. H., 125, 430n37

O'Neill, Thomas, 70, 137

L'Opinion Publique, 216, 349

Order of the United American Mechanics, 227–28

O'Reilly, John Boyle: on Americanism, 167, 193; and Irish nationalism, 181, 189, 193, 196; on self-improvement, 350

O'Reilly, Patrick T., 125, 171

O'Reilly, Tom, 111

organizational networks. See institutional networks

O'Rourke, Hugh, 299, 302, 467n66

orphanages, 63, 159, 339

Orsi, Robert, 343

Orstrom, Charles, 309

Osgood Bradley (firm), 303, 469n81

O'Sullivan, Cornelius, 252

Our Lady of Lourdes, 86, 343

Our Lady of Mount Carmel parish, 348

Our Lady of the Angels parish, 129–30, 328, 341

Our Lady of Vilna Church, 348

Overlock, Melvin, 290, 293

Palm Sunday Riot (1847), 24, 29

parades: Columbus Day, 3, 355–58; Corpus Christi, 82, 94; Fourth of July, 179; multiethnic, 342; neighborhood, 63; political, 317–19; St. Patrick's Day, 1–3, 169, 172–78,

253–56, 358, 383–86; Swedish Midsummer Festival, 287

parish missions, 83–84, 86

Parker, Alton B., 239

parks, 61

Parmalee, A. W., 233, 448n77

Parnell, Anna, 185, 187

Parnell, Charles Stewart: end of nationalist
leadership, 202–3, 266; as hero to
Worcester Irish, 196, 198; Land League
leadership of, 180, 191–92; as leader of
moderate nationalists, 135, 178, 195; and
No Rent Manifesto, 187

Parnell, Delia, 188

parochial schools: and accommodation, 133,
158–62; Catholic Church's reaffirmation
of, 204–5; growth of, 262, 335–37; as institutional networks, 262–63; in Ireland,
27–28; Irish history taught in, 272; priests'
role in opposing, 155–56, 159, 335

Patrick, Saint, 29, 68–69, 72

patriotism, 323–24, 326–27, 377. *See also*
Americanism

patronage, political, 44, 150–52, 161, 248–49,
316. *See also* government employment

Paulists, 155

Perlman, Joel, 103

Philippines, 259

Phoenix Park killings, 196, 439n126

"physical force" men, 195–96

Pierce, Jefferson, 212

"pioneer" Irish, 23–24

Pius IX, 79–80

Pius X, 331

Plan E, 380–81

plays. *See* theater

Plunket, Sir Horace, 26

Plunkett, Francis, 182, 225

Plunkett, William, 70, 137–38

police officers, 43, 149

Polish immigrants: and Columbus Day celebrations, 3, 355, 357; as competitors, 12,
15, 271–72; neighborhood patterns of,
128, 271, 287–88; and pan-ethnic Catholic

cooperation, 4, 348, 354, 377–78; political
participation of, 294, 321

politics: and city charter reforms, 225–26,
236–38, 380–81; French Canadian participation in, 148, 214, 217, 232–34, 238,
294–95, 298, 302, 320–21; Hibernians'
participation in, 247–49; Italian participation in, 295, 298, 302–3, 320–21;
Lithuanian participation in, 294; machine tactics in, 316; partisan press in,
231–32; and party re-registrations, 315;
Polish participation in, 294, 321; Swedish
participation in, 214, 220, 232, 238,
282–83, 309–10, 313–14, 321; women's
participation in, 44, 186, 317; and working-class organizations, 208, 212–13,
233–34. *See also* Citizens' Alliance; patronage, political; *specific parties or
candidates*

poor farms, 51, 57

populists, 212–13

Potato Famine, 23–24, 93

Potter, Burton W., 290

Power, John J., 127, 373, 430n37; accommodationist leadership of, 155–56, 206, 327;
and Ancient Order of Hibernians, 171; on
Bible reading in public schools, 138; and
domestic service training, 41; and hospitals, 63, 157; and parochial schools,
155–56, 159; plain style of, 80, 87; as
St. Wulstan's member, 155; temperance
leadership of, 165; wealth of, 154

Powers, William, 211

Pozetta, George, 7

Pratt, Charles, 148–52, 197

prejudice, anti-Catholic/anti-Irish. *See* anti-
Catholicism; discrimination

Prentice Brothers (machinery manufacturer), 207, 209

Presbyterian Church, 141, 328

presidential elections: anti-Catholicism in,
271, 330–31, 382; Cleveland/Butler,
150–51; Coolidge, 318; Eisenhower, 380;
Hoover/Smith, 271, 317–23, 330–31, 353,

presidential elections *(continued)*
380, 483n207; Kennedy, 382; McKinley/
Bryan, 233, 238, 318; F. D. Roosevelt,
379–80, 483n207; T. Roosevelt, 309–10;
Wilson, 297, 467n66
press, partisan, 231–32. *See also specific
newspapers*
priests: accommodationist leadership of,
152–56; advancement of, in Church hierarchy, 331–32; and Irish nationalism,
183–84, 190, 358, 362–63; political power
of, 178; as temperance leaders, 156,
163–66, 264; and women's organizations, 99, 166, 195
professional occupations, 102–3, 108–9,
112–13, 116, 350, 457n146, 485n21
Progressivism, 465n54
prohibition, 220, 292, 294, 296, 300, 308,
323. *See also* drinking; liquor license referenda; temperance movement
property ownership, 49–50, 55
Protestantism: and KKK, 306–9; lure of, 105,
271, 333; of native stock Yankees, 141–42,
285–86; of Swedish immigrants, 220, 309
Prouty, Olive, 141
pubs. *See* saloons
Pulson, Sven, 217

Quinn, J. Frank, 176, 255
Quinn, Patrick, 51, 183
Quinsigamond Village neighborhood,
219–20, 286–87, 309

radicalism, 134, 187–95, 324–26, 366–67, 377,
453n104
railroads, 20
Ratigan, John, 237
Reardon, John F., 282–83, 310
Recorder, 204–6
Reed, Alden, 379
Reed, Charles, 149, 197
Reed, Edgar, 218
Reed, F. E., 209, 448n77

Reed and Prince (manufacturing firm), 274,
279, 379
Reidy, George C., 211
Reidy, Maurice, 304–5
relief organizations. *See* charities
religious vocations, 28–29, 88, 157
Republican Party, 289–98; and Citizens' Alliance, 146–52, 230–35; and city charter
reforms, 225–26, 238; factionalism of,
238–40, 308; French Canadians and, 217,
294–95, 298; and high school controversy,
224–26; Italians and, 298; and municipal
improvements, 289, 291–92, 296–97, 300,
314–15; and nativism, 226, 229; and post-
war ills, 300; re-registrations to, 315;
Swedes and, 220, 309–10, 313–14; Yankee
dominance in, 222
revivals, religious, 229
Ribbonmen, 170–71
Richardson, George, 136, 173
Riordan, John J., 138
Robbins, Wallace, 376
Rochford, Lezime, 316
Roe, Albert, 140, 450n82
Roe, Alfred S., 223–24, 226
Rogers, John J., 251
Ronan, James, 188
Rooney, Annie, 88
Roosevelt, Franklin D., 379–80, 483n207
Roosevelt, Theodore, 310
Rosenzweig, Roy, 6–7, 35, 166, 277, 428n23,
435n71
Rossa, O'Donovan, 179, 195
Rowland, Thomas, 359
Ryan, Ed, 111
Ryan, Rosy, 408n16
Ryan, William, 336, 363

Sacred Heart, devotion to, 82–83
Sacred Heart parish: devotional revolution
in, 80; Holy Name societies in, 87; home
and exile theme in, 31; and Ladies Land
League, 183; missions in, 83–84, 86;

music and worship in, 81; organization
of, 63, 87; schools in, 159, 336; social activities in, 64–65, 74, 159; sodalities in,
84; temperance movement in, 164
saints, veneration of, 29, 36–38, 68–69, 72,
85–87, 94, 334, 343
St. Agnes Guild, 93, 342
St. Aloysius societies, 91
St. Andrew parish, 378
St. Anne's Cadets, 173
St. Anne's Hill neighborhood, 60, 271, 288
St. Anne's parish: Holy Name societies in, 87;
and Ladies Land League, 183; missions in,
86; organization of, 63; schools in, 262,
335; social activities in, 64–65; sodalities
in, 84, 93; women's support of, 400n54
St. Anne's Total Abstinence Society, 163, 265
St. Bernard's parish, 130, 363, 414n61
St. Casimir's parish, 348
St. Charles Borromeo parish, 378
St. Elizabeth's Hospital, 63, 157
St. Francis Home Aid Association, 339
St. Francis Home for the Aged, 339–40, 344
St. Francis-St. Therese Catholic Workers,
385–86
St. Jean de Baptiste Society, 348
St. John's Church, 59, 81, 87, 215
St. John's Dramatic Club, 78
St. John's High School, 75, 377, 383
St. John's parish: Corpus Christi celebration
in, 82; devotional revolution in, 80;
growth of, 127; Holy Name societies in,
87; home and exile theme in, 31; Irish
nationalism in, 363; and Ladies Land
League, 183; missions in, 83–84, 86; non-
Irish members of, 340, 378; organization
of, 63, 87; Protestant mission in, 328;
schools in, 158–59, 262, 335, 377; social
activities in, 74; sodalities in, 84, 93
St. John's Temperance and Literary Guild,
163–64; end of, 204, 255; membership of,
168, 265; minstrel shows of, 77; revival of,
263; and self-improvement, 101, 166

St. John's Temperance Cadets, 164, 167, 173
St. Joseph's Church, 215
St. Joseph's Day, 340
St. Joseph's Home for Working Girls, 41
St. Margaret Mary's parish, 341
St. Mary's parish, 348
St. Patrick's Day, 340; and Ancient Order
of Hibernians, 2–3, 134, 172–78, 253–56,
272, 385; and Clan na Gael, 254–55; home
and exile theme of, 31; in Ireland, 177;
other entertainments on, 41, 69, 239; parades on, 1–3, 169, 358, 383–86; and temperance movement, 174–77; women as
organizers, 384
St. Patrick's Temperance Society, 163
St. Paul's Lyceum (St. Paul's Total Abstinence Society), 1–2, 77, 163, 264, 265, 386
St. Paul's parish: church construction in, 127;
devotional revolution in, 80–81; financial
stability of, 159; non-Irish members of,
37, 340, 383; schools in, 336; as seat of
diocese of Worcester, 373; sodalities in,
87; women's support of, 41
St. Peter's High School, 377
St. Peter's Mutual Advancement Society, 168
St. Peter's parish: financial stability of, 159;
Holy Name societies in, 87; music and
worship in, 81; non-Irish in, 215, 340,
383; organization of, 125, 157; schools in,
336, 377
St. Stephen's parish: growth of, 127, 157;
Holy Name societies in, 87; minstrel
shows in, 77; missions in, 86; non-Irish
in, 215; plain style of, 81; schools in, 336;
sodalities in, 87
St. Stephen's Total Abstinence Society, 263,
265, 342
St. Vincent de Paul Society, 64
St. Vincent's Hospital, 127, 157–58, 339, 344,
374, 376–77
St. Wulstan's society, 155
Salisbury, Stephen: business career of,
143–44, 227; fund-raising of, 182;

Salisbury, Stephen *(continued)*
    philanthropic activities of, 139–40,
    157–58; political activities of, 225–27, 233;
    property-tax assessment of, 149
saloons, 34–36, 62, 122, 164, 251, 292
San Pedro Church, 383
Sargent, Joseph, 124
Scalpintown neighborhood, 59
Scannell, D. S., 44
Scannell, Dennis, 159, 183–84, 191, 430n37
schools. *See* education; parochial schools
schoolteachers, 149, 152, 224, 262–63
secret societies, 170–71, 227
self-improvement activities, 166, 168, 350
servants, domestic, 40–41, 46–47, 54–55,
    111–12, 218–19
sewage disposal, 61, 150
sexual morality, 333, 343
Shannon, William, 4–5, 9
Shea, Patrick C., 42
Shea, Patrick H., 42
Sheridan, Philip, 70
Shrewsbury Street neighborhood, 219, 271,
    288, 318–19, 342
Sinn Fein, 360–61, 365–66, 368
Sisters of Mercy, 37, 63, 86, 88
Sisters of Notre Dame, 88
Sisters of Notre Dame de Namur Convent,
    310–11
Sisters of Providence, 88, 127, 157, 339
Skerret, Ellen, 130
Sligo Club, 44, 241–42, 272
smallpox, 61
Smith, Alfred E., 317–23, 380; anti-
    Catholicism and, 271, 330–31; and
    Knights of Columbus, 353; popularity
    of, 483n207
Smith, Harry Worcester, 139, 299
social centers, 41, 62–65, 130
social clubs and societies, 162–72, 264;
    Americanism in, 169–70; blue-collar
    workers in, 169; of native stock Yankees,
    140, 285–86; and pan-ethnic Catholic co-
    operation, 341–43; and self-improvement,

168; white-collar workers in, 169, 265,
    457n146. *See also specific societies*
socialism, 208, 245–46, 324–26, 351, 366–67
Socialists, 212–13, 234, 282
sodalities, 28, 41, 84–87, 91–93
Sons of Temperance, 205
Soulliere, N. B., 298
Southwick, Albert, 408n14
South Worcester neighborhood, 59, 124;
    churches in, 63; non-Irish in, 215,
    219–20, 288; parades in, 63
Spence, John, 279
sports: Americanism of, 74–76, 377; and An-
    cient Order of Hibernians, 250; evangeli-
    cal disapproval of, 98, 140–41; and Gaelic
    cultural revival, 4, 26–27, 250; Knights
    of Columbus and, 351; and temperance
    movement, 166–67, 264. *See also specific
    games*
Sprague, A. B. R., 197, 232–35
Sprague, W. S. B., 182
Spy, 225, 231–32, 238
Squires, Arthur, 308, 312–13, 316
Stoddard, Elijah B., 147, 157, 189
Stoddard, H. G., 282
Stone, A. M., 209
Stott, Richard, 252
street gangs, 24, 62, 91, 219
street railways, 129, 230, 234, 301
strikes. *See* labor movements
suffrage movement, 226, 252–53
Sullivan, Charles F. "Jeff," 380
Sullivan, Humphrey, 51
Sullivan, John E., 235–36
Sullivan, John Patrick, 334
Sullivan, Peter: birthplace of, 44; and de
    Valera visit, 367; economy in government/
    tax cut policies of, 301; and Irish nation-
    alism, 366; Knights of Columbus sup-
    port for, 353; mayoral elections of, 43,
    300–306, 310; political activities of, 314,
    317, 321–22, 365–66, 474n121; and Pro-
    gressivism, 465n54
Sullivan, Robert, 154

Summer Shrewsbury Street neighborhood. *See* Shrewsbury Street neighborhood

Sumner, Charles, 467n66

survivance, 216, 288

Swedes: anti-Irish feelings of, 220, 310, 312; and city charter reforms, 380–81; as competitors, 12, 15, 46–47, 100, 102, 111, 206, 217–20, 300; immigration patterns of, 217–18; institutional networks of, 286–87; and Ku Klux Klan, 307, 309–11; and labor movements, 195; liquor license referenda support of, 220, 287, 309; nativists' approval of, 229; naturalization rate of, 44; neighborhood patterns of, 214, 219, 286; occupations of, 113; political participation of, 214, 220, 232, 238, 282–83, 309–10, 313–14, 321; and postwar depressions, 309; pro-German attitude of, 299, 468n68; Protestantism of, 220, 309

Syrian immigrants, 289

Tatnuck Country Club, 286, 337, 379, 485n21

Taves, Ann, 94

tax cut policies. *See* economy in government/ tax cut policies

Telegram, 150, 291, 312; charter reforms opposition of, 225; editorial policies of, 231; and Plan E, 380–81; and Rum Biddies, 254

temperance movement, 134, 162–68; Americanism in, 167–68; and Ancient Order of Hibernians, 171–72, 251–52, 253–56; blue-/white-collar workers in, 168; and Catholic Church, 156, 163–64, 328; collapse of, 204; and high school controversy, 224; and Knights of Columbus, 350; as Know-Nothing issue, 137; priests as leaders of, 156, 163–66, 264; revival of, 170, 263–64; and St. Patrick's Day parades, 174–77. *See also* drinking; liquor license referenda; prohibition

temperance societies, 75, 86, 91, 162–63, 341–42. *See also specific societies*

Ten Eyck, Edward Hanlan, 75

tennis, 74, 140

Tentler, Leslie, 92–93, 328

textile industries, 46, 276

Thayer, Adin, 197

Thayer, Ernest, 74

Thayer, John Alden, 235, 239, 467n66

Thayer, John R., 151–52

theater, 31, 74, 77–78, 122, 139, 249–50

Theresa of Lisieux, Saint, 29, 94, 334, 343

Thernstrom, Stephan, 103

Thomas Francis Meagher Club, 44, 241–42, 272

three-deckers, 21, 61

Thursday Noon Club, 281–83, 286, 291, 300, 365

tickets to America, 39, 41

Tinsley, John F., 102, 110, 304–5

Tolnay, Stewart, 122

Tom Moore Club, 31

Trahan, Camille, 302

Trainer, John B., 40

Trainer, Thomas B., 40

Trinity College, 114

tuberculosis, 61

Tuite, James, 262, 264

Tulloch, Mrs. Donald, 299

Ulster Irish, 307, 309

Underwood, Francis A., 257

unemployment, 51, 95, 207, 280

Union Hill neighborhood, 60, 124, 126–27

unions. *See* labor movements

Unitarian Church, 142

United Irish League, 258

United Irish Societies Convention, 2, 30, 168–69, 174, 181–82, 196, 254–56, 264

United States, foreign policy of, 258–59

United States Envelope Company, 290

vacationing, 74, 76, 140

Vatican II, 382

vaudeville, 74, 122, 139

Vaudreil, Joseph G., 339

Vecoli, Rudolf, 7

Vernon Hill neighborhood, 60, 124, 126–27
Verry, George, 182, 187
Victoria, Queen of England, 221, 247–48

Wachusett Boat Club, 74–75
wage-earners clubs, 282
Walker, Joseph ("Shirtsleeves Joe"), 124, 152, 197
Walsh, David I., 297, 314, 317, 380, 467n66, 483n207
Walsh, John J., 313
Walsh, Katherine, 76
Walsh, Lawrence, 181
Walsh, Margaret, 76
Walsh, Robert, 41, 159, 430n37
Walsh, Victor, 438n100
Walsh, William, 184
Washburn, Charles, 47
Washburn, Ichabod, 146
Washburn Moen Wire Manufacturing Company, 42, 47, 59–60, 207–8, 217–19. See also American Steel and Wire Company
Washington Club, 77, 168–70, 174, 254, 263–64, 341–42
Washington Square neighborhood, 62
Whalen, Katherine, 76
Whalon, John B., 75
Wheeler, Leonard, 158
Whipple, Robert Z., 306
Whitcomb and Blaisdell (manufacturing firm), 274, 279
White, J. E., 282
Whiteboys, 171
white-collar workers: in Blessed Sacrament parish, 129; as Catholic Women's Club members, 335; French Canadians as, 100; Irish as, 45, 50, 100–101, 111–12, 118, 159; as KKK members, 307; as Knights of Columbus members, 350; nativism of, 227–28; in Our Lady of the Angels parish, 129; political participation of, 147; in social clubs, 169, 265, 457n146; Swedes as, 100; in temperance movement, 168

whiteness, 15, 381–83
Whittal, Matthew, 220
widows and widowers, 55, 120
Wilhelm, Prince of Sweden, 287
Wilson, Henry, 136
Wilson, Woodrow, 297, 360, 363–64, 467n66
Winslow, Samuel, 151, 222, 233–34, 430n35
Winslow, Samuel, Jr., 408n14
Wobblies, 325–26
women: attitudes on roles of, 98–99, 114–16, 121, 186, 195, 252–53, 326, 343; Catholicism of, 41, 91–93, 400n54; as domestic servants, 40–41, 46–47, 54–55, 111–12, 218–19; economic conditions of, 45–46, 111–16, 186; education of, 114, 186; housing arrangements for, 40, 118–19, 333; immigration patterns of, 25; and Irish nationalism, 184–86, 190–91, 195; leisure activities of, 74, 76; political participation of, 44, 186, 317; and priests' control of organizations, 99, 166, 195; Protestant influences on, 333; as saloon keepers, 35–36; as St. Patrick's Day organizers, 384; suffrage for, 226, 252–53; and temperance movement, 166; as widows, 55. See also specific women's organizations
Wood, Rostow, 213, 461n32
Woodley, Robert, 73
Worcester Boys Club, 333
Worcester Club, 140–41, 286, 337, 379
Worcester Country Club, 337
Worcester Daily Evening News, 136–37
Worcester Music Festival, 139–40
Worcester Polytechnic Institute, 107–10, 445n53
Worcester Post, 231, 324
Worcester Safe Deposit and Trust Company, 275
Worcester Theater, 139
Worcester Trust, 275
Worcester Women's Club, 93, 99, 286, 335
working-class political organizations, 208, 212–13, 233–34

World Parliament of Religions, 205

World War I, 298–300, 307, 351–52, 359–60

Wright, George M.: mayoral elections of, 294, 303, 308, 310; movie role of, 285; municipal improvement policies of, 291–92; political activities of, 276, 282, 295

Wright, John J., 373–75, 377–78, 381

Wyland, Benjamin, 365

Wyman, H. Winfield, 109

Wyman Gordon Company (machinery manufacturer), 274, 379

Yankees, native stock: anti-Catholicism of, 136–37, 229, 327–28, 376; Catholic influences on, 95–96; and city charter reforms, 380–81; as competitors, 11; control of business by, 102, 143–44, 260, 273, 329, 379–80, 383; divisiveness among, 15, 138–46, 308; elite status of, 15, 45, 284; and Fenians, 179; fund-raising for Ireland by, 182; home and exile for, 142–43; on Irish drinking, 140, 165, 172, 285; and Irish nationalism, 4, 187–88, 197, 364–66; and leisure activities, 139–41, 285; and liquor license referenda, 285; local war effort of, 299; marriage and fertility among, 53, 116; migration patterns of, 142, 284; nativism of, 206, 222–30, 364; neighborhood patterns of, 128, 228; and Plan E, 380; Protestantism of, 141–42, 285; and St. Vincent's Hospital, 157–58; and temperance movement, 166

Young Ireland movement, 178–79

Young Men's Christian Association, 133, 333–34

Young Women's Christian Association, 141

Zunz, Oliver, 418n95

Zwickerath, William, Fr., S.J., 342

About the Author

Timothy J. Meagher is Director of the Center for Irish Studies at Catholic University. He is co-editor, with Ronald Bayor, of *The New York Irish,* winner of the James Donnelly Sr. Prize from the American Conference for Irish Studies.